WORLD HISTORY

The Easy Way

VOLUME TWO

A.D. 1500
TO THE PRESENT

Charles A. Frazee
Professor of History
California State University, Fullerton

BARRON'S

Copyright © 1997 by Barron's Educational Series, Inc.
Maps © 1997 by Barron's Educational Series, Inc.

All inquiries should be addressed to:
Barron's Educational Series, Inc.
250 Wireless Boulevard
Hauppauge, New York 11788

International Standard Book No. 0-8120-9766-1

Library of Congress Catalog Card No. 97-14772

Library of Congress Cataloging-in-Publication Data

Frazee, Charles A.
  World history the easy way / Charles A. Frazee.
      p.   cm. — (The easy way)
  Includes index.
  Contents: v. 1. Ancient and medieval times to
A.D. 1500 — v. 2. A.D. 1500 to the present.
    ISBN 0-8120-9765-3 (v. 1). — ISBN 0-8120-9766-1 (v. 2)
  1. World history.   I. Title.   II. Series.
D21.F868   1997
909.07—dc21   97-14772
                                               CIP

PRINTED IN THE UNITED STATES OF AMERICA

98765

Contents

UNIT 3   A WORLD OF NATIONS, 1914–1997

Chapter 20   World War I   373

Chapter 21   Europe Between the Wars   393

Introduction

It may be useful for you, the reader, to know the structure of this world history text. I have followed the two dimensions of time and space, placing events of the major regions of the world within a specific period. Although there is some minor overlap, the perimeters of the centuries under consideration are respected.

This book is meant to serve as a text or to supplement a standard volume on world history, which is usually more detailed. In it you will find a blend of information and analysis of politics, economics, religion, society, and the arts. A sample review of test items is at the end of each chapter.

I want to thank my wife, Kathleen, for her inestimable contribution in the preparation of this book.

Charles A. Frazee
August 1997

Acknowledgments

All maps created by Barron's Educational Series, Inc.

Photographs and art were provided by the following sources:

CORBIS-BETTMANN:
Pages 5, 6, 8, 10, 11, 13, 14, 26, 30, 31, 32, 34, 40, 42, 50, 51, 55, 58, 61, 63, 64, 71, 73, 74, 78, 82, 85, 86, 95, 96 top, 98, 100, 101, 104, 107, 108, 109, 111 top, 112, 127, 128, 130, 131, 133, 173, 179, 192, 197, 201, 202, 205, 206, 207, 208, 217, 218, 222, 230, 232, 239, 240, 241, 242, 243, 244, 245, 248, 255, 256, 257, 258, 261, 263, 264, 268, 269, 278, 279, 280, 281, 282, 284 bottom, 286, 287, 288, 289, 290, 291, 292, 294, 302, 304, 311 top, 312, 323, 324, 326, 327, 328, 337, 338, 340, 341, 342, 344, 350, 351, 352, 353, 355, 357, 358, 359, 360, 361, 363, 376, 377, 378, 380 top & bottom, 381, 383, 384, 385, 386, 394, 396, 398 top, 399, 400, 401, 402, 403, 404, 407, 408, 409, 416, 417, 419, 421, 422, 423, 424, 425, 426, 427, 436 top & bottom, 437, 439, 440, 443, 444, 449, 450, 451, 452, 453, 455, 457, 460, 461, 468, 470, 471, 473, 474, 475 bottom, 481, 482, 489, 490, 491, 493, 495, 496 bottom, 503, 505, 506, 507, 508, 510, 517, 521 top & bottom, 523, 529, 530, 539, 540, 542, 547, 549 top & bottom, 551, 552 top & bottom, 553, 555, 556, 557, 558, 560, 567, 568, 571, 572, 573, 574, 575, 576, 577, 578, 584 top & bottom, 585.

FRENCH TOURIST AGENCY: Page 72

GRANGER: Pages 43 top, 53.

NASA: Page 559

INDIA TOURIST AGENCY: Pages 143, 144.

CHARLES FRAZEE:
Pages 15, 17, 18, 20, 28, 29, 33, 35, 36, 37, 39, 43 bottom, 54, 57, 60, 75, 76, 79, 80, 81, 83, 96, 102, 103, 106, 111 bottom, 119, 120, 121, 122, 124, 125, 129, 132, 139, 140, 142, 144, 150, 151, 152, 153, 155, 156, 158, 160, 161, 162, 170, 171, 175, 176, 177, 178, 190, 191, 193, 194, 196, 199, 215, 216, 220, 221, 229, 231, 260, 266, 271, 284 top, 301, 307, 308, 309, 311 bottom, 319, 320, 321, 325, 329, 331, 365, 374, 398 bottom, 405, 462, 475 top, 477, 478, 479, 480, 488, 496 top, 497, 511, 512, 513, 518, 519, 520, 524, 525, 531, 532, 533, 534, 535, 536, 538, 586.

UNIT 1

CONTINENTAL INTERACTIONS

A.D. 1500–1789

CHAPTER 1

Reformation Europe

Europe is one of the world's smallest continents in size, yet within its circumference it holds great physical and ethnic diversity. In ancient and medieval times it passed through periods of significant accomplishment followed by periods of serious decline when invaders or disease threatened catastrophe. In the Late Middle Ages and the Renaissance it experienced new values, while old ones were questioned.

Physically northern Europe or Scandinavia was the home of Norwegians, Danes, and Swedes. The Scandinavians were once a single people, but their language and culture began to go separate ways during the 500 years preceding A.D. 1500. In 1500 the Norwegians and Danes shared the same dynasty and were ruled from Copenhagen.

The Baltic Sea separates Scandinavia from Central Europe, home of the Germans, Poles, and Baltic peoples. The land in the northern part of Central Europe is flat and sandy, the climate is cool, making herding cattle easier than farming. Proceeding southward, Central Europe touches the Alps in modern Austria and Switzerland. The Carpathian Mountains form a giant backward S as they wend their way from Romania to Bulgaria. The Czech and Slovak Republics and Hungary lie within the basin of the Danube, East Europe's longest river. Eastward the Great European Plain expands into the lands of Belarus, Ukraine, and Russia. The climate here is hot in the summer but very cold in the winter.

Much of Europe's best farmland is found in France, Belgium, and the Netherlands, nations that border the Atlantic Ocean. Across the English Channel lie two large islands. The English, Welsh, and Scots share the larger island; the Irish inhabit the smaller one.

Three peninsulas jut into the Mediterranean Sea, the southern border of Europe. To the west, below the Pyrenees Mountains, is the Iberian Peninsula, home to Spaniards and Portuguese. Italians live in the middle peninsula, cut off from Central Europe by the Alps. The third region, the Balkans, is a rugged land the size of Texas. It contains the South Slavs, Romanians, Albanians, Greeks, and some Turks living in Istanbul and its nearby region. A Mediterranean climate offers hot, sunny summers and cool, rainy winters.

In 1500 minorities of Jews and Gypsies also lived within Europe's borders. Jews made their homes mostly in East Europe, while Gypsies reached western Europe about A.D. 1200 after Muslim invasions forced them from their homeland in India.

Christianity was the religion of a large majority of Europeans, but it presented two faces. Catholic, or Latin Christians, lived in West Europe, while Orthodox Christians inhabited East Europe. Although Catholic and Orthodox beliefs were similar, their cultures were quite different. A line separating Catholic and Orthodox Christians could be drawn from the western border of the Russian and Ukrainian lands through the Balkans and then to the Adriatic Sea.

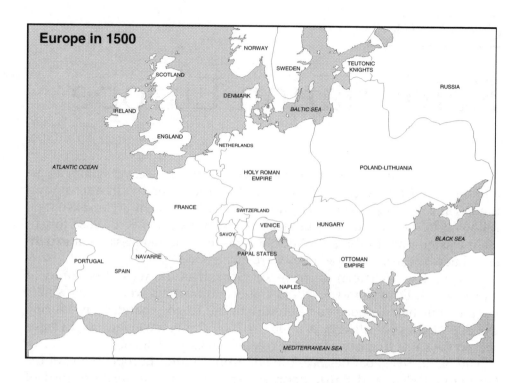

Unlike today, when religion is a personal decision, in the early sixteenth century it was very much a public matter, the concern of kings and queens. To deviate from the ruler's faith was to become suspect of treason. Monarchy was, with few exceptions, the prevailing form of government.

The economy was predominantly based on agriculture. The nobility, the great landowners, were the rich, whereas the peasantry, who actually worked in the fields, were generally quite poor. Townspeople, merchants and artisans, enjoyed a higher standard of living than peasants but were still recovering from the result of an outbreak of bubonic plague (the Black Death) in the fourteenth century. Although the signs of it were just appearing, Europe was about to become, for the first time in history, the leading civilization of the world.

The Approach of the Reformation

For close to a thousand years the Catholic church was the single most important unifying cultural force in western Europe. Within a period of 50 years, this unity was lost. Most of northern Europe adopted **Protestant** Christianity, a new expression of faith that focused on individual belief and the Bible as the only source of religious truth.

In 1500 every western European Catholic believed that Jesus, after he departed this world, intended that the apostle Peter and his successors were to head the church on earth. Peter had gone to Rome, the imperial capital, and died there a martyr. Over the centuries the bishops of Rome, known as popes since the fourth century, had played a major role, not only in religion but also in the politics of western Europe. However, in the early sixteenth century many Catholics were disillusioned with papal leadership.

Under Pope Alexander VI, born Rodrigo Borgia, the papacy was little more than a Spanish preserve, filled with the pope's children, his relatives, and friends. In 1503 the Romans were pleased when the cardinals, the papal electors, chose Giuliano della Rovere, an Italian, to succeed him. Giuliano took the papal name of Julius II. The pope had three goals: to enhance his family's fortune, to make Rome the outstanding city of Renaissance artists, and to expand the territories of the Papal States, the lands belonging to the pope in central Italy. Upon Julius's death, Giovanni de' Medici, from that wealthy and most prestigious family of Florence, followed him as Leo X.

Leo X, pictured with his nephews, made Rome the center of European culture in the early sixteenth century.

Christian men and women throughout Europe expected more from their leaders than either Alexander, Julius, or Leo provided. As Renaissance princes, the popes were superior to their Italian contemporaries in patronizing the arts. Their plans to secure the boundaries of the Papal States were generally successful. However, as spiritual leaders of the Catholic church, they were failures, for too often they allowed personal ambition and artistic distractions to shape their policies.

Because the moral tone in Rome was so lax, it is not surprising that throughout Europe bishops imitated the popes in pursuing wealth and prestige. Absenteeism was common, for the bishop of a town frequently made his residence at the royal court or lived on a family estate. A vicar served in his stead, but church revenues were transferred to the bishop. Pluralism was a common practice; many church leaders held two or more bishoprics in order to collect additional funds.

Priests who served in the Catholic parishes had no special seminary training, but half of the priests who served in Europe's urban churches were university graduates. Clergy salaries came from benefices, which acted like endowments, donated to the churches in the towns. In Germany town councils regulated the number and work of the clergy and actually had more control over them than their bishops. City magistrates also supervised the town's monasteries and convents. There were far too many clergy; one estimate counts one cleric for every 20 lay people.

The clergy in rural areas presented quite a contrast to their urban colleagues. They were poorly educated, and few were ever bold enough to preach a Sunday sermon. Most lived humbly among their peasant congregations, worked on their own plots of land, and cared for their livestock. On Sundays and holy days they presided at Mass and baptized newborn babies. They tended to reinforce, rather than reject, the superstitions of the people they served. The canonical law of celibacy was a heavy burden to keep, an ideal impossible for some and impractical for others.

At this time Europe had a number of scholars, called Humanists because of their interest in philosophy and the arts, who decried the ignorance of the rural clergy and their parishoners. The most prominent of all Humanists was Desiderius Erasmus. From 1500 to 1520 Erasmus dominated the intellectual life of Europe. Born and educated in the Netherlands, he was ordained a priest and later appointed rector at the University of Paris. He authored a series of works urging reform and better opportunities for education.

Desiderius Erasmus became the most prominent Humanist of the sixteenth century.

The Humanist critics recognized that ordinary Christians imitated their pastors and knew little of their faith. At worship they were only observers. Because the priest did not face the congregation and quietly conducted the service in Latin, now a foreign language for Europeans, the communal aspect of the Mass, the Sunday worship service, was negated.

Indulgences

A practice that many Humanists found objectionable was the use of **indulgences** as a source for church income. Indulgences did not forgive sins, only sacramental confession did that, but the distinction must not have been clear for many uneducated people. To receive absolution, a **penance** was required similar to a fine in civil court. Acts of penance in early Christianity included making a long pilgrimage or fasting on bread and water for a period of time.

Over the years, an indulgence became a common substitute for a deed of penance. In the early sixteenth century, gaining an indulgence by making a donation to the church was very popular both for the clerics who offered them and for the people who received an indulgence certificate.

Pope Julius II and most of Rome's population saw that the old St. Peter's basilica, built by the Roman emperor Constantine the Great in the fourth century, was near collapse. Over the protests of preservationists who thought it could be repaired, the pope ordered the church to be razed and commissioned plans for a new edifice, to be the largest building in Europe. The pope desperately needed money to pay for his venture, so he offered an indulgence to anyone who would contribute to the construction of the new St. Peter's.

In 1517 a papal preacher reached the principality of Saxony, a German territory within the Holy Roman Empire. The Prince of Saxony, Frederick the Wise, would not let the papal emissary into his lands, for he did not want money leaving his principality to go to Rome. He found support from Martin Luther, a teacher at the local university in Wittenberg. Luther contended that the papal indulgence was a fraud and its preaching should be stopped. His protest touched off the **Protestant Reformation.**

Martin Luther

Martin Luther was a man of strong convictions and emotions. He was also an idealist, who believed that the sixteenth-century church had seriously departed from the teaching of the New Testament, the scripture that contained the life and teaching of Jesus. Luther's own religious training made him scrupulous to an extreme, for in his own estimation he could never reach the perfection he sought in his own life.

Luther began his higher education as a law student at the University of Erfurt, but unexpectedly, and to the deep chagrin of his father, he announced his intention to join the Augustinian Canons, who served as the university's faculty. The Augustinians were delighted to receive him, and within two years he was ordained. Luther's superiors subsequently appointed him to teach at the University of Wittenberg.

While lecturing on St. Paul's Epistle to the Romans, Luther found a solution to his fears in the verse ". . . he shall gain life who is justified through faith." This text opened a totally new vision for him. Only God could offer **justification,** forgiveness of sins, and restoration to his love.

Luther wrote a document called the Ninety-Five Theses that challenged the tradition of granting indulgences. He sent a copy to his bishop, who then forwarded it to Rome. The printing press was a great assist to Luther in reaching all literate Germans.

As he published pamphlet after pamphlet, broadening the issues he found objectionable in the contemporary church far beyond indulgences, Luther became a hero to most Germans. His friends made vain efforts to restrain his charges when he decided to challenge the authority of the pope. Leo X, after considerable delay, for at first Rome did not take Luther seriously, excommunicated him for his defiance of papal authority. Luther showed how little he cared by burning the excommunication in a public demonstration of defiance.

At this point, in April 1521, the recently elected Holy Roman Emperor Charles V ordered Luther to appear at a Diet, an imperial assembly, in the city of Worms. Luther's eloquent defense of his position persuaded the emperor and his advisors that he was a dangerous man. Fearing that the emperor planned to arrest him, Luther's friends spirited him out of town and hid him in a castle under an alias. In this secluded hideaway Luther began translating the New Testament into German. Although other biblical translations existed, none came close to the vivid prose of the Reformer.

For the rest of his life, Luther never stopped preaching or writing on justification by faith alone. He continued to assert that it was faith, not good works or attendance at Mass or indulgences, that brought people closer to God. He lashed out at the privileged status the clergy held, asserting that Christ's priesthood was conferred on lay men and women as well as priests and bishops. He rejected priestly celibacy, because the New Testament made no mention of it, as well as five of the traditional seven sacraments of the church. He kept only Baptism and the Eucharist. Luther believed that his message was urgent because he thought the end of the world was imminent.

Martin Luther charged that the Catholic church of his time had departed from the teaching of the New Testament.

Many princes and town councils welcomed Luther's teaching. They threw out their bishops and took over the property of the churches and monasteries. Lutheranism reflected the values of both the urban middle class and a landed aristocracy that resented the privileges of the Catholic clergy and the great wealth that the institutional church had accumulated over the centuries. German peasants were pleased to hear that they no longer had to pay the **tithe,** the 10% of their crops that went to support the clergy.

Luther had no desire to upset the German political or social system. In 1524 he was shocked to learn of peasant revolts against the landowners. He never intended that his teaching on freedom should encourage rebellion so he urged on the landowners to battle the peasants. Within four years the princes had won, but Luther had lost many of his earlier supporters.

The Germans settled in East Europe followed Luther into the Reformation, as did the Teutonic Knights of the Baltic. In 1523 Gustavus Vasa, king of Sweden, became a convert, and in Denmark and Norway, both countries ruled by Frederick I, the Reform progressed with royal support.

Luther's last years were spent in Wittenberg living comfortably with his wife and children, surrounded by admiring students and friends. He was a man of great loves and great hatreds, a personality that admirably fitted him for his historic role.

There are several explanations for Luther's success in northern Europe. One was Luther's personality. His energy and conviction attracted many people to his cause. German nationalism rallied others. In rural areas, where people understood little of theology, the will of the prince was sufficient to make men and women Lutheran or to keep them Catholic. Politics as much as religion determined the direction of the Reformation.

Anabaptists

One group of Christians that appeared at the time of the Reformation was inspired by Luther but felt that he had not gone far enough in repudiating the practices of Catholicism. These were the **Anabaptists,** who themselves divided over a number of issues according to divergent biblical interpretations. Anabaptist means to rebaptize. One thing all Anabaptists agreed upon was that only adults, once they had faith, should be baptized. Furthermore, people who had received baptism as infants had to receive the sacrament again.

Europe's rulers were unanimous in their efforts to suppress the Anabaptists, using the excuse that some advocated polygamy and others refused to pay taxes or fight in armies. Anabaptists were hunted down, imprisoned, drowned, or burned at the stake by royal armies. Anabaptist believers tried to keep a low profile to avoid problems but vigorously held onto their convictions. They survive today as Mennonites, Hutterites, and Amish Christians.

Reformers in Switzerland

Luther's attack upon Catholic doctrine spawned similar movements in Switzerland, a small country made up of Germans, French, and Italians. Here Huldrych Zwingli took on church authorities with the same enthusiasm that marked Luther.

Zwingli was a priest in Zurich when he first started preaching against the position of the pope, the veneration of saints, and clerical celibacy. Like Luther he insisted that only the Bible could be a guide to holiness and all other traditions should be ignored unless they had the sanction of the New Testament. Within a few years Zwingli convinced a number of the Swiss of his ideas. However, the more conservative forest cantons of the country rejected them. In 1531 Zwingli led an army against the forest cantons to persuade them of their errors and died in battle.

Zwingli was soon replaced by another reformer who took on the cause of Reform. This was John Calvin, who arrived in Switzerland from his native France the same year that Zwingli was killed.

While a law student at the University of Paris, Calvin was attracted to Luther's thought and joined those of like mind until they were warned that the royal government intended to arrest anyone espousing Lutheranism. This threat caused Calvin to travel to Basel, where he immediately set to work drawing up a statement of his beliefs addressed to the French sovereign, Francis I. Entitled *The Institutes of the Christian Religion*, it soon became recognized as the major literary work of the Reformation.

In the *Institutes* Calvin stressed that God is completely transcendent, in control of all that happens in the universe. A person is **predestined** either to act correctly or not because of what God has already decided. Eternal reward and punishment is the result of predestination. The good works of Catholicism were idolatrous, for they encouraged people to believe that they merited salvation. Luther's religion was too much centered on a human decision to profess faith to suit Calvin.

John Calvin led the Swiss reform from the city of Geneva.

In 1536 Calvin moved from Basel to Geneva, which had only recently adopted the Reformed faith. The rector at St. Peter's church invited him to join in his ministry, launching Calvin on his career. Calvin preached sermons lasting several hours in which he denounced all forms of sin as well as gambling, extravagant dress, dancing, and frivolous behavior of any kind. He intended that Geneva should become a city of God on earth with its citizens devoted to reading the Bible, praying, and living with a single-minded devotion to simplicity and sobriety.

City merchants were encouraged by Calvin's notion that even in this life the chosen or predestined will be blessed by God with prosperity. Though capitalism was not invented in sixteenth-century Geneva, it certainly received a spiritual blessing there.

Calvinism proved to be more international than Lutheranism. It found converts in young men flocking to Geneva from England, Scotland, France, the Netherlands, and Hungary. When they left the city's religious schools, they returned home eager to share their faith. Their disciples became the English Puritans, the Scottish Presbyterians, and members of the French, Dutch, and Hungarian Reformed Churches.

The Reformation in England

While the continental Reformation was in progress, the Tudor king, Henry VIII, acted to keep Lutheranism from England's shores. He wrote a treatise opposing Luther's doctrine that earned him high praise from Rome and the title Defender of the Faith from the pope. Several years later Henry was to add still one more title, Supreme Head of the Church of England, but for this he received no accolades from Rome.

England's church reform was different from events on the continent. It originated with the problem that Henry had no male heir to succeed to his throne.

Henry's wife was the Spanish princess Catherine of Aragon whom his father, Henry VII, intended should wed his elder brother, Arthur. However, only a few months after Catherine's arrival in England, Arthur died. Lest the Spanish alliance be jeopardized, Henry VII requested a Roman dispensation from church law that forbade a man to marry his sister-in-law. Pope Julius II was happy to oblige, and Henry and Catherine were wed.

By 1527 Henry and Catherine had been married for 20 years. Five children were born, but only one daughter, Mary, survived infancy. Henry, accustomed to success in most matters, was frustrated. He feared that a woman would be too weak to control the factions in England that were hostile to the Tudors.

Henry VIII claimed to be head of the Church of England.

Henry let it be known that he worried over the failure of his marriage to produce a son. Perhaps it was due to the circumstance that he had married his brother's wife. The king petitioned the then-reigning pope, Clement VII, to rule that his predecessor had erred and to grant an annulment. This would have permitted him to marry Anne Boleyn, a lady of the court and the woman he counted on to have his heir. The king appointed his chancellor, Cardinal Thomas Wolsey, to persuade the pope of his opinion.

Although Wolsey energetically presented Henry's case, the times were not propitious for Rome to give an affirmative answer. Popes do not like to reverse decisions of their predecessors. More importantly Pope Clement VII was then the prisoner of Charles V's army. Charles, who happened to be Catherine's nephew, informed the pope that in no way did he want his aunt disgraced by a declaration that she and Henry were not in a legitimate marriage.

Given such a dilemma, Clement VII began a series of delays hoping that time would bring a solution. As the months went by, Henry became more impatient. He fired Wolsey, fined the English clergy for making appeals to Rome, and forced the bishops of England to recognize that he was the head of the church, "in so far as that is permitted by the law of Christ."

In August 1532 Henry appointed his friend, Thomas Cranmer, to the archbishopric of Canterbury. Several months later the king secretly married a pregnant Anne Boleyn. Cranmer, on his authority, annulled the marriage to Catherine. However, the child born to Henry and Anne was a girl whom they named Elizabeth. They hoped a second pregnancy would bear a son.

Henry now sought and received from Parliament the title Supreme Head, this time with no qualifications. The lawmakers bestowed all papal rights and income on the king. Most members of Parliament wanted stability and agreed with Henry that he must have a son. They passed an Act of Succession that declared Mary, daughter of Catherine, was illegitimate and that heirs to the throne must be Anne's children.

All English officeholders were required to take an oath stating that they supported the settlement. The vast majority took the oath, including all but one of the nation's bishops. Henry's chancellor and well-known Humanist, Thomas More, also resisted the monarch's plans. More was both scholar and politician. He shared Erasmus's passion for church reform, but like Erasmus he felt no sympathy for Luther's or Henry's way of effecting it.

After Wolsey's dismissal, Henry had named More his chancellor, only to discover that he did not share his views on the king's claim to head the church. More was charged with treason for refusing to take the oath of supremacy and imprisoned in the Tower of London. Later the king ordered his head to be cut off and displayed on London Bridge.

Henry's next move was against the monastic orders. He ordered the confiscation of the English monasteries and convents, pensioned their inhabitants, and transferred their properties to the crown. The lands were then auctioned, and the money was used to pay the debts of the government.

In 1547 Henry died, leaving as heir Edward VI, a 10-year-old boy by his third wife, Jane Seymour. Edward was hardly of an age to determine the course of the nation. This became the province of his advisors, all of whom had their own interests uppermost in mind rather than those of the young king.

Archbishop Cranmer saw to it that the church, which Henry kept Catholic, should now shift toward Protestant views. He dictated sermons to be read on Sundays that denied that the Mass was a sacrifice. The Archbishop compiled and edited the *Book of Common Prayer*, an unusually beautiful text for the services of the Church of England, or Anglican, worship. A new ordination rite for priests and the consecration of bishops became official, and celibacy was abolished. This trend toward Protestantism continued until Edward's death in July 1553, leaving England as reformed as law could make it.

Politics and Religion in Ireland and Scotland

While Henry ruled, he pursued a much more active policy in Ireland. He had no illusions about the loyalty of Ireland's Gaelic-speaking natives who still lived in a society organized around clans. One of Henry's lieutenants who was sent to Dublin reported that rebellion was so much in their blood that only "compulsion and conquest" would quiet the Irish.

The test of Ireland's fidelity to Catholicism came during Edward VI's reign when Archbishop Cranmer ordered the clergy to use the *Book of Common Prayer* for worship rather than the familiar Latin *Missal*. English bishops and priests were sent to Ireland, but they could not speak Gaelic, so their efforts failed.

Scotland was a thorn in Henry's side. In 1513 King James IV, of the house of Stuart, was husband of Margaret, Henry's sister, but this did not lessen their hostile feelings toward one another. Twice Henry warred on the Scots and made plans to join their throne to England.

The Catholic Response to the Reformation

During the difficult times that struck the Catholic church in the early sixteenth century, many of the clergy sought to find a proper response to Protestantism. The idea that most frequently was put forward suggested that the pope summon a general council of the church's bishops to discuss reform. The Holy Roman Emperor Charles V believed that such a council would bring the Lutherans back into the church.

After long delays, in 1545 Pope Paul III invited the bishops to meet in the town of Trent, located in northern Italy, to deliberate the issues the Reformers had raised.

The Catholic bishops of Europe gathered at Trent to discuss the issues raised by the Reformers.

The bishops determined that Catholic doctrine could not be changed. Faith had to be joined to good works for justification. The bishops retained the Latin Mass and a celibate clergy so as to emphasize the special status of priests. Far from lessening papal authority, the pope received more duties. Some steps were taken to improve the discipline of the church. One change demanded that bishops live in their towns and forbade them to hold more than one office. Candidates for the priesthood were to receive special training in seminaries. There were to be no more indulgences given for donations. The Council of Trent laid the groundwork for the Catholic, or **Counter-Reformation.**

Catholicism benefitted from the organization of several new religious orders in the early sixteenth century. Angela Merici, an Italian woman, formed the **Ursulines,** a group of nuns dedicated to teaching in schools for girls. A Spanish woman, Teresa of Avila, restored discipline to the existing Carmelite Order.

The most important of men's new religious orders was the Society of Jesus, or **Jesuits.** Its founder was Ignatius Loyola, a Basque soldier who had fought and been wounded in his country's wars with France. While convalescing, he decided to devote himself to religious work when he recovered. Loyola gathered several disciples about him, and in 1534 he and his companions made a vow to form a religious order of teachers and missionaries. By the time of the founder's death, the Society had over a thousand members scattered in communities across Europe.

Ignatius Loyola, founder of the Jesuits.

Catholicism had an advantage in that most of Europe's kings and queens remained in the traditional faith. The exceptions were the Scandinavian monarchs and Henry VIII, and even Henry wanted no Protestant theology in the Church of England. In countries where royal patronage was denied, the Protestant religion enjoyed only limited success, primarily in the cities among the merchant and artisan class and in the countryside among nobles who found in Lutheranism and Calvinism a way to resist royal control.

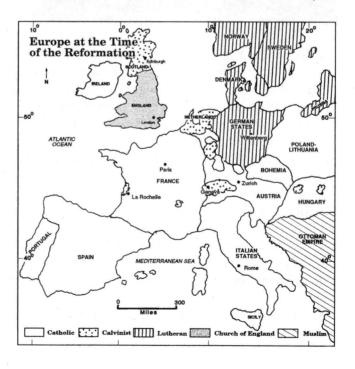

The Habsburg Ascendancy

The events that shook the religious life of western Europe took place at a time when the Habsburg family provided the major ruling house of Europe: represented by Charles I of Spain and his brother, Ferdinand of Austria. Charles's inheritance was the result of fortunate marriages between his grandparents and his parents.

Charles was born in Ghent in 1500 and always felt more at ease speaking Dutch than any other language. By the time he was 19, almost all the lands to which he had claim were his. Still, because the office was elective, Charles had to be chosen by the seven electors before he could assume the title of Holy Roman Emperor. In 1521 he was crowned at Aachen, Charles V of the Holy Roman Empire.

Charles was a staunch Catholic, and the fact that many of the German princes who resented Habsburg rule were in Luther's camp gave him sufficient reason to resist the Reformation. Although several times he went to war against princes who supported the Reformation, his victories were always fleeting. In 1529, when he ordered the laws against heresy enforced, the Lutheran princes protested, giving the name Protestant to the Reform.

Clashes between the Habsburgs and the Lutheran princes continued long after Luther's death. Nevertheless, in 1555 Ferdinand of Austria, brother of Charles V and his representative in Germany, and the Lutheran princes agreed upon a truce, known as the Peace of Augsburg. Its major provision ordered that the prince of a territory should decide the religion of his subjects.

There was no rest for Charles throughout his lifetime. The Spaniards resented his advisors from the Netherlands; at the very moment he left for the imperial coronation, the Castilians in Spain revolted. France was a constant problem. Its king, Francis I, was convinced that he must break the ring of Habsburg territories that surrounded his country. A series of wars with only short periods of intervening peace marked Charles's rule.

The royal palace in Granada was one of the many used by Charles V.

Charles also inherited the role of Christian Europe's protector against the Muslims. Spanish and imperial territories often came under attack from Islamic corsairs in the Mediterranean as well as from Ottoman armies in the Balkans.

Spain Overseas

While Charles ruled, great empires were brought down in the Americas and intrepid captains circled the world. A combination of courage and cruelty marked these early explorers who followed Christopher Columbus in their search for new lands and wealth to claim for the king of Spain.

The Portuguese were first to commence the age of European exploration, sending out expeditions to follow the coast of Africa until their ships should reach India. Within a year after Columbus's voyage, Ferdinand and Isabella requested the pope to draw a line of demarcation to separate Spanish finds from those of Portugal. In 1494 the Treaty of Tordesillas moved the line farther west, with Spain having the right to lands in the west and Portugal, to the east. This treaty placed Brazil within the Portuguese orbit.

Amerigo Vespucci, a Florentine who sailed to Brazil, gave his name to two continents, capturing the honor that should have gone to Columbus. To his credit Vespucci recognized that what he saw was not Asia, an opinion Columbus refused to accept. When the German publisher Martin Waldenseemüller published Vespucci's report, he gave the name America to the lands across the Atlantic. Further evidence that this was a wholly new world appeared in 1513 when Vasco Núñoz de Balboa crossed the Isthmus of Panama and discovered an ocean on the other side.

One of the truly magnificent voyages of all time was initiated by Ferdinand Magellan, a Portuguese in the service of Charles I. On a plea that he could reach the Spice Islands of southeastern Asia and claim them for Spain, he received limited support for his expedition. In 1519 Magellan left Europe, sailed across the Atlantic, and headed southward along the South American coast. Despite the loss of two ships, he convinced his crew to sail through the strait at the tip of South America that still bears his name.

For three long months Magellan was at sea until striking Guam. Ten days later he reached the Philippines. While there, he took sides in a local dispute on Cebu Island and was killed. His lieutenant, Juan Sebastián de Elcano, took charge of the sole remaining ship and guided it back to Spain where it arrived in September 1522. Only 35 men safely returned. The price of the expedition was high, but Europeans now knew that Asia could be reached by sailing west and that between Europe and Asia lay a huge continent and the vast Pacific Ocean. The importance of Spanish discoveries was to give Charles an immense source of wealth to carry on his many wars in Europe.

Toward the end of his life, Charles was resigned to the fact that his goals of keeping Habsburg territories intact and Catholicism preserved within them were beyond his strength. He divested himself of some responsibilities when he handed over his rule of his lands in Italy, the Netherlands, and Spain to his son Philip and made sure the imperial title went to his brother Ferdinand. In 1557 he retired to a monastery and died a year later.

Charles was an intelligent and sincere man, but he lacked the broad vision needed for leadership. The peoples he governed did not like him. They could think only of the taxes required to pay for his many wars. Spaniards were unhappy about financing an army in Germany, while Germans wondered why they should support a Mediterranean fleet.

Protestants resisted his religious policy, and the French and Ottomans constantly fought him. The vast riches of the Americas evaporated in the imperial wars. Charles tried to deal with all these problems, but each one demanded his full attention. The complexities of the early sixteenth century were beyond the abilities of Charles or anyone else to address in one lifetime.

France under Francis I

The driving ambition of King Francis I, one of the most brilliant men ever to hold the French crown, dominated politics after he came to power in 1515. Francis was the model Renaissance prince—suave, poised, handsome, and fond of display, as well as a fancier of the arts. He thought himself both a scholar and a warrior and surrounded himself with courtiers from the nobility who gladly served him. His architects covered the country with palaces to promote the notion of royal ubiquity.

Francis I commissioned the building of the castle of Chambourd.

Francis I watched religious events as they unfolded across the Rhine. Although he welcomed Luther's revolt against his archrival Charles V, because anything that gave the Habsburgs trouble promoted his own cause, it was a different story when Protestant thought came into France. The king already controlled church appointments and received a substantial income from a portion of church taxes. More importantly, he identified public loyalty to his throne with fidelity to Catholicism.

Calvinism rather than Lutheranism proved more attractive to those Frenchmen who did accept the Reform. They were called **Huguenots** and numbered less than 10% of the population, in absolute numbers about 750,000 people. Most were of urban middle class background, similar to the Genevan citizens who were Calvin's most loyal followers.

In 1521 Francis first invaded northern Spain and then sent an army into Italy against the duchy of Milan, a territory Charles claimed as Habsburg land. In 1525 the imperial army defeated Francis at Pavia, leaving him so desperate that he confessed, "Nothing is left to me but honor and life." Charles imprisoned Francis in the Alcazar of Madrid until he agreed to renounce all French claims in Italy. Released from prison and safely back in Paris, Francis retracted his promises and sought allies among the Italian city-states and the pope.

This alliance proved to be more of a disaster for Pope Clement VII than for Francis. In 1527 Charles V's victorious army marched into Rome. Many of the troops were German Lutherans, delighted to occupy the capital of Catholic Europe. The soldiers who had not been paid for months besieged Clement in the Castel Sant'Angelo and pillaged church treasures, ending the brilliant days of the Renaissance in Rome.

Italy in the Reformation Era

The exhausting struggle between the French and Habsburgs to dominate Italy sapped the strength of many of the city-states that were once so strong and independent. The resources of the city-state could not compete with the larger and more populous territorial nations.

The fate of Venice demonstrates the problem of the Italian states. Already in 1508 French and Spanish forces made common cause with both the emperor and the pope in a rare moment of cooperation to humble the once-proud city. The Venetians were severely defeated, saved from the worst only by dissension within the ranks of their adversaries.

Rome was at the center of Renaissance artistic life at the opening of the sixteenth century. Pope Julius II prized artists almost as much as military victories. He commissioned Raphael to decorate the Vatican Palace so that it might be a fitting residence for the popes. Leonardo Da Vinci was also a resident of Rome until 1517. To Julius's credit he recognized the genius of Michelangelo and set him to work painting the ceiling and walls of the Sistine Chapel. Julius also commissioned him to carve a statue of Moses to decorate his tomb.

The statue of Moses by Michelangelo.

Pope Leo X, a true Florentine, continued his predecessor's attention to music and the arts. He was a composer himself and dined to the music of wind ensembles. He was entranced by Michelangelo's work, as well he might be, for the artist had already distinguished himself with his magnificent sculptures and paintings.

In his old age Michelangelo was called upon to provide one more service to the church. Pope Paul III asked him to design the apse and dome of St. Peter's, which he wanted to be much higher than that envisaged by Donato Bramante, the principal architect.

Italy's foremost authors during the Reformation period concerned themselves with history and politics despite the overwhelming interest in art that pervaded their time. Probably the most popular book on politics ever composed was Niccolò Machiavelli's *The Prince.* It appeared in 1513 following the author's diplomatic career serving the Florentine state. *The Prince* argued that those who govern must be firm, clever, and above all pragmatic.

Peoples of East Europe in Reformation Times

The Reformation era affected the people of East Europe in different ways. For the Polish people the Renaissance and the Reformation occurred at the same time. Italian Humanists found a hearty welcome in the country where they introduced the latest Renaissance thoughts to their hosts. Painting and architecture flourished, and poets for the first time used Polish as a sophisticated literary language.

Both Lutheran and Calvinist missionaries brought the Reformation into Poland. The gentry, the small landowners, embraced Calvinism for political and economic as well as religious reasons. Allegiance to Protestantism helped them in their struggle to remain independent of royal authority and domination by the magnates, the Polish nobility.

It was for Hungarians that the sixteenth century produced the most dramatic events. In 1521 the Ottoman sultan, Süleyman II sent word to Louis, the young king of Hungary, that he expected to be paid tribute in return for allowing him to rule his country. Louis's advisors convinced him to refuse. The Ottomans then marched northward and took Belgrade. Located where the Danube and Sava Rivers meet, Belgrade was the key to any further advance into central Europe. A series of successful campaigns found the Turks in the late summer of 1526 on the plain of Mohács in southern Hungary. Louis's outmanned forces were defeated, and the king himself drowned as he fled the field. Süleyman occupied Buda in September but then withdrew to Istanbul, taking with him 100,000 enslaved Christians.

The people of central Hungary were crushed. Buda, once a thriving capital, became no more than a village. In the countryside a sullen peasantry worked for Turkish rather than Hungarian lords with little beyond the necessities of life to keep them at their task.

After Louis's death the Habsburg Ferdinand of Austria became king of Royal Hungary, a narrow corridor of lands bordering Austria. Later the Bohemian Diet, meeting in Prague, opted for Ferdinand to become their king. By midcentury Ferdinand was also elected Holy Roman Emperor, leaving no doubt that he had claim to recognition as the strongest figure in central Europe. Ferdinand I and his Habsburg descendants stood guard on Christendom's eastern border as Holy Roman Emperors and kings of Bohemia and Hungary for the next 300 years.

In the sixteenth century Russia was a strange and foreign country to West Europeans with customs more Asian than European. Its self-contained Orthodox Christianity meant foreign ideas, such as Protestantism, had no means of entry. No university or printing press had a presence there.

The Grand Prince of Moscow after 1505 was Vasily III whose father was Ivan the Great and mother, the Byzantine princess, Sophia Palaeologina. Vasily's mother gave him a claim to the heritage of the Roman Empire for she was a niece of the last emperor of Constantinople.

Selim I and Süleyman II Lead the Turkish People

Two extraordinary men held the Ottoman sultanate during the Reformation era: Selim I and Süleyman II, whom Western historians have named the Magnificent. The Ottoman Empire now ruled directly or indirectly all of the Balkan Orthodox Christians: Greeks, Serbs, Romanians, Bosnians, Albanians, Macedonians, and Bulgarians.

Selim, whom his subjects knew as the Grim, directed his attention to the Orient more than toward Europe, adding Southwest Asia and Egypt to Ottoman territories. In 1520 when the victorious sultan was poised to lead Turkish armies against his European enemies, he died unexpectedly, leaving his legacy to his son Süleyman.

Süleyman brought the Ottoman Empire to the height of its prestige and influence. His Turkish people formed an elite from Hungary to Egypt, and his capital, Istanbul, became the most populous city of the eastern Mediterranean. To further his expansionist plans, Süleyman cultivated the **Janissary Corps,** made up of Christian boys recruited from Balkan villages and converted to Islam. He also handsomely rewarded the *sipahis,* the native Turkish cavalry, with land and booty wherever Ottoman arms added new territories to his domain.

In 1529 Süleyman brought Ottoman forces to the gates of Vienna and placed the city under siege for several weeks. Then cold weather intervened and the Janissaries, not accustomed to fighting under winter conditions, insisted on returning to their camps near Istanbul.

The tomb of Süleyman the Magnificent was built next to his mosque in Istanbul.

For the Turkish people Süleyman is remembered as the great lawgiver, a ruler who sought to better the lives of his Muslim subjects. To western Europe he was viewed as the Great Lord, the intrepid challenger to Christian Europe's existence.

Conclusion

All western Europe was never united under a single political structure, but religious belief for centuries provided a bond for its people. In the early sixteenth century, that bond was broken when Luther, Calvin, and Henry VIII urged a different view of Christianity.

The Reformers asserted that the Catholic church had fallen into error in its teaching. The issue was a serious one because religious people were very much concerned about theology. If pope and bishops were, in fact, in error, then everyone's eternal destiny was in jeopardy.

The Reformation was meant to purify the Catholic faith, but it resulted in dividing European Christianity in the West. Today well over a thousand Christian churches exist, each claiming to speak in the name of Jesus of Nazareth, its founder.

At the very time the Reformation was in progress, the Habsburg brothers, Charles and Ferdinand, were consumed by constant warfare to keep their territories intact. The gold and silver brought into Spain simply passed through that country in order to finance the Habsburg armies scattered across Europe's battlefields. To the east, two able Ottoman sultans, Selim I and Süleyman, challenged not only the Habsburgs, but all Christian Europe.

CHAPTER 1 REVIEW
REFORMATION EUROPE

Summary
- There was dissatisfaction with the Catholic church in western Europe around 1500 because of inadequate leadership.
- Humanists urged that the clergy be held to a higher level of education.
- The issue of offering indulgences for donations to St. Peter's was offensive to many Catholics.
- Martin Luther's attack on indulgences provided the spark that set off the Protestant Reformation.
- Charles V, Holy Roman Emperor, sought to discourage Protestantism through military action.
- John Calvin instituted a reformation in Switzerland.
- Catholicism held on in southern Europe and Ireland, aided by sympathetic monarchs and newly founded religious orders.
- Henry VIII's reformation kept Catholic doctrine intact, but made the sovereign of England the head of the church.
- A constant battle went on between the Habsburg rulers of Europe and the French and Ottoman Turks.
- The early sixteenth century was a great age of discovery for Europeans.

Identify
People: Julius II, Leo X, Humanists, Erasmus, Luther, Emperor Charles V, Zwingli, Calvin, Henry VIII, More, Cranmer, Francis I, Michelangelo, Süleyman, Ferdinand of Habsburg, Vespucci, Alexander VI, Clement VII, Thomas Wolsey, Edward VI, Columbus, Balboa, Magellan, Machiavelli, Selim I
Places: Wittenberg, Geneva, Canterbury, Rome, Venice, Mohács, Bohemia, Istanbul, Brazil
Events: rebuilding of St. Peter's in Rome, Diet of Worms, peasant revolt, Peace of Augsburg, Council of Trent, circumnavigation of the world, Treaty of Tordesillas

Define

Protestant	tithe	indulgences
Protestant Reformation	Ursulines	penance
justification	Jesuits	Counter-Reformation
Anabaptist	predestination	
Janissary Corps	Huguenots	

Multiple Choice
1. The rebuilding of St. Peter's began while he was pope:
   - (a) Leo X
   - (b) Pius XII
   - (c) Alexander VI
   - (d) Julius II

2. Humanists were scholars who advocated
   (a) better legal protection for women and children.
   (b) reforms in the monarchy.
   (c) cheaper book prices.
   (d) reforms in the lives of the clergy.

3. Among the Humanists, the preeminent figure from 1500 to 1520 was
   (a) Erasmus.
   (b) More.
   (c) Francis I.
   (d) Julius II.

4. An indulgence
   (a) forgives sin.
   (b) allows a person to sin without guilt.
   (c) forgives the penance due to sin.
   (d) reserves a church position for a candidate.

5. Luther taught at a university in
   (a) Wittenberg.
   (b) Erfurt.
   (c) Worms.
   (d) Augsburg.

6. Luther's doctrine claimed that
   (a) good works were needed for salvation along with faith.
   (b) faith alone was sufficient for justification.
   (c) clergy and lay people were very different.
   (d) the Bible was to be interpreted through church tradition.

7. Anabaptists insisted that
   (a) infants be baptized at an early age.
   (b) infants be baptized by immersion.
   (c) faith precede baptism.
   (d) only a clergyman can baptize.

8. John Calvin's doctrine emphasized
   (a) prayer.
   (b) reading the Bible.
   (c) the sacraments.
   (d) predestination.

9. Calvin's headquarters were in
   (a) Wittenberg.
   (b) Zurich.
   (c) Bern.
   (d) Geneva.

10. Henry VIII's chancellor that first sought to have his divorce recognized by the pope was
   (a) Wolsey.
   (b) Cranmer.
   (c) Cromwell.
   (d) More.

11. She was the daughter of Henry VIII and Catherine of Aragon:
    (a) Jane Seymour
    (b) Mary Tudor
    (c) Mary Stuart
    (d) Elizabeth

12. She was the daughter of Henry VIII and Anne Boleyn:
    (a) Jane Seymour
    (b) Mary Tudor
    (c) Mary Stuart
    (d) Elizabeth

13. This treaty ended the religious wars in the Holy Roman Empire:
    (a) Cleves's Accord
    (b) The Paris Accord
    (c) The Peace of Vienna
    (d) The Peace of Augsburg

14. Calvinists in Scotland were known as
    (a) Huguenots.
    (b) Puritans.
    (c) Presbyterians.
    (d) Anglicans.

15. The French contemporary of Emperor Charles V was
    (a) Henry I.
    (b) Henry II.
    (c) Philip III.
    (d) Francis I.

16. The major defeat of the Hungarians took place at
    (a) Buda.
    (b) Pest.
    (c) Szeged.
    (d) Mohács.

17. His ships first sailed around the world:
    (a) Magellan
    (b) Drake
    (c) Dias
    (d) Da Gama

18. He gave his name to the Americas:
    (a) Vespucci
    (b) Magellan
    (c) Balboa
    (d) Elcano

19. Ignatius Loyola founded
    (a) the Loyolans.
    (b) the Jesuits.
    (c) the Ursulines.
    (d) the Dominicans.

20. The farthest a Turkish advance ever reached into central Europe failed outside
    (a) Mohács
    (b) Vienna
    (c) Venice
    (d) Budapest

Essay Questions
1. Discuss the issues raised by Luther's Reform.
2. Was the Reformation a success?
3. How did the Catholic church respond to the Reformation?
4. Why were Europeans able to make voyages of discovery in the sixteenth century?
5. What were the connections between the artistic enhancement of Rome and the Reformation?

Answers

1. d	6. b	11. b	16. d
2. d	7. c	12. d	17. a
3. a	8. d	13. d	18. a
4. c	9. d	14. c	19. b
5. a	10. a	15. d	20. b

CHAPTER 2

Europe in a Time of Dynastic and Religious Wars

Religious and dynastic problems dominated Europe in the latter part of the sixteenth century. The fallout from the Reformation was still obvious. So also were the contests among the European monarchs to enhance their territories and the prestige that went with governing more lands and collecting more revenue. Catholics fought Protestants, Frenchmen warred with Spaniards, Poles sent armies to do battle with the Russians.

In its most elementary sense the European scene presented a struggle between the House of Habsburg and all other monarchs of western Europe. The Habsburgs, nephew and uncle, Philip II of Spain and Ferdinand I of the Holy Roman Empire, seemed so formidable that the rest of Europe's monarchs feared for the future. Was it possible that western Europe would become a Habsburg preserve?

Philip II's Spain

In 1556 at the age of 28, Philip of Habsburg became King of Spain. His inheritance included large parts of Italy, the Netherlands, and all Spanish America. At this time he was married to Mary Tudor, Queen of England, with the result that Philip's interests extended over a much broader area than his own domain encompassed.

Philip II sought to keep all Habsburg territories intact.

Philip took all his responsibilities quite seriously. He had the same two goals that motivated his father: to strengthen the hold he had on his territories and to uphold the Catholic church in each of them. Philip had a crusading spirit and a devotion to meticulous detail that fitted him for the task. He was probably the most hated man in late sixteenth-century Europe, but he thought of himself as kind and patient. The great castle that he built at Escorial, with its heavy walls and dark brooding appearance, reflected the personality of the man who lived within.

To pay for his army and bureaucracy, the Spaniards groaned under heavy taxation. There was never enough money. Commerce and industry languished under a 10% sales tax. Several times the king defaulted on loans causing economic havoc in the government.

Philip was intolerant of religious dissent in Spain and used the court of the **Inquisition** to promote his views. He was especially concerned that converts to Catholicism from Judaism, **Marranos,** and from Islam, **Moriscos,** were less than sincere. Constant harassment led to a Moriscos revolt that shook the nation over years in cruel, bloody battles. While the Morisco War was in progress, Philip received word of an equally disturbing threat to his rule in the Netherlands.

Revolt in the Netherlands

Seventeen separate provinces composed the Netherlands, each accustomed to little interference with its internal affairs so long as taxes were paid. Three ethnic groups lived here: the Dutch in the north, Flemings in the central area, and French-speaking Walloons in the south. A representative body, the States General, with delegates from the provinces met to discuss common concerns. By this time a slight majority of people in the Netherlands were converts to Calvinism or the Anabaptist churches.

Opposition to Philip coalesced around William of Nassau, Prince of Orange. William became the champion of the Dutch Calvinists, although he seems to have had little personal interest in religious affairs.

Philip was convinced that peace in the Netherlands could be had only with a strong Spanish garrison in place. Therefore he dispatched the Duke of Alba with 10,000 men to secure the country. The duke presided over a court that heard the cases of political and religious dissenters. Those found guilty were so numerous that the duke's court became known as the Council of Blood.

Walls surround the Alhambra royal palace in Granada, a city that held a large number of Moriscos.

In spite of the increase in Spanish soldiers, the insurrection continued. Rebel Dutch sea captains were able to gain control of the city of Brill and its coastline. The Spanish army could not dislodge them nor do anything to counter Dutch supremacy on the seas. Philip recalled the Duke of Alba and sent a new commander to the Netherlands but to no avail. Failure to pay the Spanish forces created a mutinous spirit, and in November 1576 the city of Antwerp was savagely looted in an incident known as the Spanish Fury.

Three years later Alexander Farnese, one of Philip's lieutenants who was dispatched to the Netherlands, by persuasion and bribery regained the Walloon and Flemish provinces for Philip. In an agreement known as the Treaty of Arras, the ten provinces of the south again recognized him as their sovereign, but the seven northern provinces continued the conflict under a coalition, an alliance called the Union of Utrecht.

The trend now favored Philip because the Dutch lost their leader, William of Nassau, when he was assassinated. For a while confusion reigned in the Dutch camp until Queen Elizabeth of England sent 5,000 infantry and cavalrymen to keep the rebellion alive.

Although the end of the conflict was not to appear for another 50 years, it was obvious that the Netherlands' seven provinces of the north, would never again accept Spanish sovereignty.

Union with Portugal

The Portuguese nation fell into the hands of Philip as a result of a chain of circumstances. Because his mother was a Portuguese princess with a claim on the throne, Philip directed the Spanish army to move into

Portugal when a vacancy occurred on the throne. Philip promised that Portugal would remain autonomous and to prove his good will settled in Lisbon for the next three years. Although the nobility accepted Philip, he was never able to gain the loyalty of a majority of the Portuguese people.

Philip and the Mediterranean

Philip constantly had to concern himself with Mediterranean affairs. Each year Muslim fleets raided the coasts of Spain, Italy, and the islands of the Mediterranean carrying off thousands of hapless people to be enslaved in North Africa or in Ottoman lands.

This Venetian fortress on Corfu held out against all Ottoman attacks on the Greek Ionian Islands.

In 1570 the Spanish king commissioned a Habsburg fleet in response to an urgent appeal from the pope to form a Holy League. Cyprus, an island in the eastern Mediterranean where the Venetians provided the government but where Orthodox Christians were a large majority of the population, was under Turkish attack. Don Juan, Philip's half-brother, was called upon to lead the League's navy to aid the Venetians. The fleet came too late, and Cyprus fell. In the following year, however, the Christian fleet discovered the Turkish ships in winter quarters in the Corinthian Gulf port of Lepanto (now Naupaktos). The Ottoman admirals hastily ordered their men to return to the galleys and rowed out to meet the Christians. Don Juan's superior artillery and warships sank many of the Turkish vessels after three hours of battle, and the remainder fled. The Christian victory at Lepanto was the last great sea battle in which galleys were employed.

Philip and the Armada

Philip's experiences with England were all unfortunate. First, there was his doomed marriage to Mary Tudor; second, English pirates constantly harrowed Spanish ports and vessels in the Americas; and finally, Queen Elizabeth's troops reinforced the Dutch rebels. In 1588 Philip ordered the formation of a great Armada to put an end to English vexations. His admirals brought together 130 ships, 8,000 sailors, and 19,000 soldiers.

The navy was to sail into the English Channel to transport the Spanish army in the Netherlands to England. The Armada set sail with confidence, but the fleet soon ran into problems from heavy seas. In addition, in the Channel the large Spanish galleons were easy targets for the more maneuverable English vessels. The Armada was never able to approach the English coast but sailed around Scotland and Ireland before straggling home with the loss of 54 ships and thousands of men.

The high seas of the English Channel and the British navy kept the Armada from landing on the English coast.

In assessing the long reign of Philip, his many defeats and disappointments must be balanced against his considerable success in managing Spain and his other European possessions. His goal of preserving the Habsburg legacy intact was probably an impossible one.

Elizabethan England

In 1553 King Edward VI died, leaving as heir his half-sister, Mary Tudor. The hereditary principle was so strong in the minds of English men and women that there was little opposition, despite the law that denied her the English throne. Mary's first wish was to make England Catholic again. Shortly after her accession, she persuaded Parliament that she was not the supreme head of the Church of England. Therefore, England and Rome were once again united, and the religious, but not the economic, changes made during the reign of Edward VI were repudiated. Those who held monastic properties kept them.

Mary's religious policies were ill-advised. She actively persecuted the Puritan wing of the Anglican church, creating some 300 martyrs, among them Archbishop Cranmer of Canterbury, and earning herself the title of Bloody Mary.

Mary's political decisions were equally unfortunate. On the advice of Emperor Charles V, she agreed to marry his son, Philip. Her subjects feared that the marriage would undermine English interests in favor of Spain.

Their childless marriage was also without affection. Philip's concerns were focused on events in his native country and the Netherlands. Upon the death of his father, Philip left England to take up his duties on the continent, and Mary stood publically abandoned and disgraced. Moreover, her health was poor. She suffered from severe headaches and a rare disease that carried the symptoms of pregnancy. This contributed to periods of depression and hysteria. Her subjects felt little sympathy for her, and she died after ruling only five years. The religious settlement was once again to be overturned, for Elizabeth, the remaining daughter of Henry VIII, was a young woman whose sympathies matched those of her father.

Elizabeth, while outwardly conforming to the restoration of Catholicism, at heart had remained an Anglican throughout her half-sister's reign. Within a year of her coronation in 1559, Parliament passed legislation restoring the Anglican church and prescribing the *Book of Common Prayer* for worship.

The queen was a remarkable ruler. Elizabeth had the charisma of her father. The queen's charm allowed her to rule in authoritarian ways, keeping Parliament and the upper classes contented with financial and social privileges. The legislation she wanted adopted by Parliament was prepared in her Privy Council and then submitted to the Houses of Parliament where it received the vote of the members.

Queen Elizabeth I, sovereign of England.

The economic stability of the country can be explained by the vigor and success with which Englishmen took to the sea in the Elizabethan age. English cloth merchants anxiously looked for new markets, wherever they could be found. Captains of the age, such as John Hawkins and Francis Drake, harassed the commerce of Spain and seriously impaired its links with Mexico and South America.

The fact that the queen had no husband, and hence no direct heir, troubled many of her subjects. It was a subject that the queen herself did not care to discuss. She used her single status as a diplomatic weapon in the conduct of foreign affairs, for nearly all European princes of marriageable age were anxious to find a throne for themselves by wedding Elizabeth.

Another reason for concern was the fact that living on English soil under house arrest was Mary Stuart, former queen of the Scots. In 1568 Mary had fled for her life from her rebellious subjects and sought sanctuary under her cousin's protection. As a Catholic and the closest relative of the Tudor house after Elizabeth, she represented a significant threat to Elizabeth's throne. Conspirators against the queen used Mary as their foil. After 19 years of hesitation, Elizabeth had Mary executed for treason in February 1587.

Mary Queen of Scots lost her life because she represented a threat to Elizabeth.

A year later Elizabeth and the English nation were threatened by Philip II's great Armada. This was the single greatest menace she ever confronted, and the English victory greatly enhanced the queen's popularity.

The last years of Elizabeth's reign, from the defeat of the Armada until her death in 1603, were not so pleasant. Economic difficulties plagued the crown when the costs of the war with Spain and a rebellion in Ireland had to be paid. The gentry and merchants who now sat in Parliament were not as willing as their fathers to accept the queen's guidance. They resisted her regulating the economic life of the nation through granting monopolies and licenses. Many of these political dissenters were also Puritans who bridled at Elizabeth's retention of bishops and the *Book of Common Prayer.*

Scotland

For the Scots the events that had brought Mary, their queen, to her untimely death began unfolding some 50 years earlier. The movement leading to Mary's downfall was directed by John Knox, a faithful disciple of Calvin whose fiery denunciation of her rule proved to be the queen's undoing.

In 1542 Mary Stuart had inherited her throne while still a child upon the death of her father, James V. The kingdom was in reality governed by her French Catholic mother, who was also named Mary, a member of the Guise family. In order to hold off English threats, Scotland was increasingly linked to the continent with French armed forces stationed in Edinburgh. When it was time for her betrothal, Mary was married to Francis, son of King Henry II of France.

In 1559 Knox inspired a revolt supported by the Scots of the Lowlands. Elizabeth sent troops to aid the rebels, forcing the French to leave the country. With the French gone, the Scottish Parliament voted to abolish papal authority and to adopt a profession of faith outlined in Knox's tract, *The First Book of Discipline.*

Mary returned to Scotland but found herself isolated. A new marriage brought forth an heir, the future James VI, but her fate was sealed after she fled to sanctuary in Elizabeth's England. Mary's tragic life has given authors and playwrights ample opportunity to expand on her misfortunes ever since.

Ireland

Elizabeth's policies toward Ireland meant disaster for a majority of the Irish. Her father, Henry, the first to bear the title King of Ireland, ruled the island directly from London. Elizabeth was well aware that the Irish still held to Catholicism and regarded English officials in their country as foreigners. Irishmen were constantly making their way to Rome and Madrid to sound out the pope or the Spanish king on projects to overthrow her rule.

In 1579 Gerald Fitzgerald, Earl of Desmond, led one more attempt to oust the English. Elizabeth's troops scoured the Irish countryside, burning the villages and crops and driving off the cattle upon which the population depended for their food.

The last and final rebellion of Elizabeth's reign took place in Ulster under the leadership of the O'Donnells and the O'Neills. Prompted by Irish hatred for the queen, Hugh O'Neill moved against the English garrisons in Ulster and Connaught in the west. A contingent of 4,000 Spanish infantrymen landed in Ireland to keep the rebel army in the field. Nevertheless, Elizabeth's commander, Charles Blount, Baron Mountjoy, defeated the Irish. In the long run Elizabeth's policies in encouraging English plantations and enforcing Anglicanism did little but ensure that Ireland would constantly be a hotbed of revolution.

The Religious Wars in France

For the French people the latter half of the sixteenth century was a turbulent period that witnessed a succession of bitter civil wars between the Catholics and Calvinist Huguenots. The nation's energies were sapped by this contest in which both sides vied for the kingship, convinced that a final victory could be obtained only if a member of their own faith held that position.

The austere worship in a Huguenot church consisted of prayers, hymns, and a sermon based on a biblical text.

In 1572 Henry of Navarre, a Bourbon prince and a Protestant, was to marry Margaret of the Catholic Valois dynasty, placing him in line to succeed to the French throne. To honor the event, thousands of Huguenots streamed into Paris. The Guise party saw the marriage as an opportunity to strike at their enemies. They used the queen-mother as their intermediary, persuading Catherine to convince her son, Charles IX, that the Protestants intended to seize his throne. On the night of St. Bartholomew's feast day, August 24, the Guise soldiers joined by royal troops fell upon the unsuspecting Huguenots. All of Paris became a scene of murder and pillage.

The massacre of St. Bartholomew's Day was meant to forestall the Huguenots coming to power in France.

Both the Guise party's Catholic League and Philip of Spain were determined to block Henry's accession, for he had survived the events of August. In 1589 he claimed the kingship. One by one, Henry defeated the armies sent against him. Meeting in the Estates General, the French nobles, clergy, and prominent members of the Third Estate pondered over their choice. A solution became easier when Henry announced a conversion to Catholicism, making him acceptable to his countrymen who were still of the traditional faith. In 1594 Henry entered Paris to become Henry IV, King of France with the quip, "Paris is worth a Mass."

After 40 years of conflict, the French people desperately needed peace, and the monarchy was the only institution that could provide it. Absolutism was welcomed as an alternative to chaos. With the Spanish army driven from France, Henry felt strong enough to issue the Edict of Nantes in April 1598. This gave the Huguenots freedom of conscience, permission for public worship in specific places, and equality before the law. Certain fortresses were to be held by the Huguenots to protect themselves against attack.

In addition to bringing religious peace to France, Henry IV was faced with restoring confidence in royal government. He chose an economic advisor, the Duke of Sully, who had a clear vision of how to ensure the royal treasury's solvency. Sully found new sources of income for the state and brought order into its confused system of tax collecting.

Unfortunately for France, in 1610 these well-considered efforts came to an abrupt halt when a religious fanatic plunged a dagger into King Henry. The nation mourned him, for he had a personal charm that made him very popular. He once said of himself, "I'm gray on the outside, but gold within."

The Empire and Italy

Although Ferdinand I of Austria had planned to rule the Holy Roman Empire effectively, he was frustrated because his territories were so fragmented among its many princes and city-states. The Habsburg ruler discovered that he could do little to direct the empire's affairs. Divisions between Catholics and Protestants were so mixed with political factions that there was no way to untangle them.

The religious divisions of the Germans were not found in Italy, but the same kind of political forces prevented any kind of unification in the peninsula. Italians still thought first of their attachment to the city where they lived. The centrifugal forces dominating the peninsula were abetted by foreign powers whose partisans within Italy acted on their behalf.

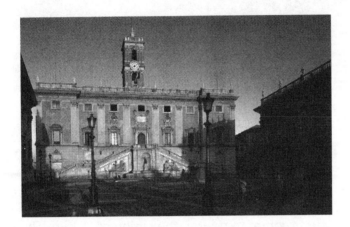

The Palazzo Senatorio was the center of Rome's administration in the sixteenth and seventeenth centuries.

A visitor to Rome would have found that city a lively one late in the sixteenth century, heartened by the gains of the Counter-Reformation. The popes acted vigorously to enforce the Council of Trent's decisions wherever that was possible. Pius V published the *Roman Catechism,* a book that became the religious handbook for Catholic education. Framed in response to Luther's *Great Catechism,* it was in use for the next 400 years.

By 1600 the religious boundaries of Europe had become fixed much as they are today. Southern Europe and Ireland remained within the Catholic church, while northern Europe was now Protestant.

The Baltic Contest

For the Danes the latter sixteenth century proved to be an unfortunate one because King Frederick II in 1563 dragged them into a conflict with Sweden. Frederick's ambition was to rule both in Stockholm and Copenhagen so for a long seven years his armies went to war to realize his plan.

Those who profited most from Danish exhaustion at the conclusion of the war were Dutch seamen who entered the Baltic with enthusiasm. The Dutch easily outdistanced the enfeebled cities of the Hanseatic League, which was once the great commercial power of the Baltic. The Dutch carried grain, furs, fish, and naval supplies from the eastern Baltic to ports in western Europe where there was great demand for those products.

Sweden's rise to political prominence was a result of the Vasa dynasty's ability not only to hold off the Danish threat to their throne, but also to expand into the eastern Baltic. The kings in Stockholm were never hesitant to dispatch their army into this region if it gave them more land to govern and advantages to their merchants in the Baltic trading zone.

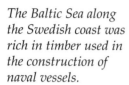

The Baltic Sea along the Swedish coast was rich in timber used in the construction of naval vessels.

Poland and Lithuania Form a Commonwealth

In 1569 Swedish and Russian intervention in the Baltic prompted the Poles and their neighbors to the east, the Lithuanians, to form a single commonwealth under a common ruler in the Union of Lublin. The Lithuanians agreed to send delegates to the Polish Diet and to look to Sigismund Augustus II as their king within the newly created state. On the other hand, the Lithuanians retained their own legal system and army. The area of Belarus was to be kept within Lithuanian administration, but Poland would manage Ukrainian affairs.

Three years after the formation of the Commonwealth, Sigismund died heirless, and with his death the medieval Polish dynasty lost its last representative. The nation's nobility and gentry proposed that the Poles elect their king. At a time when the rest of Europe saw nations moving toward stronger monarchies, Poland went in exactly the opposite direction.

For a time Poland chose a Frenchman, then a Hungarian, and finally a Swedish monarch, Sigismund III Vasa, to become the Polish sovereign. Sigismund, a zealous Catholic, aided the Jesuits in repelling Protestant inroads into Poland. In addition, the king cultivated a movement among the Orthodox bishops of Ukraine who resented what they considered interference in their affairs by the Greek Orthodox patriarch of Constantinople. In 1596 a majority of Ukrainian bishops joined the Catholic church transferring their allegiance from Constantinople to Rome.

At the close of the sixteenth century, the Commonwealth of Poland-Lithuania was the largest state in eastern Europe. It was a sprawling territory that included tens of thousands of Belarussians, Ukrainians, and Jews, none of whom enjoyed full civil rights.

The Jewish population of Poland-Lithuania grew in importance as its numbers increased. In 1551 King Sigismund Augustus reconfirmed Jewish autonomy, which allowed Jews to elect a kahal, a board of commissioners to direct affairs within their communities. A judicial and educational system appeared, supervised by rabbis charged with settling disputes and overseeing young men in the study of the Torah and the Talmud.

The Russian State under Ivan the Terrible

In 1547 Ivan IV, son of Vasily III and Helen Glinsky, was crowned tsar of all the Russias. During his minority Ivan was at the mercy of his mother and several noble, or *boyar*, families. When he came of age, he was determined to assert his independence. In 1550, to free himself from boyar interference, Ivan summoned the first Zemski Sobor, the Assembly of the Land, with personally chosen members, circumventing the boyar Duma, or council, that formerly gave the tsar its opinions.

Soon afterwards Ivan's armies went to war to bring the Tartar state of Kazan under Muscovite control. Later he overwhelmed the Astrakhan khanate on the lower Volga River, opening the whole course of the river to Russian colonization. These campaigns were such great victories that he commissioned the construction of St. Basil's church in Red Square to commemorate them.

Ivan IV had St. Basil's church built to commemorate his victories over the Tartars.

Ivan became more autocratic as he got older. In addition, he suffered from paranoia. Many of the high boyars fled to Lithuania, fearing for their lives. Dismayed at their defection, Ivan packed his belongings and left Moscow for a village 50 miles distant.

Moscow's city officials pleaded with Ivan to come back, promising that he could do as he wished to rid the country of those who opposed him. Ivan did return and appointed military officers known as *oprichniki* to scour the land and rid it of his enemies. Wearing black costumes and riding black horses with a dog's head on the saddle, the oprichniki covered the land, raiding the boyars' estates and putting suspected opponents of the tsar to death. After eight years of turmoil, the boyar class and the clergy, the two major foundations of all Russian life prior to Ivan's times, were decimated.

Terror and human suffering filled the remainder of Ivan's reign. The tsar probably was never completely insane, but neither was he mentally balanced. Despite his instability and his title "terrible," Ivan's rule was a significant one since the size of Moscow's dominions more than doubled.

In 1584 Ivan's son Feodor, who was even more eccentric than his father, succeeded him. Feodor's main interest was in church services, especially the ringing of bells. Ivan had appointed a regency council to manage the realm because even he was aware that it was quite beyond Feodor's capabilities. One of the five regents who made up the council was Boris Godunov, who had been Ivan's confidant but had never been party to his excesses. Boris married his sister to Feodor, allowing him to obtain easy access to the tsar. Other boyar families deeply resented Godunov's influence.

During his lifetime Ivan had taken seven wives. The last of these gave him a son named Dmitry, but he was considered illegitimate by the church and therefore ineligible to inherit the throne. Feodor's regency council, to be sure that the boy would cause no problems, exiled Dmitry and his mother. Seven years later, when the boy was ten years old, he died, killed on the order of Boris Godunov or accidentally, no one is sure. At the time the incident was soon forgotten, but because Feodor was childless, the dynasty of Rurik, which had ruled Russia since the ninth century, was apparently doomed.

During Ivan's time, in the frontier areas of Ukraine, between the Russians and the **Crimean Tartars** (the remnant of the Mongols who had invaded Russia in the thirteenth century), a nation of fugitives and frontiersmen led a separate existence. These men were the Cossacks, organized into several bands whose leader was known as hetman. The Cossack way of life mixed primitive farming and herding with robbery. No women were allowed in the Cossack camps. Numbers were kept up due to a stream of recruits who joined their ranks to avoid the taxation and forced labor of Muscovite lands.

The Ottoman Empire

The rule of Süleyman II the Magnificent came to an end in 1566 while the aged sultan was on campaign in Hungary, a fitting conclusion to a life that he devoted to the expansion of the Turkish lands. His legacy included an empire based upon a strong economy, an updated legal structure, and an army that was one of Europe's best. Süleyman could boast that he had purged the empire of Muslim Shi'ites, whom he regarded as heretical, just as Philip II thought of Protestants. The price the sultan paid for orthodoxy was to allow the *ulema,* the Muslim judges and theologians, to have a much stronger influence on state policy. Highly conservative and traditional in their world view, the ulema sought to keep any new ideas from entering the Ottoman world.

Süleyman's successor was the incompetent Selim II, son of his favorite wife, Roxolana. Selim's accession began a succession of sultans who were the favorites of the harem run by their mothers. In order to cope with the cost of government, offices and honors were sold to the highest bidders, and corruption was all-pervasive in the civil bureaucracy.

In 1570 Selim directed the Ottoman fleet against Cyprus, which fell to the Turks. When the Ottomans landed on the island, many of the Greeks living there were willing to take up arms against their Venetian lords. After the conquest Cypriotes who belonged to the Catholic faith either were killed or fled abroad, and their churches were destroyed or turned into mosques.

The Balkan Christians during Ottoman times continued to worship in Byzantine churches.

Life for Balkan Christians living under Turkish rule became more onerous whenever the central government's authority weakened. Local landowners were much more exacting and arbitrary than the sultan's officials. Because taxation and rents were increasingly burdensome, some villagers took to a life of brigandage in the mountains. These were the **klephts** of Greece and the **haiduks** of Serbia. They raided Turkish caravans and, when these were lacking, nearby towns. A romantic tradition surrounded them, although their actions were brutal and violent.

The Structure of Society in Sixteenth-Century Europe

In western Europe much of the economic structure of feudalism had been dismantled by the close of the sixteenth century, yet society still functioned much as it had in the Middle Ages.

At the very top of society were the Holy Roman Emperor and Europe's kings who, with their families, lived lives of leisure and luxury. Their subjects and courtiers believed that they had a mandate from above to govern wisely, and even when they did not, it was likely that excuses were made for them. Nothing could be more important to a dynasty than a favorable marriage. At times weddings affected the destinies of Europe more than war. The Austrian Habsburgs were especially adept at picking the right partners. A saying was abroad, "Others make war, but you, lucky Austria, marry."

The nobility were quite a varied group by the late sixteenth century. Descended from the knights and nobles of the Middle Ages, some had become princes of major territories, wealthy and powerful magnates who could challenge the king's power. This was especially true of the central European kingdoms. Other aristocrats barely eked out an existence, but they retained their titles. They were called barefoot nobles because for one reason or another their families had lost their land and money.

The 95% of the remainder of the population were townspeople and peasant farmers. They were Europe's laborers. Most asked little from life and, in turn, received little. Within the towns those who worked hard rose above their fellows. They formed a merchant class, the *bourgeoisie*, which in economic terms often equaled or even surpassed the nobility.

There were some improvements in society's attitudes toward women. All the Protestant Reformers believed that marriage was a public act and society had a duty to oversee its regulations. In Catholic Europe the Council of Trent's legislation forbade clandestine, or secret, unions. The law now required that husband and wife pronounce their vows before a priest and several witnesses. This protected women who formerly had been abandoned by their husbands with impunity. Trent included marriage as one of the seven sacraments. On the other hand, Luther and Calvin viewed marriage as a civil contract and felt that each state should be free to devise its own legislation on the matter.

For the single woman in Protestant countries, convent life was no longer an option. Therefore, she became more dependent than ever on her family. Reformation mores joined with middle class values to hold up the dutiful housewife, always obedient to her husband, as the model of femininity.

Cloth-making was one of the many tasks of women in sixteenth-century Venice

The life of upper class wives, whether Protestant or Catholic, continued much as before. They had to oversee the upkeep of the house, manage the servants' activities, care for the sick, and organize meal preparation. A good portion of the day was consumed in overseeing the distilling of beverages.

Homes were more comfortable. In the late sixteenth century glass windows allowed more light, and mattresses and pillows of feathers replaced the straw pallets and hollowed logs of earlier generations. Homes of the wealthy had private chapels testifying to the piety of the age.

In England and in many other regions on the continent, it was still the practice among the nobility to send young children away from home at seven or eight years of age. Friends, an uncle, or an aunt took on the responsibility for their education. This child exchange was considered essential for the strengthening of social bonds between families.

In Catholic countries children had their own special celebrations. At the time of First Communion, parents and friends showered gifts on the child. On Twelfth Night, the close of the Christmas season, children and parents enjoyed a wide range of special dishes for eating, and afterward the whole family joined in games.

Sixteenth-Century Science

It should not be thought that religion and politics were the only concerns of sixteenth-century men and women. Progress in the sciences brought better understanding of the universe and the human person in a number of areas.

The most exciting of sixteenth-century discoveries were in astronomy. A Polish cleric, Nicholas Copernicus (Kopernik), made studies that convinced him that the Ptolemaic system could not adequately explain the movement of the heavenly bodies. He contended that the earth was in motion, rotating daily on its axis and making an annual circuit around the sun. Copernicus reached his conclusions not from data obtained from direct observation, for the telescope had not yet been invented, but from plotting the path of the planets mathematically, a task that Arab astronomers before him had already accomplished.

Copernicus placed his findings in *Concerning the Revolution of the Celestial Orbs* but delayed publishing it because he feared that his conclusions were too controversial in a world convinced that the Bible was also a book of astronomy. It was only after his death in 1543 that his work circulated in Europe's scholarly circles, setting the stage for a whole new view of the physical universe.

The next step in astronomical discoveries appeared in the work of a Danish astronomer, Tycho Brahe. He studied planets, comets, and what is today called a supernova. Brahe's studies convinced him that the stars were not fixed and that the planets did not travel in perfect circles. Brahe's thorough investigations placed astronomy on a sure basis, but it was still too soon for universal acceptance of a universe in which men and women would live on a small planet circling a sun among a myriad of stars.

Growing interest in astronomical investigation in Rome made possible greater accuracy in chronology. Pope Gregory XIII is known for his reform of the calendar that bears his name. In 1582 the pope's calendar, which dropped ten days from the Julian calendar, came into use in Catholic countries. Protestant and Orthodox European states were slow to accept such a

A contemporary woodcut shows Brahe in his observatory.

radical change advocated by a pope and continued to use the Julian calendar several centuries longer.

Sixteenth-century scholars made advances in mathematics and engineering. An engineer, Simon Stevin, from his experience in designing fortifications in the Netherlands, was the first to invent a decimal system that could be used for fractions. Another practical scientist was Georg Bauer, better known as Agricola, who wrote on mining and metals, establishing a primer for early mineralologists.

In 1543 Andreas Vesalius, an instructor at the University of Padua, introduced the scientific study of anatomy. Previously doctors learned about the human body from studying Galen's text, a work written during the second century. Vesalius used actual cadavers in the classroom for his instruction, a practice soon adopted by other medical instructors.

The Arts

Italians dominated the artistic world of the late sixteenth century. From all over Europe students came to marvel at the creations of Michelangelo and Raphael. The Italians were willing to concede that they were second best only in music, behind the composers and conductors from the Netherlands.

In the field of architecture the name of Andrea Palladio ranks before all others. In his Villa Rotonda, where a massive country home was built as a cube with a low dome on top, he established a principle of construction that Thomas Jefferson used at Monticello. Palladio wrote a four volume work on architecture that had immense influence on the style known as classicism.

The most famous painter of the day worked in Spain. He was Domenikos Theotokopoulos, better known as El Greco. Born in Venetian Crete about 1541, he came to Venice to study art. As the most wealthy monarch in Europe, Philip II invited El Greco to his court.

Philip commissioned him to paint the altarpiece in the chapel of St. Maurice in the Escorial. Today this is considered one of El Greco's masterpieces, but the Spanish king found it too unconventional for his taste. Its vivid use of color, the abundance of light and shadow, and the spiraling action that takes the viewer up to heaven did not please Philip. El Greco found a new patron in the archbishop of Toledo.

El Greco's contemporary in Flanders was Pieter Brueghel, but the style of his work and inspiration could hardly have been more different. Brueghel's subdued palette pictured the Netherlands' villagers and peasants going about their daily lives—eating, working, and drinking. No triumphant saints are pictured on Brueghel's canvases, but rather the hard life that his countrymen had to endure in an age of conflict with Spain.

Brueghel's picture of a biblical scene actually portrays a Spanish force entering a Dutch village.

Opera first appeared in the late sixteenth century at Florence. It grew out of the desire to revive ancient Greek theater using themes from classical stories. Opera became popular in other Italian cities where wealthy patrons employed dramatists, singers, and experts on scenery to stage lavish productions on the occasion of important festivals.

English theater developed its distinctive style at the close of Elizabeth's reign. The first permanent locations for players to perform were built in London. One of these playhouses was the **Globe Theater,** and here in the last decade of the sixteenth century a group of professional actors known as the Lord Chamberlain's Company brought William Shakespeare into their ranks. Shakespeare proved himself to be an outstanding dramatist and a giant of English literature.

William Shakespeare, the greatest playwright of English literature.

Shakespeare composed an average of one or two plays each year until his death in 1616. He seems not to have acted himself or to have taken only minor parts. Shakespeare lived at a time when English literature excelled. He did much to make it a medium of expression never before reached in any language.

Conclusion

The second half of the sixteenth century in western Europe belongs to two able sovereigns, Philip II of Spain and Elizabeth I of England. Intense rivals, they represented their nation's ambitions to hold a dominant position on land and sea. Elizabeth's successful challenges to Philip on the Atlantic and in the Netherlands foreshadowed England's rise to the commercial leadership of Europe. War appeared to be more normal than peace, at least as long as kings and queens would not content themselves with their inheritances.

In East Europe a wide disparity existed between the upper classes and the peasantry. The latter were tied to the land of the nobility, working throughout their lives on the owner's behalf. Privileges in society were reserved for the upper class.

The Polish-Lithuanian commonwealth planned to halt Moscow's expansion, but the task was beyond it. The Ottoman Empire, so dependant on military victories for its success, suffered a major setback at Lepanto.

Copernicus's hypothesis on the position of the earth in the solar system initiated a new way of thinking about the universe, preparing the way for the scientific revolution of the seventeenth century.

CHAPTER 2 REVIEW
EUROPE IN A TIME OF DYNASTIC AND RELIGIOUS WARS

Summary
- The latter sixteenth century witnessed many conflicts over religious and dynastic matters.
- Philip II, Habsburg ruler of Spain, was the most powerful king of continental Europe.
- The people of the Netherlands rose in revolt against Philip's religious and economic policies.
- Elizabeth, daughter of Henry VIII and Ann Boleyn, was a very effective monarch of England.
- A major contest for the French monarchy kept that country in turmoil until Henry of Navarre became ruler in 1589, the first of the Bourbons to do so.
- Poland and Lithuania formed a commonwealth to balance the growing power of Russia.
- In western European society, much of the medieval feudal structure was gone, but in eastern Europe serfdom became even more onerous.
- The greatest advance in science was the publication of Copernicus's views on the solar system.

Identify
People: Philip II, William of Nassau, Mary Tudor, Mary Stuart, John Knox, Henry of Navarre, Guise family, Ferdinand I of Austria, Cossacks, Copernicus, Brahe, Palladio, Shakespeare, Elizabeth I, Ivan IV, Feodor, Godunov
Places: Antwerp, Brill, Cyprus, Ulster, Nantes, Stockholm, Ukraine, Kazan
Events: wars of Philip II, Battle of Lepanto, the Armada, St. Bartholomew's Day massacre, Formation of the Polish-Lithuanian Commonwealth

Define

Marranos	Globe Theater
Moriscos	Crimean Tartars
Inquisition	oprichniki
Puritans	ulema
Concerning the Revolution of the Celestial Orbs	klepht

Multiple Choice
1. The empire of Philip II at the beginning of his reign did not include
    (a) Spain.
    (b) the city-states of North Italy.
    (c) the Netherlands.
    (d) the Holy Roman Empire.

2. Philip's castle was called
    (a) the Escorial.
    (b) the Louvre.
    (c) the Alhambra.
    (d) the Alcazar.

3. The Netherlands sent representatives to an assembly called
   (a) the Diet.
   (b) the Parliament.
   (c) the Assembly of Notables.
   (d) States General.

4. Spain added this country to its territories during the reign of Philip II:
   (a) Portugal
   (b) Navarre
   (c) the Netherlands
   (d) Milan

5. Philip's decision to send the Armada was a result of
   (a) English attacks on Spanish ships in the Americas.
   (b) the claim he had on the throne from his marriage to Mary Tudor.
   (c) Elizabeth's aid for the Dutch rebels.
   (d) all the above.

6. The husband of Elizabeth of England was
   (a) Philip II.
   (b) Edward VI.
   (c) Francis I.
   (d) none of the above.

7. The Reformation in Scotland owes its success to
   (a) Elizabeth.
   (b) Mary, Queen of Scots.
   (c) James V.
   (d) John Knox.

8. The defeat of the O'Neills in Ireland resulted in
   (a) the introduction of English settlements in Ireland.
   (b) Elizabeth's granting Ireland to Gerald Fitzgerald.
   (c) Philip II's dispatch of the Armada.
   (d) Irish independence in the British Isles.

9. The most aggressive state in the eastern Baltic was governed by the
   (a) Habsburgs.
   (b) Tudors.
   (c) Danes.
   (d) Vasas.

10. Sweden's capital was
    (a) Copenhagen.
    (b) Helsinki.
    (c) Danzig.
    (d) Stockholm.

11. Poland's leaders decided in the sixteenth century that their ruler should be
    (a) hereditary in the Vasa family.
    (b) hereditary in the Valois family.
    (c) elected.
    (d) chosen from the Lithuanians.

12. Moscow's famous St. Basil's church was built to commemorate Ivan IV's victory over
    (a) Poland.
    (b) Lithuania.
    (c) Smolensk.
    (d) Kazan and Astrakhan.

13. The hetman was a leader of
    (a) Gypsies.
    (b) Ukrainians.
    (c) Livonians.
    (d) Cossacks.

14. Selim II used his army to conquer
    (a) Crete.
    (b) Rhodes.
    (c) Cyprus.
    (d) Athens.

15. The bourgeoisie are people who belong to
    (a) the nobility.
    (b) the clerical class.
    (c) the French Protestant church.
    (d) the urban middle class.

16. Women of the sixteenth century had to be adept at
    (a) teaching public school.
    (b) public speaking.
    (c) serving in church services.
    (d) distilling beverages.

17. Copernicus placed the center of the solar system
    (a) in the Milky Way.
    (b) on the earth.
    (c) at the sun.
    (d) in Jerusalem.

18. A reform of the calendar was promoted by
    (a) Copernicus.
    (b) Brahe.
    (c) Bauer.
    (d) Pope Gregory XIII.

19. Vesalius's name is associated with the study of
    (a) minerals.
    (b) engineering.
    (c) astronomy.
    (d) anatomy.

20. Spain's most prominent painter in the sixteenth century was
    (a) El Greco.
    (b) Brueghel.
    (c) Raphael.
    (d) Palladio.

Essay Questions
1. Why was there so much hostility toward the Habsburgs in sixteenth-century Europe?
2. What were the successes and failures of Queen Elizabeth in England?
3. Why did astronomy become the leading science of the sixteenth century?
4. Describe the class structure of sixteenth-century Europe.

Answers

1. d	6. d	11. c	16. d
2. a	7. d	12. d	17. c
3. d	8. a	13. d	18. d
4. a	9. d	14. a	19. d
5. d	10. d	15. d	20. a

CHAPTER 3

An Age of Kings

Throughout the Middle Ages nobles and churchmen had hemmed in the monarchs as best they could with limits placed on their authority. By 1600, however, the Reformation had diluted the political power of the church, and the self-interest that motivated the aristocracy was more likely to bring anarchy than ordered government. As a result, the only remaining authority that had the resources needed to field large armies, build prisons for lawbreakers, and collect taxes was Europe's kings.

There were exceptions: the condemnation and execution of their king showed that English men and women might suspend their loyalty to the monarchy. In the Netherlands, Switzerland, and Venice, republican traditions were deeply rooted. Among larger states Poland also presented an exception. Elsewhere this was the great age of monarchy, a period of European history that accelerated the process of bringing nations under a single ruler, the king.

Absolutism and Society

Because of intermarriage, nearly all European monarchs were related and were a mixture of several nationalities, but this did not stop them from making war upon one another. Even enlightened political theorists saw no reason why men should not willingly die on behalf of their monarchs. The king had become an awesome figure and received the adulation that once was given to the holy men and women of the Middle Ages.

By the end of the seventeenth century, sovereignty was understood to rest on secular rather than religious grounds. The old view, which held that the king's authority depended upon God's will, was very influential in 1600, but by 1700 monarchs did not appeal to God but to their armies to get acquiescence from their subjects.

Wealthy landowners from Ireland to Russia enjoyed a life of leisure supported by the peasants who labored on their estates. It is difficult to generalize about the nobility of Europe, but on the whole it can be said that they monopolized the important positions of church and state. Their privileges were many; their responsibilities, few. Even in this age of absolutism, local government remained almost completely in their hands.

The law in European nations was written on behalf of the landowning class, the nobles, and the high clergy. Crimes against property were severely punished. Insolvent debtors were imprisoned, at best a self-defeating measure, until they could pay up. Wealthy merchants in the towns did not count for much until they invested in a rural estate and possibly bought themselves a noble title.

The kings allowed many offices of state to be purchased. Indeed, in times of economic distress, creating new titles was one way for the royal treasury to become solvent. Seventeenth-century noblemen and women loved titles, ceremony, and majestic processions in which they could show off their finery.

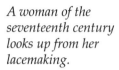

A woman of the seventeenth century looks up from her lacemaking.

Demographics

In 1600 the French and Germans were the most numerous Europeans: each group approached 15,000,000 people. Italians ranked third in population, counting about 10,500,000. Spain numbered 8,000,000 and shared the Iberian peninsula with 1,500,000 Portuguese. English men and women had increased to 4,500,000, while the Irish and Scots together were less than 2,000,000. Three million people lived in the Netherlands, which was about one-half million more than lived in Scandinavia. The mixed population of Poland-Lithuania stood at 7,000,000 of whom 750,000 were Jews. Estimates of the Russian and Ukrainian population vary widely, but 7 to 9,000,000 should be close. The Hungarians, ravaged by war, were now 3,000,000 men and women. Balkan Christians held their own at 7,500,000, while the Turkish population stood at 1,000,000 in Europe with an equal number living in Asia. A million Crimean Tartars were settled north of the Black Sea. Gypsies lived a nomadic life all over the continent, perhaps 500,000 people in all. Western Europe's largest cities were London and Paris, both holding close to 200,000 people, while Amsterdam was half their size.

Civil War in England

In 1600 England was more politically united than any state in Europe. The English people shared a common language and law with only a single parliament. The majority were of the same Anglican religion, although important minorities of both Puritans and Catholics were also present.

When Queen Elizabeth died in 1603, her next of kin was the Scottish king, James VI, son of Mary Stuart whom Elizabeth had executed. He was crowned James I but soon began to irritate his subjects because of his ideas on government. James wrote of kingship in an essay, "The True Law of Free Monarchy," in which he proposed that a ruler must be absolutely free to make decisions. This was a divine right, vested in the monarch by God himself.

James, however, ran into difficulties when he sought to put his doctrine into practice. Most Englishmen came to regard him as an obnoxious foreigner who had little knowledge of the country or its people. His blustering repelled them, and they soon agreed that James was "the wisest fool in Christendom."

King James I, first monarch of the Stuart dynasty.

A major problem for James dealt with religion. James much preferred the Anglican church over all others because he was its head. He looked to the church to assist him, and he, in turn, supported the church. As James explained the situation, "No bishop, no king." On the other hand, the Puritans claimed, "Christ Jesus is the king of the church whose subject King James is, and of whose kingdom, he is not a king, nor a lord, nor a head, but a member."

In 1604, at a meeting between the Puritans and the Anglican bishops, a number of issues were raised; one of them was a request for a new translation of the Bible. In 1611 a commission of translators completed their work and published the King James Bible. This became the standard English translation and did more to shape the further development of the language than any subsequent publication.

There was still a Catholic minority left in England, which was covertly served by perhaps 200 priests. A small group of conspirators among the Catholic gentry plotted to assassinate James in order to restore the country to the traditional faith. In November 1605 these conspirators secretly had barrels of gunpowder placed under the Parliament buildings for the moment when the king and members would be in attendance. Unfortunately for the plotters, a Catholic nobleman was warned by a mysterious letter to avoid the session. In London James's ministers were alerted. A search of the basement revealed the gunpowder and a soldier-of-fortune, Guy Fawkes, nearby with fuses. The unmasking of the Gunpowder Plot caused penalties and heavier fines to be placed on those known to be Catholics. England had reason for a new holiday, Guy Fawkes Day, in which the highlight of the celebration was to set fire to a straw image of the pope or Fawkes.

The Catholic cause fared poorly in Ireland. Soon after James's accession Hugh O'Neill offered his submission to the king. James allowed him to return to his home and estates as a landlord, not a prince. Four years later, O'Neill along with about a hundred of his followers voluntarily abandoned Ireland and left for exile on the continent. The "flight of the earls" gave the English government exactly what it wanted.

Ulster Catholics were left defenseless. James placed colonies of Anglicans and Scottish Presbyterians on confiscated lands to secure the province. The estates of the Ulster counties were parceled out to any person who would settle Protestant farmers on it and build a castle for its defense. Although Catholic Irish peasants stayed on in Ulster, the majority were dispossessed.

James's son, Charles I, inherited all the problems of his father. His personality was hardly appropriate for the task, for Charles was a quiet person who enjoyed art, reading, and hunting and found public life a burden. Born in 1600, a second son, he was never expected to rule. It was only when he was four years old that he began to talk, and throughout his life he had a speech impediment. Probably this was the result of having had rickets in his infancy, a common disease among children of the seventeenth century. Rickets also affected his ability to walk because it left him with abnormally short legs.

In 1628 under the leadership of Edward Coke and John Eliot, Parliament drafted a Petition of Right, which affirmed that the king's power did not extend to the person and property of English men and women. It further stated that the king could not tax without Parliament's consent, forbade martial law in peacetime, and prohibited arbitrary arrest.

Charles' response to this document and others like it was to dissolve Parliament and after 1629 personally to rule the country. Like his father, he had to resort to a variety of stratagems to provide revenue. One of these was the right of the king to collect ship-money from coastal towns for the upkeep of the royal navy. When Charles extended the collection to inland cities, a Puritan, John Hampden, became a hero for his refusal to pay.

A devout Anglican, Charles added to his problems by taking the advice of Archbishop William Laud to require a liturgy based on the *Book of Common Prayer* for worship in Scotland. Scottish Presbyterians vowed to form a league to defend their traditional worship and would have nothing to do with Anglicanism.

In order to respond to the Scottish challenge, Charles had no choice but to call Parliament back into session. Three weeks later, it was evident that nothing productive would be forthcoming, so Charles sent the members packing. This session has received the name, the Short Parliament, in contrast to the Long Parliament, which soon followed. Several months passed and a chastened king who now needed funds to suppress an Irish revolt and to oust a Scottish army in the north of England had no recourse but to ask the members to return. This Long Parliament was not so easily dissolved.

There was good cause to think that the Puritans might bring charges against the queen, so Charles himself made his way to Parliament to arrest six leaders whom he charged were treasonous. They escaped, leading to Charles's decision to leave London. He collected an army at York while Parliament's leaders did the same around London.

By the summer of 1645, Parliament's soldiers, the New Model Army consisting of single-minded Puritan men was ready for combat. They were ably commanded by individuals like Oliver Cromwell and soon had the royal forces on the run. Oxford, now Charles's capital, was surrounded, and in May 1646 the king had to escape from the city in disguise and seek sanctuary with a Scottish army that he thought supported his cause. Later the Scots betrayed the king and returned him to England as a prisoner.

Meanwhile, a split developed between the English Presbyterians and the Independents, one more Puritan group that identified with Cromwell. His position was so secure that he threw the Presbyterians out of Parliament. The remaining 60 Independents voted to place Charles on trial as a public enemy. The king refused to plead in his defense, was convicted, and was executed on a cold January morning in 1649. For the first time in its history, England turned toward a republican form of government, and both monarchy and the House of Lords were abolished.

An executioner displays the severed head of King Charles I.

Only in Ireland forces loyal to Charles were still in the field, but in October 1649 Cromwell's army of Puritans landed in Ireland determined once and for all to settle the country's rebel streak. The New Model Army's attack upon the Irish brought death and destruction to the inhabitants of that country. After a long and bitter siege of the town of Drogheda, a massacre that signaled the Puritans' decision to spare no one took place.

The collapse of Irish resistance allowed Cromwell to confiscate the lands of most Catholic clan chieftains and distribute them to his followers. The "Curse of Cromwell" and the inability of the remaining clan chieftains to cooperate among themselves shaped Irish history for the next two centuries.

The Growth of the Dutch Republic

The most prosperous people of Europe in the early seventeenth century lived in the seven United Provinces of the northern Netherlands. This was a remarkable feat because the Netherlands had no great natural resources. The country was mostly flat farmland that was created by pushing back the waters of the North Sea. Along the coast the Dutch turned to the sea and became the largest shipbuilders in Europe and its most enterprising merchants.

By constructing dikes along the North Sea, Dutch farmers extended their farmland.

The internal life of the Netherlands was quite distinct from other states in Europe. Religious tolerance flourished; in this part of Europe, Calvinists, Catholics, Lutherans, and Anabaptists learned to live together. The Netherlands often served as a haven for persecuted religious minorities from other countries, such as the Puritans of England. When the Jews left Portugal, many settled in Amsterdam, where their industry contributed to that city's economy, and their schools made the town a center of Jewish scholarship.

Artists from the Netherlands distinguished themselves in the seventeenth century. Peter Paul Rubens enhanced an already impressive Flemish tradition of painting in his homeland and throughout Europe. His canvases are full of pink-cheeked cherubs and gods and goddesses in swirls of color. Rembrandt van Rijn, who took up residence in Amsterdam in 1631, painted with such intensity that his work has been compared to drama.

The Rise of France

The two strongest political powers in early seventeenth-century western Europe were France and Spain. In 1600 Spain was judged to be the stronger of the two, but by mid-century their positions were reversed. The much more numerous French people, with their religious wars behind them, entered into a time of prosperity and soon outdistanced the overextended Spaniards.

The assassination of Henry IV left his ten-year-old son Louis XIII as heir to the throne. The queen-mother Marie de' Medici served as regent, but she was incompetent and put her trust in worthless favorites to direct the government. The government was soon bankrupt, forcing the queen to summon the Estates General. As many anticipated, the estates spent their time complaining.

While Marie planned his future for him, young Louis XIII was left in the charge of court servants and a physician whose constant concern was to regulate his bowel and sexual habits. His adolescence made Louis a neurotic for the rest of his life.

As Louis grew older, he and his mother had their differences. Happily for France's future the queen-mother had made one outstanding choice for the position of court chaplain, Armand du Plessis, Duc de Richelieu. Richelieu acted to moderate the tension between mother and son. In 1622 his reward was a nomination to the cardinalate, and two years later he was named chief minister of the king.

Because the king much preferred music and hunting to governing the country, Richelieu supervised the direction of the state. His aim was clear: "My first goal was the majesty of the king, the second was the greatness of the realm." To put this policy into effect, Richelieu planned three steps: to destroy Huguenot political power, to reduce the nobility to the king's authority, and to strike at the Habsburgs everywhere in Europe. France was to become Europe's preeminent nation with "One faith, one law, one king."

Cardinal Richelieu sought to enhance the power of the French king.

In 1624, the very year he assumed power, Richelieu ordered the construction of a fort near La Rochelle, the major Protestant stronghold on the Atlantic coast. Threatened by this decision, the Huguenots responded with armed resistance. Richelieu successfully isolated the town by building a wall across La Rochelle's harbor and turning back an English fleet sent to relieve the siege. In October 1628 La Rochelle surrendered. In the aftermath Richelieu confirmed Huguenot religious liberty, but all Protestant forts were ordered dismantled, and Huguenot self-government abolished.

Richelieu's goal of diminishing the power of the nobility was also effective. Using his sense of what was possible, he allowed noblemen to have a monopoly on state offices, but his spies kept watch on them to thwart any independent activities.

Richelieu's foreign policy concentrated on restricting the Habsburgs at every opportunity. Because the Austrian Habsburgs were engaged in the Thirty Years' War after 1618, the French poured subsidies into Protestant German principalities to keep the contest alive.

Richelieu's statesmanship and ruthlessness brought the country political greatness and made the power of the French king as secure as one man could ever make it. Louis XIII died soon after his minister, leaving an infant son under the regency of his wife, Anne of Austria. Anne kept in office, as chief minister, Giulio Mazarin, a Sicilian who was already a cardinal.

After a Spanish defeat at the battle of Rocroi, the cardinal's plan was to pursue the Habsburgs to the bitter end. In 1648 when the Treaty of Westphalia concluded the Thirty Years' War, Mazarin could rest content. The Holy Roman Empire remained divided, and France gained the province of Alsace. Mazarin was now free to deal with Spain. Victory did not come so easily here. The war did not end with a French victory until 1659.

The Decline of Spain

Across the Pyrenees to the south of France, the Spanish kingdom was a study in contrasts. On the exterior Spain appeared very strong, but its strength was an illusion. The particularism of its regions—Castile, Aragon, Catalonia, and Andalusia—was as firm as ever.

King Philip III was the opposite of his meticulous father in temperament. He allowed the government to be run by his ministers. When in 1622 a Dutch captain captured the whole Caribbean flotilla, the Spanish government's budget was thrown into chaos, for it depended on the annual arrival of bullion from the Americas for its survival. Even more damaging in the long run was inflation. The cost of goods purchased by Spain constantly increased at the very time its precious metal supply was falling. When debasing the coinage no longer worked, the government sold the right to collect state revenues to Genoese bankers.

Ultimately Spain's downfall occurred because of its involvement with France. In 1636, drawn into the Thirty Years' War in support of Ferdinand of Styria, his cousin, Philip IV employed the resources of his country to provide munitions and men for armies wherever they were needed.

Unrest in southern Italy, the disastrous defeat at Rocroi, and its exhausting war with France after the Treaty of Westphalia eroded Spain's remaining strength. The Spanish soldier, poorly paid and seldom on time, no longer frightened the rest of Europe. The Spanish sailor was no longer master of the seas.

In 1640 the Portuguese rose against the Spaniards while Philip IV was distracted by a Catalonian rebellion. Aided by the French, the Portuguese regained their independence.

It was said that Philip IV, born on Good Friday, only laughed three times in his life. It is easy to see why. The early seventeenth century was a melancholy time for Spain, relieved only in part by its great artists and authors.

This was the era of Miguel de Cervantes Saavedra whose *Don Quixote*, published in 1608, quickly became one of the world's most popular stories. Cervantes' contribution to literature was unique. No one else in his time approached his talent for writing fiction.

The Thirty Years' War

The worst of the conflicts that plagued this century was the Thirty Years' War, which determined the future of the German people for centuries to come. Their lands were devastated for three decades as army after army crossed over them. The toll in lives and property damage was greater than in any previous conflict in European history.

The occasion for the opening of the Thirty Years' War was an event that took place in Bohemia, although the stage was set earlier when German princes formed two leagues—one Protestant and one Catholic. Before his death in 1619, the childless emperor Matthias named his candidate for the throne, Ferdinand of Styria. In Prague resentful Czechs threw his representatives out a window, an incident known as the Defenestration of Prague.

In November 1620 Count Johann von Tilly, commander of the Catholic Union's army, met the rebellious Bohemians at White Mountain just outside Prague and defeated them. Ferdinand replaced the rebels with Habsburg loyalists from all over the empire. The first, or Bohemian phase of the Thirty Years' War, had ended with a total Habsburg victory.

Tilly then moved his army eastward, conquering several German Protestant principalities. Fearful that a united Catholic Germany was in the making, Christian IV, the Danish king, came into the war on behalf of the Protestant cause. This began the second phase of the war, but Tilly easily disposed of the Danes.

An artist has painted the horrors of the Thirty Years' War.

The war might have ended here except for a number of circumstances that came together after 1627. Cardinal Richelieu financed the Swedish king, Gustavus II Adolphus, to take up the battle against the Habsburgs. In 1630 Gustavus crossed into Germany with his Swedish army. For the next two years Gustavus's Swedes proved how capable they were. In November 1632, however, at the battle of Lützen, although the victory went to the Swedes, Gustavus Adolphus was killed. Swedish military strength never recovered from the loss.

When Ferdinand III replaced his father as Holy Roman Emperor, he genuinely wanted peace. He opened negotiations with his enemies, promising that he had abandoned any idea of actually ruling the empire. On that basis in October 1648, after more than four years of deliberation, the combatants signed the Treaty of Westphalia.

This treaty ensured that the several hundred principalities of the Holy Roman Empire were free to govern themselves and the emperor's title was to remain little more than honorific.

Italy

At a time when much of Central Europe was torn by war, the Italian city-states stood aside. There was still money in Rome to build palaces and fountains. Most of the popes' concerns continued to center on promoting their families' interests and patronizing the arts. They were elected late in life, because the cardinals did not want anyone to hold office for long.

Seventeenth-century Rome preferred the **Baroque style,** a highly decorative type of architecture, sculpture, and painting. Artists sought to capture religious sentiment in a dramatic fashion with religious figures portrayed in feverish motion, clothed in swirling drapery, and depicted with superhuman features. Soon the style moved into Europe's courts. The spectator was meant to be caught up in a frozen moment of time, dazzled by the richness of its presentation, and awed by its dynamic strength.

Gianlorenzo Bernini's work is regarded as the supreme achievement of the Baroque style. Named architect of St. Peter's, he designed the great baldachin over the main altar, its twisting bronze columns in contrasting colors asserted the weighty authority of the popes.

Bernini's baldachin over the main altar of St. Peter's Basilica is a masterpiece of the Baroque style.

Eastern Europe

The defeat of the Czechs at White Mountain hung like a cloud over that nation for the rest of the century and beyond. Ferdinand II, strengthened by an immigrant nobility of Catholic loyalists, announced that the Bohemian kingship would henceforth be hereditary in the Habsburg dynasty both in the male and female lines.

At the beginning of the seventeenth century, Jewish life remained strong in eastern Europe. The Commonwealth of Poland-Lithuania held the largest concentration of Jews in the world. These communities prospered in Poland-Lithuania when they leased estates from Polish magnates, but their very success placed them in danger. Ukrainian peasants regarded the Jews with a mixture of jealousy and hatred. They looked to the Cossacks, the frontiersmen of the steppes, for support against both Poles and Jews.

When Bogdan Khmelnicky raised a general revolt against the Poles, the Jews were caught in the middle. Whole villages were burned to the ground, their inhabitants slaughtered or sold into slavery. At the close of Khmelnicky's raids, nearly a quarter of the Jewish people of Poland-Lithuania—150,000 men and women—were dead.

Russia's Time of Troubles

The Russian people in the early seventeenth century found the period as chaotic as it was for the Germans during the Thirty Years' War. They remember the period as their Time of Troubles. When Tsar Feodor died in 1598, Boris Godunov, Feodor's guardian and father-in-law, announced his candidacy for the Muscovite succession. What Boris had not counted upon was the resurrection of Ivan IV's son, Dmitry. A rumor was abroad that the young boy had escaped his assassins and still lived in Poland.

In 1603 a "Dmitry" convinced the Polish king Sigismund Vasa that he was really Ivan's son. He requested Polish arms to return him to Moscow, promising in return to join Russia to the Catholic church. Despite all efforts made by Tsar Boris and the Orthodox Patriarch Job to discredit him, some Cossack bands and Ukrainian peasants rallied behind Dmitry. His army grew by the thousands. As he approached Moscow, Boris mysteriously died, and Dmitry entered the town. Within a few weeks, however, the pro-Polish policy of Dmitry caused a conspiracy to be formed against him. Dmitry was killed (a second time?), and his remains were shot from a cannon toward Poland. Later several other Dmitrys appeared, allowing the Poles to return to the Kremlin.

A call to defend the Russian homeland and the Orthodox faith frustrated Polish aspirations. Resistance led by the church hierarchy, and joined by several stauch Orthodox Cossack armies drove the Poles from Moscow, and in 1613 at a meeting of the Zemski Sobor, Mikhail Romanov was chosen to be tsar.

In the beginning the young tsar's advisors, his mother and the boyars, had to cope with problems created by a decade of violence and with Swedish and Polish armies that still occupied much of western Russia. In

A Russian Orthodox church can be recognized by its onion-shaped domes.

time these problems were solved when his father Filaret, a Polish prisoner until 1619, returned to Moscow to be chosen patriarch and to manage the administration of the country in conjunction with his son.

The Ottomans

The Ottomans entered the seventeenth century preoccupied with their traditional enemies, the Persians in Asia and the Habsburgs in Europe. Their position was not promising.

In 1638 Sultan Murad III abandoned the child-tribute and reorganized the Janissaries. Although their numbers were impressive, the quality of those enlisted had declined so badly that the Corps was no longer dependable. The native Turkish soldiers whose incomes came from lands leased from the sultans were reluctant to go to war, and the system of land tenure changed as their estates became their own. These were known as *chiftliks,* and could be bought, sold, or inherited. Obviously the Ottoman state needed an overhaul, but innovation was considered dangerous.

Because military victories were the lifeblood of the Turks, the advisors of Sultan Ibrahim I suggested an attack upon the Venetian-held island of Crete. In 1645 war commenced with a Turkish landing at Canea, and a number of victories followed.

Economic Life in Seventeenth-Century Europe

Governments in the seventeenth century became more interested in economic activity than ever before. The kings of Europe realized that there was a close connection between commerce and political strength. Those nations that were economically strong were able to pay for larger armies. The economic system that developed at this time is known as **mercantilism.**

Mercantilism was based on several premises: commerce and colonies exist for the sake of the mother country, exports must be maximized, and imports must be minimized. A country's wealth was determined by how much precious metal it held within its borders. A corollary of mercantilism held that prosperity for one nation meant decline for another; therefore, raw competition for increasing market share was always in progress.

Wealth came to be concentrated in a few cities where it was managed by an elite of corporate and bank executives. Early seventeenth-century Dutch and English businessmen first established the economic institutions that are now essential for modern capitalism.

In England and the Netherlands, merchants formed companies to expand the scope of their businesses. These companies paid their governments for charters that allowed them to operate as monopolies. The East India companies established in Amsterdam and London made substantial profits and demonstrated the value of cooperative ventures of this kind. A permanent company, managed by directors and financed by public subscriptions, was a vast improvement on the earlier method of doing business where individuals assumed all the risks and liabilities.

Amsterdam overtook Antwerp as the center of European commercial activity. The United Dutch Provinces brought about this shift by blockading Antwerp's port on the Scheldt River during their wars with Spain.

The Amsterdam Stock Exchange set prices on commodities for the rest of Europe.

The Dutch so dominated commerce that Amsterdam sent lists of commodity prices to other cities of Europe to guide them in setting their charges. Promise-to-pay notes were increasingly used to facilitate purchases and sales. These notes were similar to modern checks. When signed, they could be used as collateral and there was no limit on the number of endorsements permitted.

Wide disparities were the rule for the continent's farmers. In England a minor agricultural boom occurred. A significant rise in prices for agricultural commodities took place. Landowners promoted the **enclosure movement,** which either combined numerous peasant plots into a single field or took less productive land out of farming and put it into pasture with a subsequent drop in the number of laborers needed. Therefore landowning gentry and aristocrats could charge higher prices for grain.

Elsewhere from France to Russia life was not so prosperous for those who tilled the soil. Many farmers on the continent were subject to days of forced labor and multiple dues and fees carried over from medieval feudalism.

Serfdom was the lot of most East European farmers and was made more onerous because the demand for grain in western Europe kept increasing. To reach a higher level of production, more days of work were required on the landlord's property. Grain yields were poor and breeding of animals was haphazard so that the possibility of famine was always close by.

The Scientific Revolution

The great scientists of the seventeenth century laid the foundation for the world in which we live, with all its conveniences and machines, its computers and technology. Do not think that those who were responsible for this growth in scientific understanding were always aware of what was happening. Many held to the superstitions of the past at the very time they were making their discoveries. It was their good fortune to experiment with hypotheses other than those put forward by Aristotle or Ptolemy, until then considered so authoritative on scientific matters that their word was final.

Copernicus's and Brahe's discoveries had first caused doubts to be raised concerning the accepted wisdom on motion that divided movement into two categories: that found in the heavens and that found on earth. The former was considered to be more perfect because it was circular, and the latter, less perfect because it was linear. Seventeenth century astronomers not only proved Copernicus and Brahe right but also demonstrated that there was no distinction to be made between all motion in the universe.

Johannes Kepler, a German astronomer, in his search for a single explanation for movement in the universe discovered that the path of the planets was elliptical rather than circular and that their speed of revolution varied as a function of their distance from the sun. Kepler made it possible for astronomers to predict mathematically the positions of the earth, sun, and planets. Thanks to him, the hold of the Ptolemaic system on western astronomy was broken.

Invention of the telescope in the Netherlands about 1608 made possible further discoveries. In particular, publication of the work of Galileo Galilei on astronomy created great controversy within the scientific community. A professor of mathematics at the University of Padua, Galileo put the telescope to practical use.

In 1613 Galileo published his research in a book called the *Sidereal Messenger*, in which he described the mountainous terrain of the moon and showed that its light was a reflection of the sun. All the universe, he proposed, follows the same natural laws. Galileo claimed that there was no doubt that Copernicus's description of the universe was the correct one.

Galileo pleads his case before the Court of the Inquisition.

Ecclesiastical authorities feared that he was challenging scriptural truths, although Galileo contended his discoveries had nothing to do with revelation. He took his telescope to Rome to let astronomers look through it to see for themselves. They argued that to accept Galileo's premises was to destroy the ordered Aristotelian system held in reverence for centuries and to call into question scriptural verses placing the earth at the center of the universe. Later church authorities agreed that he could publish his thoughts on the Copernican system, but only as an unproved hypothesis.

In 1632, however, Galileo returned to print despite the warnings he had received. His new publication once more upheld the Copernican view of the universe as a proven fact. This so disturbed church officials and professors at the University of Rome that Galileo was summoned before a Court of Inquisition made up of ten cardinals. A majority agreed to force Galileo to recant anything in his writing contrary to the Catholic faith. He was also sentenced to live under house arrest for the rest of his life.

The struggle between Galileo and the church caused many people to believe that science and religion must be impossible to reconcile, which was an unfortunate misunderstanding because the questions raised at Galileo's trial were not about science but rather biblical interpretation. Does the Bible have only a literal sense?

Galileo was also a great physicist as well as an astronomer. Early in his career he studied how the pendulum's movement was a useful device for understanding motion. He researched the force of gravity in objects, invented a thermometer, and constantly worked on improving the telescope. In what was a major break with Aristotelian physics, he argued that, in spite of appearances, all bodies fall at a uniform rate of speed.

Major advances were made in mathematics during this century. Scholars introduced logarithms for the first time. René Descartes invented analytic geometry, paralleling the work of Pierre de Fermat, who quite independently made the same find. In 1642 Blaise Pascal, at 19 years of age, assembled the first machine that could add and subtract figures.

The great thinkers of the day were usually men with broad interests. The Englishman Francis Bacon, like René Descartes, addressed the question of knowledge. How do men and women know things and to what extent can they approach certainty? Bacon posited that quoting authorities was not sufficient. Only investigation, observation, and experimentation offered solid proof. Truth must be arrived at through trial and error and could be found only at the end of a long process known as induction, the reasoning from individual cases to general laws. For Descartes, knowledge was had only after stripping away everything people think they know until they arrive at the certainty of their own thinking selves. "I think, therefore I am" was Descartes' view of the human person.

Descartes argued that certainty began with the thinking self.

Descartes was basically a mathematician. He believed that extension and motion were the two great realities in the universe and only things that could be explained mathematically offered certainty. He was frustrated in trying to explain emotion and admitted that he could not understand how thought influences physical matter. Troubled by problems in his native France, Descartes left the country to make his home in the Netherlands. Later he accepted an invitation from Sweden's Queen Christina to go to Stockholm, took ill, and died soon afterward.

Descartes might have lived longer if he had given greater attention to medicine, which was another of his interests. But unfortunately people still trusted charms and incantations rather than hard facts about disease and the human body. It is true that more attention was given to the medicinal qualities of herbs and chemical substances. In 1628 the one great medical advance of this age was William Harvey's discovery of blood circulation. That such a basic factor in understanding anatomy took so long to appear shows how medicine lagged behind the accumulation of knowledge in other sciences.

Religion

The seventeenth century was a religious age. Church attendance and concern for morality was as high or even higher than it had been during the Reformation. Writing on religious subjects found a broad audience, and even collections of sermons were in demand.

In England, William Laud, bishop of London and later archbishop of Canterbury, was recognized as the leading Anglican churchman of the age. Laud sought in every way possible to promote Anglicanism in England, Scotland, and Ireland.

Robert Bellarmine, a Jesuit cardinal theologian, and the church historian Cesare Baronio represented Catholic scholarship during this era. Both lived and worked in Rome for many years in the service of the popes. Another Catholic, Vincent de Paul, capitalized on a revival in French Catholicism to found a religious order of men and women to furnish teachers and missionaries. Vincent's Daughters of Charity opened hospitals, orphanages, and shelters for the aged, displaying an active social concern in a world that often shunted the poor and handicapped aside.

The issue of who could be saved was the most divisive dispute among seventeenth-century Calvinists, although many other matters were hotly debated during this period. The question of interpreting Calvin's doctrine of predestination strictly or moderately was the issue. On one side was Jacob Harmensen (Arminius), a theologian of Leyden, who argued that an absolute understanding of predestination was too harsh. On the other side was a colleague, Franz Gommer, who believed that Calvin's austere doctrine could not be modified in any way. In 1618 a synod at Dort ruled against Harmensen, but his followers did not concede. Arminianism became a strong force for change within the Dutch church and other Calvinist communities.

Unfortunately a search for witches continued to agitate the religious consciousness of both Catholic and Protestant Europeans. People saw the hand of God in every human event. He was always giving signs and omens through natural phenomena, but Satan was believed to be just as active, forming covenants with people to spread sickness and cause crop failures or childlessness. Happily, after 1650 the witch craze began to fade.

Conclusion

The early seventeenth century was Europe's age of kings. It had important consequences for political development in future decades. The kings' enhanced authority meant less power was in the hands of Europe's numerous nobility. The businessmen of European cities much preferred to deal with a royal ministry and therefore found good reason to support absolutism.

The trend was not universal; England's regicide is proof that religious issues were still very much alive and could result in the death of a king. The rise of France had been long delayed because of internal conflicts. The eventual ascendance of the nation was predictable because of its large population and the fertility of its soil. Cardinal Richelieu prepared the way for its kings to be the most powerful rulers in Europe.

For the German people, the Thirty Years' War was devastating and its consequences lingered for decades. The Treaty of Westphalia guaranteed that the Germans would remain a divided people, nullifying the advantage of their large numbers.

Artists of the period embraced the Baroque style with enthusiasm. The exuberance of this style reflected very well the magnificence of the age of kings.

CHAPTER 3 REVIEW
AN AGE OF KINGS

Summary

- The early seventeenth century began a period when the kings of Europe claimed to rule by divine right.
- The rulers, although claiming to be absolute, had to depend on the nobility to act on their behalf.
- The Stuart dynasty replaced the Tudors in England when James I came to London.
- Civil war began between King Charles I and the Parliament, now in Puritan hands.
- Charles was executed by the leaders of Parliament.
- The Netherlands was noted for two things: tolerance and a commercial empire.
- France replaced Spain as the major continental power under Louis XIII's minister, Cardinal Richelieu.
- The Thirty Years' War, fought to determine whether the Habsburg emperors could rule effectively in Germany, came close to destroying the country.
- The artistic style of the seventeenth century is known as Baroque.
- Russia went through its Time of Troubles.
- Mercantilism was the prevailing economic theory of government.
- The beginning of modern science started in the seventeenth century creating enough changes to be called a revolution.
- Pietism dominated the religious views of many seventeenth-century Protestants.

Identify

People: James I, Guy Fawkes, Cromwell, Rembrandt, Louis XIII of France, Philip IV of Spain, Cervantes, Ferdinand of Styria, Bernini, Khmelnicky, Kepler, Descartes, Bacon, Laud, Charles I, John Hampden, Rubens, Henry IV, Richelieu, Mazarin, Philip III of Spain, Ferdinand II, William Harvey, Bellarmine, Baronio, de Paul, Arminius

Places: Oxford, Drogheda, La Rochelle, Canea, Amsterdam, Prague

Events: Short and Long Parliaments, Richelieu's advance of the French monarchy, Thirty Years' War and the Treaty of Westphalia, Russia's Time of Troubles, trial of Galileo

Define

absolutism	King James Bible	Baroque style
enclosure	Zemski Sobor	enclosure movement
mercantilism		

Multiple Choice

1. One of the goals of seventeenth-century merchants was
   - (a) the privatization of the economy.
   - (b) the use of gold as currency.
   - (c) to secure a landed estate and title.
   - (d) to obtain a place at court.

2. Divine right of kingship means that
   (a) the king is God's appointee to rule.
   (b) the king has the right to govern the church.
   (c) the king should appoint bishops.
   (d) the king must initiate all laws.

3. During peacetime government depended on
   (a) issuing bonds.
   (b) income taxes.
   (c) subsidies from the merchant class.
   (d) the king's personal income.

4. The largest number of people in seventeenth-century Europe were
   (a) Poles and Russians.
   (b) Spaniards and Portuguese.
   (c) English and Irish.
   (d) French and Germans.

5. The largest cities in seventeenth-century Europe were
   (a) Berlin and Vienna.
   (b) Paris and Lyons.
   (c) London and Dublin.
   (d) London and Paris.

6. James I of England was also monarch of
   (a) the Netherlands.
   (b) France.
   (c) Hungary.
   (d) Scotland.

7. Guy Fawkes was associated with a plot to
   (a) infiltrate the Spanish court.
   (b) destroy the Bank of England.
   (c) blow up the king and Parliament.
   (d) drive the English from Ireland.

8. The Petition of Right affirmed
   (a) individual rights.
   (b) the need for judicial reform.
   (c) the legitimacy of absolute monarchy.
   (d) the right of a people to revolution.

9. Scottish Presbyterians in the seventeenth century resisted the plans of
   (a) Archbishop Cranmer.
   (b) Mary Tudor.
   (c) the Short Parliament.
   (d) Archbishop Laud.

10. The English Civil War resulted in a victory for
    (a) Cromwell.
    (b) James I.
    (c) Charles I.
    (d) absolute monarchy.

11. The East India Company was formed in
    (a) the Netherlands.
    (b) Paris.
    (c) London.
    (d) Antwerp.

12. "One faith, one law, one king" was the slogan of
    (a) James I.
    (b) Ferdinand II of the Holy Roman Empire.
    (c) Cardinal Mazarin.
    (d) Cardinal Richelieu.

13. The economy of Spain depended on
    (a) an annual supply of bullion from the Americas.
    (b) a tax on merchants.
    (c) an income tax.
    (d) the king's private wealth.

14. The Defenestration of Prague was the first event in
    (a) the War of the Pyrenees.
    (b) the Seven Years' War.
    (c) the Thirty Years' War.
    (d) the Habsburg wars with the Turks.

15. The battle of Lützen was a Swedish victory, but
    (a) the army of Tilly escaped.
    (b) too many Swedes were killed so that this was the last battle of their army.
    (c) Gustavus II Adolphus was killed.
    (d) the Danish king assumed defense of the Protestant cause.

16. The Treaty of Westphalia
    (a) kept the Holy Roman Empire divided.
    (b) united the principalities of the Holy Roman Empire.
    (c) denied France the Rhineland.
    (d) ended Habsburg hold on the imperial title.

17. The largest concentration of Jews in the world lived in
    (a) Spain.
    (b) the Holy Roman Empire.
    (c) Russia.
    (d) Poland-Lithuania.

18. At the close of Russia's Time of Troubles, the delegates to the Zemski Sobor chose a tsar from the family of
    (a) Vasa.
    (b) Habsburg.
    (c) Rurik.
    (d) Romanov.

19. Mercantilism determined that wealth was principally found in
    (a) natural resources.
    (b) gold and silver.
    (c) manufacturing.
    (d) agriculture.

20. Merchants spread liability for losses by opening their companies to
    - (a) government officials.
    - (b) stockholders.
    - (c) employees.
    - (d) lawyers.

21. A promise-to-pay note resembled
    - (a) a check.
    - (b) a stock certificate.
    - (c) gold coinage.
    - (d) a bond.

22. The Scientific Revolution's first advance was in
    - (a) physics.
    - (b) mathematics.
    - (c) geography.
    - (d) astronomy.

23. Galileo's trial was over his publications supporting
    - (a) Kepler.
    - (b) Aristotle.
    - (c) Ptolemy.
    - (d) Copernicus.

24. Induction is a method of gaining knowledge based on
    - (a) authority.
    - (b) generalizations.
    - (c) mathematics.
    - (d) experimentation.

Essay Questions
1. What were possible good effects, if any, of royal absolutism?
2. What should the Stuarts have done to preserve their crown?
3. A balance of power dominated the plans of European statesmen. How was this illustrated by the Thirty Years' War?
4. What were the positive and negative aspects of mercantilism?
5. Who were the pioneers of the Scientific Revolution? Why did it not come before the seventeenth century?

Answers

1. c	7. c	13. a	19. b
2. a	8. a	14. c	20. b
3. d	9. d	15. c	21. a
4. d	10. a	16. a	22. d
5. d	11. c	17. d	23. d
6. d	12. d	18. d	24. d

CHAPTER 4

Louis XIV's Europe

In the latter part of the seventeenth century, one man dominated the European scene, Louis XIV, King of France. Never before had the power of a European monarch reached such dimensions. The eyes of all the other rulers on the continent fastened on the style of the French court. Louis's every move and decision was followed with a combination of awe and irritation. The French king's flair for the magnificent might attract or repulse but could hardly be ignored. The monarch's absolutism further weakened the authority of the clergy and nobility, the two classes that had the most to lose in the accentuation of royal power.

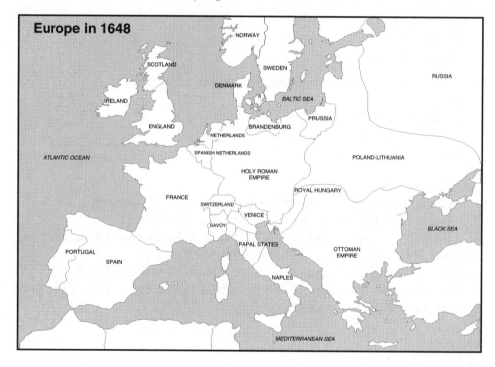

Europe in 1648

Louis XIV, the Sun King

Louis XIV did not have a promising childhood. In 1643, at nine years old, he became king, upon his father's death, but was under the tutelage of his mother, Anne of Austria, and her minister, Cardinal Mazarin. Together they concentrated the power of the state in their own hands. They neglected Louis's education, even though he had a quick mind and could have profited from better training. Louis had strong emotions, but the young prince learned to keep them under control. He appreciated the challenge of kingship. The king once described his occupation as "grand, noble, delightful."

On the day following Mazarin's death in 1661, Louis XIV, then 22 years old, announced that there would be no replacement for his chief minister. He intended to take the administration of the state entirely into his own hands. Louis believed that God had given him absolute authority to rule in France and that he was subject to no one but his own conscience.

A number of councils—financial, military, and commercial headed by secretaries—directed the national government. The king placed able men in the top positions of these offices. Jean Baptiste Colbert, a holdover from Mazarin's tenure, held office in both financial and commercial councils. His assistants called him the North Pole because of his ability to oversee all the affairs of the realm. Colbert worked hard to raise the monarchy's revenues by enforcing the tenets of mercantilism.

Unfortunately, much of the wealth garnered for king and country by Colbert was dissipated in Louis's attempts to find glory in military adventures. Expenditures were lavished on an army numbering 300,000 men, a size never before seen on the European continent.

Louis XIV, the Sun King.

Louis's army was used on four occasions, principally against the Dutch in an effort to have France replace the Netherlands as the leading commercial nation of Europe. The last of his military adventures, the War of Spanish Succession, extending from 1701 to 1713, was fought to place Louis's grandson, Philip of Anjou, on Madrid's throne. Other European sovereigns viewed this as a serious threat to the balance of power among the European states. The Treaty of Utrecht, which concluded the war in 1713, provided that Philip of Anjou should go to Madrid as King Philip V, but the two crowns of France and Spain were never to be joined. Louis had made his point. Today a Bourbon, not a Habsburg, sits on Spain's throne.

In his pursuit of power in France, Louis wanted to exercise complete control over the Catholic church, which, because it had its own leadership, represented a rival to his authority. His court preacher, Bishop Jacques Bossuet of Meaux, led the king's assault speaking in favor of an autonomous French church.

The king also had a group of religious dissidents whom he felt he must curb. These were the **Jansenists,** rigorous Catholics whose dogmatic views and strict morality placed them very close to the Calvinists. They took their name from Bishop Cornelius Jansen, whose book, the *Augustinus,* gave the movement its scripture.

The Huguenots provided the country with many of its industrious and better-educated citizens. In the eyes of the king, however, they were dangerous because they reserved the right to worship God in their own, rather than the king's way. As a result, in 1685, contrary to the moderation that had previously characterized his religious policy, Louis revoked the Edict of Nantes, which his grandfather had so wisely decreed. Thousands of Protestants were now in jeopardy and, contrary to expectation, preferred leaving the country to acquiescence.

In 1665 Louis decided on the reconstruction of the palace of the Louvre in Paris, but by the time of its completion, the king was already thinking of a move to Versailles, a town just outside the capital. Here he envisioned a completely original structure to provide a fitting residence. The architects planned a large complex of buildings surrounded by formal gardens and stately fountains.

Versailles, the palace of Louis XIV.

At Versailles royal etiquette demanded that Louis be surrounded by hundreds of servants. Gossip over the king's mistresses, gambling, tennis, and hunting only partially removed the boredom. Life was one large ceremony, which delighted those who were willing to play the courtier for all its worth. Its artificiality in dress, dance, manners, and general deportment appear somewhat vulgar today.

It was Louis who began wearing a wig, introducing a trend in men's fashions that soon swept all Europe. By contemporary standards, Louis XIV was magnificent, and the grand style evoked at Versailles inspired jealousy and feeble attempts at emulation everywhere in Europe. The French language spread to every court, and diplomats were mute without it.

In 1715 Louis died at 77 years of age. By that time his popularity in France was in decline as a result of a turn to piety and the heavy costs of his wars. Louis brought France to the pinnacle of grandeur, but both for his successors and the nation he governed, he left a burdensome legacy.

The Search for Stability in the British Isles

In 1653 Cromwell grew tired of those members of Parliament who dared challenge his autocracy. He dismissed them, "Your hour has come, the Lord hath done with you.... You are no Parliament, I say you are no Parliament." An **Instrument of Government** drawn up in that year made Cromwell lord protector and established a one-house Parliament for England, Scotland, and Ireland. The importance of this instrument lay in the fact that it offered England its first written constitution with a separation of governmental powers.

Oliver Cromwell dismisses Parliament.

In 1658 Cromwell died with his protectorate cracking at the seams as English men and women chafed under Puritan rule. Two years were enough for Richard Cromwell, his son and heir (Tumbledown Dick to his critics), to prove his lack of administrative qualities. A newly elected Parliament asked that Charles II return from exile and restore the Stuart dynasty.

Charles entered London amid shouts of joy that the Puritan interlude was at an end and the atmosphere of "Merrie England" had returned. Charles did not press his advantage. He agreed to let Parliament retain most of its powers to avoid religious controversy and to abstain from levying any new taxes without its consent. The Anglican bishops returned to their posts and urged Charles and Parliament to require all English men and women to use the *Book of Common Prayer.*

Charles's allies formed a party known as Tories, which later developed into England's first true political organization. Opposition to the Tories was found in a group given the name Whigs. Its policies were based on a general mistrust of Stuart government.

In 1665 the city of London suffered from an attack of the plague that carried off tens of thousands of people. In the following year, to compound the capital's problems, a great fire burned several days destroying many of the city's landmarks. Fortunately Charles could count on the abilities of Sir Christopher Wren to plan the reconstruction of the city and to replace the old St. Paul's cathedral with a new structure. Wren's magnificent design was carried out so that the church towered over London and became its most familiar landmark.

Upon Charles's death, the succession passed to his brother James II. Unlike Charles, James found it difficult to work with Parliament. James was a convert to Catholicism, and few English men and women were pleased about that. A majority in Parliament feared that a Catholic dynasty would mean a return to the days of Mary Tudor. In 1687, by a Declaration of Indulgence, James sought to better the condition of the small Catholic minority by granting tolerance to all faiths. Seven Anglican bishops, judging this to be the first step toward reestablishing Catholicism, went to the Tower rather than support the king.

As long as James's two daughters, Mary and Anne, were Protestant and in line to inherit the crown, a Catholic succession was remote. Then, in June 1688 a son was born to James's queen, Mary of Modena. The Whig party made common cause with the Tories that the king must go. Contacts were made with Mary and her husband, William III of Orange, inviting them to come to England.

The crown of England is offered to William and Mary.

In November 1688 backed by a "Protestant wind," William, who saw an opportunity to bring England into a coalition against Louis XIV, landed at the head of 14,000 Dutch troops. The startled James threw the Great Seal of the kingdom into the Thames and scurried out of the country for France where Louis XIV offered him asylum. This allowed Parliament to declare that he had abdicated and to invite William and Mary to assume the throne as joint sovereigns. English men and women called this transfer of power the **Glorious Revolution.**

The Stuarts in Ireland and Scotland

The Irish Catholic chieftains remained loyal to the Stuarts and joined James's army when he landed in their country. James laid siege to Londonderry, a Protestant stronghold in Ulster but was unable to take it after three months. An English force then relieved the town. The last act in the drama took place in July 1690 on the Boyne River. At the Battle of Boyne, the English defeated James's forces, and the dethroned king had to flee back to France.

The Dublin Parliament, consisting entirely of Anglo-Irish Protestant members, now enacted laws that banished priests and made it illegal for Catholics to gain admittance to the university or enter the professions.

In Scotland many of the chieftains among the Highland clans were James's partisans and became known as Jacobites. They sought to aid him by an uprising when he made his landing in Ireland to regain the crown. Among traditional Scots, who still held to a view of society based upon an unqualified allegiance to their clan chief, it was a shameful act of disloyalty to abandon the Stuart house.

In this field, next to the Boyne River in Ireland, James II lost his battle to stay in power.

The Rule of William and Mary

After William and Mary were in London, Parliament wanted to be sure that the new monarchs understood their position. In a Bill of Rights, Parliament required that all legislation be approved by its two houses and that no army could be raised or taxes imposed without its consent. The Glorious Revolution turned England away from absolutism and toward constitutionalism and placed the Anglican church in a commanding role in the nation.

The reign of William and Mary was a prosperous one for the country. Although William never lost interest in his homeland, he did not neglect his adopted country especially after his wife's death. He managed affairs through a small group of men who formed his inner circle. These were drawn from the House of Lords and served him well.

In 1702 William died, and the succession passed to his sister-in-law, James's second daughter Anne, who was then married to a Danish prince. In 1707, while the War of Spanish Succession was in progress, Parliament joined Scotland and England into a single nation, Great Britain. The union required that the sovereigns of Scotland would also descend through the heirs of the Protestant Stuarts and that Scottish lords and commoners would sit in a joint Parliament with the English. The union was easily accepted by the Anglicized Scots of the Lowlands, but in the Highlands loyalty to James Edward, son of James II, remained strong.

When Queen Anne died in 1714, she was without an heir. Although she had 18 pregnancies, no children survived her. The crown, therefore, passed to her nearest relative, George I, who held title to the German principality of Hanover.

Two Englishmen, Thomas Hobbes and John Locke, made major contributions to political philosophy in the seventeenth century. The English experience, which had witnessed one king killed and another sent into exile, obviously caused thoughtful men to ponder the validity of absolutism and to look for the roots of sovereignty. For the Royalist Hobbes, author of *Leviathan*, which was published in 1651, absolutism made sense. Mankind's existence would be "solitary, poor, nasty, brutish, and short," unless men and women handed over their freedom in return for the security that only unlimited monarchical power offered. Government, "the Leviathan," totally secular in its origins, had the duty to deliver human society from anarchy.

Hobbes's argument on the secular origins of the state was universally accepted by later political thinkers, but another Englishman, John Locke, challenged his apology for absolutism. Locke criticized Hobbes for positing such a pessimistic view of humanity. He contended that the Glorious Revolution proved his thesis that rebellion often brought positive results. Locke believed that people had natural rights to life, liberty, and property.

The Atlantic States

In 1650 the Dutch people continued to hold an economic edge over all other European nations. This very prosperity attracted the envy of the more populous states. The first attack on Dutch commerce occurred when Cromwell's Parliament passed a Navigation Act. It required that only English ships could serve English ports.

William III of Orange took charge of Dutch resistance to Louis XIV's plans to occupy the Netherlands. He built up his forces by alliances with other nations, and his advantageous marriage to Mary, daughter of James II, ensured England's support. Continued Dutch participation in the conflicts with the French cost the country so heavily in men and resources that it brought an end to the Netherlands' supremacy in commerce and shipping.

Spain's position in the latter seventeenth century was not enviable. Although once the leading country among western European nations, it now was powerless to resist becoming a center of foreign intrigue and unable to control its own destiny.

Much of Spain's gold had left the country. That which remained in the country went into church decoration.

In 1655 upon the death of Philip IV, the succession passed to his four-year-old son, Charles II. While in his minority, affairs of state were managed, or rather mismanaged, by his mother Maria Anna. The Spanish nobility, who looked upon the queen-mother as too weak to resist the advice of her counsellors, forced her into exile when the king was but 11 years old. Already Charles gave evidence of thyroid and mental handicaps; throughout his life he was expected to die each day.

As Charles grew older and more feeble, demands were made on the childless monarch to settle his estate. Finally, he was forced to choose between an heir from among cousins in Vienna or the Frenchman Philip of Anjou, also a relative and a grandson of Louis XIV. The expectation of a Bourbon sitting in Madrid, as well as in Paris caused the 14-year War of Spanish Succession. When the Treaty of Utrecht brought the war to a conclusion, its conditions required that Spain give up the Southern Netherlands, Luxembourg, Gibraltar, and its possessions in Italy and that Philip V take over the throne, hardly a fair exchange.

The Germans under Habsburgs and Hohenzollerns

While Leopold I was emperor in 1683, Turkish forces reached as far as Vienna, the Habsburg capital, for the second time. Pope Innocent XI sought to persuade other European monarchs to come to Vienna's rescue. In response, the Polish king, Jan III Sobieski, brought a contingent of 25,000 Poles into Austria, rescuing the Habsburg capital.

Leopold then directed his general, Charles of Lorraine, to pursue the demoralized Ottomans. He struck into Turkish-held Hungary where for a century and a half the people had lived under the Ottomans. By 1686 Buda and Pest were regained. Later Prince Eugene of Savoy, the most able military leader of the day, assumed command of the Habsburg armies and kept the Turks on the run. His gains prepared the way for the 1699 Peace of Karlowitz. By this treaty the sultan's government ceded territory to the Habsburgs for the first time in their long history of conflict.

The successful defense of Vienna and the series of victories won by Eugene of Savoy breathed new life into the Habsburg monarchy. The decline of Austrian fortunes that had followed the Treaty of Westphalia was reversed. The Habsburgs were now the strongest power in Danubian Europe, attracting talented civilian and military officials from all over the continent.

In 1711 the imperial crown passed to Charles VI. He sought to make Habsburg sovereignty permanent by issuing the Pragmatic Sanction of 1713. In it Charles proclaimed that all Habsburg lands were indivisible and that his line of heirs would provide the only legitimate sovereigns in the years ahead. The document was circulated through the courts of Europe where monarchs signed with great ceremony but smiled in private, well aware that the Pragmatic Sanction could very easily become little more than a scrap of paper.

Although it was not possible for the Habsburgs to see into the future, it would have been well for them to consider that Prussia with its Hohenzollern rulers was fast advancing as a state with the potential to challenge Habsburg primacy.

Schönbrunn palace was the residence of the Austrian Habsburgs.

The Thirty Years' War had been a disaster for most Germans, but at its conclusion Prussia's young ruler, Frederick William, actually gained more territories. Known as the Great Elector, Frederick William decided that his possessions could be secure only if he created the strongest army in northern Europe. German soldiers from all his domains were enlisted in the Prussian army, and a tradition of military service as the paramount duty of the citizen was impressed on all. The **Junkers,** the landed aristocrats, who were owners of the large Prussian estates, thought of no other occupation but that of officers in the army.

Italy

Italy in the latter seventeenth century was politically divided into several large and small states, many under the political control of foreigners. Venice, once the proud mistress of the Adriatic, continued its efforts to stave off disaster as the Ottomans encroached upon its few remaining eastern Mediterranean possessions. The Cretan war now centered on a siege of Candia (Iraklion), which lasted for a long 11 years, but in the end the Venetians had to admit defeat and leave the island.

In 1684 the Venetians took advantage of Turkish discomfort after their failure before Vienna. Francesco Morosini, an able Venetian general, landed an army in the Peloponnesus and soon brought the whole peninsula under his control. He then moved across the Corinthian Isthmus and laid siege to Athens. During this encounter, a Venetian cannon ball landed in the Parthenon on the Acropolis, where the Turks had stored ammunition. The beautiful temple to Athena, which had survived for almost two millennia, was severely damaged.

Sweden and Poland in the Baltic

In 1654 Charles X, successor to Queen Christina who had abdicated, had no intention of limiting his career to Sweden. His one interest in life was leading armies. He opened hostilities against Poland with seasoned veterans of the Thirty Years' War. The Poles put up little resistance, the nobility believing it was the king's business, not theirs, to defend the nation.

The advance of the Swedes encouraged the Russians and Prussians to hurry and join forces against the hapless Poles lest they lose out on a contemplated partition of the country. A weak monarchy and a large Polish upper class, increasingly dominated by powerful magnates with their private armies, meant that the king could never field a national army strong enough to hold off the country's enemies.

The Warsaw palace of Poland's kings was rebuilt after World War II.

By the winter of 1655 only Gdansk and Lvóv, among the larger cities, were still in Polish hands. At the monastery of Czestochowa, a small force of soldiers and monks refused to capitulate to the Swedish forces. Despite overwhelming odds, Czestochowa held out, and its remarkable deliverance signaled a Polish revival. Since that time, Czestochowa has become a Polish national shrine, and the painting of its Virgin has become the most venerated object of Polish devotion.

The Diet of 1674 chose Jan III Sobieski to be king. Sobieski was a proven leader, with a French wife whose ties to Louis XIV were considered an excellent asset for the beleaguered country. In 1683 his battle plan had saved Vienna and forever ended the threat of Ottoman expansion into the heart of Europe. Sobieski was the last able king to rule Poland.

It was obvious to everyone that the country needed reforms if the resurgence it enjoyed under Sobieski was to be retained. The Diet was more and more at the mercy of foreign powers and the hobbling *liberum veto*, which allowed a single member to stop debate, strangled effective action.

A failure to accept reform was demonstrated when Russian and Prussian partisans in the Diet united to choose the weakest candidate available as Sobieski's successor. He was the German Elector of Saxony, Augustus II. In order to fulfill his personal goals, he brought Poland into one more bloody conflict, the Great Northern War. Augustus planned with the Russian tsar, Peter the Great, and the Danish king, Frederick IV, to force the Swedes from the Baltic.

Instead of a quick victory, the unlikely alliance of the three kings soon discovered that Charles XII, the Swedish monarch, was more than a match for them. In November 1700 Charles first destroyed a Russian army and then turned on the Poles. For the next six years Swedish armies marched the length of Poland until Augustus admitted defeat and resigned.

The Smolensk kremlin passed back and forth between Poles, Russians, and Swedes.

Charles then turned once more against Peter the Great who had consolidated his position in the interim. When Charles sought to break through to the south, Peter caught and defeated the Swedish army at Poltava in July 1709. Charles had to flee to the Ottoman Empire where he spent his time convincing the Turks it was to their advantage to attack the Russians.

After Poltava, Russian armies restored Augustus, and Poland became subject to the whims of the tsar. In 1717 Peter forced a new constitution on the Poles, which reduced them to the status of a satellite of Russia.

Russian Tsars and Ottoman Sultans

In 1645 Tsar Alexei, the young son of Mikhail Romanov, came to rule the Muscovite state. Alexei had received only a smattering of schooling but strong indoctrination in the Orthodox faith.

The government of Alexei's advisors required that the boyars furnish a certain number of men for the armed forces and pay taxes for their support. Yet there were constant complaints from the landowners that they did not have sufficient manpower on their estates. A plan had to be devised to keep the peasants from moving about. In 1649 Alexei's advisers drew up a proposal that placed even greater burdens on the serfs. No limit was put on the time a runaway peasant might be forcibly returned to his or her master, and landlords could appeal to the government for assistance in tracking down fugitives.

The landowners also lost their freedom to the extent that all were required to perform military service. Russia's people were universally organized in a system meant to provide a privileged way of life for the few who held power in the state or church.

One of Alexei's favorites was Nikon Minin, a monk whom the tsar nominated to the patriarchate. Nikon wanted to change certain church practices that the Orthodox Academy of Kiev pointed out as contrary to Byzantine Orthodoxy. These included the misspelling of Jesus' name and making the sign of the cross with two fingers rather than three. In 1653 Nikon ordered the Russian clergy to conform to Byzantine practice or face deposition and arrest.

These orders were opposed by some of the church's most dedicated clerics. One of them, Avvakum, courageously argued that to accept these modifications was to admit that the Russian church had been in error for centuries. He and thousands of others, called Old Believers, were arrested and sent into exile. Avvakum spent the rest of his life in Siberia where cold, hunger, beatings, and imprisonment did nothing to shake his resolve. At the end of his ordeal, authorities ordered his return to Moscow where he was sentenced to die by burning at the stake. The martyrdom of Avvakum simply strengthened the Old Believers' determination. Avvakum wrote a book about his trials, the first autobiography in the Russian language.

Russian monasteries often served as fortresses.

The Cossacks, once Moscow's partisans in Ukraine, soon grew restless under the tsar's administration. In 1670 Stenka Razin rallied the Don Cossacks and joined by thousands of desperate serfs marched upon Moscow. Razin's army collapsed, however, and he was caught and executed, joining in death 100,000 followers who shared his fate. Stenka Razin became a folk hero to the Russian serfs, but a demagogue to the landowners who were always fearful of another rising that might topple them.

In 1682 Peter the Great inherited the tsar's crown. He had grown to be a giant of a man, fully 6 feet 8 inches in height, with enough eccentricities to match his frame. He had a terrible temper, enjoyed drinking bouts that lasted for days, and had nothing but contempt for the ceremonies of the court. As a child he had learned to play the drum, and this continued to interest him more than any formalities that were expected of him.

When he came to power, Peter was determined to make the Russian army the strongest in Europe. In 1695 Peter led his army against the Ottoman Turks, who held the port of Azov at the mouth of the Don River. This first campaign failed, but in the following year a combined land and sea attack forced the Ottomans to capitulate, and Azov surrendered to the Russians. Peter returned to Moscow for a victory parade in which the tsar marched behind the Russian generals, playing his drum.

Peter realized that if he was to keep the momentum for Russian expansion, his military forces needed the better weapons and technology of the

West. He decided upon a personal trip to western Europe, the first Russian ruler ever to do so. The Grand Embassy departed Russia for the Netherlands in March 1697 apparently headed by a Swiss commander who had in his employ a noncommissioned officer, Peter Milhailov, who was the tsar in disguise.

Because Peter was especially interested in Dutch shipbuilding, for four months he examined the Amsterdam shipyards. Next, he visited London and Vienna, but there word reached him that a mutiny had broken out in the army. He hurried back to Russia to sit in judgment on the rebels, 2,000 of whom were executed, some by Peter himself.

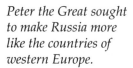

Peter the Great sought to make Russia more like the countries of western Europe.

Peter's goal as a participant in the Great Northern War was to gain a port for Russia on the Baltic, bringing to an end its landlocked position. Peter placed the Swedish naval base at Narva under siege, only to suffer a crushing defeat as a result of the swift attack of Charles XII. While the Swedes spent the next six years fighting in Poland, Peter rebuilt his forces. After the battle of Poltava, the Russians had things their own way. In 1721 Peter signed the Treaty of Nystad with the Swedes, thereby joining Livonia (Latvia), Estonia, and Karelia to Russia.

Peter is justly famous for the reforms he inaugurated in the internal affairs of Russia. Already his father Alexei had changed Muscovite custom when he allowed women to attend his court. Peter went further than his father for he invited women to attend parties and wear Western-style dress-es. He disliked the beards his courtiers wore and ordered the men to shave them off or pay a tax of a hundred rubles. Men were to divest themselves of the bulky caftans worn in Moscow and to adopt Western-style trousers.

In order to confirm the Westernization of Russia, Peter transferred the country's capital from Moscow, with its traditions linked to the past, to St. Petersburg on the Gulf of Finland. Tens of thousands of people were employed under the most difficult conditions to construct the city on a European model. In 1714 the government moved to St. Petersburg.

St. Petersburg was a beautiful city, filled with canals and spacious stone houses, but the price paid in human suffering was terribly high. This was of little concern to the tsar who, like Louis XIV, felt the whole world should turn on his will.

In 1725 Peter died at 53 years of age leaving an impressive record. Russia has always remembered Peter, for he brought the country out of the past and destroyed its isolation.

St. Petersburg in the eighteenth century.

Although Russian strength expanded late in the seventeenth century, there were signs that the Ottoman Empire remained in serious difficulty. The sultans, who in theory were the absolute rulers of the empire, were ill-equipped for their occupation. In past centuries the law of fratricide required the ruling sultan to kill his brothers on his accession to thwart any possibility of rebellion. This practice was now abandoned, and close relatives of the ruler were given the dubious alternative of incarceration within the Grand Serai, the sultan's palace. Here potential sultans spent monotonous years of enforced confinement in reading and writing, with no one to speak to except palace eunuchs. Then, if the ruling sultan died, one would be called forth to assume the duties of governing the state as best he could.

Naturally, the weakness in the sultanate permeated other offices in the ruling institution. Bribery became the key to advancement, and provincial governors often felt confident they could ignore orders from the capital.

The pool of the Grand Serai in Istanbul's harem.

Social and Economic Factors in Europe

The increased cultivation of the potato was of major significance during the age of Louis XIV. Of all foods that came from the Americas, the potato was the most valuable. It was easy to grow, even in cool climates with marginal soil; highly nutritious when eaten; and easily stored and transported.

At first Europeans did not eat it but rather used it as an ornamental plant in gardens or for animal feed. The Irish were the first to grow it for human consumption.

Ireland's population exploded as potato production spread across the island. Despite the loss of life in Cromwell's wars, the Irish population increased to 2,500,000 people by 1715, thanks to the potato.

The Russians were second in the rate of population growth, fed by an increase in rye production that was the staple of their black bread. More steppe lands were plowed and new villages founded so that by the early eighteenth century Russian and Ukrainian numbers reached 15,000,000 people. The Ottoman Empire, Poland, Spain, parts of Italy, and almost all the German lands had net declines from 1650 to 1700 as a result of famine and the consequences of war. Disease kept life expectancy below 35 years of age for those Europeans who survived childhood.

Society had changed some of its notions on children's care and education. In France it was popular for women who could afford it to give their babies to wet nurses rather than care for them at home. Infants drank little milk after weaning. People avoided fruits and vegetables because they were believed to cause illness. The diets of children consisted of little else than bread, meat, and fish.

Latin schools were opened in France, primarily to train choristers. In them, students learned singing, arithmetic, reading, writing, and etiquette. It was still general practice for girls to study at home. By the eighteenth century nearly all the urban population in northern Europe was literate. In the Mediterranean region literacy lagged far behind. It was thought quite remarkable when, for the first time in history in June 1678, a woman, Elena Lucrezia Piscopia, received the Doctor of Philosophy degree from the University of Padua.

Economic life in the age of Louis XIV expanded as competition for both foreign and domestic markets encouraged the production of more goods. In order to insure their businesses, the merchants of western Europe expected national governments to fight their battles. By the start of the eighteenth century, the merchant vessels of England were fast approaching the number sent out from the Netherlands. The London government was intent upon providing a navy to defend its interests.

Science

The latter seventeenth century was a time when the pioneers in science began to have their work appreciated and expanded upon. The hypotheses of earlier scientists had destroyed the closed world view of the Middle Ages, and now there was need to provide a new synthesis. Rather than in the universities, where curricular change was so difficult, it was in academies or scientific societies, chartered by interested monarchs, that new theses were presented and discussed.

New names appeared on the roster of those whose thought has shaped the modern world of science. In astronomy Christian Huygens was first to describe Saturn's rings and later to invent the pendulum clock for the accurate measurement of time. Edmund Halley charted the skies, mapped the trade winds, and gave his name to the world's best known comet. Robert Boyle's name is associated with the properties of air and gases. He built a pneumatic pump to demonstrate the relation between pressure and volume. Boyle rejected the axioms of Aristotle on elements and put forward the idea that corpuscles explain the composition of matter.

Antony van Leeuwenhoek, a Dutch naturalist and lens maker of Delft, described the complexity of living matter and the multiple forms of life unseen by the naked eye. He was the first to see blood cells, find bacteria in humans, and examine sperm under the microscope. His research dispelled the common belief in spontaneous generation of life that had mislead biologists up to his day.

Disease, especially typhus and smallpox, was a terrible scourge on the European population of the seventeenth century. Millions of people died from smallpox, and other millions were disfigured for life by the scars it left on the body. Doctors were unable to find a cure for smallpox.

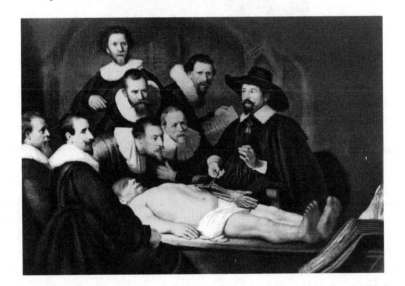

A Dutch doctor conducts an anatomy lesson.

Gottfried Wilhelm Leibniz improved upon Pascal's adding machine some 30 years after its invention when he created a more sophisticated device that could also multiply and divide, with the comment, "It is unworthy of excellent men to lose hours like slaves in the labor of calculations...." Leibniz independently published a work on calculus at the same time that Isaac Newton was studying the same problem. Leibniz's interests extended over mathematics, philosophy, and theology, and his efforts led to the founding of the Berlin Academy.

Without doubt, Isaac Newton was the most outstanding scientist of his age. Born in 1642, the very year Galileo died, some saw the latter's spirit reincarnated in Newton. It was he who at last made the world understandable with a new synthesis. Newton's versatility was demonstrated in many areas. He invented a new form of calculus, discovered the composition of white light, constructed a reflecting telescope, and when named to head the English mint devised a new coinage system.

All these accomplishments pale in comparison to his discovery of the law of gravity. Building upon the work of Galileo and Kepler, both of whom had written on the principles of celestial and terrestrial motion, Newton completed their studies by describing in mathematical terms the motion of sun, earth, moon, and planets. He drew geometric figures to illustrate how gravity works to attract physical bodies and hold them in position. This meant that tables could be constructed that accurately predicted natural phenomena centuries in advance. Newton's discoveries were to stand the test of time until Albert Einstein proposed his theory of relativity.

Sir Isaac Newton, England's foremost scientist.

In 1687 Newton published his research in the *Mathematical Principles of Natural Philosophy,* which has been called the most important book of the century. It made obsolete all previous explanations of astronomy and physics.

By the opening of the eighteenth century, science was making such advances that the world view of educated Europeans had completely changed from what it had been two centuries earlier. It was science that now was treated with reverence, and the truths it gave were accepted as dogma.

Sports and Leisure

People in the seventeenth century had a wide variety of interests. This was especially true of the leisured upper class for whom manual labor was unthinkable. Hunting was still considered the way for a gentleman to spend the afternoon. Here was found excitement, companionship, and a chance to demonstrate one's skills as a horseman. The physical exercise helped to keep Europe's aristocrats in shape, for they were notoriously heavy eaters and drinkers.

Nearly everyone enjoyed different kinds of ball games. One aristocratic favorite was golf. In the early seventeenth century the English Society of Golfers at Blackheath started regular play. Scotland was the birthplace of the sport, where it dates from the late 1400s, so it is not a coincidence that its popularity rose when the Scottish Stuart dynasty came to London. A similar game appeared in the Netherlands where it was called *het kolven.*

Most of the words used by today's golfers are of Dutch origin, such as *tee* and *putt*. *Golf* is the word for a club.

Another game kings and aristocrats enjoyed was tennis. Its origins were in France where it was known as the palm game and differed from modern tennis because it was played on inside courts. In 1697 Paris counted 114 courts, and Charles II, when he returned to London, refurbished the one built at Hampton Court in the days of Henry VIII. Louis XIV spent every afternoon either on the tennis court or hunting.

During the Middle Ages swimming fell out of favor. Late in the seventeenth century a few daring people took to the water again, and one Frenchman wrote a book on *The Art of Swimming*. Personal cleanliness suffered as a result of Europeans' aversion to bathing. As late as 1672, an Italian gentleman who sent a German lady a bar of soap also had to send instructions on how to use it.

Throughout Europe and among all classes, people enjoyed such sports as boxing, wrestling, horse racing, and archery. Some regions had local favorites: bull fighting in Spain, hurling the stone in Scotland, and bowling in the Netherlands.

Quieter games played at home included checkers, chess, and cards. Chess is the older game, well known throughout the Middle Ages. The names used for the pieces demonstrate a medieval origin, and to checkmate the king is to kill the sheikh, an Arabic phrase.

Upper and middle class people gathered in the evening to sing, dance, or produce skits within the family circle. Performing and listening to music was always an attractive activity.

Gambling was extremely popular among both children and adults, outside of Calvinist regions. It was said that Anne of Austria, queen-mother of Louis XIV, did nothing all day in her later years except to gamble and say her prayers.

Ballet and dance occupied many nights for European courtiers in the seventeenth century. Theater and operatic performances that combined both acting, singing, and extravagant spectacle fitted aristocratic taste. Masques at court were rivals to the opera and allowed nobles and even queens and kings to take parts. In 1669 Louis XIV inaugurated the Royal Academy of Music and patronized Jean Baptiste Molière as playwright of the French court.

Conclusion

The latter seventeenth century produced winners and losers on the map of Europe. Louis XIV will always have his admirers for he brought his nation a grandeur never before reached. Although much of his life was spent in playing a role, it appears that he at least recognized it to be theater and in this regard ranks above many of his contemporaries.

Kings could be popular one day, Charles II comes to mind, and then have fortune turn on them violently, as happened to his brother James II. In England Parliament found Puritanism too narrow, but it also feared a king who might return England to Catholicism and place in jeopardy the gains made by its members.

Poland, still a large nation on the European map in the seventeenth century, masked a powerlessness to change direction to prevent a perilous descent. Its neighbors found its internal weakness inviting and an enticement for them to intervene. The Ottoman Empire was on a similar course, governed by those who lacked the will to strengthen the state because it meant changing traditional ways of thinking and acting.

Peter the Great placed Russia into the rank of seventeenth-century winners because he did not fear change but rather welcomed it. If Moscow's institutions stood in the way of Westernization, then they had to be abandoned.

The latter seventeenth century's politics demonstrates how important it was for the rulers of Europe to make adaptations. People ordinarily resisted change and shunned innovation, but stubborn resistance to new ideas put those so inclined into the ranks of the losers. Poland and the Ottoman Empire illustrate the point.

CHAPTER 4 REVIEW
LOUIS XIV'S EUROPE

Summary
- Louis XIV, King of France, in the latter seventeenth century was known as the Sun King because of his style, which brought royal absolutism to its height.
- The wars of Louis XIV dissipated much of the country's wealth, especially in the War of Spanish Succession, which sought to place a grandson on the throne in Madrid.
- Louis's lasting monument to France is his palace at Versailles.
- In England Cromwell's Puritans created a commonwealth, but a majority of people welcomed a restoration of the Stuarts.
- The last Stuart king lost the allegiance of his subjects and his daughter Mary, wife of the Dutch ruler, William of Orange, ensured a Protestant succession.
- The Austrian Habsburgs had a remarkable recovery in the Balkans in the late seventeenth century.
- The Hohenzollerns made Prussia an important state by building up its army.
- The Swedes and Russians took advantage of Poland's weakness.
- The Romanov tsars had problems with Old Believers and Cossacks until Peter the Great effectively began to rule the country.
- Peter's goal was to bring Russia into conformity with Western ways.
- European farmers benefited from new crops, especially the potato, from the Americas.
- Scientists of the period discovered more about the physical world.
- Newton's discovery of the law of gravity was the most important development of the age.

Identify
People: Louis XIV, Colbert, Bossuet, Charles II of England, Wren, William and Mary, Hobbes, Locke, Sobieski, Frederick William the Great Elector, Charles X of Sweden, Avvakum, Peter the Great of Russia, Piscopia, Boyle, Leeuwenhoek, Philip of Anjou, Richard Cromwell, Leopold I, Tsar Alexei, Stenka Razin, Halley, Leibniz, Newton
Places: Versailles, Czestochowa, St. Petersburg
Events: War of Spanish Succession, battle of the Boyne, Great Northern War, the discoveries of Newton, Habsburg gains against the Turks, discovery of the law of gravity, Treaty of Utrecht, Peace of Karlowitz, Treaty of Nystad

Define

Jansenism	England's Instrument of Government
Junkers	Glorious Revolution
Old Believers	Cossacks

Multiple Choice

1. Royal absolutism put a check on the power of
   (a) merchants.
   (b) nobles and clergy.
   (c) the middle class.
   (d) farmers.

2. Louis XIV's chief financial minister was
   (a) Colbert.
   (b) Sully.
   (c) Mazarin.
   (d) Richelieu.

3. The war of Spanish Succession was fought to gain the Spanish throne for
   (a) William of Orange.
   (b) Henry of Navarre.
   (c) Mazarin.
   (d) Philip of Anjou.

4. A Jansenist was
   (a) an Old Believer.
   (b) a French Protestant.
   (c) a Jacobite.
   (d) a Catholic with Calvinist tendencies.

5. The revocation of the Edict of Nantes
   (a) gave freedom to Huguenots.
   (b) took away the forts of the Huguenots.
   (c) caused many Huguenots to leave the country.
   (d) none of the above.

6. The new palace of Louis XIV was built at
   (a) Versailles.
   (b) Rouen.
   (c) Paris.
   (d) Lyon.

7. This English leader preferred the title of Lord Protector:
   (a) Laud
   (b) Hampton
   (c) Charles I
   (d) Cromwell

8. The Stuart restoration brought him back to London:
   (a) Charles I
   (b) Charles II
   (c) James II
   (d) William

9. A seventeenth-century Whig favored
   (a) the Puritans.
   (b) the Tudors.
   (c) the House of Orange.
   (d) the Stuarts.

10. William and Mary's arrival in London is known as
    (a) the Restoration.
    (b) the Commonwealth.
    (c) the Glorious Revolution.
    (d) the Great Restitution.

11. Parliament put a check on William and Mary's authority through enacting
    (a) a provision for impeachment.
    (b) an Instrument of Government.
    (c) an Act of Succession.
    (d) a Bill of Rights.

12. After the death of Queen Anne, British sovereigns came from
    (a) Hanover.
    (b) Scotland.
    (c) the Netherlands.
    (d) Bavaria.

13. His ideas supported the Glorious Revolution:
    (a) Hobbes
    (b) Locke
    (c) Laud
    (d) Bentham

14. Prince Eugene of Savoy directed Habsburg armies against
    (a) Poland.
    (b) Prussia.
    (c) Russia.
    (d) the Ottomans.

15. The Pragmatic Sanction of 1713 sought to
    (a) preserve Habsburg claims to all its lands.
    (b) secure the throne of Spain.
    (c) overturn the Treaty of Karlowitz.
    (d) guarantee the borders of Prussia.

16. The Great Elector ruled in
    (a) Austria.
    (b) the Netherlands.
    (c) Hanover.
    (d) Prussia.

17. The Parthenon of Athens suffered major destruction during a war between the Ottomans and
    (a) Austria.
    (b) Russia.
    (c) Turkey.
    (d) Venice.

18. Czestochowa was a turning point in a war between Poland and
    (a) Austria.
    (b) Sweden.
    (c) Prussia.
    (d) Russia.

19. The *liberum veto* was a device used in the Polish Diet to
    (a) question the king's ministers.
    (b) elect the monarch.
    (c) stop debate.
    (d) elect a prime minister.

20. An alliance of East European monarchs to limit Swedish control of the Baltic began the
    (a) Thirty Years' War.
    (b) Great Northern War.
    (c) Seven Years' War.
    (d) War of Polish Succession.

21. Tsar Peter the Great built a new capital at
    (a) Moscow.
    (b) Novgorod.
    (c) Smolensk.
    (d) St. Petersburg.

22. The largest percentage growth of population in Europe resulted from
    (a) corn production in France.
    (b) wheat production in Ukraine.
    (c) potato growing in Ireland.
    (d) corn production in Russia.

23. Edmund Halley's name was attached to a
    (a) star.
    (b) supernova.
    (c) meteor.
    (d) comet.

24. This Dutch lens maker first saw bacteria in a microscope:
    (a) Steno
    (b) Huygens
    (c) Boyle
    (d) Leeuwenhoek

25. *The Mathematical Principles of Natural Philosophy* dealt with
    (a) astronomy.
    (b) biology.
    (c) gravity.
    (d) relativity.

Essay Questions

1. Assess whether Louis XIV deserves the title of Sun King.
2. Compare the Puritan Commonwealth with that of the rule of the Stuarts in England.
3. What determined the conflict between Habsburgs and Hohenzollerns in seventeenth-century Europe?
4. What were the causes of Polish weakness?
5. What were the factors affecting Europe's farmers in the seventeenth century?

Answers

1. b	6. a	11. d	16. d	21. d
2. b	7. d	12. a	17. d	22. c
3. d	8. d	13. b	18. b	23. d
4. d	9. c	14. d	19. c	24. d
5. c	10. c	15. a	20. b	25. c

The European Enlightenment

The period of the European Enlightenment derives its name from writers who believed that they were entering a new period of European history. Reason, broadly understood, would in the future guide the actions of governments and other social institutions. Because of the progress made in science, the authors of the Enlightenment were convinced that they had found laws that were applicable to all areas of human behavior.

Voltaire sounded the call of the Enlightenment in his statement, "This century begins to see the triumph of reason." He and other writers of the age were quite a different breed of thinkers than those who led the Renaissance, Europe's last great intellectual movement. Renaissance scholars looked for truth through an examination of the literature of ancient Greece and Rome. The Enlightenment drew its inspiration from the work of the seventeenth century's mathematicians and scientists. For them the discoveries of this period were of such magnitude that they demanded reexamination of human existence.

Personalities of the Enlightenment

The proponents of the Enlightenment were a talented elite to whom the French word *philosophes* has been given. To be a philosophe was to be a lover of wisdom, to belong to an international community of scholars anxious to "enlighten" their fellow men and women. They corresponded with one another to compare their latest views and to announce their most recent publications. Frequent travel was another mark of the Enlightenment's thinkers that enabled them to make their observations.

Most of the philosophes were French, with a generous sprinkling of Englishmen, Scots, Germans, and Italians. Few were found in Spain, Scandinavia, or East Europe where there was less interest in reforming society. Many of the philosophes gathered in the salons of Paris where wealthy women supervised the discussions of their guests.

The most influential of the early philosophes, Charles Louis de Secondat, the Baron de Montesquieu, was a many-sided man. A lawyer of Bordeaux, he was an avid reader of Isaac Newton and John Locke. In 1721 he published anonymously *The Persian Letters,* a fictional account of two Persians traveling through France and their observations on the country's government and religion.

Baron de Montesquieu urged a division of power in government.

To Montesquieu, the British Parliament was a model of good government. In 1748 he published *The Spirit of the Laws,* in which he argued that Great Britain's separation of powers between executive, judicial, and legislative branches of government was the key to British political achievement.

One of France's best-known philosophes was Jean-Jacques Rousseau. Born in a watchmaker's family of Geneva, his relatives raised him without much supervision. At 16 he ran away from home, arriving in Paris without a job. He and his mistress, Thérèse Levasseur, had five children; all of them were placed in foundling homes.

Rousseau gained sudden fame when he was given a prize for his essay, "Discourse on the Arts and Sciences," in which he held that civilization corrupted people. He lived under the motto, "Everything is naturally good if left alone." Rousseau idealized the past when, he believed, civilization and its institutions had still not corrupted men and women. For him the "noble savage" was the ideal, free to choose his or her way of life untrammeled by laws and traditions that other people wanted to impose.

Rousseau was a strong advocate of universal education, believing it to be the foundation of a nation's prosperity. Although hardly a model for parenting himself, in *Émile, or an Essay on Education,* he urged that children find their own way, only learning things when they have an interest. Above all, no memorization should be required of a child.

Rousseau's *Social Contract* became one of the most influential political works ever written. His political theories attacked the monarchical principle, holding that all citizens are equal. The accident of birth that brought European kings to power was rejected as contrary to reason. The *Social Contract* later provided the slogan for the French Revolution, the struggle for "Liberty, Equality, and Fraternity."

François Arouet, better known as Voltaire, was another of the Enlightenment's popular authors. Voltaire was a man of great energy and a prodigious writer. His works fill over a hundred volumes on a wide variety of subjects: drama, history, poetry, politics, and religion. During his youth he spent time in prison for attacks on Louis XV's regent, an incident that turned him to call vigorously for a reform of the French government. Much of his life he spent abroad on the Swiss frontier, for it was too dangerous for him to live in France. In his essays he loved to heap scorn and satire on his opponents.

Voltaire sought a society free from authoritarian institutions.

Many of his essays singled out the church in France as an institution that needed reform at the least, destruction at the best. He blamed it for purveying myths and superstitions that kept people ignorant of the truth. He and Rousseau both died in 1778, just a decade before many of their ideas prompted the French people to revolution.

An enduring monument of the French Enlightenment was the publishing of the *Encyclopedia*, a multivolumed work that emerged over a period of 14 years, from 1751 to 1765. The editor of the *Encyclopedia* was Denis Diderot, who sought pieces from sympathetic authors from all over France. Within articles that seemed innocuous on the surface, in order to escape governmental censors, writers generously criticized French society.

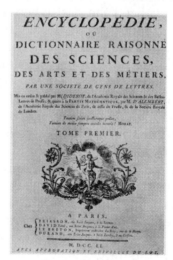

Title page of the Encyclopedia.

David Hume was a Scottish essayist, born in 1711 in Edinburgh. When he was a teenager, he became a skeptic and throughout his career published essays on religious, social, and economic issues. His most famous treatise, *An Essay Concerning Human Understanding,* explored the acquisition of knowledge.

Hume advanced the idea that all religions were of little value, arising out of human hopes and fears, the product of imagination. Only one area of human knowledge was certain, because it rested on evidence that could not be challenged. This was mathematics. Otherwise, all else was uncertain, for evidence was neither sufficient nor convincing.

Prussia's contribution to the Enlightenment came from Immanuel Kant, a teacher of philosophy in the city of Königsburg (now Kaliningrad in Russia). Kant published his ideas in two volumes, *The Critique of Pure Reason*, printed in 1781, and *The Critique of Practical Reason*, a work that appeared seven years later. While acknowledging that information comes from sense perception, Kant believed that reason, an innate quality, was alone responsible for conceptualization. Certain concepts were absolute, "whose truth or falsity cannot be discovered or confirmed by any experience." Priority was given to the categorical imperative of duty. A person's most impelling motivation depends on doing what one must. Kant defined duty as "the necessity to act out of reverence for the law."

Cesare Bonesana, Marchese of Beccaria, an Italian jurist and economist, took up another issue of concern to Enlightened thinkers. How should penal laws be reformed? His work *On Crimes and Punishment* urged a reform of the harsh and strict laws that punished so many minor crimes against property.

Although the major individuals of the Enlightenment have already been listed, dozens of others espoused the reforms advocated by these dominant thinkers. The only idea that appealed to all was abiding skepticism toward established institutions.

Basically, the Enlightened critics wanted a political reform that ensured that all men, but not yet women, should be treated equally before the law and their rights as citizens acknowledged. They urged that ethics replace religion, democracy supplant absolutism, and education of all male citizens dislodge the general governmental indifference to learning.

It is important to note that none of the prominent Enlightened authors had a political career but preferred to follow a private life of writing. Their most important legacy was to appear in the future, in the American and French Revolutions, which drew from them their guiding principles.

Politics in the British Isles

The British government enjoyed remarkable stability during the eighteenth century, despite a series of ineffective kings of German ancestry from Hanover. Parliament was in control, with landowners and merchants lining up in either the Whig or Tory parties.

The elections that entitled members to a seat in Commons were hardly fair. Some districts were "owned" by individuals; others were won because of bribery. Half the seats were controlled by a handful of people. Interest groups saw to it that candidates supporting them would not lose, donating sums of money to guarantee that result.

The House of Lords, made up of titled nobles and the Church of England's bishops, was generally Whig in sentiment, filled with the descendants of those who effected the Glorious Revolution. They supported the

Hanoverian succession with enthusiasm. In the House of Commons the Tories sometimes were strong enough to gain a majority. Actually party labels did not count for much because the large majority of Parliament's members had the same goals: keeping the Hanoverian dynasty on the throne and the nation's economy strong.

Under George I, Robert Walpole became the major figure in Parliament, skillfully managing patronage so as to hold power. He is credited with becoming Great Britain's first prime minister. Walpole was the architect of the cabinet system, where members who also served as ministers reported to the full house on their activities and assumed responsibility for their decisions.

Robert Walpole initiated the cabinet government in Great Britain.

Walpole sought to keep Great Britain out of war because paying for armed forces was the major cause of high taxation. His policies were successful until 1739; then the country entered a 20-year period of constant conflicts.

There were still British men and women who believed that the Stuarts were the rightful rulers of the country. Twice Stuart pretenders landed in the British Isles, once in 1715 when James Edward sought to claim the throne of his father, and again in 1745 when his son, "Bonnie Prince Charlie," arrived on the Scottish coast. In April 1745 German mercenary troops brought by Britain from Hanover met his army at Culloden.

The MacDonalds, angered at the position they had been assigned in the ranks, refused to fight and allowed the British force to overrun them. Charlie narrowly escaped capture by hiding in the Highlands until he was rescued by a French ship. Lest the Highlands should rise again, the London government arrested their chiefs, banned the kilt, and effectively destroyed the clans that had organized Scottish life for centuries.

During the reign of George II, William Pitt provided the leadership of the House of Commons. His policies brought the nation notable victories over France in the Americas and in India. After 1763 Great Britain was the undisputed victor in the colonial wars and sat comfortably as the leading economic power of the world.

Pitt did not easily work with King George III, who came to the throne in 1760. George was the first Hanoverian brought up in England and, therefore, took much more personal interest in the affairs of state that once were handled by the prime minister.

After 1770 Lord Frederick North was in charge of Parliament as the king's minister. Edmund Burke led the opposition, calling for Parliament to act independently of the king. One pressing issue was how to deal with the growing independence movement in the British colonies of America. Those who rejected criticism argued that the reformers's constant complaints over the vacillation of the king and the corruption in Parliament were bound to encourage American separatism.

The issue was to be settled by force of arms in the American Revolution. At its conclusion, William Pitt the Younger became the Parliamentary prime minister. In 1788 George was incapacitated by a rare illness, porphyria, which was caused by too much pigment in the blood. He held on to the throne but lived the rest of his life in fear of a relapse.

For Irish Catholics the eighteenth century continued bleak. Penal laws that discriminated against them in many ways remained on the books. The Dublin Parliament excluded them, so they had no political voice. Catholics were forbidden to hold public office, and they could not become lawyers nor purchase land from a Protestant. Failure to pay rental fees on time meant confiscation of farmers' land, and absentee landlords, many living in England or Scotland, raised the rent on their properties as they pleased.

Crime and brigandage became common, thanks to the wretched condition of the peasant population. The upper class left the country when they could, leaving the Catholic bishops and priests to represent the population. The Catholic clergy therefore assumed a political as well as a religious role.

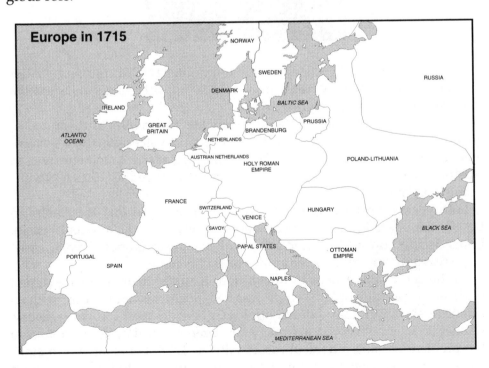

Europe in 1715

France in the Old Regime

Louis XIV's great-grandson, who was then but five years of age, succeeded him as Louis XV. Much as in London, Parisian politics was the domain of vested interests. The nobility that Louis XIV had tried to keep in check flocked back to Paris and political office.

After the failure of the Mississippi Bubble, a failed scheme to shift the nation's debt into private hands, the court gave the leadership of the government to the aged Cardinal André Fleury, then 73. He held office as the king's chief minister until his retirement at 90 years of age.

Like the Hanoverians in London, Louis XV found himself increasingly the butt of criticism. The *parlements* of the country acted as if they, rather than the king, decided legislation. Frustrated with their independence, Louis abolished them in 1771. Obviously more of his subjects were angered by this action than were pleased, and inspired by the philosophes' writings, indignation swept the nation.

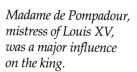

Madame de Pompadour, mistress of Louis XV, was a major influence on the king.

It is said that Louis recognized his unpopularity and quipped, "After me, the deluge." He may never have said it, but it certainly reflected the inheritance he left his own grandson.

In 1774 Louis XVI entered the kingship. He was honest and wanted to govern well but lacked the intelligence needed to steer the royal government through the troubled times ahead. His wife, Marie Antoinette, was an Austrian Habsburg, and the unpopular marriage stirred up French patriots against the king.

Four years after becoming ruler, Louis was advised that the American Revolution offered France a golden opportunity to strike at Great Britain. Louis decided on intervention with both men and money. French assistance was a determining factor in the American success.

At the end of the American Revolution, with the treaty of peace signed in Paris, the prestige of France was restored. Such was not the case with its financial situation. Huge debts now weighed down the royal treasury. Louis's finance ministers tried many stratagems, but they could not solve the problem of state indebtedness. Finally, in 1788, Louis agreed to summon the Estates General, little realizing that this was to be the first step toward revolution.

The Germans under Habsburgs and Hohenzollerns

The Habsburg Holy Roman Emperor, Charles VI, thought that he had ensured the succession for his daughter, Maria Theresa, upon his death. In 1740, however, upon her father's death, Maria Theresa did not just inherit the crown but a pack of troubles from neighboring countries. The Elector of Bavaria intended that he, rather than a Habsburg, should become Holy Roman Emperor. Frederick II, King of Prussia, cast his eyes on the province of Silesia, and King Louis XV of France considered annexing the Austrian Netherlands, modern Belgium, to his country.

A woman of less ability may well have been overcome by the many challenges that the War of Austrian Succession commenced. Instead, Maria Theresa resisted. She appeared before the Hungarian Diet, holding her infant son Josef in her arms, and implored the nobles to raise an army in her defense. The eloquence of the queen changed the usually reluctant Diet to come to her assistance.

Maria Theresa sought to better government in the Habsburg lands.

Despite the addition of Hungarian troops, the Habsburg armies could not remove the Prussians from Silesia. Therefore, in 1745 Maria Theresa accepted the loss of the province.

In domestic affairs Maria Theresa was intent upon centralizing the government and making it more efficient. She also gave her attention to providing more schools for her subjects and improving medical facilities. She managed to govern while at the same time giving birth to 12 children.

One of them, Josef, had received the crown of the Empire in 1765, but as long as his mother lived he had to show restraint in his plans to radically reform the Habsburg administration. In 1780, upon the death of Maria Theresa, Josef finally had his opportunity.

In the next ten years Josef put into law the changes that he long contemplated to modernize the Holy Roman Empire. Josef's legislation in many ways was admirable. He abolished serfdom and granted full citizenship to Jews and members of all Christian churches. He required the nobility to pay taxes. Less commendable was an edict that made German the only official language in the empire and a compulsory class in all its schools.

The emperor wanted to put the Catholic church in his state under his sole authority. He would head the church, not the pope. His interest in church affairs caused him to close many monasteries and convents, to limit priests to offering only one Mass a day, and to regulate how many candles could be lit for Mass.

The vast majority of his subjects had little sympathy with Josef's reforms. They went too far and came too fast. The emperor's epitaph summed it up, "Here lies a man who, with the best intentions, never succeeded in anything."

While the fortunes of the Austrians fluctuated, Prussian strength continued to grow under its Hohenzollern kings, Frederick William I and Frederick II, whom his subjects called the Great.

Frederick William was known throughout Europe for his fascination with military affairs. The rather meager revenues that came to Berlin were used to increase the army to the same size as the armed forces of France and the Holy Roman Empire. The king especially delighted in his elite unit, the Potsdam Guard, which enlisted only men over six feet in height.

Despite his father's strict moralistic training, his son and heir apparent, Frederick, showed little interest in the army. His concerns as a young man were in art, literature, and playing the flute. His father responded to these activities by beating Frederick, locking him up, and taking away his books. Once the young Frederick and a friend tried to run away. They were caught, and the king ordered his accomplice beheaded while the young prince watched in horror.

Slowly Frederick's father weaned him away from the arts, and in a tribute to his father's perseverance, Frederick shifted his attention to statecraft. The crown prince was given his own regiment to drill and after a while discovered it to his liking.

In 1740 Frederick succeeded his father as Prussian ruler and immediately sought to expand his nation's borders with an attack on Habsburg Silesia. Next Frederick's ambition led him into the Seven Years' War, which extended from 1756 to 1763. A coalition of Austrians, Saxons, Russians, Swedes, and French sought to teach the upstart Prussian ruler a lesson.

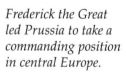

Frederick the Great led Prussia to take a commanding position in central Europe.

Frederick struck first into Saxony and then into Bohemia, where he put Prague under siege and occupied the town. In 1757 he defeated a French army and then an Austrian one. The Russians in 1759 reached Berlin and occupied the Prussian capital, but they withdrew when Frederick bribed its commander.

Frederick was then saved through a stroke of good fortune. In 1762 Tsarina Elizabeth, under whose command the Russians fought, died, and the succession passed to Peter III, a great admirer of Prussia and its ruler. Peter ordered the Russian soldiers to leave Prussia. A year later the Seven Years' War ended with all Frederick's possessions intact and the other European states grudgingly acknowledging his gains.

East Europe

For the Poles, the eighteenth century was one best forgotten. Once the largest state in East Europe, in this period the Polish-Lithuanian Commonwealth disappeared from Europe's map.

The problems of Poland were many. The elected Polish kings were usually foreigners, Germans from Saxony. The nobles who ran the country were indifferent toward the fate of the monarchy.

In 1764 the Russian choice for the Polish crown was Stanislaw Poniatowski, formerly a lover of Catherine the Great. He arrived in Poland to discover that some nobles actually were willing to limit the chronic problems brought on because of the *liberum veto.*

The Poniatowski palace in Warsaw was built during the last years of independent Poland.

Civil war erupted, and Russian armies marched into Poland. The Ottoman Turks then joined the fray announcing that they intended to help the Poles against the Russians. Maria Theresa in Vienna feared that the Russians were making too many gains and threatened to send her army into Poland. As a general war over Poland hovered over Europe, Frederick the Great suggested a solution: partition Poland lest a general war break out.

Therefore, in 1772 Poland-Lithuania lost one third of its territories and one half of its population. Russia took all of what is now Belarus, Austria gained Poland's southern region, and Prussia annexed Pomerania on the Baltic.

Russia

Following the death of Peter the Great in 1725, the Russians had seven rulers in the next 37 years. Although two were complete outsiders, without any relationship to Peter, the others were his descendants or related to him by marriage. Most were quite content to leave the actual management of the state in the hands of advisers. These court officials were frequently Germans who had become Russian citizens after Peter's conquests in the Baltic.

While the court had every luxury, the condition of the serfs worsened. Taxation had to cover the ruler's growing expenses in peacetime and the costs of the army during war. Recalcitrant serfs suffered public beatings or exile to Siberia. Many fled of their own volition to escape the heavy burdens of the tax collector.

During the rule of Peter the Great's daughter, Tsarina Elizabeth, the Germans at court lost their influence. Elizabeth acted with a firm hand, making her own appointments and setting her own policies. Elizabeth put Russia on the side of the Habsburgs during the Seven Years' War, but upon her death the new Tsar Peter III gave up all the Russian gains.

Peter's fondness for Frederick has an explanation. He himself was German, born in the small state of Holstein. An alcoholic at 11 years of age, his future did not look promising. Court officials found him a wife in Princess Sophia Augusta of Anhalt-Zerbst, who was brought to St. Petersburg where she changed her name to Catherine.

Peter had nothing but contempt for his wife whom he humiliated as often as possible. Catherine was not above ingratiating herself with officers of the Imperial Guard. In their barracks, they acclaimed Catherine as sovereign, and rejected Peter. She led them to her husband's residence where the tsar agreed to yield the throne so long as he could keep his mistress, his dog, and his violin. Catherine agreed, but a week later the Guard killed Peter, and Catherine was left supreme.

A young Catherine the Great sought ways to reform the Russian state.

Catherine is another Russian ruler who has had Great added to her name. Although a foreigner, she took on the management of the Russian state with zest. She was an avid reader, especially of the philosophes whom she greatly admired, corresponding with Voltaire and providing a pension to Diderot. She thought herself "enlightened," as did Frederick the Great of Prussia and Josef II of Austria. There is no doubt that she proved to be conscientious, sometimes working 12 or 15 hours a day in administrative matters.

On Catherine's direction, jurists were put to work to rationalize the nation's law code that had reached an impossible size and complexity. She personally drew up the *Nakaz*, a set of instructions for the reform with ideas taken from Beccaria's works on crime and punishment. The new code forbade the use of torture, established equality before the law, limited capital punishment, and offered toleration to religious dissenters from the Orthodox church.

Despite changes in the law, serf revolts became more common during Catherine's reign. They were put down with great brutality and generally with little trouble. However, in 1773, Emilian Pugachev, a Don Cossack who claimed he was Peter III, gathered an army of serfs, Cossacks, Tartars, and Asian tribesmen. For a time government troops sent to put down his revolt were routed. Wherever Pugachev marched, he burned the landlords' manors and freed the serfs. For two years Pugachev terrorized the countryside, until at last he was captured, brought to Moscow in a cage, and there beheaded.

The problem of serfdom simply would not go away, yet Catherine preferred to ignore it because she could not afford to lose the support of the nobility. In fact, life for the men and women who were serfs, well over half the population of the country, was increasingly difficult. In a **Charter of the Nobility,** issued in 1785, landowners were allowed to sell their serfs or give them away with no restrictions attached. Their owners might flog them, force them into military service, or exile them to Siberia with impunity. All the labor of the serfs, if it brought profits, benefited their masters. It is true that Catherine lightened the taxes that fell on state-owned serfs, but they remained subject to the whim of government officials.

The Ottoman Balkans

For the Greeks of the Ottoman Empire, the eighteenth century provided further opportunities to enhance their position as junior partners of the Turks in managing the government. They held many important and lucrative offices in Istanbul.

A key to Greek success was western education and ability to converse in European languages. Many children of the **Phanariotes,** the Christian upper class, attended universities abroad, especially in Italy.

The Orthodox patriarchs also enhanced their authority in the eighteenth century. Patriarch Kyrillos V issued an edict, the *Oros* of 1755, that required the baptism of converts to Orthodoxy from any other religion. The Oros of 1755 broke any communion with the western churches, for in effect it denied the validity of their sacraments. This statement, rather than the events of 1054, marks the true schism between the Christian East and West.

In 1774 the Ottomans agreed to a peace with Russia in the Treaty of Küchük Kainarji, after one more war between these traditional enemies. The Ottomans lost some territory in the Crimea and the Black Sea regions and gave to the Russians, according to St. Petersburg's interpretation, the right to protect Orthodox Christians in the Ottoman Empire.

A kiosk stands in the Grand Serai of the sultans.

Science in the Eighteenth Century

While the science of the seventeenth century had been largely one of discovery and experimentation, that of the eighteenth century was mainly one of assimilation, classification, and the application of new data.

Because of Newton's contributions, the fields of astronomy and physics experienced the most progress. Astronomers of the century were chiefly interested in testing the validity of the Newtonian synthesis.

William Herschel, originally a German organist, moved to England where he educated himself in astronomy. He built his own telescope with which he identified sun spots, mountains on the moon, and the snow caps of Mars. He discovered the planet Uranus and mapped the stars in the Milky Way. His sister, Caroline Herschel, discovered eight comets while working independently of her brother.

The most important advances in physics concerned the study of electricity. In 1746 scientists at the University of Leyden in the Netherlands invented the Leyden jar, which was used to store electricity. Alessandro Volta, a professor at Pavia, constructed the first practical battery. In his honor, the electrical unit volt received its name. Benjamin Franklin, on the western side of the Atlantic, demonstrated that lightning was an electrical discharge in the atmosphere.

A number of inventions during the eighteenth century assisted the growth of physics. Gabriel Fahrenheit, a German merchant living in the Netherlands, constructed a thermometer of mercury in a sealed tube. The scale of temperatures he devised are still in use in the United States. The Swedish astronomer Anders Celsius built the centigrade thermometer named for him, with 0 as the freezing point and 100 at the boiling point.

The most outstanding chemist of the century was Antoine Lavoisier. He correctly explained the process of combustion and demonstrated that respiration and combustion were both forms of oxidation. His research demolished the theory of phlogiston, which held this substance caused combustion.

Antoine Lavoisier and his wife. Lavoisier made many contributions to the physical sciences.

A Swedish doctor, Carl Linnaeus, was first to classify plants systematically based on their organs of reproduction, stamens and pistils. Not content with identifying over 12,000 plants, he also classified animals, minerals, and even diseases. Linnaeus devised a system of nomenclature that gave each plant and animal a generic and a specific name.

Learned societies encouraged governments to finance voyages of discovery in the national interest. These expeditions included specialists in many diverse fields. Naturalists examined strange flora and fauna and described and classified them.

Religion and the Enlightenment

Although the philosophes had a critical attitude toward all social institutions, they were especially impatient with religious structures. The established churches in western Europe, especially in England and France, found their systems of belief under vigorous attack. The philosophes wanted to convert Christianity into a belief in a God of nature. They rejected the Bible's story of creation as unscientific, opposed revelation as a source of knowledge, and claimed miracles to be fantasy. At most the proponents of the Enlightenment, known as **Deists,** would allow God only responsibility for the initial creation.

Deists held that the only true belief was a natural religion common to all men. Religion had a certain social validity when it stressed morality, but all the rest was expendable. Although Deism was popular with the intellectuals of the eighteenth century, it failed to gain wide appeal among any other class.

Freemasonry helped to spread Deism. In 1717 a number of secret societies, patterned after the medieval guild of stone masons, formed a Grand Lodge in London. Its constitution stressed belief in a God of nature and sought to appeal to men of all beliefs.

The greatest success of the critics of Christianity resulted in the suppression of the strongest element in the Catholic church, the Society of Jesus. Members of this group were the educators of Europe's upper class, and in numbers they were the largest of religious orders. A campaign against the Jesuits began in Portugal and spread through the other Catholic states of Europe, until it reached all the way to the papacy. In 1773 Pope Clement XIV issued a decree dissolving the Society of Jesus in an effort to pacify the rulers of Europe who had turned so antagonistic to it.

Among many Protestants of the eighteenth century, questions about the formalism of the established churches proved to be a problem. The result was a strong pietist and evangelical movement that first appeared in Germany. A number of Lutheran pastors stressed a revived personal spirituality and less concern over theological issues. Pietism influenced Count Nikolaus Zinzendorf, a German nobleman to organize the church of the Moravian Brethren.

In Great Britain the Methodist church represented the move to Pietism. Charles Wesley and his brother John, while students at Oxford, along with other sympathetic young men, devoted themselves to regular times of prayer, reading the Scriptures, and pursuing acts of charity. They were so methodical in their religious activities that they were called Methodists.

John Wesley, founder of the Methodist church.

For a time both brothers went as missionaries to colonial Georgia in America but returned disillusioned with frontier life. Back in Britain the Wesleys preached fervent open-air sermons and stressed the singing of gospel hymns, many of them Charles's compositions.

Traveling on horseback through England and Ireland, John Wesley supervised the growing Methodist congregations, especially among the British working class for whom the Anglican church's ritual seemed distant. The hostility of bishops to his movement forced John, ordained a priest of the Anglican church, to form a separate organization and a church independent of the Anglican communion.

On a positive note, the secular spirit of the Enlightenment encouraged greater toleration of all religious faiths. The Deists furthered this trend by their complete indifference to religious commitment of any kind. Pietists also assisted religious toleration because they minimized the importance of dogmas and creeds. Their emphasis was on leading a moral life, not on doctrinal orthodoxy. Jews were the special beneficiaries of the toleration of the times, as they entered the main stream of the western European states.

Economic Activity in the Eighteenth Century

The European economy continued its momentum. All other societies, for better or worse, could not resist the impact of Europeans in their midst.

The circumstances that allowed Europeans to increase their preeminence and wealth is a complex story, with many aspects to be considered. To begin, Europe's access to science and the technology that flowed from discovery gave its citizens a significant advantage over men and women on other continents. An ability to organize time was another favorable factor. Better ships, navigational devices, and especially the development of superior armaments propelled the European advance into the far reaches of the world.

Europe also had banking and credit facilities to provide the capital that its merchants required. Gold and silver bullion poured into European mints to be stamped into coinage that held its value because it was based upon precious metals. The easy flow of currency greased the wheels of entrepreneurs seeking to expand their businesses.

Men and women who had money in Great Britain invested in raw materials and then "put them out" to peasant farmers. In their cottages men, women, and children worked to fashion these materials into marketable products. Many of the families who worked in these cottage industries were farmers who used the work to supplement their incomes during the winter months.

Textiles, especially those made of wool in England and Scotland, were the most important products of the cottage industries. Besides woolens, the British farm household fashioned cotton goods, but in the eighteenth century, even linen production was more important. Small shops that had furnaces forged copper, iron, and lead containers as well as porcelain and glass.

Farmers in France thresh grain in a barn.

For many merchants, domestic markets appeared too limited, and therefore they set their eyes upon international trade. Here greater risks also brought enhanced profits. The French dominated commerce in western continental Europe and in the Ottoman Empire. The British were ahead in the Americas and East Asia.

Many businessmen were convinced that governments' enthusiasm for mercantilism was flawed. When merchants were free to buy and sell as they chose, profits increased and contributed to the wealth of the nation. An argument developed for free trade, or **laissez-faire capitalism.**

Both David Hume and Adam Smith argued the case for deregulation in Great Britain. In 1776 Smith, a Scottish economist, published *An Inquiry into the Nature and Causes of the Wealth of Nations.* Few other books have had such an influence on economics and politics. Smith contended that restrictions on trade and industry were counterproductive. Wealth was not in precious metals but in a country's resources.

Society in the Eighteenth Century

During the eighteenth century, life expectancy for the average European improved. Demographers give credit to the greater abundance of food. Poorer people were often healthier than the rich for they lived on grains and vegetables rather than meat. Both rich and poor ate little fruit and suffered vitamin deficiencies.

Sickness was all-pervasive, with the common notion still prevalent that either bad air or evil spirits caused disease. Druggists were many, selling herbal cures that sometimes helped and sometimes did not.

Surgeons were of the opinion that if a person had a broken bone, amputation was a sure cure. Anesthesia did not yet exist, so operations were very painful. No one knew the importance of sterilizing instruments beforehand, so infection often accompanied any kind of surgery.

When a person became ill, blood-letting was thought to be one of the best prescriptions. This was often done by applying leeches to the body, a practice that has now been discovered to have some benefit. Another solution to illness consisted of digesting large amounts of laxatives so as to purge the body of its foreign elements.

Mentally ill people suffered from the common view that madness must be the fault of those who had it. London's asylum for the insane, named Bethlehem, was so chaotic that the word *bedlam* has entered the English language.

Four out of five people could be expected to contract smallpox sometime in their lifetime. Edward Jenner, a British physician, attacked this scourge. He took the serum from cowpox, a related disease, and used it to inoculate people against smallpox. The success of Jenner's work finally convinced the public of the safety of vaccinations, and the long road to destroy smallpox began. Early in the 1900s smallpox disappeared throughout the world in what is surely one of medicine's greatest accomplishments.

Marriage in the eighteenth century took place when the man was often in his thirties and the woman in her twenties. Large numbers of people never married. Economic considerations explain this phenomenon. Until a man had enough money to move from his parents' house, or in some localities until his father died, marriage was out of the question. To build up their finances, young boys were apprenticed to craftsmen and merchants, but wages were very low. Young girls served as domestic servants.

An eighteenth-century bakery produced a variety of breads and provided a small mill for customers to grind their own grain.

As economic security increased, so too did the number of births, both in and out of wedlock. In the average family, six pregnancies were considered the average. Of that number, perhaps four children might survive childhood. The number of deaths of infants and women in childbirth was high, and as a result men in the eighteenth century lived longer than their wives.

Rich parents sent their children to school at an early age because elementary schools were now found all over western Europe. The study of the Bible and the catechism took up much of the school day. As early as 1717, the Prussian government encouraged elementary schooling for all children.

For the upper classes, the Age of the Enlightenment provided a good life. Many lived in large and spacious homes where servants waited upon them day and night. Portraits of ancestors hung on the walls to remind them of their obligations to keep the family properties intact. To fill in the day's hours, many of the gentry class took up scientific studies of one kind or other.

When not bothered by business, members of the upper class hunted, gambled, and drank large amounts of beer and whiskey. While French men and women gathered in salons, British men preferred coffee houses and pubs.

Malahide, a land-owner's house in Ireland.

The gap between rich and poor remained evident even in the midst of the boom times of the century. For the poor the standard of living continued to be low, and the hopelessness of their situation meant a serious rise in alcoholism. In London gin was the preferred drink, and an astonishing number of poorer people were addicted to it.

Literature, Art, and Music

French cultural dominance was so complete during the eighteenth century that most educated Europeans slavishly copied everything that came out of Paris. Nowhere was this more true than among the Germans. Educated men and women wrote and conversed in French, although Latin remained the language of the university classroom.

Johann Wolfgang Goethe became the first figure in German literature. His influence on the German language rivals Shakespeare's impact on English. Goethe is best known for *Faust,* which portrays the dilemma of a man who sells his soul to the devil in return for knowledge and power.

In England the novel became immensely popular. Daniel Defoe's *Robinson Crusoe* reads like a first-hand report of this most famous of island castaways and retains its status as one of the most popular stories in the English language.

The emergence of periodicals and newspapers first occurred in Great Britain in the eighteenth century. By 1750 London had seven dailies, ten weekly newspapers, and numerous periodicals. Most of these journals catered to the tastes of the general public, but some were serious literary publications that provided publishing opportunities for young writers.

The Age of the Enlightenment was a great epoch in the history of symphonic music. There was a notable increase in the number and quality of instruments. Antonio Stradivari fashioned violins to standards that have never been surpassed. In 1710 Bartolomeo Cristofori invented the piano, which gradually replaced the harpsichord and clavichord among keyboard instruments. In 1767 the world's first public piano concert was given in London.

George Frideric Handel, composer of the Messiah.

Two great composers of the century were both born in the German Saxony in 1685. George Frideric Handel went to England as court musician to George I. Although Handel produced many operas, he is most famous for his 32 oratorios, the sacred counterpart of the opera. Of these, Handel's *Messiah* is his most commonly recognized oratorio. While Handel basked in the musical center of the English court and society, his countryman, Johann Sebastian Bach, lived in relative obscurity as a church organist. Although he composed many forms of music, Bach's true musical vocation was in the service of the church.

Wolfgang Amadeus Mozart was the greatest figure in music in the Habsburg Empire. As a small child, his genius was recognized as he traveled about with his father and sister, Maria Anna. Before he reached ten years of age, he had published two symphonies and ten violin sonatas. Mozart's career required him to live in numerous European cities to serve his many patrons. He never escaped poverty for long. By the time of his premature death at 35 years of age, he had over 600 works to his name. He was then so poor that he was buried in an unmarked grave in Vienna.

Among Italian composers, the eighteenth century produced Antonio Vivaldi, a creator of concertos, sonatas, and operas in abundance. A Catholic chaplain at a girl's orphanage in Venice, he required from his pupils extraordinary skill on the violin. The *Four Seasons,* written in 1725, has become his most famous piece.

Conclusion

For the masses of European workers and farmers, the discussion of the Enlightenment on the place of nature, reason, government, and economic institutions were far removed from their daily concerns. Providing shelter, food, and clothing for survival and a degree of comfort required long hours of work in western Europe, while in the eastern part of the continent where serfdom still held forth, there were no rewards for equally hard labor. It was life without satisfaction.

Ideas do have consequences and move events along, but the concepts of freedom, toleration, and democracy took decades to evolve from the written word into action. When that happened, these ideas sparked the French Revolution, and Europe was never the same again.

Among the European nations there were improvements in education and health care, but even this was limited to the privileged in the upper and middle classes. The notion of human equality was often found in the writing of the philosophes, but even they did not extend this principle to the female members of the human race. It was an enlightened age for the few, but not for the many.

It was certainly a sign of progress that religious toleration played a more influential role. For the past two centuries, European monarchs were convinced that they must impose their religous views on their subjects, lest treason sweep the land. In the eighteenth century freedom of conscience scored some gains as governments learned to separate political from religious loyalty.

CHAPTER 5 REVIEW
THE EUROPEAN ENLIGHTENMENT

Summary
- Eighteenth century Britain was a time of stability with Parliament's power in the ascendancy.
- Cabinet government developed under the first prime minister, Walpole. A succession of able prime ministers followed.
- Penal laws continued to discriminate against Irish Catholics.
- Louis XV found it difficult to govern because of parlements, while his successor Louis XVI fell into financial difficulties.
- Prussia became the leading German power, putting Habsburg Austria into second place.
- The neighbors of Poland began its partition.
- Catherine the Great managed to expand Russia's borders and to reform some of its internal institutions, but did not eliminate serfdom.
- The thinkers for whom the Enlightenment is named urged that reason and nature must guide governments and human life.
- Natural science advanced in physics, chemistry, and botany.
- The Enlightenment put religion on the defensive.
- Europeans dominated economic activity in world trade.
- Medicine made progress, but illness, especially smallpox, remained a terrible scourge.
- The royal court and language of France dominated the cultural life of Europe.

Identify
People: Walpole, Bonnie Prince Charlie, King George III, Louis XV of France, Maria Theresa, Frederick II of Prussia, Poniatowski, Catherine the Great, Phanariotes, Montesquieu, Rousseau, Voltaire, Kant, Lavoisier, Wesley, Jenner, Mozart, Diderot, Hume, Bonesana, William Pitt, Fleury, Frederick William I of Prussia, Tsarina Elizabeth, Pugachev, Kyrillos V, Herschel, Linnaeus, Goethe, Defoe, Handel

Places: Silesia, Berlin, Königsberg, Leyden

Events: Seven Years' War, Pugachev's rebellion, publication of the *Encyclopedia*, development of capitalism

Define

parlements	Charter of the Nobility
Deism	laissez-faire capitalism
freemasonry	development of symphonic music
liberum veto	

Multiple Choice
1. Thinkers of the Enlightenment found truth in
   (a) quoting authorities.
   (b) the laws of a nation.
   (c) church doctrine.
   (d) reason and nature.

2. Britain's House of Lords was made up of
   (a) elected representatives.
   (b) hereditary nobles and Anglican bishops.
   (c) prime ministers.
   (d) the king's deputies.

3. The battle of Culloden was a disaster for
   (a) the Stuarts.
   (b) the Tudors.
   (c) the Hanoverians.
   (d) the Windsors.

4. He was king during the years of the American Revolution:
   (a) George I
   (b) George II
   (c) George III
   (d) none of the above

5. The parlements of France contended that they had a responsibility to
   (a) check on the church.
   (b) supervise education.
   (c) give assent to new laws and taxes.
   (d) administer colonial legislation.

6. The wife of Louis XVI was
   (a) Catherine de'Medici.
   (b) Maria Theresa.
   (c) Marie Henrietta.
   (d) Marie Antoinette.

7. Austria lost this province to Prussia in 1745:
   (a) Silesia
   (b) Saxony
   (c) Bavaria
   (d) Hanover

8. Jews were given full citizenship in Habsburg lands by
   (a) Maria Theresa.
   (b) Josef II.
   (c) Charles II.
   (d) Frederick II.

9. The Potsdam Guard with its tall soldiers was the creation of
   (a) Frederick William I.
   (b) Frederick II.
   (c) Ferdinand II.
   (d) William I.

10. The Seven Years' War ended with
    (a) Prussia partitioned.
    (b) Prussia intact.
    (c) a French army stationed in Prussia.
    (d) a Russian army stationed in Prussia.

11. Frederick II suggested that the partition of the Ottoman Empire should be replaced by
    (a) partition of Hungary.
    (b) economic sanction of Russia.
    (c) partition of Poland.
    (d) trade agreements with Saxony.

12. Catherine the Great was born in
    (a) Poland.
    (b) a German principality.
    (c) Russia.
    (d) Prussia.

13. The leader of a rebellion against Catherine's rule was
    (a) Dmitry I.
    (b) Razin.
    (c) Poniatowski.
    (d) Pugachev.

14. Baron de Montesquieu believed that good government came from
    (a) a strong king.
    (b) a wise foreign policy.
    (c) a centralized economy.
    (d) separation of powers.

15. The ideal of Rousseau was
    (a) the polished gentleman.
    (b) the scholarly clergyman.
    (c) the well-mannered lady.
    (d) the noble savage.

16. The *Encyclopedia* was a work that promoted
    (a) Pietism.
    (b) Protestantism.
    (c) freemasonry.
    (d) enlightened thought.

17. David Hume might be called a
    (a) politician.
    (b) skeptic.
    (c) theologian.
    (d) physicist.

18. Kant's categorical imperative was based on
    (a) duty.
    (b) religion.
    (c) philosophy.
    (d) law.

19. Caroline Herschel is famous for her discovery of
    (a) new stars.
    (b) Uranus.
    (c) Pluto.
    (d) comets.

20. Celsius is famous for his
    (a) Leyden jar.
    (b) thermometer.
    (c) telescope.
    (d) mathematical tables.

21. Botanical classifications were the work of
    (a) Fahrenheit.
    (b) Lavoisier.
    (c) Linnaeus.
    (d) Franklin.

22. Deists thought of God as
    (a) a redeemer.
    (b) transcendent.
    (c) the great architect.
    (d) personified in the Hebrew scriptures.

23. The Methodist church owes its foundation to the
    (a) Grimms.
    (b) Romanovs.
    (c) Jesuits.
    (d) Wesleys.

Essay Questions
 1. Discuss the work of the major natural scientists of the eighteenth century.
 2. Were the Enlightened thinkers too optimistic about their view of humans? Explain your answer.
 3. What were the factors that allowed parliamentary government to develop in England?
 4. Explain the rise of Prussia.

Answers

1. d	6. d	11. c	16. d	21. c
2. b	7. a	12. b	17. b	22. c
3. a	8. b	13. d	18. a	23. d
4. c	9. a	14. d	19. d	
5. c	10. b	15. d	20. b	

CHAPTER 6

Southwest Asia in Early Modern Times

Southwest Asia extends along the eastern Mediterranean from Anatolia to the southern coast of the Arabian Peninsula and inland to the eastern border of Iran. In ancient times it was the birthplace of the urban and agricultural revolutions. Here about 5,000 years ago civilization first appeared in the valley of the Tigris and Euphrates Rivers. For centuries Southwest Asian peoples contributed to the great empires of the ancient world, from the time of the Persians through the Romans.

Here major religious leaders, Moses, Zarathustra, Jesus, and Muhammad first preached their messages. The last of these, Muhammad, so inspired the Arab peoples that they spread throughout Southwest Asia indelibly imprinting on it the Arabic language and the Islamic faith.

It is, for the most part, an arid world, where the climate makes every drop of rain important. Much environmental damage has occurred, limiting the amount of land that can feed its population. It was always a crossroads, where East and West met to exchange their products.

Two major Muslim kingdoms dominate the history of Southwest Asia in early modern history. One is the Ottoman Empire; the other, Persia. Despite a common religion, Islam, and a universal esteem for the Qur'an, the book that all Muslims revere as God's revealed word, there was no love lost between the two kingdoms. Because the Ottomans straddled both Europe and Southwest Asia, they appear in the history of both regions.

The Ottoman Turks belonged to the **Sunnite** branch of Islam, while Persia represented the **Shi'ite Muslims.** This division, centuries old, principally resulted from a dispute over who should lead the Muslim community. The Sunnites held that any male Muslim could be elected Muhammad's representative, or caliph. The Shi'ites believed the leader must be a descendant of Muhammad, through his son-in-law, Ali and the Prophet's wife, Fatimah. Many wars were fought over this issue in the Middle Ages, and in 1500 no solution was yet in sight.

The Ottomans had come into Anatolia in the eleventh century and assimilated many in the Greek and Armenian populations that preceded them. In the fourteenth century they crossed into Europe and quickly made the southern Balkans part of their domain. In 1453 Sultan Mehmed II conquered Constantinople, bringing to an end the Byzantine period of Roman history and establishing his capital there, renaming the city Istanbul.

Mehmed II constructed Anadol Hisar to cut off supplies to Constantinople.

Ottoman Government

The Ottoman government was an absolute monarchy. In theory the sultans owned all the land, and everyone who served in the administration held office because of the sultan's command. The Muslim *ulema*, the religious establishment of the Ottomans, consisted of teachers of the Qur'an, *imams* who led Friday worship, *kadis* who were Islamic judges, and **muftis** who interpreted the law.

Despite the sultan's power, there were limitations on his decisions. Some limitations were the result of the difficulties of transportation and communication, which remained primitive throughout the period. Governors in distant provinces had a way of ignoring the central bureaucracy when it suited them. Other boundaries on the sultan's authority were the result of Islamic tradition that said all law had to be based on the Qur'an. Therefore every edict promulgated in the sultan's name had to receive the approval of the *sheik ul-Islam*, the highest ranking Muslim official of the state. His assent, issued in a document called a *fetva*, assured everyone that the sultan's proclamation conformed to the Qur'an.

An advisory council, the **divan,** consulted with the sultan on policy. Its major figure was the Grand Vizier. While the sultans personally attended meetings of the divan in early Ottoman history, later they were content to listen in on the discussions, seated behind a grill on the second floor of the meeting room in the Grand Serai, the sultan's palace in Istanbul.

Istanbul, capital of the Ottoman Empire.

Everyone who worked in the Grand Serai was expected to come into the sultan's presence only when requested. Silence was the rule, for no one could speak unless the sultan began the conversation. A large number of his personal aides were deaf mutes.

The sultan's army had two major divisions. The cavalry was made up of native Turks, the *sipahis,* but the infantry was recruited from the **Janissaries.** Born into Christian Balkan families, the Janissaries were therefore considered the sultan's slaves. Brought into army camps, where they were forced to become Muslims, they received the best military training available. Those who excelled moved into the Ottoman administration, some of them attaining the rank of Grand Vizier, the highest office a sultan could confer.

From the mid-seventeenth century onward the Janissaries were out of control. Unwittingly the Ottoman state had created a body of men who were so powerful that they could challenge the sultans themselves. When the Janissaries grew angry, they gathered outside the main gate of the Serai, turned over their lunch pails, and began to beat on them with spoons. Sometimes it was for better rations or for less interference in their private lives, or perhaps they demanded the head of an unpopular minister of the divan.

Barbarossa was the architect of the Ottoman navy. His efforts created the sultan's fleet so as to compete with Venice and Spain.

The Ottoman government was chronically in debt, thanks to corruption among its officials who drew a salary but did little work to justify their position. Only a portion of taxes collected in the provinces ever reached Istanbul. To better the financial health of the state, monopolies were awarded on the payment of a fee, and gradually tax collecting was put up for annual contracts with individuals or families. Using tax farming guaranteed a regular amount of income, but in the countryside the peasant population resisted paying taxes in every way possible.

Social Classes in Southwest Asia

The importance of the extended family can hardly be emphasized enough in the culture of Southwest Asia. It was the duty of the present generation to uphold the position of the family and to keep intact all its possessions so that they might be passed on to their children.

Large landowners, government officials, and military commanders made up the upper class and held the most property. They lived in spacious homes where dozens of servants waited upon them. When the work day ended, there was time for hunting, horse racing, and an occasional game of polo. Turkish wrestlers, covered with grease, were popular attractions for spectators on Ottoman holidays.

Ottoman society's main divisions were between those who worked for the government in some capacity, the *âskeri*, and the *reaya*. The former were exempt from taxation, while the latter, both Muslims and non-Muslims, had financial obligations to the sultan's government. Over time the burden of taxes fell more heavily on those who were not Muslim.

The most important of these taxes was the *cizye*, a tax upon every non-Muslim male of military age. While in the sixteenth century, the cizye was moderate, it grew to be set in an arbitrary way, so as to become a crushing burden on the Christian peasantry in Anatolia and the Arab lands. The land tax, the cizye, and frequent extraordinary levies kept the Christian peasantry poor. The central government did nothing to stop rapacious governors or tax farmers from squeezing every bit of revenue possible from their subjects. Poor Muslims and Christians suffered from too little, not too much, government from Istanbul.

Wealthy Muslims preferred to live in the cities where they could have access to the mosque, the Islamic school, known as the *medrese*, and the amenities of urban life, leaving the countryside to the reaya. In the towns merchants were both Muslim and non-Muslim and made good livings. They provided the capital for a variety of businesses, and although Islamic law forbade loaning money at interest, a number of strategies provided ways to avoid the prohibition. In fact moneylenders became an essential class, in an atmosphere where farmers often fell into debt after a bad harvest.

Wealthy Turks built houses along the Bosporus.

The pilgrimage to Mecca, the *hajj*, was a goal for every Muslim who could afford the expense. It was an experience never to be forgotten. If the journey to Mecca was out of the question, then a visit to Jerusalem or the nearby tomb of a holy person was always possible.

Muslim men, who could afford to do so, married up to four wives. Even though they could marry Christian women, no Christian man could legally take a Muslim woman for his wife. The children of these families were raised in the Islamic faith. The penalty for apostasy to Islam was death. Such measures ensured a constantly expanding Muslim population.

Women went veiled when they left the privacy of their home, for shopping, going to the baths, or visiting relatives. Their lives were almost entirely spent within the family and neighborhood. Certain laws protected them. Legally they kept the dowries they brought with them at the time of their marriage, they could own property, and they played a major role in the education of the family's children.

In the Grand Serai hundreds of women were kept in the ruler's harem. Four were the sultans' wives; the rest, his concubines. Guards made certain that no one entered the harem. These guards were African eunuchs and therefore unable to produce any children likely to have political ambitions.

The woman who directed life in the harem was the sultan's mother. Having her son on the throne gave her privileges no one else enjoyed. She had her own staff and revenues, and her influence with her son allowed her to make suggestions on appointments and policy. Nevertheless, she was prohibited from assuming any political office, as were all women in the patriarchal society of the Ottoman world.

Slavery was a common feature throughout both the Turkish and Persian empires. In Istanbul 2,000 slave merchants carried on their trade. Many slaves were prisoners of war; others were young men and women captured in slave raids in Africa, Ukraine, or the Caucasus Mountains.

The number of slaves, nearly all kept in domestic service, showed how wealthy a person was. At one time over 20,000 slaves lived in the Grand Serai to serve the needs of the palace.

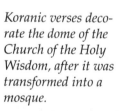

Koranic verses decorate the dome of the Church of the Holy Wisdom, after it was transformed into a mosque.

The Qur'an asserts that Christians and Jews have a respected place within Islamic society. They kept their churches and synagogues and were governed by their own community's private law, and their religious leaders represented them before Ottoman officials. On the other hand, they could build no new places of worship and needed permission to make repairs on old ones.

Although a common opinion once held that Mehmed II laid down the rules that applied to the Christian reaya at the time of the fall of

Constantinople, placing them in *millets* or nations, it is now certain that the organization of the reaya was worked out piecemeal over the centuries. Mehmed II simply adopted the Muslim traditions governing Orthodox Christians, Armenians, and Jews as he found them.

The Greek Orthodox patriarch was considered the most important reaya of the Ottoman world. All Orthodox believers were his responsibility, legally and morally, and it was his duty to speak for them before the Ottoman government. Because making "gifts" to Ottoman officials was the only certain way to obtain high office, the Greek patriarchs paid huge sums of money to obtain the patriarchate. Their tenure was brief, for as soon as one person became patriarch, others were waiting in the wings to unseat him.

The major Christian communities beside the Orthodox and Armenians were the Syrian churches: the Melkite, Jacobite, and Maronite. The Melkites were scattered throughout Syria and Palestine, the Jacobites lived in northern Syria and southeastern Anatolia, and the Maronites shared Mt. Lebanon with a Muslim group known as the Druzes. All were now Arab-speaking.

In the seventeenth and eighteenth centuries, French Catholic missionaries set up churches loyal to Rome among the Melkites, Jacobites, and Armenians. The Maronites were Catholic since the time of the Crusades. The French acted as protectors of the Catholics in the Ottoman Empire, giving any Christian who joined the church certain privileges, such as a European passport.

In the Persian territories the Christians belonged to the Church of the East, now known as the Assyrian church. A small group of Mazdaists, belonging to the ancient religion of Persia still existed, but the majority had moved to India where they were called Parsees. Jews were found in all the major Ottoman cities, and most were merchants. Istanbul held a large community of Jews, and in Thessaloniki, Greece, Jews were a majority in the population.

Each of the Ottoman cities had separate quarters, sometimes walled, for the members of the different religious communities. These were the *mahalles*, and at night their gates were closed to outsiders. In every mahalle the mosque, church, or synagogue was the center of public life. Even though members of all faiths intermingled in the public life of the town, family activities centered in the quarter. Women hardly ever left their mahalle.

The countryside was a world of villages where headmen made decisions for their communities. The office of headman was usually hereditary, passed on from father to son over generations. The landlords, the richer merchants, members of the Muslim ulema, and sometimes Christian clerics met in local councils to form policy. They served as administrators, judges, and tax assessors for their villages. Another important task was to allocate pasture lands to the nomadic herders who lived in the countryside. Quarrels over pasture and water rights might end in violence, if the decisions were unfair.

The male population spent a major part of every day at the coffeehouse. Here conversation on politics, society, and economics competed with backgammon for the patrons' interest. Smoking water pipes at the coffeehouse became popular after the introduction of tobacco from the Americas.

The Cappadocian countryside in Turkey.

Wealthy Muslims frequently donated property to be used as an endowment for the upkeep of a mosque, public bath, fountain, or hospital. These gifts were known as *waqfs,* and every town and village depended on them for money to support public works and aid the poor.

In the Arabian peninsula during the eighteenth century, a reaction against the luxurious life of too many wealthy Muslims appeared in the teaching of Abd al-Wahab. His view of Islam demanded strict austerity and no compromise with anything that departed from Qur'anic law. The Bedouin of the desert sympathized with this view because their opportunities for indulgence were few. Wahabi theology still has an impact on public life in modern Saudi Arabia.

The Economic System

The wealth of the Ottoman and Persian empires came from agriculture and commerce, as in all pre-industrial societies. After the conquest of a region, Ottoman officials were quick to take a census of the people and their lands. Taxes fell upon households according to religion: Muslim, Christian, or Jewish. The recording of property also provided a base for allocating lands to the Turkish cavalry, the *sipahis,* or to the Janissaries.

Scribes at work in this building in modern Ankara.

In 1500 large grants of land, *timars,* and smaller ones, *ziamets,* were parceled out to Turkish sipahis in return for military service on a lifetime lease. Revenues were meant to be large enough to support at least one soldier and his retainers on campaign. So long as the empire expanded, a growing amount of territory was available for making new grants to the military. The reverse was true after the close of the seventeenth century, when the empire began to contract. Efforts were put forth to keep peasants on the land, due to recurring labor shortages.

Merchants were an important part of the economy for in the 1500s the Ottoman world became a part of the network of international trade that extended from Europe to China. Unfortunately for the Turks, much of the trade in their own empire was in the hands of Christian or Jewish reaya. Christians and Jews had contacts abroad and were anxious to learn the European languages Turks held in disdain. Christian Greeks attended Western universities and learned of improved opportunities to expand their businesses.

In the sixteenth century France was the first European nation to obtain trading privileges in the Ottoman Empire through treaties known as **Capitulations.** The Capitulations were often renewed with Paris, and new ones were signed with England and the Netherlands. The ambassadors of these countries in Istanbul came to exercise considerable influence at the Ottoman court.

The main market of Istanbul, the *bedestan,* lay directly on top of its predecessor of Byzantine times. In its narrow passageways merchants tended their small shops where negotiating the price was an art. Grocers, jewelers, spice merchants, craftsmen making shoes, or tailors sewing garments were also located here.

Every craftsman had to belong to a guild that checked the quality of the products, set a price, and controlled competition. Guilds also dispensed welfare to disabled members, provided social activities, and marched in colorful procession on festival days. The guilds gave their members an identity.

Those guilds involved in importing goods from outside the empire were less regulated and therefore enjoyed higher profits. There was a large demand for European hardware, watches, and clocks. Huge amounts of grain arrived at Istanbul's docks to feed a population of close to 700,000 people.

In Anatolia, Bursa and Izmir were busy places, as were Damascus, Aleppo, and Beirut in Syria. Each city had a specialty, such as steel in Damascus and silk in Bursa and Beirut. Damascus was important for it was in this city that pilgrims assembled to set off on the hajj to Mecca.

The pilgrim road to Damascus.

In the 1700s the hold that the ulema had over the government was a major reason for Ottoman economic decline. The ulema resisted any change that its members perceived as a threat to Islamic orthodoxy. Therefore there was no scientific research in the Ottoman or Persian lands as there was in the West. Innovations in technology were rejected out of hand if they originated in Christian countries. It was only in 1727 that a printing press was permitted to open. Dissemination of new ideas was not welcome; only an adherence to the past was allowed.

The Janissaries were reluctant to employ weaponry imported from the West, an attitude that Turkish opponents were pleased to foster. However, enough muskets and artillery made their way into the empire that the armed forces were far ahead of Persia. This explains the limited victories the Turks enjoyed on Asian battlefields.

One further economic factor that hampered the Ottomans was the use of silver rather than gold currency. Because large silver imports from the Americas gave western Europe as much silver as it needed, the Ottoman currency lost much of its value, and prices of imports rose significantly. The government was unable to hold back inflation while the worth of silver declined.

Developments in Ottoman History

In 1500 the Ottoman sultan, leader of the Ottoman Turks, was Bayazid II, son of Mehmed II. His rule extended over two continents. In Europe the Turks were in control of the southern Balkans, whereas in Asia the Anatolian lands were theirs. Only Venice still held important bases in the East Mediterranean.

In 1512 the sons of Bayazid sparred with each other for the right to succeed their ailing father. After Selim prevailed he forced his father to abdicate. Selim was ruthless; he proceeded to kill his brother and rival the following year, thus establishing himself as undisputed ruler of the Ottoman Empire.

Selim I was an ambitious man. His people knew him as Selim the Grim because of his stern temperament. He certainly did not intend to tolerate Persian gains in eastern Anatolia. The sultan organized the Ottoman army and marched eastward against those Turkish tribes that had accepted Shi'ism as their faith.

These Shi'ite Turks were known as *kizil bashi,* or red heads, because they wore red turbans to distinguish themselves. Despite a spirited defense, they proved no match for Selim's well-trained forces. As Selim expected, Shah Isma'il of Persia came to the aid of the kizil bashi. In 1514 the two armies met at Chaldiran, a city east of the Euphrates River.

The battle was fought with intensity, for both sides believed that the winner would determine whether Turks or Persians should dominate Southwest Asia. Selim emerged the victor, because his infantry had muskets and artillery, which the Persian side lacked. Isma'il's forces depended on cavalry charges that were effective in past engagements, but they were now suicidal.

When eastern Anatolia and northern Mesopotamia, the region of Kurdistan, were firmly in his control, Selim had but one more major competitor for supremacy in Southwest Asia. This was Mamluk Egypt's leader,

Kansu al-Gauri. The Mamluks were a dynasty drawn from slaves recruited in the Caucasus mountains for the army and then brought to Egypt.

In 1516, two years after Chaldiran, Kansu al-Gauri took his army into Syria. Selim's forces met him north of Aleppo in Syria, and once again the Ottoman army prevailed. Selim occupied Damascus and other Syrian towns, incorporating them into his territories. At this point Selim offered the new Mamluk sultan, Tuman Bey, a chance to make peace. The Mamluk sultan refused, so Selim continued his march, taking Cairo in January 1516. The Turkish leader killed Tuman Bey, but he allowed local government to remain under the control of the Mamluks.

A Persian army battles its enemies riding horses and elephants.

Because the Sunnite caliph lived in Cairo, he became Selim's subject. The sultan ordered the caliph to Istanbul where, according to some reports, he transferred the caliphate to Selim. This joining of the sultanate with the caliphate gave the Ottoman rulers powerful prestige throughout the Sunnite Muslim world. The caliph was the head of all believers, and now it was one of the prerogatives of the Ottoman sultans.

To further enhance the religious dimension of the sultanate, the keepers of the Islamic holy places in Mecca and Medina offered their submission to Selim. This gave the Ottomans the role of guardians of Islam's most sacred shrines and added still one more title of respect to the rulers in Istanbul. Secular authority, which the sultans enjoyed as commanders of the Muslim armies or *ghazzis,* was combined with the religious power that came from the caliphate.

Even though the Ottomans were now the major power in Southwest Asia, the Persians were only down, not out. When Süleyman I the Magnificent succeeded to the Istanbul sultanate, he again sent Ottoman armies against the Persians. They captured Baghdad and other major towns in Mesopotamia.

Turkish armies, however, did not like fighting a long distance from home; consequently, the garrisons left to retain Ottoman conquests were not large or strong enough to hold what had been gained. Each Persian shah worked to regain the initiative in Mesopotamia with the result that the frontier constantly shifted back and forth. Peace treaties were signed with great ceremony only to be torn up as soon as an advantage seemed to appear for one side or the other.

Süleyman the Magnificent, greatest of the sultans.

As old age approached, Süleyman suffered the growing distrust of his sons and possible heirs. The eldest he had strangled, only to witness a battle between two younger ones that ended with one of the sons fleeing to Persia. Süleyman sent money to the shah to have him killed, and the Persian leader was happy to oblige.

This left Selim II to become ruler after Süleyman's death. After power, Selim preferred life in the harem and strong drink to governing the huge empire he inherited. He turned over the administration to Mehmed Sökullu, his Grand Vizier. Historians date the start of the Ottoman decline with the sultanate of Selim II.

The Sixteenth Century in Persian History

The foundation of early modern Persia begins with the Safavids, who formed a dynasty that long influenced the country's destiny. Key to Safavid success was its alliance with a **Sufi** brotherhood. This brotherhood was one of the many mystical orders that appeared in Islam and energized its devotees after Timur Leng's disastrous invasion of the Muslim world in the late fourteenth century.

The Safavids first appeared in Azerbaijan, a region to the west of the Caspian Sea. They were followers of those Shi'ites who believed that after Ali there had been 11 more legitimate rulers of the Muslim community. However, the twelfth imam, or leader, disappeared and intends to return only at the end of time. Until that occurs, representatives of the hidden imam are to govern Shi'ite believers.

The Safavid rulers identified themselves as the deputies of this hidden imam. With such extraordinary prestige, they could demand unquestioned obedience from their followers. On the local level, *mullahs,* the Shi'ite clerics, actively supported this claim.

The early Safavid movement was remarkably successful in gaining converts from among Azerbaijani Turks, Kurds, and Persians who looked upon them as the only true Muslim leaders in the world. In the Safavid devotion to their cause, they were quite willing to shed their blood against Ottoman Sunnite heretics. Wearing their red turbans, they charged into battle convinced that death would propel them into the immediate joys of eternity.

A Persian Sufi summons his followers.

In 1501 the head of the kizil bashi, Isma'il, took Tabriz away from another tribal leader and assumed the title of shah. He then declared that the Shi'ism of the Safavids was the official Persian religion. Isma'il's armies covered the countryside, bringing the whole of the Iranian plateau under his control. His armies were equally successful against the Uzbeks who lived to the north of Persia, defeating them in 1510 at Mary.

Four years later, Isma'il learned that his forces at Chaldiran were too antiquated to hold the line against Selim I's Turks. The defeat at Chaldiran jolted Isma'il, but he ordered a scorched-earth policy so that the Ottomans obtained little plunder after their victory. The conquered Shi'ite population refused to accept the Turks as their masters and resisted conversion to Sunnite Islam.

The Persians were now aware of a much broader world, not only because of contacts in war with the Turks but also because of the Portuguese presence at the port of Hormuz at the mouth of the Persian Gulf. The Persians had something to learn from both.

From the Ottomans they learned the necessity of modernizing their army. Therefore, they were pleased to receive two English brothers, Anthony and Robert Sherley, who came to Persia to assist in training the armed forces. From the Portuguese they learned of new products and the ideas that came with them from Europe.

This occurred during the high point of Safavid rule, when Abbas I was shah, from 1588 to 1629. His capital at Isfahan became one of the great cities of the Muslim world, making it the architectural and cultural center of Southwest Asia. A man personally noted for his cruelties, Abbas saw to it that his kizil bashi chieftains lived up to their promise of undivided loyalty to him. The chiefs and their retainers were assigned locations in the provinces where they personally gathered and retained the taxes levied on the population in return for military service.

Shah Abbas won several notable victories over both the Uzbeks and the Turks during his long tenure on the throne. Especially rewarding was a defeat of the Turks near Lake Urmia in 1602 that regained several important towns in the region for Persia: Kars, Shirwan, Mosul, and Baghdad.

Abbas learned from the example of the Ottoman Janissaries the importance of a slave army. Recruiters took young boys from the Christian Caucasian tribes and enlisted them in the Persian forces to the military's great benefit.

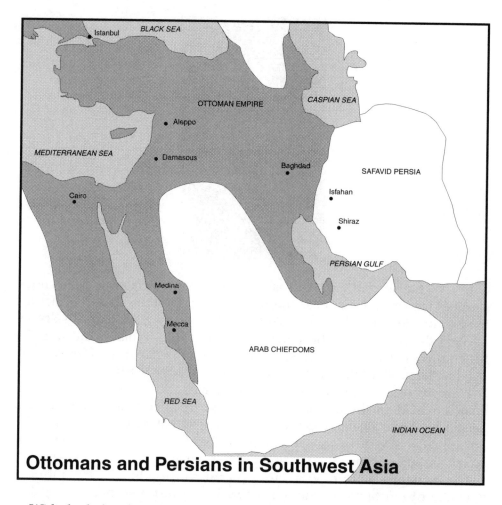

Ottomans and Persians in Southwest Asia

With the help of the English, Abbas's army marched on Hormuz, defeated the Portuguese, and opened up that port to commerce with the East India Company. Soon Hormuz joined Surat in India as a major port of entry for European goods into Southwest Asia.

Shah Abbas governed Persia from Isfahan during one of its most prosperous times.

Ottomans and Persians Continue to Battle

There were still Ottoman victories to be won in the seventeenth century. In 1635 the Turks recaptured Yerevan and Tabriz from the Persians and three years later took back Baghdad. In 1638 Murad IV made the fateful decision to allow native Turks to fill the ranks of a reduced and presumably more docile Janissary Corps.

This did not function as planned. In 1640 the Janissaries overthrew the unfortunate Sultan Ibrahim I, blaming him rather than themselves for Ottoman problems. For two decades there was war and anarchy in Istanbul until Mehmed Köprülü became Grand Vizier. Born in Albania, Köprülü brought order to the country through thousands of executions of those who were, or potentially were considered to be, enemies of the sultan. His son Ahmed followed him in office, retaining his father's policies.

Interest in European affairs produced a lull on the Persian frontier for a time. Then in 1730 Nadir Shah resumed hostilities and regained the Caucasus region for Persia.

In the Ottoman heartland of Anatolia, the central government met increased opposition from local chieftains, the *derebeys,* who refused to pay attention to Istanbul when its directives did not suit them. For the Ottomans the latter eighteenth century was to become a time of peril as the inroads of the world economy, represented by European merchants, eroded their economic structure.

The Persian shahs also suffered from separatist movements in the eighteenth century. In 1709 an Afghan chieftain, Mir Vais, created a separate state, resisting an attempt to make his nation Shi'ite. Within a few years the Afghans grew so strong that their army was large enough to invade Persia. The Afghan leader, Mir Mahmud, marched into Persia, announcing that he was now shah.

Persian mosques are noted for tall, elaborate entrances.

In St. Petersburg the war between Afghans and Persians played into Russian hands. Peter the Great sent his armies into Azerbaijan and the Caspian regions and annexed them to his empire. Peter then proposed to the Ottoman sultan that each take a part of the Persian lands for themselves. Mir Mahmud was in no position to resist, having fallen into a severe mental illness that, among other decisions, caused him to order all Persian nobility to be executed. The shah's instability plunged all Isfahan into chaos.

In 1736 Nadir Shah, despite being ethnically a Turk and a Sunnite by faith, came to power in Persia. The shah went on the attack against both Russians and Turks and then directed his armies into India.

Three years later the Persians captured Delhi in a campaign that resulted in a huge loss of life among the city's inhabitants. An agreement between the shah and the Moghul emperor left the latter in Delhi on the condition that he pay Nadir Shah a handsome indemnity and cede to him all territory north and west of the Indus River. Among Nadir Shah's prizes were the Peacock Throne of the Moghuls and the Koh-i-noor diamond, at that time the largest in the world. Both were taken back to Persia.

Nadir Shah's armies reached as far as Bukhara in Uzbekistan, demonstrating the impact of Persian arms on the country's neighbors. However, Nadir Shah's campaigns were organized on the often undependable loyalty of tribal armies. Moreover, the Persian peasants had to work day and night to pay the taxes imposed on them. In 1747 an assassin struck down the Persian monarch, issuing in a period of anarchy.

Eventually Karim Khan Zand came out on top and established a new dynasty in Persia. Karim Khan receives good marks as a monarch, ruling from his capital of Shiraz. The Zand shahs gave Persia a more quiet time in which to explore peace with its neighbors.

Culture and Arts

The early modern period in Ottoman and Persian history is noted for its many arts. Ottomans excelled in architecture, especially in the construction of mosques. The great Ottoman architect, Sinan, constructed over 300 structures during the time of Süleyman. The most impressive was the mosque where his patron now lies buried. He promised Süleyman, "I have built you a mosque that will remain on earth to the Judgment Day." The only mosque to have six minarets is the Sultan Ahmed, or Blue Mosque, built early in the seventeenth century to rival in size the Church of the Holy Wisdom.

The Blue Mosque in Istanbul was built to rival Justinian's Church of the Holy Wisdom.

The interior spaces in the mosques of Istanbul were covered with tiles, especially made in the kilns of Iznik. It was also a time for building aqueducts, roads, and bridges throughout Ottoman lands.

Poetry was considered the highest form of literature among the Ottomans. Abd ul-Baki is best remembered for his lament on the death of Süleyman. An author of poetry that arose out of the Sufi tradition, Mehmed ibn-Süleyman Fuzuli, wrote of the intense love of God that he shares with a mystic. Historians, essayists, and biographers were in abundance at the court and the homes of wealthy nobles.

Puppet shows provided villagers with stories of mighty warriors fighting the forces of evil, identified as the sultan's enemies. Music and dance were always a part of the entertainment at festivals.

The greatest of the sultans' many garden parties occurred during the spring Tulip Festival. All Istanbul shut down to enjoy the blooming of tulips and to march in processions honoring the change of seasons. Turtles with candles on their backs wandered among the palace tulip gardens to illuminate the night.

Persian arts flourished at their highest point in the mid-sixteenth century. Safavid shahs brought architects to Isfahan to decorate the city with mosques, fountains, gardens, baths, and other public buildings. Ceramic tiles, resembling the colors of a garden, embellished the exteriors of the buildings, noted for their massive entrances. Persian artists excelled in illuminating manuscripts and producing miniatures of court life and stories of the Persian past.

Persian artists, experts at the illumination of manuscripts, picture women making purchases at a bazaar.

Persian literature included works on history, philosophy, and religion. Poets in Isfahan were as honored as those in Istanbul, as were the calligraphers who made copies of their works. Ironically, for a long time Turkish was the preferred language of the Isfahan court, even though Ottoman calligraphers used Persian models for their manuscripts.

Tapestries and carpets were produced in village and city workshops all over the Southwest Asian world and became a major export to Europe. Each region had its own style of carpet. Months and even years of work were required to finish a carpet. Utensils of brass and silk materials were in demand both at home and abroad.

Conclusion

Southwest Asian culture of the sixteenth and seventeenth centuries, whether Turkish or Persian, was heavily influenced by the Islamic faith. In fact, one way of speaking about Muslim law is to call it the *shari'ah*, meaning the path that leads men and women into following God's will. Unlike their European counterparts, the elite of the Ottoman and Persian worlds were not troubled by religious doubts.

There was conflict between Ottomans and Persians, colored by their allegiance to the Sunnite and Shi'ite forms of Islam, but basically the interminable wars in Anatolia and Mesopotamia were contests for political and territorial gain. Those who fought for the sultan or the shah enlisted in the armed forces hoping to share in the rewards that victory brought.

The Ottoman state was remarkable for providing an internal world where Muslims and Christians coexisted, if not on an equal level, at least on one that tolerated differences. There were always some western Europeans who emigrated to Istanbul because they believed that fortunes could be made within the sultan's bureaucracy or serving in his army. In its government, the Ottoman world was unique in keeping native Turks from office, allowing the sultan's slaves to run affairs. Because a born Muslim could not be enslaved, a major opportunity existed for men born Christian to find a role in the empire.

Southwest Asia's weakness was in economics. The physical environment, the aridity of so much of its land, kept agricultural production static. The merchants of the region thought in terms of local demand and missed out on the expansion of trade into worldwide markets. The region supplied raw materials and markets for European goods, but it failed to develop its own commercial network.

CHAPTER 6 REVIEW
SOUTHWEST ASIA IN EARLY MODERN TIMES

Summary
- Bayazid II, Turkish sultan in 1500, directed his armies against Persia, the major enemy of the Ottomans.
- Selim II defeated the Persians at Chaldiran, opening a period of Turkish domination of much of Southwest Asia.
- Selim also disposed of his last major rival, the Mamluk sultan of Egypt.
- The Ottoman victories allowed the Ottoman rulers to assume the title of caliph and to become guardians of the Muslim shrines in Mecca and Medina.
- The ascendancy of the Safavid dynasty in the person of Shah Isma'il begins the early modern period of Persian history.
- Much of Safavid strength was the support given them from an alliance with a Shi'ite Sufi brotherhood.
- The reign of Abbas I from 1587 to 1629 was the high point of Persian fortunes.
- The failure of the Janissary Corps to retain its military effectiveness caused its decline in Southwest Asia.
- Nadir Shah's rule marked a resurgence of Persian fortunes.
- Southwest Asian society, divided between nobles and commoners, was based on family relations.
- Islam, the religion of the great majority of the people of Southwest Asia, dominated the cultural life of the region.
- The economic life of Southwest Asia often was determined by local guilds and European merchants.
- The greatest of Ottoman architects, Sinan, built over 300 structures in his lifetime.

Identify
People: Mehmed II, Abd al-Wahab, Bayazid II, Selim I, kizil bashi, Shah Isma'il, Kansu al-Gauri, Süleyman I the Magnificent, Abbas I, Nadir Shah, Mir Mahmud, Sinan, Tuman Bey, Ibrahim I, Mehmed Köprülü, Mir Vais, Karim Khan Zand, Abd ul Baki, Fuzuli

Places: Istanbul, Isfahan, Mecca, Bursa, Izmir, Damascus, Tabriz, Azerbaijan, Uzbekistan, Baghdad, Medina, Yerevan, Delhi

Events: decline of the Janissaries, battle of Chaldiran, rise of the Safavids in Persia, wars between Turks and Persians

Define

Sunnite and Shi'ite Muslims	âskeri	reaya
Janissaries	cizye	medrese
Capitulations	Sufi	hajj
millets	mufti	mullah
divan	mahalle	

Multiple Choice

1. The only serious challenge to Ottoman control of the eastern Mediterranean came from
   - (a) Portugal.
   - (b) France.
   - (c) Venice.
   - (d) Persia.

2. This Ottoman sultan brought Southwest Asia under Turkish control:
   - (a) Bayazid I
   - (b) Süleyman the Magnificent
   - (c) Murad IV
   - (d) Selim I the Grim

3. A Shi'ite Muslim believes that the caliph, the leader of the Muslims, must
   - (a) live in Baghdad.
   - (b) be elected by the ulema.
   - (c) lead the hajj to Mecca.
   - (d) be a descendent of Ali.

4. The preeminent Islamic holy places are located in
   - (a) Mecca and Medina.
   - (b) Damascus and Aleppo.
   - (c) Isfahan and Mecca.
   - (d) Bursa and Konya.

5. The key to Safavid success in Persia was its support from
   - (a) the caliph in Cairo.
   - (b) the use of modern weaponry.
   - (c) a Sufi brotherhood.
   - (d) merchant guilds.

6. A Shi'ite cleric is called a
   - (a) mullah.
   - (b) mufti.
   - (c) caliph.
   - (d) sultan.

7. Two Englishmen who aided the Safavids were
   - (a) the Anthonys.
   - (b) the Joneses.
   - (c) the Sherleys.
   - (d) the Browns.

8. Hormuz, a port on the Persian Gulf, became a center of trade between Persia and
   - (a) the British East India Company.
   - (b) the Dutch West India Company.
   - (c) the Muscovy Company.
   - (d) the French East India Company.

9. The families of Balkan Christians provided soldiers for the
    (a) Ottoman bureaucracy.
    (b) Persian army.
    (c) Ottoman sipahi cavalry.
    (d) Janissary Corps.

10. Nadir Shah briefly held the Indian capital of
    (a) Isfahan.
    (b) Tabriz.
    (c) Surat.
    (d) Delhi.

11. The most beautiful mosques of Istanbul were designed by
    (a) Süleyman.
    (b) Selim.
    (c) Sinan.
    (d) Sinbad.

12. The tiles from the kilns of this Ottoman town were known for their colors and design:
    (a) Bursa
    (b) Izmir
    (c) Istanbul
    (d) Iznik

13. The major division in Ottoman society was between
    (a) Janissaries and sipahis.
    (b) âskeri and reaya.
    (c) mullahs and muftis.
    (d) soldiers and civilians.

14. A medrese is a Muslim
    (a) mosque.
    (b) palace.
    (c) courtyard.
    (d) school.

15. The hajj is
    (a) a prayer.
    (b) a donation.
    (c) the leader of a prayer in the mosque.
    (d) the pilgrimage to Mecca.

16. The most powerful woman in the harem of the Grand Serai was
    (a) the sultan's chief wife.
    (b) the oldest woman in the harem.
    (c) the youngest woman in the harem.
    (d) the sultan's mother.

17. The head of Orthodox Christians in the Ottoman Empire was
    (a) the chief mufti.
    (b) the Patriarch of Constantinople.
    (c) the Patriarch of Antioch.
    (d) the chief reaya.

18. The law of fratricide required a new sultan to
    (a) kill his brothers.
    (b) dismiss members of the former divan.
    (c) appoint a new Grand Vizier.
    (d) send his brothers into exile.

19. Capitulations allowed special privileges in the Ottoman Empire to
    (a) the ulema.
    (b) Persian merchants.
    (c) European merchants.
    (d) Jews.

20. A reform movement in Arabia originated with
    (a) the sheikhs of the Bedouin.
    (b) al-Ghazzali.
    (c) al-Wahab.
    (d) the ulema.

Essay Questions
1. Why were the Ottoman and Persian Empires at war throughout most of the early modern period?
2. Compare the role of the Muslim religious leadership in Southwest Asia with that of Christians in Europe.
3. Discuss the possible reasons for the decline of the Ottoman Empire after the seventeenth century.

Answers
1. c	6. a	11. c	16. d
2. d	7. c	12. d	17. b
3. d	8. a	13. b	18. a
4. a	9. d	14. d	19. c
5. c	10. d	15. d	20. c

CHAPTER 7

Mughal India

The land of India dominates South Asia. Shaped like an inverted triangle, it has the Indian Ocean on both sides. The island of Sri Lanka lies off the southern coast. Mighty mountain chains, the Himalaya and Hindu Kush, cut India off from the rest of Asia, but passes allow people to travel back and forth. From the melting snow of these mountains, the nation's major rivers, the Ganges and Indus Rivers, receive their waters.

Horsemen cross through the mountains of Kashmir, which lie on the border between India and Inner Asia.

India's climate is usually very warm, especially before the monsoons arrive in the spring, bringing relief as well as life-giving rain. Rain does not fall equally on the land, and western India is so arid as to be a desert. South of the Ganges Plain is one more dry region, the Deccan plateau, a countryside of flat grassland and shrubs. Because of tropical rainfall, the southern coastal areas are covered with lush vegetation.

India's history begins in ancient times when people settled the Indus Valley, creating dozens of cities where traders and farmers exchanged their goods. Apparently, about 1500 B.C. Aryans, an Indo-European people, poured into the region. They brought with them their language, Sanskrit, and their religion that evolved through the centuries into Hinduism.

A distinctive aspect of Aryan society was the division of people into four major classes and thousands of castes. The caste system ranked every one according to occupation and social prestige, with the highest the Brahmins and the lowest the Untouchables. In no other world society were the lives of people so ordered because of their birth.

To complete early India's religious past, it was the country where the Buddha taught his path to enlightenment, and Mahavira founded the Jains. Christianity also appeared in communities on India's south coast.

The most important religious and ethnic invasions occurred in the early Middle Ages, when Muslim Arabs first came on the scene. They imposed their rule over part of the Hindu population, converting several million people, but failed to convince the vast Hindu majority that Islam was a better religion.

After the initial Muslim appearance in India, a succession of tribal peoples of Inner Asia moved into the country, often with destructive force. Some were Turkish, and some were Mongol, but the most fearsome was a combined army led by Timur Leng that left the north of India reeling at the close of the fourteenth century. After Timur's departure the throne fell into the hands of mercenary soldiers, who began their lives in servitude and were therefore known as the Slave Dynasty of Delhi. In 1500 a representative of that dynasty governed the north of India.

In 1526 the armies of the Delhi sultan were unprepared to meet a new onslaught of invaders that plunged into India from the north. Neither were the maharajahs in the south ready to deal with the Portuguese who arrived at Calicut (now Khozikoda) in 1498. A new page in the history of India was beginning.

The Kingdom of the Mughals

The leader of the northern invasion was Zahir-ud-Din Muhammad, known to his followers as **Babur** (the Lion). Like other conquerors in India's past, Babur had his origins among the Turkic–Mongol peoples of Inner Asia. In fact, Timur Leng was a distant relative. Babur's army was quite a bit more sophisticated, for he brought with him soldiers bearing muskets and cannon. He was a big man, known for his personal strength; "Babur never hit a man he did not knock down."

Advancing from Afghanistan, Babur's soldiers took Delhi and Agra, the two major cities of the north. Like his predecessors, he chose Delhi for his capital, where he kept a court of extensive civil and military officials. The dynasty he founded is known as **Mughal.**

A minaret of Delhi's main mosque.

While Babur was busy consolidating his rule, a new faith came on the Indian scene. This was the religion of the **Sikhs** (Disciples). Its founder was Nanak, who stressed the notion of a single God, the Creator, as Islam taught, but combined it with the Hindu goal of union with the deity. Nanak's teaching caused Baybars and his Mughal successors to try as best they could to stamp out Sikhism. For Muslim believers, there can never be a prophet after Muhammad. Nanak, and the **gurus,** leaders of the Sikh community after Nanak, were denying one of Islam's basic beliefs.

Mughal persecution brought forth a militant response from the Sikhs. They became soldiers, always carrying arms to defend themselves. The men took the name Singh, which means lion, and the women, Kaur, lioness.

Akbar's Rule

The grandson of Babur became the Mughal dynasty's most impressive ruler. When he was but 13 years of age, Akbar inherited the Mughal throne, which he held for half a century, from 1556 until 1605.

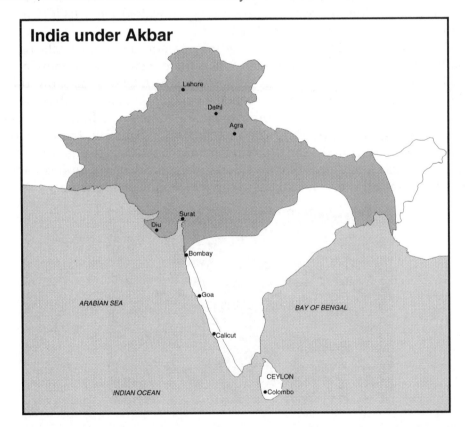

India under Akbar

Akbar's ambition was to become a great warrior, and he lived up to his own expectations. He fought the Hindu Rajput maharajahs of western India, who proved no match for his well-trained forces. Akbar, wearing a suit of gold-plated armor, personally led his troops riding into battle on an elephant. After their defeat, Akbar treated the Rajputs well, for he did not want to make them lasting enemies. By the time of his death, his kingdom held all northern India including the Deccan plateau.

The court of Akbar.

What made Akbar different from other Mughals was his tolerance of all Indian religions. The usual disdain for Hindus that marked Muslim rulers in India was not a part of Akbar's character. He invited representatives of the different faiths to present their case before his court. After hearing from them all, he decided to begin his own religion, called *Din i-Ilahi* (Divine Faith), and appointed himself the teacher.

Akbar incorporated Hindus into his administration and removed the hated poll tax that fell upon non-Muslims. When there were years of famine, he absolved people of paying any taxes. However, the tolerance he showed for other religions as well as his own creation, the Din i-Ilahi, died with Akbar.

Akbar's son, Jahangir, soon proved his incompetence. In a move that drove a wedge between the Mughals and their subjects, the emperor restored the usual taxes on the Hindus and treated them as inferiors. Jahangir became an alcoholic and dependent on drugs. His incapacity forced his Persian wife, Nur Jahan, to run the country in his name.

The Rajput palace in Jaipur, built by the maharajah of the city.

The Mughal Empire reached its golden age when the son of Jahangir came to the throne. This was Shah Jahan, who ruled from 1628 to 1658. The Mughal Empire grew so wealthy that Shah Jahan could afford to have three capitals: Lahore, Delhi, and Agra. In all these cities he commissioned forts to be built of red sandstone, which also served as palaces. Jahan's most important monument is India's best-known building, the **Taj Mahal.**

The white marble Taj Mahal was built over the tomb of his wife, Mumtaz Mahal, during the years from 1632 to 1649. Shah Jahan wanted her burial place to be the most beautiful in all India and planned to build a similar one for himself of contrasting black stone. Shah Jahan's plans did not happen. His ambitious son Aurangzeb overthrew his father and imprisoned him for eight years until his death in the Red Fort at Agra. From his prison window Shah Jahan could see the Taj Mahal in the distance. Needless to say, his tomb was never built with such grandeur.

The Taj Mahal, Mughal India's most famous building.

Aurangzeb, a stern man, restored the Mughal policies of harshness toward the Hindus. In 1669 he ordered the destruction of many temples throughout India, causing great distress to his Hindu subjects. He also levied heavier taxes on them. His wars against the Sikhs and the Hindu maharajahs of the Deccan, the Marathas, brought the Empire little gain but much grief.

After Aurangzeb's death in 1707, the Mughal emperors showed little ability. The Europeans were now in India, anxious to trade for cloth and spices in the port cities. The small principalities once joined to the empire went their own way because the central government no longer frightened the maharajahs.

The palace of the maharajahs of Hyderabad, one of India's largest cities.

Europeans in India and Sri Lanka

In 1498 the Portuguese captain Vasco da Gama became the first European captain to cross the Indian Ocean. An Arab pilot who knew the route from East Africa was willing to show him the way. Da Gama made a fabulous profit on the spices he brought back to Lisbon. The news that a direct route by sea existed between Europe and India sparked the imagination of every Portuguese sea captain. Several years later, in 1508, Portuguese sailors also reached Colombo, the capital of Sri Lanka.

At first the Portuguese met little opposition. Neither the Mughals or the Maratha states in the south had navies. Therefore, the Portuguese simply filled in a vacuum after they disposed of the Arab fleets that formerly sailed the Indian Ocean.

In 1510 Afonso de Albuquerque took the port of Goa on the western coast of India and turned it into the administrative capital for the Portuguese in India. Goa retains its European character to this day. From Goa the ambitious Albuquerque continued to sail the eastern seas, setting up stations in Malacca, the major Malaysian port, and Hormuz at the entrance to the Persian Gulf. In 1542 Francis Xavier, the most respected of Jesuit missionaries to India, landed at Goa and made the city his headquarters.

The Catholic cathedral of Goa. For centuries this city was the center of Portuguese administration in India.

Portugal was a small country and could hold its monopoly on the Indian Ocean trade for little more than a century. Then the Dutch took most of their empire away from them. Later the French and British arrived in India, each of them trying as best they could to gain an advantage with the native Indians. The colonial powers wanted to import Indian cotton to keep their weavers busy at home. They were equally concerned about expanding markets for their countrymen to sell products made in Europe. India had become part of the world market created by Europeans.

By the early eighteenth century British and French merchants were in competition to become the primary traders in India, organized in East India Companies. Time after time, British forces defeated the French and their Indian allies. Both sides used natives, **sepoys,** in their armies.

One of the most memorable battles in India involved Robert Clive, the East India Company's chief military official in India, and the Muslim ruler of Bengal. In 1757 the armies met at Plassey. Despite their superiority in numbers, the Bengali leader's army proved no match for the British and their sepoys. The successful use of artillery was a deciding factor in the western victory.

After the Bengali conquest, the French no longer were a concern to the agents and military forces of the East India Company, who marched forward collecting Indian states throughout the nation. Mughal officials simply had no resources to stop the European advance. From the major seaports of Surat, Calcutta, Bombay, and Madras, which had been under European control since the seventeenth century, agents of the company moved into the interior. Often there was no need to displace the local maharajah as long as the company dictated economic policy.

The British East India Company

By 1757 the British East India Company controlled areas around Bengal, most of southern India, and the Ganges Valley in the north. The company remained a private concern with the London government simply overseeing its activities.

In 1770 a major famine broke out in Bengal, the result of mismanagement by company officials. Hundreds of thousands of people died. Obviously reform was needed among the corrupt company employees. In response to this abuse, Parliament enacted a series of laws to rein in the free-wheeling antics of the company. To restrain its ambition, London forbade its agents to intervene in local conflicts.

Three years after the famine, the London government agreed to give the British East India Company a monopoly on trade in India. It was not easy for the directors of the company in London to know exactly what was happening so far away in India. Constant conflict was the rule between the small states of the country, and these wars, despite Parliamentary prohibition, often drew the East India Company's agents and their armed forces into siding with one side or the other. They believed this to be necessary in order to protect their interests.

In the 1790s Lord Cornwallis, of Yorktown fame, went off to India to supervise the company's administration. He succeeded in limiting the abuses of its personnel and established a much more responsible court system.

Conclusion

Many of the majestic monuments of modern India were built in Mughal times. Palaces, mosques, and massive gardens were constructed to delight the Mughals. With the exception of Akbar's rule, however, Hindus and India's other religious groups did not enjoy the good life provided the Mughals.

Mughal authority was not strong enough to deal with the European merchants who arrived in the country, eager to buy cotton and to sell products made in European workshops. Many maharajahs were quite willing to become a part of the European commercial network.

Why was British expansion in India so successful? As in most parts of the Asian and African world, superior weapons and organization made the difference. Moreover, neither the Indian princes nor the Mughal emperor could compete against the better pay and living conditions offered sepoys in British employ. India was a region that still had no sense of political unity.

CHAPTER 7 REVIEW
MUGHAL INDIA

Summary
- Zahir-ud-Din Muhammad, known as Babur, invaded India, beginning the kingdom of the Mughals.
- The Mughal Empire's most famous ruler was Akbar, a man noted for his courage and tolerance.
- Shah Jahan commissioned the building of the Taj Mahal, the finest example of Mughal architecture.
- The Portuguese were first to create a series of trading stations in India.
- The British and French later replaced the Portuguese and commenced a contest for India.
- The British East India Company represented the interest of its merchants in the country.

Identify
People: Babur, Akbar, Jahan, Aurangzeb, Francis Xavier, Vasco da Gama, Albuquerque
Places: Delhi, Agra, Lahore, Sri Lanka, Goa, Bengal
Events: founding of the Sikh religion, Europeans come to India to trade, economic domination of the British East India Company

Define
Taj Mahal   sepoys   Sikhs   gurus

Multiple Choice
1. The two main cities of northern India were
    (a) Delhi and Agra.
    (b) Bombay and Calcutta.
    (c) Delhi and Jaipur.
    (d) Madras and Jaipur.

2. The Mughal dynasty's Shah Jahan is remembered for
    (a) his conquests of the south.
    (b) the founding of the Mughal dynasty.
    (c) the founding of the Sikh religion.
    (d) the building of the Taj Mahal.

3. The religion of Din i-Ilahi was promoted by
    (a) Nanak.
    (b) Akbar.
    (c) Babur.
    (d) the Rajputs.

4. The Marathas were the Hindu maharajahs of
    (a) northern India.
    (b) the Deccan plateau.
    (c) the southern coastline.
    (d) Afghanistan.

5. The first European traders in India were the
   (a) French.
   (b) Spaniards.
   (c) Dutch.
   (d) Portuguese.

6. Robert Clive served as an employee of
   (a) the French.
   (b) the London government.
   (c) the East India Company.
   (d) the British Foreign Office.

Essay Questions
1. Why was India attractive to the Portuguese?
2. Why do Akbar and Shah Jahan stand out among Mughal rulers?
3. Discuss the role of the British East India Company.
4. If you were at Akbar's court, how would you react to the emperor's religious policies?

Answers
1. a   4. b
2. d   5. d
3. b   6. c

CHAPTER 8

East Asia Meets the Outside World

East Asia, the most populous region of the world, had certain features that gave it a distinct culture. Two world views—Confucianism and Buddhism—which can be understood either as religions or ethical systems, heavily influenced the people living there. Confucianism, the older of the two systems, taught the Chinese and their neighbors the value of following traditional authority in the family and in public life. Buddhism presented a view that encouraged men and women to seek enlightenment, to focus with serenity on all that comes their way.

Geography of China

The land of China extended over a large territory in East Asia. The people living there thought of themselves as inhabiting the Middle Kingdom, the center of the universe, surrounded by other lands, whose inhabitants were considered to be barbarians. The Chinese were convinced that they alone possessed true civilization and all other peoples would do well to acknowledge their superiority.

China has two major regions: the north around the Yellow River where there are four seasons each year and the tropical south where the Yangtze River flows. The Yellow River was tempestuous. From the beginning of history, the Chinese tried to tame it, building earthen dikes to keep the river within its channel. Without constant care of the dikes, the river overflowed, spreading over hundreds of square miles and leaving lakes one or two feet deep that rotted the plants in the fields. The Yellow River has received the name China's sorrow.

The Yangtze is much gentler. Boats can navigate its waters deep into the interior of the country. Along its course it has several lakes that have served as reservoirs in times of drought.

The north of China is mostly a flat plain that in the winter is subject to strong cold winds that carry a great amount of dust, causing the sky to turn yellow. This dust, called **loess,** makes the plain very fertile for it lays down a rich layer of topsoil. In the north farmers in medieval times planted millet, which was the staple grain of the region.

South China is both warmer and wetter, a land of two seasons: dry and rainy. From the monsoons it receives up to 60 inches of rain each year. The warmth and humidity combine to make this rice-growing region of China one of the most productive areas of agriculture in the world.

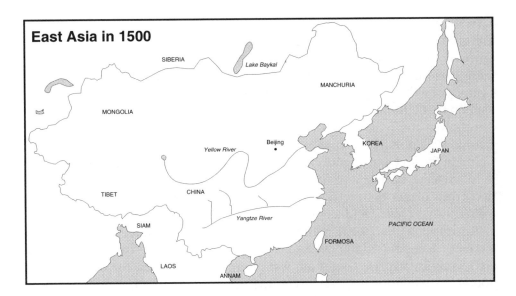

East Asia in 1500

Therefore China's two distinct geographic regions allow regular production of various food crops, making it possible for the country to feed the largest population in the world. When China entered the early modern period, it had over 100,000,000 people, and by 1800 its population numbered 150,000,000.

The Last Days of Ming China

The Chinese measured time according to dynasties because they were convinced that their rulers were not mere mortals. They were chosen by Heaven, another name for God, to be its sons. Therefore, these Sons of Heaven ruled with a divine mandate, and the overturning of a dynasty was a major event in history. When affairs went badly in the country, the mandate had obviously been withdrawn; therefore, it was time to confer it on a new dynasty. This occurred in 1368 when the Ming dynasty took the throne of China.

The inauguration of the Ming emperors brought China new prosperity. They proved to be able administrators and oversaw a country that had great human and natural resources. It was also a government that possessed an elite body of scholars who provided a pool of talent for public service unequaled in the world. China's gentry class, living in the countryside, served local government in an efficient, albeit authoritarian manner, following the dictates of Confucius. At that time China had the world's most advanced technology, and its engineers possessed skills that made the country a marvel to the few travelers who had the opportunity to visit it.

Beginning in 1403 the Ming emperors sent out seven great expeditions into the Indian Ocean that called at ports from India to East Africa. The purpose of the expeditions was to demonstrate how strong the emperors of China had become and to let foreign peoples know that acknowledging them as the world's most powerful figures was a good idea. Those countries close to China were persuaded to continue, or to begin, paying tribute to these emperors.

In the fifteenth century China was on the brink of expanding its civilization into a much broader world in South and East Asia. Suddenly in 1433, however, the expeditions stopped, for reasons not altogether clear. Possibly there was fear of a Mongol attack or the money required for imperial projects sapped the navy's resources. Had these expeditions continued, it might well be that China, not the small states of Europe, would have dictated the direction of the world's future. China was remarkably self-sufficient, while Europe was not. This explains the reason Europeans sailed all the way to China in the sixteenth century, rather than the Chinese sailing to Europe.

In 1514 the Portuguese first reached China, breaking the country's isolation from direct contact with Europe. The natives found the foreigners from the West hairy and smelly, not at all to their liking.

An imperial ban kept merchants from overseas trade, so the Chinese were not accustomed to new and strange products. The Portuguese discovered to their surprise that there was no market in China for their cache of goods. However, European silver was in great demand, for the Chinese, despite their invention of paper money, used only silver coins after 1450.

The Ming emperors did not want Europeans to have the right to trade wherever they wanted or to settle among them with their disturbing ways. Therefore, after 1555 Macao, a town on the southern coast, became a base for the Portuguese. Later Canton (now Guangzho) also served as a center of exports.

Besides silver, several agricultural imports brought on European ships interested the Chinese. These new food crops entered China from the Philippines: corn, white and sweet potatoes, and peanuts. These plants adapted well to the Chinese environment and soon found a place in people's diet.

Government in the Forbidden City

The Ming emperors were very anxious to have a palace complex worthy of rulers who considered themselves Sons of Heaven. They therefore commissioned major improvements in their Beijing capital. In the heart of the city, architects laid out a series of buildings separated by courtyards. This complex was known as the Forbidden City because only those on official business could enter. A wall and moat encircled the palace area, which extended two miles around.

Inside the Forbidden City of Beijing, residence of China's emperors.

The emperor lived inside the Forbidden City with hundreds of officials. Many of them were eunuchs, for they were supposed to be low on ambition because they could have no heirs for their position or wealth. Certain eunuchs gained the ear of the emperors and frequently gave advice that promoted only their own interests.

In addition to the males of the Forbidden City, hundreds of women, wives or concubines, lived within the palace complex. Except for serving the emperor, they had little to do, living an existence of permanent boredom.

The Ming emperors of the sixteenth century were in theory absolute, but their power was nothing like it had been in the past. The luxurious life they led in the Forbidden City sapped their energy. Their councilors frequently led them into paths that enhanced their influence but did little for the country.

The entrance into Beijing's Tiananmen Square.

The imperial fleet, once so powerful, was allowed to decline, and the army did not receive its monies. About 1570 the Ming emperors made major restorations on the Great Wall, but afterward its maintenance was neglected.

Outside the capital, the number of government administrators was actually too few. One estimate counts only 2,000 officials. This small figure meant that revenues from land taxes could be "lost" or not collected, state monopolies on salt and tea could be easily avoided, and labor service on roads, dikes, or defenses could be unenforced. Less money for the central government weakened its effectiveness, but this was not observed outside of China.

A host of states offered tribute to the imperial court in Beijing. At times Korean, Vietnamese, Burmese, Tibetan, Laotian, and Philippine states sent ambassadors to Beijing to offer gifts and pay tribute to the Chinese emperors. Ceremony was rigid and required that they *kowtow* before this supreme ruler of the East Asian world. In return for their acknowledgment of imperial omnipotence, the ambassadors returned home with promises of Chinese benevolence toward their own princes.

Because the south coast of China found itself under constant attack from Japanese, Korean, or even local pirates, instead of strengthening port defenses, one emperor ordered all coastal settlements relocated 30 miles inland. To stop piracy of Chinese ships at sea, his solution was to prohibit their voyages. Such self-defeating measures were obviously an invitation for economic disaster. However, because enforcement was lax, ports remained open, and merchants continued to send out ships. Smuggling was a way of life for many Chinese traders.

The Ming emperors had revived the examination system that required candidates for office to pass before they could enter imperial service. About half the positions in the administrative apparatus were filled by those who succeeded in taking the tests. The content of the examinations depended on a student's ability to memorize Confucian classics rather than to suggest innovations.

The street of animals before the Ming tombs.

Every two or three years young men who had prepared for years to take the examinations appeared at local testing centers. The exams covered several days, and only the best scores allowed a candidate to proceed to the provincial level. Once more the less able lost out, and successful candidates moved on to the next step in Beijing where only the top students of all China gathered for several grueling days of testing. Of those who started the process, 1 in 100 passed the final examinations. As a reward, these students received major posts in governmental offices and were a respected elite throughout the nation.

Unfortunately, although the examination system should have given the Chinese empire the wisest civil servants in the world, in practice it did not. The study of Confucian classics was too narrow a base to provide a general education for the practical problems that officials faced. The educated civil servants also had to compete with the eunuchs who surrounded the emperor and fawned on him. Incompetent decisions were the result as was frustration within the ranks of those who saw their nation stagnate.

The Wan Li emperor, who ruled from 1572 to 1620, was almost completely indifferent to government. Content to let his officials run the administration, he spent his time in the harem and in other diversions. Because the Wan Li emperor accepted the court's advice to put all taxes into a single tax to be paid in silver, it was necessary to import silver in still larger amounts, and the value of the metal skyrocketed.

In 1582 the Ming court, usually unfriendly to Europeans, made an exception and welcomed a Jesuit missionary, Matteo Ricci, to Beijing. Ricci came with a strong background in science and astronomy, which allowed him access to the government's inner circle. He and the Jesuits who followed adopted the Chinese way of life, dressed like them, and became well versed in Confucian wisdom. The Jesuits revived the intellectual curiosity of the Ming court. They explained the working of clocks, the use of astronomical instruments, and corrected the Chinese calendar.

Matteo Ricci stands next to one of his converts.

Ricci, in his reports, noted that the empire was no longer what it had been. Relatives of the officials received favored treatment, secret police struck fear into the hearts of citizens, states that used to pay tribute now had tribute paid to them. Ricci described the military as having low morale because their pay was infrequent and their rations inadequate. Court squabbles among the noble families whose daughters were in the imperial harem were never ending.

Ricci and his successors made some progress in converting the Chinese to Christianity. For the emperor and most of his court, whatever religion came from outside China, by its very nature, was inferior.

Society in Sixteenth-Century China

The indifference of the last Ming emperors toward government made life difficult for the nation's peasants. The emperor's officials abandoned any effort to control rapacious landowners from taking over the farms of the peasants. The landowners threw free peasants off their farms, causing them to wander the countryside as day laborers. Moneylenders cooperated with the landlords, foreclosing on farmers who could not pay back their loans. Often the peasants had no choice but to turn to banditry in order to survive.

Many of the landlord families had relatives among government officials and through bribery could count on their support. Their servants carried the wealthy class of Chinese in sedan chairs as they visited one another, without a glance at the peasants working in the fields.

The life of Chinese women followed a certain pattern. As a young bride, a woman was introduced into the home of her husband where she found herself under the absolute authority of her mother-in-law. For years she labored as her mother-in-law directed, waiting for the day when she might proceed to that position herself. Often her husband, if wealthy enough, took another wife or a concubine. Women entertainers for the upper class enjoyed more freedom than any wife did.

Culture in Ming China

The late Ming period was rich in cultural activities. Both men and women wrote poetry and made ink brush paintings. Portraits and landscapes were the favorite subjects along with birds and other animals. Ceramics, colored blue and white, were also in fashion. The tableware of Ming China has seldom been equaled in quality and design. It found a ready market in Europe.

Literature of the time was extensive. Two novels, *The Water Marquis* and the *Golden Lotus*, have made their way into anthologies of world literature. Thanks to a growing reading public and more print shops using wood blocks, a large number of books appeared, including mystery and detective stories. Buddhist religious texts were also popular.

Composers of opera were kept busy because this musical form became a popular entertainment for Chinese audiences. Over 300 operas appeared during the last years of Ming China.

Qing China

In the middle of the seventeenth century rebellion swept over China because of peasant desperation. The imperial government seemed paralyzed. In 1644 the last Ming emperor hanged himself rather than fall into the hands of the rebels.

To the north of China, the Manchus watched the struggle with interest, ready to take advantage of the country's weakness. One of their chieftains, Nurhachi, officially a vassal of the Mings, managed to form a coalition of tribes loyal to him and anxious to enlist in his armies. Nurhachi established a capital at Mukden (now Shenyang). At this time Chinese culture was so strong in Manchuria that, except for language, it was difficult to distinguish Chinese from Manchus.

A Manchu army now arrived at the gates of the Forbidden City. Its commander, Dorgon, son of Nurhachi, broke into the Forbidden Palace and established Manchu control over the capital. In the following years he extended his rule over the outlying provinces, and in 1683 the island of Taiwan, the last holdout of Ming loyalists, was taken.

The Manchu rulers took the Chinese word *Qing*, meaning pure, to describe their dynasty. They were pleased that their conquest had been relatively easy because their numbers were very few in comparison to the Chinese. The Manchus were but a ruling elite, approximately 2% of the total population.

The Manchus did not disturb the forms of government inherited from the Ming. What they changed were the appointees to office, putting one Manchu and one Chinese into major positions of state. The examination system for government office continued in force, allowing native Chinese to get ahead and serving as a safety valve against rebellion. Nevertheless, the Chinese were reminded that they were subjects, for men were required to wear their hair in long pigtails, and Manchus were forbidden to intermarry with native Chinese.

A street scene in Beijing in 1713 depicts the many activities of the citizens of the Chinese capital.

The Qing rulers in the first decades of their rule provided good government, and the country's economic strength returned. Taxes once more filled the imperial treasury. Neighboring states, such as Korea and Vietnam, resumed tribute to the Forbidden City in recognition of the emperor's power.

The second of the Manchu rulers was the Kangxi emperor, whose long reign extended from 1661 to 1722. The Kangxi emperor was a major patron of the arts and Confucian scholarship. He kept the intellectuals in the capital busy putting together huge encyclopedias for his library.

The Kangxi emperor's measures to aid the peasant class included lowering taxes and limiting the days that farmers had to work on government projects. Public works continued to receive his attention. The Yellow River dikes were always in need of repair as were the irrigation ditches that distributed the river's water.

The Manchus were reluctant to make the needed changes in the countryside that would limit the authority of the landlord class over the peasantry. Therefore, the owners of the land, dressed in silk and cultivating long fingernails to demonstrate that they never needed to work, continued to rule arbitrarily the peasants who worked on their estates. China remained a nation of few rich families and many poor ones.

The Qing emperors continued Ming commercial policies. They kept the Europeans isolated in Macao, although the Kangxi emperor did permit opening four more ports to Western merchants. He also kept a watchful eye on the commerce of native Chinese. Merchants financed voyages abroad, as long as government port officials took their share of profits. Europeans were always anxious to import silk, tea, and porcelain, products that they paid for in silver.

The Chinese easily absorbed the huge amounts of metal that were minted in the Americas. Between 1500 and 1800 the amount of silver arriving in China was 80% of world production, amounting to 150,000 tons. The abundance of currency in circulation brought both prosperity and rising inflation in the port cities of the country.

In matters to the north of China, the Kangxi emperor's officials worked out an arrangement with Peter the Great establishing a boundary with the Russians who now had reached the Pacific. A treaty signed with the tsar's ambassadors was the first ever between the Chinese and a European nation. The emperor also annexed both Mongolia and Tibet to his territories, demonstrating the return of vigor to Beijing's armies.

After the long rule of the Kangxi emperor, the Manchu rulers no longer were of the same caliber of leadership. Once more the court, filled with eunuchs, began to exert its influence over the emperor. Even some candidates for the civil service were found cheating, and other families sent bribes to guarantee their son's success.

Emperor Qien Lung receives a gift of Mongolian horses.

The motivation for public service was simply to enrich the families whose sons occupied the major positions in the bureaucracy. Monies were so diverted to personal fortunes that, as in Ming times, the army and navy were denied funds to maintain their strength. The Yellow River dikes that had been so carefully repaired in the 1600s developed leaks that were temporarily and haphazardly mended.

Despite all these problems, and to some extent because of them, the country's population increased to 200,000,000 people. More mouths to feed put great pressure on Chinese farmers to produce more and more. Mountainsides, once lush with native vegetation, were covered with terraces to increase the amount of arable land.

Landless peasants flocked to the Chinese cities in hopes of finding work, but towns did not offer that many jobs. Silver coins slowly lost their value, declining to one third their original worth. Inflation made it impossible for the emperors to buy the guns and ammunition needed to upgrade the army and navy, making China an easy target for European intervention in the nineteenth century.

Japanese Geography

The nation of Japan is made up of a chain of islands in the Pacific that lie over 100 miles from Korea. This distance was far enough to keep Japan isolated from many events that affected the Asian mainland, but close enough to allow it to take those elements of Chinese civilization that it wanted.

The four main islands of Japan are Honshu, Kyushu, Shikoku, and Hokkaido. The islands are mountainous, with only about 20% of the land available for farming. Its topography turned Japan to sea, making fish rather than meat a staple part of the national diet.

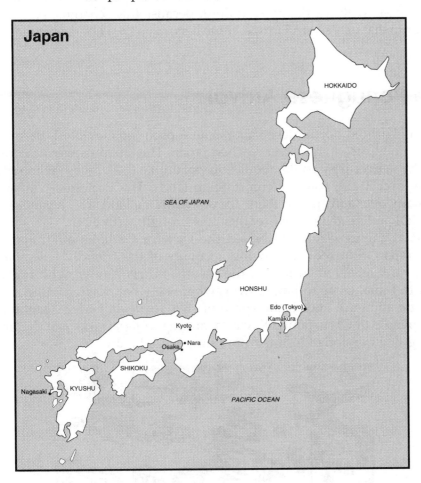

The Japanese climate varies according to the seasons, with most of the rain coming in summer monsoons. In the winter stiff winds from the north bring clear, sunny days. Unfortunately for the Japanese, their country, on the Pacific Rim, is frequently shaken by earthquakes that can cause tremendous damage.

The Culture of Japan

The Japanese received much of their culture from China in their early history. From that country they learned writing, painting, and architecture. Buddhism, the major religion of East Asia, came into Japan in the sixth century A.D. from Korea. It did not replace the indigenous religion, known as Shinto, but coexisted with it. The Japanese were very tolerant in their religious views.

The government of Japan was in theory in the hands of an emperor, who reigned but did not rule. Actual policy-making lay with prime ministers, later *shoguns,* drawn from strong families among the aristocracy.

The Japanese nobility, the *daimyo,* had a professional warrior class at its disposal. These soldiers were the *samurai,* who devoted their lives to the service of their lord. They had their own code of honor, *bushido,* that drew strict rules for combat. A samurai would not fight with anyone he thought below his social equal.

The daimyo lived in great palaces on estates that peasants farmed. Peasant farmers did not own the land but, in return for their labor, shared in the harvests with the daimyo landlord. Because this economic system was similar to that of western Europe, some historians speak of it as feudalism.

The Portuguese Arrival

In 1542 three Portuguese sailors came onto Japanese soil. Before this event, no European had ever reached Japan. The Japanese were anxious to learn whatever they could about Europe, unlike the Chinese who rejected nearly everything coming from foreign lands. The Portuguese answered the many questions put to them about their homeland. The Japanese were especially interested in the firearms they brought with them.

The Portuguese sailors opened the way for Catholic missionaries to enter Japan. Spurred by glowing accounts of the friendly welcome the Europeans received in Japan, the Jesuit Francis Xavier, who formerly lived in India, came to Japan. Everywhere he went, Xavier found a sympathetic audience and in the space of two years converted several hundred people to Christianity. Xavier's landing in Japan was just the first of an ongoing mission of Jesuits from Europe into Japan.

A Japanese screen depicts a meeting with the Portuguese.

Warrior Rulers

In 1573 a veteran soldier, Oda Nobunaga, pushed aside the ruling shogun and took over the government of Japan. Nobunaga's authority rested on the firearms that the Japanese learned to make from Portuguese models. The samurai who opposed him did not believe that their swords were no longer effective, but Nobunaga taught them that their way of fighting was now obsolete.

Oda Nobunaga was followed by another general, Hideyoshi. His title was *taiko* because, like Oda Nobunaga, his ancestors were not of the nobility; he had risen through the army to his position.

Hideyoshi was careful not to trouble the wealthy daimyo, so in order to raise state revenues he placed even more taxes upon the peasants. He disarmed any peasants who had weapons and announced a policy requiring every individual to remain in his or her occupation.

For the first time, due to Hideyoshi's strict rule and taxation, Japan had a uniform government throughout all the islands. From his Osaka castle, which he had built for his family, he could be well pleased with his accomplishments.

However, the taiko's ambition did not permit him to be content with these accomplishments. In 1592 he sent armies against Korea with plans to incorporate that nation within his lands to use as a stepping stone for an invasion of China. The Koreans, with Chinese help, resisted the invaders, and upon Hideyoshi's death the Japanese gave up the project.

Hideyoshi early in his career often met with the Jesuits in Japan. He had no use for Buddhism and looked upon Christians as allies in his efforts to control the Buddhist monks who often resisted his policies. Later he turned on the Christians because he received information that the missionaries from Europe were preparing the way for a foreign conquest. He ordered the missionaries to leave Japan but did not enforce the rule.

Nevertheless, in 1597 Hideyoshi ordered the arrest of six Spanish missionaries and their companions and had them crucified. This opened a new period of fear for those Japanese who had become Christians, now numbering about 300,000 in a nation of 20,000,000.

The last of Japan's strongmen of the early modern period was Ieyasu Tokugawa. In 1603 Ieyasu became shogun, beginning a dynasty that lasted until 1868 when the office of the shogunate was abolished. Ieyasu's noble ancestry allowed him to take the shogun title.

Ieyasu was anxious that there should be no opposition to his family's hold on the government. Two things stood in his way: the European Catholic missions with their Japanese converts and the power still held by the local daimyo. In 1613 he sought to solve the first problem when he ordered that all Christians return to the Buddhist religion. Some agreed, but others did not.

To further Christian isolation, the shogun sought to break all connections between Japan and the outside world. He ordered that no merchant ships could be built in Japan to sail abroad and that no Japanese were allowed to travel outside the country. Japanese who lived in a foreign land could not return. In effect, after 1642, except for a Dutch vessel permitted in the Nagasaki harbor, Japan became a closed country to foreigners.

Then Ieyasu began to deal with the daimyo problem. He commanded that the daimyo, then numbering about 250, swear an oath of loyalty to him. There were few who refused because Ieyasu could expand or reduce the size of their territories.

Osaka castle, built at the time of Hideyoshi, the warrior ruler of Japan.

In 1637, at a time when his son ruled, a Christian daimyo in Kyushu called for an uprising against the Tokugawa family. He probably had hopes of getting aid from European nations, but none appeared, and the rebellion failed. About 37,000 Catholics were killed; some of them crucified. The few families that survived went into hiding.

Ieyasu Tokugawa and his descendants made their residence in Edo (modern Tokyo). To keep an eye on the daimyo, the shoguns required that the daimyo live in Edo for a certain period of time each year. When the daimyo returned to their lands, their families were held hostage in Edo.

The Tokugawa solution to the civil wars and constant battles of the past was to rule with a strong arm. It served their purpose well. The samurai, with no wars to fight, turned to study or ink painting. Confucius, who had been known for centuries, now appeared as a special sage to the Japanese. His stress on obedience to superiors and strong parental authority was just what the Tokugawas wanted.

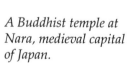

A Buddhist temple at Nara, medieval capital of Japan.

Peasant farmers labored under the weight of obligations to the shoguns and daimyo. On the other hand, the merchant class made great fortunes during Tokugawa times. Living in prosperous towns, there was sufficient domestic business to allow them to enjoy life as never before. Foreign competition was slight, and with their protected markets, artisans produced quality goods, rivaling those of China.

Japan along with Europe supplied China with silver from its mines. Because the Tokugawa shoguns controlled Japan's silver production, the profits they gained from it enabled them to keep their armed forces well supplied.

Japanese population, as in China, expanded in the sixteenth and seventeenth centuries. Then about 1710 the environment put limits on the amount of farmland available for farming, and taxation and population growth leveled off.

Korea

The Korean people live on a peninsula that juts into the Pacific. Their land is a beautiful country, much of it mountainous. In the north the winters are very severe, making the growing season relatively short.

The Koreans speak a Uralic-Altaic language, which is similiar to Mongolian and Japanese but quite different from Chinese. Yet it has been China that has always had a profound influence over Korean culture. The Koreans welcomed the gifts of their Chinese elder brothers but at the same time held at arm's length any possibility of assimilation into China.

In 1392 the Yi dynasty of monarchs came to power in Korea and provided the country with rulers until the twentieth century. By 1500 the Yi kings, governing the nation from Seoul, had developed Korean imitations of the Chinese civil service and an examination system meant to fill it. Confucian ethics dominated the world view of the Korean upper class that served the state, and Buddhism, as in China, offered a religion. Yi kings sent tribute to Beijing to guarantee that the emperors would not attempt direct rule of their nation.

A Korean woman offers rice for sale.

Factions at the court caused a series of crises in the 1500s that ceased only when a threat to Korean independence emerged. Hideyoshi's Japanese invasion unified the Korean factions to resist. The Chinese emperor also sent his soldiers to help repulse the Japanese, and after six years of war that left much of the country in ruins, the Japanese withdrew. Much of the credit for the Korean defense went to an admiral who covered his ships with metal plates to ram the Japanese fleet.

The next decades were spent in rebuilding the damage from the war. Landowners, the highest class in society, resumed their hereditary positions in the government, both national and local. Merchants traded Korean products such as ceramics, metal work, and books with foreign traders. The Koreans invented their own phonetic alphabet, which distinguished it from Chinese characters, and were the first Asians to use movable metallic type.

A Buddhist temple in Korea overlooks a valley.

The Philippines

The Philippines are composed of over 7,000 islands, and until the sixteenth century each was a world to itself. Most of the people shared a common Malay language, survived on subsistence farming, and traded with neighboring islands, but no major state had ever developed. Chinese and Japanese traders came to the Philippines looking for ways to open commercial ties with the islanders, but their importance was minimal.

Muslim traders from Indonesia arrived on Mindanao, planting Islam on this southern island. On other islands animistic religions prevailed, leaving people there open to Christianity once Europeans arrived.

The Spaniards in the Philippines

The first contact with Europeans took place in 1521 when Ferdinand Magellan's tiny ship arrived in the Philippine islands during the first circumnavigation of the world. Magellan's involvement with an internal conflict cost him his life on the island of Cebu. Magellan had claimed the Philippines for Spain, and in 1565, when the first settlement was established on Luzon, the island archipelago received its name from the Spanish sovereign, Philip II.

World trade across the Pacific commenced in 1571 with the foundation of the city of Manila. After that date, regular merchant ties between the Americas and Asia increased every year. Manila became the place of exchange for silver going to China and silk coming from it. Ships from Acapulco, Mexico, carrying tons of silver destined to satisfy the Chinese insatiable appetite for the metal anchored in Manila's harbor. By 1650 there were 42,000 people in the city: 20,000 Filipinos, 15,000 Chinese, and 7,000 Spaniards. They were busily engaged in warehousing the products that moved both east and west on an annual voyage.

As in Latin America, Spanish friars established missions that attracted thousands of Filipino converts. Their presence has made the Philippines the only East Asian nation to have a Christian majority.

Southeast Asians

Among the Indonesian archipelago of 3,000 islands, Java held a predominant position. Fertile soil provided wealth to its people and high revenues to the sultans who ruled there. On other islands small states appeared only to collapse and reform as one ruler rose to power only to be toppled by a neighbor.

On most islands Islam had replaced earlier Hindu or Buddhist beliefs. An exception was the island of Bali, which retained its Hindu religion. Muslim traders from India, many of them members of Sufi brotherhoods, persuaded both rulers and their subjects of the spiritual and material advantages of conversion to Islam.

The Indonesians shaped Islam to their own culture, softening its requirements to fit their native traditions. Therefore, women rejected veiling and seclusion, and the fast of Ramadan was kept in a relaxed manner. Nevertheless, Islam struck deep roots, making Indonesia the world's most populous Muslim nation today.

The islands' most important products were spices. Almost the whole world's supply of cinnamon and cloves was grown there. Malacca, a city of the Malay peninsula, was the center of trade, for it lay on the narrow straits that merchant ships had to use to travel between the islands and all points west.

Vietnam, Cambodia, and Laos were the countries with the largest populations on the Southeast Asian mainland. Dozens of other people, original settlers, were either displaced or replaced by the expansion of these people. The Hmong are a good example of indigenous people who were forced into the mountains as the Vietnamese expanded.

There were two Vietnams: one in the north with its capital at Hanoi and the other in the south with Hue as its leading city. The history of North Vietnam was a constant struggle against Chinese political domination. Sometimes the Vietnamese were successful; at other times they had to endure Chinese occupation. Although political rule of Ming and Qing emperors was vigorously rejected, Chinese culture, as in Korea, shaped the Vietnamese character.

In the south, in the Mekong River delta, the Vietnamese expanded at the expense of the Khmers, or Cambodians. The country here was excellent for rice cultivation, allowing a native kingdom, Annam, to appear. Chinese culture was also present in Annam, but it was never as strong as in the north.

The Khmer were at one time the dominant people of Southeast Asia. They were the builders of the city of Angkor Thom, the largest town of Southeast Asia for centuries, and of nearby Angkor Wat, the largest temple complex ever constructed in world history. In 1431 their Thai neighbors destroyed Angkor Thom, and the better days of Cambodia disappeared. About 1500 a rebuilt capital was located at Phnom Penh.

Both the Thai and the Burmese people settled in Southeast Asia after migrating from China. The Burmese came first, about A.D. 800, and the Thais arrived later, about 1600. Both people engaged in nearly constant warfare with indigenous peoples and with each other. The major cultural influence on both was Theravada Buddhism, but its pacific influence did little to inhibit Burmese and Thai rulers from marching their armies into each other's territories.

Early in the 1500s the Burmese gained the upper hand, but a Thai recovery occurred in the late eighteenth century. In 1782, at the new capital of Bangkok, the present Thai ruling dynasty came to power.

Conclusion

It was difficult for the people of East Asia to understand the reason the Europeans wanted into their world. They did not want into the European world.

Although from Roman times forward, as Chinese silk traveled across the Great Silk Road, no Chinese ever went so far as to accompany it to its final destination. Marco Polo's famous journey to the Mongol emperors in Beijing was not even noted in a single Chinese source. Therefore the Portuguese arrival on the coast of China and Japan and other parts of Southeast Asia was a mutual revelation for both discoverers and the discovered.

Unlike in the Americas, the Chinese and Japanese could resist the European diseases, and their population was dense enough to ward off any thought of conquest. If the Europeans wanted to trade, it was on the terms set by the East Asian rulers, not on those set by the westerners. Except in the Philippines, European religion was given only a limited welcome.

The structure of Chinese society, which placed the government in the hands of men trained in Confucianism, was both a strength and a weakness. On the one hand it kept Chinese culture intact, but on the other hand the failure to appreciate the importance of western technology eventually would put China at a great disadvantage.

Japan withdrew into itself in Tokugawa times, but not so much that its rulers were cut off from new developments in the outside world. The spice trade of Malacca and the tons of silver brought into Manila made those cities hubs for European trade and places where Asian and European cultures met.

CHAPTER 8 REVIEW
EAST ASIA MEETS THE OUTSIDE WORLD

Summary
- China's geography has determined much of its history.
- The coming of the Portuguese meant direct, but limited, contact between China and Europe.
- The emperors lived in the Forbidden City, a complex of buildings in Beijing.
- The examination system continued to provide recruits for government officers, but it did not function sufficiently well to prepare the Chinese for the impact of the Europeans.
- Chinese society was principally one of impoverished peasants whose work provided a leisured life for the landowning class.
- The Qing dynasty was of Manchu origin. It continued the structure of the Mings.
- The nation of Japan profited from its island position and its proximity to China.
- The Japanese nobility, the daimyo, were served by a class of soldiers, the samurai.
- Warrior rulers, the shoguns, came to power late in the sixteenth century.
- Christianity had a strong presence in Japan until persecution practically destroyed it.
- Japan became a hermit nation under the Tokugawa shoguns.
- Spain entered the Philippines, shaping the culture of the islands.
- Both the Chinese and Japanese considered Korea a prize worth fighting over.
- The islands of Indonesia came under Muslim cultural and European economic influence.
- The Southeast Asian mainland was shared by Vietnamese, Cambodians, and Laotians.

Identify
People: Ming emperors, Wan Li, Ricci, Dorgon, Qing emperors, the Kangxi Emperor, Xavier, Oda Nobunaga, Hideyoshi, Ieyasu Tokugawa, Yi kings, Nurhachi
Places: Macao, Forbidden City, Manchuria, Edo, Manila, Bali, Bangkok, Hanoi, Canton, Seoul, Phnom Penh
Events: Chinese examination system, Jesuits in Beijing, isolation of Japan, spice trade of Indonesia

Define

loess	kowtow	daimyo
samurai	shogun	taiko

Multiple Choice
1. The great river of North China is the
   (a) Wei.
   (b) Yangtze.
   (c) Mekong.
   (d) Yellow.

2. The staple grain of North China is
   (a) corn.
   (b) wheat.
   (c) rye.
   (d) millet.

3. Chinese emperors claimed their right to rule came from
   (a) Heaven.
   (b) election.
   (c) hereditary succession.
   (d) nomination by the army.

4. Local government in China was provided by
   (a) the gentry class.
   (b) imperial bureaucrats.
   (c) military governors.
   (d) members of the imperial family.

5. Chinese currency in Qing times was
   (a) paper.
   (b) gold.
   (c) copper coins.
   (d) silver coins.

6. The Portuguese base on the Chinese coast was at
   (a) Canton.
   (b) Shanghai.
   (c) Beijing.
   (d) Macao.

7. The residence of the emperors was in Beijing's
   (a) Golden Palace.
   (b) Forbidden City.
   (c) Shantung district.
   (d) Silver Palace.

8. Many officials in China were eunuchs because
   (a) they scored better on the state examinations.
   (b) they were often relatives of the emperor.
   (c) they were more efficient.
   (d) they could have no heirs.

9. Problems for merchants on China's south coast came from
   (a) government taxation.
   (b) piracy.
   (c) climatic changes.
   (d) currency inflation.

10. Entry into the imperial service required
    (a) years of prior military service.
    (b) relatives who had influence.
    (c) passing examinations.
    (d) the knowledge of several languages.

11. The most prominent Jesuit to live in Beijing was
    (a) Ricci.
    (b) Loyola.
    (c) Xavier.
    (d) Rodriguez.

12. The head of domestic affairs for wives in a Chinese family was
    (a) the mother-in-law.
    (b) the chief butler.
    (c) the oldest sister-in-law.
    (d) the father of the family.

13. Chinese potters favored these colors in their ceramics:
    (a) black and white
    (b) green and blue
    (c) blue and red
    (d) blue and white

14. Nurhachi was a Manchu chieftain who
    (a) united the tribes under his rule.
    (b) invaded China.
    (c) captured Beijing.
    (d) extinguished Chinese culture in Manchuria.

15. The wearing of a pigtail was a sign that you were
    (a) Laotian.
    (b) Korean.
    (c) Chinese.
    (d) Manchu.

16. European merchants in China were primarily
    (a) importers of European goods.
    (b) importers of Indonesian goods.
    (c) exporters of Chinese products.
    (d) exporters of Indonesian goods.

17. China and Russia agreed on a boundary during the time of
    (a) Kangxi and Peter the Great.
    (b) Wan Li and Catherine the Great.
    (c) Bodi and Peter the Great.
    (d) none of the above.

18. The native religion of Japan was
    (a) Buddhism.
    (b) Confucianism.
    (c) Hinduism.
    (d) Shinto.

19. A samurai is a Japanese
    (a) ruler.
    (b) religious leader.
    (c) prime minister.
    (d) soldier.

20. Hideyoshi sponsored this type of government:
    (a) authoritarian
    (b) democratic
    (c) monarchical
    (d) aristocratic

21. The capital of Tokugawa Japan was
    (a) Nagasaki.
    (b) Kyoto.
    (c) Kobe.
    (d) Edo.

22. World trade between Asia and the Americas extended from
    (a) Acapulco and Macao.
    (b) Mexico City and Edo.
    (c) Kobe and Acapulco.
    (d) Acapulco and Manila.

23. Seoul was the residence of this dynasty:
    (a) Manchu
    (b) Qing
    (c) Ming
    (d) Li

24. The religion of most Indonesians became
    (a) Christianity.
    (b) Hinduism.
    (c) Buddhism.
    (d) Islam.

25. A native kingdom in South Vietnam was
    (a) Hue.
    (b) Hanoi.
    (c) Annam.
    (d) Angkor Thom.

Essay Questions
1. How did the Forbidden City epitomize the foreign policy of China?
2. Compare the role of the nobility of China with that of Japan.
3. What was the fate of Christianity in East Asia?
4. Why did the leaders of the East Asian nations fear opening their countries to westerners?
5. Why can it be said that world trade began with the opening of Manila?

Answers

1. d	6. d	11. a	16. c	21. d
2. d	7. b	12. a	17. a	22. d
3. a	8. d	13. d	18. d	23. d
4. a	9. b	14. a	19. d	24. d
5. d	10. c	15. c	20. a	25. c

CHAPTER 9

African Peoples

Africa is a very large continent, at its farthest points stretching east and west about 5,700 miles and north to south 6,000 miles. The great Sahara Desert creates the continent's two regions: North Africa and Sub-Saharan Africa. Because of cultural and ethnic differences, they are very diverse places, with histories in the early modern period that took different directions. Large parts of Sub-Saharan Africa for the first time came into direct contact with Europeans in the sixteenth century.

African Geography

North Africa's climate is very similar to that of the Mediterranean region with hot, dry summers and cool, moist winters. The coastal areas of North Africa get rain in the winter as winds blow across the Mediterranean, picking up moisture that then falls as rain or snow in the mountains. These regions average about 30 inches of rain each year, while the Nile delta only gets about 10 inches.

The Atlas Mountains are a dominant feature of the landscape in Morocco and Algeria. They have always provided security to the tribespeople of North Africa who hoped to escape from the restrictions and taxes of a central government.

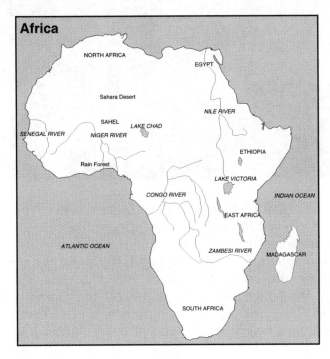

Egypt is at the far east of North Africa, and is a land whose history extends back 5,000 years. Unlike the region of western North Africa, Egypt and its neighbor Libya are predominantly desert. Egypt, however, is much more fortunate than Libya, for the Nile River, the world's longest, passes through it. In the past the Nile's annual flood deposited an inch or more of topsoil on Upper Egypt and carried fertile earth into the delta region, or Lower Egypt.

Because winter rains provide enough moisture, North African farmers of the 1500s grew dates, olives, and grapes along the coastline. Wheat was the staple grain crop of the region.

Herding peoples, such as the Tuareg, followed their sheep and goats as they migrated in search of pasture land. In the summer they went into the mountains, and in the winter they returned to the grasslands of the plains.

In the Sahara there are vast empty lands, where only sand and rocky gravel cover the ground. The Sahara is the largest desert in the world, covering 3,500,000 square miles. Here and there oases appear where springs bring water to the surface. The **sahel,** lying south of the Sahara, is the transition zone between desert and rain forest.

South of the Sahara, the major landform is a region of plateaus, separated from one another by slopes or cliffs. Much of the African continent is about 2,000 feet above sea level.

A major feature of East Africa is a crack in the surface, the Rift Valley, that runs from southern Africa all the way to the Dead Sea. This valley has sides a mile high and its floor often reaches 20 miles across. Most of Africa's lakes lie within this depression: Lakes Malawi, Tanganyika, and Victoria.

A felucca provides transportation on the Nile.

Rivers are the great highways of the African interior. The Nile and its tributaries, the White Nile and the Blue Nile, which meet at Khartoum in the Sudan, comprise the continent's major waterway. The Nile passes through a great swampy region, the Sudd, in the southern Sudan on its way to Khartoum. In central Africa the Congo is the major river, while in the northwest the Niger and in the southeast the Zambezi drain major basins. One of the world's great waterfalls is on the Zambezi: Victoria Falls tumbles from a height of 335 feet.

The rivers of Africa on their way to the sea must pass over rapids or fall from plateaus to the coastal lowlands. Ocean-going ships cannot navigate them, and this factor contributed to the isolation of the interior. Shifting currents at the rivers' outlets created sandbars, so few good harbors were to be found along the coast.

A great tropical rain forest covers the Congo basin, the western coast-lands, and the eastern side of the island of Madagascar. In these areas the forests, supporting a great variety of wildlife, are forever dripping, since up to 100 inches of rain falls each year.

On the African plains, or savannas, both to the north and south of the rain forest, the natural vegetation turns to high grasslands and open tracts of woods. There is more wildlife in Africa than anywhere else in the world. For centuries African hunters have taken advantage of the thousands of animals that make the savanna their home.

A pride of lions after dinner.

North Africa

Egypt received new leadership in 1517 when the Ottoman sultan, Selim I, occupied Cairo, putting to death its last Mamluk ruler, Tuman Bey. He appointed an Ottoman governor to oversee the taxation of the country and preserve domestic peace. For the most part, Turkish rule did not affect local government; the Mamluks up and down the Nile remained in place. They monopolized the wealth of the country and continued to make the life of the ordinary Egyptian peasant difficult, showing no restraint in their collection of rents. The 10% of Egyptians who were Christians of the Coptic church had to pay an additional tax, the *cizye*, for remaining faithful to their religion.

In the region from Algeria to Libya, Ottoman fleets fought with the Spaniards for control of the main coastal cities. Tunis passed back and forth between the Turks and the Habsburgs as did several Algerian towns until a Turkish victory decided the issue late in the sixteenth century. In fact, local rulers, supported by pirates, had more to say about events on the Barbary Coast than either the kings of Spain or the Ottoman sultans. This period was the great age of piracy in the Mediterranean, when

Muslim and Christian buccaneers sought to gain captives and booty to enrich themselves at the expense of merchants of every land.

Of all the North African states, Morocco was the scene of a decisive contest between Europeans and Muslims. In 1578 King Sebastian I of Portugal decided to be the last of the Crusaders. The Moroccan army crushed his forces, and he lay dead on the battlefield. The victor, Ahmed al-Mansur, then began the Sharifian dynasty, which gave the country strong central government and a determination to preserve its independence. Ottoman administration never reached as far as Morocco.

West African History

In 1500 the major West African kingdom was Songhai. The Songhai state had its base on the edge of the sahel, the transition zone between the desert and the savanna. Its capital, Gao, on the Niger River, was a hub for the caravan trade between the desert, the savanna, and the rain forest. Its most flourishing city was the fabled Timbuktu, in 1500 a town of 50,000 people pursuing a large number of trades.

Songhai, like the sahel kingdoms that preceded it, was predominantly a Muslim community. Thanks to trade with Arabs and Berber Muslims, Islam gained many converts in preceding centuries. Timbuktu had dozens of Muslim *medreses,* schools where Islamic studies flourished. A major export of the town was books, laboriously copied by hand in the workshops of the town.

Side by side with the Muslim elite were African peoples who remained faithful to their traditional animistic religions. The rather easy-going Muslims of the sahel were not overly anxious to convert all their neighbors to their belief.

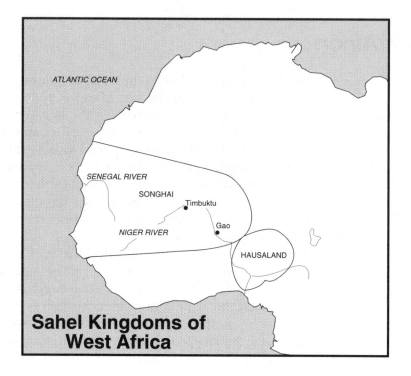

Sahel Kingdoms of West Africa

Songhai's authority extended to many tributary states that offered its rulers gifts, especially gold, so as to retain control of their own internal affairs. The rulers in Songhai kept a fleet of ships on the Niger, the first African navy. The kings lived apart from ordinary citizens, preferring a life of isolation so as to lend an aura of mystery to their person. An Arab traveler reported that in Gao the beating of drums announced that the king was eating in the palace. Men and women had to wait until he finished before they could resume their business.

Songhai reached its height midway through the sixteenth century. Then in 1591 a Moroccan army of Tuaregs accompanied by Spanish and Portuguese mercenaries descended upon the Songhai lands and destroyed Gao. The invading army had muskets, and the Songhai ruler did not. After this defeat Songhai's prosperity passed to the Hausa people nearby.

Kano, the Hausa capital, now became the major city of the sahel region and, like Timbuktu, a center of Muslim life in Africa. The Hausa rulers used cavalry to ensure tribute from nearby peoples, but it was not easily done, for riding horses in the rain forest was a difficult task.

The Yoruba and Ibo peoples, living to the south of the Hausa, developed kingdoms in West Africa in the region of modern Nigeria and Benin. Markets that exchanged forest products for exports from drier regions soon grew into towns. Cloth, ivory, metal, kola nuts, and especially gold were the chief products bought and sold. Both Yoruba and Ibo kings continued the now-established tradition that they should live in royal towns separated from their subjects.

The Yoruba rulers of Ife sponsored artists to cast bronze sculptures of them and thus began in the region a strong artistic tradition that then passed to Benin. From 1550 to 1690 artists of Benin crafted copper portraits of their kings to be used at royal funerals. They also cast plaques to hang on the columns of the royal palaces. Today they are considered some of Africa's finest examples of art.

A copper cast of a Benin king.

The Bakongo were located on the Atlantic coast of the Congo Republic with a capital at Mbanzakongo. Within Bakongo's borders as many as 2,000,000 people made their homes. However, large kingdoms like Bakongo were hard to maintain in the rain forest regions of Africa where the more usual political system depended on chiefdoms of limited size.

Ethiopia

In the Horn of Africa, to the east of the sahel, the Ethiopian kingdom was dominant. Successor to the ancient state of Axum, a dynasty of rulers in the country extended back over a thousand years, claiming to be the descendants of a royal wedding between King David of Jerusalem and the Queen of Sheba. Besides its dynasty, the distinguishing mark of the Ethiopian kingdom was its Christian religion, adopted as early as the fourth century. The Ethiopian Christians depended on the Coptic patriarch of Alexandria, who in 1500 was living in Cairo, to send them their bishop, whom they called the Father of Peace.

In 1500 the advance of Muslims in the Sudan and in Somalia threatened to destroy the Ethiopian kingdom. Then in 1542 a Portuguese army arrived on the scene to come to its aid. Their newly found European allies for a time convinced the Ethiopians to join the Catholic church, and Jesuit missionaries arrived in the country. However, the move to Rome was unpopular, and the Ethiopians came to resent the foreign presence. In 1632 the king expelled the Jesuits, and Ethiopia returned to its traditional self-contained Christianity.

East Africa

South of Ethiopia, the coastline of the Indian Ocean was lined with towns that for centuries were part of the commercial zone of the Indian Ocean. Here busy harbors took in goods from as far away as China. Many of the merchants were Arabs, Persians, or Indians who had settled here to trade ivory, gold, palm oil, tortoise shell, rhinoceros horn, and iron ore. Kilwa Island, located off the coast of modern Tanzania, was one of Africa's busiest ports.

The native blacks were mostly Bantu-speaking, belonging to a language group that identified them as part of a migration that began centuries earlier. The original homeland of the Bantu was along the Atlantic, in modern-day Nigeria and Cameroon. Over the decades they had traveled all the way to East Africa, some as farmers and others as herders. They cultivated food crops introduced from Southeast Asia: bananas, coconuts, rice, and yams. A knowledge of iron-making gave the Bantu an advantage over the peoples they displaced.

Another migration, from the north, brought tall Nilotic peoples into the area. They were cattle herders, ancestors of the Tutsi and Masai. One group, the Luo, formed a strong state called Baganda near Lake Victoria.

Austronesians, kin to the natives of Indonesia, crossed the Indian Ocean to settle the island of Madagascar.

As in West Africa, the upper class in the port cities of the east coast were Muslims, while most of the local people remained animists. Zanzibar was one center of brisk trade. Its sultan supervised the export of gold, ivory, and slaves to Southwest Asia. On the island plantations slave laborers worked at growing cloves.

Mt. Kilimanjaro, East Africa's tallest mountain, always has a snowcap.

To communicate in this very cosmopolitan world, a language called **Swahili** was spoken from Mogadishu in the north to Sofala in the south. When written, Swahili used the Arabic alphabet.

South Africa

The Bantu migration did not stop in East Africa but carried on to the south of the continent. Here the original settlers, the San and Khoi Khoi, were pushed southward, for they lacked the numbers, iron weapons, and cohesion of the newcomers.

A considerable impediment to settlement in southern Africa and throughout the continent was the tsetse fly. This insect, which resembles a horse fly, carries sleeping sickness to both animals and people. Cattle bitten by the tsetse fly would soon die; therefore, herders had to avoid those areas where infestation was a problem. Malaria was another serious disease that plagued Africa, carrying off thousands of men, women, and children each year.

By 1500 Great Zimbabwe, once the capital of several Bantu kingdoms, was in decline. What made this town so distinctive was its use of granite to build a palace complex and a solid stone tower. A wall surrounded Great Zimbabwe, 30 feet tall and 820 feet in length.

Society and Culture

In West Africa the mixed population of the sahel regions resided in villages. Because polygamy was accepted as the norm for marriage, families were very large. The number of children guaranteed the parents that they would be provided for in sickness and old age. Villagers lived in houses of mud brick or reeds with thatched roofs and kept small gardens that grew the plants they needed for food.

Families belonged to clans that claimed a common kinship and worshipped their own deities. A clan might trace relationship on either the mother's side, the father's side, or both. When boys or girls reached puberty, an elaborate ceremony introduced them into full clan membership. At the time of marriage, some people were patrilocal, whereas others required the man to come live with his wife's relations.

In the capitals of the larger African states, the population was divided into an elite of the royal family, the ruler's counselors, and his army commanders. The artisans and the lesser city officials, with the religious leaders, formed a second tier within society. Muslim scholars did not care much for the freedom that women enjoyed in the city's public life, without veils or, as in the town of Jenne, with no clothes at all.

Special privileges went to members of the armed cavalry that guarded the king and moved about his territories enforcing the law and collecting taxes. Ownership of horses and guns demonstrated the wealth and position that gave them significant prestige. When a professional cavalry existed, the king became more powerful. He did not have to depend on local chieftains to appear with their forces whenever he went to war.

The ruler of Benin, the oba, *in procession.*

Much of African art depended for patronage from the royal court. Weavers fashioned the king's wardrobe so that he and his officials could dress in elegance. Wood carvers made masks for ceremonies, and bronze casters made utensils for the court. Carving in ivory was a well-established tradition.

African peoples loved music, and dancing accompanied every festival from the capital to the village. Drums beat out rhythms that brought everyone into the celebration. Story telling was another art form that preserved African folk traditions among every people.

The Europeans Come to Africa

The Portuguese, on the Atlantic coast of Europe, first took an interest in sailing down the African coast in the 1400s. Their interest was in reaching the gold mines of West Africa. They came on **caravels,** ships well fitted for both ocean and river navigation. A Portuguese prince, Henry the Navigator, directed and financed the expeditions.

In 1482 the Portuguese placed a fort on the West African coast, calling it St. George of Mina. Further voyages southward reached the tip of South Africa and the Cape of Good Hope, and in 1497 the Portuguese captain Vasco da Gama sailed all the way to India.

A Portuguese caravel, a type of ship used to explore the African coast.

Da Gama's fleet called at the coastal towns of East Africa, checking out the potential for the Europeans to take over the Indian Ocean trade. The Portuguese intended to make the Indian Ocean their own, placing garrisons ashore to protect their interests. Muslim traders, who for centuries controlled the markets between East Africa, India, and the Spice Islands of Indonesia, were pushed aside. The gold from the Zambezi River region became a Portuguese monopoly.

The Portuguese held onto their bases in East Africa until the eighteenth century when the Arabs and Persians returned. Only Mozambique remained a Portuguese territory until the twentieth century.

When the Portuguese came to Africa, one of their goals was the conversion of the people to Christianity. They were successful in the Bakongo kingdom where the ruler took the Portuguese name Afonso I. During his rule, from 1507 to 1543, Afonso made a major effort to convert his whole nation to Christianity, and his son was named a Catholic bishop.

The Portuguese presence in West Africa became a nightmare for the native Africans after Brazil developed a plantation economy, resulting in a great demand for slaves. Luanda, the Portuguese station in Angola, developed into a center for the export of blacks, and the area about Bakongo became a battleground. By 1660 Bakongo was no more, and the region of Angola returned to wilderness as a result of severe depopulation.

Portugal was too small a country to ensure that African trade would retain its monopoly for long. First Dutch and then English and French ships arrived on what came to be called the Gold Coast and to the east, the Slave Coast.

The captains of the European ships were anxious to buy slaves to transport to the West Indies and the British colonies in America to work on sugar and tobacco plantations. In 1637 the Dutch ousted the Portuguese from St. George of Mina, and the Netherlands soon came to be the dominant slave-trading nation of the world. The Dutch held this position for about a hundred years. After that time, English traders replaced them on the West African coast. In 1713 the *Asiento*, a provision in the treaty ending the War of Spanish Succession, gave the British the right to sell slaves in the Spanish colonies of the Americas.

Afrikaners in South Africa

In 1652 the Dutch, under Jan van Riebeeck, landed at the Cape of Good Hope with the intention of providing a supply base for ships of the East India Company on their route to the islands of Indonesia. The Khoi Khoi people who then lived in South Africa were herders of sheep and cattle and at first welcomed the foreigners.

The few Dutch settlers were happy to discover that the Cape had neither the tsetse fly nor malaria but enjoyed a climate similar to the Mediterranean. It was a land where Europeans felt at home, compared to the hot, humid climate of other parts of Africa. Staunch Calvinists, the Dutch were joined by French Huguenots when Louis XIV expelled them from France.

The Dutch greet the Khoi Khoi in South Africa.

At the beginning the **Afrikaners,** as they came to be known, planted wheat, grapes, and vegetables. Then they turned to cattle ranching, with huge regions of land used for pasture. Slaves tended the animals.

The Afrikaner expansion threatened the Khoi Khoi way of life resulting in two frontier wars during the seventeenth century. The Khoi Khoi lost their pastures to the whites, and many had no choice but to move to the towns where they found work as domestic servants or craftsmen and -women.

The next blow suffered by the natives occurred when a ship from Europe arrived in the Cape Town harbor infected with smallpox. The Khoi Khoi fell victim to the disease by the thousands. After the plague abated, the Khoi Khoi were so decimated that they never recovered. Their descendants of mixed ancestry survive as the **Cape Coloured** in modern South Africa. The San hardly fared better, for they were pushed into the inhospitable Kalahari Desert.

The African Economy and the Slave Trade

Africa in the early modern period was a continent of farmers and herders, but this does not mean that cultivating plants was easy. The soils of both the rain forest and the savannas are generally thin and lack the nutrients to make agriculture profitable. Subsistence farming was the rule.

The introduction of plants from the Americas and Southeast Asia gave an important boost to African farmers. Importing cassava, corn, and manioc from the Americas and bananas, sweet potatoes, and yams from Southeast Asia created food surpluses, which resulted in a significant jump in the population. Herders of the sahel and in East Africa depended on cattle. They were so important that popular opinion judged the wealth of a family by the number of its animals.

Artifacts made in the villages were brought for exchange on market days. The gold trade was the most lucrative of commodities, but in addition traveling merchants bought and sold cloth, grain, salt, and slaves.

After the Europeans came to Africa, people on both coasts were drawn into the world economy. Eventually even the population in the African interior was affected. The guns and horses that the Europeans brought in ever-increasing quantities soon became the major articles of trade within African kingdoms.

African cloth merchants display their products at a market.

The practice of enslaving criminals and prisoners of war taken from neighboring peoples was common in Africa long before the coming of the Europeans. African kings kept enslaved men and women as domestic servants to show their importance. The more slaves a king had, the greater his prestige. The kings might sell some of their slaves to North African traders who took them to Muslim countries where there was always a demand for household workers. Women were preferred so as to work in the houses of the wealthy and to join their harems.

In 1441 European participation in the slave trade began when a small number of blacks were brought to Portugal. The Europeans found that the kings of the coastal kingdoms were quite willing to trade in slaves. Those who were captives feared for their lives because they believed that the Europeans were cannibals and intended to eat them.

The major impetus for the growth of slavery appeared when European sugar plantations were started in the Americas. Growing sugar was a labor-intensive industry that needed many workers. Most of the slaves brought to the Americas were young men capable of hard work in the cane fields and sugar mills.

The sources for slaves varied through the decades. At first the slaves came from regions of modern Congo and Angola, but then the source shifted northward to the kingdoms on the Bight of Benin, where the African continent shifts westward. African kings were intent upon gaining the largest share possible of the slave trade. Therefore, constant warfare was the norm along the West African coast, and raids into the interior supplemented the prisoners of war obtained through battles.

The European traders did not usually go into the interior of the country to get slaves. They bought them from African kings or merchants along the coast who leased them the **stations** or factories where the Europeans had their markets. A tax was paid to African kings for every slave purchased. The Europeans were not allowed to own land on the West African coast. In return for the slaves, at first the Europeans gave the African kings cloth, brass or metal goods, and cowerie shells before the trade shifted to guns and horses to equip royal African armies.

The slave trade, from the seventeenth through the nineteenth century, was profitable enough to limit any other type of African commerce. There were some plantations in the Canary and Cape Verde Islands of the Atlantic, but these were exceptions. Exports of ivory, peppers, and gold still went to Europe, but the amount of trade in these commodities was dwarfed by the slave trade.

It is impossible to know how many people were transported to the Americas. Estimates vary from 14,000,000 to 9,000,000. One historian suggests that in the 1500s there were 900,000 taken to the Americas. During the 1600s the number was 2,750,000; in the 1700s it was 7,000,000; and finally in the early 1800s there were 4,000,000.

For every slave who survived the passage to the Americas, it is estimated that another died or was crippled in Africa. Another student of the slave trade holds that one out of five persons died while on the ships crossing the Atlantic. The long voyage to the Americas frequently caused disease to spread among the captives. Conditions were sometimes so bad that captives sought to escape their fate by committing suicide or by organizing hopeless mutinies.

Despite this loss of people, surprisingly there was no serious depopulation of West Africa. With the exception of Angola, the population was able to absorb the losses because of the high birth rate among African families.

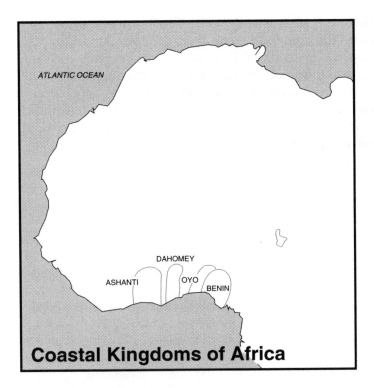

Coastal Kingdoms of Africa

Several African kingdoms prospered along the Gold and Slave Coasts during the height of the slave trade. These included the Yoruba kingdoms of Oyo and Benin and the Fan state of Dahomey. The armies of these kingdoms, armed with guns sold to them by the Europeans, preyed on the peoples of the interior. Captives were torn from their homes, marched to the coast, and sold to the waiting slave traders.

Each kingdom sought to gain captives in its own way. In Dahomey only the king could export slaves, for the Fan people had a strong ruler who wanted no competition from independent merchants. In Benin, the ruler, the *oba*, limited the number of people taken, preferring to trade pepper and ivory. The Ashante, members of the Akan nation, were also wealthy enough to unite under a king whose **Golden Stool** was the symbol of his authority over other chieftains. Kings Osei Tutu and Opuku Ware were two of Africa's strongest leaders early in the eighteenth century thanks to the armies they could outfit with European firearms.

Conclusion

The coming of the Ottoman Turks into Egypt and North Africa created new leadership in that part of the world. What was remarkable was how little it changed matters. Egypt and the North African states now sent a portion of the taxes they received to Istanbul, and as long as those revenues arrived, the Ottoman sultans were content.

The opening of the European slave trade in West Africa was the direct result of changes in European society. The relationship between Europeans drinking coffee that needed sweeteners and the opening of sugar plantations in the Americas that required a large labor force may not be immediately evident, but such was the case. The European initiation to smoking also increased the demand for cheap labor on the American plantations.

The coastal kingdoms of West Africa cooperated with the European slavers because it brought them greater wealth and power. With guns and ammunition, which were manufactured only in Europe, local rulers could extend their territories into much broader areas. A mutual dependence between African rulers and European slave merchants endured until early in the nineteenth century.

CHAPTER 9 REVIEW
AFRICAN PEOPLES

Summary
- The geography of Africa varies from tropical rain forest to desert.
- In 1517 Selim I, the Ottoman sultan, killed the Mamluk ruler of Egypt, placing the country under Turkish rule.
- Morocco, under the Sharifian dynasty, remained independent of the Ottomans, although most other North African towns became tributaries to Istanbul.
- Songhai was the major state of West Africa in 1500.
- Coppersmiths of Benin fashioned bronze portraits of their kings, the finest art of the period.
- Ethiopia, a Christian nation, came under attack in the seventeenth century from its Muslim neighbors.
- The coastal towns of East Africa grew wealthy from the Indian Ocean trade.
- African societies were based on families organized in clans.
- The Portuguese were the first Europeans to reach the African peoples south of the Sahara.
- Europeans sought gold and slaves in their trade with West Africa.
- The Dutch made a permanent settlement at the Cape of Good Hope.

Identify
People: Ahmed al-Mansur, Yoruba, Hausa, Bantu, San, da Gama, van Riebeeck, Ashante, Khoi Khoi, Austronesians, Tutsi, Masai, Luo, Ibo, Bakongo

Places: Sahara Desert, Rift Valley, Sudd, Madagascar, Algeria, Gao, Timbuktu, Kano, Ethiopia, Great Zimbabwe, Kalahari Desert, Songhai

Events: Turkish capture of Egypt; Moroccan defeat of the Portuguese; Benin artists make copper portraits; Portuguese arrival in West Africa; slave trading in Africa

Define
oba	Asiento	Afrikaners	Cape Coloured
sahel	Swahili	caravels	

Multiple Choice
1. North Africa gets rain from
   (a) monsoons.
   (b) winds blowing across the Mediterranean.
   (c) the Atlantic winds.
   (d) the Arctic.

2. The largest desert in the world is the
   (a) Sahara.
   (b) Kalahari.
   (c) Mojave.
   (d) Gobi.

3. The major river of central Africa in modern Congo is the
   (a) Nile.
   (b) Zambezi.
   (c) Niger.
   (d) Congo.

4. The local government of Egypt after the Ottoman conquest was in the hands of
   (a) Turkish governors.
   (b) Bedouin chiefs.
   (c) Hausa chiefs.
   (d) Mamluk landowners.

5. The Barbary Coast was noted for its
   (a) export of gold.
   (b) spices.
   (c) gold.
   (d) pirates.

6. The capital of Songhay was
   (a) Gao.
   (b) Timbuktu.
   (c) Kano.
   (d) Dakar.

7. The dominant religion of the sahel region was
   (a) Islam.
   (b) Christianity.
   (c) Buddhism.
   (d) Mazdaism.

8. The artists of Benin worked in
   (a) gold.
   (b) silver.
   (c) stone.
   (d) copper.

9. Ethiopian Christians received their bishop from the patriarch of
   (a) Rome.
   (b) Constantinople.
   (c) Antioch.
   (d) Alexandria.

10. Tutsi and Masai people belong to a group known as
    (a) Nilotes.
    (b) Bantu.
    (c) Swahili.
    (d) Khoi Khoi.

11. The language of trade on the East African coast was
    (a) Portuguese.
    (b) Arabic.
    (c) Swahili.
    (d) Dutch.

12. This insect carries sleeping sickness:
    (a) the horse fly
    (b) the house fly
    (c) the mosquito
    (d) the tsetse fly

13. A stone city in southern Africa was at
    (a) Mogadishu.
    (b) Mozambique.
    (c) Madagascar.
    (d) Great Zimbabwe.

14. The first Portuguese fort in North Africa was called
    (a) the Cape of Good Hope.
    (b) the Senegal.
    (c) St. George of Mina.
    (d) St. James of Compostela.

15. The principal impetus for slavery in South America developed out of a need for slaves to work
    (a) on sugar plantations and in silver mines.
    (b) on wheat farms.
    (c) on ships that carried bullion to Europe.
    (d) on pineapple and cocoa farms.

16. The *Asiento* gave the British
    (a) the right to sell slaves to the Spanish colonies.
    (b) mining rights on Africa's west coast.
    (c) title to the gold mined in West Africa.
    (d) a monopoly on African ivory.

17. The first expansion of the Afrikaners was at the expense of
    (a) the Bantu.
    (b) the Nilotes.
    (c) the Khoi Khoi.
    (d) the Angolans.

18. These American plants were introduced into Africa:
    (a) potatoes and beans
    (b) corn and manioc
    (c) wheat and barley
    (d) tobacco and barley

19. European slave traders usually
    (a) led expeditions into the interior to find slaves.
    (b) bought slaves from pirates of the North African coast.
    (c) bought slaves from the Muslim coastal cities.
    (d) bought slaves from the rulers of West African coastal kingdoms.

20. The Golden Stool was the symbol of power for the chieftain of
    (a) Dahomey.
    (b) Benin.
    (c) Togo.
    (d) the Ashante.

Essay Questions

1. Compare the role of the Chinese potter with that of the African copper-smith in the sixteenth century.
2. List the similarities of the Portuguese merchant's role in China and Africa during the sixteenth century.
3. Explain how the geography of Africa influenced the social and economic growth in the region.
4. Discuss the impact of slavery on the African people.

Answers

1. b	6. a	11. c	16. a
2. a	7. a	12. d	17. c
3. d	8. d	13. d	18. b
4. d	9. d	14. c	19. d
5. d	10. a	15. a	20. d

CHAPTER 10

North America

Isolated by two oceans from the rest of humanity, the Indian populations of the Americas developed their own unique cultures for thousands of years before the Europeans intruded, uninvited, into their world. It was a traumatic event; until the arrival of Columbus, native Americans had no idea that there were other people on the earth.

Indian peoples were ill prepared to meet the Europeans who came with their guns, horses, and diseases. Technology had not advanced so far in the Western Hemisphere where metals were only sparingly used as tools, bows and arrows remained the major weapons, and the wheel was still not employed for any practical purpose. More importantly, the peoples of the Americas had never developed the antibodies carried by the Europeans and Africans that gave them partial immunity against smallpox, measles, tuberculosis, and influenza. These diseases proved deadly to millions of Indians, accounting for a loss of human life unprecedented in the history of the world.

Geography

North America extends from tropical Panama to frigid Alaska with a great variety of climatic and topographical differences. North America's weather tends to be more moderate, whereas much of South America is tropical.

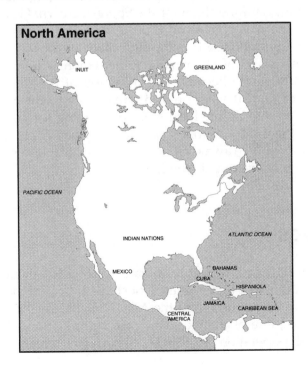

The Rocky Mountains and the Sierra Madres of Mexico run north and south through the continent. The mighty Mississippi drains much of the lands that now form the United States, and the Great Lakes are one of the world's largest reservoirs of fresh water. Many of the Caribbean Islands are the peaks of submerged volcanic mountains.

Deserts exist in North America's western interior, a major contrast to the rains that fall in the Caribbean. Plateaus make up the lands of much of Mexico and the western United States, while rain forests that cover rolling hills dominate Central America.

It was in this world in 1500 that the majority of Indian populations were either still in hunting and gathering societies or in an agricultural economy that produced a limited food surplus. Mexico was the exception. Here the first Indian civilizations had their origins, and in the sixteenth century the great Aztec empire flourished, completely unaware that within a half century the world its people knew would disappear forever.

The Caribbean

Christopher Columbus first landed on a Caribbean island of the Bahamas and named it San Salvador. The peaceful Arawak Indians were there to greet him and his sailors.

The Arawak were themselves under intense pressure at the time because the Carib Indians of the South American coast of Guiana had invaded their homeland. The Carib were fierce warriors, who traveled from island to island in large dugout canoes, preying upon the Arawak. Because Carib Indians often ate their victims, the English word *cannibal* comes from the name that the Spaniards called them. More obviously, they gave their name to the Caribbean Sea.

Over the following ten years, Columbus sailed among the many islands of the West Indies, claiming them for the Spanish crown. He called the people Indians, for he was convinced that he had reached the Indies of the Orient. In 1496 Columbus settled the first town of the New World, Santo Domingo, on the island of Hispaniola. Other colonies followed on Puerto Rico, Jamaica, and Cuba because the attraction of finding gold on these islands, small though it was, proved irresistible to the Spaniards. The Indians were forced to do the hard labor of panning for gold in the rivers and digging in the mines, so that soon they perished from either illness or overwork. Today the Arawak are extinct, and only one small group of Caribs survive on the island of Dominica.

The Aztecs

In the heart of Mexico, the Aztec Indians, who called themselves *Mexica*, had created a capital that they named Tenochtitlán. In 1500 their empire covered a distance that extended from the Atlantic to the Pacific and held up to 20,000,000 people, one of the world's densest populations. In comparison with the Spanish population of 7,500,000, Mexico was three times larger.

Early Aztec history records an unimpressive beginning. About A.D. 1200 the Aztecs were but a small nomadic people who were part of the shifting population on the northern plateau of Mexico. Their language, Náhuatl, linked them to other Indian peoples of the region. Their religion focused on the war god, **Huitzilopochtli** (the name meant left-handed hummingbird), who would guide them to a permanent place to settle.

According to Aztec belief, Huitzilopochtli told them to look for a place where an eagle, holding a snake in its beak, would be perched on a cactus. They discovered this sign on an island in Lake Texcoco, located in the heart of a region known as the Valley of Mexico. Here they founded their city, Tenochtitlán.

A reliable food supply supported a great increase in population and permitted the Aztecs to set out on the road to conquest. The Indian peoples of the Valley of Mexico were first to fall; then other peoples on the Mexican plateau were conquered. Only their larger neighbors, the Tarascans and Tlaxcalan people, proved too strong for Aztec subjugation.

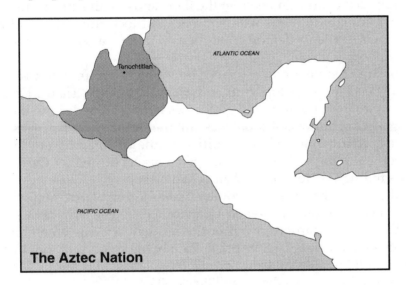

The Aztec Nation

The Aztec motivation for empire is not entirely clear. Some historians see it as a result of growing population pressure in the Valley of Mexico, a limited area hardly able to support an estimated 200,000 people in Tenochtitlán and an equal number outside the capital. Other students of Aztec society argue that war was constant because of the need for human victims to be sacrificed to the Aztec gods and goddesses. To die in battle while pursuing an enemy for use in a sacrifice was the ideal death for a male Aztec.

So long as subject states provided their quota of women and men to the Aztec rulers, local elites were left in place. There was no occupation of Aztec armies among foreign peoples because the threat of what could happen to them if they resisted was enough to keep tributaries in line. Marriage of Aztec princesses with foreign rulers was another, more benign way to keep subject states loyal to Tenochtitlán.

Aztec society was highly stratified. At the top was the emperor, Moctezuma II, whose status was semidivine because he represented the gods to his people. Moctezuma's title was Great Speaker. He lived in a magnificent palace in the heart of the capital. In 1502 a council of high officials had chosen him from among his brothers to hold office.

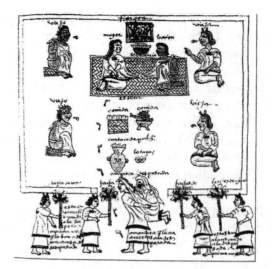

*An Aztec marriage
ceremony.*

The imperial court numbered in the thousands, with a prime minister at its head. Ordinary humans who approached Moctezuma first had to put dirt on their heads to demonstrate their humble status compared to his exalted role.

His palace stood close to a huge 200-foot high pyramid and twin temples dedicated to Huitzilopochtli and another divinity, Tlaloc. Dozens of other temples to Aztec gods and goddesses were scattered about the city as were smaller whitewashed palaces for the nobility and priests. Giant causeways that connected Tenochtitlán to the mainland were thronged with people coming and going. Two open markets existed for the exchange of goods through barter, for the Aztecs had no coinage.

Canals, rather than roads, were the main thoroughfares, reminding the first Europeans to compare Tenochtitlán to Venice. The city was very clean and full of flower gardens, even in the residential areas where ordinary people lived in houses of adobe brick. Each of the sections of the city, called *calpulli,* had its own administration, lands, schools, and temples. Its male residents also fought together in military units.

A noble class of warriors lived in luxury and held private estates for their support. Their families were large because, like the emperor, they were polygamous. When they appeared in public, their clothes and jewelry identified them as people of importance. An artisan and merchant class also existed, but they had no hope of entering the upper class no matter how wealthy because entry to that group was through hereditary descent. Carving jade and making golden jewelry and elaborate feathered ornaments occupied many craftsmen. Little industry existed.

Women in Aztec society fell into the class of their husbands. Those in the nobility enjoyed a leisured existence, whereas women in the lower classes spent their days caring for children, cleaning house, weaving cloth, and up to six hours a day laboriously grinding corn to make flour. Women owned property in their own names and served as professional midwives. A woman dying in childbirth was honored equally as a warrior in battle.

About one third of the Aztec population owned no land and had to find employment as day-laborers in farming or construction. Slavery was the lot of debtors and criminals, but this group was very small in comparison to the rest of the population.

The Aztec religion dominated people's lives, and death was a major factor in its worship. More than in any other world society, human sacrifice was integral to the Aztec system of belief. The gods and goddesses demanded the most precious gift of all, human life, lest they lose their strength and go out of existence, causing the world to end. To give the deities the power to maintain the world, Aztec priests offered dozens of sacrifices each day. They would plunge a knife into the chest of a victim and then offer up the bloody heart to the gods.

Quetzalcóatl was the feathered-serpent god and patron of learning for the Aztecs.

At special festivals honoring the gods, a day-long series of human sacrifices totaled in the thousands. Ceremonial cannibal rites followed with the eating of arms and legs, but never the hearts. Estimates of the need for 15,000 victims a year kept the Aztec armies in constant campaigns to supplement the men and women victims collected from other Indian nations.

The Aztecs had a ceremonial calendar of festivals that, in addition to human sacrifice, demanded songs, dances, and processions. Poets composed works to the gods but also speculated on such matters as life after death. The calendar was on a 52-year cycle. At the end of the period, officials extinguished all the fires of the empire. As the whole population waited in darkness, a priest in Tenochtitlán kindled a flame in the chest of a victim. When he succeeded, it guaranteed life would continue for another 52 years. Runners from Tenochtitlán then spread out across the empire with the new fire.

In November 1519, Moctezuma, who was still in the process of consolidating his empire over several new subject peoples, received disturbing news. Bearded foreigners with strange beasts had landed on the Atlantic coast and wanted to approach the capital. Moctezuma possibly thought that their leader was the god Quetzalcóatl; therefore, he sent him sacred objects from the god's temple in Tenochtitlán. In fact, it was the Spaniard Hernán Cortés, and he had every intention of marching to the capital whose wealth was well known in Cuba, his Spanish base in the Caribbean. Cortés burned his ships behind him to demonstrate his resolve.

With his small army of 553 armored men, horses, and even a small cannon, Cortés marched first against the Tlaxcalans. Stunned by a type of warfare they had never seen, the native warriors were easily defeated, and subsequently the Tlaxcalans became allies of Cortés. Their hatred of the Aztecs made this an easy decision. With great audacity Cortés entered Tenochtitlán, which was surrounded on all sides by thousands of Moctezuma's warriors. Through interpreters Cortés and Moctezuma discussed the reasons for the Spanish intrusion. Fearing a trap, Cortés took Moctezuma prisoner and forced him to speak on behalf of the Spaniards.

Cortés meets Moctezuma II entering Tenochtitlán.

In the weeks that followed, Cortés had to leave the Aztec capital to fight off a new army sent by the governor of Cuba to arrest him for insubordination. That done, he returned with a larger force, 1,300 men, but found that in his absence his lieutenant had so angered the Aztecs that his position was in jeopardy. The brother of Moctezuma, Cuauhtémoc, had declared himself emperor, which made their hostage less important. As he sought to reestablish his authority, Moctezuma died on June 30, 1520, after he was hit by a stone hurled by an Aztec warrior. The Spanish garrison in *la noche triste* was forced from the city with a loss of two thirds of its men. Cortés, however, survived, recruited a new army, and once more marched on Tenochtitlán. Smallpox preceded him, killing tens of thousands of the natives who had no natural resistance to the disease.

After a 3-month siege the Spaniards took the city and became undisputed masters of the Aztec empire. The use of firearms and horses coupled with the able leadership of Cortés gained Charles I a nation larger than Spain itself with a vast amount of wealth, which was now transported to Spain.

Spanish America

After their conquest of the Aztecs, the Spaniards tore down the buildings of the capital and rebuilt it along European lines, naming it Mexico City. It became the capital of New Spain, with a viceroy and his officials in charge. The viceroy reported to the Council of the Indies in Spain.

Large towns such as Mexico City looked much like European towns, with churches, plazas, shops, public buildings, and the homes of public officials and wealthy landowners and mine operators. Schools opened, and children attended classes much as in Spain. Mexico City's university dates from 1551. The capital and the larger provincial towns were lively places as artisans, soldiers, clerics, businessmen, and Indian servants jostled each other on market days. Festivals were frequent and colorful, especially on the days dedicated to patron saints.

Spaniards tore down Aztec temples, replacing them with Christian cathedrals.

Life in mining centers in the north was quite a contrast to the genteel ways of the capital. Here tough mine owners and their laborers made their homes in frontier towns where individuals had to furnish their own law and order. The death of so many natives immediately after the conquest caused a chronic labor shortage.

Because few Spanish women migrated to Mexico at first, men took women for wives and mistresses from the Indian peoples, creating mixed families, the *mestizos.* The mestizos soon formed a large segment of the colonial population. Later, when Spanish women began to emigrate in larger numbers, it was usually as the spouses of officials. As best they could, they recreated the life they knew in Spain.

Preferred marriages were arranged for daughters among families who belonged on the same economic level. Young widows were fortunate because by law they inherited one half their husband's estate. Daughters often preferred life in a convent to marriages that would require them to live isolated on ranches far from the cities.

Relatively few African slaves came to Mexico because a plantation economy did not exist there. Those who did come were usually employed as domestic servants. Unlike the English and Dutch, the Spaniards encouraged marriage among slaves, and it was against the law to separate husbands and wives. Nevertheless, Africans had a low birth rate and high mortality resulting in a sparse African population in Mexico and Central America.

European whites held an advantage over every other Mexican group, especially if they were born in Spain. This resulted from the *fuero,* a package of privileges that no one but a person in the upper classes enjoyed. Recent arrivals, known as *peninsulares,* formed part of this group, who thought themselves quite superior to those Europeans born in the Americas, the *crillos,* or *creoles.* Mestizos, and of course the Indians, had little opportunity to be treated as equals.

A social gap broadened as more emigrants arrived from Spain with their families. Many in the creole class were wealthy, but it also held poor farmers living in remote rural regions sharing a life of poverty with the Indians who worked on their ranches.

Individual settlers in Spanish America held land grants called *encomiendas* and Indians to work on them. The encomiendas varied in size; some holdings were in the hundreds, while others were in the thousands of acres. Slowly the landscape changed as raising cattle, wheat, and vineyards replaced growing corn as in Aztec times. Sheep, goats, and horses also became staples on the huge ranches of Mexico and Central America.

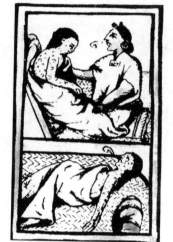

Smallpox devastated the Aztec population in Mexico.

Because the Indians were unfamiliar with a money economy, paying their taxes was a heavy burden. The solution was to sign on the labor force of a **hacienda,** or cattle ranch, which provided a sense of security, because the owner of the hacienda took on the fiscal responsibilities of his workers. Authorities encouraged Indians to settle in villages to enlarge the supply of laborers on the haciendas. It was only a matter of time until the Indians fell into debt, which meant that they or their children could never leave the hacienda where they worked.

Religion in New Spain

The Spaniards considered their conquest to be a sign of God's favor and were convinced that they had an obligation to convert the Indians to Christianity. Catholic friars, Franciscans, Dominicans, and Augustinians were soon at work all over Mexico and Central America catechizing the Indian populations. Priests often baptized thousands of converts in a single week. Later, members of the Society of Jesus arrived in the Americas.

The clergy treated the Indians much as parents might treat their children. Although baptized, they did not receive communion or enter the priesthood. Catholic clergy considered Indian temples idolatrous and destroyed them whenever they had an opportunity. They put up churches in their place, similar to those they knew in Spain.

After several generations the church in Mexico, and throughout Central America and the Caribbean, became wealthy from inheriting large grants of land. Some of its officials used their positions to become bankers. It was also evident by this time that even though many Indians were nominal Christians, they also retained faith in the religion of their ancestors.

Catholic missionaries were the first who sought to protect the Indian laborers from the harsh hours of work that most endured in the mines or in the fields of the Spanish settlers. Bishop Bartolomé de las Casas of Chiapas was vigorous in his protests to the Spanish court over injustices done to the Indians. Because of las Casas's insistence, in 1542 Charles I's government checked the Indians' unlimited labor obligations and taxes. In the future the natives were required to work on the farms and ranches of the Spanish settlers only 45 days a year.

Of course, it was one thing to legislate and another thing to enforce the law. Consequently, the lives of most Indians changed very little. The ban on Indian slavery unintentionally turned the Spaniards of the Caribbean to Africa for workers, beginning the infamous trade in blacks that lasted through the next centuries.

Because mercantilism was the prevailing economic theory in Europe, it is hardly surprising that the Spanish government kept its colonies tied closely to the homeland. Spanish law forbade direct trade with any other nation. Seville, and later Cadiz, were Spain's only ports of entry for American goods. Products could only leave the New World on convoys to Spain that departed annually from Veracruz in Mexico or Panama, on the isthmus connecting the two Americas. Silver production destined for the Far East left Acapulco for Manila and then was shipped to China, its final destination.

One fifth of all the gold and silver mined went to the crown. Because mercury imported from Spain had to be used in processing the ore, and this was a government monopoly, the miners were kept forever in dependency. Such restrictions invited smugglers and pirates to have a field day in finding ways to support themselves outside the law. English, French, and Dutch pirates prowled the coasts of Spanish America.

Mining was the most important factor in the economy. Gold but chiefly silver flowed back to Spain in enormous amounts. The European economy eagerly absorbed these precious metals because there was a severe shortage of bullion prior to the discovery of the American deposits. Charles I and the Spanish kings who followed him needed money desperately, and the ability to pay their debts rested upon a continual delivery of precious metals from the New World. Prices doubled in Spain from 1500 to 1550, and in another 50 years they rose four times again due to the influx of bullion.

European settlement in the Americas resulted in a massive exchange of plants between Europe and the rest of the world. After Columbus's second voyage Europeans planted sugar cane on the Caribbean Islands, and it soon became the major crop of the West Indies. From the New World came corn, beans, and potatoes to change the diets of millions of people in Europe; smoking tobacco was also adopted by the Europeans with enthusiasm.

North of the Rio Grande

North of the Rio Grande, in what is now the United States, Spanish explorers had hoped to discover the gold and silver that their countrymen found in Mexico. Instead, they found wilderness, desert, and an Indian population that was in a hunting-gathering economy with some peoples also engaged in primitive agriculture. They had no wealth to interest the Spaniards.

Demographers estimate that the number of native Americans north of the Rio Grande in 1500 was about 1,000,000 men and women. At least 200 languages were spoken in this very diverse population, but none were written. Some Indian nations numbered in the thousands; others, in the hundreds. The great Mississippi society of earlier times was now but a memory, leaving the Anasazi people of the Southwest as the most advanced of Indian cultures.

The Taos pueblo reflects the Anasazi buildings of the American Southwest.

Many Indians on the Great Plains were nomads, following the animals they hunted with bow and arrow. People in the East lived in wigwam villages, united by common ancestors and religion. Men hunted deer and small game, while women raised corn, beans, and squash to supplement their diets. Some Indians preferred fishing or collecting crustaceans to hunting.

Hernando De Soto and Francisco Coronado are associated with first exploring Spanish America north of the Rio Grande. De Soto's expedition covered much of what in the future became the United States' Southeast. Coronado fruitlessly marched about the Southwest in the years from 1539 to 1542 looking for seven cities of gold that were rumored to exist there.

In 1565 the Spaniards first put down a permanent settlement at St. Augustine in Florida, making that city the oldest in the present United States. By 1630 missionaries had formed up to 40 settlements of Christian Indians in the region.

There was even more activity among the Franciscan friars in New Mexico. In 1630 a missionary reported 60,000 Pueblo Indian converts. Then, 50 years later during a Pueblo uprising, the missions literally went up in smoke as the Indians rejected all things Spanish. Later they reopened, and the friars returned. In neighboring Texas, the Apaches and Comanches found little reason to become Christians.

Florida Indians used canoes for transportation.

The Franciscan Junipero Serra led the most successful attempt to make converts of the Indians of the Spanish borderland. In 1769 he founded the first California mission in San Diego. In all, Serra organized nine missions on the Pacific Coast. His successors added 12 more, so that a traveler could find a mission within a day's walk along the route from San Diego to San Francisco.

The Franciscans believed that the best way to make the Indians practicing Catholics was to collect them into mission compounds where they could be clothed, instructed, housed, and taught European ways. The friars set up a daily schedule of instruction and work that was quite foreign to the temperament of the natives. Although some Indians accommodated themselves to the regimen, many others perished from illness or overwork. Those who sought to escape could count on pursuit by the Spanish garrisons attached to the missions.

The California missions carried on a lively trade with the ships of all European nations. Large ranches provided meat and hides, and Indian craftsmen became very skilled. Yet in the perspective of the present, although not the past, the mission system effectively destroyed the California Indians' way of life and many of the people whom it was meant to help.

Mexico and Central America in the Eighteenth Century

The coming to power of the Bourbon dynasty in Spain in 1713 had a profound effect on Spanish America. King Philip V wanted Spain to play a role in Europe that would restore it to the rank of a Great Power. Spanish colonies were expected to provide the impetus that had been lacking under the feeble administrations of the last Habsburgs.

The Bourbon plan was to knit the colonies much more closely to mainland interests by sending out more peninsulares, completely loyal to the crown, and to make certain revenues came to Spain in ever-increasing amounts. The Bourbon kings took direct charge of affairs in Spanish America, ignoring the views of the Council of the Indies. Over the decades this council, founded to administer the colonies, had learned what could or could not be expected.

The rigid policy of the Bourbons was in sharp contrast to the flexibility of earlier regimes that allowed the creoles to hold most appointments in the New World and were content with moderate tax revenues. The government now managed the collection of the *alcabala,* the sales tax. It upset the pattern of trade through the addition of more monopolies that included gunpowder and alcohol. Peninsulares, up to 100,000 of them, crowded out the creoles from positions that had been theirs for generations.

All these changes met either passive or violent resistance. Creole uprisings shook Spanish America in protest. Nevertheless, in 1765 King Charles III sought to extend royal control over Mexico even further. The royal court in Madrid reorganized the country into twelve *intendencias,* all under a single commandant, who bypassed the viceroy and reported directly to Spain. Moreover, the law added tobacco production to the already large list of royal monopolies.

To make sure that the crown received all the revenues due it, the king ordered a much larger Spanish garrison to take up quarters in the country. Two years later, the Jesuits, who had been strongest in asserting the rights of the Indians, were expelled, leaving civil authorities with unchecked power.

The members of the Mexican creole society found their social and economic position further in decline. Like their English counterparts to the north, they read Rousseau, Voltaire, and the other writers of the Enlightenment. They began to wonder why they should tolerate the peninsulares, the Spanish-born administrators who jealously held on to the highest privileges of Mexican society.

Central America

In the early sixteenth century Spanish *conquistadors* brought the Central American lands under their control. The Maya and many other Indian nations were struck by disease or were enslaved and deported to the Caribbean Islands. In 1570 the government of Philip II set up an administrative unit, an *audiencia,* in Guatemala that held authority over all Central America with the exception of Panama, which was still subject to Mexico City's viceroy. Much of the government remained in local hands because the region's few sources of gold and silver made Central America less important than Mexico. Spanish plantation owners introduced banana and coffee as viable economic crops, while the Indian population was content to grow corn and beans on small farms in the mountains.

Panama was important because of its strategic location and its ports. Spaniards in Panama built a paved road across the isthmus for the transit of goods from the Atlantic to the Pacific.

Mayan temples rise above the rain forest.

The West Indies

When it became obvious that the West Indies were not a land of gold and silver, Spanish colonists turned to agriculture and shipping. Caribbean ports became bases for the cargo that went off to Spain. Their wealth attracted Dutch, British, French, and even Danish pirates to the Caribbean, forcing the Spaniards to fortify their towns. Some of the less defended smaller islands were lost to Spain. The French took Guadeloupe and Martinique, the Dutch captured several islands off the South American coast, and the English took Barbados. In 1655 Jamaica fell to a British force in the Caribbean, while Oliver Cromwell ruled in England.

By 1673 Barbados was the primary source of sugar for England, producing it in hundreds of tons. During the eighteenth century Jamaica replaced Barbados as the major supplier of sugar to Europe, and its plantations established it as the richest of England's colonies.

The French in the New World

Early in the 1500s the French monarch, Francis I, took note of Columbus's discovery with interest. Visions of gold and silver flashed before his eyes. He certainly did not intend that his archenemies the Spaniards should get it all. In 1523 he commissioned a mariner, Giovanni Verrazano, to cross the Atlantic. Verrazano brought back no gold or silver, nothing but a claim that France could act upon in the future for its share of America.

French interest in the New World increased as a result of the rich fishing grounds off the Canadian coast. In 1534 a new expedition set out for North America under Jacques Cartier. Sailing into the Gulf of St. Lawrence, Cartier announced that the neighboring lands were now the possession of the king of France. Two more visits followed; one reached as far as modern Montreal.

French fishermen, after their boats were filled with cod, dried their nets on nearby coastlands, where they encountered Indians who wanted to trade furs for the tools of the fishermen. The French brought back mink, otter, fox, and especially beaver pelts, which were made into hats that became required fashion for the well-dressed gentlemen of Paris.

In 1603 plans were completed for a permanent French colony in North America. A year later an expedition settled in Acadia, in the Canadian province now known as Nova Scotia. The most intrepid French explorer was Samuel de Champlain who founded Québec on the banks of the St. Lawrence River. Québec remained a small isolated outpost in New France for many years. Both the English and the Iroquois Indians wanted it removed, and they constantly launched attacks against it.

Louis XIV determined that he must be the Sun King not only in Europe but also in New France. The weakness of the Québec colony was no longer to be tolerated. French soldiers were sent across the Atlantic to deal with the Iroquois, and merchants accompanied them to expand the fur trade. French frontiersmen, *coureurs de bois*, penetrated deep into the interior reaching the Great Lakes in a relentless pursuit of furs. Incentives for farmers to emigrate were sufficiently persuasive to populate New France with about 7,000 people by 1673.

In that year two explorers, the fur trader Louis Joliet and the Jesuit missionary Jacques Marquette, sailed the Mississippi as far as the Arkansas River, claiming the area for France. In their wake more merchants and missionaries followed, putting up forts on the Mississippi, Illinois, and Wabash Rivers. In 1682 René-Robert Cavelier, Sieur de La Salle, sailed to the mouth of the Mississippi River on the Gulf of Mexico, expanding the lands of New France deep into the North American interior. He named these lands for his king, calling it Louisiana.

French and British interests were bound to clash because both intended to expand their territories in North America. Conflicting claims caused a series of wars during the eighteenth century, sometimes beginning over issues raised in Europe, at other times starting in the New World. The wars usually ended with British victories. In 1713 Louis XIV's agreement reached at the Treaty of Utrecht transferred Newfoundland, Nova Scotia, and the Hudson Bay region to London's control.

In 1756 the Seven Years' War on the European continent spilled over to North America, where it was known as the French and Indian War. It was an unequal struggle because the French population was only 65,000 people whereas 1,000,000 English citizens lived in the Thirteen Colonies. British armies were better supplied and had the aid of the Iroquois.

In 1759 a British force under James Wolfe faced the French general, Louis-Joseph, Marquis de Montcalm, on the Plains of Abraham outside Québec. Both generals died during the battle, which ended in a British victory. A year later the capture of Montreal, the second city of New France, sounded the colony's death knell. In 1763 the Peace of Paris gave most of what remained of New France to Great Britain.

A British governor-general arrived in Québec to ensure the region's control and impose British law on the citizens. This meant that French Catholics, the majority of the people living there, could not hold public office or participate in any political decisions. The Catholic church lost its privileged position.

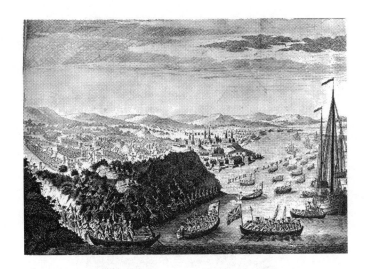

General James Wolfe's British troops sail down the St. Lawrence River to attack Québec.

British governor-generals wanted to gain the loyalty of the French Catholics and urged Parliament to reverse the discriminatory laws that kept Catholics out of government. In 1774 Governor-General Guy Carleton succeeded in his efforts to have Parliament accept the Québec Act, granting the French Canadians full civil and religious liberty. This was a wise move because when the Thirteen Colonies revolted against the British in 1776, the French remained loyal to London.

At the close of the American Revolution, about 40,000 Loyalists chose to move to Canada rather than live in the United States. Most settled in western Québec or in Nova Scotia, where the London government created the province of New Brunswick for their homeland. Those who settled in Québec demanded more self-government, which resulted in the **Constitutional Act of 1791.** This divided Canada into Lower Canada, French and Catholic, and Upper Canada, British and Protestant. Each kept its own distinctive legal and property systems.

France still held Louisiana, the region south of the Great Lakes, and its fur trappers were found all the way to the Pacific. However, French America's days were numbered.

The Thirteen Colonies

When the English king, Henry VII, learned of Columbus's discovery, in 1497 he commissioned John Cabot, an Italian captain in his service, to sail to the New World to bring him information on what he found. Although he discovered little to interest the Tudor monarch, Cabot's voyage established an English claim in the Americas. It was acted upon only a hundred years later.

At that time, in 1585, Sir Walter Raleigh put down a colony on Roanoke Island off the coast of what is now North Carolina. When a supply ship sought it out three years later, it found the site abandoned, with no satisfactory answer to what happened to its settlers. Only a mysterious word, CROATAN, carved on a tree provided a clue to its fate. This so discouraged this generation of Englishmen that no settlements were attempted for the next 20 years.

When British settlers arrived in Virginia, they discovered Indian villages sheltered by a stockade.

During the rule of King James I, two English companies of merchants formed to make a commercial success of an American adventure. James chartered them both, the London and Plymouth Companies. In 1607 the first to succeed was the London Company's Jamestown.

About a hundred colonists set down anchor in the James River of Virginia. Their purpose was to find gold, but instead they found winter and starvation. Thirty-eight survivors were left after a year, and despite further additions, the colony barely escaped destruction.

The salvation of Jamestown was found in the production of tobacco. Europeans found smoking much to their satisfaction, and the gold of Jamestown came to be recognized in the yellow leaves of this plant that proved so easy to grow. In 1619 a Dutch ship arrived with indentured blacks on board to initiate an even easier way to grow tobacco, to let others do the hard work. The London Company promised 50 free acres to every settler, and an additional amount to everyone else whose way was paid.

That same year saw the beginning of representative government in North America when the Virginia **House of Burgesses** first met in session. Its powers expanded when James I revoked the London Company's charter in preference for direct royal rule. Distant rule from London gave the colonists a taste of self-government.

Englishmen of an adventurous spirit poured into Virginia, accompanied by indentured servants who signed on for a period of up to seven years. Some of these servants were from the very poor of England; others were convicts or Irish prisoners of war, who like Africans did the labor on the tobacco plantations. The difference for the whites was that they could live in hope of freedom, whereas most blacks could not.

North of Virginia, a religious group known as **Separatists,** made up the Plymouth Colony's settlement in Massachusetts. Known today as Pilgrims, their ideology required them to live apart from other religious groups to keep their community and its faith intact. Later other Protestant groups of Puritans joined the Pilgrims in the Massachusetts Bay Colony. Their numbers grew so rapidly that three other colonies spun off the parent community: Connecticut, Rhode Island, and New Hampshire.

Individuals, **proprietors,** also sought charters from the king. In this way the Calverts, an English Catholic family, found a refuge for their co-religionists in Maryland. Pennsylvania had a similar origin, when William Penn received a charter on behalf of the Quakers. The proprietors did all they could to recruit settlers for their colonies, painting life in North America as a primitive Garden of Eden. Farming was the major occupation of the settlers, and in time fishing, carpentry, and brick making became small industries.

Hardships were many, diseases were often fatal, and attacks from hostile Indians were always a possibility, but settlers continued to pour into North America. The promise of land ownership and political and religious freedom were powerful magnets to draw people across the Atlantic. Villages became small towns; schools, churches, and roads were built; and British America was on the threshold of a promising future. The colonials were remarkably egalitarian. There were no aristocratic peninsulares in British America.

For a time English settlers were not alone on the Atlantic coast. Colonists from both the Netherlands and Sweden appeared. New Netherlands occupied the site of today's New York and northern New Jersey. In 1624 the purchase of Manhattan Island was the first step in organizing the town of New Amsterdam. Swedish settlers established themselves in Pennsylvania

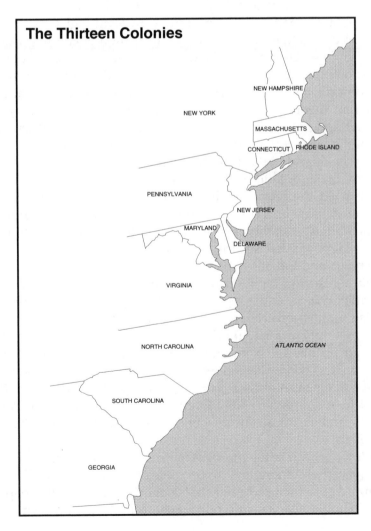

The Thirteen Colonies

and Delaware. A multinational Atlantic coast dissipated when in 1664 James, Duke of York, later King James II, squashed the Dutch and Swedes, incorporating their colonies into British America. New Amsterdam then became New York City.

A year earlier King Charles II had awarded the Carolinas to proprietors, and in 1733 the last of the Thirteen Colonies, Georgia, completed the number. A major difference was evident both here and in the other southern colonies, for the cultivation of rice, indigo, and tobacco on large plantations required many more laborers than the farms of the northern colonies. The result was a continual stream of Africans brought to the South. In 1753 blacks were 20% of the total population of the British colonies, which then stood at 1,500,000 men and women. Philadelphia became the second largest English-speaking city in the world. Only London had more people.

Great Britain and the Colonies

Great Britain's government was remarkably easy going with the colonies in an age when mercantilism was still the principle upon which governments modeled their economic policies. This meant that the colonies enjoyed a great amount of self-government and economic opportunity. American political leaders were permitted to form legislative assemblies and to set up courts that mirrored those of the mother country. Democratic ideas prompted elections to be held for seats in these assemblies where men, accustomed to speaking their minds, freely discussed issues.

British officials allowed American merchants to ignore mercantile regulations that, in theory, were the law of the land. Smuggling was rampant along the Atlantic coast. New England merchants and Southern planters agreed that the laws of Parliament should not apply to them.

On the other hand, Americans were anxious to have garrisons of the British army on their side of the Atlantic. Just as in the mother country, people regarded the French as both political and economic rivals. New France loomed large as a threat in the popular imagination. Indians who were French allies in the interior were also assumed to be enemies of the colonists. Americans felt secure because the presence of British soldiers kept the French and Indians at bay.

The fighting during the French and Indian War proved very expensive for the British crown, and King George III and Parliament agreed that, if the colonists wanted protection, they should pay for it.

Not surprisingly, many Americans professed outrage at this decision. When the government in London sought to impose the **Sugar Act** of 1764 on the colonists, there were howls of protest. The Sugar Act actually reduced the taxes on molasses and sugar that were produced in the West Indies and then shipped to New England. However, this time Parliament was serious, and customs officers were encouraged to pursue the tax's collection actively.

The following year after the passage of the Sugar Act, King George's ministers placed one more levy upon their overseas citizens. This was the 1765 **Stamp Act,** which required that legal documents, newspapers, and other items should bear a stamp purchased from the government.

The colonists responded to what they considered an infringement on their liberties by refusing to purchase British goods. Resistance gathered support in committees called **Sons of Liberty.** Opposition to these measures was so great that Parliament backed down and repealed the Stamp Act, but the victory of the Americans was short-lived.

London's Chancellor of the Exchequer, the man who had to pay the nation's bills, thought up a new way to reach into the pocketbooks of the colonists. He insisted upon new duties on such items as paper, tea, lead, and glass. Once more the response of the colonists was to boycott British goods that required the hated levies.

In March 1770 Boston became the scene of violence when British troops were sent to keep order in that city. Some Bostonians who were watching the soldiers parade pelted the soldiers with snowballs. In response, the red-coated troops opened fire, and four people were killed. Their spilled blood caused word to spread through the colonies that the British were guilty of a massacre in Boston.

British soldiers fire into a crowd, an event known as the Boston Massacre.

In London, meanwhile, there was a problem for the East India Company had too much tea that it could not sell. The company's directors proposed to Lord Frederick North, the Prime Minister, that the company should take its tea to the American colonies and sell it there, provided that the tax was removed. The tea arrived, but the colonists would not buy it. In December 1773 Samuel Adams, one of Great Britain's strongest critics in Massachusetts, recruited a group of Americans, dressed them like Indians, and had them board the three ships in the Boston harbor carrying cargoes of tea. They dumped the contents overboard.

The **Tea Party** caused the members of Parliament to strengthen their resolve anew. They could not afford to let the Americans succeed in thumbing their noses at British law. American patriots argued that so long as no colonist sat in the British Parliament, it could not legislate for the colonies.

Lord North determined that the situation demanded one more exertion of Parliament. His measures, passed in 1774, became known to their opponents as the **Intolerable Acts.** They took away almost all the powers of Massachusetts' legislature and closed Boston harbor.

The Revolution Begins

In September 1774 at Philadelphia the First Continental Congress gathered to seek ways to redress what the delegates considered the wrongs inflicted on them. They were not yet ready to call for independence, but they did expect London to recognize their grievances.

In April 1775 a British company of soldiers sent out from Boston to look for hidden arms met a body of local volunteers, the **minutemen,** at Lexington and then on Concord bridge. Shots were exchanged and the soldiers of George III fell back on Boston, all the time dodging musket balls discharged from the rifles of colonists. This action caused the Second Continental Congress to assemble.

On July 4, 1776, Thomas Jefferson's **Declaration of Independence** eloquently stated the causes of the conflict. The Second Continental Congress adopted it as the official statement of the new nation.

Delegates from the colonies sign the Declaration of Independence.

The Revolution

Throughout the next several years a succession of British armies sought to suppress the American Revolution. They were hindered by the great distance troops had to be brought across the Atlantic. After they got here, quartermasters had the problem of supplying them. British soldiers were trained in the stilted tactics of continental Europe and were unprepared for the American style of fighting. On the other hand, the British were aided by the lack of unity demonstrated in the colonies. Many legislators proved reluctant to approve the form of government, the **Articles of Confederation,** that the Congress adopted. This left the American government weak, without a chief executive, a system of courts, or an adequate system of taxation.

The skill of George Washington in keeping the Continental Army in the field does much to explain American success. The British could win significant and important battles and keep large sections of the country under their control, but Washington's resolve never allowed them to claim victory.

French assistance also helped to keep the Americans in the conflict. At first the French were hesitant to commit themselves, painfully recalling their defeat in the Seven Years' War. Thanks to Benjamin Franklin's able presentation of the American cause to the court of Louis XVI coupled with the American victory at Saratoga in the fall of 1777, the French decided on war.

In 1778 the French-American alliance brought men, money, and munitions to the colonies in sufficient quantities to allow the Americans to take the offensive. In addition, at French insistence, Spain and later the Netherlands also joined in the contest against the British. In 1781 the American army, in conjunction with the French navy, surrounded the British infantry led by Lord Charles Cornwallis at Yorktown. Cornwallis saw no way of escaping defeat. When he surrendered his sword, the American Revolution was won.

The warring nations, their muskets unloaded, negotiated the peace in treaties signed by their delegates in Europe. The Treaty of Paris confirmed the Thirteen Colonies, now the United States, to be independent and sovereign.

George Washington, first president of the United States.

Forming the United States

After the war concluded, it became evident that the Articles of Confederation were outdated. In 1787 a call went out to the states to send delegates to a **Constitutional Convention** to meet in Philadelphia.

Most delegates supported the notion of a government of three branches: executive, legislative, and judicial. This they wrote into the Constitution. Each branch had specific powers given it so that there would always be checks and balances, averting the danger of too much authority in a single unit.

After the ratification of the Constitution, Congress legislated the **Bill of Rights,** adding the first ten amendments. These amendments offered a remarkable list of individual guarantees. The Constitution provided for later emendations but wisely made the process very difficult. Frequent amendments were seen as promoting instability. Because of its clarity, brevity, and flexibility, the Constitution of the United States still provides the political framework for the United States.

Independence Hall, Philadelphia, the site of the Continental Congress.

The Constitution was the work of the upper class of the colonies and, as expected, reflected its views. Framers of the Constitution accentuated property rights for electors, and delegates to an Electoral College, rather than the people, were to choose the president.

With the adoption of the Constitution by the states, the United States entered a new era of history. Democracy, although limited, had triumphed.

Conclusion

In the space of a few decades, the Spaniards in Mexico and Central America rolled over the Indian populations that had no way to resist the weaponry of the invaders. Even more deadly were the diseases they brought. A precipitous decline in the native population commenced that lasted for a full century and a half.

Mexican Indians discovered that they were now subjects of the king of Spain and owed obedience to his officials instead of to leaders of their own ethnic background. The Catholic church set the cultural pattern for the vast majority of the population.

British and French settlers put down roots on the Atlantic side of North America, which became the Thirteen Colonies and Canada. Their interests clashed, with the result of almost constant conflict as both London and Paris sought to gain the upper hand.

It was agriculture and fur trapping that lured the British and French to the Americas, for the Atlantic coast had no precious metals. Both British and French who lived on the American frontier lived in a very egalitarian society, with none of the class differences found in Mexico.

The culture of New Spain mirrored the homeland, where people thought in terms of royal absolutism. The concept that the king is always right was vigorously resisted in the Thirteen Colonies. Politicians there decried any attempt of Parliament or King George to collect taxes from them unless they had a say in the London government. The American Revolution settled the issue when the United States took its place as an independent nation.

CHAPTER 10 REVIEW
NORTH AMERICA

Summary

- In 1500 most Indians of the Americas were in hunting and gathering societies, subsistence agriculture, or, as in Mexico, farming that produced large surpluses.
- The Aztec Empire, located in the Valley of Mexico with its capital at Tenochtitlán, was the most vigorous imperial power in North America.
- Because the Aztecs' religion demanded human sacrifice, they sought victims through constant war with their neighbors.
- In 1500 the Aztec ruler was Moctezuma II.
- Cortés, with the help of Indian allies, captured Tenochtitlán.
- The Spaniards tore down Tenochtitlán and on its foundations built Mexico City. Smallpox and other diseases wiped out millions of Indian men and women.
- Spanish men soon arrived in Mexico seeking to make their fortunes in mining or by raising cattle.
- A class structure developed between the wealthy Spanish officials and the mestizos whose mothers were Indian women.
- Friars from Spain converted millions of native Indians to Catholicism.
- Explorers north of the Rio Grande were disappointed with the meager wealth of the Indians living there.
- In the eighteenth century the Bourbon kings of Spain tried to centralize the government.
- British, French, and Dutch settlers joined the Spaniards in the West Indies in producing sugar.
- French and British interests clashed in Canada and the interior of what is now the United States.
- British settlers came to the Atlantic coast north of Florida and founded the Thirteen Colonies.
- Large numbers of settlers, for economic, religious, and political reasons, settled in the colonies.
- When Parliament sought to make colonists pay taxes to support their army in the Americas, the colonists started the American Revolution.
- The Thirteen Colonies, after their victory over the British, formed a new nation, the United States.

Identify

People: Aztecs, Moctezuma II, Cortés, las Casas, De Soto, Serra, Cartier, Pilgrims, Sons of Liberty, Jefferson, Washington, Arawak, Coronado, de Champlain, Iroquois, Cavelier, Anasazi, Cabot, Sir Walter Raleigh, Calverts, William Penn, Cornwallis

Places: Tenochtitlán, St. Augustine, San Diego, Panama, Hispaniola, Barbados, Québec, Jamestown, Philadelphia, Yorktown, Santo Domingo, Nova Scotia

Events: Cortés's capture of the Aztec Empire; establishing a Spanish government; silver mining in Mexico; settlement in the West Indies; French and Indian War; Québec Act of 1774; foundation of the Thirteen Colonies; formation of the United States

Define

Huitzilopchtli	fuero	creoles
peninsulares	mestizos	encomiendas
hacienda	proprietors	coureurs de bois

Multiple Choice

1. In population numbers the Aztec Empire was
   (a) the same size as Spain.
   (b) twice the size of Spain.
   (c) smaller than Spain.
   (d) three times larger than Spain.

2. The Aztec capital was located
   (a) on a plateau.
   (b) on an island in Lake Texcoco.
   (c) on the coast near modern Acapulco.
   (d) on the Rio Grande.

3. Tribute to the Aztecs came in the form of
   (a) grain.
   (b) metals.
   (c) cattle.
   (d) people.

4. Much of women's time in Aztec society was spent
   (a) grinding corn.
   (b) carving jewelry.
   (c) shopping in the market.
   (d) attending religious services.

5. At the end of a 52-year cycle in Mexico
   (a) all buildings were torn down.
   (b) all fires were extinguished.
   (c) a sacrifice of hundreds of men and women took place.
   (d) the emperors were sacrificed.

6. Cortés gained these Indians as allies:
   (a) the Tlaxcalans
   (b) the Maya
   (c) the Chichimecs
   (d) the Mississippians

7. In their occupation of Mexico City, the Spaniards were aided by
   (a) fierce storms.
   (b) the spread of disease.
   (c) demoralization of the Indian population.
   (d) their superior numbers.

8. A mestizo is someone who has
   (a) a Spanish mother and Indian father.
   (b) a Spanish father and Indian mother.
   (c) two Indian parents.
   (d) two Indian grandparents.

9. A peninsulare had to be born in
   (a) Cuba.
   (b) Central America.
   (c) Hispaniola.
   (d) Spain.

10. A land grant in New Spain was called
    (a) an encomienda.
    (b) an audiencia.
    (c) a fief.
    (d) a plantation.

11. The most severe problem for mine owners in Mexico was
    (a) a lack of equipment.
    (b) a labor shortage.
    (c) a lack of capital.
    (d) government restrictions on exports.

12. The great defender of Indian rights was
    (a) Las Casas.
    (b) Cortés.
    (c) Charles V.
    (d) De Soto.

13. The bullion shipped to Europe was used in Spain
    (a) to pay for the Habsburg armies.
    (b) to build churches.
    (c) to set up a social security system.
    (d) for public works.

14. The most advanced Indians north of the Rio Grande were the
    (a) Comanche.
    (b) Anasazi.
    (c) Apache.
    (d) Sioux.

15. He was founder of the California missions:
    (a) Kino
    (b) Marquette
    (c) Serra
    (d) Cartier

16. Centralization of authority in eighteenth-century Mexico was
    (a) an effort of the Bourbons to restore Spanish greatness.
    (b) the idea of Charles I.
    (c) an effort to get more money from plantations.
    (d) an attempt to strengthen hacienda owners.

17. Creoles were always resentful of the
    (a) English laws.
    (b) peninsulares.
    (c) churchmen in New Spain.
    (d) Indians.

18. The French in America were especially interested in exporting
    (a) grain.
    (b) furs.
    (c) silver.
    (d) bourbon.

19. This treaty transferred Nova Scotia to Great Britain:
    (a) Paris
    (b) London
    (c) Westphalia
    (d) Utrecht

20. The victor in 1759 in the battle for Québec was
    (a) Wolfe.
    (b) Abraham.
    (c) Cleves.
    (d) Montcalm.

21. Roanoke Island was the first American colony of the
    (a) Spaniards.
    (b) French.
    (c) Dutch.
    (d) British.

22. Representative government in North America began in
    (a) Virginia.
    (b) New York.
    (c) Massachusetts.
    (d) New Jersey.

23. After London, the largest English-speaking city in the world in the eighteenth century was
    (a) New York.
    (b) Savannah.
    (c) Philadelphia.
    (d) Trenton.

24. The Declaration of Independence was the work of
    (a) Washington.
    (b) Adams.
    (c) Jefferson.
    (d) Hamilton.

25. The first ten amendments to the United States Constitution were called
    (a) the Bill of Rights.
    (b) the Bill of Attainder.
    (c) the Charter of Liberties.
    (d) the Articles of Confederation.

Essay Questions
  1. What were the forces that shaped Spanish America?
  2. How do you explain the class divisions of Spanish America?
  3. What was the role of the French in North America?
  4. Were the problems of the Thirteen Colonies sufficient to call for revolution? Explain why.
  5. What developments in the United States called for a Constitution?

Answers

1. d	6. a	11. b	16. a	21. d
2. b	7. b	12. a	17. b	22. a
3. d	8. b	13. a	18. b	23. c
4. a	9. d	14. b	19. d	24. c
5. b	10. a	15. c	20. a	25. a

CHAPTER 11

South America

The Indian societies of South America proved just as fragile as those in the north. The Inca Empire was no more prepared to hold off the Spaniards than the Aztecs were. Elsewhere in South America, except in the intractable Amazon basin, one by one the relentless march of the conquistadors continued.

Geography

The landscape of South America is one of the most diverse in the world, a pattern of extremes. The continent holds the longest mountain chain in the world, the Andes, which extends 4,000 miles down its western coast, effectively cutting off communication with the interior. Its highest peak, Aconcagua, rises over 22,000 feet high.

The Empire of the Incas

The Amazon River, with 200 tributaries, drains the earth's largest rain forest, comprising 2,400,000 square miles. South America also has the highest major lake in the world, Titicaca, and its highest waterfalls, Angel Falls of Venezuela. On the west coast of Peru and Chile is a desert that hardly ever gets rain, while in parts of the Amazon the rain is constant. Much of the land is high plateau, such as Bolivia's *altiplano* or the grassland in Patagonia, a region shared between Chile and Argentina. The Indians of South America created a way of life remarkably suited to their environments, living in harmony, not in contest, with nature.

The Incas

Far to the south, a decade after the Mexican conquest, another Spanish expedition overran the huge Inca Empire also incorporating it into the territories of Charles I. The **Incas,** like the Aztecs, had themselves been conquerors in the fifteenth century and extended their political rule from modern-day Ecuador to central Chile, a distance of 3,000 miles. At its height it contained from 8 to 13,000,000 people.

The Inca Empire was built in little over 30 years after 1438, thanks to the military accomplishments of the warrior king Pachacuti. His armies, supplied by pack trains of llamas, using either persuasion or war, brought almost the whole of the western coast of South America under his rule. When other Indian nations submitted, he welcomed their army units into his own forces, for Pachacuti's aim was to integrate his empire. Therefore, he imposed the Incan language, Quechua, and its religion upon his tributary states.

Pachacuti removed rebellious peoples from their homelands and settled Incas in their place. He also created a huge bureaucracy to collect the taxes that flowed into the Incan capital of Cuzco in southern Peru. Engineers used these revenues to build massive stone structures, temples, and palaces in the city. Incan skill in shaping stone had no equal anywhere in the world in the fifteenth century.

The land system of the Incas divided properties into those that belonged to the gods, those that were the possession of the government, and those that were farmed to provide food for the peasant population. Harvests were not so bountiful in the Andes or along the Pacific coast so that South American cities never reached the population levels of Mexico. Cuzco, the Incan capital, held a population of only 100,000 men and women. Irrigation works and the terracing of mountains extended the amount of arable land, but farming was always a risk. Because no draft animals were available for farming, everything from plowing to harvesting was done by humans.

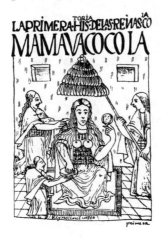

The Incan coya is attended by her servants.

The society of the Incas bore some resemblance to that of the Aztecs. At its peak was the emperor, whose title, Inca, has given its name to the whole society. A ruling Inca designated his successor from among his close male relatives. People thought of the Inca as absolute, for he was considered divine, a descendant of the sun, and his principal wife a child of the moon. All subjects were his children over whom the Inca and his queen, called the *coya*, ruled.

Although many other wives shared the royal palace, the coya enjoyed many privileges. When the Inca was on campaign, she ruled in his absence, and for one month of the year, usually September, she was regularly in charge.

The Incan religion had a strong interest in ancestors. Therefore, each Inca had to concern himself with his predecessors who were mummified and carried in procession on festive occasions. Their bodies were kept in the great Temple of the Sun in Cuzco. Because an elaborate worship was required after the death of an Inca, every ruler had to be sure that he made enough new conquests to support his cult after death. This may help to explain the constant expansion that the Incan rulers pursued.

The Incan nobility were also military officers, gathered into ten royal clans. The Spaniards called them Big Ears because their custom was to wear huge earplugs of gold and silver as part of their dress. Their orders while on campaign allowed no pillaging so that conquered people were more likely to submit, but despite this policy, rebellions were frequent.

Ordinary people belonged to kinship groups called *ayllu*, organized under a chieftain who directed farming activities and work on government projects. These included road building, repair of temples, and, the worst task of all, work in gold and silver mines. Women had to provide huge amounts of cloth so that weaving consumed all the time they could spare from preparing meals and caring for children. They owned property in their own name and rights to pasture and water for their animals.

The corpse of a dead Inca, carried in a religious procession.

When children were born, their mothers put them in a cradle that was strapped on their back, so that the work of the mother was not interrupted. To strengthen them, little children were given cold baths. Only when it was evident the child would survive, at two or three years of age, did the parents give it a name.

The Incas had a well-developed social security program. Government warehouses supplied a person with necessities when he or she became too ill or too old to work. No one needed to become a beggar in Incan society.

The economy supported few merchants, for each province was supposed to be self-sufficient after it paid its taxes to Cuzco. Artisans in the towns included potters, jewelers in precious metals, and tool and leather makers. Transportation in the mountains was very difficult, another reason for the paucity of merchants.

This did not mean that road construction was neglected. Quite the contrary, Incan emperors were anxious to weld their lands together through a complex system of highways that included suspension bridges over canyons. Because no wheeled vehicles existed, paving was not necessary. Inns and warehouses were located along the roads at a day's journey from one another. The extent of the system can be appreciated for the Incas built 10,000 of these inns.

The religion of the Incas based itself on the worship of the sun and moon. A creator god, Viracocha, also had his temples. Holy places and temples were scattered all over the empire where priests received people's offerings and sacrifices of grain and animals.

In 1493 the Inca, Huayna Capac, began his rule. Despite the tradition of locating the capital in Cuzco, he decided to make his residence in the north, in Ecuador. As a result people in the southern region of the empire developed a separatist movement that in 1525 resulted in a civil war. Two sons of Huayna Capac vied for leadership. One Huáscar, the legitimate heir, fought Atahualpa, a child of his father by a concubine. The civil war was a deadly contest and explains the weakness of the empire at the time the Spaniards arrived in Peru in November 1532. At that moment Atahualpa had just defeated his half-brother and executed him along with all his family and officials.

Pizarro's Conquest

Only a few months later, Atahualpa met Francisco Pizarro and his small army. Unlike Cortés, Pizarro had but 200 men and no Indian allies. Atahualpa arranged to see Pizarro at a hot springs where he was used to bathing. He suspected that Pizarro was the god Viracocha, so Atahualpa treated Pizarro with great respect. Smallpox had preceded the Spaniards, wiping out many of Atahualpa's people and demoralizing his army.

Atahualpa, the Inca emperor at the time of Pizarro's conquest.

Atahualpa was unarmed except for a cortege of his nobles. The Spanish captain easily took Atahualpa prisoner. In return for his freedom, the Inca promised to fill a room with gold. The gold was delivered as promised, but the Spaniards treacherously refused to free their prisoner; they baptized and then strangled him.

The vast majority of Incas then accepted a ruler selected by the Spaniards, another son of Huayna Capac. However, after some soldiers had raped his wives, the new Inca formed an army to push them out of Peru. Despite the fact that he raised a force of 60,000 warriors, he failed to take Cuzco, now occupied by Pizarro. Fleeing to a mountain retreat, the Inca was betrayed and later executed. Two other Incas tried to rally their subjects against the Spaniards, but in vain. In 1572 the last, Tupac Amarú, was caught and killed.

Tupac Amarú, last of the Incas, adopted Spanish dress.

This was not the end of Indian resistance. The native population of the Andes held on to its language and culture and continues to do so to this day.

In the rest of South America, away from the influence of Peru, Indians remained in hunting-gathering societies. Often they were quite isolated from each other. In the Amazon region, as on the islands of the West Indies, the tribal peoples cultivated manioc, a root that can be eaten only after its poisonous properties are washed out. Some Indians in the Amazon were headhunters, a gruesome custom that continued into the twentieth century. Many Indians had a taste for drugs, especially in the high Andes, where chewing coca leaves gave people a defense against the cold. Tobacco juice was also drunk as a narcotic.

The Spanish conquest proceeded to expand in South America, southward into Chile and northward into Ecuador and Colombia. Other conquistadors moved into Argentina from expeditions based in Peru.

Many explanations combine to account for the success of the Spaniards. These include superior weaponry, the use of horses, the ruthless character of the soldiers, and the skill of the commanders. Probably the capture of the Incan leader, who alone could give orders, hampered Indian resistance in Peru. The most important factor was disease. The Indians had no resistance to the many sicknesses that the Europeans unwittingly passed on to them, causing millions of Indian men, women, and children to die.

By 1622 demographers estimate that the native population of North and South America combined had dropped 90% or more from what it had been in 1500. The emigration of more people from Spain and the importation of African slaves saved the countries of Spanish America from complete depopulation. In 1650 the population began to increase as the Indians who survived the conquest developed immunities to the deadly plagues that killed their ancestors. Since then the birth rate has dramatically increased.

The Indians did get one bit of revenge. They probably gave the Spaniards a deadly form of syphilis, which first appeared in Barcelona in 1494 and then spread across Europe killing several million people along the way.

The Spanish Administration

King Charles I and his successors owned all the newly discovered land and were responsible for its government. Charles deputed the Council of the Indies to manage the administration of his Spanish possessions. Unfortunately many men who sat on the council had no experience with Spanish America and based their legislation on what they knew of European government. Nevertheless, the council enjoyed all legislative, judicial, and executive powers over the Spanish possessions of the Americas.

Colonial Latin America

The council appointed royal viceroys in Lima to represent the crown. Governors who were responsible to the viceroys sat in the more important towns, employing a large number of bureaucrats and office holders modeled upon the government of Spain itself. They collected the taxes, built public works and saw to their maintenance, and provided security against those Indians who still resisted European rule.

Under the governors, smaller units of administration, *audiencias,* judicial districts and their courts, and town councils, *regimientos,* administered the land, frequently with overlapping jurisdictions. To increase its revenue the Council of the Indies sold some offices to the ambitious. Candidates were second- and third-generation Europeans born in the Americas, the creoles. Because holding public office did not really pay well, corruption among lesser officials was rampant.

The viceroys were so far away from Spain that they soon learned to make their decisions fit the circumstances. The number of Spanish soldiers stationed in the Americas was relatively small, forcing administrators to use force only as a last resort. The most highly regulated regions were mining areas, for it was principally precious metals that the Spanish court wanted from the New World.

In 1545 Spanish prospectors discovered the richest silver mine in the world at Potosí in Bolivia. It was at such an altitude that nothing would grow, so there were no settlements nearby. When it was known how rich the discovery was, the population went from zero to 160,000 people. From 1550 to 1600 this single mine produced 60% of the total silver production in the whole world and provided the Spanish empire of Philip II with the means to carry on its many military campaigns in Europe.

In 1590 silver production peaked and then went into decline. Silver's monetary value also decreased because so much of the metal was in circulation. The Ming dynasty in China had been the major customer for South American silver, but because of its own problems, it could no longer afford to import the metal. Many mine owners fell into bankruptcy, and in Spain the government's ability to pay its bills from the sale of silver came to an end. The effect of the silver trade on China and Spain, geographically so far away from each other, demonstrates at this early date the interdependence of the world economy.

The silver mine of Potosí was the richest in the world.

The Jesuits became the advocates of the South American natives after they began their work in the New World. In Paraguay missionaries built settlements for the Indians to remove them from the usual exploitation of European settlers. This did not sit well with either the mine owners or the government, and in 1767 the Jesuits were expelled and the Indian towns were dispersed.

The same kind of rivalry as occurred in Mexico repeated itself in South America between the creoles and the peninsulares. In the eighteenth century tensions increased and violent uprisings broke out, joined by Indians whose grievances were in fact much more serious. Venezuela and New Granada (now Colombia) had a series of clashes with Spanish troops. *Mestizos,* Indians, and slaves marched on Bogotá, demanding a relaxation of taxes and threatening to cut the throats of the peninsulares, who were paid from the revenues squeezed out of their pockets.

In Peru another Tupac Amarú, claiming royal descent from the first of that name, battled Spanish soldiers for control of the country in a war that left 100,000 dead. A British blockade in the late 1700s cut off supplies of mercury, shutting down the mines and throwing an already anemic economy into depression.

The social classes of Spanish America pictured on a cup: an Indian, a Spaniard, and a black man.

Despite the unrest in South America, potential revolutionaries found little agreement on what should be done. For 300 years Spain had decided policy for Spanish America and discouraged any thoughts of self-government or cooperation among the creole elites. There was no training for political organization or for the compromises needed to forge a mass movement. Rigid class distinctions further impeded united action.

Brazil

In 1500 Portuguese claims to Brazil originated from the unintended discovery of the region. Pedro Alvares Cabral, sailing under the Portuguese flag, was blown off course as he sought to follow the African coast on a voyage to India and instead touched the coast of Brazil. The land fell within the territories awarded the Portuguese crown in the Treaty of Tordesillas of 1494.

For the first four decades after its discovery, Brazil received little attention from Lisbon because the Asian colonies of Portugal were so much more valuable. No gold or silver could be found. The only commercial activity carried on was the exportation of wood containing a special kind of dye in demand in Europe. The tree producing the dye was called brazilwood and gave its name to the country.

In 1532 the Lisbon government of King Joâo III offered grants of land to members of the nobility who would establish plantations along the Brazilian coast. Few proved successful because raising capital for these ventures was so difficult.

Portugal found Brazil a great deal more important when coffee drinking in Europe created a more pressing need for sugar. Settlers introduced cane into Brazil and found its climate ideal for its production, equal to the Caribbean Islands.

Those plantation settlements that did succeed in Brazil attracted more colonists from Portugal. A string of small towns began to dot the coastline, with the capital of the colony at Salvador. While at first Indian labor provided workers on the plantations, both for legal and economic reasons the planters turned to Africa for their work force. Slavery soon supplied Brazil with its workers. By 1600 there were 30,000 Europeans and 15,000 Africans in Brazil. A hundred years later the Europeans and Africans were an equal number at 150,000 people. By 1800 the number of blacks in the country stood at 2,500,000.

Portugal divided the country into captaincies, each of them reporting directly to Lisbon. Brazil, unlike the Spanish colonies, had no printing press or university. People lived in a rugged frontier society. The country was much more dependent on events occurring in Europe than the Spanish colonies were.

Because the colonists took wives from among the Indians and Africans, Brazil in the past, as well as today, held a large population of people of mixed ancestry. In Brazil and other Portuguese colonies, skin color was not a reason for discrimination as much as class structure.

In the eighteenth century demand for sugar kept rising and with it the number of Africans who were transported to Brazil, about 20,000 yearly. The slave population did not reproduce in sufficient numbers, so the plantation owners had to depend on a constant stream of Africans to make up for their losses. The slaves planted and harvested the cane and worked in the mills processing the sugar cane juice.

Workers process sugar in a small Brazilian mill.

In 1695 Brazilian life became even more tempestuous when prospectors discovered gold. News of the find brought a strong flow of Portuguese immigrants into the country. From 1735 to 1760 Brazil became the leading gold-producing country in the western world, and fortunes were made and lost in a matter of days. Much of the gold made its way to Portugal, but that country was so dependent on British trade that it profited very little. In addition to gold and sugar, Brazilian exports included tobacco, hides, and cotton.

Conclusion

The effect Spanish invaders had on the Incan Empire was similar to the impact they had on the Aztec population in Mexico. At a time when both empires were still young, the Spaniards came on the scene and brought them down.

Lima, like Mexico City, became the seat of a Spanish viceroy whose major task was to ship the precious metals of the New World back to Spain. Here the bullion was used not for productive causes but to finance the many Habsburg armies at war all over the European continent.

The Portuguese claim on Brazil required the Spaniards to share the South American continent. Here most fortunes were made from sugar plantations as well as from mining. To grow sugar, large numbers of workers were needed, and growers turned to African slaves to supply their needs.

Latin America always was torn by class conflict, for those who were creoles resented the presence of the peninsulares, as well as their wealth and their claims to social preferment. This became a more serious problem when a movement for independence began late in the eighteenth century.

Summary
- South America is a continent of great extremes in landforms and climate.
- The Incan Empire extended along the length of the coastal region of the Andes.
- The Inca, the emperor, ruled in a very autocratic manner over subject populations.
- Pizarro effected the Spanish conquest of the Incas.
- Disease was the ally of the Spaniards in South America as it had been in Mexico.
- The Spanish crown set up a viceroy in Lima to govern its new possessions.
- The richest silver mine in the world opened at Potosí in Bolivia.
- In colonial society, peninsulares and creoles had conflicting interests.
- The Portuguese colony of Brazil prospered from its plantations worked by African slaves.

Identify
People: Atahualpa, Pizarro, Tupac Amarú, Pachacuti, Cabral, Viracocha, Huayna Capac, Joâo III

Places: Andes, Cuzco, Amazon, Potosí, New Granada, Brazil, altiplano, Aconcagua, Bogotá

Events: Growth of the Incan Empire; treaty of Tordesillas; administration of the Council of the Indies; importation of slaves into Brazil

Define
coya   Inca   ayllu

Multiple Choice
1. The highest waterfalls in the world is
   (a) Niagara.
   (b) Victoria.
   (c) Angel.
   (d) Yosemite.

2. The creator of the Incan Empire was
   (a) Pachacuti.
   (b) Atahualpa.
   (c) Quechua.
   (d) Huayna Capac.

3. The Inca was considered
   (a) an absolute ruler.
   (b) a descendant of the sun.
   (c) divine.
   (d) all the above.

4. The Inca's wife was the
   (a) alcalla.
   (b) quipu.
   (c) quechua.
   (d) coya.

5. Women were constantly working to provide taxes in the form of
   (a) coins.
   (b) pottery.
   (c) cloth.
   (d) carpets.

6. Incan roads were narrow because
   (a) most travel was by riding horses.
   (b) travel was on rivers.
   (c) there were no wheeled vehicles.
   (d) travel was in small, narrow carts.

7. The Spaniards came upon the Incas
   (a) just after a civil war.
   (b) in the midst of a festival.
   (c) just after an invasion of Amazon Indians.
   (d) during the enthronement of the Inca.

8. In Spain the administration of the colonies was in the hands of the
   (a) Inquisition.
   (b) Alcabala.
   (c) Council of the Indies.
   (d) queen's courtiers.

9. The single richest silver mine in the world was in
   (a) Peru.
   (b) Bolivia.
   (c) Argentina.
   (d) Brazil.

10. The Jesuits formed large settlements of Indians in
    (a) Paraguay.
    (b) Bolivia.
    (c) Peru.
    (d) Uruguay.

11. In the eighteenth century he led the last Inca revolt:
    (a) Tupac Amarú
    (b) Pachacuti
    (c) Viracocha
    (d) Cabral

12. This treaty awarded Brazil to Portugal:
    (a) Tordesillas
    (b) Utrecht
    (c) Paris
    (d) Lima

13. The great agricultural wealth of Brazil went into the production of
    (a) cotton.
    (b) cattle.
    (c) sugar.
    (d) tobacco.

Essay Questions
1. Compare the Portuguese colony of Brazil with that of the Spanish colonies.
2. Describe the conquest of Pizarro.
3. Why was mining so important to Spanish America?

Answers

1. c	6. c	11. a
2. a	7. a	12. a
3. d	8. c	13. c
4. d	9. b	
5. c	10. a	

CHAPTER 12

Peoples of the Pacific

The Pacific Ocean covers one third of the earth's surface and contains about 25,000 islands. Some are very large and once were attached to nearby continents. When glaciers lowered the sea level, it was possible for land bridges to form, allowing the migration of plants and animals to come from the Asian mainland. Good examples are found in the flora and fauna of Australia and New Guinea. Underwater volcanos threw up some islands, and still more were formed when coral grew inside the rims of submerged volcanos, constructing atolls.

The apparently limitless sea, where only a few specks of land interrupted the wind and waves, shaped the island view of the world. Whichever way island residents sailed, they expected to find uninhabited land, and over the centuries they were proved correct.

Ancient Australia

Australia is the world's smallest continent, in extent 3,000,000 square miles. It lies entirely in the Southern Hemisphere fairly close to the equator. Its vast interior is a great desert, and only about 8% of the land is arable. On the eastern side of Australia the skeletons of animals that make up coral have created the Great Barrier Reef, the largest in the world.

The Aborigines who lived in Australia for thousands of years before the arrival of the Europeans were expert hunters of the animals of the continent, especially the kangaroo. Their weapons were of stone and shell. A rich religious and artistic tradition was handed down from generation to generation. The Aborigines, like the American Indians, thought themselves to be the only people in the world until European explorers sailed into their world.

A recent find of a carved sandstone pillar in northwestern Australia is thought to be 75,000 years old. If this date is verified, then the Aborigines of Australia will take the title of the world's oldest artists from the Cro-Magnons of France. The thousands of carvings on the pillar will far outdate the paintings of European caves.

The Austronesians

Anthropologists divide the native peoples of the Pacific into Melanesians, Micronesians, and Polynesians. The Melanesians usually have darker skin color and are related to the people of New Guinea. They inhabited also the Solomon Islands, New Caledonia, and Fiji. The

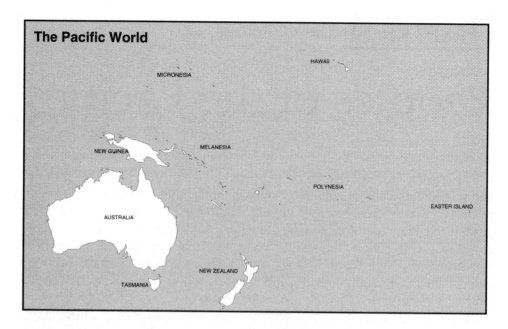

The Pacific World

Micronesians made their homes on the small islands close to the Asian mainland, including Guam, the Marianas, and the Marshall Islands. The lighter-skinned Polynesians lived within a triangle that extended from New Zealand to Hawaii and, at its farthest extension, Easter Island. Recent researchers have suggested using the terms Near Oceania and Remote Oceania because they more accurately reflect the history of Pacific settlement.

The peopling of Near Oceania occurred much earlier than that of Remote Oceania. Australia and New Guinea received human settlers as early as 80,000 years ago. A wave of Melanesians sailed to the islands of their homeland beginning about 9000 B.C., whereas the populations of Micronesia and Polynesia reached the islands they claimed in an emigration beginning only 3,500 years ago. The most recent emigration brought men and women to New Zealand about A.D. 900.

The languages of the Pacific belong to the **Austronesian** family. It is thought that the original home of the Austronesians was in southern China. For proof linguists point to the indigenous people of Taiwan, who speak an Austronesian language. As their numbers increased, the Austronesians sailed to New Guinea and to Fiji, Tonga, and Samoa. In the latter two island groups, a distinctive Polynesian culture first originated. From here other adventurers went on to the Cooks, the Societies, and the Marquesas. Other Austronesians turned to the west, crossed the Indian Ocean, and made their homes on the island of Madagascar.

Contrary to popular opinion, the Pacific islands were not rich tropical oases. Many were poor with thin soil. Fresh water was hard to come by, and few plants and animals were found that could benefit humans. The closer the islands were to the mainland, the more species they held. Reptiles and birds were abundant, but the islands held no mammals. Easter Island had only 30 plant species, none of them edible.

Because native plants and animals had evolved with no predators to speak of, they became easy prey for the first humans. Many soon disappeared, hunted to extinction. On some islands, sanctuaries were established where hunting was off-limits, or reserved for the royal family, in an effort to halt the rapid loss of animals. **Taboos** on gathering crustaceans

Polynesians who settled Hawaii after A.D. 500 entered an island world untouched by humans.

and fishing in lagoons and reefs during certain periods of the year helped to sustain animal life in the sea. Religion and magic fortified the prohibitions on hunting and fishing.

These efforts at halting environmental decline, for the most part, did not work. It is a false myth to think that Pacific islanders lived in harmony with nature, rather than trying to exploit every resource open to them. Scarcity left them no choice.

The Austronesian invention of the ocean-going canoe made human voyages possible. To give them a large enough capacity to hold both people and cargo, they had to be built in generous dimensions. Keeping them stable in heavy seas required floats on one or both sides of the boat. The sailors navigated using the location of the sun and stars, the pattern of wave motion, and the flight of sea birds.

A Polynesian canoe carried men, women, plants, and animals needed for setting up their new home.

The Austronesians carried in the canoe hulls the plants and animals they kept for food. These were bananas, coconut palms, yams, taro, and breadfruit. Somehow the Austronesians also had the South American sweet potato, but how and when it became cultivated in the islands remains unknown. The islanders also brought pigs, chickens, dogs, and rats with them. The rats made short work of the flightless birds or those that nested on the ground.

The Austronesians carried another tool to use on the islands besides their stone weapons. This was fire. In order to clear the land for planting, they set fires in the lowlands, destroying the vegetation for fields. In the highlands slash-and-burn techniques cleared the trees but made the hillsides vulnerable to erosion. When lush hill soil washed down into the sea, cropland disappeared as well. Soon weeds, unconsciously carried in their canoes, appeared among their crops, creating even more problems for island farmers.

Island societies were organized in chiefdoms. The ruler was generally the eldest male of the royal clan. Second sons did not inherit, which prompted some to take to the sea to form their own colony with kinsmen and women.

Even though the food supply on larger islands was adequate, this did not prove true for the smaller islands. Food storage was also difficult. On certain islands drought was a constant problem, forcing engineers to design extensive irrigation works. Hunger within an increasing population often passed into famine, resulting in low life expectancy. Occasionally food became so scarce that abortion, infanticide, and driving weaker clans into the sea to be drowned was a desperate response to overpopulation.

One example of the destruction of life on the islands makes the environmental story clear. This is the story of Easter Island or *Rapa Nui,* the most isolated locality in all of Polynesia, 1,500 miles from the nearest island and 2,300 miles from the South American coast. How it was discovered is one of the fascinating mysteries of Polynesia.

Archaeologists believe that the first Austronesians arrived on Easter Island about A.D. 400. An unknown number of men and women came ashore to begin their new life. At the time a forest of palm trees covered Easter Island, so the settlers began clearing the land by using fire to destroy the trees. With the forest cover gone, the ever-present wind quickly dried out the poor soil, and eventually only a few valleys were fit for agriculture. The Easter Islanders had to live on sweet potatoes, the chickens they brought with them, and little else.

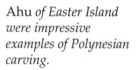

Ahu *of Easter Island were impressive examples of Polynesian carving.*

One of their chiefs decided on the carving and placement of stone statues, called **ahu,** all over the island. Having only stone tools, however, made carving a challenge. To put the ahus in the right place required rolling them on palm tree logs, a technique that soon consumed all the remaining palms and made survival even more difficult. Warfare between the clans over farmland became common with the result that the population diminished from about 8,000 people in 1600 to 2,000 men and women in the eighteenth century. They were also trapped, for there were no more trees to build boats. Angered at their plight, the Easter Islanders toppled their statues and must have looked out longingly to the sea's horizon in hope of rescue.

Hawaii

Polynesian colonists between A.D. 600 and 950 reached the Hawaiian Islands. The settlers brought much of the food supply they had known in their original home. They used fire to clear the lowlands and began planting their crops. The population spurted upward, so that to increase the land under cultivation became an urgent necessity. Irrigated taro fields answered the need for a time. Population estimates vary from 125,000 to a million at the height of Hawaiian prosperity.

Society became highly stratified under rulers who married within the royal clan. Warfare was constant as one chief fought another for control of an island or even part of an island. A court surrounded the chief with administrators, attendants, and warriors.

New Zealand

The Polynesians of New Zealand, the Mâori, accomplished the last settlement in the Pacific, coming ashore about A.D. 900. They found the islands too cold for the tropical plants they used to grow but were saved through the introduction of the sweet potato. Up to 1200 the population growth was very slow, until a major clearing of the forests caused a spurt in population.

A Mâori house was large enough to hold a number of people.

This put a great strain on New Zealand's resources, resulting in ousting weaker clans from food-producing areas. In 1769, on the eve of the European discovery of their homeland, the Mâori population stood at about 100,000 men and women.

The Europeans Arrive

In 1532 Ferdinand Magellan's ships, in the first around-the-world cruise, took 3 months and 20 days to cross the Pacific Ocean. After his ship accomplished this feat, other European explorers followed, and the route that carried silver from Acapulco to Manila became the most traveled in the Pacific. Europeans did not want to settle on the islands, rather like modern travelers from Los Angeles to Tokyo, they wanted to get across the Pacific as quickly as possible and regarded its size an inconvenience.

The single exception to European indifference was the island of Guam, for this offered a stopping place for the Manila galleons. The natives of Guam, the Chamorro, soon paid a heavy price for welcoming the Spanish sailors. They picked up the usual European diseases of smallpox, influenza, and meas.es. The native Chamorro declined from 50,000 people to about 1,300 in 300 years.

In the eighteenth century, French, British, and Dutch navigators sailed into the Pacific, reflecting a great interest in science and exploration, part of the legacy of the Enlightenment. First to come into Australian waters was the Dutch captain William Jansz. Other Dutch sailors followed. Abel Janszoon Tasman took his ships around Australia without ever seeing it, but he did land on the island off the southern coast that now bears his name, Tasmania.

The most important explorer was the British naval captain, James Cook. His three voyages through the islands mark the true opening of the Pacific to Europeans. Cook had the advantage of knowing his position, for by the time of his first voyage in 1769, instruments could determine longitude. Cook made the first accurate maps of the Pacific, destroying the myth of a large continent that geographers thought existed somewhere in the mid-Pacific.

At the time Cook arrived in Hawaii imported European diseases had already swept away so many natives that only 50,000 men and women were left. In 1779 Cook himself died in Hawaii during a battle with the natives.

On this ship, Captain James Cook explored the Pacific Islands.

Cook was responsible for putting Australia on the map. In 1770 he had discovered the eastern coast and saw its potential, naming it New South Wales. In London his discoveries prompted the government to dispatch a convoy of about 730 prisoners, men and women, and their guards to Australia. The ships arrived in 1788, setting up a colony on Botany Bay.

Conclusion

The islands of the Pacific were the last part of the world to receive human settlement. The process was a slow one, for island-hopping required extraordinary navigational skills and a great deal of good luck. Setting out in a canoe crowded with humans, plants, and animals for an unknown destination across a seemingly endless sea speaks well of the courage or of the desperation of the Austronesian sailors who populated the Pacific.

The European intrusion into the Pacific world, as in the Americas, caused a serious disruption in the life of the islanders with much the same effect. By the time of the European arrival, it was already evident that the fragile environment of the islands was deteriorating as a result of human habitation.

CHAPTER 12 REVIEW
PEOPLES OF THE PACIFIC

Summary
- The Aborigines lived in Australia as hunters and gatherers for thousands of years.
- The island peoples of the Pacific are the Melanesians, Micronesians, and Polynesians.
- The islands when settled often offered harsh environments for hunting and fishing.
- The courage of the Austronesians is proved by their willingness to travel great distances in open canoes.
- Island forests were damaged by fire.
- The last settlement in the Pacific was the Mâori colonization of New Zealand.
- The first islanders to experience European contact were the Chamorro of Guam.

Identify
People: Aborigines, Melanesians, Mâori, Tasman, Cook, Micronesians, Polynesians, Chamorro, Jansz
Places: Near Oceania, New Guinea, Samoa, Madagascar, Easter Island, Hawaii, Guam, Remote Oceania, Fiji, Tonga
Events: settlement of Australia and the Pacific Islands; efforts to provide food on the islands

Define
Austronesians   taboo   ahu

Multiple Choice
1. The number of islands in the Pacific is about
    (a) 10,000.
    (b) 30,000.
    (c) 25,000.
    (d) 35,000.

2. A recent find of carving on a sandstone pillar makes these people the world's first artists:
    (a) Mâori
    (b) Hawaiians
    (c) Polynesians
    (d) Aborigines

3. The predominant languages of the Pacific belong to this family:
    (a) Austronesian
    (b) Arawak
    (c) Uralic-Altaic
    (d) Hawaiian

4. One feature of the Pacific Islands was the lack of
   (a) flightless birds.
   (b) flying birds.
   (c) reptiles.
   (d) land mammals.

5. A taboo is
   (a) an invitation.
   (b) a prohibition.
   (c) a doll.
   (d) a dance.

6. To clear the land of the islands, people used
   (a) fire.
   (b) stone axes.
   (c) metal saws.
   (d) machetes.

7. The ahu are famous statues of
   (a) the Marquesas.
   (b) the Marshalls.
   (c) Easter Island.
   (d) Hawaii.

8. Spaniards reached Guam on their journey to
   (a) China.
   (b) the Philippines.
   (c) Japan.
   (d) Mexico.

9. The most important of British expeditions into the Pacific were made by
   (a) Tasman.
   (b) Cook.
   (c) Cleve.
   (d) Rhodes.

Essay Questions
1. How did European contact affect the island cultures?
2. Discuss the methods and means of navigation used by island sailors and compare them with those of the Europeans.

Answers

1. c	4. d	7. c
2. d	5. b	8. b
3. a	6. a	9. b

UNIT 2

A PERIOD OF EUROPEAN DOMINATION
A.D. 1789–1914

CHAPTER 13

The French Revolution and Napoleonic Europe

The French Revolution of 1789 begins the modern history of Europe. Essentially the French Revolution swept away the political and social structure of the Middle Ages and replaced it with a new order that promised greater social justice and political equality. The slogan of the revolutionaries, "Liberty, Equality, and Fraternity," summed up their goal.

Background

Toward the close of the eighteenth century, France held 24,000,000 people, making it the most populous country of Europe. It was also the most prosperous, with a significant number of people now in the middle class, but an unequal distribution of wealth kept the peasantry poor. It was the middle class, the *bourgeoisie*, who had been touched by the thought of the Enlightenment. What they read made them very unhappy that the king of France acted as if the nation was his personal property and the nobility, exempt from taxation, had all the privileges and none of the responsibilities for paying the country's bills.

Many also thought something should be done to make Catholic churchmen, equally privileged, to contribute more to the nation. Most French bishops were from families of the nobility and preferred life at the Court of Versailles or on family estates to spending time overseeing their churches. The parish priests, however, were present to serve their congregations. They were far removed from the frivolous scene surrounding the king and court.

The clergy made up the **First Estate;** the nobility, the **Second Estate. The Third Estate** was composed of everyone else. This Third Estate encompassed a very diverse group of people. Some were wealthy bourgeoisie, who made their living as merchants and craftsmen or as professionals, such as engineers, bankers, lawyers, or doctors. Members of the bourgeois class also held local offices in towns and provincial governments. Despite their importance to the country's administration, no one in the middle class had any decision-making role at the upper level of government. The nation's policies rested entirely in the hands of the king and his appointees from the nobility.

Rural peasants were also part of the Third Estate, but politics was not their concern. Their homes were poor and cold, their hours in the field were long and tedious, and opportunities for educating their children were practically nonexistent. Yet they had to pay high rents to the landlord and fees for selling their produce and using his mill to grind grain for their bread. The church took a tenth of what was left at the end of the harvest season. For a certain number of days each year they were also enlisted in the *corvée*, labor on the roads or on improvements of the royal lands.

The Government's Economic Crisis

The temptation for France to enter the American Revolution against the British had proven too strong to resist. Even though the French and the colonists gained the victory in America, the British won battles against them in the West Indies and India. In 1783 the Peace of Paris gave the United States its independence, but France had little to show for its efforts except a huge debt that the war created.

In 1783 the king was Louis XVI, a man whose personality was pleasant, but he lacked the qualities of a strong leader. Rather than enjoying public life, he preferred to spend his time at his hobby, making locks.

Louis failed to grasp the severity of the financial crisis, shifting the task of finding a solution to his ministers. They valiantly tried to borrow enough money to meet the needs of the budget. In 1787 a convention of the two upper estates met to see if they would agree to be taxed. The bishops and nobles rejected outright the idea that the debt was their problem and dispersed without accomplishing anything.

One more time Louis's finance minister sought a loan, but the high court of Paris, the **Parlement,** defiantly refused to register it, although in the past this had been little more than a formality. At last his ministers advised Louis that to solve the country's difficulties he should summon the **Estates General.** The Estates General was the medieval French assembly that gave advice to the king, but since 1614 it had never met.

Excited preparations commenced all over France for the Estates' convocation. The bourgeoisie intended to seize this opportunity to demand a thorough reformation of the French political and economic system.

In May 1789 delegates from the three estates gathered at the royal palace of Versailles. The Third Estate held the most representatives, more than the other two estates combined, so that its leaders demanded a one-man, one-vote electoral system. The king resisted, knowing that the preservation of his privileges was safer if the estates voted as a bloc. Louis counted on the clergy and nobles to resist radical tinkering with the structure of his government.

National Assembly

On June 17 the members of the Third Estate, fed up with the stalemate over the voting issue, proclaimed themselves a **National Assembly.** Its leaders invited the nobles and clergy to join them. A group of sympathetic priests and a smaller number of nobles accepted. This allowed the National Assembly to claim that it now actually represented all classes of the French nation. Three days later, locked out of their meeting room, the members of the National Assembly gathered at an indoor tennis court. There they swore an oath that they would not adjourn until they had written a constitution for the nation. This decisive action on the part of the National Assembly was answered by no response on the part of the king and his ministers. Louis had yet to decide what to do.

The Oath of the Tennis Court turned the Estates General into a National Assembly.

Throughout France the report of events occurring at Versailles energized the country. There were rumors that the king had called the army closer to Paris to prepare to disperse the National Assembly. A great fear and apprehension swept over France.

On July 14 a mob in Paris surged through the streets to the royal prison, the Bastille. Rumor had it that the king had imprisoned his opponents inside. The crowd besieged the Bastille and took it, but found no political prisoners. This no longer mattered. The capture of the Bastille had great symbolic value: the people of Paris had challenged the king's power and won.

During August the National Assembly passed a series of laws to make France a constitutional monarchy and provide a more democratic society. The National Assembly abolished the privileges and titles of the two upper estates. All elements of serfdom were repealed. In the countryside peasants took matters into their own hands, burning the documents that listed their feudal obligations.

What was the king to do? Obviously he needed to act, yet one more Paris demonstration seized the initiative. Armed with clubs and shouting "Bread," a group of demonstrators marched on Versailles. They seized Louis and his family, put them in a cart, and returned to Paris with their royal prisoners. The shout went out, "We have the baker and the baker's wife and the little cook boy. Now we shall have bread." The National Assembly followed them to Paris, where it became subject to the raw emotionalism of the crowd.

The National Assembly continued to remake France. One of its accomplishments was the **Declaration of the Rights of Man,** which proclaimed "Men are born free and equal in rights." Its members also reconstructed the administration system. It abolished the former provinces and put in their place 83 departments. Officials in the departments were to be elected rather than appointed. To solve the country's financial problem, the assembly delegates confiscated church lands and, using these properties for security, issued paper money.

Storming the Bastille demonstrated the anger of the Parisians against their king.

The delegates went beyond taking away the church's properties when it issued the **Civil Constitution of the Clergy.** It reduced the member of bishoprics to 83, one elected for every department, and made the church an arm of the state. The clergy were required to take an oath to support the new constitution. All over France Catholic bishops and priests were placed in a dilemma, to take the oath or to refuse it. In the end, only seven bishops and fewer than half the priests agreed, so that conservative Catholics lost much of their interest in further revolution and took up arms against the government in Paris in several regions of the country.

Legislative Assembly

By 1791 the Constitution was finished and Louis had signed it. The Constitution reduced the powers of the king and permitted him only to suspend action for a time but not to veto a law passed by the legislature. A one-house **Legislative Assembly,** elected by male taxpayers, was to govern the country.

The king, a prisoner in his Paris palace, sought ways to blunt the revolution's progress. He looked to Vienna for support, where his brother-in-law was the Holy Roman Emperor. Louis contacted officers in the army to check their loyalty. Then, impatient over the speed of events, he decided to escape. In late June, disguised as servants, Louis, his queen Marie Antoinette, and two of their children, left the palace in a coach for the border. At midnight the next day, officers sympathetic to the Assembly recognized the king and stopped the royal flight. His captors returned the family to Paris under guard where they were put back under house arrest.

The next period of the revolution, from October 1791, found the Legislative Assembly in session, moving the country farther along the path of change. Radicals, led by Jean Paul Marat, Georges-Jacques Danton, and

Maximilien Robespierre wanted a complete revision of the country's laws. They operated out of clubs, the most important as well as the most revolutionary was known as the **Jacobin.**

Maximilien Robespierre was responsible for much of the work of the Legislative Assembly and the Convention.

Outside of France the monarchs and nobility in the rest of Europe viewed events occurring there with apprehension. If the king of France was now a captive of his subjects, would crowns all over Europe soon topple? They commenced preparing their armies for action.

In April 1792 the Legislative Assembly, with the approval of the king, declared war on the Holy Roman Empire. The army, weakened by desertions, did poorly. Nor did the National Guard, led by the Marquis de Lafayette, once an officer in the American Revolution, fare any better. A state of crisis hung over the nation.

The Convention

Paralyzed by foreign conflict on French borders and civil war at home, the Legislative Assembly voted to turn over its powers to an Executive Council. A new assembly, the **Convention,** would then meet. Danton and Robespierre, members of the Committe of Public Safety, intended to promote the revolution by ridding the nation of its enemies, and enemies it had in abundance. When the Convention met for the first time in September 1792, it proceeded to abolish the monarchy and named King Louis a traitor to the nation. He was put on trial, found guilty, and taken to the guillotine where he paid with his life for opposing the revolution. Marie Antoinette, his wife, later shared his fate.

By 1793 all the major states of Europe, in the **First Coalition,** were at war with the French. In Paris itself mobs demanded that more and more victims be taken to the guillotine. Anyone who showed the least bit of reserve could be charged with treason and jailed. Many of these paid for a lack of enthusiasm with their lives. The goal of making France a republic disappeared in the face of the Terror. The Jacobins, once the Revolution's radicals, fell victim to even more extremists. Hauled before tribunals and judged guilty of betraying their ideals, the guillotine finished the lives of the Jacobin leaders. The revolution was eating its own children.

The executioner displays the head of King Louis XVI.

Despite these internal convulsions, the armies of France, filled with recruits drafted to increase its numbers, pushed back the country's enemies. Soldiers fought with nationalistic enthusiasm never before seen on the continent.

The days of the Terror at last wound down as moderates decided enough blood had been shed. Finally a new constitution set up a structure for the country, placing it under five directors. Their task was to restore order and at the same time to preserve the gains of the revolution.

Partitions of Poland

While all eyes were on events happening in France, the neighbors of Poland saw an opportunity. It had become obvious even to the Polish nobility that their government needed reform, if their nation was to survive. Therefore, in 1791 the members of the Diet agreed to a new constitution that established a hereditary monarchy and abolished the *liberum veto.* Because these measures were meant to strengthen the nation, Catherine the Great of Russia determined to stop them from taking effect. She proposed one more partition and invited the Prussians to join her. This second partition left Poland with only a core area that was still its own, and even there a Russian army of occupation kept guard.

Appalled at what had happened, a Polish officer, once a brigadier general in Washington's army during the American Revolution, Tadeusz Kosciuszko, called on the Poles to resist. Fortune was not with the Poles. The Russians defeated Kosciuszko, and Poland suffered a third partition that erased it from the map of Europe.

The Directory and Napoleon

Often historical events hinge on the appearance of a personality who is present at the right time and in the right place. Such was Louis Napoleon Bonaparte, a Corsican general in the service of the revolution. In 1795 it was troops under his command that put down "with a whiff of grapeshot" the last rioting in Paris and provided him with a reputation for dependability. French politicians found a man whom they thought they could trust.

The directors decided to give Napoleon an army to strike at Great Britain, at that time the one remaining country still at war with France. The other members of the coalition against France, one by one, had dropped out of the contest so that only the British still felt it worth the cost. In 1798 Napoleon, realizing a frontal attack on Great Britain was out of the question, made a peculiar decision, which he thought would break his enemy's supply line with India. He shipped off with a French army to Egypt so as to stop commerce coming from the Orient into the Mediterranean and thence to England. Napoleon rather easily defeated the Mamluk armies of Egypt, but in October 1799 the British destroyed the French fleet.

An idealized Napoleon rides over his Egyptian enemies.

Napoleon was not about to let the precarious state of his army, now marooned in Egypt, get in the way of his personal ambition. He returned to France, leaving his soldiers behind, just in time to find that Paris was ready for one more revolution. On November 9, 1799, soldiers loyal to Napoleon surrounded the Directorate's legislature. The members decided it was in their interest to choose Napoleon to be the First Consul of the Republic.

The French Revolution now produced a new ruler, far more powerful than the king who preceded him. Democratic values had proven too shallow for the country, and unlike what happened in the United States, leadership passed so quickly from hand to hand that most French men and women were again ready to accept the authority of a single ruler. Stability seemed preferable to the continual series of wars that the revolution set off.

Napoleon acted as though the ideals of the revolution were still alive despite the fact that he ignored them when it was to his advantage. He recognized that there was a new spirit abroad in France propelled by a very powerful emotion, **nationalism.** Although Napoleon filled his armies with recruits of every ethnic background, he encouraged them to think of themselves as Frenchmen.

Gone were the churchmen and nobles along with the king who once had given France its elite. Now it was the secular state and the middle class that replaced them. Napoleon was prepared to use the bourgeois class to create a new France, with an army convinced that it was fighting to bring liberty, equality, and fraternity to the rest of Europe.

Napoleon Comes to Power

Napoleon Bonaparte was born in Ajaccio, Corsica, just a few weeks after the island fell to the French. Corsica had formerly been under the control of Genoa. Napoleon's early education was given by a priest tutor, but while still not quite ten years of age his father took him and his brother, Joseph, to France. Here his father enrolled him in a military school. Because of his Italian accent when speaking French, his classmates called him "the boy with a straw in his nose."

At 15 he transferred to the Military School of Paris, but his grades were not good. He graduated forty-second in a class of 48. Nevertheless, he was commissioned a second lieutenant in the artillery. For a time he went back to Corsica to await events.

In 1789 the revolution broke out, and Napoleon returned to his regiment. He decided to cast his lot with the revolutionary party, commenting, "It is better to eat, than be eaten." He secured a position in the army of General Jacques Dugommier and was present when Toulon, an important royal naval base, fell to the revolutionaries. Several months later a grateful government in Paris named him general, with a command in the Army of Italy.

During this period of his life, his accomplishments were few because the Army of Italy spent most of its time looking for enough to eat. In May 1795 he returned to Paris. When the Paris **Commune,** representing the Parisian radicals, sought to turn out the Convention, his friends called on him to lead the troops defending that body. His success, shooting point blank at the Commune's supporters and killing 600 people, caused the Convention to hail him as the hero of the day. It was this show of force that propelled him into his second command in Italy.

Napoleon Bonaparte claimed to extend the goals of the French Revolution through his wars in Europe.

The Austrians who occupied northern Italy fell back before Napoleon's army, now fighting under the slogan, "We have come to break your chains." Turin, Milan, and then Rome were taken. Napoleon offered to make peace with the Habsburg emperor provided France should determine the status of northern Italy. The result was the establishment of a puppet state, named the Cisapline Republic. A treaty with Venice also transferred its possessions to France.

Then had come the Egyptian expedition that in fact was a disaster for the French, but Napoleon, after his return home, turned it into a personal victory. In 1799 Napoleon, only 30 years old, became the head of France. What no one knew at that time was the general's ambition. France was not to enjoy peace as long as Napoleon ruled.

The Consulate

As **First Consul,** Napoleon set about reorganizing the country, centralizing authority in his own hands. Censorship and state control over publications thwarted any opposition. The army and police took their orders from him or his appointees. On the economic front, he set up the Bank of France to restore confidence in the currency. Napoleon could boast, "Citizens, the revolution is established upon the principles that began it. It is ended."

The First Consul solved the religious problem when he and Pope Pius VII signed a **Concordat,** an agreement that allowed Napoleon to nominate bishops as long as the pope invested them in their office.

Napoleon's greatest accomplishment was a thorough reform of the civil and criminal law. This **Code Napoleon** was clear and fair, a model for other legal reforms throughout Europe. It promised equality before the law, religious toleration, and the abolition of privilege and serfdom. The code has had a lasting impact on the legal systems of continental Europe and other parts of the world; it is a serious competitior to the common law tradition of Great Britain and the United States.

When Napoleon came to power, the major powers of Europe, Great Britain, Austria, and Russia were still at war with France. Little by little this **Second Coalition** of allies directed against France began to fall apart. Russia withdrew, and a campaign against Austria forced that nation out of the coalition, leaving only Great Britain to fight on. In March 1802 Napoleon and the British agreed to the **Peace of Amiens,** so that for the first time in over a decade France was not at war.

The Emperor of the French

Napoleon's success both in domestic and foreign affairs to this point was outstanding. In 1804 the consul's soaring popularity allowed Napoleon to construct a new Constitution. This document named him Emperor of the French. Believing that it would add to his grandeur, Napoleon invited the pope to come to Paris to attend his coronation. Despite objections from all the other royal families of Europe, Pius VII went to Paris where he officiated at the emperor's coronation in Notre Dame. The pope only watched as Napoleon put the crown on his own head. The emperor did not want anyone to get the idea that he was dependent upon the church.

After his own coronation, Napoleon places a crown on his empress Josephine.

The Emperor's Wars

The Peace of Amiens did not last a year. There were too many unresolved issues remaining between Napoleon and the British. London feared French control over the Netherlands. Here Napoleon had established the Batavian Republic, which was no more than a satellite of Paris. French puppet states on the continent meant that British interests were in danger of vanishing.

Napoleon planned an invasion of England, but Admiral Horatio Nelson's victories at sea doomed it. In 1805 at the battle of Trafalgar, Nelson's fleet sent a joint French-Spanish squadron to the bottom of the sea.

Napoleon's response was to inaugurate an indirect attack upon the British. He established the **Continental System,** an embargo on British trade in all markets of the continent. The British struck back with **Orders in Council,** which prohibited any ship from going to a French port without first stopping at one of their ports.

The advantage lay with London because England had an effective navy and France did not. In addition, all other world markets were open to the British, so rather than facing economic disaster, the Continental System did little damage. Britain's trade actually increased instead of declining.

In London the government of William Pitt considered several ways to cause Napoleon trouble on the continent. Plans were approved to furnish money to any nation willing to take on France. As a result of British influence, a **Third Coalition,** made up of Austria, Russia, Sweden, and Prussia united against the French.

In a series of campaigns, Napoleon defeated each of his opponents in succession. French armies marched eastward into Vienna, Berlin, and

Warsaw. On a raft in the Niemen River, which separated Russian territory from conquered Prussia, Alexander I, tsar of Russia, met with Napoleon. The two emperors agreed on peace after the tsar promised to honor the Continental System.

In January 1808 it appeared that Napoleon's star was still on the ascendant. Most of Europe was either directly under French rule or had joined with France as an ally. A **Confederation of the Rhine** brought together the southern German states, while in northern Germany Napoleon's brother Jerome ruled over the newly created **Kingdom of Westphalia.** Two other brothers were also enthroned: Joseph in Spain and Joachim in Naples.

This mighty empire, however, was not to last. In Spain nationalists rose against the French occupation army and drove Joseph from Madrid in August 1808. The Duke of Wellington landed in Portugal with a British army that encouraged resistance for the next five years, until the French were finally expelled.

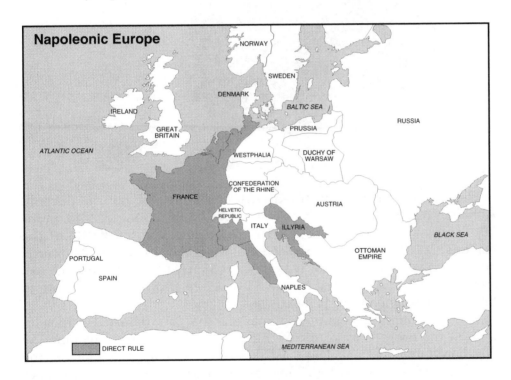

In St. Petersburg general dissatisfaction with the Continental System caused Tsar Alexander to permit British merchants to return to Russia. Napoleon had to make a decision. Either he had to force Russia to cooperate or he had to give up the Continental System. The emperor chose war.

On June 22, 1812, Napoleon's troops crossed into Russia with an army of 600,000 men. The *Grand Armée,* the largest ever recruited for one of his campaigns, was only half French, for recruits were conscripted from all over Europe.

Russian strategy was to avoid an open fight, but to withdraw before the French, leaving a scorched earth behind. To supply such a large force without resources to live off the land caused Napoleon's army serious problems. When at last the French occupied Moscow, they found it a hollow shell. Alexander gave orders to set the city on fire rather than to let its buildings be used for stationing the French invaders. Napoleon expected the tsar to surrender at this point. For days, he waited for Alexander's emissary to meet him in the Kremlin, but no one came.

It was now obvious that the army could not winter in Russia, so Napoleon gave the order to retreat. The once proud Grand Armée headed westward, harassed constantly by Russian attacks but even more by ice and snow. The Russian winter meant total misery and starvation for the troops. By the time the army reached friendly territory in early December, half a million soldiers lay beneath the ground, covered by Russian snow. It was one of the world's greatest military blunders.

The Grand Armée retreats from Moscow.

The Russian army, now filled with confidence began the pursuit. Although Napoleon won a victory at Lützen in the spring of 1813, in the fall of that same year he suffered a major defeat in the **Battle of the Nations.** Only a few months remained for the French to raise another force, but the magic of the emperor was gone. In March 1814 Paris surrendered, and Napoleon resigned the throne. The victors allowed him to retire to Elba, a small island off the Italian coast.

The statesmen representing the nations that had defeated Napoleon invited the brother of Louis XVI, then living in exile, to resume the Bourbon throne in Paris. Louis XVIII returned to Paris and replaced the flag of the revolution, the red, white, and blue tricolor, with the lily banner of Bourbon France. All over Europe, with the exception of Sweden, Napoleon's appointees fell from power, and the royal houses he had ousted took back their thrones.

Road to Waterloo

On Elba a bored Napoleon plotted a return to France. On March 1, 1815, he landed on the south coast and in five days entered Paris as Louis XVIII fled. Napoleon promised that he was a changed man. There would be no more wars, and France should have a new constitution. Many French men and women were willing to believe him, but the leaders of the nations who had allied against him were not. Armies were put in motion to return to France.

Napoleon led a hastily recruited force to Waterloo, in Flanders, to meet a combined force of British, Dutch, and German soldiers commanded by the Duke of Wellington. At the end of the battle, the French had lost. Napoleon once more resigned. This time his place of exile was St. Helena, a far-away island in the Atlantic off the African coast. In 1821 he died there.

Conclusion

The Battle of Waterloo brought a close to this revolutionary epoch in European history. The clock was turned back, but not all the way. Many of the ideas of the French Revolution and the Napoleonic reforms remained.

Respect for individual rights and toleration of different religious opinions remained a legacy of the revolution. Kings in Europe had to recognize that arbitrary power was no longer acceptable. The importance of the middle class was heightened because its members were no longer subjects but rather citizens of their nations.

Most of all, nationalism received a tremendous assist. In France, and in the lands the French troops occupied, the idea that the nation was supreme became predominant. People who shared a similar language, culture, religion, and history came together as never before. This set a pattern that today makes nationalism the strongest force in the world.

CHAPTER 13 REVIEW
THE FRENCH REVOLUTION AND NAPOLEONIC EUROPE

Summary
- France was the most populous nation of Europe, having a large middle class.
- The bourgeoisie were very much influenced by the thought of the Enlightenment.
- French participation in the American Revolution landed the government deeply into debt.
- King Louis XVI agreed to summon the Estates General.
- The Estates General announced that it was a National Assembly with the right to draw up a constitution.
- During the Convention, the Terror struck France, as hundreds of men and women were guillotined.
- Napoleon came to power as a general of revolutionary France.
- Napoleon initiated many internal reforms in France, professing them to be the fulfillment of the goals of the revolution.
- France's neighbors went to war with Napoleon to curb his ambition to rule the continent.
- Napoleon's downfall occurred because he could not defeat the British navy or the Russian winter.

Identify
People: Louis XVI, Marie Antoinette, Robespierre, Jacobins, the directors, Napoleon, Duke of Wellington, Tsar Alexander I, First Estate, Second Estate, Third Estate, Marat, Danton, Catherine the Great, Kosciuszko, Pope Pius VII, Nelson, Louis XVIII

Places: Bastille, Trafalgar, Niemen River, Waterloo, Batavian Republic, Kingdom of Westphalia

Events: economic crisis in France; summoning the Estates General; formation of the National Assembly; the Terror; partition of Poland; rise of Napoleon; wars of the Emperor; Battle of Waterloo; Battle of Trafalgar; Battle of the Nations

Define

Parlement of Paris	Declaration of the Rights of Man
Commune	Civil Constitution of the Clergy
Code Napoleon	Continental System
Grand Armée	nationalism
National Assembly	Peace of Amiens
Legislative Assembly	Jacobins
Confederation of the Rhine	First Consul
The Convention	First Coalition
Orders in Council	

Multiple Choice

1. The privileged classes of France were
   (a) nobility and clergy.
   (b) bourgeoisie and clergy.
   (c) courtiers and soldiers.
   (d) soldiers and nobility.

2. The Catholic bishops in France formed the
   (a) First Estate.
   (b) Second Estate.
   (c) Third Estate.
   (d) none of the above.

3. Lawyers and doctors were to be found in
   (a) the First Estate.
   (b) the Second Estate.
   (c) the Third Estate.
   (d) all the above.

4. The Peace of Paris gained this territory for France:
   (a) Nova Scotia
   (b) Louisiana
   (c) Florida
   (d) none of the above

5. The economic problems of the royal government were aggravated by the
   (a) Parlement of Paris refusing to register a government loan.
   (b) piracy in the Atlantic.
   (c) deflation of the currency.
   (d) inflation.

6. The storming of the Bastille symbolized
   (a) the failure of the Estates General.
   (b) the rise of the bourgeoisie.
   (c) the weakness of the king.
   (d) reaction to British interference in France.

7. "Men are born free and equal in rights" was a sentence taken from
   (a) Rousseau.
   (b) Voltaire.
   (c) Jefferson.
   (d) the Declaration of the Rights of Man.

8. The Legislative Assembly
   (a) enhanced the power of the king.
   (b) allowed the king only to suspend action.
   (c) gave the king the right to veto legislation.
   (d) none of the above.

9. In the early days of the revolution, they were the most radical:
   (a) the Dominicans
   (b) the Girondists
   (c) the Jacobins
   (d) the National Guard

10. The nations that partitioned Poland were
    (a) Russia, Sweden, and Prussia.
    (b) Austria, Sweden, and Prussia.
    (c) France, Austria, and Russia.
    (d) Russia, Prussia, and Austria.

11. The dominant figure in the Convention was
    (a) Marat.
    (b) Robespierre.
    (c) Danton.
    (d) Napoleon.

12. Napoleon's birthplace was in
    (a) Paris.
    (b) Sardinia.
    (c) Genoa.
    (d) Corsica.

13. Napoleon's original title was
    (a) First Consul of the Republic.
    (b) Director.
    (c) General of the Army of Flanders.
    (d) Minister of Public Safety.

14. Napoleon capitalized on this emotion that drew upon the legacy of the revolution:
    (a) liberalism
    (b) democracy
    (c) conservatism
    (d) nationalism

15. The Cisalpine Republic was located in
    (a) northern Italy.
    (b) southern Italy.
    (c) Switzerland.
    (d) France.

16. Napoleon settled the religious opposition to the revolution through
    (a) the Treaty of Rome.
    (b) a Concordat with Pope Pius VII.
    (c) persecution of the church.
    (d) reaching an agreement with the Archbishop of Paris.

17. The reform of the law effected by Napoleon was the
    (a) Justinian Code.
    (b) Common Law.
    (c) Peace of Amiens.
    (d) Code Napoleon.

18. In 1804 Napoleon took a new title:
    (a) President
    (b) King of France
    (c) Emperor of France
    (d) King of Italy

19. Napoleon's efforts to cut off outside trade with Great Britain was known as the
    (a) Orders in Council.
    (b) London Embargo.
    (c) Continental System.
    (d) Atlantic Blockade.

20. On a raft in the Niemen River, Napoleon came to terms with
    (a) Russia.
    (b) Prussia.
    (c) Austria.
    (d) Poland.

21. Napoleon's defeat in Russia was caused by
    (a) superior arms of the Russians.
    (b) winter and lack of supplies.
    (c) Tsar Alexander's victory at Borodino.
    (d) Alexander's victory at Smolensk.

22. Napoleon's first place of exile was
    (a) St. Helena.
    (b) Elba.
    (c) Vilnius.
    (d) Warsaw.

23. The victor at Waterloo was
    (a) the Duke of Wellington.
    (b) the Marquis of Portugal.
    (c) the king of Prussia.
    (d) Tsar Alexander I.

Essay Questions
1. Explain the coming of the French Revolution.
2. Compare the American Revolution with the French Revolution.
3. What happened in France to explain the rise of Napoleon?
4. Why is the French Revolution a turning point in European history?

Answers

1. a	6. c	11. b	16. b	21. b
2. a	7. d	12. d	17. d	22. b
3. c	8. b	13. a	18. c	23. a
4. d	9. c	14. d	19. c	
5. a	10. d	15. a	20. a	

CHAPTER 14

Politics in Europe from 1815 to 1914

After the Napoleonic wars it was time to mend Europe. In 1814 states-men and diplomats converged on Vienna to put the world back together following the pattern of the eighteenth century. Legitimacy and compensa-tion were the two guiding principles. Monarchs ousted by Napoleon were put back on their thrones. Where boundary changes were in order, diplo-mats looked for ways to offer compensation. The goal was to keep a bal-ance of power among Europe's Great Powers.

Congress of Vienna

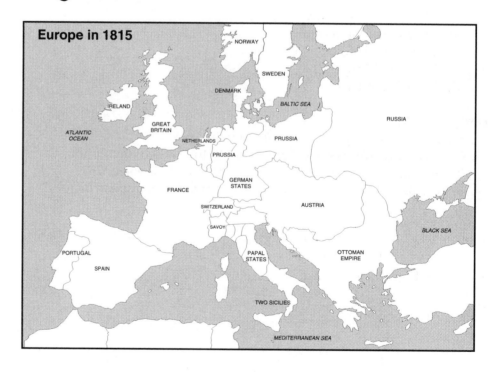

Included in the visitors to Vienna for the Congress were six monarchs, their advisors, and a host of servants totaling in the thousands. Vienna, a city noted for its music and good eating, filled with soldiers from all European armies, draped in the dazzling colors of full dress uniforms. At nightfall the theaters and cafes opened to capacity crowds. Ludwig van Beethoven was present to direct Mozart's concerts. In the theater the plays of Johann von Schiller delighted audiences. High stake gambling was a major diversion.

The Austrian Foreign Minister, Prince Klemens von Metternich orchestrated the Congress in the name of his sovereign, Francis I. In 1806 Francis, who had divested himself of the title of Holy Roman Emperor and was content to become Emperor of Austria, also agreed to give up the Southern Netherlands. In return Austria regained its primary position in the German Confederation. Austria would head this body of 38 members. Prussia was the second most important state, and its gain of Rhineland territories gave it a hold in western as well as eastern Germany.

The Russians, represented by Tsar Alexander I, secured major territorial additions. Finland was taken from the Swedes, and the province of Bessarabia secured from the Ottomans, one time allies of the French. The tsar added most of Poland to his dominions, permitting him to claim that he was now King of Poland.

Metternich addresses the delegates to the Congress of Vienna.

The British picked up several colonies in the Caribbean and Central America, the island of Malta, and Cape Town in South Africa. London diplomats were most anxious to keep a balance among the continental nations to ensure a lasting peace. Therefore, Viscount Robert Castlereagh, the British foreign minister, argued that the French should be treated with leniency. He did not want to make the position of the restored Bourbon monarch, Louis XVIII, too difficult. While in their deliberations, Napoleon left Elba for his "one hundred days," putting a scare into the Viennese diplomats. Waterloo ended the crisis.

Liberalism and Conservatism

Two contrasting philosophies dominated the 1800s. One was **liberalism.** Liberalism in this age stressed individualism, freedom from oppressive government, and the right for men and women to speak, publish, and worship as they wanted. Liberals believed that monarchical governments had too much power. A charter or constitution should put limits on what kings could do. Continental liberals judged the written constitution of the United States and the unwritten constitution of Great Britain to be models of political good sense.

The nineteenth-century liberal believed in liberty but not in equality. Basically a middle class phenomenon, liberalism held that the lower classes were a danger to good government. People who had little wealth were apt to threaten those who held property if they were allowed to get into positions of power.

In England Jeremy Bentham taught that society should aim to provide "the greatest good for the greatest number." He represented the English liberal opinion "that government that governed least, governed best." On the continent, liberals made common cause with nationalists. This was especially true among Germans and Italians, who remained politically divided without a center around which to unite.

Conservatives, of course, reacted against liberals, arguing that tradition was more important than change, the safe path better chosen than the unknown. They thought of the French Revolution as a bad dream. In Europe after 1815, the conservatives held the positions of power.

The painter Delacroix portrays Liberty leading the French people against tyranny.

Metternich was very concerned to keep a lid on potential troubles caused by liberals and nationalists in central Europe. His first challenge came as soon as 1817 when German students organized a protest to conservative rule. The Austrian Foreign Minister in response sponsored the **Carlsbad Decrees,** a series of laws that banned secret societies and censored all publications. The next eruption against the system occurred in Spain. A revolution there toppled King Ferdinand VII. Ironically a French army marched into Spain and rescued his throne; then attention focused on Greece.

Greek Revolution

In 1821 the Greeks in the Peloponnesus rose up against Turkish rule in a series of attacks upon army barracks and the homes of Muslim landowners. The Peloponnesian revolt coincided with an invasion of a Greek army into the Ottoman province of Moldavia. This army, captained by Alexander Ypsilantis, was raised on Russian soil and counted on the support of Tsar Alexander I. The invasion, however, was a total failure militarily and the tsar, conscious of his role as the pillar of stability in Europe, disavowed any interest in the Greek cause.

Throughout Europe educated people were trained in the classics, and their admiration for ancient Greece created an outpouring of sympathy for their descendants. Governments might wince, but the press and public opinion were unanimous in urging intervention. Lord Byron, the most romantic of the English poets, went to Greece to join the rebellion and died there.

The Ottoman sultan, Mahmud II, sent his army into Greece each spring, but the rebels simply melted into the mountains. The sultan became well aware of the Janissary decline and his soldiers' unwillingness to stay the course in Greece during the winter. Consequently, the sultan appealed for help from Egypt.

An Ottoman army's massacre of the population on the island of Chios stirred up sympathy for the Greeks.

The Egyptian governor, Muhammad Ali, agreed to send a force to Greece. In European capitals the Egyptian invasion was regarded as particularly offensive. The governments of Great Britain, France, and Russia finally concluded that they must act. An allied fleet sailed into the Bay of Navarino, the base for the Egyptian-Turkish flotilla, and sank almost all its vessels. A Russian declaration of war on the sultan followed.

Diplomats finally prevailed upon the Turks to permit an independent Greece. However, they drew the borders of the new state very narrowly, leaving a majority of Greek people under the sultan's sovereignty. Nevertheless, in 1830 the creation of a Greek state first broke down Metternich's system for preserving the territorial integrity of all European countries.

Nationalist Revolutions in the Netherlands and Poland

Hardly had the Greek revolt been resolved, when an uprising took place in the Southern Netherlands. The leaders of this rebellion wanted to break away from the seven United Provinces of the Netherlands. The rebels, Flemings and Walloons, first demanded home rule. When they did not receive it, they took up arms. Their cause succeeded, and a new country, Belgium, appeared on the European map.

A revolt in Poland was next. Nicholas I, tsar after 1825, harbored an intense dislike of Poles. In 1830 his policies brought them to the point of rebellion. At first Polish armies met with success, but without outside money and munitions, their effort to force out the Russians was doomed. At length, in September 1831 the Russians captured Warsaw. The tsar proceeded to annex the Polish territories to Russia, and a vigorous suppression of nationalist sentiment became the rule for the next several decades.

France

There was a feeling in Europe that if the French sneezed, all Europeans caught a cold. Therefore, the uprisings in Poland and the Netherlands were blamed on the French, for in 1830 the people of Paris had descended into the streets demanding the ouster of the reactionary Bourbon monarch, Charles X. Charles called on the army to resist the protestors, but it refused.

Even though many leaders of the revolution wanted the restoration of a republic, realists recognized that a monarchy would be more acceptable to the rest of Europe. At the news of the fall of Charles, Tsar Nicholas proclaimed, "Gentlemen, saddle your horses, the French are in revolt." Therefore, a better solution was to enthrone a relative of the Bourbons, Louis Philippe, Duke of Orleans. Louis Philippe gave the country a good bit of latitude, dressed like a French businessman, and promoted economic development in preference to political change.

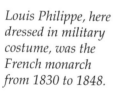

Louis Philippe, here dressed in military costume, was the French monarch from 1830 to 1848.

Reform in Great Britain

In 1815 Great Britain stood out as the country that had been the major factor in Napoleon's defeat. An era of tranquility and peace seemed to lay in the future. Yet there were problems. The Tories, the dominant party in Parliament, proved unwilling or unable to solve the employment problems of the veterans of the Napoleonic Wars. The soldiers returned home to find no work. Moreover, Tory politicians saw to it that Parliament voted to protect their interests from competition from cheaper foreign grain in a series of acts called the **Corn laws.**

Reform came slowly in a number of ways. Robert Peel, a Tory leader, sponsored legal reform, mitigating the barbarous practice of beating a prisoner or putting a person to death for small crimes. Peel placed policemen on London's streets, and the name they still carry, **bobbies,** is a testament to his efforts. Eventually in 1846 the Corn laws were repealed.

The migration of workers from rural areas into new cities and the expansion of older urban areas created a demand for political change. The new cities had no representatives in Parliament, whereas many rural areas were so depopulated that they were known as rotten boroughs. In these boroughs a handful of voting landowners decided elections. The Reform Act of 1832 increased the electorate by 50%, and the cities finally received representation. Now more manufacturers and businessmen took their seats in the House of Commons.

The Peoples of Central Europe

The Germans were well aware that the system of Metternich kept them divided and politically weak. As a nation they could not speak with a single voice. Therefore nationalists, to Metternich's dismay, kept up pressure for a united Germany. In the forefront of the movement were academics, journalists, and other professionals.

Progress first appeared in the economic sphere. Prussia, the strongest state of northern Germany, invited other German principalities to join in a common customs union, the **Zollverein.** In 1834 the union held 17 members with a population of 36,000,000 people. Trade passed back and forth freely within the union. The fact that Austria did not join the Zollverein allowed the Prussians to assume the economic leadership of the German states.

Russian Empire

Russian prestige reached a new height after Tsar Alexander I's armies turned the tide against Napoleon. Russia was the largest of European states, reaching from the Baltic to the Pacific, including Alaska. In all, one sixth of the inhabited surface of the earth was a part of this great empire.

What distinguished Russian society was the great gap between rich and poor. At the top of the social order, a group of aristocrats, the landowning class, were dominant. Men in this class served in military careers and filled the bureaucracy. The other 90% of the people were serfs, barely able to eke out a living.

Within the small class of noblemen and women were those whose travels and western education caused them to dream of political and economic reform. For a time, it appeared that Alexander was open to change. He allowed the landowners of the Baltic provinces to free their serfs. However, after 1815 his actions became so inconsistent that his commitment to any policy was hard to discern.

In this kind of atmosphere, a number of military officers planned how they might change Russia for the better. Attracted by democracy and the freedom from arbitrary rule that existed in western Europe, they organized secret societies.

In December 1825 Alexander died, although a persistent rumor claimed that he disappeared into a monastery. His younger brother, Nicholas, was named heir. This arrangement passed over Constantine, an elder brother. In St. Petersburg, soldiers gathered to take an oath of allegiance to the new ruler. Their officers planned to challenge Nicholas on the occasion. They encouraged their troops to cry out for, "Constantine and Constitution!" Apparently, most soldiers thought Constitution was the name of Constantine's wife.

Nicholas led loyal troops to the square and sought to disarm the rebel regiments. The conspirators, whom history knows as the **Decembrists,** fought back. It was an unequal struggle. Nicholas' troops either killed the Decembrists or took them prisoner.

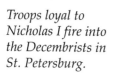

Troops loyal to Nicholas I fire into the Decembrists in St. Petersburg.

This experience so unnerved the new tsar that reaction marked his long rule. He was convinced that conspiracies were everywhere and created a secret police force, the **Third Section,** to infiltrate any group bent on reform. It was so effective that the Decembrist movement did not survive.

The government made no move to ameliorate the poverty of the masses of serfs. During the 30 years of Nicholas's rule, Russia moved backward, not forward. Its institutions failed to change, and in remaining static Russia lost the prestige it enjoyed after the Napoleonic wars.

1848 Revolutions

The movement to remedy the Congress of Vienna occurred 33 years later, in the year of revolution, 1848. At that time revolts broke out in every major city of central Europe. What prompted these events? Principally, it was a joining of liberals and nationalists demanding change. So long kept out of political power, the sons of the Napoleonic generation demanded that they be included in the policy-making of the government. In countries where ethnic minorities were present, the uprisings were demands for independence and self-determination. The revolts fed on each other. When news of demonstrations in one city reached another, it sparked action there.

One more time, France led the way. The colorless Louis Philippe became increasingly unwelcome among French citizens. By 1848 nearly everyone agreed Louis Philippe was dull, and the French could not tolerate dull leaders. In February 1848 revolutionaries of many stripes demanded that the king step down. He agreed and left for British exile. The leaders of the revolutionaries set up a provisional government in Paris. Most were republicans, inspired by the events of 1789. The economic rebels wanted more than political change. Louis Blanc, their charismatic leader, promoted the idea that the government had a duty to respond to the needs of the unemployed. As a result, **National Workshops** were established but were badly managed and underfunded. This experiment to help the poor earn a living soon became discredited.

In April a constituent assembly, elected by the vote of 9,000,000 Frenchmen, drew up a constitution that cancelled all the efforts of the Parisian followers of Blanc. For three days Paris was the scene of battles between the army and those supporting reform. The military then gained the upper hand. When the election for president took place in December, it was a Bonaparte who won, proving that magic was still associated with the name. This was Louis Napoleon Bonaparte, a nephew of the famous emperor. Like his uncle, Louis Napoleon had ambitions, but at this moment they lay hidden.

In the various German states the news that the French were in a revolutionary mood caused liberals and nationalists to break into a fever. Rather quickly a number of princes decided that prudence dictated that they come up with constitutions. More difficult to attain was the task that nationalists set before themselves, the quest for a united Germany.

Revolutionaries in Berlin took to the streets in August 1848 to demand a constitution.

The hopes for this new nation rested in a convention that met at Frankfurt. The **Frankfurt Assembly** included a majority of academics and professionals. In theory its members represented the various states of the German Confederation. Unfortunately, few had any practical experience.

As the debate on creating a unified German nation opened, the Austrians found themselves on the defensive and walked out. The delegates therefore offered the crown of a united Germany to the Prussian king, Frederick William IV.

Frederick William was none too anxious to respond. The constitution makers insisted that the new "Emperor of the Germans" should be dependent on popularly elected representatives, but Frederick William claimed he was king by divine right. Therefore, he rejected the title and, in time, the members of the Frankfurt Assembly went home. Frederick had made his point. A united Germany under a parliamentary democracy would have to wait.

In Vienna everyone seemed to be after Metternich's head. He fled the Habsburg capital, his house in flames, leaving Emperor Ferdinand I to promise reforms. Throughout the empire demonstrators marched in the streets. In Prague the Czechs and in Budapest the Hungarians demanded autonomy, if not complete independence. Revolts in Italy were also initially successful. The distressed Ferdinand abdicated in favor of a nephew, Franz Josef.

Conservatives among Franz Josef's advisors urged him to use the army against the protestors, and this proved effective everywhere but in Hungary. In Budapest the nationalists were strong enough to declare independence, draw up a constitution, and form a national army. The leader of the revolution, Louis Kossuth, organized the Hungarian resistance for several months. Then 80,000 Russian troops struck Hungary from the east. It marked the end of the revolution. The Russian general sent a note to Vienna, "Hungary is at the feet of Your Majesty."

Two years after they began, the revolutions of 1848 were at an end. They failed because the middle class liberals and nationalists were too few in number. The majority of central Europe's peasant farmers remained untutored about politics and nationalism, so they withheld their support.

The Creation of Italy

Nowhere was nationalism so fervently held among university students than in Italy. Not since the final days of the Roman Empire had the peninsula really been a single state. "Italy was," according to Metternich, "but a geographical expression."

The Congress of Vienna allowed Austria to hold a predominant position in Italy. Vienna directly ruled the northern provinces of Lombardy and Venetia. The monarchs in the smaller Italian states only governed with Austrian consent. An exception was the kingdom of Sardinia-Piedmont, for it was actually free of Habsburg oversight. The Papal States occupied central Italy, and the kingdom of Naples, the poorest part of Italy, was in the south.

Secret revolutionary societies flourished in this atmosphere. The largest was the **Carbonari.** Members enlisted a large number of political activists to its cause. Giuseppe Mazzini provided intellectual leadership to this movement. He authored a large number of tracts and pamphlets to fuel ambition for a unified nation, calling his organization, **Young Italy.**

Camillo di Cavour was the architect of a united Italy.

Complementing Mazzini's publications were the policies of Count Camillo di Cavour, the prime minister of Sardinia-Piedmont. Cavour used every opportunity to strengthen his nation's claims to the leadership of all Italy. His most significant success came when he enlisted the aid of Louis Napoleon Bonaparte for his cause. The emperor promised French military aid to Sardinia-Piedmont to drive the Austrians from Italy.

In 1859 a brief but decisive campaign brought the combined French and Piedmontese armies partial success. The area around Milan, the Lombard region, was taken, but the Austrians still held Venice and its nearby territories. Uprisings in other Italian states enabled a declaration of Italian nationhood to be made in Turin, the Sardinian capital.

Giuseppe Garibaldi leaves Genoa on his expedition to overthrow the Bourbon king of Naples.

At this moment a new actor, Giuseppe Garibaldi, came on stage. For much of his life, Garibaldi had pursued the career of soldier of fortune. He was now prepared to do the same in his native country. Garibaldi organized an army of Red Shirts and with it invaded Sicily. He toppled the Bourbon king of Naples making Garibaldi the dominant leader in southern Italy. Then Cavour convinced Garibaldi to add his conquest to the Italian state in the north. Rome still remained outside Italy, but in 1870 the Italian national army marched into the city, declaring it the capital of a single national government. Pope Pius IX and his successors refused to acknowledge the loss of the Papal States and retreated into the Vatican in a gesture of protest.

Germany Becomes a Nation

The architect of German unification was Otto von Bismarck, chancellor of Prussia from 1862 until 1890. Called to that office during a period of crisis, the new chancellor laid his cards on the table, "The great questions of the time cannot be solved by speeches and parliamentary majorities—that was the mistake of 1848 and 1849—but by blood and iron." Bismarck saw to it that the army lacked nothing in keeping abreast of the latest weaponry.

In 1866 Bismarck used a conflict in the northern duchies of Schleswig-Holstein to trick Austria into war. In June 1866 Bismarck dispatched troops into Austrian-occupied Holstein. Franz Josef's generals then blundered into a war against Prussia. The contest was over in seven weeks, for the Prussians easily rolled over the Habsburg armies. The peace treaty added 5,000,000 new subjects to Prussia. The southern German states, however, remained wary of Prussia. What Bismarck needed was a French attack, so that he might come to their "rescue."

Once more the Iron Chancellor, as Bismarck was known, engineered a provocation. Emperor Louis Napoleon Bonaparte fell into the trap. The French declared war without considering Prussia's military strength and new weapons. Once again a Prussian tide crushed an opposing army. Louis Napoleon and his army had no choice but to surrender.

In May 1871 Bismarck chose the Hall of Mirrors in the Versailles Palace to declare a unified German empire. The southern German states now clamored to get inside. The Germans also annexed the French province of Alsace-Lorraine and forced Paris to agree to a large indemnity.

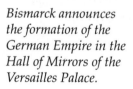

Bismarck announces the formation of the German Empire in the Hall of Mirrors of the Versailles Palace.

Bismarck's Germany made the state the most important institution of the nation. Hence, the chancellor, in the name of the government, began a campaign against the Catholic church. Bismarck rightly judged that members of this church also held an allegiance to a worldwide community. This struggle with the church is known as the **Kulturkampf.**

In 1878 Bismarck determined that Socialists had become more dangerous than Catholics, therefore, he sponsored legislation to outlaw the Socialist Party, but its candidates, under another label, continued to win elections to the Reichstag, the German parliament. In order to wean the workers from Socialism, Bismarck sponsored social legislation that made Germany the first welfare state in Europe.

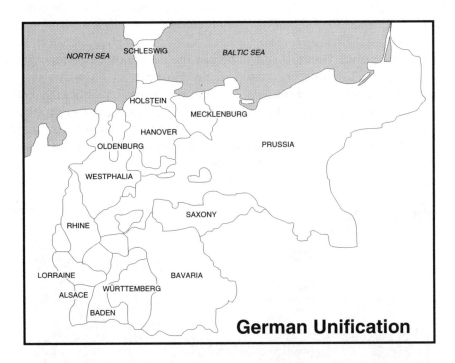

German Unification

France Searches for a New Beginning

When Louis Napoleon Bonaparte became president of France, he announced, "The name of Napoleon is in itself a program. It stands for order, authority, religion and the welfare of the people in internal affairs, and national dignity in public affairs." Apparently this was what the French electorate wanted. In 1852 a plebiscite offered Louis Napoleon the title of emperor.

Over the next two decades the emperor followed a course that gave France renewed optimism for the future. Manufacturing prospered as did banks and agriculture. The emperor also embarked on a major renovation of Paris. Broad boulevards replaced narrow medieval streets. New bridges crossed the Seine, and the city sparkled with its fresh look.

The emperor's search for brilliance in foreign affairs, however, was not so successful. First there was the Crimean War. Louis Napoleon insisted that the Turks allow the Franciscan friars, not the Orthodox, to control the

Christian churches in Jerusalem and Bethlehem. The Russians supported the Orthodox claims and went to war with the Ottomans rather than negotiate a settlement. Both the French and British regarded the conflict as one more example of St. Petersburg's plan to destroy the Ottoman Empire, and this they resolved to resist. Fought in the Crimea, the war's main action was a siege of the Russian naval base of Sevastopol. In this conflict, France, although on the winning side, lost 100,000 men and millions of francs.

Other military ventures kept the French army busy. In 1859 it had assisted the unification of Italy. In 1861 Louis Napoleon ordered troops into Mexico, a venture that ended six years later, with his candidate to lead that country executed. His last and final mistake was his commitment to the Franco-Prussian War. When released from captivity, he went into exile in Great Britain.

In Paris the population refused to accept the reality of a German victory. Led by the city's officials organized in the **Commune,** Parisians went to war with the national government. Now in its Third Republic, the French army battled the Communards. Even though the Parisians fought bitterly, the Republic's army was so much stronger that the issue was never in doubt. At the war's conclusion some 20,000 people lay dead and another 10,000 were arrested, shot, or sent into exile.

A firing squad prepares to execute members of the Commune of Paris.

Within the Chamber of Deputies, the French parliament, monarchists and republicans were constantly bickering. A good indication of the division within the country between Right and Left grew out of the arrest for treason of Alfred Dreyfus, a Jewish officer in the French army. In 1898 Dreyfus was accused of betraying military secrets, convicted, and sentenced to Devil's Island, the notorious prison of French Guiana. The conservative forces in France, noted for anti-Semitism, lined up for Dreyfus' conviction. The republicans wanted acquittal. As it turned out, Dreyfus had been framed and was later exonerated.

European Jews

The growing force of nationalism in France, and throughout all of Europe in the late nineteenth century, made life difficult for minorities. No group suffered quite as much as the Jews, although the Gypsies were not far behind.

Since the Middle Ages life in Europe was burdensome for Jews. Discrimination followed them wherever they went. In an era of nationalism, they did not fit in. On the theoretical level, racism received support from a French diplomat, Arthur de Gobineau. In his *Essay on the Inequality of Races* Gobineau argued, "The racial question overshadows all other problems of history. It holds the key to them all. The inequality of the races from whose fusion a people is formed is enough to explain the whole course of its destiny." Published in four volumes between 1853 and 1855, its message was often repeated in the work of other authors.

Those Europeans who were unemployed or were stuck at the bottom of the social ladder looked for a scapegoat and found it in a "Jewish conspiracy." Politicians, noting its popularity, ran for office on a program directed against Jews. In France the Dreyfus trial demonstrated the depth of this agitation.

Great Britain in Victorian Times

The British escaped the turbulence of the 1848 revolutions on the continent. The nineteenth century continued to bring peace, except for the interlude of the Crimean War. London was very prosperous, at the center of international banking and insurance. In 1851 the British put on a public display of their accomplishments in the world's first great international exhibition, the **Crystal Palace.**

The palace was actually a giant greenhouse, 1,848 feet long, 460 feet wide, and 600 feet high. A million square feet of glass covered the expanse. Inside were exhibits from all over the British empire and other participating nations.

Since 1837 the nation's queen was Victoria, a lady of sober, moral dignity. She was, until her death in 1901, the model monarch. The two great statesmen of the era were William Ewart Gladstone, head of the Liberal Party, and Benjamin Disraeli, the leader of the Conservatives. The Tories were now called Conservatives and the Whigs, Liberals.

The single most intractable problem in Parliament was what to do about Ireland. In the 1840s a terrible famine struck that nation, killing a million people and forcing another million to leave their homeland or starve to death. Yet British landowners, heavily represented in the House of Lords, were adamant that they would do nothing to alleviate the distress of Irish tenants. Although many Catholics and Protestants in the south of Ireland wanted **Home Rule,** the Presbyterians in Ulster firmly rejected separation from the British crown.

The interior of the Crystal Palace held exhibits from all over the British Empire.

The Irish problem caused a major change in the way the British nation was governed. Even though Commons three times passed bills permitting Home Rule, the House of Lords voted them down. The result was the Parliamentary Act of 1911 that limited the House of Lords to a temporary delay over legislation that the House of Commons passed. The House of Lords became a debating society.

Untouched was the issue of women's suffrage. Although it was often talked about, little had been done about it. Women's lobbying, the circulaton of petitions, and the sympathetic writings of John Stuart Mill, the nation's eminent philosopher, brought few converts to the issue. A faction of suffragettes, Emeline Pankhurst and her daughters, took more active measures. They heckled politicians at public meetings and chained themselves to the railing before the prime minister's residence. Women in sympathy with them smashed windows and started fires. The British public both admired and were angered at their methods to obtain the vote.

A suffragette distributes literature supporting women's rights.

Spain and Portugal Fall Behind

The leading nations of the sixteenth century, the peoples of Spain and Portugal, had little impact on continental events of the late 1800s. The farmers of both nations toiled on the estates of the great landowners who dominated the political and economic life of the countries. The only stable institutions were the church and the army, and the views of the leaders in both were steeped in reaction. As a result challenges to their authority appeared out of the small middle class. One of these was **anarchism.** Anarchists held an ideology that argued all government was evil and should be abolished. The result was riots, revolts, and assassinations that the authorities brutally suppressed.

In 1898 Spain lost its last colony in the Americas when the United States claimed the right to intervene in Cuba. The Spanish-American War was mercifully brief. At its conclusion, Spain lost Cuba along with Puerto Rico, Guam, and the Philippine Islands to the United States.

The Portuguese held on to their colonial empire more successfully than did the Spaniards. The backwardness of the country, however, paralleled that of Spain.

Austria-Hungary and Its Nationalities

If a person looked at a map in 1850 it would have been obvious that the Austrian Empire was *the* great power of central Europe. What they would have seen was deceptive, however, for although its borders were extensive, in an age of growing nationalism, Austria was an anachronism. The Hungarian Revolution of 1848 not only proved the unhappiness of a major nationality within the empire, but also showed that without Russian help the government in Vienna could not have repressed it.

Franz Josef, emperor after 1848, proved to be the longest reigning sovereign of any European state in modern times. He himself was anything but modern. He refused to ride in an elevator or use a telephone. His interests were in government detail.

Franz Josef, emperor of Austria-Hungary, represented the conservative view of East European monarchs.

The Catholic church held an important role in the empire and promoted loyalty to the dynasty. In return, Franz Josef gave the church control over education. The army also acted to cement the various peoples of the empire. Its language was German so that no matter the origin of conscripts, officers required them to learn enough to be able to follow commands. Finally, the vast imperial bureaucracy contributed to a sense of unity.

In 1866, after the Prussian defeat of Austria in the Seven Weeks' War, the government of Franz Josef decided that a major political shift was needed. Either the Hungarians or the Slavs had to be brought into the empire as full partners, rather than subjects. The government decided to elevate the status of the Hungarians. Henceforward, the empire became known as Austria-Hungary. For the disappointed Habsburg Slavs, the choice confirmed the saying, "The Habsburgs never remember anything and never learn anything." It was Slavic armies that helped Franz Josef defeat the Hungarian rebels only 13 years earlier.

Scandinavian Countries and Switzerland

The three nations of Denmark, Norway, and Sweden, in the far north of Europe, kept their distance from the international scene in the nineteenth century. Earlier large numbers of people migrated to the United States, but after 1870 living conditions improved. Denmark became a world leader in the production of dairy products and livestock breeding.

In 1905 Norway voted to end its union with Sweden and to set off on its own. Lacking the rich agricultural soil of Denmark, the Norwegians turned to the sea. Fishing and whaling were the mainstays of the economy. Sweden's wealth proved to be in its forest industries and iron mines.

In all three Scandinavian nations, political parties sponsored social legislation to protect workers, women, and children from exploitation. The Scandinavian people were ahead of all other European states in their respect for civil rights. Norway was Europe's first nation to grant universal suffrage to all its citizens. In 1913 the law gave women freedom to run for political office.

Switzerland, like the Scandinavian states, stood apart from Great Power politics as much as possible. Its government was a federation of cantons that found Germans, French, and Italians cooperating. The Swiss had both Europe's highest literacy rate and per capita income.

Ottoman Balkans

The Ottoman Empire, like Austria-Hungary, appeared to be one of Europe's strongest nations, but its structure was hollow. It earned a distasteful title, the Sick Man of Europe. Even the Turks themselves realized that they were ill, but they hoped that they would not be allowed to die. They were fortunate that their doctors, the Great Powers, could not agree on how the sick man's estate should be divided among them.

The Balkan peoples, however, were not about to wait for permission to fight for their independence. Inspired by the Greek example, Serbia continued to explore ways to expand its autonomy, which was grudgingly recognized in Istanbul. The Romanians received independence at the end of the Crimean War, and in 1887 Bulgaria became an independent nation.

Abdul Hamid II's Dolmabaçe Palace was built on the shores of the Bosporus.

The last Ottoman sultan of the nineteenth century was Abdul Hamid II. In order to keep his popularity and distract the Turkish population from the real economic and political problems facing the country, he stirred up his Muslim subjects against Christians.

In 1913 a coup toppled the sultan when three military officers, known as the Young Turks, came to power. Unfortunately the Young Turks also espoused extreme nationalism, causing severe discontent among Ottoman minorities.

The Russian Experience

Russia was the third great empire of eastern Europe. In 1850 the majority of Russian people were still bound to the land as serfs. Alexander II, who succeeded his brother Nicholas I, not only inherited the lost Crimean War but an even more serious problem, what should be done about serfdom? Riots in the countryside showed that action had to be taken soon.

A boat on a Russian river employs serfs to pull it upstream.

In 1861 the tsar issued his Edict of Emancipation. This decree allowed the serfs to move about freely and to hold a tract of land that a family could farm. However, each household had to compensate the government for its land through the village community called the *mir*. The peasant, therefore, had a new master, the mir. In order to pay the landowners, the government issued bonds.

Other reforms dealt with local government and education, but none really changed the social situation. As a result, secret societies formed to be rid of the tsar. In 1881 one of these assassinated Alexander. A wave of terror followed, initiated by the army and police in the name of the next tsar, Alexander III. His ministers also sponsored measures meant to break the nationalist movements among the minorities living in Russia. No group suffered as much as Jews. **Pogroms,** riots against Jews, sprung up throughout Belarus and Ukraine.

Late in the century the Russian economic situation improved. Railroad building was especially intense, thanks to an infusion of capital from investors in western Europe. The most famous of the railroads was the Trans-Siberian, completed in 1903 after 12 years of labor. This railroad opened up Russia's Far East to new settlers and industries. It also, however, frightened the Japanese who were equally intent upon expansion in that area. The result, the Russo-Japanese War of 1904, proved to be a disaster for the Russian armed forces.

With the army licking its wounds, reformers in 1905 prevailed upon the tsar to allow a representative assembly, the **Duma** to be elected. For a time the Duma seemed to hold promise, but Nicholas II, tsar after his father's death in 1894, soon learned to harness it and thwart the move to democracy.

Conclusion

The political history of Europe during the nineteenth and early twentieth centuries was a contest between liberals and conservatives, both of them arguing that their view of society was better. The liberals wanted to keep the fruits of the French Revolution while conservatives looked upon this event with extreme suspicion. Had not the revolution ushered in two decades of war?

France, Great Britain, and most other western states made progress in democratic reforms and the protection of human rights that liberals advocated. However, in the Iberian peninsula and in eastern Europe monarchs, propped up by the army, police, and religious authorities, continued to rule with few checks on their power.

Everywhere nationalism captured the allegiance of the middle class. As ties to religious faith waned, nationalism bound people together. Newspapers, magazines, and textbooks used in public schools trumpeted the past glories of the nation.

The period was a time of significant material progress as the standard of living rose for most people in all the states of western Europe except Ireland, Spain, and Portugal. Technology, based upon scientific inventions, created a more comfortable world for the middle class of Europe, who presumed that progress was unstoppable. Few realized that national hatreds could lead them into a catastrophic war.

CHAPTER 14 REVIEW
POLITICS IN EUROPE FROM 1815 TO 1914

Summary

- After the Napoleonic Wars, the leaders of the major states of Europe met in Vienna to restore "legitimate" sovereigns and to redraw some of the boundaries of the European nations.
- Liberals of the nineteenth century believed that every nation needed limited and democratic governments.
- Conservatives of the period supported monarchies and the police, army, and church that upheld them.
- The Greek Revolution of 1821 broke down the system of authoritarian rule when the Greeks rose up against the Ottoman government.
- Britain experienced a period of parliamentary reform.
- The Russian Empire, ruled by autocratic tsars, was the most powerful state in Europe.
- In 1848 liberal and nationalist revolutions broke out in central Europe.
- Italy became a single nation under the leadership of Sardinia-Piedmont.
- Germany united under Prussian leadership with Bismarck its architect.
- The latter nineteenth century in Europe, Great Britain's Victorian Age, was a period of growing democracy and economic expansion.

Identify

People: Metternich, Alexander I of Russia, Louis XVIII of France, Nicholas I of Russia, Peel, Decembrists, Kossuth, Mazzini, Garibaldi, Bismarck, Louis Napoleon, Dreyfus, Victoria of Great Britain, Abdul Hamid II

Places: Frankfurt, Sardinia-Piedmont, Alsace-Lorraine, Sevastopol

Events: Congress of Vienna; revolutions of 1848; unification of Germany and Italy; Franco-Prussian War; struggle for home rule in Ireland; emancipation of Russian serfs

Define

Frankfurt Assembly	Corn laws	Kulturkampf
liberals	Zollverein	Duma
conservatives	Carbonari	pogroms
Carlsbad Decrees	bobbies	Third Section
National Workshops	Young Italy	Commune
Crystal Palace	anarchism	Edict of Emancipation

Multiple Choice

1. The host for the Congress of Vienna was
   - (a) Franz Josef.
   - (b) Louis Philippe.
   - (c) Bismarck.
   - (d) Metternich.

2. He took the title King of Poland after the Congress of Vienna:
   (a) Franz Josef
   (b) Stanislaw Poniatowski
   (c) Alexander I
   (d) Frederick William IV

3. After 1830 he ruled in France:
   (a) Charles X
   (b) Louis Blanc
   (c) Louis Philippe
   (d) Napoleon III

4. Someone who thought that "government that governed least, governed best" in the nineteenth century was known as a
   (a) nationalist.
   (b) conservative.
   (c) liberal.
   (d) communist.

5. The Carlsbad Decrees were meant
   (a) to suppress student dissent in Germany.
   (b) to bring Austria and Hungary into a dual monarchy.
   (c) to encourage free speech in Austria.
   (d) to form a customs union among the German states.

6. Navarino's battle guaranteed
   (a) Serbian independence.
   (b) Belgium's independence.
   (c) autonomy for the Romanian principalities.
   (d) Greek independence.

7. Corn laws in Great Britain favored
   (a) consumers.
   (b) exporters.
   (c) landowning farmers.
   (d) London merchants.

8. In the nineteenth century Austria contained three major ethnic groups:
   (a) Poles, Germans, Croatians
   (b) Austrians, Hungarians, and Slavs
   (c) Hungarians, Italians, Austrians
   (d) Poles, Germans, Slovenians

9. The Decembrist Revolt in St. Petersburg sought
   (a) the depostion of Alexander I.
   (b) Constantine and Constitution.
   (c) the enthronement of Nicholas I.
   (d) the emancipation of the serfs.

10. National workshops were the idea of
    (a) Louis XVIII.
    (b) Mazzini.
    (c) Louis Napoleon Bonaparte.
    (d) Louis Blanc.

11. The leader of the Hungarian revolutionaries in 1848 was
    (a) Mazzini.
    (b) Kossuth.
    (c) Deak.
    (d) Metternich.

12. The intellectual leader promoting a united Italy was
    (a) Cavour.
    (b) Garibaldi.
    (c) Mazzini.
    (d) Louis Napoleon.

13. The pope's response to Italy's seizure of Rome was
    (a) to leave the city.
    (b) to call on help from Austria-Hungary.
    (c) to become a prisoner in the Vatican.
    (d) to flee to Naples.

14. The Franco-Prussian War was planned ahead by
    (a) Frederick William IV.
    (b) Franz Josef.
    (c) Bismarck.
    (d) Kossuth.

15. As a result of the Franco-Prussian War, France lost
    (a) Alsace-Lorraine.
    (b) Provence.
    (c) Nice.
    (d) Brittany.

16. The German parliament was known as the
    (a) Riksdag.
    (b) Reichstag.
    (c) Diet.
    (d) Parlement.

17. The Dreyfus Affair caused French conservative public opinion
    (a) to demand changes in the military.
    (b) to demand a return of the monarchy.
    (c) to support the officer's conviction.
    (d) to demand Dreyfus's release.

18. Zionism became a program for
    (a) Franz Josef.
    (b) Dreyfus.
    (c) Gobineau.
    (d) Hertzl.

19. Home rule for Ireland was not welcomed by
    (a) Ulster politicians.
    (b) members of the House of Lords.
    (c) both of the above.
    (d) neither of the above.

20. Emeline Pankhurst is remembered for her struggle to
    (a) improve Britain's hospitals.
    (b) raise the opportunities for education among poor school children.
    (c) improve London slums.
    (d) get women the vote in Great Britain.

21. After the Seven Weeks' War with Prussia, Franz Josef made them equal partners with Austria in his empire:
    (a) Croatians.
    (b) Bosnians.
    (c) Czechs.
    (d) Hungarians.

22. In 1913 the Young Turks toppled
    (a) Mahmud II.
    (b) Mehmed II.
    (c) Abdul Hamid II.
    (d) Ahmed I.

23. In Russia attacks on Jews were known as
    (a) soviets.
    (b) dumas.
    (c) pogroms.
    (d) mirs.

Essay Questions
1. Discuss the positive and negative features of the Congress of Vienna.
2. Why did the Revolutions of 1848 fail?
3. Compare the goals of Russia with those of Austria in the nineteenth century.
4. Discuss the diplomacy of Bismarck.

Answers

1. d	6. d	11. b	16. b	21. d
2. c	7. c	12. c	17. c	22. c
3. c	8. b	13. c	18. d	23. c
4. c	9. b	14. c	19. c	
5. a	10. d	15. a	20. d	

CHAPTER 15

Industrialization, Urbanization, and Colonialism

After 1830 an era commenced that allowed Europeans to dominate the world politically and economically for just over the next hundred years. The Industrial Revolution was a major cause of Europe's predominance. Armed with new technology, Europeans moved out into the world, settling in the Americas, South Africa, Australia, and New Zealand in the largest migration in world history. In much of Asia and most of Africa, Europeans established control over native peoples.

The Industrial Revolution Begins

Essentially, the Industrial Revolution of Europe meant a steady change that shifted work from human and animal energy to machines powered by steam, electricity, and the combustion of gasses. This revolution became possible thanks to the seventeenth-century scholars who first learned about matter and motion beyond what Aristotle taught his students in ancient Athens. These scientists examined nature and physics with instruments that allowed them to see through telescopes and microscopes and to measure quantities with an accuracy never before possible.

Other changes, actually moving too slowly to be called revolutions, occurred in agriculture and commerce. Landowners learned how to farm using more efficient methods that brought them greater profits. Merchants became more wealthy as overseas trade expanded. The riches gained from increased food production and commerce created a reservoir of money that could be used for investment elsewhere.

Why did the Industrial Revolution not come sooner? People have always been interested in technology that might help them get work done more easily and efficiently. The many inventions of both the ancient and medieval world prove this. For the most part, however, cheap or even free labor prohibited an intensive search for better ways to manufacture a product or harness new sources of energy. Before 1780 the water wheel remained the most efficient form of mechanical energy.

The first essential ingredient for an industrialized society was **capital,** money that can be put at risk to build a railroad, steamboat, or factory. At the beginning of the Industrial Revolution, capital was in precious metals and coinage minted from gold and silver. The production of gold and silver and the profits accumulated from mining added to that of commerce and agriculture meant that capital in Europe was readily available to finance industrialization.

Wealthy people invested their money to build factories, railways, and utility plants in the hopes of making a profit. Credit was available in the form of bank loans and bonds. Businessmen who took their companies public sold stock as another means of capital expansion. Ownership passed to the stockholders, but there was no guarantee of a profit. This kind of economic system is known as **capitalism.**

A second major requirement for industrialization was an adequate labor force, hiring women and men to work in the offices, factories, mines, or railroads. In early capitalist systems, businessmen and factory owners were interested in maximizing profits, and one way to do this was to keep wages as low as possible. The excuse they used for paying so little was that no one was being forced to take a job in their establishments. Yet many people, if they did not want to starve, had to find work wherever it was offered.

A third factor in building a capitalist economy demanded a market for the goods manufacturers offered. When there was not a sufficient number of customers at home, businessmen readily sought foreign consumers, intimately tying colonialism to industrialization.

Great Britain Comes First

Soon after 1780 the Industrial Revolution began in Great Britain, more than two generations ahead of all other European countries. British landowners and merchants, many of them living in Liverpool, who once made their fortunes in the slave trade, were anxious to find new places to put their wealth. During the years accompanying the French Revolution and the Napoleonic Wars, the government demanded more and more products. Uniforms and military supplies, such as sailcloth and cannons, were in short supply.

A woman tends a spinning jenny as it makes thread.

The need for textiles explains why manufacturing first appeared in this industry. Up to the eighteenth century thread-making and weaving were done in thousands of farmers' homes, during the winter, when the weather made it impossible to work in the fields. The whole family was involved, with raw wool or flax brought by a merchant and then collected after it was woven into cloth or linen. During the Napoleonic Wars, British businessmen built factories for cloth-making where large numbers of workers tended the looms that made cloth much faster and of a standard quality.

Before there could be factories to replace the individual weaver, owners had to purchase machinery needed to make the cloth and to find a way to power it. This led to the engine that first produced that energy, the steam engine.

The Steam Engine

The earliest use of the steam engine was not to make cloth but to pump water from mines. When a certain level beneath the earth was reached, water seeped into a mine making it difficult to continue work. As early as 1712 Thomas Newcomen came up with the idea of creating an engine that would take advantage of the power created when hot water becomes steam and expands in a cylinder. In 1769 Newcomen's engine was improved upon by the Scotsman James Watt, who patented a new form of the device. He used gravity, rather than cooling, to have the cylinder's piston fall. Moreover, by adding a series of gears and levers, Watt's engine was able to turn vertical into rotary motion.

There were still problems connected with Watt's invention. Unless the piston fit exactly into the cylinder, the steam leaked, and the engine lost much of its efficiency. It was not until a way was found to cut metal exactly on a lathe that Watt's engine functioned well.

After that happened, cloth merchants throughout England were delighted. They constructed their factories inland near coal mines, because burning coal produced the steam that powered the mechanical looms. Production increased enormously. British wool, linen, and later cotton textiles became so cheap that they replaced individual weavers as far away as India and China.

At the pithead of a coal mine, workers load coal onto pack animals.

The first of the countries on the continent to experience industrialization was Belgium. In 1830 this was a new country whose existence owed much to British foreign policy, and fortunately it had an abundance of coal and metal ore. As a result, British investors and engineers sought positions in Belgian development. Railroads were built, coal mines were opened, and iron and steel mills were put under construction. Belgium's dense population offered an attractive labor supply. Other western European countries experienced their industrial revolutions only after 1870.

Improvements in Transportation and Communication

As the Industrial Revolution developed in Great Britain, finding a better means of transporting goods was essential. First of all, raw materials had to be shipped to the manufacturing site. Second, all the savings from efficient factories were useless unless the finished goods could be distributed to potential consumers. In the latter part of the eighteenth century, the British met this problem by improving roads and investing in canals. In fact, the British became so efficient in digging canals that no part of the island was more than 70 miles from water transportation.

The world's first iron bridge spanned the Severn River in Scotland.

The steam engine proved more versatile than its inventors first imagined. In 1807 the American Robert Fulton put one on board a boat on New York's Hudson River, opening a whole new era of water transportation. European shipbuilders then began the construction of steamboats to ply the rivers of the continent.

The next frontier was the ocean. In 1838 a steamship, the *Great Western*, crossed the Atlantic in 15 days. Two years later Samuel Cunard's line started regular service to the United States from Europe. By 1870 over 3,000 steamships registered under the British flag. Remarkably there was still an equal number of sailing vessels, for tradition died hard on the sea. From 1815 to 1890 the elegant clipper ship ruled the waves. Then the steel hull and screw propeller made sailing vessels obsolete.

If the steam engine could contribute so much to water transportation, it is not surprising that it was also possible to use it on land. In 1825 a stationary engine was used to pull cars on rails. Four years later George Stephenson discovered how to put an engine on wheels. In this way the first railroad made its appearance. The Liverpool and Manchester Railway traveled between the two cities at what was then the breakneck speed of 16 miles per hour. The advantage the railroad offered, moving people and bulky goods quickly and efficiently over long distances, guaranteed the future of the locomotive. By 1851 there were 6,000 miles of track crisscrossing England and Scotland. The obvious superiority of the railroad brought an end to the era of canal building.

At the inauguration of the Liverpool-Manchester Railroad, passengers with cheap tickets rode in open cars, whereas those with the more expensive ones rode in covered cars.

Progress in communications paralleled the advances in other fields. In 1837 the telegraph first appeared, proving that a message could travel on a wire over long distances. Soon afterward technology was sufficiently advanced that it became feasible to lay a cable across the Atlantic. Its success, demonstrated in 1866, brought Europe and North America together, allowing information to pass between the two continents in a matter of minutes.

Manufacturing

Inventions tend to build upon one another. When a better way was found to make a new invention or to increase efficiency in one field, the technology breakthrough was transferred to other means of production.

By far the iron and steel industry profited most from technological improvements. Between 1830 and 1845 British mills increased their output 300%. This advance can be traced to the use of coke rather than coal in smelting the ore. Coke caused the ore to liquify much faster. Later Henry Bessemer improved the process, creating a hotter furnace, so that steel production increased even further. By 1870 factories in Great Britain turned out 500,000 tons of metal as orders for the commodity multiplied.

Along with the continuing increase in steel production, demand for other metals soared. Copper, used since ancient times to alloy bronze and brass, became essential for making wire in the electrical industry. Lead and zinc, also known for centuries, had new uses. In 1883 aluminum, made from bauxite ore, came on line. Tin, when covered with iron, made the tin can indispensable in every household. Although most of these metals were found in Europe, some were not. As they became essential to industry, the western nations sought them in distant lands, contributing to the search for colonies.

A by-product of steel making was coal gas. By 1830 British housewives cooked with gas, and in a few years cities throughout Europe and the Americas used it to light up the night.

Other industries developed at a fast pace, making products more plentiful, cheaper, and usually better. Among these were farm vehicles, shoes, printing presses, glass, and food products.

In 1839 photography developed thanks to Louis Daguerre's experiments. Charles Goodyear, in that same year, discovered how rubber could be used to make a large number of household objects. The armaments industry so expanded with the invention of new weapons and munitions that warfare took on a much more deadly dimension. Petroleum products, for use in making kerosene and cleaning fluids, then appeared on the scene. In 1870 the world consumed 5,500,000 barrels of oil, and only ten years later that number reached 30,000,000 barrels.

Industrial Cities

The urbanization of European life was a direct consequence of the nineteenth-century Industrial Revolution because the first factories were located near the coal fields that fired the machinery. Workers had to live in the immediate location of the factories, drawn there by the jobs that they offered.

For the first two generations of industrialization, working conditions were very harsh. The day might extend from before dawn until 9 or 10 o'clock at night. Girls and women hauled coal from deep in the mines to the entrance in baskets, sometimes forced to crawl the whole way. Factories were often dirty and unhealthy, and safety features were unknown. When workers went home to the tenements where they lived, life was not much better. Crime, alcoholism, and disease were ever present.

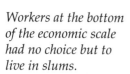

Workers at the bottom of the economic scale had no choice but to live in slums.

Thomas Malthus sought to explain the poverty of workers. He blamed it on the large number of children in their families. With an ever-increasing number of mouths to feed, parents' incomes could not possibly improve.

The theory of **economic liberalism** supported the idea that there should be no regulation of working conditions. Another name for economic liberalism is *laissez-faire* economics. Laissez-faire is French for "Leave it alone." First found in Adam Smith's *Wealth of Nations,* a book that attacked the prevailing mercantilism of European nations, the idea was put forward that government should keep out of economic matters. The balance between supply and demand should determine prices, wages, and labor conditions.

The profits gained from manufacturing went to the factory owners, enabling them to live in spacious homes, eat well, and travel abroad. They could send their children to private schools. Their mansions were quite a contrast to the slums of the workers in the cities.

Over the objections of many factory owners, in the 1830s the British government decided that it had a responsibility to regulate working conditions, mainly to protect women and children from exploitation. Acts of Parliament limited the working hours of women and children and provided for factory inspection. This legislation was expanded in 1842, when Parliament forbade mine owners to hire women or boys under 10 years of age to work underground. Five years later a law established a maximum of 60 hours a week for this same group.

Social critics seldom spoke of the miserable houses of peasants and the squalor of rural life. On the other hand, observers noted the terrible living conditions of the early industrial city in all countries. People lived in attics and cellars and even slept in the streets. Walls in tenements were often paper-thin, and the rooms were impossible to heat. Running water was a luxury for the few.

Although Thomas Crapper perfected the flush toilet in 1837, chamber pots were the only facility available in the tenements. They were emptied out the window into the street, which served as a sewer. Dogs, pigs, chickens, and even people rooted in the garbage. Nearby packing houses, glue factories, laundries, and breweries dumped their refuse into rivers.

Voices of Protest

The impetus for the passage of laws protecting workers first came from humanitarian and religious figures. Methodist clergy were especially active in urging reform. There was also the example of the Scottish industrialist, Robert Owen, who paid his laborers a decent salary and provided them with housing as an example to fellow factory owners. He hoped to prove that it was possible to both make profits and treat workers with dignity. Owen wrote on his ideas in hopes of convincing other businessmen of the soundness of his program.

Another line of protest arose from authors who believed **socialism** was the answer. For them it was the ownership of income-producing property that was at fault. As long as individual owners controlled raw materials, banks, factories, and mines, they argued that the lot of the worker would never improve.

Robert Owen's factory, New Lanark Mills, was meant to be a model for other manufacturers.

Some early advocates of change were Frenchmen who were known as **Utopian Socialists** because they believed that people would adopt their program through persuasion. A much more revolutionary socialism, or **Communism,** appeared in the writing of two Germans who lived much of their lives in England. These were Friedrich Engels and Karl Marx. Together they collaborated on a pamphlet, the *Communist Manifesto.* In it they predicted that the working class, increasingly more desperate, would in time rise up in revolution and seize the property of the ruling class, the bourgeoisie.

The *Communist Manifesto,* published in 1848, threatened not only the economic order as it was then known, but also religion, government, and social stability. Marx claimed that these were projections of the ruling class's domination of wealth and deserved to be abolished or greatly reformed.

The Manifesto discussed the relationship between the workers, called the **proletariat,** and the Communist Party:

> *The Communists disdain to conceal their views and aims. They openly declare that their ends can be attained only by the forcible overthrow of all existing social conditions. Let the ruling classes tremble at a Communist revolution. The proletarians have nothing to lose but their chains. They have a world to win.*
> *WORKING MEN OF ALL COUNTRIES, UNITE!*

Karl Marx, the father of Communism.

Marx spent many years working on a three-volume book in German that he entitled *Das Kapital.* In it Marx thought he had shown, at least to his own satisfaction, that the only solution to workers' poverty was to form a classless society. In this society the means of production were to be held in common; therefore, exploitation would end. In many ways Marx was an idealist whose ideology makes him the last of the thinkers of the Enlightenment. One thing he did not consider sufficiently was another path to a better life through workers' organizations.

Labor Unions

Although some workers were inspired by Marx to form revolutionary groups, others sought less violent means to effect change. After 1825 there had been sporadic attempts for labor organizations to be established in England, but these were limited to a few individuals. Only the prosperity of the 1850s allowed the first major organization, the Amalgamated Society of Engineers, to appear.

Engineers were the people who ran the factories, supervised the businesses, and hired and fired employees. Often they were themselves part of the working class, practically oriented, who actually made the inventions that spurred on the development of industry. One of the necessities for successful businesses was organization. The engineers provided it.

Soon other unions, especially of skilled workers, appeared on the scene. Their weapon, rather than revolution, as Marx contended, was the strike. During a strike the workers sought to shut down a factory or business by refusing to work. Owners, of course, sought to break a strike by hiring new employees or soliciting the government to furnish police or army units to break the will of the strikers.

In 1889 dock workers were sufficiently organized to shut down the port of London. In the next decade, membership in unions grew so rapidly that by 1900 there were 2,000,000 people in the British labor movement.

Life Improves

Concern for the urban environment and life for most workers developed more favorably during the latter part of the 1800s. Wages were more adequate, housing more plentiful, and laborers became more independent as hours of work declined. Because young people obtained jobs at an earlier age, they also married much earlier than they had in a rural setting. There were some significant improvements in city life: the construction of municipal sewer systems that improved sanitation, better streets and lighting, and land being set aside for public parks.

Life in the city influenced the family in several ways. Households had to adapt to the industrial workers' new schedules. The clock instead of the sun came to dictate the routine of the family. However, a number of technological improvements altered family life and the role of women.

The first important changes in the home came from improved ways of heating. Traditionally, the kitchen fireplace not only served as the oven, but it also provided what heat the living quarters possessed. Before the fireplace the entire family gathered to eat and rest. Cast iron stoves for both kitchen use and heating came on the market and by 1850 were commonplace. It was then but a short step to install a single large furnace in the basement of a home with ducts taking heated air to upstairs rooms. After 1870 homes of the rich and upper middle class enjoyed both hot water and steam heat.

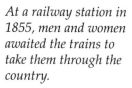

At a railway station in 1855, men and women awaited the trains to take them through the country.

New means of transportation also made life more pleasant. In 1828 horse-drawn trams first appeared in Paris and soon were common on the streets of British cities. The perfection of the pneumatic tire in the 1880s led to the popularity of the bicycle as a means of transportation, and soon afterwards the streetcar appeared. During the first decade of the present century, major cities built extensive subways that have outlasted the appearance of the automobile.

Women in Industrial Society

The impact of urban living in the early 1800s was profound for women. For recent arrivals the new and often strange environment, overcrowding, and polluted water and air often were overwhelming. Their husbands were usually absent from the home for most of the day, and they were left to care for the children in tenements holding dozens of families. Many women also held jobs in factories. If they had to stay home with small children, women used their spare time to embroider, do needlework, or make artificial flowers and umbrellas. Children could sell these objects on the streets.

It was middle class women who felt the full impact of the shift from domestic to industrial production. Such wives were left free to assume full control of their households, the rearing of the children, and even the finances of the household. One consequence of this newly found authority of middle class women was to limit the size of their families. The adoption of improved birth control methods led to fewer children.

Wealthy and upper middle class women became increasingly the directors of vast households. They not only had the care of the children but also had to supervise many servants. In fact, status within society was determined by the number and kinds of servants one could afford. Male servants such as a butler or a coachman were signs that a family had arrived. It was not unusual for wealthy families to have ten female servants. In 1911 half of all working English women were in domestic service.

The daily routine of women considerably changed when two new inventions came onto the market. These were the sewing machine and the typewriter. Although both were perfected by Americans, inventors from many nations contributed to their final success.

In 1846 Elias Howe patented the sewing machine. By this time cloth was cheap, but women still had to sew clothes using a needle. Only in households that could afford a seamstress did wives escape this drudgery. Tailors made the outer garments for men, but did nothing about underwear. A middle class wife with a number of children could spend all her waking hours with needle in hand.

At first sewing machines were large and complex, intended for tailor shops and factories. The introduction of the sewing machine into the factory made possible the ready-made garment industry. Women then found jobs running the sewing machines in the factories. In 1856 the Isaac Singer Company began selling smaller versions on the installment plan. Sewing machines crossed the Atlantic and were soon in homes across Europe.

The typewriter was the other invention that changed the position of women in the nineteenth century. As early as 1875 a typewriter advertisement declared "no invention has opened for women so broad and easy an avenue to profitable and suitable employment as the typewriter." Throughout Europe the typewriter made possible women's introduction into the business world.

Leisure in Urban Society

Prior to 1800 farming people in Europe enjoyed frequent holidays and festivals. Often men and women combined pleasure with work. The church calendar with its seasonal feasts also provided ample opportunities for recreation. This type of amusement lost much of its meaning in the city. Baptisms, weddings, and funerals were still occasions for reunions, but it was often difficult for all the relatives to come together as in the past.

Edouard Manet painted men and women attending a Paris concert.

After the middle of the century, working class men and women turned to a different kind of recreation. They were attracted to amusement parks with merry-go-rounds and roller coasters, to dance halls, and to theaters. Special events such as band concerts, balloon ascensions, and boxing matches were staged to attract customers. Many workers drifted away from church attendance, preferring to spend Sundays relaxing.

The British were first to introduce organized sports. The idea caught on and quickly spread to the continent and North America. Horse racing drew many fans because it also offered people a chance to gamble. Cricket and rugby remained sports of the upper classes. Soccer attracted mass participation and spectator audiences in Britain and in time throughout western Europe.

Much social life for men was spent with friends at a pub or tavern. Ordinary Europeans did plenty of heavy drinking before the age of the city, and urban life gave it more prominence. From 1830 to 1914 the yearly intake of alcohol more than quadrupled.

The leisure activities of the upper classes were less influenced by city life. Those with country estates still spent much time hunting, fishing, riding to the hounds, or giving lavish entertainments. When trains and steamships made travel to distant places possible, this became the expected activity for part of the year. Many of the rich and famous spent the summer at the seashore. In Germany this was the age of the great health spas with the wealthy trying to improve their physical condition by "taking the waters."

The Arts

Often considered the greatest of composers, Ludwig van Beethoven, dominated music in the early nineteenth century. His nine symphonies raised instrumental music to a height that has never been surpassed. A prodigious composer, Beethoven included piano sonatas, string quartets, and vocal music in his works.

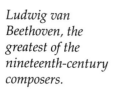

Ludwig van Beethoven, the greatest of the nineteenth-century composers.

Romanticism dominated the great operatic composers of the time: Giuseppe Verdi and Giaccomo Puccini. Claude Debussy, Maurice Ravel, Igor Stravinsky, and Arnold Schoenberg took modern concert music in quite different directions. In 1913 when Stravinsky's *Rite of Spring* was presented, it so outraged the audience that a riot broke out.

The German public preferred poetry and romantic composers such as Felix Mendelssohn, Johannes Brahms, and Franz Liszt. Richard Wagner offered opera lovers a new dimension in music. Béla Bartok in Hungary and Bedrick Smetana and Antonin Dvořák in Bohemia ably represented the musical composers of Austria-Hungary.

Paris was the center of the late-nineteenth-century art world. **Impressionism** was in vogue. This style sought to portray a moment in time in the life of ordinary people. Paul Cézanne, Edouard Manet, Claude Monet, and Auguste Renoir were recognized masters of impressionism.

Vincent van Gogh and Paul Gauguin experimented with vivid light and color. Van Gogh's *Starry Night* captures the artist's intensity. Gauguin offered colorful scenes of South Pacific islanders. Later painters moved into **expressionism,** where depicting emotion became the thrust of the work.

Vincent van Gogh's Starry Night *is ablaze with movement.*

Every nation had its favorite authors and poets in an age where romanticism flourished in literature. Writing in English were the novelists Charles Dickens, Charlotte Brontë, and William Makepeace Thackery. The Scotsman Robert Louis Stevenson entertained readers with his adventure stories, while the poetry of Alfred Lord Tennyson and Elizabeth Barret Browning reached an appreciative audience. French writers of note were Gustave Flaubert, Émile Zola, and the short story author, Guy de Maupassant.

Medicine

The nineteenth century offered significant advances in medicine. The importance of hospital cleanliness and the use of ether and chloroform to anesthetize patients made operations less painful and reduced the danger of infection. Louis Pasteur investigated why milk spoiled. He discovered the cause in the microscopic organisms he named bacteria. His name is now attached to the heating process, pasteurization, that makes milk safe to drink. Sigmund Freud's investigation into the subconscious laid the basis for modern psychiatry.

In 1898 the French husband and wife team, Marie and Paul Curie, published their investigations into radioactivity. They discovered two new elements, radium and polonium, which laid the groundwork for today's use of nuclear medicine.

Scientific Thought

Numerous scientific advances burst upon the world. Few captured the attention of people more than the 1859 publication of Charles Darwin's *The Origins of Species by Means of Natural Selection.* In his work Darwin, a biologist, argued that the huge variety of plants and animals in the world is the result of competition between individuals and species. Some survive, while others disappear. Why? Because the survivors possess some quality that gives them an edge over their competitors.

Because most religious Europeans thought they must take the account of creation as given in the Bible's Book of Genesis literally, Darwin's thesis met much opposition. In 1871 Biblical literalists were more upset when Darwin moved his thesis further to include humans in *The Descent of Man.* In this work Darwin placed people into nature's pattern of the survival of the fittest. He theorized that over time earlier life forms gave birth to the humans that now inhabit the earth.

Charles Darwin's books caused a revolution in biological thought.

By 1900 a consensus among biologists accepted Darwin's evolutionary theory, even if Biblical literalists did not. Darwin never used the term *evolution,* but others applied it to his work.

Following on Darwin's biological thesis, several social scientists took up his argument as a means of understanding societal structure. They held that women were inferior to men because they were weaker and mentally inferior. Some races were stronger than others. The more powerful, which these authors identified with white males, had a natural right to rule over others. **Social Darwinism** conveniently justified women's exclusion from public life as well as European colonialism.

Gregor Mendel, an Austrian botanist, discovered through experimentation in crossbreeding peas, that certain traits are passed on from one generation to another following a pattern. His pioneering work, not appreciated until after his death, gave birth to the study of genetics.

Physicists and chemists participated in a more sophisticated understanding of matter. Often their work overlapped. Max Planck proposed the **quantum theory** of energy. John Dalton published his findings that all matter is made up of tiny particles that he called atoms. The Russian, Dmitry Mendeleyev, organized a **Periodic Table** that arranged elements according to the specific weight of the atoms that composed them.

Although the political structure of Europe had its boundaries, science ignored them. Scholars from all over the European world studied and improved upon one another's work and borrowed ideas from research wherever produced.

Europe's Changing Scene

After 1870 there was a second stage of industrialization that resulted from new inventions and the increased use of power. The most important of the new discoveries was electricity. Zenobe Gramme developed the first dynamo to produce electric power. In the mid-nineteenth century there had been some promising experiments, but it was principally the genius of Thomas Edison, an American inventor, who made the light bulb a reality. His discovery enabled towns everywhere in Europe to replace gas with electricity to provide illumination at night.

In the decade from 1880 to 1890 big business, as we know it today, was born in Europe and the United States. This was due to the establishment of **corporations.** A corporation is a very large business, managed by a number of executives who are responsible to a board of trustees. Corporations could be publicly owned through the sale of stock, or privately owned if an individual or family put up all the capital themselves. The corporation, rather than the individual, is a legal entity, and in case of a disaster of some kind, it is held responsible. Three great corporations were Vickers-Armstrong in Great Britain, Schneider-Creusot in France, and Krupp in Germany. In the United States the Rockefellers and Carnegies founded equally prosperous businesses.

Workers in a mill forge steel.

The automobile made its appearance when two German inventors, Karl Benz and Gottlieb Daimler, put the gasoline combustion engine on wheels. In 1890 Daimler opened his motor company that produced cars. He named them Mercedes, for this was the name of a friend's daughter. By 1900 Europe and America had 13,000 autos on the road.

The invention of the airplane was to change the world, opening a new and exciting means of transportation. In 1903 Orville and Wilbur Wright flew the first heavier than air machine at Kitty Hawk, North Carolina. In 1908 Wilbur Wright took a new model of his airplane to Paris. Here he delighted thousands of people flying circles around the Eiffel Tower for two hours. Telephones and radios also made their appearance early in the twentieth century.

European Migration

The nineteenth century witnessed a huge movement of people in Europe from farms to cities. There was one other migration, as European men and women moved to every other continent bringing their culture with them.

Demographers estimate that nearly 60,000,000 Europeans left their homes from 1815 to 1914 to settle in foreign places. This was the largest emigration known to history. Not all stayed abroad. Fully 20% later returned home. Great Britain, Ireland, Italy, Austria-Hungary, and Germany, in that order, were the countries that supplied the largest number of emigrants crossing the oceans. The chosen destinations were principally the United States, Argentina, Canada, Brazil, and Australia. In the other direction, approximately 7,000,000 Russians moved eastward into Siberian and Inner Asian homes.

The underlying causes of migration were the result of personal decisions of millions of people that life would be better somewhere other than in Europe. By 1850 serfdom was abolished, except for Russia, so men and women were free to move. Governments put no hinderance in their way. The building of railroads and the abundance of steamships offering cheap tickets made the journey possible for the masses. At this time in history, all countries welcomed new arrivals because there was employment for everyone willing to work.

Irish immigrants, fleeing poverty and repression, arrive in New York

After 1900 trade between the continent and the overseas Europeans created a vast world market. Manufactured goods were exchanged and emigrants, who often arrived in new homes with little but a suitcase and a few coins, by the end of their lives enjoyed a level of prosperity that placed them in the middle class.

Capital followed the emigrants' path outside of Europe. London bankers set the pattern for investment through the free exchange of currencies based on the gold standard. Even small investors in Britain, France, and Germany were willing to buy bonds of foreign governments or to purchase stock in companies operating abroad.

The New Imperialism

The mood of Europeans and the attitude they took toward the rest of the world swung back and forth like a pendulum during the nineteenth century. At one time journalists and authors counted on a public eager to hear stories of far away places. At another, Europeans became much more concerned with matters closer to home. Late in the nineteenth century, the hesitation stopped. All over Europe politicians suddenly decided that colonies were necessary for any country aspiring to be a world power.

This movement is known as **colonialism** or the **new imperialism,** for it was not just a matter of trade that became important. Along with European economic interest went colonies of settlers into Asia and Africa.

Wealthy and middle class businessmen, railroad builders, and factory owners eagerly pursued growth. Growth meant looking for new sources of raw materials and for customers in other parts of the world. Bankers and insurance company executives were just as eager to invest in countries abroad as at home.

Military officers constituted another group of Europeans who awakened to world concerns. Generals and admirals, whose task was to guarantee the security of their nation, worried that another country might take the lead in acquiring foreign bases and controlling essential raw materials. Most vocal citizens believed that the military was entirely right and that they deserved the support of the country.

A religious dimension was also linked to the new imperialism. The nineteenth century for the first time found Protestant missionaries in Africa and Asia competing with Catholics for converts. In this case the flag followed the cross. David Livingstone, the most celebrated missionary of the century, was known throughout Great Britain. His popularity was so widespread that when he died in 1873, the government brought back his body to England for burial in Westminster Abbey.

Looking at a map of the world, every school child in Britain could see where red covered the territories over which the Union Jack, their flag, was flying. Every little French student checked the areas that were green. After 1880 each nation, with its color assigned by a consensus among mapmakers, felt a surge of pride when looking at the schoolroom map and knowing that, "We are there."

It is somewhat astonishing to realize that the era of colonialism did not catch on earlier than 1880. Yet in Great Britain, the Liberal Prime Minister

Protestant missionaries first arrived in Africa in the nineteenth century.

Edward Gladstone resisted any further extension of what was already a large British empire. The Liberals were known for their lack of enthusiasm for any more colonies. He and his Cabinet were quite content with a "Little England."

In 1830 the French government set up its first African colony in Algeria. Although it kept a major interest in Algeria, the French were less than enthusiastic about further overseas commitments. At the close of the Franco-Prussian War in 1871, the government of the Third Republic offered to exchange all its colonies in order to retain Alsace-Lorraine. Otto von Bismarck, the German Chancellor, only smiled at the offer.

This attitude changed dramatically only a decade later. In 1882 advocates of expansion formed the German Colonial Society. The argument was thought to be compelling. Germany was a crowded nation. Colonialism would mean the ability to ship surplus population out of the country. For Germans, and for the people among whom they settled, colonization should offer untold benefits.

In London a Royal Colonial Institute paralleled the German society. More importantly, Benjamin Disraeli assumed the leadership of the Conservative Party. Often holding the prime ministry in the late nineteenth century, Disraeli's plan committed the Conservatives to a "Big England." He fervently believed that it was Great Britain's role to lead the European world into the unclaimed lands of Asia and Africa.

France also had its exponents for a large empire. One of its leading economists urged, "Colonization for France is a question of life or death. Either France will become a great African power, or in a century or two, she will be no more than a secondary European state." The same sentiments found echoes in the Belgian, Dutch, and Italian press. Only East Europeans kept apart from the colonizing fever.

Conclusion

There is little doubt that the first period of industrialization was extremely painful for millions of European workers. Low wages and difficult conditions of labor placed their lives only a notch above survival.

However, when unions formed and governmental bodies began to regulate the conditions of labor, prosperity increased. There were booms and busts, and unemployment continued to be a problem, but with all its drawbacks, industrialization meant a better way of life for the descendants of those first workers. There is no way that the world could support the population it now holds without the Industrial Revolution. This event changed people's lives more than anything else since the invention of farming.

The migration of large numbers of Europeans into the Americas, Australia, and other parts of the world was the other major event of the century. Colonization in Africa and Asia transformed life in those lands, for they became bound economically and politically to Europe. The political hegemony of Europe was to last little more than a century in Africa and Asia, but European culture sank its roots so deeply in those lands that it appears to be permanent.

CHAPTER 15 REVIEW
INDUSTRIALIZATION, URBANIZATION, AND COLONIALISM

Summary
- The Industrial Revolution allowed Europeans to shift work from human and animal energy to machines.
- Essential ingredients for industrialization were capital, labor, and markets.
- The first nation to become industrialized was Great Britain.
- Improvements in transportation and communication assisted industrialization.
- The rapid expansion of cities followed upon the construction of factories.
- Voices of protest rose over the plight of the factory workers who remained impoverished.
- One of the most strident of protests against capitalism came from the pen of Karl Marx and Friedrich Engles, who collaborated on the *Communist Manifesto.*
- Women found a place in industrial society working outside the home.
- Charles Darwin's theories on evolution challenged previous ideas on biology and anthropology.
- The migration of millions of Europeans created a very different population shift in the Americas and Australia.
- Colonialism became common in parts of Africa and Asia as Europeans took control.

Identify
People: Newcomen, Watt, Fulton, Cunard, Goodyear, Malthus, Owen, Marx, Singer, Beethoven, Pasteur, Freud, Darwin, Verdi, Benz, Dickens, Disraeli
Places: Liverpool, Belgium, Siberia, Argentina
Events: start of Industrial Revolution in Great Britain; canal and railroad building; women enter the labor market; formation of labor unions; growth of corporations; migration of Europeans; beginnings of the new imperialism

Define

capitalism	socialism	colonialism
laissez-faire	Impressionism	proletariat
economic liberalism	strike	Romanticism
expressionism	new imperialism	Social Darwinism
quantum theory	Periodic Table	corporation

Multiple Choice
1. Before there could be an Industrial Revolution there had to be
   (a) an agricultural boom.
   (b) devaluation of precious metals.
   (c) the end of mercantilism.
   (d) a Scientific Revolution.

2. Before 1780 this was the most efficient form of mechanical energy:
   (a) the windmill
   (b) the water wheel
   (c) the sail
   (d) the raft

3. Credit for building factories came from
   (a) bank loans.
   (b) selling bonds.
   (c) selling stock.
   (d) all the above.

4. An impetus for industrialization resulted from the needs of
   (a) the American Revolution.
   (b) the Napoleonic Wars.
   (c) the War of Spanish Succession.
   (d) the Seven Years' War.

5. Watt is given credit for
   (a) improving the steam engine.
   (b) inventing the steam engine.
   (c) discovering the screw propeller.
   (d) discovering electricity.

6. The first continental nation to industrialize was
   (a) France.
   (b) the Netherlands.
   (c) Denmark.
   (d) Belgium.

7. Before the railroad became the major means of transportation within Europe there were
   (a) canals.
   (b) caravans.
   (c) mule trains.
   (d) clipper ships.

8. The credit for inventing the railroad belongs to
   (a) Watt.
   (b) Newcomen.
   (c) Goodyear.
   (d) Stephenson.

9. The name of Louis Daguerre is associated with
   (a) the iron and steel industry.
   (b) aluminum.
   (c) electricity.
   (d) photography.

10. Economic liberalism wanted
    (a) government regulation of factories.
    (b) standards on production.
    (c) monopolies on essential products.
    (d) no government regulations on business.

11. Robert Owen believed that factory owners must
    (a) fight government regulation.
    (b) pay workers a living wage.
    (c) maximize profit through paying low wages.
    (d) avoid borrowing money to build factories.

12. The *Communist Manifesto* blamed poor working conditions on
    (a) the government.
    (b) religious leaders.
    (c) the army.
    (d) the bourgeois class.

13. One way to determine women who were wealthy was to count the number of their
    (a) household servants.
    (b) pets.
    (c) children.
    (d) new formal gowns.

14. The first large labor organization was the
    (a) Amalgamated Society of Engineers.
    (b) United Coal Workers.
    (c) Teamsters.
    (d) United Dockworkers.

15. Freud's contribution to medicine was in the field of
    (a) psychiatry.
    (b) chemistry.
    (c) optometry.
    (d) dentistry.

16. Natural selection was Darwin's explanation for the
    (a) extinction of certain species.
    (b) survival of certain species.
    (c) rise of primates.
    (d) connection between reptiles and birds.

17. Matter, according to Dalton, was composed of
    (a) the four elements.
    (b) mixtures of gasses and liquids.
    (c) atoms.
    (d) chemical compounds.

18. The *Starry Night* painted by van Gogh is an example of
    (a) expressionism.
    (b) romanticism.
    (c) classicism.
    (d) impressionism.

19. Inventors of the automobile were
    (a) Ford and Chrysler.
    (b) Goodyear and Bessemer.
    (c) Benz and Daimler.
    (d) Orville and Wilbur Wright.

20. The major impetus for European migration in the nineteenth century was
    (a) religion.
    (b) politics.
    (c) adventure.
    (d) economics.

21. After 1890 the European Great Powers began 30 years of colonialism, principally in
    (a) the Americas.
    (b) Asia and Africa.
    (c) Australia.
    (d) India.

22. In England Prime Minister Gladstone favored
    (a) a large empire.
    (b) a little England.
    (c) complete occupation of India.
    (d) none of the above.

Essay Questions
1. What are the essentials for an industrial society?
2. Were women adversely or positively affected by the opportunity to work outside the home? Explain why.
3. How did the *Communist Manifesto* view the world?
4. Discuss the importance of Darwin to the world of science.
5. What explains the migration of Europeans to other parts of the world? How has this affected world history?

Answers

1. d	6. d	11. b	16. b	21. b
2. b	7. a	12. d	17. c	22. b
3. d	8. d	13. a	18. d	
4. b	9. d	14. a	19. c	
5. a	10. d	15. a	20. d	

CHAPTER 16

Imperialism in Africa

In 1800 there were approximately 700 different ethnic groups living in Africa. Each had its own language and culture with its own political system. Some were ruled by absolute kings; others were aristocracies. Many were Muslims, a few were Christian, but the majority were animists who held to traditional religions.

The most prosperous of the African kingdoms were the Ashante and Dahomey on the Atlantic, who were rich because of their participation in the slave trade, and the sultanate of Zanzibar on the Indian Ocean coast. Because new tropical plants from the Americas and Southeast Asia were now grown, the population was on the increase as the food supply expanded.

In the late nineteenth century European governments found Africa a continent ripe for colonization. The impetus for this concern had many sources. Businessmen developed economic pursuits, both for raw materials and markets, and Christian missionaries sought to end, or at least limit, the slave trade and to spread their faith, while politicians thought to enhance their prestige by accumulating vast territories to add to the national domain, a work that their country's nationalists acclaimed.

Egypt under Muhammad Ali

The title, founder of modern Egypt, belongs not to a native of the country, but to an illiterate Albanian general, Muhammad Ali. Born in Kavalla, in 1801 Ali arrived in Egypt as an officer of an Albanian battalion in the Turkish army. He was part of the force that the sultan sent to oust what remained of the French military expedition that had come with Napoleon. When the French were gone, Egypt was thrown into chaos, for the local Mamluk nobility had no desire to allow Ottoman governors back into their country.

Ali shifted his Albanians from one rebel Mamluk to another until, after four years of clever diplomacy and plenty of good luck, Ali could declare himself Pasha of Cairo. A reluctant sultan in Istanbul had no choice but to recognize his claim.

Ali now took on the task of creating an efficient administration and fostering financial institutions to support it. He enlisted Christian Copts and French advisors to aid him in his plan. Muhammad Ali found one cause or another to confiscate most of the land held by the Mamluks. The financial burdens fell principally, as usual, on the peasants, the *fellahin,* who in order to increase their production were "hanged, buried alive, beaten, and loaded with chains."

Because the Mamluks in 1811 still represented a potential threat, Muhammad Ali threw a dinner for several hundred of them at the Citadel of Cairo, his palace. The doors were then locked, and the Pasha's Albanians went through the hall killing them off.

With this problem solved, Muhammad Ali sought to implement his plans to bring Egypt into the nineteenth century. He wanted a native Egyptian army, a reform of agriculture with attention focused on raising cotton, a school system modeled on Europe, and a class of Egyptian administrators trained in western management.

Muhammad Ali greets a visiting British colonel and several French engineers.

Muhammad Ali first used his army against the Saudis in Arabia. He defeated them, pushing them out of Mecca and Medina and, therefore, allowing him to pose as the champion of Islam. In 1820 his soldiers marched southward into the Sudan, where he intended the formation of a slave army of blacks. When this met with such resistance, he resorted to the conscription of fellahin. Anyone so taken never returned. Ali's son Ibrahim commanded the force, and when Sultan Mahmud sought help against the Greek revolutionaries, Ibrahim's army came to his aid. For his services to the sultan, Muhammad Ali demanded that the Ottomans turn over the province of Syria to his control.

When they refused, the Egyptian army marched into Syria. It performed exceptionally well in several battles and was on the brink of toppling the Ottoman dynasty when the Russians intervened and forced Muhammad Ali to forego a march on Istanbul. The Egyptians held Syria for the next eight years, but when war with the sultan's government again threatened, this time the British and French forced him to leave his Asian possessions.

Muhammad Ali spent much of his time in Alexandria, making it his capital and overseeing its buildings so as to make it again one of the great cities of the Mediterranean. Toward the end of his life, his mind failed and his son Ibrahim ruled with the title of khedive. Ali's rule of Egypt was considered to be the most constructive since the time of the Ptolemies.

The relatives of Muhammad Ali who succeeded him had none of his qualities. They lived in luxury, and although they professed the goal of modernizing the country, they ran up so many bills that Egypt's government was mired in debt. One solution to bankruptcy was to find a new source of revenue. Ferdinand de Lesseps, a French engineer, proposed building a canal through the Suez Isthmus to unite the Mediterranean and Red Seas. He convinced Khedive Sa'id that revenue from a canal would rescue the government's finances.

De Lesseps formed the Suez Canal Company and sold shares at a moderate price to investors. Sa'id bought 92,000 shares himself. In 1859 work began on the project with 25,000 fellahin working at a time in shifts both day and night. They had to move 100 miles of dirt, rock, and sand in the desert sun. It was an immense task, rivaling the building of the pyramids, that caused hundreds of its laborers to die of exhaustion.

Ten years after construction started, on November 17, 1869, ships entered the canal. De Lesseps and the French Empress Eugénie were on the first vessel. The Austrian Emperor, Franz Josef, was on the second. The then ruling khedive, Isma'il, spent $280,000,000 on the festivities surrounding the event, including the first operatic performance of Giuseppe Verdi's *Aida.* He obviously forgot that the canal was to raise money for Egypt, not to put it deeper into debt.

Opening day of the Suez Canal brought dignitaries from all over the world.

Isma'il's spending habits brought the nation to the point of bankruptcy. He thought of mortgaging the government's shares in the canal to France, but the British Prime Minister, Benjamin Disraeli, offered to buy them, effectively making the London government guarantor of the canal.

The inevitable financial collapse of the Egyptian government was delayed but a year. In 1876 a joint British-French team took over the ministries of finance and public works. Three years later the son of Isma'il, Tawfiq, assumed power only to meet with rebellion in the armed forces led by a colonel, Ahmad Urabi Pasha. In July 1882 a joint British-French naval squadron appeared off Alexandria in order to protect Europeans whom rioters, agitated by Urabi, had put in danger.

The British, but not the French, shelled Alexandria for ten hours and then landed troops. They defeated Urabi and his army, and subsequently exiled him to Sri Lanka (Ceylon). For all practical purposes the British took charge of the government and the army, although Egyptian officials stayed in place at the lower level.

Lord Cromer, Evelyn Baring, represented Great Britain, with the title of Resident and Consul-General, from 1883 to 1907. He and his aides directed all the important Egyptian ministries. Later other residents were not so firm, recognizing that a strong nationalist movement, opposed both to Europeans and the khedives, required concessions. Then came World War I, and in 1914 the British announced that Egypt was to become their protectorate.

North Africa

The Ottoman sultan was the nominal head of the North African territories west of Egypt, the Barbary Coast, but, in fact, officials from Istanbul were little more than ornamentation. Real power was in local leaders, called *deys,* who ran affairs much as they saw fit.

To support themselves, the deys worked hand in hand with the pirates who operated from their ports. These Barbary pirates openly engaged in seizing ships on the Mediterranean, subjecting the crew and passengers to a life of slavery. The United States' Marine hymn notes the action of the corps in trying to suppress piracy on the high seas, by action taken "on the shores of Tripoli."

In 1830 a French expedition invaded the city of Algiers and, after a series of long and difficult campaigns, occupied the interior. European colonists began to buy property in the countryside and in Tunisia as well, thanks to a French protectorate over that country.

Morocco remained an independent sultanate, but after the 1890s the sultan had no control over the tribespeople of his nation. Once more the French intervened and, with a 1904 agreement in hand, appeared ready to assume a protectorate over that country.

At this moment, in March 1905, the German Kaiser Wilhelm II arrived in Morocco, speaking loudly of Moroccan independence and creating a diplomatic crisis between Berlin and Paris. Despite an agreement that gave France a "special position" in Morocco, tension remained, and a second crisis arose in 1911. The Germans once more backed away from upholding Moroccan independence in return for concessions elsewhere in Africa.

Meanwhile, the new nation of Italy, anxious to create an African empire, cast its eyes across the Mediterranean to Libya. After a short war with the natives and the Ottoman garrison located there, in November 1911 Italy declared its protectorate over that country. Strong Libyan resistance continued for several years.

At the beginning of World War I all Muslim North Africa was in one way or other under European control. Native peoples had to accept westerners living in their midst, people who had little sympathy with their traditions and Islamic culture. Lacking the stimuli of industrialization, the university and school system, the financial resources, and a much more benign climate, North Africans were at a great disadvantage dealing with the Europeans. They did recognize that their leaders were no longer so important. There was a new elite, and it was foreign and nominally Christian.

The Sudan

The clash of European and African Muslim culture was dramatically evident in the Sudan, immediately to the south of Egypt. In northern Sudan the people were Muslim, but in the southern region of the country, tribal people who were Nilotic blacks knew Muslims only as slave hunters. The two parts of the Sudan, then and now, had little to bind them together.

In 1820 Hussein, a son of Muhammad Ali, led an Egyptian army into the Sudan in order to establish his father's rule there. It was a difficult task for the Egyptians to control the whole of the Sudan or to recruit its people into the army. Many tribesmen preferred to die rather than accept conscription into Muhammad Ali's army, which they considered to be only a prolonged sentence of death.

In 1870 a British officer, commanding a battalion of soldiers, moved far into the southern Sudan. Everywhere he announced there would be no more slave trading. Several years later General Charles Gordon established his residence at Khartoum, where the Blue Nile joins the White Nile. Gordon ruthlessly sought out slave dealers and had them arrested.

In the interior of the Sudan, unknown to the Egyptians or the British, one Muhammad Ahmad was at that moment recruiting followers for an army. Ahmad claimed that he was the *Mahdi*, the long-expected leader of Islam, who was to lead it in the last days of the world. He announced that God had chosen him to purify the practice of the Sudanese Muslims and to drive unbelievers from the country. A British-Egyptian force sent to arrest him failed, allowing the Mahdi to attack Khartoum in February 1884.

Gordon received instructions from London to evacuate the country, but he stayed on in Khartoum. For 11 months the city was under seige while Gordon awaited reinforcements. They did not come in time. The Mahdi's soldiers took the city in January 1885, massacring its citizens and killing Gordon. Overnight Gordon was vaulted into the ranks of British heroes. The Mahdi did not enjoy his triumph for long. He died, probably of typhus, the same year.

British troops defeat the Mahdi at Obdurman.

The Mahdi's followers continued the fight for the next decade, generally with success to the embarrassment of London. In 1896 the British government decided to send General Horatio Kitchener to reconquer the Sudan. Kitchener met the Mahdi's army at Obdurman and easily defeated it; once more the Egyptian flag flew over Khartoum. The British were also there, hence the name adopted in 1899, the Anglo-Egyptian Sudan.

Kitchener then had to deal with a French occupation of Fashoda, which threatened to start a conflict between Great Britain and France over the exact boundaries of their African possessions.

South of the Sahara

When the nineteenth century opened, European settlements were limited to the African coast. The interior of the continent was both unknown and feared. Because of its vast distances, the harsh terrain, and above all the many tropical diseases of Africa, few Europeans ventured far from their bases.

European geographers, adventurers, and scientists, nevertheless, were intent to learn more about the African world. As a result a number of explorers set out to map the continent's interior. In 1805 the earliest, a Scotsman, Mungo Park, followed the course of the Niger River, until he drowned in the attempt. A Frenchman, René Caillié, in 1827, became the first European to make a journey across the Sahara.

The most famous of explorers was the Scottish missionary, David Livingstone. He made several travels into the African interior and in 1853 crossed the continent following the Zambezi River and thence into Angola to Luanda.

The search for the source of the Nile occupied every European geographer's mind, for it was one of the great unanswered questions for mapmakers. During the years from 1861 to 1863 the expeditions of John Speke and James Grant found the answer when they discovered the Nile's outlet on Lake Victoria.

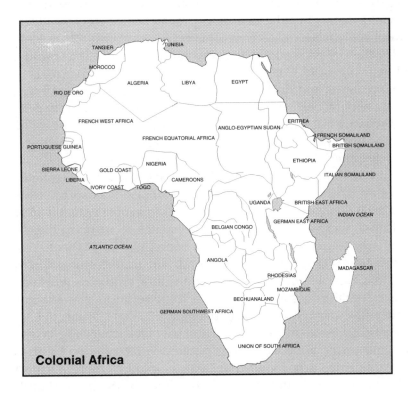

Colonial Africa

West Africa

In the sahel region of West Africa, a number of Muslim reformers made their appearance early in the nineteenth century. One of these, Usuman Dan Fodio, a Fulani, contended that the rulers of Hausaland were no longer practicing Islam correctly. With his Fulani disciples he set up a territory of emirs that stretched from his capital at Sokoto across northern Nigeria all the way to the Atlantic Ocean.

Among coastal peoples the Ashante nation was increasingly more powerful. Its ruler, the Ashanthene, succeeded in amassing a considerable fortune from cooperation with the Europeans. He employed a large bureaucracy and surrounded himself with an elaborate court ceremonial. Artists found patronage at his court in Kumasi, the Ashante capital. His slaves worked in the mines digging out the gold that he sold to the traders. The growing of corn, transplanted from the Americas, gave Ashante farmers new prosperity and helped feed the nation's increased numbers.

The Ashanthene had at his disposal a large military force that was well armed with European firearms. The use of guns made it easy for the Ashante and other coastal nations to prey upon the peoples of the interior for captives that could be sold into slavery; trade in humans was still a major factor in West African life. As many as 4,000,000 people were taken across the Atlantic in the early nineteenth century, while traders crossed the Sahara with another 1,000,000 men and women destined for markets in Egypt, North Africa, and Southwest Asia.

Wealth in West Africa was in people, not land. When in 1807 the British officially ended slave trading in West Africa, the Ashante economy was dealt a serious blow. A number of British and other Europeans still traded on the Gold Coast, but the heat and prevalence of tropical illnesses kept their numbers small.

In 1874 the British decided that it was in their best interest to establish control over the Gold Coast. Therefore, a force of British soldiers invaded the Ashante lands and destroyed Kumasi. A colonial governor became the head of the Gold Coast, although the Ashanthene was permitted his court.

The British built a railroad between the coast and the gold mines, dredged a deep water port at Accra, and constructed a road system. All this activity benefitted European, not African, interests.

The introduction of the cocoa palm to the Gold Coast was one positive contribution of the colonial rulers. The climate was so favorable to its growth that it soon replaced gold as the nation's most valuable export.

The British were also in Sierra Leone, which was set up like Liberia to be a home for returned African slaves. Soon in other parts of West Africa, the British flag was hoisted. Colonial administrators enjoyed remarkable success. In a typical colony, civilian and military officers worked hand in hand. A colonial governor supervised the operation that extended from the capital all the way to the local level.

Principal duties of the administration involved collecting taxes, providing law and order, and overseeing public works initiated by the colonial power. Authorities demanded that taxes be paid in money, introducing a new economic system that changed the lives of people unfamiliar with working for wages. Many Africans had no choice but to labor on European-owned plantations or in mines in order to pay their obligations.

British officials who came to the colonies remained aloof from the African people among whom they lived. As much as possible, they continued the way of life they knew in Europe. High officials brought out their wives and families from England or Scotland and settled in quite comfortable homes where native servants waited upon them.

The Europeans usually recruited natives for the local militia but were reluctant to allow a native African to reach the status of an officer. Colonial administrators did not usually directly interfere with local African traditions or laws, as long as these did not conflict with their authority.

The king of Benin, dressed in his ceremonial robes.

The French were also interested in creating a tropical empire in West Africa. French traders on the Senegal River offered their nation a foothold that allowed it to expand along its banks and establish a presence in the Ivory Coast and in the sahel, which became known as French West Africa and Equatorial Africa. These territories were actually larger than those held by the British, but they were not as valuable.

Generally European government officials were content to keep out of educational matters. These were considered to be in the province of churches and their religious organizations. Direct government participation in economic affairs, much as in Europe itself, did not happen.

East Africa

In 1800 East Africa had its own native wealthy rulers and merchants. In addition to slaves, ivory, hides, and agricultural products were exchanged. The latter were principally cloves and palm oil, for a plantation economy existed here, much as in the American sugar and tobacco industries. On the small island of Zanzibar, 100,000 men and women slaves worked the fields that gave the region its wealth.

On the savannas of East Africa many people were on the move in the nineteenth century. Those who kept cattle jostled with farming populations. Bantu, Nilotic, and Kushitic languages demonstrated the different historic origins of the people who spoke them. The Nilotic ethnic groups, predominantly cattle herders, were often successful in establishing themselves as elites over Bantu farmers. The Tutsi, a Nilotic people, for example, dominated the Hutus in Rwanda.

Buganda, located near Lake Victoria, was a large kingdom noted for its prosperity. It became troubled late in the nineteenth century over conflicts among Christians, Muslims, and animists; this unrest gave the British an excuse to set up the colony of Uganda.

The progress of the British in East Africa was principally a result of the effort to stop the slave trade in that part of the continent. Moving beyond the prohibition of slave trading, in 1833 Parliament abolished slavery in all British colonies. However, the demand for slaves in North Africa and Southwestern Asia continued to keep the trade in humans alive. British abolitionists continually pressured their government to intervene.

In East Africa the natives showed relatively little opposition toward European occupation. Without any sense of property as held by Europeans, African chieftains affixed their marks or signed their names to treaties with little understanding of the consequences. Because the European colonial governments did not tamper with the power of the chiefs and their councils, there was room for accommodation.

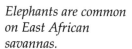

Elephants are common on East African savannas.

African climate and diseases, more than military opposition, hampered European colonial officials. Wherever the tsetse fly flourished, sleeping sickness was a serious deterrent to colonial expansion. In 1900 in Uganda, 100,000 people were stricken and died. Many colonial soldiers were infected with malaria only a few years or even months after arrival and perished.

Following a decade or more of European rule, white settlers arrived in the East African highlands where the climate was cooler. Some were farmers, especially in Kenya, where they bought the best land for growing crops. Other colonists, as in Rhodesia and South Africa, were engineers who went into mining. Soon they shared the comfortable lives similar to the European administrators and officers stationed elsewhere in Africa. Everywhere the white colonists were a small minority compared to the larger native population.

The British and French had designs on making their territories contiguous in East Africa. Cecil Rhodes, the most famous of British empire builders in Africa, envisioned a British north-south axis, "from the Cape to Cairo." The French planned an east-west corridor, from Senegal on the Atlantic to their Red Sea port of Djibouti.

While others clamored for more colonies in Africa, within Germany Chancellor Bismarck remained aloof. What he did not want was a conflict in Africa that would spread to Europe. For this reason, in 1885, he convoked a conference on Africa to meet in Berlin. Delegates from all the interested parties came together to discuss the formation of a state in the Congo and to sort out the procedure Europeans should follow in the acquisition of territories in the continent.

At the Berlin Conference, European diplomats divided the African territories.

Despite Bismarck's reluctance, other Germans were not so aloof. Karl Peters, founder of the German Colonial Society, led an expedition into East Africa that enabled his country to establish a presence in what is now Tanzania. On the Atlantic coast the Germans annexed any territories free of other European powers. These were Togoland, Cameroon, and Southwest Africa.

The Italians, latecomers on the imperial scene, staked a claim in Ethiopia. What they had not planned for was a vigorous resistance from the natives. King Menelek, the Ethiopian king, recognizing that his nation was alone in preserving its independence, invested in the purchase of modern arms. He raised an army of 100,000 soldiers, who were ready for the Italians when the expected invasion in 1896 occurred. The Ethiopians won, and Italy had to content itself with Eritrea and Somalia.

Central Africa

The Congo had its own unique experience. Here in the heart of Africa a journalist on the New York *Herald*, David H. Stanley began to search for the "lost" Livingstone. Livingstone was not lost, but looking for him made a good story for the newspaper. When his mission was over, for he found Livingstone, Stanley proceeded to Europe to find investors to develop the Congo region.

In 1878 King Leopold II of Belgium joined Stanley in his project, the **International Congo Association.** The association was a private venture, with no connection with the Belgian government. Stanley then returned to Africa to enlist native chieftains in his scheme.

In 1885 the association's territories, renamed the Congo Free State after the Berlin conference, became one of the world's major sources of rubber, but at the expense of the natives. European overseers forced them to work in the rubber plantations under threats of harsh punishments. Despite all efforts to make the Congo an economic success, nothing worked. Leopold borrowed from the Belgian government treasury to keep the project afloat.

When he died in 1908 the debt was still outstanding. Accordingly the Brussels government inherited the king's property, and the Congo Free State became the Belgian Congo.

Despite the agreements reached in Berlin, conflicting plans for African empires nearly brought the European states to the brink of war at the close of the nineteenth century. In 1898 a French officer and his men occupied a post at Fashoda, in the southern Sudan. Three years later Kitchener's British detachment, marching from the north, reached Fashoda and told the French that they were trespassers. For a moment there was a standoff. The commanders awaited instructions from London and Paris. It was the latter that backed down. France ordered an evacuation, for in Paris politicians considered German, not British, expansion the greater threat.

What allowed the Europeans success in Africa? The same factors were there as those present during the age of discovery. The Europeans had vastly superior technology, were united under a single national administration, and possessed managerial skills that assisted them in their penetration of Africa. Conversely, the native Africans were weakened by disunity, low technological skills, and a viewpoint on the purposes of life that contrasted with that of the Europeans.

South Africa

Compared to all other regions of Africa, the far south has an abundance of natural resources. Its farmlands are the most fertile, and beneath the surface deep in the earth are the richest areas of the world in gold and diamonds. South Africa, moreover, has a temperate climate, much like that of the Mediterranean with hot dry summers and cool rainy winters.

Throughout the eighteenth century, Bantu peoples were on the move southward from central Africa, bringing their cattle with them. The Bantu people prospered in South Africa, setting up several powerful states. Among these nations were the Swazi, Zulu, Xhosa, Sotho, and Ndebele.

Their leaders were chieftains of great authority, and their societies were well integrated. What they lacked in their competition with the Europeans was weapons. In 1818 one of the Zulu chieftains, Shaka, built up a large centralized state that included many other peoples.

Shaka's disciplined army used a short stabbing spear for their weapon. Soldiers lived apart, in their own villages, so as to keep their morale and training high. Although Shaka himself was killed in 1828, his successors built upon his institutions, making the Zulus the most formidable army in South Africa. Zulu attacks on other African peoples weakened resistance to the approach of the whites.

By 1800 the Afrikaners or Boers, in families or in larger groups, had pushed into the South African interior in ever greater numbers in search of pastures and farmland. Their material possessions were few, but because all were at least nominal members of the Reformed church, they believed themselves to be an elect. Many thought that God had given them a command to make this part of the world on the tip of the African continent a new Europe. Cape Town became a bustling city of several thousand people with a look that resembled towns in the Netherlands.

In 1824 Boers met with Shaka, the Zulu chief.

The British Arrive

Events in Europe now were to affect the Cape Colony. In 1795, when Napoleon's French army successfully invaded the Netherlands, the British government sent a garrison to occupy Cape Town. For a time the Dutch reclaimed their settlement, but in 1806 British troops once more returned and added the Cape Colony to the empire. The British changed the official language to English and introduced their currency. However, the Boers still spoke their own language, Afrikaans, an offshoot of Dutch.

With Great Britain in control, settlers from England, Scotland, and Ireland looked to South Africa to start a new life. During the 1820s they arrived in such great numbers that Cape Town took on an English flavor. Continued unrest along the frontier gave British army commanders reason to move farther inland. A group of Coloureds, who were denied citizenship, also moved northward into the region of the Orange River.

A Cape Coloured dresses in European style.

The Great Trek

In 1835 the **Great Trek** began. This was a movement of the Boers still farther northward, out of the territory governed by the British. Traveling in covered wagons, the Trek was similar to the migration of Americans into the Indian territories of the West.

The Zulus recognized this migration as a threat. Small battles took place between Zulu warriors and the Dutch *voortrekkers,* or pioneers. In 1838 the voortrekker leader, Andries Pretorius, led an army against the Zulus and defeated them badly at Blood River. The Zulu defeat meant that more land was available for the European settlers.

There were some Boer settlements in the valley of the Orange River and others in the Transvaal region. In 1843 the British announced that Natal on the Indian Ocean side of South Africa should be added to the Cape Colony. At the same time London recognized the independence of the two Afrikaner republics: the Orange Free State and Transvaal. The Boers drew up constitutions and set up parliaments in both countries.

By 1860 the white population in South Africa reached 300,000 people. The Bantu were probably close to 3,000,000, but were unable to unite in the face of the European expansion. In the 20 years between 1870 and 1890 all the Bantu nations collapsed, and their chiefs lost their power. At this same time immigrants from India began to enter Natal where they worked on sugar plantations.

Economic issues now appeared to bring rapid change to South Africa. Even though farming, herding, and the growing of grapes preoccupied the Cape Colony, in 1867 the discovery of a large diamond field along the Vaal River caused many farmers to abandon agriculture for mining. In 1889 the **DeBeers Consolidated Mines Company** took over diamond production, creating a monopoly that it holds to this day.

A large number of new immigrants from Europe now arrived on the scene. Many disputes broke out over property rights, and the London government for obvious reasons argued that the British must restore peace. Government troops moved against the Transvaal government but met determined opposition until a truce was effected.

The search for gold spurred on a migration of Europeans into South Africa.

In 1886 another discovery, this time of gold, brought more thousands of immigrants into the Boer republics. These *uitlanders* were not welcome. The

Afrikaner president of Transvaal, Paul Kruger, tried to limit immigration, especially in the area of Johannesburg. A decade later a British adventurer, Leander Jameson, led a raid into the Transvaal that gave the British an excuse to take action. The Boer War was the result. It lasted from 1899 to 1902 and was bitterly fought on both sides until the British prevailed.

United South Africa

At the conclusion of the conflict, the London government dissolved the two Boer Republics. The Orange Free State and Transvaal were annexed to the Cape Colony. In 1908 a convention in Durban agreed on the unification of South Africa's four colonies: Cape Colony, Natal, the Orange Free State, and Transvaal. The country became the Union of South Africa.

An Afrikaner, Louis Botha, was elected the country's first prime minister. Most of his fellow Afrikaners were not reconciled to British rule and remained bitter over their defeat. Botha did not believe that it was in the nation's interests to continue reliving the war's events. Botha wanted to work with London in developing the country. Sharing his views was Jan Christian Smuts. Together they dominated the South African Party, the dominant political force after the foundation of the union.

In 1914 opposition coalesced around a distinctive Afrikaner Party. Its leader was James Herzog and his appeal was to Afrikaner nationalism and opposition to British rule.

Conclusion

By 1914 colonialists allowed only two African territories to remain untouched. One was Liberia, under the United States' protection. The second was Ethiopia, a country that had narrowly escaped Italian conquest.

Assessments of the colonial experience in Africa vary considerably. One colonial administrator asserted, "The processes now called colonialism have been, beyond question, the most beneficent, disinterested, and effective force that has ever been brought to bear on Africa in all its history." This was especially true for primary education and matters of public health.

On the other hand, African peoples and their lands were exploited. Various peoples found themselves divided and ruled from European capitals, and the national rivalries of Europe were exported into Africa. Government in London, Brussels, Paris, and Berlin drew boundaries to suit themselves, with no consideration for the people who lived there.

The peoples of North Africa found themselves in much the same position as those south of the Sahara. Colonial administration did improve transportation and communication systems, and medical care did become more widespread. However, the political ambitions of the rising middle class were frustrated by French, British, or Italian officials who saw their task to make these regions serve first the interests of Europe, not of the local residents.

Chapter 16 Review
Imperialism in Africa

Summary
- Muhammad Ali founded modern Egypt.
- The British took over the administration of Egypt in the latter nineteenth century.
- The first North African colonial expedition brought Algeria under the control of France.
- The Sudan was the scene of a war between the Mahdi and the British.
- The most famous of Christian missionaries in Africa was David Livingstone.
- The Ashante were the dominant people of West Africa.
- The British moved into the Gold Coast and Nigeria, setting up a colonial administration.
- France also began its own empire in West Africa.
- European powers incorporated East Africa under their control.
- King Leopold II made the Congo region his personal preserve.
- Zulus and Afrikaners sought to control South Africa.

Identify
People: Muhammad Ali, de Lesseps, Urabi, Gordon, Kitchener, Livingstone, Shaka, Zulu, Boers, Ashante, Dahomey, Mungo Park, Speke and Grant, Cecil Rhodes, Karl Peters, Menelek, David Stanley, Leopold II, Xhosa, Sotho, Ndebele, Pretorius, Kruger, Jameson, Botha, Smuts, Herzog
Places: Alexandria, Algiers, Morocco, Libya, Khartoum, Kumasi, Sierra Leone, Zanzibar, Kenya, Congo Free State, Tunisia
Events: Muhammad Ali's rebuilding Egypt; digging the Suez Canal; British occupation of Egypt and West Africa; French, Germans, and Italians establish other African colonies; Great Trek of South Africa; discovery of gold and diamonds in South Africa

Define

fellahin	Ashanthene	voortrekkers
International Congo Association	Great Trek	DeBeers Consolidated Mines Company

Multiple Choice
1. Muhammad Ali originally came to Egypt
   (a) in the Ottoman army.
   (b) to fight the British.
   (c) to fight the Sudanese.
   (d) none of the above.

2. Ali's goal was to break the power in Egypt of the
   (a) Mamluks.
   (b) Mahdi.
   (c) British.
   (d) Berbers.

3. Ali's successors in Egypt became famous for
   (a) their battles against Libyan tribesmen.
   (b) running up debts.
   (c) building a dam at Aswan.
   (d) distributing land to the fellahin.

4. The Suez Canal unites
   (a) the Mediterranean and the Nile.
   (b) the Red Sea and the Persian Gulf.
   (c) the Red Sea and the Nile.
   (d) the Red Sea and the Mediterranean.

5. The dominant European power in North Africa west of Egypt was
   (a) Spain.
   (b) Great Britain.
   (c) Italy.
   (d) France.

6. Italy sought to create an African empire in
   (a) Libya and Ethiopia.
   (b) Libya and Sudan.
   (c) Ethiopia and Uganda.
   (d) Ethiopia and Djibouti.

7. The Mahdi and his followers led a successful seige on
   (a) Cairo.
   (b) Fashoda.
   (c) Algiers.
   (d) Khartoum.

8. The credit for identifying the source of the Nile belongs to
   (a) Livingstone and Stanley.
   (b) Speke and Grant.
   (c) Kitchener and Gordon.
   (d) Baring and Gordon.

9. A close relation existed between slave raiding and
   (a) the British occupation of the Gold Coast.
   (b) the foundation of Sierra Leone.
   (c) the discovery of gold in West Africa.
   (d) importation of guns by coastal African kingdoms.

10. Western education was brought into Africa principally by
    (a) colonial administrators.
    (b) the British army.
    (c) Christian missionaries.
    (d) the Afrikaners.

11. Nilotic peoples in central Africa had an economy based on
    (a) growing palm trees.
    (b) cultivating cotton.
    (c) herding elephants.
    (d) herding cattle.

12. Cecil Rhodes planned on British territories joining
    (a) the Cape of Good Hope to Cairo.
    (b) Alexandria to Cairo.
    (c) Rhodesia to Kenya.
    (d) Zanzibar to Accra.

13. The Congo Free State impressed laborers to work on plantations producing
    (a) palm oil.
    (b) rubber.
    (c) cocoa.
    (d) millet.

14. At Fashoda in 1901 a standoff occurred between
    (a) French and British forces.
    (b) German and French forces.
    (c) Zulus and Xhosa.
    (d) Kruger and Rhodes.

15. In 1818 the Zulus were ruled by
    (a) the Ashantene.
    (b) the San.
    (c) the Khoi.
    (d) Shaka.

16. The Cape Colony was occupied by the British
    (a) in 1762.
    (b) as a result of the Peace of Utrecht.
    (c) as a result of the Peace of Paris.
    (d) during the Napoleonic Wars.

17. The battle of Blood River in 1838 was an Afrikaner victory over
    (a) the Xhosa.
    (b) the Ndebele.
    (c) the British.
    (d) the Zulus.

18. The great diamond monopoly in South Africa is managed by
    (a) Kruger.
    (b) Smuts.
    (c) Rhodes.
    (d) DeBeers.

19. At the conclusion of the Boer Wars these regions were annexed to the Cape Colony:
    (a) Orange Free State and Transvaal
    (b) Orange Free State and Kenya
    (c) Natal and Transvaal
    (d) Transvaal and Botswana

20. The first prime minister of the Union of South Africa was
    (a) Smuts.
    (b) Herzog.
    (c) Botha.
    (d) Kruger.

Essay Questions
1. Why is Muhammad Ali considered the founder of modern Egypt?
2. What was the motivation for Europeans seeking African colonies in the late nineteenth century?
3. How did African peoples respond to European colonialism?
4. What events occurred in South Africa that gave it a unique history?

Answers

1. a	6. a	11. d	16. d
2. a	7. d	12. a	17. d
3. b	8. b	13. b	18. d
4. d	9. d	14. a	19. a
5. d	10. c	15. d	20. c

CHAPTER 17

Europeans and Asians

The story of imperialism in Asia differs considerably from the African experience. Asian populations were much more dense, and native rulers exercised their authority with a much firmer hand. In Southwest Asia, the Ottomans and Persians still held on to their empires, but Western inroads were making an impact that could not be denied. Ambassadors of the European Great Powers at the courts of the sultans and shahs were much more than observers of the local scene.

This was the great age of British India, with India becoming Great Britain's most important colony. The British also moved eastward into Burma, and their influence and ambassadors reached as far as remote Nepal and Tibet.

In China and Japan indigenous civilizations had long been in place. People in these societies felt that they had nothing to gain from Europeans except military technology and reliable supplies of precious metals. For centuries the Japanese ruling class limited relations with the West to a single ship in the Nagasaki harbor. Chinese emperors also confined western merchants to stations along the southern coast of the country.

Southwest Asia

The British, French, Russians, and Germans had designs on establishing a presence in Southwest Asia. These countries proceeded along those lines because of the weakness of both the Ottomans and the Persians. Although the courts of the Muslim monarchs of these countries did not betray it, their political survival demanded the support of one or the other of the European Powers. Ottoman foreign policy caused the sultans to become allies of the French at one time and their enemies at another time.

As the century opened, the Ottoman Empire's sultan was supreme over all political and religious events in theory, but in practice competing interests surrounded his throne. Often he was at their mercy, especially the generals of the Janissary Corps. In 1808 Mahmud II became sultan. He had to cope with nationalist movements in the Balkans that resulted in on-going conflicts with Greeks, Albanians, and Serbs as well as a realization that whenever the Great Powers wanted to intervene in the foreign affairs of Istanbul, he could do little to resist their interference.

Mahmud determined that he must try to create a modern military force as the first step toward Turkish modernization. With the help of western military advisers, in 1826 he announced the creation of a New Style Army. Mahmud wanted to eliminate the inefficient and unruly

Janissary Corps, and their leaders played into his hands. As expected, they rebelled rather than accept Westernization, allowing Mahmud's New Style Army to train their artillery on the Janissary barracks. In a matter of minutes, the guns of the sultan's loyal forces decimated the Janissaries. The Corps was eliminated from the Turkish scene.

After 1830 Mahmud began his program of modernization in Istanbul. The red fez replaced the turban, beards were shaved, and a frock coat known as the Stambuli jacket became the fashion instead of Oriental dress.

Istanbul is a city of minarets.

Mahmud's foreign policy remained subject to decisions made in London, Paris, and St. Petersburg. This became obvious when Muhammad Ali's Egyptians passed through Palestine and occupied Syria. Had it not been for Russian help in 1832 and British assistance in 1839, the sultan could well have lost his throne.

After 1840 British prime ministers were convinced that they should support the integrity of Ottoman lands and the authority of the sultans. In return they expected reforms in Ottoman administration.

In 1839 the son and successor of Mahmud II, Abdul Mejid, issued a decree, the **Hatti Sherif of Gulhane,** which promised equal justice for all citizens—Christians, Jews, and Muslims. It was a code of laws that took no consideration of religious affiliation. Regular and fixed collection of taxes sought to remove local abuses, and a new system of political appointments gave consideration only to merit. This was highly idealistic because the Hatti Sherif challenged centuries of traditional Islamic supremacy over the non-Muslim population in Anatolia, Syria, and Palestine.

Throughout the mid-century Christians and Jews made substantial progress in social and political life, supported by the laws that grew out of the Ottoman reforms. The **millet** system was now in full force, giving each religious community its own leadership. This was especially important for those Arab and Armenian Christians who had become Catholics or Protestants.

The house of a wealthy merchant of the nineteenth century stands abandoned today.

A check on religious harmony in the sultan's lands occurred as a result of a conflict that broke out between the Franciscan friars and the Greek Orthodox clergy over control of the Church of the Holy Sepulchre in Jerusalem. The French emperor, Louis Napoleon III, demanded that the Franciscans regain those rights that the Orthodox churchmen who shared the church had taken. The Russian tsar, Nicholas I, patron of the Greeks, warned the sultan not to make any move that would threaten the Orthodox position in Palestine.

When Abdul Mejid refused the tsar's demands, the Russian fleet bombarded the Ottoman navy in the Black Sea, and troops entered the Principalities in the Balkans. The British and French came to Ottoman aid, commencing the three-year Crimean War that extended from 1853 to 1856. Because this war resulted in a Russian defeat, London and Paris were again in a position to demand even more from the sultan's government. The result was the second document of the Ottoman reform, the **Hatti Humayun of 1856,** which emphasized the end of all religious discrimination in the army, schools, and civil service.

The third and final reforming document for the Ottomans was the Constitution of 1876, which was issued over the signature of Sultan Abdul Hamid II. In effect, it was to make the Ottoman Empire a constitutional monarchy, with a guarantee of personal freedom for all its citizens. A popularly elected two-house parliament was to sit in Istanbul with a prime minister heading the government. However, the outbreak of war with Russia in 1877 allowed Abdul Hamid to suspend the constitution.

During these years Ottoman government debts rose to astronomic proportions. In 1881 the sultan had no choice but to allow the formation of the Ottoman National Debt Administration, which was run by Europeans. Economic fiscal control over Ottoman administration was now complete.

The sultan's humiliation turned to despotic moves against anyone who opposed his authoritarian regime. Opponents all over the empire were arrested, tortured, and shot. Abdul Hamid stirred up the populace against

Armenians, the most comfortable but the least defensible of the Ottoman Christians because their homeland was in eastern Anatolia, outside the view of western diplomats. In the 1890s the Armenian massacres, which were to lead to the genocide of World War I, commenced.

The sultan's government found a friend in the German Kaiser, Wilhelm II. In 1903 Wilhelm proposed a Berlin to Baghdad railroad. German officers came to train the Ottoman army, and everywhere German merchants settled in Ottoman cities.

A building in the Grand Serai offered the sultan a quiet place to relax.

In 1908 a rebellion, initiated by a group of dissident army officers, overthrew the sultan's government. These rebels joined the broader-based Committee on Union and Progress to demand the restoration of the Constitution. However, as events unfolded, the government of the **Young Turks** became a political triumvirate of three men: Talat Bey, Enver Pasha, and Jemal Pasha. Their attention was focused on retaining what was left of Turkish territories in the Balkans and leaving the peoples of Southwest Asia to go their way. These priorities would change dramatically during World War I when the Turks joined the Central Powers.

Persia

The Persian kingdom, despite its distance from Europe, could hardly escape European involvement in the nineteenth century. The Kajar shahs, like the Ottoman sultans, were often pulled one way or the other by representatives of the Great Powers.

The loss of Persian territory was one factor. In the beginning of the nineteenth century, there was almost constant warfare in Afghanistan and on the Caucasus border with Russia. Both the British and French sought to bolster the Persians against Russian influence, but they were not strong enough to prevail against the tsar's armies. Azerbaijan and Armenian territories fell to St. Petersburg as the Persians were forced to pull back.

The most able of the Kajar shahs was Nasir ud-Din, who, much like the Ottoman sultans, sought to modernize the bureaucracy and army. During his long reign, from 1848 to 1896, he visited Europe three times.

While Nasir ud-Din ruled, a new world religion was born. First had come Sayyid Ali Muhammad, who claimed in the Sufi tradition to be the Bab (the Gate) to a new interpretation of Islam. In 1850 his claims to be a prophetic voice resulted in his execution, and his followers dispersed. One of them, Baha Ulla, took up his cause, broadening the Bab's appeal and developed the religion known as **Baha'i.**

In December 1905 a popular revolution against the Persian royal government broke out. Much of its inspiration was the work of Jamal ud-Din al Afghani, a popular Muslim reformer who urged a return to a purified Islam. The revolutionaries were able to prevail upon Shah Muzaffar ud-Din to call for an election of a popular assembly, the Majlis, to meet in Tehran, the Persian capital.

Worried over an increased German presence in Southwest Asia, the British and Russians decided to call off their rivalry in Persia. In August 1907 negotiators awarded the northern part of Persia to Russian tutelage and the southern part to Great Britain. Neither party was concerned that the Persians themselves should have a say in their own future.

Efforts were put forward to straighten out the financial situation of the Persian government in the intervening years. An American, W. Morgan Shuster, came to Tehran, but the Russians, who did not want his mission to succeed, frustrated his plans. Then came World War I, and despite the shah's proclamation of neutrality, foreign armies operated at will on Persian territories.

India

The military conquest of the vast land of India with its hundreds of millions of people was completed by the beginning of the nineteenth century. The British East India Company managed the relations of most of the continent through its agents and the private armies they had at their disposal.

As investments poured into India, the British East India Company's management sought new avenues for profitable economic gain. In the process increasing numbers of Indian farmers grew cotton and poppies for opium, which could be sold for cash rather than food.

The colonists in India formed an elite known as **nabobs.** They lived in ornate houses, with dozens of servants. These homes often resembled the palaces of the maharajahs, constructed so as to avoid the worst heat of the tropics. Many British East India Company officials also learned to live like the maharajahs, traveling about the country on elephants. Because most expatriates were single men, Indian women frequently became wives of the company's employees.

Early in the nineteenth century there was a clamor for Britain to play a much more active role in India. The push came from two directions. One was from the missionary-minded Evangelical movement, especially Methodist clerics. They resented the British East India Company's policy of preventing Christian missionary activity in India. The other impetus came from popular English writers, who believed that the superiority of British culture should be shared with the Indian elite. They wanted this elite to receive a Western education and be introduced to Western science so as to "improve" India.

Although this feeling of Englishmen and women that they had a better way of life could be contested, some particular changes in Indian life did make sense. For example, British authorities put an end to the activities of a Hindu sect that was so destructive that its name, *thug,* has come into the English language to describe brutality. Even more in line with humanitarian reform was the effort to eliminate *sati,* the custom that expected Hindu widows to die by burning to death on the funeral pyres of their husbands. In the 1830s the British enforced its elimination.

Despite all that the British East India Company did to monitor its agents' activities, it was never enough. This was evident when, in 1857, the Sepoy Rebellion took place. The Sepoys were the native Hindu and Muslim soldiers who served under British officers.

The Sepoy Rebellion pitted native Hindus and Muslims against the British.

The revolt failed, but in assessing its cause, the London government reformed its policy and in 1858 assumed the direct control of India. By that time nearly all the native states and their maharajahs were under British control.

The British Crown Rules India

Of all British overseas colonies, India was the most highly prized as a source of raw materials and a market for goods produced in Great Britain's factories. Government policy now encouraged Indians to learn western customs and ways. Schools offered education in the English language. The building of roads and telegraph lines as well as railways and port facilities worked to transform India's economy.

In economic terms Indian exports were increasingly drawn into a global trading pattern. The exports were principally raw materials, especially jute and cotton. Rather than fields planted with food crops, farmers turned toward the production of cash crops. This was a major change in the way Indian agriculture was practiced.

For India's peasants, there was little economic progress. They remained poor, and the poorest of them all, the untouchables, did not move out of the direst sort of poverty.

A by-product of the British occupation was the creation of an Indian middle class. These were the people who took over the roles of middle managers, doctors, lawyers, Christian clergy, and employees in the civil service and army. This in large part was a result of the education that the sons of India's upper classes, and less frequently the daughters, received in English language schools. A common bond between these educated Indians existed because the school curriculum was the same all over the country.

British families traveled in camel carts in nineteenth century India.

The British and Indian elites found that they had mutual interests. What Great Britain had not counted on was a change in attitude within the Westernized elite that made them restive. Why should Indians be paid lower salaries than Europeans? Why should the president of a bank always be a European? It was evident that as long as India had its British *rajas*, native people could never aspire to be masters in their own houses.

In 1885 Indian nationalists, both Hindus and Muslims, formed the **Congress Party** to promote equality in the civil service. Several years later, in 1906, a group of Muslims created their own organization, the **Muslim League.**

Indian nationalists demanded that they, rather than the British, should profit from India's trade with the rest of the world. For this to happen, India had to become independent. However, when World War I started, all thoughts of independence had to be shelved. India, important in peace-time, was doubly essential to Great Britain during the war.

China

In the nineteenth century the increased power of the British and the decreased authority of the Chinese emperors confirmed the view of merchants that they had an absolute right to trade with anyone, anywhere. They broke down the restrictions placed upon them by Chinese officials because the government was too weak to enforce its laws.

The British East India Company, rather than provide scarce gold for Chinese goods, hit upon the idea to pay for them in opium. Poppies grown in India produced the opium that was brought into China. By 1833 the value of this trade between Britain and China exceeded £15 million.

Alarmed at the amount of drugs within the country and the terrible effect it had on the population, in 1839 an energetic Chinese official seized and burned the opium stored in the warehouses of southern China. As a result, British merchants lost huge fortunes.

The outraged merchants called upon British naval vessels cruising in the South China seas to come to their defense. The European superiority in weapons made resistance put up by the Chinese futile. The Opium War was altogether one-sided, thanks to the skills of the British navy and its marines. Port after port fell into British hands. An ironclad British **gunboat** easily swept the wooden Chinese junks from the sea.

In 1842, in the **Treaty of Nanking,** the Chinese government recognized that further warfare was no longer possible. The emperor's government agreed to lease the area of Hong Kong to Great Britain and allowed consuls to make their homes in five other ports. The Chinese promised to limit taxation to 5% on goods leaving their country. The Manchu government also granted the British **extraterritoriality rights.** These privileges gave Europeans access to courts that tried cases according to British, not Chinese, law.

Despite this generous settlement, European merchants working in China were still not satisfied. They wanted to expand their business to other ports and to have greater access to inland markets. Again the Chinese sought to resist, and once more their efforts failed.

Eight years after signing the Treaty of Nanking the Daiping Rebellion challenged Manchu rule in Beijing. For 14 years revolutionaries led by Hong Xiuquan, a charismatic leader who adopted many ideas from Christianity, fought imperial forces. A catastrophic loss of life and property occurred before the Manchu forces suppressed it.

Canton's harbor was filled with western ships in the nineteenth century.

In 1860 French forces joined the British in forcing one more concession from the Chinese. A contingent of western soldiers marched into Beijing and demanded that the Manchu court allow foreign ambassadors to make their residence in the imperial capital and that more ports be opened to foreign merchants. The ambassadors' task was to make sure that the Chinese government did nothing to jeopardize European interests.

The final humiliation of the Chinese was yet to come. This time it was fellow Asians, the Japanese, who pounced upon them. The Japanese had quickly adopted Western weapons and military skills and were anxious to expand Japanese territories on the Asian mainland.

In 1894 their armies moved into Korea, a country then loosely attached to China. Victories over the Chinese armies sent to defend Korea opened the door to Japan. By the Treaty of Shimonoseki, Beijing agreed to pay an indemnity and recognize Korean independence. In addition, the Chinese turned over the island of Formosa, now Taiwan, as well as the Shandong Peninsula to Japan.

When the European governments reviewed the treaty, they forced a revision. They believed that Japan had taken too much. Therefore, the western statesmen demanded that the Japanese return the Shandong Peninsula to Chinese control.

A Japanese army battles the Chinese in the Sino-Japanese War.

Wherever the Chinese looked in the last decade of the nineteenth century, they saw their empire slipping away. Despite the nominal independence of Korea, Japan now dominated the country. The Russians were also expanding their presence in Manchuria and the French, in Indo-China. Britain held Hong Kong and dominated southern Chinese trade. China was now a nation subservient to the West and Japan, carved up into spheres of outside influence.

European gunboats patrolled the Yangzi and other rivers, a highly visible symbol of western domination over China. Foreign consuls were more powerful in the cities than the officials sent out from Beijing. In Shanghai, Europeans set up an International Settlement based upon a western style of life. Here European merchants and their families lived as if they were in their own homelands, in a gated community with its own police. No Chinese native was allowed to live within its precincts.

It was obvious to all educated Chinese that something was wrong. The European Powers and Japan were picking away at the bones of the country. The imperial government seemed altogether powerless to protect its interests. Why was this happening?

Much of the blame may be placed upon the reactionary class of Chinese officials who remained contemptuous of western ways. All their training still centered on Confucian ethics, which taught a disdain for merchants and foreigners. China, in their view, was supreme in culture and civilization. Any accommodation to change was promptly dismissed, even in this era that gave ample proof of impending disaster.

A European web of trade now penetrated the nation's interior, resulting in the growth of Chinese middlemen. These merchants took advantage of the European presence; they became the contacts between buyers and sellers on the local scene and created a native Chinese elite as had happened in India. From this class, sons and daughters went abroad to enroll in western universities. This experience caused many Chinese to reject the values of Confucianism and to adopt western ways.

Those natives who attended schools within the country also came in contact with Europeans. The opening of Christian missionary schools, Protestant and Catholic, offered an education that was altogether western. Graduates of these schools often became converts and looked upon the West with admiration and envy. At the same time, especially among university graduates, a strong nationalistic bent developed. Activists wanted the Chinese to assert themselves, to reject the European domination of the nation's economy.

The dowager empress, Cixi, cared for little beyond keeping the status quo. Although she had little of the authority that earlier emperors enjoyed, she held onto the perception that nothing was different and saw to it that the emperor, her nephew, should follow her orders. The royal court rejected every reform movement because its members rightly judged that such a transformation meant the end of their privileges and positions.

There was a long tradition of anti-foreign sentiment among ordinary Chinese people. They believed that many of their woes were the result of the European presence. Activists formed anti-foreign groups; the most prominent of them was known as the **Boxers.**

Groups of Boxers began to attack European establishments and Christian schools. The upshot was a joint American-European intervention. In 1900 several of the European Powers, along with the United States, sent armies into China to assert protection over their nationals. The Boxers fought back, but despite vigorous resistance, the foreign soldiers put them down. The use of force once again ensured that the western presence should remain unchallenged.

U.S. troops march through Beijing's Forbidden City at the conclusion of the Boxer Rebellion.

Eleven years later unrest, centered in numerous secret societies, again swept the country. Students and soldiers joined together to demand that the court dismiss its incompetent ministers. Puyi, the last of the Manchu emperors who was a young boy at the time, gave up the throne. A Chinese student at the University of Honolulu, Sun Yat-sen, took advantage of the confusion. He returned to China where he set about organizing a nationalist party, the **Guomintang.**

On the eve of World War I, in 1911, Sun Yat-sen was elected president by the assembly, known as the Revolutionary Alliance. Military power was in the hands of one of the army generals, Yuan Shikai. Sun governed as president for a time, but Yuan and other former generals, now turned **war lords,** held much of China in military fiefdoms and had no intention of taking orders from him. Force or threats of force were all that mattered. Sun, resigned to the fact, allowed Yuan to assume the presidency until 1916, when a coalition of his enemies forced Yuan from office.

Japan Enters the Modern World

Japan was every bit as isolated as China from the European world until the nation was pried open. The Americans played the same role in Japan that the British played in urging the Chinese to accept foreign trade.

Commodore Matthew Perry sails into the Edo harbor.

In July 1853 Commodore Matthew Perry sailed into Tokyo Bay to confer with Japanese officials concerning their policy toward shipwrecked sailors and to obtain a treaty opening the country to commerce. (The capital of the country, then called Edo, is today Tokyo.) Japanese policymakers, the shogun and his advisors, decided that it was time to reverse their isolationist stance. When Perry returned to Japan in May 1854, the Japanese were ready to sign a treaty opening their markets to United States' exports. This was a major turning point in Japanese history. Seventy Japanese delegates came to the United States for a parade up New York City's Broadway.

The American treaty paved the way for other nations—Great Britain, France, the Netherlands, and Russia—to follow. Unlike China, which always had large segments of society that resisted Westernization, almost all elements of Japanese society quickly came to appreciate western technology. The powerful heads of the Japanese clans recognized the impossibility of business as usual.

In 1868 a coup toppled the shogun of the Tokugawa clan. Its leaders restored the Meiji emperor to the status enjoyed by his ancestors. This event received the name, the **Meiji Restoration.** In fact, the clan leaders did not allow the emperor to become too powerful, for this would have challenged their own positions.

A samurai was a professional Japanese soldier.

Shinto, the native Japanese religion, profited from the emperor's rehabilitation because it deified him. A wave of nationalism swept through the country. This served the purpose of the Japanese generals, anxious to create a military force along western lines armed with European weapons. The Germans arrived in Japan to advise on the creation of a modern army, recruited through conscription. The British were called in to direct the formation of a navy.

The Japanese ruling class was anxious to set up a public educational system according to western models. They welcomed foreign teachers and commenced secondary schools and universities throughout the nation. Graduates, who could afford to do so, sought education abroad.

Western investment and factory managers assisted the formation of Japanese companies. Certain powerful families often controlled these businesses. Unlike in the United States, the Japanese favored monopolies because they made industrial production more efficient. The government sponsored a program of high taxation in order to raise money to improve ground transportation and port facilities.

Industrialization progressed rapidly in Japan with factories constructed throughout the country.

In 1889 the government produced a constitution making Japan a parliamentary democracy. This was more on paper than in fact. The heads of prominent families, who held positions in the executive branch of the government, retained power over the **Diet,** the Japanese parliament. The Japanese were now self confident enough to demand that the foreign powers amend the inequalities in the treaties signed in the aftermath of Perry's appearance.

Japan's leaders then turned to imitate the colonialism of the West. The Japanese first decided on challenging the fading Chinese control in Korea. This precipitated the Sino-Japanese War of 1894 that brought the Japanese onto the Asian mainland. Easy victories won by the nation's armies made the European Powers take notice. When they demanded that the Japanese return the Shandong Peninsula, the national leaders obliged. The army was not yet prepared to take on a western force.

A few years later, the Japanese were ready. It was quite obvious that the Russians, who had their own plans for expansion into Korea and Manchuria, intended to put limits on the Japanese. In 1904 an incident between the two armies touched off a war between the Japanese and Russians. In a matter of months, the Japanese army routed their opponents on land, and their fleet sent a Russian armada, having sailed halfway around the world, to the bottom of the sea. This Japanese victory alerted the West that one Asian nation was well on the way toward becoming a country able and willing to compete in the imperial scramble.

Colonialism in Southeast Asia

The Dutch continued their dominance over the islands of Indonesia throughout the nineteenth century. Local loyalties and island peculiarity assisted them in holding on to their political power and economic dominance.

In the Philippines, after the Spanish-American War, the United States staked out its first Asian colony. In the United States, nationalist sentiment strongly asserted the need for the country not to be left out of Asian affairs, and holding the Philippines provided access to Asian markets.

France made several advances on the Asian mainland. In this case it was Catholic missionaries who came first; then the flag followed. The Chinese, nominal rulers of Indochina, passively watched their influence erode. In 1883 a treaty between France and China allowed that the Europeans should henceforth govern Vietnam, Cambodia, and later Laos.

The British, meanwhile, had moved from bases in India into Burma and set their eyes on further expansion in the region. The French had the same intention. Rather than stir up a conflict, London and Paris agreed to allow Siam (now Thailand) to remain independent. This country provided a buffer between British and French colonies. Siam was the only Southeast Asian nation to escape European rule in the age of imperialism.

A Vietnamese emperor had to deal with French colonials.

Conclusion

The British insistence on paying their bills in China in opium rather than in precious metals demonstrates the extent of how far colonial powers were willing to go for economic gain in Asia. China was at the mercy of westerners and the Japanese. Some historians blame Confucius and his ethical system for this state of affairs, but in reality the stubborn resistance to change held by the Chinese officials who profited from their privileged positions was more at fault.

Japan's rapid adaptation to industrialization and mobilization of its military forces demonstrates what a contrast existed between Japan and China. The upper class in Japan accepted change with enthusiasm. Its members recognized that the country's Westernization was to their advantage.

Great Britain's direct control of India after the Sepoy Rebellion demonstrated the importance of India to the mother country. Queen Victoria was hailed as Empress of India, a title that she enjoyed very much.

The question of a successful reform in the Ottoman Empire was also seen in China. The very people expected to effect the changes, however, were those most likely to be damaged if they came about. Without the prodding of the European Powers, no sultan would govern differently than his predecessors. In the villages of the Ottoman Empire, as in China, life was comfortable for those who held power, and they resisted any effort to move into the contemporary world.

Europeans and Asians met each other in the nineteenth century on an unequal footing. As a result, Europeans and their American cousins assumed a remarkable feeling of superiority. The western political presence would last for about one hundred years, a small amount of time in the history of the world. A growing educated middle class from the Mediterranean to the Pacific would see to that.

CHAPTER 17 REVIEW
EUROPEANS AND ASIANS

Summary
- In the Ottoman Empire, Mahmud II began reforms to better administer his empire.
- A period of reform commenced in the Ottoman Empire.
- The Crimean War was fought to determine which European power would dominate the Ottoman Empire.
- Persia had to give up claims to territory in Inner Asia as Russia expanded.
- After the Sepoy Rebellion of 1857, London took direct control over India, displacing the British East India Company's officials.
- China, in an attempt to stop the opium trade, fought a losing war with Great Britain.
- Everywhere the borders and sovereignty of China were under pressure from outsiders.
- Sun Yat-sen formed a nationalist government based on his party, the Guomintang.
- Commodore Perry opened Japan to American merchants.
- The Meiji Restoration took power from the shoguns and returned it to the emperor.
- The Japanese took the path of imperialism, adding Korea to their sphere of influence.
- The war between Russia and Japan demonstrated that an Asian country could defeat a European power.
- Southeast Asia, with the exception of Siam, was divided between the British and French.

Identify
People: Cixi, Sun Yat-sen, Perry, Mahmud II, Abdul Mejid, Young Turks, Nasir ud-Din
Places: Nepal, Burma, Hong Kong, Korea, Shandong Peninsula, Shanghai
Events: Opium war; European interference in China; the Meiji restoration; Russian-Japanese War of 1904; Sepoy rebellion, British crown assumes the administration of India; the Ottoman reform; the Crimean War

Define

millet	Hatti Humayun	Muslim League
Guomintang	Boxers	Meiji Restoration
gunboat	Baha'i	extraterritoriality rights
nabobs	Congress Party	Hatti Sherif of Gulhane

Multiple Choice
1. In the early nineteenth century, the one point of entry for Europeans into Japan was
   (a) Edo.
   (b) Kamakura.
   (c) Nagasaki.
   (d) Kobe.

2. In the early nineteenth century British merchants in India paid their bills in
   (a) paper money.
   (b) gold.
   (c) silver.
   (d) opium.

3. The Treaty of Nanking granted this area to Great Britain:
   (a) Hong Kong
   (b) Macao
   (c) the Shandong Peninsula
   (d) Taiwan

4. In Manchuria the Chinese watched as this country's influence grew:
   (a) Korea
   (b) Great Britain
   (c) Japan
   (d) Russia

5. One major way European and United States' influence entered China was through
   (a) education provided by missionaries.
   (b) Chinese officials' visits to Europe.
   (c) Admiral Perry's fleet.
   (d) Chinese officials' visits to the United States.

6. The Boxer movement in China supported
   (a) ridding China of foreigners.
   (b) more monetary aid to China from Europe.
   (c) opening up more ports to outsiders.
   (d) closing the port of Hong Kong.

7. The leader of the Guomintang Party was
   (a) Chiang Kai-shek.
   (b) Mao Zedong.
   (c) Sun Yat-sen.
   (d) Yuan Shikai.

8. The isolationist policy of Japan began to crumble after
   (a) the Meiji restoration.
   (b) Shintoism was abandoned.
   (c) Perry sailed into the Edo harbor.
   (d) Sun Yat-sen returned from Honolulu.

9. The Sino-Japanese War of 1894 allowed the Japanese a foothold in
   (a) Korea.
   (b) Siam.
   (c) Burma.
   (d) Tibet.

10. The British East India Company
    (a) managed the economic life of India.
    (b) governed India from Delhi.
    (c) managed the trade coming from Indonesia.
    (d) was an agent for the British Parliament.

11. In India the British tried to eliminate sati, the practice of
    (a) human sacrifice.
    (b) warfare among the villagers.
    (c) conflict between Muslims and Hindus.
    (d) widows throwing themselves on the funeral pyres of their husbands.

12. A middle class developed in India as
    (a) owners of factories.
    (b) landlords.
    (c) middlemen between the British and natives.
    (d) governors of provinces.

13. In an effort to gain equality, in 1885 native Indians formed
    (a) the Muslim League.
    (b) the Congress Party.
    (c) the Hindu League.
    (d) the All-India Party.

14. India's principal export was
    (a) wool.
    (b) silk.
    (c) cotton.
    (d) forest products.

15. The Spanish-American War gained the United States the nation of
    (a) Siam.
    (b) Okinawa.
    (c) Taiwan.
    (d) the Philippines.

16. The French in Indochina governed
    (a) Laos, Cambodia, and Vietnam.
    (b) Siam, Vietnam, and Laos.
    (c) Burma, Cambodia, and Vietnam.
    (d) none of the above.

17. The only Southeast Asian country to escape colonial rule was
    (a) Burma.
    (b) Cambodia.
    (c) Siam.
    (d) Indonesia.

18. Mahmud II of the Ottoman Empire succeeded in
    (a) defeating the Persians at Tabriz.
    (b) sending an Ottoman army into the Sudan.
    (c) destroying the Janissary Corps.
    (d) ridding the Ottoman Empire of European merchants.

19. After 1840 this European nations' foreign policy was to keep the Ottoman Empire intact:
    (a) Russia
    (b) France
    (c) Germany
    (d) Great Britain

20. The Crimean War began over a conflict in
    (a) the Crimea.
    (b) Azerbaijan.
    (c) Ukraine.
    (d) Jerusalem.

21. The 1876 Ottoman Constitution tried, but failed, to
    (a) make the Ottoman Empire a democracy.
    (b) solve the problem of debt in the royal treasury.
    (c) depose the Sultan Abdul Hamid II.
    (d) set up a protectorate over Egypt.

Essay Questions
1. Why did Europeans want in, and the Chinese and Japanese, want them out of their nations?
2. What were Russian interests in East Asia?
3. How do you explain the rapid progress of Japan in the late nineteenth century?
4. Describe the reasons the British took over the direct rule of India.
5. What prompted the reform movement in the Ottoman Empire? What was its fate?

Answers

1. c	6. a	11. d	16. a	21. a
2. d	7. c	12. c	17. c	
3. a	8. c	13. b	18. c	
4. c	9. a	14. c	19. d	
5. a	10. a	15. d	20. d	

CHAPTER 18

Latin America in the Nineteenth Century

During the colonial period of Latin America, the Spaniards, Portuguese, French, Dutch, and British colonists who occupied the region south of the Rio Grande and around the Caribbean islands developed their own consciousness. Known in Spanish America as **creoles** they distinguished themselves from the **peninsulares,** those emigrants who left the home country to serve in Latin America. Both Madrid and Lisbon reserved the highest positions in both government and church for the peninsulares. Little by little, as happened in the British colonies of North America, groups of colonists considered how they could break the ties that bound them to Europe.

The Struggle for Independence

The creoles operated the business life of Latin America. From their ranches and mines came sugar, hides, grain, and silver. Such products brought wealth to Latin America, especially in the eighteenth century. Creoles, however, deeply resented Spanish trade policies and sought to circumvent them by smuggling. Their protests eventually led Spain to liberalize its restrictive trade policies, but the changes came too late.

The creoles were also irked by a program of discrimination that made them second-class citizens in their own homelands. They knew that the peninsulares would never accept them as social and political equals.

The example of the successful American Revolution evoked a strong response among the creoles. If it was possible for a colonial people to rebel in the north, why could it not happen in the south?

Not all Latin Americans, however, even among the creoles, thought that revolution was a good idea. For 300 years their political, religious, and economic destiny had rested in the hands of European statesmen and monarchs. Many had prospered and built up large fortunes and were unsure of what independence might bring.

The idea of independence seemed less attractive when the first revolution in Latin America turned slaves against their masters. In 1791 the slaves and mulattoes of Haiti rose in rebellion against the French elite in that country. The leader of the blacks, Toussaint L'Ouverture, guided the insurrection until he was treacherously betrayed. This warned the creoles in the rest of Latin America that a political revolution might produce dire unforeseen consequences, making it a struggle of the poor versus the rich.

In 1791 a slave revolt commenced in Haiti.

The Revolutions

When Napoleon Bonaparte's armies entered Spain and overthrew the king, the moment for action had come. In South America the initial center for rebellion was in Venezuela where for many years Francisco de Miranda sought to ignite a struggle for independence. One effort failed in 1806 and another, in 1810. Miranda was imprisoned and died an early death. Simon Bolivar continued the struggle and ultimately freed the modern nations of Venezuela, Colombia, and Ecuador. Bernardo O'Higgins led the quest for independence in Chile, and Jose San Martin provided leadership in Argentina. In December 1824 the last Spanish army fought Bolivar and lost to him in the Peruvian Andes.

The independence gained in these wars did not give Latin America stability. The victorious creoles experienced little harmony because factions developed. Dispute arose over the form government should take, the status of the church, and economic policies. No one seemed exactly sure where the boundaries of the new states should be drawn. Therefore, wars between countries and within them often brought Latin America to the brink of total chaos.

Simon Bolivar, liberator of Venezuela, Colombia, and Ecuador.

European links were still strong, despite the virulent nationalism that developed after the wars of independence in the creole elite that now governed the Latin American states. The Catholic church, the major cultural influence in the region, still depended on Europe. The Latin American economies relied on European trade. Latin America remained a part of the European economic system long after political independence was attained.

Brazil Takes a Different Course

By the nineteenth century there were two major groups among Brazil's European population, just as there was in the Spanish colonies. One consisted of Portuguese born in Brazil, while the other was made up of those born in the mother country. The latter emigrated to Brazil as civil and military officials and churchmen. For the most part the two groups cooperated with each other. Compared to other Latin American colonies, Brazilian politics were relatively peaceful; there was not the same intense passion for independence.

In 1807 Napoleon's armies invaded Portugal. King João VI and his court, rather than accept life in an occupied country, sailed off to Brazil, to Rio de Janeiro. This city then became the new capital of the country. The king announced that henceforth Brazil would enjoy the same status as that of Portugal. Culturally, the presence of royalty in Brazil gave the nation a strong social uplift.

In 1820, with Europe back to peaceful ways, the king decided that he should move back to Lisbon, a decision he reached with some regret. Rio de Janeiro was now a thriving metropolis with schools, a printing press, and a busy port; in fact it was the capital of Portugal's Asian and African empire. In his place João named his son, Don Pedro, to the regency. He offered him the advice that if the independence movement should become strong enough, he should lead, not follow it.

Don Pedro I, emperor of Brazil.

Within two years, the Brazilians cut their ties with Portugal. Don Pedro followed his father's advice, declaring on September 7, 1822, "Independence or Death!" His reward was to become Pedro I, Emperor of Brazil, making him the first monarch ever to reign in the Americas. For the next nine years Pedro ruled, but as the years passed he lost the public's favor. In 1831 he stepped aside for his son, Pedro II.

During Pedro II's reign, Brazil's economy continued to flourish, although much of the trade was in the hands of British merchants. The upper class, made up of the great landowning families, was reluctant to spend money on anything except the purchase of more slaves and improvements to their sugar mills. The lower class of Europeans lacked any political or economic power, allowing few to rise to a better status. As in most South American nations, the failure to develop a middle class was a serious misfortune for the country.

As the century progressed, world opinion and a few native Brazilians called on the government to abolish slavery. The large landowners protested, but in 1888 slavery became illegal. The monarchy did not long survive its disappearance. A year later the Brazilians ousted Pedro II and declared their country a republic.

The Brazilian Republic

In the latter part of the century, the number of European emigrants swelled. They came not only from Portugal but also from Italy and Germany. A settlement of several hundred U.S. Confederates moved to Brazil rather than be governed from Washington. The new immigrants fit into an economy that now depended more on growing coffee than on producing the sugar to sweeten it.

After the declaration of its republic, Brazilian politics changed very little. The same wealthy landowning families determined the course of the country. The population continued to increase, and cities grew larger, but the rigid class lines remained very much in place. One new emigrant wave came from Asia, when Japanese arrived in Brazil, looking for opportunities to enjoy a better life.

The Independence Movement in Mexico

The events that finally crystallized the independence movement in Mexico occurred in Europe. In 1808 French armies occupied Spain, forcing the royal family to abdicate in favor of Napoleon's brother, Joseph Bonaparte. With a French king in Madrid, how should Mexico City respond? Where was its loyalty? Politicians in Mexico, especially the creoles, decided it best to pledge their allegiance to the viceroy, Jose de Itturigaray, an official nominally loyal to the deposed King Ferdinand VII. The peninsulares were suspicious of anyone supported by the creoles. They forced out Itturigaray, putting one of their own into power.

The next few years, marked by high inflation, drought, and the deflation of real estate values, saw the level of discontent rise throughout Mexico. Two Catholic priests, Miguel Hidalgo and Jose Maria Morelos, now took the lead in organizing a rebellion.

Before his ordination Hidalgo had been a Jesuit student, but after that religious order was expelled from the country, he finished his studies under the Franciscans. His first assignment was in the town of Dolores, where he organized discussions on politics and economics. Out of this background Hidalgo and his peasant sympathizers decided to act. On September 16, 1810, they shouted out the Cry of Dolores, "Long live Our Lady of Guadalupe! Death to corrupt government!"

Miguel Hidalgo first raised the flag of revolt in Mexico.

Since then, September 16 has been Mexico's Independence Day. Our Lady of Guadalupe refers to the account of an Aztec peasant who claimed to have seen an apparition of Mary, mother of Jesus, in the early sixteenth century. Our Lady of Guadalupe became the nation's patroness and was extremely popular among the poorer people, for she appeared as an Indian woman, not a Spaniard.

Indians and mestizos composed the majority in Hidalgo's army. It marched on Guanajuato, expelling the government garrison and continued to move from victory to victory until it reached the outskirts of Mexico City. Here the rebellion stalled. For unknown reasons the army turned north, only to be crushed in an ambush. The rebel leaders, including Hidalgo, were captured, tried, and executed.

The flame of revolution now passed to Hidalgo's former student, Morelos. Two years after Hidalgo's death, Morelos summoned representatives from all over Mexico to attend a meeting that agreed on a platform of democratic government, universal male suffrage, the abolition of slavery, and an end to government monopolies. Such far-sighted proposals captured the imagination, but Morelos' attempts to topple the viceroy collapsed even more swiftly. He met his end, like Hidalgo, before a firing squad.

Creole society in Mexico was still not sure that its members wanted to support a political revolution that might also turn into a social one. Yet Mexicans were still not happy to learn that the restored Bourbon dynasty in Madrid wanted to return to rule Mexico as if nothing had happened.

In 1821 a new and unlikely revolutionary, General Agustin de Iturbide, appeared. Once a military commander in the Spanish army, Iturbide decided to change sides when he learned a new government had come to power in Spain. He joined forces with those promoting revolution in a proclamation called the **Three Guarantees.** These were the establishment of a constitutional monarchy, a promise of full recognition for the Catholic church, and equality between creoles and peninsulares.

The declaration caused Madrid to send out an army from Spain. However, in recognition of Iturbide's popularity among the upper classes, the Spanish viceroy agreed to avoid a battle. In February 1821 the viceroy announced that he would recognize Mexican independence.

Iturbide was named regent until a sovereign was named. However, Iturbide saw to it that his supporters elevated him to the role of emperor. With his new title he became Agustin I, Emperor of Mexico. Iturbide had no use for the Congress with whom he was meant to share power so he dismissed it. The emperor soon revealed his incompetence, and a group of opponents forced him from office. They declared Mexico to be a federal republic. Later Agustin I was executed.

In 1829, as a result of a change in heart in Madrid, an expedition arrived on the Mexican coast, but it soon dispersed. A major assist for the Mexican response grew out of the **Monroe Doctrine** of 1823, which stated that the United States looked unfavorably upon any more European colonies in the Americas. It was, of course, a bluff because the United States had no way to enforce such a ban. Great Britain did, and it was in British economic interests to nurture the new Latin American republics. It was now Great Britain, rather than Spain, whose trade dominated Mexican imports and exports.

Antonio Lopez de Santa Anna surrendered to a wounded Sam Houston, commander of the Texan army.

In 1833 Antonio Lopez de Santa Anna, a figure who had been among the detractors of the Iturbide empire, became president. For the next 20 years Santa Anna dominated Mexican politics. He was a true *caudillo*, a military strongman, who alternated between bravery and action, vanity and cruelty.

Santa Anna's first concern dealt with Texas. Here North American settlers had arrived in such numbers that they easily outnumbered the Mexican population. In March 1836 the Texans from the United States felt themselves confident enough to secede, declaring themselves the Texas

Republic. Santa Anna took the Mexican army northward and won the battle of the Alamo, but he did not have the military strength to bring Texas back into Mexico. In fact, in April of that year, Santa Anna fell into the hands of the Texans and had to agree to the secession.

In 1845 Congress agreed to join the Texas Republic to the United States, precipitating a war between the United States and Mexico. It was a very one-sided affair. American troops occupied the port of Veracruz in March 1847 and entered Mexico City the following month. The final battle of Chapultepec took place within the city. Mexicans remember it well; impressed by the bravery of the cadets in the Military Academy who chose to die by jumping off the Chapultepec precipice rather than surrender. The **Treaty of Guadalupe Hidalgo** ended the war and forced Mexico to give up almost half its territory, from California to Colorado. The United States paid Mexico $15,000,000 and settled individual claims against the Mexican government in return.

Reform movements in Mexican history resemble waves of the sea. They rise, crest, and then crash and collapse, but a new wave is always on the horizon. Santa Anna's wave finally crashed in 1855. This time the reform had as its leader a Zapotec Indian, Benito Juarez. Juarez had studied law and then decided on a political career. He organized the Liberal Party, which followed Santa Anna's regime, rewriting the constitution and taking away much of the church's lands and its influence over education. The constitution now rejected the long-standing *fuero* for the upper classes.

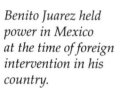

Benito Juarez held power in Mexico at the time of foreign intervention in his country.

Obviously the Mexican conservatives fought back as best they could, raising an army to oust Juarez. This War of the Reform lasted for three years with the final victory going to Juarez. He assumed the presidency in January 1861. The new president was not without problems. The war had exhausted the state treasury. He informed Mexico's debtors that the nation could not pay, a move that outraged Europeans who had loaned money to the country.

Foreign Intervention

Spain, France, and Great Britain argued that they were acting on behalf of their citizens when they landed an army at Veracruz. The French emperor, Napoleon III, had more ambitious plans for Mexico than collecting a debt. After the British and Spaniards withdrew, he ordered the French army to advance on Mexico City. On May 5, 1862, General Ignacio Zaragoza won a major victory over the French at Pueblo, but the Mexican win was not long lasting. The French occupied Mexico City, Juarez fled, and the French candidate, a Habsburg prince, Ferdinand Maximilian of Austria, was declared emperor.

Napoleon III had convinced Maximilian that he would be welcome. In fact, Juarez's opponents were happy to have him on the scene, until they learned that Maximilian did not intend to abolish Juarez's reforms. The United States was also hostile to Maximilian, but Washington could not protest too forcefully because it was involved in the Civil War. In November 1866, with the Civil War at an end, the United States, in conformity with the Monroe Doctrine, demanded that the French army leave. The French evacuated their forces from Mexico, leaving Maximilian on his own. Shortly afterward, his enemies captured and then executed him. Maximilian was a well-meaning ruler, but the odds for success were against him. Juarez returned to power until his death in 1872.

The Government of Porfirio Diaz

In 1877 Porfirio Diaz governed Mexico at a time when the country sought a return to stability. For almost 40 years Diaz stayed in power, with a brief interruption of four years. There was, without doubt, an economic boom, the result of Diaz's efforts to attract foreign investment for the country's infrastructure: railroads, highways, and port facilities. These improvements gave Mexican exports an opportunity to enter the world market. From 1877 to 1900, trade doubled with the outside world.

Diaz's government also sought to raise the country's educational level. His budget financed many schools in the towns, but in the rural areas educational facilities remained practically nonexistent. Women in Mexico were confined to roles of wife and mother and were completely excluded from public life. Actually poorer women had more freedom than those in the upper class because these women were often at the center of buying and selling on market days in the countryside. Indian women, whether willingly or not, remained tied to tradition with only a very few breaking out of the mold.

Upper-class families were the greatest beneficiaries of government policies. They gathered most of the profits from the export of hides, copper, steel, and silver.

There was a special police force, the *rurales,* whose duty was to keep the countryside quiet. It was no easy task in remote areas where power rested in the hands of local strongmen with private armies that allowed them to ignore laws they did not care for. Life was especially difficult for miners, whose standard of living was little more than survival.

The price Mexicans paid for order was to agree to Diaz's program. He did not allow a free press nor the organization of opposition parties. His government was a classical case of authoritarian rule.

The Revolution of 1910

The emerging Mexican economy brought forth an equally emerging middle class that chafed under the rule of Diaz. Once more the banner of revolt was raised, first by workers, and then by the population at large. Diaz resigned, and in January 1911 a new alliance of reformers appeared, supported by a populist army. For a time the government was in the hands of a succession of strongmen, many of them in power for but a few months claiming to be saviors of the people and out to purge Mexico of corruption. Rebel armies appeared; among them were Poncho Villa and Emiliano Zapata.

An army of the Zapatistas prepare for an engagement against government troops in 1914.

The United States claimed the right to intervene in defense of its interests. When an expedition of Villa crossed into New Mexico, President Woodrow Wilson dispatched an American force into Mexico.

When at last the fighting receded, an assembly of Mexican politicians deliberated plans for a new constitution. This Constitution of 1917 secularized education, forbade the ownership of land by foreigners, restored some of the Indian lands taken in Diaz's days, and provided for universal suffrage. In the economic sphere, the Constitution recognized unions, and the eight-hour day was written into the law of the land.

From 1910 to 1920 Mexico lost a half million people because of civil war. The result was the impoverishment of the people, especially the peasants, and the loss of any type of economic security.

Successive presidents made some efforts at land redistribution, but the process of breaking up the large estates proved slow and tedious. The establishment of credit facilities and irrigation projects in various localities did aid some in the peasant class, but for the most part apathy and resistance to change won out over those who wanted a different kind of Mexico.

Conclusion

The conflict between creoles and peninsulares in Spanish America marked the social life of the region from the seventeenth century. As the creole population increased, its members became more vocal over what they considered the injustices of the Madrid government. However, instead of moving in that direction, the Bourbon dynasty made decisions that increased economic restrictions on Spanish America and closed off access to the political offices that the creoles had come to expect as belonging to them.

The revolutionary spirit of South American creoles used events occurring in Napoleonic Europe to spark it into action. In Mexico the revolution was more the result of the poverty and frustration of the poorer classes. In Haiti it was a conflict between slaves and masters. Ironically, at the very time that rebellions swept Spanish America, Brazil welcomed their king into safe exile.

Revolutions, however, are always difficult. They involve great risk. In order to attract followers, revolutionaries must make extravagant promises about the future in order to have people sacrifice for the present. After the guns are silent and the soldiers go home, they await the fulfillment of their dream for a better world. Then reality sets in, and the golden age must be postponed. Many times Latin Americans learned this lesson in the nineteenth century.

CHAPTER 18 REVIEW
LATIN AMERICA IN THE NINETEENTH CENTURY

Summary
- Creoles, who produced the wealth in Latin America, resented the peninsulares, who came from Europe to hold the best political positions.
- The first revolution in the late eighteenth century broke out in Haiti.
- Years of revolution happened in the Spanish colonies while Napoleon's armies occupied Spain.
- Brazil's experience was different, for the king of Portugal was exiled to Rio de Janeiro.
- Brazil later opted for independence and became a republic.
- Hidalgo and Morelos led the independence movement in Mexico.
- In 1821 the Spanish viceroy in Mexico City declared Mexican independence.
- Santa Anna became the dominant political figure of early nineteenth-century Mexico.
- Texas and much of the Mexican northwest was lost after a war with the United States.
- In 1910 a revolution brought a new party to power intent on removing the influence of foreigners and the church in Mexican life.

Identify
People: L'Ouverture, Hidalgo, Bolivar, San Martin, Joâo VI, Don Pedro II, Morelos, Iturbide, Santa Anna, Juarez, Ferdinand Maximilian, Diaz, Villa
Places: Venezuela, Colombia, Rio de Janeiro, Chapultepec
Events: growth of the independence movement; revolutions in Latin America; signing the Treaty of Guadalupe Hidalgo; French intervention in Mexico; Diaz's rule in Mexico City; Revolution of 1910

Define

Monroe Doctrine   rurales   Treaty of Guadalupe Hidalgo

Multiple Choice
1. The productive class in Latin America was
   (a) the peninsulares.
   (b) the creoles.
   (c) the Indians.
   (d) foreigners.

2. Leader of the Haitian revolution was
   (a) San Martin.
   (b) Bolivar.
   (c) Manet.
   (d) L'Ouverture.

3. The country of Colombia owes its independence to
   (a) San Martin.
   (b) O'Higgins.
   (c) Bolivar.
   (d) Miranda.

4. Even after independence, Latin America was linked to Europe because of
   (a) economic and religious ties.
   (b) peninsulares who continued to enter the country.
   (c) the Monroe Doctrine.
   (d) the need for silver.

5. The king of Portugal went into exile in
   (a) Colombia.
   (b) Venezuela.
   (c) Brazil.
   (d) Cuba.

6. "Independence or Death" became the Brazilian slogan of
   (a) Joâo VI.
   (b) Don Pedro I.
   (c) Pedro II.
   (d) Bolivar.

7. With the demise of slavery in Brazil in 1888,
   (a) no more sugar was produced.
   (b) no more coffee was grown.
   (c) the monarchy collapsed.
   (d) the Amazon Indians took the place of Africans.

8. Dolores was the site of the first Mexican call for
   (a) the return of Ferdinand VII to Madrid.
   (b) the resignation of Viceroy Itturigaray.
   (c) revolution.
   (d) Indian independence.

9. The issuing of the Three Guarantees was supported by
   (a) Viceroy Iturbide.
   (b) Morelos.
   (c) Hidalgo.
   (d) Santa Anna.

10. The victor at the battle of the Alamo was
    (a) Santa Anna.
    (b) Iturbide.
    (c) Crockett.
    (d) Houston.

11. California and much of the American Southwest was lost to Mexico by
    the treaty of
    (a) Guadalupe Hidalgo.
    (b) Austin.
    (c) Paris.
    (d) Mexico City.

12. May 5 is a holiday for Mexicans because of a victory at Pueblo over
    (a) Spanish troops.
    (b) French troops.
    (c) Juarez.
    (d) Zaragoza.

13. The 1910 Revolution in Mexico was a victory for
    (a) secularists.
    (b) the church.
    (c) foreign corporations.
    (d) United States' interests in Mexico.

Essay Questions
1. What occasioned the revolutions in Latin America against Spain?
2. Why was the experience of Brazil different from events in Spanish America during the revolutionary period?
3. What were the events that shaped Mexican history in the nineteenth century?

Answers

1. b	6. b	11. a
2. d	7. c	12. b
3. c	8. c	13. a
4. a	9. a	
5. c	10. a	

CHAPTER 19

The United States and Canada

The two countries north of the Rio Grande developed rapidly into modern nations in the period from 1789 to the beginning of World War I. Both went through a period of expansion westward as millions of emigrants from Europe crossed the Atlantic to seek new opportunities in North America. Even though the Thirteen Colonies threw off British rule prior to 1789, the Canadians remained loyal to the crown.

The history of the United States is very different from other world societies. It was truly a new world, with no king or emperor, no nobility, and no religious traditions that regarded outsiders as hostile enemies, and it was relatively free from the danger of foreign invaders. It was also a land of immense natural resources, lightly populated by native Americans who were no match for European numbers and technology.

Growth of the United States

The United States Finds Its Way

With the adoption of the Constitution, the United States entered a new era of its history. The problems facing the United States now seem small compared to those of other world societies, but to those involved they needed urgent attention. In 1789, the very year the French Revolution began, George Washington was elected the first president of the United States under the newly ratified Constitution. The president assumed office in New York City.

The most serious question before Congress and the president was to find a way to finance the administration. A large debt to bondholders still had to be paid for the Revolutionary War, but not everyone agreed on how this should be done. On the one side was Thomas Jefferson whose supporters opposed the government's assuming too many responsibilities.

Thomas Jefferson, third president of the United States.

The opponents of Jefferson followed the leadership of Alexander Hamilton. They believed that the federal government must assume all the debts of the states that they had incurred during the Revolutionary War and pay them off using revenues collected from custom duties and taxes. They wanted a national bank to be set up to facilitate the government's finances.

In 1791 Congress agreed to the establishment of the bank. The votes of Southerners were won over on a promise to locate the capital in the South, on land on the border of the states of Virginia and Maryland, to be called the District of Columbia. In 1800 the capital, named for Washington, began to function as the nation's administrative center.

Not all Americans were pleased with the government's taxing power. In Pennsylvania farmers who were used to making whiskey resisted all attempts to collect revenues on their products. President Washington felt that supporting federal law was essential and sent an armed force to demonstrate his conviction, initiating a precedent that the federal government has the right to intervene in state matters.

Because the new nation had to conduct its affairs while Europe was in the throes of a revolution in France and, subsequently, while Napoleon was in power, foreign affairs played a major role in the activities of the first president. Neutrality, with a tilt toward the British, became the chosen path.

American diplomats signed treaties with both the British and the Spaniards that settled outstanding issues between the countries. Dealing with Revolutionary France was not so easy, but the second president, John Adams, despite French provocations against American ships on the Atlantic, refused to be pulled into a war with that nation.

Although the Constitution said nothing about them, political parties developed around the two major figures of the nation: Alexander Hamilton and Thomas Jefferson. The followers of the former became known as Federalists, whereas Jefferson's party was called the Democratic-Republicans.

Because of a misguided attempt by the Federalists to quash dissent when their majority in Congress passed the harsh and unpopular Alien and Sedition Acts, Jefferson won the presidency for two terms, beginning in 1800. Even though it was against his principles for government to take on a major role, Jefferson decided to purchase Louisiana, the region between the Mississippi River and the Rocky Mountains, from Napoleon's government. The annexation of the Louisiana Purchase added over 800,000 square miles of land to the United States. In 1819 Spain would agree to sell Florida, increasing the size of the country still further.

Monticello was the Virginia residence of Thomas Jefferson.

The young nation also had to devise a way to handle disputes within the government. In this regard, the Supreme Court, the nation's highest judiciary, took the initiative in claiming the right to oversee the legislation of Congress to make certain that it did not conflict with the Constitution. Chief Justice John Marshall had a major role in defining the relationship between the federal and state governments in favor of Washington.

While James Madison governed the country, the War of 1812 was fought with Great Britain over that country's taking American seamen off their ships on the high seas and forcing them onto British ships. For two years the battles went on. The most notable event was the British seizure of Washington and the burning of the Capitol and the White House. Fortunately, Dolley Madison, the President's wife, saved many of the House's heirlooms from destruction.

The United States soon recovered and entered into a period known as the Era of Good Feelings. It was characterized by harmonious relations between the citizens and their government. After 1816 the Federalist Party declined, accused of lack of devotion to the Union. There was a succession of Jeffersonian Democrats in the presidency and Congress until 1841 when William Henry Harrison, the Whig candidate, was elected.

Dolley Madison was the First Lady during the War of 1812.

Americans took their place in literature and the arts during the early nineteenth century. Washington Irving, James Fenimore Cooper, and Ralph Waldo Emerson were men of letters who gave respectability to the new nation's literature. Among artists, the lithographs of Nathaniel Currier and James Ives became popular in home decor.

During this period Congress maintained a protectionist attitude. Such politicians as Henry Clay asserted that the United States needed high tariffs to protect its young industries and their employees from foreign competition. It was the old argument of mercantilists in new form. Congress rechartered the national bank so as to better control the finances of the country from Washington.

Settlers on the eastern coast in the original 13 states were anxious to move into the West in the 1820s, for here they hoped to find land to farm and achieve a better life. They followed the National Road, which extended from Maryland to Illinois and provided an artery of transportation to thousands of European settlers moving westward. Often the hardships of frontier life were great. The native Americans were too few and they lacked the superior firearms of the settlers to offer much resistance, but weather, disease, the dense forests, isolation, and housing that was little better than shacks took a heavy toll, especially among women and children.

Although most settlers wanted to farm, others were anxious to build towns west of the Mississippi and in the Northwest Territories, the modern Midwest. Towns offered women and men opportunities to pick up supplies, to sell their crafts, to read a newspaper, and to visit a tavern. Doctors, lawyers, clergy, and their families joined the wagon caravans that continued the march westward.

For religious reasons in 1847, the Mormons, followers of Joseph Smith, found their way to Utah. Brigham Young, then their leader, made Salt Lake City the headquarters of the Mormon pioneers.

As the West filled in, the number of territories admitted into the United States increased. In the period from 1820 to 1849, eight new states became part of the country.

Brigham Young led the Mormons into Salt Lake City.

Two regions that held Americans were still outside its frontiers in the 1830s. These were British Oregon in the north and, in the south, the Mexican lands that extended from Texas to the California shore. Spurred by a sentiment known as **Manifest Destiny,** the American pioneers of the West sought to find a way to join the United States.

In 1835 Americans in Texas revolted against the Mexican government and set up an independent republic. Within a decade the ultimate desires of the Texans were fulfilled when their land became a state. Soon afterward, in 1846 war commenced with Mexico over the position of the Texas boundary.

Within two years the better-armed Americans defeated Mexico, and in the treaty signed after the war, American representatives secured the transfer of thousands of square miles of northern Mexico to the United States. This annexation included lands that are now the states of California, Utah, Nevada, Arizona, New Mexico, and parts of Colorado. Later the Gasden Purchase brought more Mexican land under United States sovereignty. Expansion of the nation was not a blessing for all, especially for the American Indians and the slaves who were brought into the new states when settlers from the South staked out their plantations.

Dispossessed Indians had no choice but to find new homes in the western United States.

Immigrants

Great Britain sent a steady stream of its men and women into the United States early in the nineteenth century. An estimated 11,000,000 people immigrated to North America. In proportion to its population, Ireland provided the largest number of its people. Long living in poverty and despair from failed rebellions against British rule, the United States appeared to be a promised land. When the Great Famine of 1846 and 1847 occurred, the emigration from Ireland swelled, with over a million people, one seventh the population, fleeing their homeland. By 1900 half of Ireland's population had left their country for homes across the Atlantic.

German liberals joined the European exodus after the revolutions of 1848. Later immigrants were farmers and townspeople who hoped to make a new start in North America. By 1890 approximately 6,000,000 men and women had come to the United States.

Economic Expansion

The rich agricultural land of the United States was one of the major reasons men and women wanted to establish homes in this country. At first the pioneers were content with subsistence farming, but this soon developed into producing crops that could be sold in a market. Planting corn and wheat and raising livestock kept farmers prosperous in the North. In the South, cotton and tobacco growing, a plantation economy, resulted in an increase in slavery.

Better farm machinery helped agricultural expansion. The cotton gin sped up the separation of the seed from the fiber, while the reaper of Cyrus McCormick made grain harvesting much more efficient.

Mining provided opportunities for many new citizens to the United States. The lure of quick wealth through prospecting for gold attracted thousands of people to California. The timber industry also hired its share of workers to fulfill the demand for wood products.

To transport the goods produced by farmers, miners, and lumberjacks, new inventions came into play. In 1807 Robert Fulton's steamboat made its first trip on American waterways. Soon steamboats crowded the rivers of the United States delivering goods efficiently and cheaply to the towns of the new nation. A rash of canal building also helped connect centers of trade. In 1825 the Erie Canal opened a passage from the Hudson River to the Great Lakes. Traffic took the manufactured goods of the East to the West, while grain and animal products moved the other direction. After 1830 railroads replaced the canals to accelerate the flow of goods in both directions.

Horses pulling a barge on the Erie Canal.

Politics and Society

In 1828 United States citizens voted for Andrew Jackson as president. Unlike all high-born predecessors, Jackson was born in a log cabin on the American frontier and had obtained the notice of the public because of his military exploits. Jackson claimed that his political decisions would reflect the concerns of ordinary people, not those of the Eastern Establishment. Jackson dismissed many of the appointees of earlier presidents so as to effect his policies. He wanted nothing to do with the national bank and vetoed its rechartering.

Women's rights occupied some of the nation's reformers. In the United States laws forbade women to own property in their own name, and they could not stand for public office or vote in elections. Opportunities for higher education were nil until, in 1835, Oberlin College in Ohio first permitted women to enroll, breaking down a barrier to women entering the professions.

In 1848 the situation began to improve, when New York state legislation changed the law to allow women to own property in their own names. In Seneca Falls, New York, Lucretia Mott and Elizabeth Cady Stanton summoned the **Women's Rights Convention,** which passed resolutions demanding better opportunities for women.

There was also a movement for providing public education to young people. Horace Mann proved himself an able advocate for universal education and a curriculum that stressed the basic three Rs: reading, 'riting, and 'rithmetic. Soon state legislatures, lest their citizens be left behind, appropriated money for public elementary and high schools as well as universities. Colleges, which were usually church sponsored, opened throughout the country to train students to become teachers.

Of all social issues confronting the United States in the early nineteenth century, the question of slavery was paramount. Even though most northern states had enacted laws to prohibit it, in the South, planters growing tobacco and cotton argued that it was essential for their economy that slavery be maintained. Congress was equally divided between free states and slave states, 11 each, until 1819. The request by the Missouri Territory for statehood in that year obviously meant this balance would be disturbed.

The **Missouri Compromise** quieted the divisions in Congress when Maine became a free state and Missouri a slave state. However, the compromise also specified that there should never be slavery in any territory of the Louisiana Purchase north of Missouri's southern border.

In the 1830s William Lloyd Garrison, a journalist, led the cause of those known as **abolitionists** who demanded the complete abolition of slavery. Garrison's newspaper, *The Liberator,* caused many a Southerner to become even more defensive over the right to own slaves. The attacks of Garrison and the black orator, Frederick Douglass, made many in the South determined not to back away from their policies.

Coming of the Civil War

The emotionally charged issue of slavery would not die. In 1850 Henry Clay again tried to find a solution lest the Union come apart, but this time Congress ignored him. Legislators passed laws to allow the people living in the two territories of Kansas and Nebraska to vote on whether to admit slavery. This violated the provisions of the Missouri Compromise that "forever prohibited" slavery there.

In 1854 outraged anti-slavery citizens formed a new political party, the Republicans, to contest the election. Older political parties campaigned on a platform that tolerated slavery. Although the Republicans did not win the presidential election that year, the party's strength continued to grow.

In 1857 a major blow was dealt to the abolitionist cause. The Supreme Court passed the Dred Scott Decision, which ruled that slaves were not citizens and that laws forbidding slavery in any state were, in fact, unconstitutional. This happened at a time when pro- and anti-slavery partisans were making Kansas a battleground.

Two years later, an abolitionist, John Brown, led an attack on the government arsenal at Harpers Ferry, Virginia. Brown's raid, actually a hopeless venture, was meant to touch off a slave rebellion, but federal troops easily suppressed it. Brown was sentenced to die by hanging, but he became a martyr to many in the North, more powerful dead than alive.

When the election of 1860 took place, the nation was altogether divided. Abraham Lincoln, the Republican candidate, was the victor. Southerners expected that he would ban slavery, and rather than wait for him to take office, South Carolina legislators voted to secede from the United States. They were followed later by five other states who declared themselves the Confederate States of America. Subsequently six other states joined them, making 11 states in all that withdrew from the Union.

On April 12, 1861, soldiers of the Confederacy opened an attack on Fort Sumpter, a U.S. government post in the harbor of Charleston, South Carolina. For the next four years war raged between those Americans who wanted the Union preserved and those who wanted to set up a separate nation in the South.

President Abraham Lincoln meets with General George McClellan, commander of the Union Army.

The Southern armies, under General Robert E. Lee, were smaller and less able to make up losses. Over half a million people, on both sides, died in the conflict before Lee realized the South could not go on. At Appomattox Court House, Virginia, he surrendered to the Union commander, Ulysses S. Grant. While the war was in progress, in 1863 President Lincoln issued the **Emancipation Proclamation,** freeing all slaves living in Confederate territory.

After the War

The period following the Civil War is known as the Reconstruction Era. Unfortunately the wisdom of Lincoln was not there to guide the nation through these difficult times. An assassin, John Wilkes Booth, shot and killed the president during the same week that Lee surrendered.

Vice President Andrew Johnson was given the task to reunite the nation, but he had few of Lincoln's presidential qualities. Reconstruction passed into the hands of the **Radical Republicans,** whose goal was to make the Confederate states pay a high price for their rebellion. Johnson came close to removal from office, since the Republicans in Congress impeached him for not following their policies.

By the Thirteenth Amendment to the Constitution, all slavery was abolished. Black people became full citizens by the Fourteenth Amendment, and male blacks, according to the Fifteenth Amendment, were given the right to vote.

Throughout the South, opportunists called **carpetbaggers** assumed control of state government along with emancipated blacks. Some white Southerners struck back, joining organizations such as the Ku Klux Klan, whose goal was to deny black men and women equality through intimidation. Through the efforts of the Klan and other less obvious methods, white supremacy remained the rule in the South.

Home of a black family in Kentucky in 1892.

The North actually increased its manufacturing potential during the Civil War as a result of the wartime material demands. From 1870 to 1914 the United States, especially in the northern states, experienced its own industrial revolution. From a nation of farmers, the United States developed into an urban country where workers found jobs in industry and business.

Businessmen who owned the factories of the United States were fortunate to have inventors who constantly came up with new ideas for products and solutions for problems affecting industry. A good example of how the United States benefitted from inventions is the story of barbed wire. Before the 1870s cattlemen and farmers were always at one another's throat in the burgeoning West. Cattle roamed at will on the Western plains and often invaded the farmers' fields. This caused a great deal of friction and at times bloodshed. While branding helped identify ownership, it did not stop cattle from wandering.

In 1873 Joseph Glidden invented barbed wire. Soon it was possible to control cattle grazing, and the range wars came to a satisfactory conclusion. Fences with barbed wire protected the farmers' crops; consequently, the cattlemen no longer had to fight range wars to protect their cattle.

New Immigrants

Immigrants continued to pour into the United States. Another 25,000,000 entered the country from 1870 to 1916. Scandinavians were attracted to the United States by its free homestead policy. Most were farmers who found it too hard to earn a living in their homelands. Letters from pre-Civil War immigrants along with elaborate advertising by steamship and railroad companies brought whole Scandinavian districts to the New World. Some 2,000,000 Swedes, Norwegians, and Danes were attracted to the fertile prairie lands of the upper Mississippi Valley.

Until the last quarter of the nineteenth century, people who left Europe were usually from the northern or western parts of the continent. The pattern then changed. Immigrants now came from southern and eastern

Europe. By 1900 the earlier migration lessened as the British, Scandinavians, and Germans tended to stay home. However, between 1900 and 1910, there were 3,600,000 Italian immigrants; Austria-Hungary sent 1,100,000, and Russia, 900,000.

In the early part of the nineteenth century, most Italians went to Brazil and Argentina. After 1900, however, they came to the United States where they settled largely in big cities. Most were unskilled workers who found employment in the mines, factories, or in construction. They were forced to live in crowded tenements, and many were so unhappy with their situation that they saved their money to return home as soon as possible.

Like the Italians, the Slavs did not emigrate in large numbers until after 1900. Czechs, Slovaks, and Slovenes came from the Austro-Hungarian Empire, many fleeing from political repression. This was also true of Poles living in Russian lands, especially after 1881 when efforts were made to stamp out ethnic nationalism. The Slavic migration was similar to that of the Italian in that most people congregated in large cities where they filled the need for cheap labor. Before 1914 some 5,000,000 Slavs arrived in the United States and Canada.

A large number of Jewish emigrants crossed the Atlantic, leaving the oppression they found in Europe. In 1881 Tsar Alexander III embarked on a brutal policy of repression that destroyed what little economic and political rights Jews had in Russia and Russian-controlled Lithuania and Poland.

Urban Society

As the United States turned from a nation of farmers to workers in businesses and factories, American cities had a tremendous growth. The number of city dwellers went up by 25% from 1870 to 1914.

A wealthy class of citizens now appeared on the social scene. They made their money through owning factories, developing land for housing, or setting up banks. Building railroads and utilities was another path to success. Because there was no income tax and little regulation of business, profits soared for the wealthy. The owners of certain businesses did whatever was necessary to stifle competition through cut-throat deals.

Consuela Vanderbilt, a representative of the new wealthy families in the United States.

More impressive than the growth of the 5% of the people who were very well off was the increase of people who could be considered middle class. They enjoyed a living standard that enabled them to have nearly everything they needed or wanted. Usually families worked hard in businesses or were self-employed as doctors, lawyers, or shopkeepers. Millions were found in the small towns of the United States, their homes lining elm-shaded streets.

Once a month or more they took the train into the larger towns to shop at the big department stores such as Marshall Field of Chicago and R. H. Macy of New York. Outings to lakes or rivers for Sunday picnics or, after 1900, watching the local ball team play provided entertainment. Visiting the circus was always popular as was the annual county fair. Silent motion pictures became a new form of entertainment during the early twentieth century.

The United States also had its poor, people who for one reason or other had difficulties making a decent life. Recent immigrants were handicapped if they did not speak English and frequently had to take low-paying jobs. The most severely handicapped were those who suffered from racism. Black men and women had few opportunities to hold jobs that allowed them to enter the middle class. Often they had no choice but to find work as domestic servants or field hands. Blacks' homes were located in the poorest sections of the towns where they lived.

In the South, cotton-pickers received a share of the crop for their labor in the fields.

On the West Coast, Chinese laborers who came to work on the Union Pacific Railroad were in no way accepted as equals by whites. Certain areas of towns were set apart as Chinatowns. Chinese were the last hired and the first fired during any economic slowdown. Their children, forced to work at an early age to support the family, frequently had little or no education.

The Progressive Movement

Despite the general feeling that the United States was a land of opportunity, the fact that not everyone could have a share in its wealth meant that critics, calling themselves **Progressives,** sought to change the economic structure. Progressive women sought political equality, principally the right to vote. Led by Susan B. Anthony, the **National Woman Suffrage Association** agitated for inclusion. In 1869 the suffragettes scored a victory when the Wyoming Territory legislators allowed women's suffrage.

Susan B. Anthony led the fight for women's right to vote in the United States.

Labor leaders wanted to organize farmers and workers to balance the power of management. In 1886 Samuel Gompers founded the American Federation of Labor for skilled laborers. Farmers had their own groups, the National Grange and the Farmers' Alliance.

The Knights of Labor, another workers' organization, in contrast to the American Federation of Labor, sought to recruit unskilled workers into its ranks. In 1886 at a meeting in Chicago's Haymarket Square, someone exploded a bomb, causing a disturbance that resulted in the death of eight policemen. Opponents blamed the Knights of Labor leadership, resulting in a major decline in membership.

During the administration of President Ulysses S. Grant from 1869 to 1877, corruption in politics at the national level reached a new high. Critics urged that a reform on political appointments was necessary. Congress responded, passing the Civil Service Act of 1883, which made many federal positions open to people because of merit, not political favoritism.

Economic Development

Railroad construction provided a major impetus for economic development. By 1900 the rail system in the United States reached 200,000 miles. Grain from Minnesota could now be shipped to the bakeries of New York City in a matter of days.

In 1869 the whole nation was thrilled when near Ogden, Utah, a golden spike was driven into a rail tie to complete the first transcontinental railroad. Now it was possible for people and goods to move from coast to coast.

The growth of big business and corporations was one more factor affecting life in the late nineteenth and early twentieth centuries. Investors bought the stocks and bonds of these companies, allowing them to build new industries and secure new markets. Dividends went to shareholders willing to invest their capital. The New York Stock Exchange on Wall Street became the scene of transactions totaling thousands of dollars on a single day.

The location of industry was not spread universally throughout the nation. Wealthy Americans preferred to put their factories in New England, the Mid-Atlantic states, and the Midwest. They avoided the South, which remained predominantly rural, with small farms the rule. Many southern farmers, especially blacks, were tenants who rented their land through sharecropping. To be a sharecropper meant that a farmer had to give a portion of the harvest to the landowner. In years of slim harvests, both were forced into debt.

In the West, miners, farmers, and cattlemen settled the Great Plains. The American Indians were swamped in the process. For those who lived from hunting buffalo, the slaughter of the herds by white men meant the end of their way of life. There were no more buffalo. Federal troops saw to it that the American Indians were settled on reservations that doomed them to lives of poverty and hopelessness.

Political Life and Reform

The Progressive Movement in the late nineteenth century succeeded in gaining political support from members of both the Republicans and Democrats. A Populist party appeared as a further goad to reform.

Local government took on additional responsibilities toward the poor and the health of citizens. Cities enacted regulations for building, housing, and the workplace and paid for inspectors to check on enforcement.

The federal government acted to support **free trade.** Congress passed the Sherman Antitrust Act to prohibit monopolies and trusts, and President Theodore Roosevelt eagerly saw to the implementation of the legislation. In 1911 the largest oil corporation, John D. Rockefeller's Standard Oil Company, had to be broken up as an illegal monopoly.

During a strike against coal mine owners, Roosevelt was the first president to act on behalf of workers. He also promoted regulation of meat, food, and drugs in laws passed by Congress in the Federal Food and Drugs Act. Roosevelt and his successors urged additional reforms through Constitutional amendments, which gave the government the right to initiate a graduated income tax.

Foreign Policy

In the 1890s the United States was sufficiently strong and wealthy to take its place in world affairs. The nation first flexed its muscles against Spain. When revolt broke out in Cuba, one of the few remaining Spanish colonial possessions, American nationalists demanded that the United States support the cause of the revolutionaries. Assisting their activist policy was the destruction of the battleship *Maine* off the Cuban coast.

Although no one knew the exact cause, the interventionists used the incident to blame Madrid, and President William McKinley requested that Congress declare war on Spain.

Teddy Roosevelt leads the Rough Riders into action in Cuba.

The Spanish-American War lasted but a few months, from April to December 1898, because the United States had a significantly stronger military force. At the treaty that ended the war, Spain ceded the Philippines, Guam, and Puerto Rico to the United States. The United States now had an empire. One further territory was added to the nation when Congress annexed the Hawaiian islands.

Theodore Roosevelt, famous for his statement that a guide to foreign policy-making should be "Speak softly and carry a big stick," advocated a major commitment to an increase in the military and threatened to go to war if denied the right to build the Panama Canal.

Digging the Panama Canal required ten years' labor, from 1904 to 1914.

Canada

The population of Canada increased after the War of 1812 as settlers from Europe, especially the British Isles, poured into the country. With them came a desire for greater self-government.

French Canadians were wary of the influx of English-speaking immigrants. They resented the fact that policies were determined by the crown's British appointees, who ignored the wishes of the French Canadians. Rebel groups tried unsuccessfully to overturn the government.

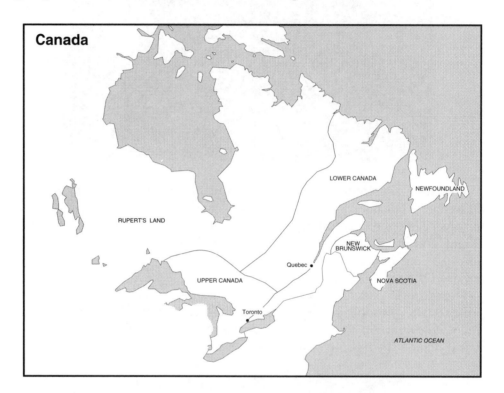

Canada

LOWER CANADA

NEWFOUNDLAND

RUPERT'S LAND

NEW BRUNSWICK

Quebec

UPPER CANADA

NOVA SCOTIA

Toronto

ATLANTIC OCEAN

In 1841, with the assent of the Parliament in London, Canada's two divisions, Upper and Lower Canada, became a single nation, the Province of Canada. The main concern of politicians of the day was to secure local self-government.

In March 1867 the London Parliament passed the **British North America Act,** which gave Canada dominion status. The British monarch was head of state and appointed a governor-general, and London managed foreign affairs, but in all other matters, Canada became a parliamentary democracy with a political system similar to that of Great Britain.

Canada's first prime minister was John A. Macdonald. His immediate goal was to expand his nation to the West, to annex the territory then known as Rupert's Land, an area that the Hudson's Bay Company owned. The Canadian government also acquired the large Northwest Territory, and British Columbia joined the Canadian Federation in 1870, bringing Canada's territories to the Pacific Ocean.

Immigrants in Canada head westward for homes on the prairies.

Two parties developed, the Conservatives and Liberals, who contested the elections. Much of government policy surrounded the building of a cross-continental railroad, which was finished only in 1885. The completion of the railroad brought thousands of settlers to Canada's plains where they became wheat farmers. Economic investment in steel, textiles, and flour milling also aided economic expansion during the ministry of Wilfrid Laurier, the first French Canadian to hold office.

Canada's role in the British Empire was a point of contention between the English-speaking and French-speaking population. In the crises that became a part of the early twentieth century, English-speaking Canada felt the nation should stand behind the London government unconditionally. French Canadians generally saw no reason to get involved.

Canada had one more problem—the United States. How could a separate Canadian identity remain intact when so many ties existed with its large neighbor to the south?

Conclusion

The strength of the United States had grown at a phenomenal rate from the days of Washington to 1914, when Woodrow Wilson was president. From a small agrarian nation, the United States had developed in the space of a century into a world power. Its economy had shifted from farming to manufacturing, and its society, from frontier values to those of a sophisticated populace. The Civil War had divided the nation, but with the passing of the generation that experienced the war, the wounds it inflicted began to heal.

For millions of people the United States was seen as a land of opportunity, a haven for those who wanted to find political and social freedom. In 1914 America still had its dispossessed, but their status compared well to the poor in many other world societies. Canada also was a land of prosperity, its vast resources waiting to be tapped by new immigrants.

CHAPTER 19 REVIEW
THE UNITED STATES AND CANADA

Summary
- How to finance the government was the most pressing problem for the United States.
- A two-party system developed between Federalists and Democratic-Republicans.
- A major move of President Thomas Jefferson was to purchase the Louisiana Territory from France.
- People from the Atlantic coast began to move inland to farm.
- Expansion continued as Oregon, Texas, California and the lands in between were added to the United States.
- A large number of men and women continued to cross the Atlantic to make their homes in the United States and Canada.
- Women leaders agitated for equal political and economic rights.
- The issue of slavery in the South was one that seriously divided the country.
- Anti-slavery advocates formed the Republican Party.
- In 1861 the Civil War commenced after South Carolina seceded from the Union.
- Reconstruction after the war made the South bitter over its treatment.
- A new wave of immigrants, this time from southern and eastern Europe, poured into the United States after the Civil War.
- Progressives urged economic and political reforms to spread wealth more evenly in the country.
- Canada became a British dominion and a single country, but tensions between English and French speakers remained.

Identify
People: Washington, Jefferson, Hamilton, Clay, Jackson, Mormons, Mott, Lincoln, Lee, Grant, Theodore Roosevelt, Macdonald, Laurier
Places: Washington, D.C., Louisiana, Erie Canal, Kansas
Events: parties arose in the Federalist period; War of 1812; westward movement; immigration from Europe; Civil War and Reconstruction; United States became an urban society; Canada became a parliamentary democracy

Define

Manifest Destiny	Emancipation Proclamation
Women's Rights Convention	Progressives
Missouri Compromise	Dred Scott Decision
abolitionists	British North America Act
Confederate States of America	

Multiple Choice
1. Washington took the oath of office as first president in
    (a) the District of Columbia.
    (b) New York.
    (c) Philadelphia.
    (d) Trenton.

2. One of the arguments early in the history of the United States involved
   (a) the establishment of a national bank.
   (b) establishing a common currency.
   (c) how congressmen should be elected.
   (d) the powers of the president.

3. Federalists were likely to support the ideas of
   (a) Washington.
   (b) Jackson.
   (c) Jefferson.
   (d) Hamilton.

4. This president made the Louisiana Purchase:
   (a) Washington
   (b) Madison
   (c) Monroe
   (d) Jefferson

5. The White House was burned during
   (a) the American Revolution.
   (b) the Civil War.
   (c) the War of 1812.
   (d) the Whiskey Rebellion.

6. The National Road was built between
   (a) Maryland and Illinois.
   (b) Maryland and Indiana.
   (c) New York and Washington.
   (d) Washington and Philadelphia.

7. The Mormon leader who brought his followers to Utah was
   (a) Young.
   (b) Smith.
   (c) Jackson.
   (d) Johnson.

8. The immigration of men and women from this country expanded after a great famine:
   (a) Great Britain
   (b) France
   (c) Spain
   (d) Ireland

9. John Brown, an abolitionist, led an attack on an armory at
   (a) Richmond.
   (b) Pittsburgh.
   (c) Harper's Ferry.
   (d) Harrisburg.

10. The first Republican president was
    (a) Johnson.
    (b) Grant.
    (c) McKinley.
    (d) Lincoln.

11. He led the Confederate armies:
    (a) Lee
    (b) McClellan
    (c) Hooker
    (d) Taylor

12. The Ku Klux Klan advocated
    (a) economic change in the South.
    (b) election of carpetbaggers.
    (c) expulsion of the Union army from the South.
    (d) white supremacy.

13. Scandinavian immigrants to the United States tended to settle
    (a) in the South.
    (b) on the Atlantic coast.
    (c) in the northern plains.
    (d) in Oregon.

14. Builders on the Union Pacific Railroad were predominantly
    (a) Mexicans.
    (b) Chinese.
    (c) Irish.
    (d) Italians.

15. The territory that first allowed women suffrage was
    (a) Dakota.
    (b) Nevada.
    (c) Arizona.
    (d) Wyoming.

16. He founded the American Federation of Labor:
    (a) Garrison
    (b) Grant
    (c) Stanton
    (d) Gompers

17. The nation was united by a transcontinental railroad when a golden spike was driven into a railway near
    (a) Reno, Nevada.
    (b) Ogden, Utah.
    (c) Sacramento, California.
    (d) Omaha, Nebraska.

18. American Plains Indians had to change their way of life after
    (a) the destruction of the forests.
    (b) the great horse plague.
    (c) the election of U. S. Grant to the presidency.
    (d) the destruction of the buffalo herds.

19. John D. Rockefeller's company was
    (a) United States Steel.
    (b) Colgate-Palmolive.
    (c) Mobil Oil.
    (d) Standard Oil.

20. The first prime minister of Canada was
    (a) Macdonald.
    (b) Frazer.
    (c) Laurier.
    (d) McCarthy.

Essay Questions
1. What compromises held the United States together in its early history?
2. Why was the Westward Movement such a major factor in the United States?
3. Historians often claim that Lincoln was the best president the United States ever had. What supports this view?
4. Why was Reconstruction such a difficult period for the South?
5. What were the major problems that the Canadians had to solve in the nineteenth century?

Answers

1. b	6. a	11. a	16. d
2. a	7. a	12. d	17. b
3. d	8. d	13. c	18. d
4. d	9. c	14. b	19. d
5. c	10. d	15. d	20. a

UNIT 3

A WORLD
OF NATIONS
1914–1997

CHAPTER 20

World War I

In 1914 Europe stood poised on the brink of a devastating war, yet the statesmen of the age seemed oblivious to the risks involved. They ignored the fact that a complicated alliance system divided the continent into two armed camps, which meant a conflict was unlikely to be localized. They also disregarded the much more sophisticated and lethal weaponry that was now available to the military forces of all nations. There were no compelling reasons for Europe to plunge into conflict in 1914, yet this happened with terrifying results.

Background to the War

Causes for World War I are multiple. Probably the greatest blame should be placed upon the alliances that bound individual nations to one another. What might start as a limited conflict between two nations threatened to drag other countries, willingly or not, into war.

The alliance structure originated in Bismarck's Germany. The chancellor, after three brief and successful wars that he engineered to unify Germany, believed that his nation was satisfied. To preserve what he gained required that nothing should challenge the German predominance in Europe. Therefore, Bismarck planned to link Germany with other nations so that France, potentially his nation's most serious enemy, would find no friends among the other European states.

In 1872 Bismarck commenced building a wall around France when he produced the **Three Emperors' League,** which brought together the rulers of Russia, Austria-Hungary, and Germany. The problem with this arrangement grew out of the rivalry between Russia and Austria-Hungary in the Balkans. After only seven years it became obvious that the league could not hold together. Bismarck abandoned the Russians and tied Germany to Austria-Hungary. Should Russia attack either state, the other would come to its aid. This remained the cornerstone of German foreign policy up to the outbreak of World War I.

Later, Italy joined the two **Central Powers** after France angered the Italians when the French seized control of Tunisia. With three members now aboard, it was possible to call the arrangement the **Triple Alliance.**

In 1890 all Bismarck's intentions collapsed after he was forced out of office. The new German monarch, Kaiser Wilhelm II, wanted to make his own foreign policy decisions. He showed the chancellor the door. Because Wilhelm had no love for the Russians, he allowed a treaty with them that needed periodic renewal to lapse. French diplomats, aware of this breach, immediately made tracks to St. Petersburg. Russia desperately required investment capital, and the French proved willing to provide it. Three years after Bismarck's dismissal, a secret treaty between France and Russia pledged that if either were attacked by Germany, the other would come to its assistance.

Kaiser Wilhelm II, emperor of Germany.

In 1904 diplomats of Great Britain and France signed the *Entente cordiale,* an agreement of mutual understanding that pledged cooperation between the two countries. Diplomats in Paris and London later convinced the Russians to join them. Tsar Nicholas II agreed, paving the way for what became known as the **Triple Entente.**

Such a charged atmosphere produced grave consequences for the security of all the European nations. Every country's generals believed it their obligation to clamor for more money to increase the size of their armies and to purchase the latest in military equipment. Soon Europe plunged into an arms race. Continental armies filled with young men, drafted for two or even three years of military service. Only the British continued to rely on volunteers.

Imperialism and economic rivalry were two further considerations that prompted nations to start on the road to war. In several instances the European urge to create overseas empires brought them into conflict with one another, especially in Africa. The rivalry between the British and Germans became increasingly bitter as a result of their competing claims on that continent. Germans arrived late on the scene in the quest for colonies and tried hard to make up for lost time.

By 1900 the industrialization of Germany had reached the point that it surpassed Great Britain's economy. In London, German economic progress was looked upon as a major threat to Britain's markets overseas. The British were very critical of Kaiser Wilhelm and Ottoman Sultan Abdul Hamid II's plans to build a railroad that would unite Berlin with Baghdad. The London government judged this as a direct threat to their lucrative Suez Canal.

The Balkan Question

The Balkans were Europe's major area of conflict. The chief antagonists were Russia and Austria-Hungary, but there were also minor players who wanted their share of Balkan territories. After a war between Russia and the Ottomans that concluded in 1878, the Viennese government assumed the administration of the two Ottoman provinces of Bosnia and Herzegovina. The population there was overwhelmingly Slavic in origin, but about 40% of the Bosnians were Muslims, and under the Ottomans they made up the upper class of landowners. Christian Serbians and Croatians in Bosnia comprised the peasant class.

Next to Bosnia the small Serbian state, weak in numbers but strong on nationalism, deeply resented the Austrian protectorate. From the point of view of Serbia's politicians, the Austrian annexation had destroyed the dream of a **Greater Serbia.** The Russians also were aggrieved because they thought of the Serbians, who shared the same Orthodox Christian faith, as their little brothers.

In 1908 Austria-Hungary annexed Bosnia and Herzegovina directly to their empire. The Austrian move brought forth bitter protests both from Belgrade, the Serbian capital, and St. Petersburg. Because the Russians were still smarting from their defeat at the hands of the Japanese in the Pacific, they were in no position to challenge the Austro-Hungarian annexation at this time. The crisis blew over, but not without making the tsar's advisors decide that never again would Russia allow Vienna to make further gains in the Balkans.

The ever-restive region did not stay quiet for long. The Great Powers might have thought themselves able to control events here; however, every politician in the Balkan states thought otherwise. Each of these countries had its eyes focused on Macedonia, a region still held by the Ottomans. In 1912 an opportunity to gain Macedonia appeared when the Italians, in a bit of empire building, attacked the Turks. This was the signal for the Balkan nations—Serbia, Greece, Bulgaria, and the small principality of Montenegro—to send their armies into Macedonia.

With so many opponents, the Turks went down, but like scavengers over a corpse, the victors quarreled over the spoils. A second round commenced with everybody pouncing on the Bulgarians who had won the most territory in the First Balkan War. This time it was the Bulgarians who collapsed.

A new nation, Albania, appeared in the Balkans. The Austrians and Italians sponsored its independence to thwart the Serb march to the sea. The creation of Albania and the results of the Second Balkan War were now facts of history. Nevertheless, no nation felt secure, nor was any Balkan politician content. A third Balkan War would ignite World War I.

The Storm Breaks

As 1914 began, in every European country military preparations were in progress, tensions were rising, and the kings of Europe were poring over maps outlining the strategies of their generals. In Washington, Colonel Edward House, advisor to President Woodrow Wilson, reported to him, "Everybody's nerves are tense. It only needs a spark to set the whole thing off."

Archduke Franz Ferdinand and Sophie, his wife, leave a Sarajevo church a few moments before they are killed.

That spark was struck on June 28, 1914, when a Serbian nationalist shot and killed Archduke Franz Ferdinand and Sophie, his wife, in Sarajevo, the Bosnian capital. The archduke was a nephew of Franz Josef and heir to the Habsburg throne.

Franz Ferdinand had demonstrated a willingness to give the Habsburg Slavs a greater role in the Austro-Hungarian Empire. Serbian nationalists, especially those in a group called **Union or Death,** or the Black Hand, wanted no contented Slavs in the Austro-Hungarian Empire. The Black Hand formed a plot on the archduke's life because he would be an easy target at the time he made a state visit to Sarajevo on the national holiday of Serbia.

A series of assassins positioned themselves along the archduke's route, but had it not been for his driver's error in making a wrong turn, the royal couple might have survived. As it turned out, Gavril Princip, a member of the Black Hand, had his chance to shoot Franz Ferdinand and Duchess Sophie to death.

Immediately there was a crisis. The Austrian government was convinced that the Serbian government had a hand in the assassination and demanded that Belgrade allow it to conduct an investigation in Serbia. The Serbians refused and rejected the ultimatum. It is now known that the Serbian prime minister, Nicola Pasić, was not actually aware of the plot, but it had been the work of a unit in the army acting on its own in supplying and training the conspirators.

In Vienna the Habsburg generals did not intend to wait. They welcomed a chance to teach the Serbians a lesson. It was thought that a brief war would head off any Serbian thought of further expansion.

At this moment the alliance system, with its complex web, was poised to throw Europe into a cataclysmic war. Russian representatives warned the Viennese government that it intended to support its Serbian ally. France, in turn, assured the Russians that their commitment remained firm. In Berlin, the kaiser's advisors urged unconditional support for Vienna, unwisely offering it a **blank check.** This meant that Germany would follow, not lead, Austro-Hungarian foreign policy. Only Great Britain urged mediation.

War Begins

German military plans were found in the **Schlieffen Plan,** a strategy that the German High Command had drawn up in preparation for a two-front war. The plan called for a swift charge into France, while army reserves and the Austrians delayed the Russians on the eastern front. After France had capitulated, the bulk of the German forces were then to be transferred to fight the Russians.

Kaiser Wilhelm and Emperor Franz Josef review their troops.

The key to the success of the Schlieffen Plan was its timing. The German generals feared that if the tsar's armies mobilized quickly, then the strategy would not work. As a result, on July 30, when the St. Petersburg government gave orders for mobilization, the Germans felt that they must respond immediately. On August 1, the Germans declared war on Russia. That same day, the French, as expected, activated their plans for mobilization. Two days later the kaiser's government declared war on France.

The Schlieffen Plan called for an invasion of France through Belgium. The Berlin government requested that the Belgians allow the passage of German troops through the country. The Belgians, not surprisingly, refused. On August 4 German armies crossed the border, guns firing. In London, the British cabinet, hesitant to this moment, felt it had no choice but to honor its treaty guaranteeing Belgian independence.

Campaigns of 1914

The war commenced in all European countries with celebrations. Patriotism was at such a peak that it carried everything else before it. Both governments and popular opinion shared the misconception that the conflict would be over in several weeks.

The German advance through Belgium, however, did not proceed on schedule. For a period of 10 days, at Liège, the army was held in check.

This pause in the advance permitted the British to transport their army across the English Channel. Despite these Allied reinforcements, German troops resumed the momentum. By September the Germans reached within 25 miles of Paris. Here the Allies held the line along the Marne River. The German generals' plan for a quick victory collapsed.

Meanwhile, on the eastern front, the Russians mobilized much faster than the Germans believed possible. Their armies overwhelmed the poorly led Austrians, frightening the Berlin government into changing its strategy of a delaying action on the eastern front. Two German generals, Paul von Hindenburg and Erich Ludendorff, took command with troops diverted from the French lines. In late August they successfully stopped the Russian push into Prussia.

War of the Trenches in the West

As the winter of 1914 approached, the western front became a stalemate. The Germans and Allies pounded each other with artillery followed by suicidal infantry charges. The machine gun gave defenders a decisive advantage over attacking forces. The airplane, however, was primarily used for observation, its potential as a weapon undeveloped. The war in the West was so evenly balanced that neither side could force a breakthrough. Millions of men dug miles of trenches from Switzerland to the Atlantic. Life in these trenches was miserable, especially in the winter rain.

British soldiers stand inside a trench.

Frustrated with military action, diplomats sought another way to gain an advantage. Both sides tried to convince Italy to join them. The Italians, although members of the Triple Alliance, did not commit themselves until after secret negotiations. By the **Treaty of London** the Italians joined the Allies. The Italians opened a front against the Austrians, but as in the west, little movement occurred on either side.

Other Fronts

With the armies bogged down in mutual attrition, the London government thought of changing the course of the war through an attack on the Ottomans. The Turks had become belligerents on the German side, thanks to decisions made by the Young Turks. They stood by when German warships flying the Turkish flag bombed Russian Black Sea ports. This brought an expected Russian declaration of war. With Turkey and later Bulgaria joining the conflict, the number of Central Powers was complete.

Winston Churchill, then British Naval Secretary, suggested that the Allies capture the Dardanelles from Turkey. This would open an all-water route to Russia's Black Sea ports. In April 1915 a landing took place at Gallipoli. For the next several months the Allied forces were pinned down on their beachhead, unable to advance any farther. Finally the decision was made to withdraw; the Gallipoli campaign had proven a disaster.

In the Caucasus, Russian and Turkish troops battled inconclusively with both sides winning, and then losing, the advantage. The Turks and British fought their battles in Iraq for control of the Tigris-Euphrates Valley.

After a delay Greece entered the war on the Allied side because its traditional enemies, Turkey and Bulgaria, fought with the Central Powers. Romania thought to wait until a winner appeared but made the wrong choice, acting too quickly. Germany and Austria occupied the country, soon after the Romanian government decided to fight with the Allies.

One of the British stratagems meant to cause trouble for the Turks was to incite the Arabs to revolt. An unlikely hero of this effort was Thomas E. Lawrence, better known as Lawrence of Arabia. Lawrence, a one-time historian and archaeologist, lived among the Arabs, encouraging them to attack the Turkish forces stationed in Southwest Asia.

Lawrence of Arabia, a romantic figure of the war in Southwest Asia.

In East Asia the Japanese came into the war in order to win the German Pacific territories. They met little resistance. German forces fared better in their African colonies. However, far away from the homeland, and unable to receive supplies, German military units in Africa went under.

War at Sea

For the most part, the German admirals decided that caution was the better policy. They kept their large warships anchored in North Sea ports. Finally at the end of May 1916, the Germans moved out and encountered the British fleet in the **Battle of Jutland.** The British counted 151 British warships and the Germans, 99. They were the largest fleets ever to face each other in world history. The two-day battle was a stand-off. The British navy lost more ships, but in the long run the victory was theirs. The Germans never again sought to challenge it at sea.

Germany's use of the submarine produced a much different result. In 1914 the German navy held about 40 submarines. None had ever been tried in actual combat, so there was no way to be sure of their potential. In September 1914 a submarine first gave evidence of its worth when it sank a British cruiser. Flushed with success against warships, submarine commanders then went in pursuit of merchant vessels.

German submarines were very effective early in World War I.

In May 1915 the most sensational sinking of the war occurred. A German submarine torpedoed the passenger ship *Lusitania* with the loss of almost 1,200 lives. Among that number were 128 American citizens, many of them women and children. President Woodrow Wilson sent a vigorous protest to Berlin. It was so strongly worded that the Germans agreed that its submarines would never target passenger liners again.

American public opinion now shifted strongly to the Allied side. Repeated German assurances that submarine warfare would respect neutral passenger ships proved untrustworthy. German leaders were placed in a dilemma. On the one hand they discovered that the submarine was the most efficient weapon in keeping supplies from reaching the Allies. On the other, to allow the submarines to return to torpedoing unarmed ships threatened to bring the United States into the war.

United States Enters the War

By the fall of 1916 it was obvious to Berlin policymakers that a British naval blockade of Germany was strangling the war effort. Severe shortages of food and supplies appeared. American aid to the Allies crossing the Atlantic meant that the United States had abandoned any pretense of neutrality. The German generals decided to gamble; they would return to a policy of unrestricted submarine warfare.

In January 1917 Germany warned that all ships entering the war zone, even those from neutral countries, were subject to submarine attack. After several American ships were sunk, on April 6, 1917, President Wilson asked Congress for a declaration of war. His request was greeted with enthusiasm. The entry of the Americans came at a crucial moment because Russia had started on its path to revolution.

Much sooner than expected, American troops, under the command of General John J. Pershing, went into action on the western front. American destroyers joined Allied vessels in forming convoys to protect merchant ships and troop transports across the Atlantic.

A wasteland stands where a World War I battle took place.

Last German Offensive

By the close of 1917, the German leaders were convinced that to win the war they must break through the battle lines on the French front. In March and April massive German infantry assaults hammered the Allied lines. By early August the fighting forces of Germany were exhausted. Hundreds of troops surrendered as others retreated. Germany's allies, the other Central Powers, were no longer in the war. On September 30, Bulgaria surrendered. In October Turkey did the same, followed a week later by Austria-Hungary. On November 11 the Germans signed the **armistice** that ended the fighting on the western front. Kaiser Wilhelm abdicated and went into exile.

Home Front During the War

In all the nations engaged in World War I, the governments took on an increasing amount of control. Food production, raw materials, and manufacturing were put at the service of the war effort. For the first time in history, women played a major role as industrial workers, recruited in large numbers to work in factories.

Because of the British blockade, people in Germany faced major shortages. Germany and all the Central Powers lacked sufficient petroleum reserves, copper, and tropical products such as rubber and cotton. Even more serious was a food shortage. German farmers lost their horses to the army, and food production declined with both farm workers and draft animals in short supply. Potatoes became the staple for everyone.

For the French and British, life was not so bleak. There was serious inflation and some shortages, but overall the civilian population remained comfortable. A series of governmental controls over wages, prices, labor, and profits appeared.

Russian Revolution

Of all the Great Powers in 1914, Russia was the least able to fight a prolonged war. Although the country was rich in natural materials, industrialization remained far behind other major nations in Europe. Russia's political institutions were even weaker than its economy. Tsar Nicholas II was supreme, and all cabinet members served at his pleasure. The legislative body, the *Duma,* was packed with his cronies. Nicholas' wife, Alexandra, was German by birth, and throughout the conflict people suspected her of favoring the Central Powers.

A strange religious sectarian, Grigory Rasputin, had gained great influence over the royal family. Through hypnosis, he was able to control the hemophilia of their son. Alexandra was convinced that Rasputin enjoyed some divine power. Actually, he disguised his real character, for he much preferred vodka to prayer. Rasputin made both political and military decisions that did great harm to the prestige of the monarchy. To be rid of him, in December 1916 a group of officers succeeded in shooting Rasputin and threw his body, not quite lifeless, into a river.

Tsar Nicholas II and his wife Alexandra sit for a photograph with their family.

Despite many obstacles, the Russian army fought well in the first months of the war. Then serious shortages of munitions developed. Many of its junior officers died because tradition demanded that they lead the troops in an attack.

In June 1917 General Alexander Brusilov launched an offensive on the eastern front. The Russian general staff planned that it should force the Austro-Hungarian army out of the war. However, the Habsburg armies did not disintegrate. Discouraged at their failure, many Russian soldiers decided that they had enough of war, and they went back to their villages.

As Russia's military capacity disintegrated, the capital, with its new name Petrograd, filled with rumors of treason and corruption. There was nothing in the stores and nothing in the shops to buy; there was no work for the workers in the factories. In March 1917 a riot broke out when people demanded food, and army units, called in to supress the rioters, joined them.

Russian generals sent a message to the tsar: to restore confidence he must abdicate. Reluctantly Nicholas complied. In Petrograd the capital's military and civil servants, doctors, lawyers, and professionals set up a **Provisional Government.** Unfortunately, those who set policy for the Provisional Government believed the war could still be won. They refused to recognize that the situation was hopeless.

From the very moment of its creation, the Provisional Government had to share power with councils, *soviets*, that had sprung up in Petrograd. The leaders of the soviets were inspired by Marxist doctrine. They recognized the possibility that the sorry state of the nation opened a window of opportunity for putting that doctrine into practice. The soviets formed a government with its own officials, the Petrograd **Soviet of Workers and Soldiers Deputies.**

Not all was peace and harmony within the Soviet. The majority were members of the Social Revolutionaries, but other smaller groups existed. Their size did nothing to keep them quiet. The **Bolsheviks** were one faction of the Social Democrats; Mensheviks made up the other wing of the party. Ironically *bolshevik* means the majority and *menshevik*, the minority, but in actual numbers the Bolsheviks were the smaller of the two.

When the war started, most Bolshevik leaders were in jail or in exile. They drifted back to Russia as soon as the Provisional Government came to power. The most prominent of the Bolshevik leaders were Nikolai Lenin and Leon Trotsky.

Both Lenin and Trotsky planned to bring about a socialist revolution *now*. While others wrangled and debated endlessly what should be done, the Bolsheviks urged immediate action. That action contained three elements: peace at once, bread for everyone, and land to the peasants. For millions of Russians, the Bolshevik program seemed to offer a solution to the chaos and misery that beset their country.

Nikolai Lenin addresses soldiers of the Red Army.

After one more failed offensive ordered by the Provisional Government, the Bolsheviks were ready to act. On November 7, 1917, the Red Guards, the military arm of the Bolsheviks, burst through the gates of Petrograd's Winter Palace, scattering the Provisional Government's officials to the wind. Said Lenin, "I feel dizzy." With the government now in his hands, Lenin had to deliver on the promises he had made. He contacted the Germans with a promise that Russia was ready to talk peace.

The two sides met at the border town of Brest-Litovsk. The Bolshevik negotiator was Trotsky. When the Germans presented their demands, they stunned Trotsky by demanding that Finland, the Baltic states, Belarus, Poland, Ukraine, and Bessarabia become independent. In agreeing to these terms, Bolshevik Russia would have to start its existence with the loss of a third of its population and farmland, a fourth of its railroads, four-fifths of its iron ore, and 90% of its coal production.

Trotsky believed that these terms were so harsh that he refused to sign a treaty with the comment that "There will be neither war nor peace." He returned to report to the Bolshevik leadership. After months of debate, for Lenin was convinced that Russia had to have peace no matter the price, the Bolshevik government signed the **Treaty of Brest-Litovsk.**

Russia's travail was not over. The Bolsheviks were only a small minority among the population as a whole. Other parties resented Lenin's high-handed operations and began to resist. Generals and their armies, once loyal to the tsar, were unlikely prospects for recruitment to the Bolshevik cause. Liberal democrats, members of the Social Revolutionary Party,

Orthodox churchmen, and a host of others openly urged the overthrow of the Bolshevik regime. Russia plunged into civil war.

The contest was between the Bolshevik government and its Red Army, organized by Trotsky, and the **Whites,** the opposition. Outside Russia, the Allied governments viewed events with great apprehension. First, Russia had withdrawn from the war, easing the pressure on Germany because it no longer was required to fight a two-front war. Second, the prospect of a nation as large as Russia in the hands of revolutionaries appeared truly frightening. On the excuse that military supplies might be diverted to the Germans, troops of Britain, France, the United States, and Japan took up positions in Russian port cities.

Foreign intervention in the civil war gave Lenin the excuse he needed to brand his enemies as traitors to Russia. Allied intervention, meant to strengthen the Whites, ended up a burden.

Red Army soldiers rally support for their cause in Siberia.

Both Red and White armies fought with appalling ferocity. Anyone thought to be on the side of the enemy was arrested, imprisoned, and frequently shot. The tsar and his family suffered that fate. Nicholas, Alexandra, and their children were placed under house arrest and then executed, on the suspicion that they might try to escape.

World War I in Southwest Asia

During the years of World War I, battles took place in the Caucasus Mountains between the Turks and Russians. In these engagements several Armenian units fought with the Russians. This gave the Young Turk leadership the excuse they needed to destroy the Armenian population of the country. As many as 1,500,000 Armenians died in this first genocide of the twentieth century.

On the diplomatic front, events moved swiftly. The Allies planned to partition the Ottoman Empire when the war finished. The British, French, and Russians would each obtain their share. The later **Sykes-Picot Agreement** between diplomats in London and Paris made the division of Turkish spoils more specific. The Bolshevik Revolution in Russia forced a rethinking of Asian policy, for western leaders had no intention of allowing the communists into equal partnership.

A British army allied with Arab forces broke through to Damascus. In the city Amir Faisal, son of the Arab leader Sherif Husain, proclaimed a nation based upon the conquest. British and French statesmen had cynically promised whatever was expedient to both Jews and Arabs.

The War Ends

After the signing of the armistice, a German delegation made up of civilian politicians represented their country to the Allied governments. They were drawn from Germany's prewar parties. Later public opinion turned on them for "selling out" the nation. The Allies chose Paris for the site of the peace conference where belligerents, victors, and vanquished should meet. Russia, a nation that had fought for so long, was ignored and uninvited because its Bolshevik rulers were now in charge.

During the war President Wilson outlined the American goals for peace in a document known as the **Fourteen Points.** Most Allied governments apparently accepted these same goals. The Germans presumed that this document would become the basis for negotiations in Paris.

British and French public opinion, however, called for retribution and revenge, and their governments' representatives at Paris reflected that anger. Their interest in the Fourteen Points was lukewarm at best. They looked upon Germany as a nation guilty of the mass slaughter that accompanied the war. A million British soldiers were dead or wounded for life. The French lost 2,000,000, and the Italians, 600,000. The German delegation found itself isolated in Paris. Its members passed their time in hotel rooms, while the Allies decided Germany's future.

Paris Treaties

Despite the fact that Allied leaders professed to be waging war in the name of democracy, in fact three men and their diplomatic staffs decided how the torn European continent should be mended. These three were President Wilson of the United States; Georges Clemenceau, the French premier; and David Lloyd George, the British prime minister.

President Woodrow Wilson went to Paris to direct U.S. participation in the peace conference.

Several concerns guided Wilson. He wanted a "peace without victory" and believed that self-determination should solve boundary disputes. His primary goal was the creation of a **League of Nations,** an international organization to make sure that there should never again be such a war.

Lloyd George and Clemenceau thought that Wilson was too much the idealist. Clemenceau made harsh demands. He wanted Germany crippled so that it should never again threaten Europe's peace. Lloyd George occupied a middle position. He did not want Germany so wounded that it could not recover. All three accepted compromises that were written into the **Treaty of Versailles.**

Historians judge the treaty to be both too harsh and too easy on the Germans. This analysis is correct. Germany lost very little territory. France regained the province of Alsace-Lorraine. Belgium and Denmark nibbled at areas near their German borders. Poland, a nation swept off Europe's map in the late eighteenth century, was resurrected, and a corridor linked it to Danzig, the major port on the Baltic Sea. This meant that 1,500,000 Germans found themselves unwilling citizens of the new Polish state. The League of Nations placed the Saar region of Germany, rich in coal, under its control for 15 years.

The Allies sought to cripple Germany's potential to make war. They allowed no fortifications in the Rhineland, the territory immediately adjacent to France. Germany's army was limited to 100,000 soldiers, and the navy, to 15,000 sailors. Germans could not build any submarines and had to give up all their colonies.

The question of reparations became extremely controversial. The British, Belgian, and French governments demanded that Germany make up all the economic damages that their countries had suffered. Germany was declared guilty of starting the war; therefore, it must pay the costs. It was impossible to agree on a sum acceptable to all, so the total was left blank. Justification for the reparations was written into **Article 231** of the Versailles Treaty. In it Germany accepted the responsibility for the war, although no one in its delegation, or for that matter anyone in Germany, believed that their country was the only one at fault.

On June 28, 1919, the German representatives, over protest, signed the Versailles Treaty. The British and French also ratified the agreement. Ironically, the United States Senate, with its constitutional powers to act on foreign agreements, rejected the treaty. The Senate had a Republican majority and resented the fact that Wilson invited none of its members to accompany him to Paris. Within the United States, war-weariness had set in, and most American senators feared that a League of Nations would endanger the nation's sovereignty.

The Allies and the other Central Powers also signed treaties, taking their names from the Paris suburbs where the delegations convened. Austria suffered a huge loss of territory and population in the **Treaty of St. Germain.** The **Treaty of Trianon** left its partner Hungary with only one-third of its prewar size. The Allies treated Bulgaria more gently in the **Treaty of Neuilly.** Although the **Treaty of Sèvres** was meant to partition the Ottoman Empire, armed resistance in Turkey prevented it from ever taking effect.

Conclusion

Much of what happens in human affairs often occurs without planning, or decisions that are made have consequences that were not intended. Certainly the statesmen of Europe were pleased at the sight of larger and better-equipped armies. They felt secure because of the alliances that they had made with other nations' politicians to guarantee security. Therefore, in 1914 when the Bosnian crisis erupted, they failed to see what the outcome would be if Europe charged into a general war. Someone has said that the twentieth century begins and ends in Sarajevo.

Germany planned a quick victory in the West, but it failed to reckon with French resistance on the Marne. From then on, the war became a stalemate because the sides were too evenly matched for either to gain the upper hand. Then came two unexpected events: revolution in Russia and the intervention of the United States on the Allied side.

Few observers would have expected the Bolshevik rise to power in Russia. It was a very small group, looking at the size of the population, that composed Lenin's party. The lesson to be learned from its success is the importance of a single program that answered the needs of a war-weary people for whom the goals of the tsar and the Provisional Government were quite different from their own.

The entrance of the United States into the conflict demonstrated that the ties of Americans were still close to Europe. The Atlantic proved to be smaller than people imagined. To an idealistic audience, President Wilson promised that this would be "the war to end all wars," and Americans responded with enthusiasm. The League of Nations, the president's dream, did not enlist the same enthusiasm and failed to keep the peace. In the final analysis, Europe did not gain peace but a 20-year truce. National rivalries and hatreds survived World War I and prepared the way for World War II.

CHAPTER 20 REVIEW
WORLD WAR I

Summary
- Causes of the First World War were multiple, with nationalism and the alliance system principally to blame.
- Russia and Austria-Hungary had conflicting interests in the Balkans.
- A Serbian secret group killed the Habsburg archduke and his wife in Sarajevo, igniting the forces for war.
- Germany's plan for a quick victory over France stalled at the battle of the Marne.
- In the West, the war became a stalemate, with neither side able to achieve a breakthrough.
- German submarine warfare brought the United States into the war on the Allied side.
- A revolution in Russia resulted in Lenin and the Communist Party coming to power.
- The war ended when a civilian government in Berlin replaced the kaiser and sought an armistice.
- The goal of President Wilson was to create a League of Nations to arbitrate all future conflicts.
- The treaties of Paris decided the fate of the defeated nations.

Identify
People: Bismarck, Wilhelm II, Franz Ferdinand and Sophie, Churchill, Lawrence of Arabia, Wilson, Nicholas II, Lenin, Trotsky
Places: St. Petersburg, Balkans, Serbia, Bosnia-Herzegovina, Albania, Sarajevo, Princip, Gallipoli, Dardanelles
Events: preparations for war; Balkan conflict; assassination of the Archduke and Duchess; War of the Trenches; Russian Revolution; signing the Paris treaties

Define

Three Emperors' League
Central Powers
Triple Alliance
League of Nations
Fourteen Points
Treaty of Versailles
Soviet of Workers and
   Soldiers Deputies

Triple Entente
blank check
Schlieffen Plan
Bolsheviks
Treaty of Brest-Litovsk
Armistice
Provisional Government
Sykes-Picot Agreement

Multiple Choice
1. The first of Europe's major alliances, the Three Emperors' League, was the work of
   (a) Alexander III.
   (b) Louis Napoleon III.
   (c) Bismarck.
   (d) Frederick William III.

2. The fall of Bismarck resulted from the
    (a) Treaty of Paris.
    (b) the unification of Germany.
    (c) Wilhelm II's desire to shape his own policies.
    (d) breakup of the Central Powers.

3. Before 1914 Britain was principally concerned over
    (a) Germany's build-up in naval vessels.
    (b) Germany's alliance with Austria-Hungary.
    (c) Germany's alliance with France.
    (d) the dismissal of Bismarck.

4. A general presumption about war in Europe supposed that
    (a) it would be a short, easy conflict.
    (b) none of the nations had enough ammunition.
    (c) the generals would be prepared to fight for years.
    (d) it would not involve more than two countries.

5. A commercial rivalry for economic expansion in the Ottoman Empire existed between
    (a) Great Britain and France.
    (b) Germany and France.
    (c) Russia and France.
    (d) Great Britain and Germany.

6. After 1878 these Balkan provinces were occupied by Austria-Hungary:
    (a) Bosnia and Herzegovina
    (b) Bosnia and Macedonia
    (c) Serbia and Macedonia
    (d) Serbia and Bulgaria

7. A reason for the birth of Albania was
    (a) to compensate Serbia for the loss of its eastern provinces.
    (b) to give Serbia access to the sea.
    (c) to keep Austria-Hungary out of the Balkans.
    (d) to keep Serbia from access to the sea.

8. On June 28, 1914, these two Austrian royalty were killed:
    (a) Franz Ferdinand and Sophie
    (b) Franz Josef and Marie
    (c) Ferdinand II and Theresa
    (d) Ferdinand II and Marie

9. The advisors to Kaiser Wilhelm thought it wise after Sarajevo to
    (a) quickly head off the crisis by urging Austrian restraint.
    (b) unconditionally support Austria-Hungary.
    (c) put pressure on Vienna to break its alliance.
    (d) support Austria only with conditions.

10. The German army planned an attack on France through
    (a) Austria.
    (b) the Netherlands.
    (c) Switzerland.
    (d) Belgium.

11. The battle of the Marne River
    (a) was a Russian victory.
    (b) stopped the German advance on Paris.
    (c) kept Belgium secure.
    (d) allowed the Germans to march to Marseille.

12. During World War I the airplane was used principally for
    (a) observation.
    (b) bombing raids behind the lines.
    (c) coastal patrol.
    (d) dropping paratroopers behind the lines.

13. Gallipoli was Churchill's destination for a landing that would benefit
    (a) France.
    (b) Belgium.
    (c) Italy.
    (d) Russia.

14. The battle of Jutland was fought between
    (a) Danes and Germans.
    (b) French and German warships.
    (c) Russians and Austrians in Poland.
    (d) British and German warships.

15. The United States entered the war as a result of
    (a) Germany's using submarines against its ships.
    (b) Germany's invasion of Russia.
    (c) the stalemate in the West.
    (d) Italy's entry into the war.

16. During the war, Germans suffered from lack of imports because of
    (a) a British blockade.
    (b) a French blockade.
    (c) Britain's control of the Suez Canal.
    (d) failure of the Ottomans to send them supplies.

17. Rasputin was revered by the Russian royal family because of his
    (a) reputation as a holy man.
    (b) military skills.
    (c) healing powers.
    (d) relationship to the tsar.

18. After the tsar abdicated, in St. Petersburg there was
    (a) a provisional government.
    (b) a constitutional convention.
    (c) a government of the tsar's son, Alexei.
    (d) none of the above.

19. The Bolshevik plan for Russia was
    (a) to make it a communist state.
    (b) to continue the war until victory was won.
    (c) to continue the war until the nation's prewar borders were reached.
    (d) to make it a Fascist state.

20. The Treaty of Brest-Litovsk saw many gains go to
    (a) France.
    (b) Russia.
    (c) Germany.
    (d) the Ottoman Empire.

21. The head of the first Soviet government in Russia was
    (a) Trotsky.
    (b) Lenin.
    (c) Stalin.
    (d) Malenkov.

22. The British delegation to the Paris treaty-making assembly was
    (a) Churchill.
    (b) Macmillan.
    (c) Clemenceau
    (d) Lloyd George.

23. Article 231 of the Versailles Treaty placed the blame for the war on
    (a) Austria-Hungary.
    (b) Serbia.
    (c) Russia.
    (d) Germany.

24. Hungary lost one third of its territory in the Treaty of
    (a) Versailles.
    (b) Neuilly.
    (c) Sèvres.
    (d) Trianon.

Essay Questions
1. List the reasons why World War I occurred.
2. Why did the Germans think submarine warfare would bring them victory?
3. Why did the war in the West develop into a stalemate?
4. What enabled the Bolsheviks to come to power in Russia?
5. Some historians have claimed that the Peace of Versailles was both too hard and too easy on Germany. How do you explain this view?

Answers

1. c	9. b	17. c
2. c	10. d	18. a
3. a	11. b	19. a
4. a	12. a	20. c
5. d	13. d	21. b
6. a	14. d	22. d
7. d	15. a	23. d
8. a	16. a	24. d

CHAPTER 21

Europe Between the Wars

The catastrophe of World War I hovered over Europe for the next generation. Men and women questioned the values of western civilization as never before. New discoveries of science did little to brush away the pessimism that pervaded life during the postwar years.

Despite their efforts, it seemed that the democracies of the world were unable to solve their economic and political problems. Instead of a world made safe for democracy, World War I gave rise to authoritarian states in Italy, Germany, the Soviet Union, and most of the new countries of East Europe. For a time, in the 1920s, it seemed that a stable world order might be created through international cooperation, but all that optimism came down, shattered by the Great Depression and the aggression of Germany and Italy.

Germany in Defeat

In 1919 of all the people in the western world, the Germans were most depressed. The **Versailles Treaty** underscored that they had lost World War I, and everyone's losses and hardships were futile.

In 1919 the democratic parties met at Weimar and drew up a constitution. Unfortunately the politicians who gathered at Weimar did not have the support of the country as a whole. Extremist groups were everywhere. In 1919 several communist-led attempts were made to overthrow the government in Berlin and Bavaria.

None of the rebellions were successful because the number of German communists was still not large. What these outbreaks accomplished was to spread fear in the rest of the population that Germany might take the same path as Bolshevik Russia, and few wanted that.

On the right, partisans of authoritarian rule recruited private armies for their cause. They were disgusted with the slow response of the Reichstag to find solutions to the postwar crises. In 1923 the leader of one unsuccessful coup was a returned veteran, Adolf Hitler. The court ordered Hitler jailed, but it was well known that many Germans sympathized with his goals.

Hitler never hid his views on what the German future should be. The following selection comes from his book *Mein Kampf* and illustrates his appeal to German nationalism:

> *The National Socialist movement must strive to eliminate the inequality between our population and our territory . . . . The strength of our nation is founded, not on colonies, but on the soil of our European homeland. Never regard the nation as secure, unless for centuries to come, it can give every one of our people his own parcel of soil. Never forget that the most sacred right on this earth is a man's right to have earth to till with his own hands, and the most sacred sacrifice the blood that a man sheds for this earth.*

The Weimar government faced some daunting problems. There was mass unemployment and fiscal instability. Many of the raw materials that the nation's industry needed were in foreign hands. Alsace-Lorraine, the Saar, and Upper Silesia, centers of iron and steel production, were cut off from German factories. The Allies seized large numbers of merchant vessels, railroad locomotives, and flatcars to make up for their war losses.

A woman burns Germany's worthless currency in her oven.

The most vexing problem for the government, one that kept it from having any economic stability, came from the inability of the Allies to come up with a figure for reparation payments. There was considerable dispute over how high the bill should be, with the French insisting that Germany should pay for all the damage done to that country during the war. Because payments were supposed to be supported by Germany's gold reserves, the value of paper money went into a tailspin.

In May 1921 the German mark was valued at 62 to the dollar. By November 1923 the mark had fallen to 4,000,000,000 to the dollar, taking with it all the savings of middle-class Germans. People were reduced to bartering what they produced for life's necessities. A deep gloom settled over the nation, and the Weimar government stood accused of ruining the economy.

The government told the Allies that it simply could not pay any further reparations and requested a moratorium. The French were skeptical, believing that there was still enough hard cash hidden away so that payments could continue. The Versailles Treaty allowed the Allies to occupy the industrialized Ruhr Basin if the Germans defaulted. Acting on that premise, French and Belgium armies moved into the Ruhr, but their efforts to carry off the production of the factories located there did little more than pay for the expenses of the occupation. The occupation lasted until 1925.

It was now time for compromise. The U.S. government intervened, sending the banker, Charles Dawes, to Berlin to work out a schedule of payments that was reasonable. By 1924 the mark was stabilized, and investors flocked back to Germany. By 1929 the German economy reached the same level of production it held in 1914.

The government was also able to restore the international reputation of Germany. It signed non-aggression treaties with its old enemies and assured them that no unilateral decisions would be made concerning border disputes. Germany became a member of the League of Nations and pledged to cooperate fully with decisions made in that body. It was almost too good to be true, and it was. On the horizon hovered the Great Depression and Adolf Hitler.

Great Britain Seeks Recovery

The British people breathed a sigh of relief when the war ended. The nation emerged victorious on sea and land, and with France and Japan, the British divided the German colonial empire. The League of Nations also gave Britain mandates in Southwest Asia, charging it with administering these areas in its name.

The immediate postwar euphoria did not last. Returning soldiers found that the jobs they left when they enlisted were no longer there. British factories during the war were converted to the production of war materials. Now with the weapons of war no longer needed, the transition proved extremely difficult. Once-British markets fell into the hands of Americans and Japanese. Miners, formerly the major suppliers of coal in Europe, were laid off. Higher prices and competition from oil caused the pits to close.

Widespread unemployment swept the country, and with it protests and strikes by people who found themselves unable to make a living. Workers joined the Labour Party, which promised legislation to benefit them. The Liberal Party, in office during the war, practically collapsed. Despite the growth of the Labour Party, the strong tradition of Conservative rule was never quite overcome. Middle- and upper-class voters in Britain preferred to vote for the Conservatives, and in 20 years Labour formed only two governments.

Ireland Looks for Home Rule

There was some success in solving the nagging problem of Ireland. For a century Irish members in Parliament caused no end of problems for British governments. Like the man holding on to the tail of a tiger, politicians in London refused to let go. In the late nineteenth century, the Liberal Party came to espouse **Irish Home Rule,** but could not overcome the negative votes in the House of Lords. Then the First World War put everything on hold and Home Rule was delayed.

Ireland's peculiar mix of religions bedeviled finding a solution. Even though the overwhelming number of Irish were Catholic, a minority of Presbyterians lived in Ulster, in the northeastern part of the country. They were the descendants of Scottish and English colonists who had come over to Ireland in the seventeenth century. The Ulster Protestants, a dominant elite in this one region, wanted no part of an Ireland in which Catholics would be a majority. Their slogan, "Ulster is right and Ulster will fight," rallied the Protestants and their friends in Parliament.

During Easter week of 1916, militant nationalists of the Irish Republican Army (IRA) had seized the Dublin central post office and proclaimed an independent government. Overwhelming British force then crushed the **Easter Rebellion.** The survivors among its leaders were tried and executed. This made them martyrs for the cause of Ireland's freedom and drew many more to the cause of the IRA.

British troops behind street barricades fire on Irish rebels during the Easter Rebellion.

As hostilities came to an end on the continent, the British shifted forces to Ireland to put down the fighters of the IRA. At length, in 1921, Parliament agreed to give Ireland dominion status as the Irish Free State, but six counties of Ulster where Protestant strength was strongest, were not included. A civil war commenced in Ireland between those willing to accept London's offer and those in the IRA who wanted to continue resistance. Relations with Great Britain remained tense until 1938, when an agreement was reached that reduced tariffs between the two countries.

Frustrations of the Third French Republic

France's position at the end of the war was ambiguous in the extreme. On the positive side, the French were victors. They regained the Rhine province of Alsace-Lorraine and avenged the humiliating defeat of the Franco-Prussian War. It was their commander, Marshal Ferdinand Foch, who led the Allied armies on the western front to victory.

But the war devastated France. The northeastern part of the country, where the battle of the trenches was fought, presented a scene impossible to describe. Roads, bridges, and railroads were all in need of rebuilding, as were the closed mines and abandoned farms of the region. Towns and villages stood empty, their buildings smashed to the ground.

Under the Treaty of Versailles, the Germans were required to pay for the reconstruction. The government launched a massive effort to restore the region on the assumption that German reparations would pay the bills. However, when the reparations were suspended and the French occupation of the Ruhr proved fruitless, the government fell into a financial crisis.

In an effort to guarantee security against any future attack from Germany, the army insisted on building an expensive, and as it turned out worthless, series of forts along the Rhine River. This was the **Maginot Line,** a tribute to military planners who thought any future war must follow the course of World War I.

The politics of France were as depressing as the economic condition of the country. A host of political parties ranging from communists on the Left to monarchists on the Right clamored for attention. Because no one party could command a majority in the Chamber of Deputies, instability was the rule. Generally the premiers came from conservative parties, but in 1936 a socialist Popular Front ruled for a year.

French diplomacy aimed at keeping Germany as isolated as possible. Therefore, the Paris government created a bloc of nations to the east of Germany that were meant to thwart any plan to expand in that direction. These new countries—Poland, Czechoslovakia, Romania, and Yugoslavia—were taken under the French wing. Yet Paris ignored the reality that when Germany and the Soviet Union recovered from the war's trauma, the alliances that France constructed would not survive. France alone had to carry the burden of standing guard over the European peace, but most French men and women lacked the will to assume that responsibility.

New States of Eastern Europe

At the close of World War I, a number of new states appeared in East Europe. Their birth resulted from the principle of self-determination maintained so vigorously by President Wilson. The largest was Poland, returned to Europe's map after disappearing for over a century. In the European center, Czechs, Slovaks, and Ruthenians formed Czechoslovakia. Three South Slavic peoples put together a confederation, called Yugoslavia, which the Serbs and their dynasty dominated. In Europe's Baltic region, Finland, Estonia, Latvia, and Lithuania took their place.

Marshal Jósef Pilsudski led the government of Poland after 1918.

At the beginning all the governments of these new countries professed that free elections should determine their leadership. They promised respect for civil rights, as well as equal opportunities and safeguards for minorities within their borders.

It was not long, however, before democratic ideals began to fade. Because all these countries had multiple parties, political stalemate resulted. Governments were first pulled to the Right and then to the Left because no coalitions lasted long. The same pattern was found in the Balkan countries. In Romania, Greece, Bulgaria, Yugoslavia, and Albania, kings asserted themselves more and more, and royalist supporters clamored for rule with a firm hand.

Only two East European nations were exceptions to the shift toward authoritarian government, Finland and Czechoslovakia. In these countries, parliamentary government actually worked.

The Senate building in Helsinki, seat of Finland's legislature.

Troubled Italy

Italy emerged from World War I as a very unhappy victor. For all its sacrifices the country received few rewards, and the postwar period brought galloping inflation, unemployment, and labor unrest. Into this turmoil stepped Benito Mussolini.

Mussolini's career had taken him first into socialism, but he then made a radical turn to extreme nationalism. He formed the **Fascist Party** with a hard core of disenchanted war veterans.

Mussolini's Fascists marched under the banner "Believe, Obey, Fight!" The party's philosophy rejected democracy for strong, authoritarian government. It supported the **corporate state** where the government managed but did not own the means of production. In 1922 the Fascists were strong enough "to march on Rome." Actually, Mussolini rode in a train. The king and parliament stood aside while Mussolini organized the government.

It was now the Fascist Party rather than the government that set policy for the nation. The party made the decisions, and the government carried them out. Guiding the country was the Fascist Grand Council, with its leader, Mussolini, the *Duce.* All newspapers, radio, and movies came under Fascist control. In the schools, textbooks taught the glories of Mussolini's regime.

Italy became the first western European state to fall victim to **totalitarianism.** Every effort was made to submerge the individual into the machinery of the all-powerful state.

There was opposition from socialists and communists, but Mussolini's thugs beat them up and sent them to prison. Many Italians were grateful that discipline had returned to the cities and felt it worth the loss of civil liberties. Foreigners were amazed that for the first time in history, trains ran on time.

One other center of potential dissent was present in the clergy of the Catholic church. In Italy, homeland of Catholicism, the church was a political force. Since 1870 the popes had refused to leave the Vatican in protest over the loss of Rome, but Pope Pius XI was now prepared to seek an accommodation with Mussolini. For his part the Duce wanted to break the stalemate that existed between church and state. In 1929, after months of negotiation, delegates of the two parties signed the **Lateran Treaty.**

Benito Mussolini addresses his followers.

This agreement opened the door to reconciliation. It made Catholicism the official religion of Italy, declared the Vatican a sovereign state, and offered compensation for the occupied Papal States. On paper the impasse between church and state was broken, but the reality proved far different. Fascist ideology did not square with Catholic practice on many points. Fascism insisted that individual rights were always subservient to the demands of the state.

Forging the Soviet Union

In Europe's East a new nation-state, the Union of Soviet Socialist Republics, appeared. It was the work of Nikolai Lenin and his Bolshevik Party. (In 1921 the party took the name Communist.) Soon this state became the most totalitarian nation in all Europe.

By 1921 the Communists routed their enemies on the battlefield. The White forces, never able to work together, collapsed before the communist Red Army. Because Lenin knew well that there was still a great deal of opposition to Communist rule, he gave the secret police, the *Cheka*, a free hand to search out dissenters. The result was mass executions, imprisonment of tens of thousands, and the flight of millions. Such was the fate of all whom the Communists defined as counterrevolutionaries.

Similar to the Fascists in Italy, the party made policy, and the government simply carried out its decisions. In the Soviet Union, however, the terror and efficiency of the Communists far surpassed the Fascists at their worst. The Russian Orthodox church lost all its property, and its patriarch was jailed. Its bishops were executed or sent to Arctic labor camps, and its priests were denied citizenship. Political leaders of prewar Russia suffered the same fate.

All Soviet life came under the management of the state. Privately owned industry ceased to exist. Workers and farmers were enlisted into communist-led organizations. Ironically, Soviet legislation forbade strikes, although according to Marxist theory, the factory worker was the supreme model of the new Soviet man and woman.

Leon Trotsky was expected to follow Lenin as head of the Soviet Union's Communist Party.

Lenin dominated the executive committee of the party, as head of the **Politburo.** As long as Lenin was alive, no one dared challenge him. In 1923, however, Lenin suffered a stroke, allowing the more ambitious members of the Politburo to jockey for the succession. After his death a year later, it seemed probable that Leon Trotsky would be next in line. Even though Trotsky made speeches and wrote articles for the newspapers, a rival, Josef Stalin, slowly but surely gained support. Stalin's attention focused on the local level, placing his partisans in key positions throughout the nation. When a showdown took place, the victor was Stalin. Trotsky went into exile, and in 1940 one of Stalin's agents murdered him.

Lenin had shown that he could be flexible when he saw the post-civil-war economy in shatters. In what was known as the **New Economic Policy,** Lenin allowed farmers to sell their produce on the market and permitted small private entrepreneurs to run their own businesses. By 1927 the Soviet Union fully recovered from its wars.

Stalin, on the other hand, felt compelled to follow Marxist prescriptions for a socialist society. In 1928 he launched the first **Five Year Plan,** in which he intended to industrialize the manufacturing sector of the country completely and to collectivize its agriculture.

The price paid for Stalin's orthodoxy was unbelievably severe. Landowning peasants, the *kulaks,* preferred death to giving over their livestock and grain. The army obliged them. Millions were killed; even more were deported to labor camps. Resistance was especially strong in Ukraine, so that the peasants here suffered disproportionately. One estimate is that, overall, some 14,000,000 died or were exiled to labor camps in Siberia.

Russian peasants demonstrate against the kulaks.

By destroying the productive kulaks, famine ravaged the land. The impassive Stalin, immune to human suffering, made no concessions. As long as he controlled the army and secret police, he felt omnipotent.

The Great Depression

From 1925 to 1929 the European economy flourished, principally because of an influx of investment capital from the United States. Then in 1929 an unexpected series of events shook the world's financial markets. It all began with the failure of an Austrian bank. All over the world creditors demanded their money. Soon tills were empty of cash, and banks locked their doors. In New York the stock market crashed, wiping out the investments of thousands of people. The **Great Depression** was here.

World leaders were ill-prepared to cope with the crisis. In fact, according to capitalist theory, it was not the government's problem. This was an oversimplification. Politics and economics are always strongly linked to each other. A problem for one becomes a problem for both.

In the United States and the industrialized European countries, unemployment reached a proportion of the labor force never before seen. Fully 25% of the world's workers had no jobs. Without employment, there was no money to buy the products of factories, creating a further downward spiral of economic distress. Great Britain had 23% unemployment, but Germany's rate reached 30%.

Britain's unemployed rally for jobs in a 1934 demonstration in Trafalgar Square, London.

Governments at last began to act, but not very effectively. Throughout the world, tariffs were raised on imports in an attempt to protect local producers. These measures only brought on trade wars that did nothing to solve the problems created by the Great Depression. Many governments turned to massive public works to create jobs for the unemployed, but most of these were temporary so that a feeling of insecurity continued to hover over the world.

Rise of Hitler

In Germany one man and the party he led took advantage of the general demoralization to claim that he had an answer to the country's economic woes. This man was Adolf Hitler, and the ascent to power of his Nazi, or National Socialist Party, changed the course of history. In January 1933 President Paul von Hindenburg called upon Hitler to become the nation's chancellor.

Hitler's coming to power was due to many factors. He promised jobs to the unemployed. He told Germany's wealthy and middle-class citizens that he would suppress communism. He appealed to nationalists, still smarting over what they considered the unjust, dictated peace of Versailles.

Hitler announced that he had no intention of keeping the Treaty of Versailles with its admission of German guilt and the requirement for reparations. To all Germans, he offered a program of law and order, suppressing the crime wave that plagued the cities. Although German Jews were but 500,000 people, Hitler took advantage of latent anti-Semitism to blame them for everything that was wrong in Germany. Above all, the Nazis promised action, not endless talk, which had come to afflict the politicians of the Reichstag.

Elections in Germany never gave the Nazis more than 44% of the vote, so one of Hitler's first tasks was to destroy his political opposition. He cleverly persuaded the heads of opposition parties to dissolve their organizations allowing the chancellor to rule alone. Hitler got away with his plans because the Center Party, made up of Catholic Germans, was beguiled by Hitler's promise to sign a **Concordat** with the Vatican. Of course, Hitler, a very astute liar, had no intention of keeping its provisions, but at the time no one was aware of this.

Adolf Hitler, chancellor of Germany's Nazi government.

Hitler began a massive public works and rearmament program to provide jobs for Germany's unemployed. Decrees were issued forcing women to give up jobs outside the home so that men could take their places.

Soon all the elements of the totalitarian state fell into place. Anyone opposing the regime was branded a traitor. Many arrests followed, and concentration camps filled with men and women who were thought to be unfit to live. Racism was at the root of Nazi ideology, so in order to produce the "superior race" hundreds of handicapped and mentally ill men and women were killed. Nazis took control of the press, the theaters, and the radio, skillfully using the media to propagate the party line. Hitler's outdoor rallies, where he gave his speeches with such dynamism, gathered support to him. Even the army generals were cowed by the apparent success that came to the *Führer*, the leader.

Jews suffered the most from Hitler's policies. It was sufficient for one grandparent to be Jewish for a person to be considered an enemy of the German people. In 1935 the **Nuremberg Laws** deprived Jews of German citizenship. Then in November 1938 a Jewish student in Paris killed a German diplomat. This provided the excuse for a violent series of attacks on Jews and their property. Legislation prohibited Jews to hold jobs in most occupations, and this was only the beginning of measures that would lead to the Final Solution, the Holocaust.

Italian Fiasco

Mussolini's Italy was only muddling through in the 1930s. Unlike Germany, Italy's economy remained mired in the doldrums. The Duce decided that an attempt to build an overseas empire might distract the population from problems closer to home. His target was Ethiopia, one of the two independent countries of Africa. In 1896 it had been the scene of Italy's first attempt at empire.

The Ethiopians fought the Italians who arrived in 1936 with the weapons at their disposal. The League of Nations protested what was obviously a flagrant aggression against another people, but it was not willing to use force to stop the invasion.

Italy's next victim was closer to home. Crossing the Adriatic Sea, Italian forces entered Albania, one of Europe's smallest countries. Italy's empire now included two of the poorest nations on earth, little compensation for the sufferings endured for the sake of national glory.

By 1936 Mussolini and Hitler found common cause in their goals, creating a **Rome-Berlin Axis,** which later included the Japanese. These states snubbed their noses at the notion of collective security in the League of Nations. The postwar settlement created at the Paris Peace Conference was crumbling, but the democratic nations were hesitant to act on behalf of either Ethiopia or Albania. Europe's large nations did not yet feel threatened because their own interests were not yet jeopardized.

The Soviet Union under Stalin

Throughout the 1930s the Russian dictator, Josef Stalin, remained obsessed with the idea that if the Soviet Union failed to industrialize rapidly, the capitalist states would crush his nation. Factories, steel plants, a great dam on the Dnieper River, and a canal linking the Baltic with the White Sea were impressive accomplishments of the first Five Year Plan. The Soviets proved willing to hire engineers and technicians from abroad to assist them in this massive building program. In order to gain credits for industrial expansion, grain and other food products were exported despite the needs of the population.

A poster of Stalin looks down on a Russian street.

An immense slave labor force worked on many of these projects. The inmates of the camps built to hold prisoners overflowed with those arrested for real or imagined crimes. As many as 10,000,000 people were imprisoned. In all these camps living conditions were terrible; the food was barely enough to sustain life. About 10% of the prisoners died each year.

The paranoia of Stalin, convinced that enemies abounded, resulted in the condemnation of even those closest to him. Communist Party officials joined generals of the army in trials where they confessed to spying and treason. From 1936 to 1938 the elite of the Soviet Union came under suspicion.

The Soviet Constitution claimed that women had equal rights, with the same economic opportunities as men, and more women did enter the universities. It remained unexplained why they still held the lowest paying jobs. It was grandmothers who swept Moscow's streets and shoveled its snow.

Theoretically communism and fascism were deadly enemies. Yet in practice their goals and methods were remarkably similar. Both were totalitarian systems ruled by a single party that used terror to intimidate their citizens. Both demanded extraordinary sacrifices from their populations so that the armies and the police would be well served. It is no wonder that the mood of thinkers turned bleak in the 20 years between World War I and World War II.

Civil War in Spain

There was a rehearsal for World War II when civil war broke out in Spain. In July 1936 the army in Spanish Morocco rebelled against the Republican government in Madrid. This government was bitterly resented in army circles because it held large numbers of socialists and communists. The rebel general, Francisco Franco, drew his support from the landowners, the church, and the conservative factions of the Spanish people. The Loyalists, the party supporting the government, received aid from the Soviet Union, whereas Franco, whose policies paralleled the Fascist program, received assistance from Germany and Italy.

The Valley of the Fallen holds the graves of Spanish soldiers who fought on both sides of the civil war.

Volunteers came to fight on both sides, and the weapons and strategy of the struggle offered the armies of Europe an opportunity to judge their efficiency. By March 1939 Franco's forces were the victors, and Spain entered into a period in which fascist ideology dominated the country.

Tensions Increase

Step by step Hitler continued on his path to dismantle the Treaty of Versailles. This was not welcomed by the German army chiefs of staff who feared his unilateral moves. In 1936 when he announced his intention to send troops into the Rhineland, a decision specifically prohibited in the Treaty of Versailles, the generals believed that France and England would not permit it. However, the two wartime allies did nothing.

With his notable success in occupying the Rhineland, Hitler turned his attention to the annexation of Austria. In March 1938 this was accomplished, and once more the rest of the world stood by and watched. After Austria was joined to the **Third Reich,** the name Hitler gave to his empire, the Nazi *Führer* turned on Czechoslovakia. He claimed that the Germans of the Sudetenland, the borderland adjacent to Germany, were suffering terrible discrimination at the hands of the Czechoslovak government. Hitler massed troops on the border to intimidate the Czechs.

France had a treaty with Czechoslovakia; it promised that, in case of invasion, the French would come to the aid of the Czechs. In Paris, however, there was a strong defeatist sentiment because the French government feared that its army was simply unable to match the rebuilt German one.

In an effort to defuse the situation, British Prime Minister Neville Chamberlain flew off to Germany hoping to ascertain Hitler's plans. The discussions, with Hitler ranting and raving over the Sudetenland, astonished the very proper Chamberlain.

At this juncture Mussolini intervened to suggest a conference at Munich with the major players: Germany, Great Britain, France, and Italy. The Soviet Union was not invited, nor the Czechs, except as observers. Hitler carried the day; he would get all the areas of the Sudetenland that held a majority of Germans.

The Czechs were given this information to take back to Prague. Chamberlain got off the plane in London announcing "peace in our time." French Premier Edouard Daladier saw a large crowd gathered at the Paris airport. Even though he thought it was an angry mob, he left the plane to its cheers. He told an aide, "The fools, don't they realize what has happened?"

The sentiment against a return to war ran very deeply in Great Britain and France. Although today, many historians blame Chamberlain and Daladier for appeasement, they certainly reflected popular opinion at the time.

The Czechoslovak government, convinced it could not hold off the Germans without outside help, reluctantly agreed to let the Sudetenland go. All their fortifications were located here, leaving the country defenseless. In March 1939 Hitler made new demands. This time he insisted that

Prime Minister Neville Chamberlain returned from Munich, holding the agreement reached there that promised Europe peace.

the Czech part of the nation become a German protectorate. One more time the Prague political leaders felt they had no way to resist and gave in. Slovakia became independent in name, but it was a Nazi puppet state in fact. The Hungarian army occupied Ruthenia, with Hitler's permission.

Now German propaganda in the press and on the radio turned against Poland. The charges were similar to those against the Czechs. Berlin accused the Polish government of persecuting the German minority in the Polish Corridor and Danzig. Danzig held an international status under the League of Nations, but Poland supervised its administration. The Poles refused any border changes.

At this juncture German Foreign Minister Joachim von Ribbentrop approached the Soviets on an agreement to divide eastern Europe between them. Stalin was interested. The two countries reached an arrangement in the **Molotov-Ribbentrop Pact.** (Vyacheslav Molotov was the Soviet Foreign Minister.) The pact spelled doom for East Europe. Hitler was now free to attack Poland without antagonizing the Soviet Union.

The New Science

The postwar world proved unsettling for many people because it emphasized the lack of certainty in the natural world. For centuries Isaac Newton's thesis that the universe was governed by strict laws of cause and effect was not questioned. Now, Albert Einstein challenged this idea with his theory of relativity. Einstein showed that time and space were not absolutes, but relative.

Tremendous popular interest greeted Einstein's discovery. In the scientific world a determined group of researchers went to work to prove or disprove his thesis. When Einstein's work was combined with that of Freud, the public was even more confused about the nature of physical reality and the standards that governed human behavior.

Albert Einstein's theory of relativity demanded a reconsideration of the world of physics.

Changes in Social Life

The most profound social transformation of the people of western Europe between the wars lay in the changing role of the family and the status of women. The urban family steadily decreased in size as children became liabilities rather than economic assets. Congested urban housing further discouraged large families.

The decline in family size was greatest in the larger cities and among the more prosperous families. In all nations of West Europe, average family size dropped. In Britain during the 1870s the average family contained five children. In the 1930s the number was two. Exceptions appeared in the two totalitarian states of Germany and Italy. There governments encouraged large families, and subsidies were offered to the parents of newborn children.

In most European countries the position of women improved from 1919 to 1939. Educational opportunities increased as did employment outside the home. Women had the right to vote in most western countries and to hold political office. In the home, washing machines lessened the drudgery of doing laundry, while gas and electric stoves made preparing meals easier. Grocery stores offered foods from all over the world at remarkably inexpensive prices.

New Leisure

In 1900 most industrial employees labored about 75 hours a week and usually had only Sunday to themselves. During the 1920s Saturday also became a day of relaxation. In 1936 France enacted a law establishing the 40-hour work week.

The radio brought entertainment and mass culture into the home. It made both the world of reality and the world of make-believe a part of the daily lives of men, women, and children. From early morning until far into the night one could effortlessly listen to music, news or weather reports, drama, and sports. From modest beginnings in 1920, within ten years the radio was found in millions of homes.

The automobile revolutionized the use of leisure time. The car furnished an easy means to transport the family from the country to the amusements of the city, or from the city to the sports and outdoor activities of the country. For millions of people, the automobile brought the soccer game or the beach within reach. It made possible holiday picnics in the country and weekend trips to hunt or fish.

The automobile offered families opportunities for travel.

All over Europe patrons flocked to movie theaters to enjoy stories of heroes, heroines, and villains. Movie stars became the model of popular success, and their lives became objects of intense interest.

Conclusion

For statesmen, waging war can be easier than agreeing on a fair peace treaty. In the Paris suburbs where experts were called upon to redraw the map of Europe, there were both realists and idealists. In the realist camp were those who feared a resurgent Germany that, once recovered, could again seek to expand its territories. On the other hand, the idealists believed a peaceful Germany, with only limited sanctions imposed upon it, would take its place among a stable European community of peoples. European nations divided over those who were satisfied with the treaties ending World War I and those who wanted revision, for they believed the diplomats had wronged them.

Two events spoiled the dream of the idealists. One was the Great Depression, the other was the rise of Hitler and Stalin to power in the two strongest continental states. Western European governments always presumed that it was possible to do business with Hitler, for there was a tinge of guilt over the German minorities in Czechoslovakia and Poland that contradicted President Wilson's goal of self-determination. What they did not realize was Hitler's insatiable appetite to create a German state in East Europe that would involve the destruction of the Slavic nations.

A studied effort sought to contain Stalin's Soviet Union and its communist form of totalitarianism. The western democracies preferred to ignore Moscow as far as that was possible. The Soviet dictator received no invitation to Munich despite Soviet interests in central Europe.

One of the most regretable mistakes of the 1920s and 1930s was the unwillingness to build a country on citizenship rather than nationality. Majorities in each country beat the drums of nationalism, pushing to the side minorities that came from a different ethnic or religious background. Democracy in eastern Europe proved especially fragile, as nation after nation sought out a strong man who was supposed to lead the country to greatness.

Obviously the Great Depression contributed to Europe's turn away from democracy and toward totalitarianism. The unemployed worker is not satisfied by parlimentary debate but expects action. Unfortunately, action often meant a turn toward military adventure and factories better equipped to produce armaments than farm implements. The period from 1918 to 1938 was a restless time and was to conclude with Europe, once again, plunged into war.

CHAPTER 21 REVIEW
EUROPE BETWEEN THE WARS

Summary
- The Germans believed that the Treaty of Versailles had treated them unjustly.
- German money became worthless in the midst of uncontrolled inflation.
- Great Britain's economy was plagued by high unemployment.
- Ireland's goal of Home Rule was made difficult because of the Protestant demand in the North to remain part of Great Britain.
- France faced a difficult period of rebuilding, and too many political parties meant constant instability.
- In East Europe several new nations appeared due to the breakup of the Austro-Hungarian, Russian, and German Empires.
- A fascist government under Mussolini appeared in Italy.
- The communist government of the Soviet Union launched a massive industrialization program while imposing a terrorist regime on all its opposition.
- In Southwest Asia the British and French set up colonial regimes through League of Nations' mandates.
- The coming of the Great Depression thwarted all the efforts of the European states to recover economically.
- Hitler seized upon the discontent in Germany to come to power.
- Germany and Italy formed an Axis to pursue a common foreign policy.
- Scientific discoveries and new inventions continued to provide more leisure for the middle class.

Identify
People: Hitler, Dawes, Mussolini, Franco, Chamberlain, Einstein, Trotsky, Stalin
Places: Weimar, Ruhr Basin, Czechoslovakia, Finland, Baltic states
Events: collapse of the German currency; Mussolini comes to power in Italy; Hitler's Nazis rule Germany; Stalin's communists sponsor rapid industrialization in the Soviet Union; the Great Depression; Germany's Nuremberg Laws; the impact of the automobile

Define

Irish Home Rule	Maginot Line	Fascist Party
Politburo	Lateran Treaty	communism
Easter Rebellion	corporate state	kulaks
totalitarianism	New Economic Policy	Rome-Berlin Axis

Multiple Choice
1. The peace treaty between Germany and the Allies was signed in
   (a) Trianon.
   (b) Sèvres.
   (c) Neuilly.
   (d) Versailles.

2. A German democratic constitution was drawn up at
   (a) Weimar.
   (b) Berlin.
   (c) Nuremburg.
   (d) Potsdam.

3. *Mein Kampf* was authored by
   (a) Kaiser Wilhelm II.
   (b) Heidigger.
   (c) Ludendorf.
   (d) Hitler.

4. Reparations were demanded from Germany by France
   (a) to repair war damage.
   (b) to finance the Paris government.
   (c) in fulfillment of pre-World War I debts.
   (d) but not by any other European country.

5. The working class in Great Britain joined the Labour Party in hopes of solving
   (a) the unemployment problem.
   (b) the reparations problem.
   (c) the immigration problem.
   (d) soaring inflation.

6. Protestant politicians in Ulster that remained under British control feared
   (a) Catholic rule in Dublin.
   (b) the Irish Republican Army.
   (c) the Easter Rebellion.
   (d) all the above

7. During the interwar period the French government was the
   (a) Second Republic.
   (b) Second Empire.
   (c) Fourth Republic.
   (d) Third Republic.

8. French foreign policy had as its major goal
   (a) keeping an alliance with Great Britain.
   (b) isolating Germany.
   (c) keeping an alliance with the Soviet Union.
   (d) keeping Algeria as a French possession.

9. After 1920 this country returned to the map of Europe:
   (a) Czechoslovakia
   (b) Romania
   (c) Serbia
   (d) Poland

10. The three Baltic nations were
    (a) Serbia, Romania, and Bulgaria.
    (b) Serbia, Albania, and Yugoslavia.
    (c) Greece, Albania, and Romania.
    (d) Estonia, Latvia, and Lithuania.

11. These two nations of East Europe had viable democracies in 1938:
    (a) Poland and Romania
    (b) Finland and Czechoslovakia
    (c) Finland and Yugoslavia
    (d) Greece and Serbia

12. The Fascist slogan in Italy was
    (a) "All power to the people."
    (b) "Workers of the world unite."
    (c) "Forward for the Fatherland."
    (d) "Believe, Obey, Fight."

13. Italy's system of corporate state industry
    (a) put ownership of factories into government hands.
    (b) put ownership of factories into the hands of labor unions.
    (c) kept private ownership, but management was in government hands.
    (d) put only individual capitalists in charge of production.

14. The Lateran Treaty created the independent state of
    (a) Vatican City.
    (b) San Marino.
    (c) Monte Carlo.
    (d) Sardinia.

15. A civil war in Russia was fought between
    (a) Whites and Mensheviks.
    (b) Whites and Reds.
    (c) Reds and Bolsheviks.
    (d) Mensheviks and Bolsheviks.

16. After Lenin's incapacity, observers thought a likely successor to be
    (a) Stalin.
    (b) Malenkov.
    (c) Khrushchev.
    (d) Trotsky.

17. He killed more people in the twentieth century than any other European ruler:
    (a) Gorbachev
    (b) Hitler
    (c) Mussolini
    (d) Daladier

18. The Great Depression's most obvious effect was in
    (a) jobs.
    (b) investment.
    (c) inflation.
    (d) devaluation of the currency.

19. Hitler's program in its early years included
    (a) an end to Reichstag debate.
    (b) the end of crime.
    (c) the suppression of the Jews.
    (d) all the above.

20. The Nuremberg Laws
    (a) deprived Jews of German citizenship.
    (b) expelled the Jews from Germany.
    (c) closed all synagogues.
    (d) forced Jews to live in certain towns.

21. Mussolini's building an empire was
    (a) ignored by the other European states.
    (b) encouraged by other European states.
    (c) the League of Nations' first military exercise.
    (d) dealt swift retribution by the League of Nations.

22. Stalin's paranoia caused
    (a) the trial and execution of the Crimean Tartars.
    (b) the trial of Germans living in the Soviet Union.
    (c) the execution of many communist officials and Red Army generals.
    (d) the death of all his relatives.

23. The intellectuals of Europe between the wars were immersed in
    (a) optimism.
    (b) indifference.
    (c) interventionism.
    (d) pessimism.

24. Einstein's great discovery was in the field of
    (a) astronomy.
    (b) chemistry.
    (c) mathematics.
    (d) physics.

25. The birth rate fell in countries where
    (a) women were poorly educated.
    (b) women and men lived under democratic governments.
    (c) totalitarian regimes existed.
    (d) dictators encouraged birth control.

26. The most revolutionary invention to give most people mobility in the 1930s was
    (a) the streetcar.
    (b) the railroad.
    (c) the airplane.
    (d) the automobile.

Essay Questions
1. What were the burdens placed on the German government under the Weimar Constitution?
2. Why did Mussolini come to power in Italy?
3. Why did the League of Nations fail to keep the peace?
4. Compare Hitler's Germany to the Soviet Union under Stalin.
5. Discuss the diplomatic efforts to find peace between the wars.

Answers

1. d	4. a	7. d	10. d	13. c	16. d	19. d	22. c	25. b
2. a	5. a	8. b	11. b	14. a	17. a	20. a	23. d	26. d
3. d	6. d	9. d	12. d	15. b	18. a	21. a	24. d	

CHAPTER 22

World War II

The most destructive war in the history of the world began on September 1, 1939. On that date, the German army crossed into Poland, and planes of the German air force commenced the bombing of Warsaw. Hitler was gambling. He did not expect the British and French to support the Poles despite their alliances with that country. Two days later, however, the British Parliament and the French Chamber of Deputies declared war on Germany.

The cause of the Second World War is easy to define. Adolf Hitler long had plans to invade Germany's eastern Slavic neighbors. He intended to destroy these nations so that the Germans might expand to the east. A Nazi victory was considered essential so that the Germans would have *lebensraum,* living space, for themselves. Nazi ideology taught that pure Aryans, like the Germans, were a super race, requiring that their superior culture should be spread. Jews would be exterminated and the Slavic people either wiped out or enslaved.

In Asia the Japanese also believed in their own racial superiority. Their leaders were convinced that it was their destiny to expand into other parts of East Asia. A long military tradition, a revival of Shinto, the religion of Japan, and a psychology that taught that victory was the result of sacrifice contributed to the fighting spirit of the Japanese soldier. It was in this context that the Japanese attacked China and planned to place that country under its rule.

The 20-Year Truce

The **Peace of Paris** divided Europe into two camps, winners and losers. Those states that gained territories naturally wanted to keep the boundaries of the nations on the continent intact. At the same time the notion of self-determination militated against such a settlement because in every nation of East Europe large minorities existed. Each of these minorities was well aware that had the boundaries been drawn differently, they would be joined to a much larger and more powerful state; there they would be part of the majority.

Unfortunately, for those who determined the boundaries after World War I, the different peoples of East Europe did not live in compact clumps. There was no way that a line could be drawn through a village to separate Germans from Poles or Hungarians from Romanians. Therefore throughout the postwar period there was always agitation for change that would better accommodate ethnic minorities.

Two areas of Europe were especially troublesome: the **Sudetenland** of Czechoslovakia and the corridor of land that linked Poland to the sea. In the Sudetenland Germans once a part of the Austrian Empire made their home. The **Polish Corridor** also contained a large German minority. Hitler took advantage of these Germans, proclaiming that they were oppressed and he was only trying to help them to obtain self-determination. There were few facts to show how much oppression there was, but Hitler had no need of them. He knew well that putting all Germans into a single state was just the first step toward putting all eastern Europe into his empire.

The German minorities in other countries were not alone. Several million Hungarians found themselves inside Romanian borders. Millions of Belarussians and Ukrainians had, not by choice, found themselves inside Poland.

The League of Nations spent much of its time hearing complaints of discrimination against minorities. However this body had no way to enforce its decrees to stop harassment. The political leaders of Germany, Italy, and Japan were well aware that verbal sanctions were poor weapons and took advantage of the League's impotence to pursue their goals. In time they quit the League, when its members voted to censure them.

Hitler Triumphant

The German attack on Poland was so overwhelming that within the month resistance ended. The Germans introduced a new kind of warfare, the *blitzkrieg* or lightning war. This involved using tanks and air power to first attack enemy positions, followed by infantry units brought to the front in trucks. The blitzkrieg demonstrated the value of airpower as never before. Bombs rained down on Polish bridges, railroads, and communication centers. By striking at cities, civilians were meant to be terrorized into submission.

According to the plan of the **Molotov-Ribbentrop Pact,** the Russians moved into the eastern half of Poland, reclaiming large areas of Belarus and Ukraine. The Warsaw government fled into exile.

Mussolini, Hitler, and the Italian foreign minister Count Galeazzo Ciano plan strategy for the Axis powers.

Meanwhile British and French generals did little to cause the Germans to divert forces to the west. No military moves took place on the ground. The only losses were British ships that proved vulnerable to submarine attacks.

The war then passed to Scandinavia after Hitler ordered an invasion of Denmark and Norway. Although the British assisted the Norwegians, the navy did not stop the crossing from Denmark.

The battle with France now commenced with German troops overwhelming the Netherlands and Belgium and then pouring into northern France. The British army in France was cut off and withdrew toward ports on the English Channel. From Dunkirk the British successfully evacuated over 300,000 men.

With the French army in retreat, Mussolini declared war on France. In June 1940 the fighting came to an end. By the terms of surrender, Germany occupied the upper two thirds of the country. The bottom third received a collaborationist government headed by General Henri Pétain. Pétain was one of France's heroes during the First World War and believed that he was saving at least part of the country from occupation. The government's capital was in the town of Vichy. In Britain another French general, Charles de Gaulle, vowed to fight on, commanding an army of **Free French.**

Battle of Britain

By July 1940 Hitler was master of most of West Europe, but Great Britain remained defiant. After the fall of Norway, the office of prime minister passed to Winston Churchill, a man of extraordinary ability. He rallied the British people to resist Hitler, even though they were now his only enemies. Actually the British were not that isolated, for the policy of President Franklin D. Roosevelt was to move the United States to actively support their war effort.

In August 1940 as the Germans gathered their forces for an invasion across the channel, the German air force began attacks on British cities. Fortunately, the defenders were equipped with radar, a new detection system that allowed fighter pilots to learn the position of the German planes before they arrived. Although the cities of England suffered from severe bombing attacks, the Royal Air Force was the victor in the **Battle of Britain.**

Winston Churchill, wartime leader of Great Britain.

Mediterranean Theater

The Italian army in Libya crossed the Egyptian border, so as to attack the British defending the Suez Canal. However, the British held their ground. Later a German army arrived in North Africa but the canal remained in Allied hands.

Mussolini felt that Hitler was doing as he pleased without informing his Axis partner of what he intended. Therefore, the Duce decided to attack Greece with the comment, "Hitler will read about it in the newspaper." Moving out of bases in Albania, in October 1940 the Italians crossed into Greece only to find themselves pinned down by mountains, winter, and a determined Greek army. Hitler did read about it in the newspaper and was furious because the Italian attack caused the British to land an army supported by its air force in Greece. Hitler did not want a British presence in the Balkans because the German führer was then planning an invasion of the Soviet Union.

Because the Italians were stymied, in April 1941 the Nazi armies first struck Yugoslavia and then Greece. This diversion of German forces delayed the Soviet invasion until late June, rather than an early spring attack as had been planned.

When the Germans advanced into the Soviet Union on June 22, 1941, Josef Stalin refused to believe it. Was there not the Molotov-Ribbentrop Pact? Hitler had acquiesced in a Soviet war with Finland and the absorption of the three Baltic states of Estonia, Latvia, and Lithuania into Stalin's empire. For several days Stalin gave no orders to his generals, who had to resist as best they could. This meant withdrawing their armies eastward, making sure that the earth was scorched so that nothing of value was left for the invaders. This policy worked against Napoleon in 1812, and remarkably it would succeed again in 1941.

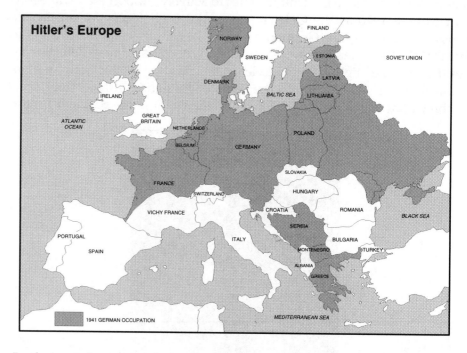

In their push eastward the Germans surrounded Leningrad, the major Russian city in the Baltic, but were never able to take it. Nazi invaders also reached the suburbs of Moscow, but Stalin held his ground and stayed in the capital as his generals, assisted by the bitter winter, stood firm.

In the summer of 1942, the Germans again marched forward, but this time the advance bogged down at Stalingrad. For months the Nazi and Soviet forces attacked and counterattacked in that devastated city. It was the bloodiest battle of the war, and also its turning point. In the end, the Soviets prevailed. During the following year the Red Army took the offensive.

Japan Attacks the United States

In 1937, the Japanese government's plan to expand in Asia, after its success in Manchuria, turned against China. The Japanese joined the Axis, as official German propaganda decided that the Japanese must be Aryans. With the nations of Europe in conflict, Tokyo believed it had great possibilities to pursue its plan to become the dominant country of East Asia.

The western countries were in no position to defend their colonial possessions in the region. After the collapse of France, the Japanese entered French Indochina and occupied the country. Burma became the next target, and finally an attack was planned on the oil-rich Dutch East Indies.

Tokyo's leaders were unsure that they could proceed against the East Indies without the intervention of the United States. With that in mind, the military chiefs decided to take action against the American naval base at Pearl Harbor, Hawaii. On December 7, 1941, Japanese bombers attacked the American fleet. Many ships were damaged, a few were sunk, but unfortunately for the Japanese, the American aircraft carriers were at sea.

President Roosevelt addressed Congress asking that its members support a war against the Japanese. The Congress and the nation, shocked by what they learned of the Pearl Harbor attack, united behind the president.

Japanese bombs fall on U.S. warships in Pearl Harbor.

Hitler fulfilled the provisions of the Axis alliance when he declared war on the United States. He had a strong personal hatred of Roosevelt for the aid he offered Britain so that it could keep up its resistance. The war was now truly global.

At first the Japanese gained easy victories in the South Pacific. Their army was well trained for the attack according to plans made years before. Japan was also fortunate that Washington decided that Hitler was the greater menace and that the war in the Pacific must play a secondary role.

The Japanese took the Philippines from the Americans and the East Indies from the Dutch, but their war in Burma and China did not reach a conclusion. The need to keep occupation forces in place all over East Asia meant that Japanese armies were spread very thin.

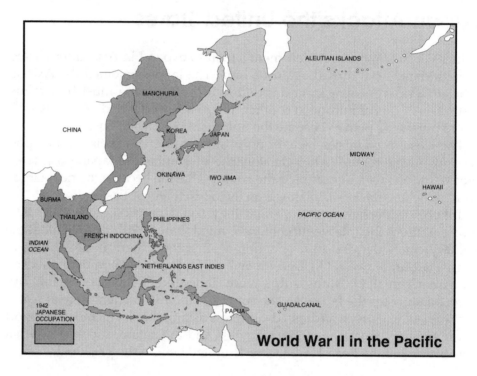

World War II in the Pacific

In June 1942 the Americans challenged a Japanese fleet in the battle of Midway and won a great victory, sinking four aircraft carriers. On the island of Guadalcanal, for months Americans and Japanese fought bitterly over every foot of ground. In the end, the Americans proved successful.

Liberation of Europe

The first step in Europe's liberation took place in Africa. In the beginning Erwin Rommel, Hitler's most able general, used his tanks in the Sahara to great advantage. Rommel's supply line to Germany, however, was subject to Allied bombers operating from Malta, an island in the middle of the Mediterranean. In November 1942 a joint American-British force landed in Morocco and pushed back the Germans until they surrendered.

Next came an Allied invasion of Sicily and a drive up the Italian peninsula, a strategy preferred by the British who were reluctant to attack the Germans head-on in France. The Italian campaign did not go well because the terrain favored the defenders, causing heavy losses. Various partisan bands fought behind the lines to assist the Allies. One of these captured Mussolini and hanged him.

The U.S. chiefs of staff were convinced that a frontal attack on the Germans in France was necessary to win the war. Under General Dwight Eisenhower, now supreme commander, on June 6, 1944, the invasion commenced with a landing on the Normandy beaches. This was D-Day. It caught the Germans off guard; they did not expect an attack at this location. With complete control of the air, the Allies pushed back the German forces. By early September most of France and Belgium was liberated, and the Allies were on the verge of victory.

United States and Soviet soldiers join hands as Germany's defenses crumble.

In early spring 1945 the Americans reached the Rhine River and seized a bridge that retreating troops failed to destroy. A British army crossed the lower Rhine several weeks later. On April 25, 1945, American and Soviet troops met on the Elbe River. Although Hitler gave orders to fight to the end, the army generals knew that further resistance was impossible and surrendered. Hitler and several top Nazis committed suicide in a Berlin bunker rather than be taken prisoner.

Ever since Stalingrad the Soviet army had taken the offensive, pressuring the German army out of Poland, Romania, Hungary, and Czechoslovakia. The Soviet offensive, at the cost of heavy losses, was one of history's most impressive military successes. The Germans and Italians also pulled out of the Balkans when they realized that their position could no longer be sustained.

The Holocaust

A human tragedy of massive dimension, the **Holocaust** took place during World War II when Nazi racism reached a climax. Hitler proposed a **Final Solution,** the extermination of all Europe's Jews. Wherever the German armies were in occupation, Jewish men, women, and children were arrested and packed like cattle into railroad cars. Without food, water, or heat they were shipped to concentration camps, with scores dying along the way.

Nazi soldiers rounded up the Jews of Europe to be sent to concentration camps on the first step of the path to the Holocaust.

In the camps, some were put on work details, others were used for medical experiments, but most were destined for the gas chambers. Told that they were going to a shower, the unfortunate victims were even given a bar of soap to carry with them into sealed rooms. The gas jets were then turned on, and they perished. Fully 6,000,000 Jews died as a result.

Jews were not alone in their suffering. Gypsies, homosexuals, and large numbers of Slavic peoples were also victims of Nazi atrocities. In absolute numbers Ukrainians lost the most men and women during the war.

War in the Pacific

General Douglas MacArthur, the United States commander in the Philippines when the war commenced, had been forced to surrender his army but promised, "I shall return." By October 1944 the U.S. forces allowed MacArthur to make good his promise.

The costliest campaign in the Pacific was fought over Okinawa, an island thought essential for the final attack upon the Japanese homeland. After Okinawa was secured, relentless air attacks commenced on Japanese cities that easily burned because of their wooden construction.

Throughout the war American physicists were at work to create the most deadly weapon ever contemplated, the **atomic bomb.** By the summer of 1945, two bombs were ready. President Harry Truman, who had succeeded to the nation's highest office upon the death of Roosevelt in April 1945, made the decision to use the bombs. He reasoned that it was better to employ them than to suffer the casualties expected if the United States made a frontal attack on the Japanese islands. On August 6, 1945, the first bomb dropped on the city of Hiroshima. Two days later a plane over Nagasaki unloaded the second bomb. Never before had a single weapon been used to kill so many people, nearly all civilians.

The horror was enough. On August 14 the Japanese government sought an armistice and several weeks later surrendered. In the final days of the war, Stalin brought the Soviet Union into the conflict against Japan, and by prior agreement the Soviets now occupied Manchuria.

The atomic bomb devastated the city of Hiroshima.

Home Front

War has always acted as a catalyst to speed up changes in society. World War II, with its total mobilization of the people and resources of the nations involved, worked a profound influence upon individuals and institutions.

The Axis leaders envisaged the war as an opportunity to destroy a decadent western civilization and to rebuild a New Order. The Nazis and Fascists intended to replace the humanist concern for individual rights with the concept of an all-powerful state. Winston Churchill pointed out the danger, "If we fail, a new dark age will descend upon Europe."

During the war, men and women all over Europe joined the **Resistance,** groups that furnished information to the Allies and worked to sabotage railroads and bridges. Their aid was also a major factor in directing Allied commanders to bombing targets.

National governments during the conflict took over all decision making, reducing state and local authorities to rubber stamps. Even in the democracies executive decisions went into effect without consulting legislative bodies. Within the democracies there was never the atmosphere of fear that pervaded totalitarian societies. Secret police in Germany and the Soviet Union saw to it that dissenters did not long exist.

In order to make up for a shortage of workers, the Germans turned to slave labor camps. Authorities ordered millions of people from their homes in occupied countries and settled them in the industrial centers of the Third Reich. Their presence was a major factor in maintaining production during a time when Allied bombing was taking its toll.

Of all the major powers in World War II, Japan had the most limited resources. When ships, planes, and munitions were destroyed, it became increasingly difficult to find replacements.

Consequences of the War

In many ways World War II was a replay of the First World War. Yet there were significant differences. The Nazis were guilty of mass slaughter and genocide never before seen on the European continent.

The costs of the war were staggering. Estimates of battlefield casualties are 17,000,000 soldiers. Some 20,000,000 civilians must be added to this number to appreciate the extent of the losses. Not since the Black Death of the fourteenth century were so many lives snuffed out prematurely.

The material damage was equally monumental, for the destruction amounted to $3,000,000,000. Hundreds of thousands of square miles of farmland was laid waste, and millions of animals lay dead. Towns and villages were shattered if they were caught in the line of fire and subjected to aerial bombardment. Bombing leveled Warsaw, much of Coventry in England, and Berlin and Dresden in Germany. Fire storms left many Japanese cities in ashes.

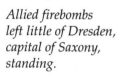

Allied firebombs left little of Dresden, capital of Saxony, standing.

Prisoners of war became targets of abuse and brutalization on both sides. Up to 95% of German prisoners of war in the Soviet Union were never accounted for. The same was true for the Soviets in German hands. Stalin's own son was among those killed. Japanese soldiers in Manchuria, 750,000 men taken in the Russian occupation, simply disappeared into Soviet work camps at the end of the war.

The task of reconstruction in the postwar era proved to be a massive one. After the guns were silenced, the immediate problem was to feed the millions of people who were without the basics for life. A second task was to rebuild the shattered European economy. The third was to recreate viable political institutions to replace those swept away by the war. One hope was to form an international organization to preserve the peace.

United Nations

In the short-lived era of good feelings immediately after the war, world leaders tried once more to construct an international force to preserve the peace. Delegates from all over the world came to San Francisco to create a charter for this body, the **United Nations.** In some ways it was similar to the formation of the League of Nations that followed World War I. In its charter, a clause not found in the League's constitution, the United Nations was empowered to use military force against nations that threatened peace.

New York City became the home of the United Nations.

The United Nations provided for a **General Assembly** and a **Security Council.** All nations had an equal vote in the General Assembly, but the more powerful nations sat in the Security Council. There were five permanent members: China, France, Great Britain, the Soviet Union, and the United States. Another six members were elected by the General Assembly for two-year terms. Each of the five permanent members was given a veto power. In practice the use of the veto stymied much of the Security Council's work. On matters involving military force, a unanimous vote of the Council was required.

Since its inception in 1945 the United Nations has been effective in dealing with crises among small countries. Its weakness appeared when the large nations of the world had interests to protect. The General Assembly became a sounding board to rally one side or another in an attempt to sway world public opinion. Since the General Assembly's formation, it has grown five-fold with the entry of numerous small nations into its membership.

Cold War Origins

At the close of the war, President Harry Truman met with Churchill and Stalin at Potsdam, in defeated Germany, to review the decisions made at other Allied conferences during the war. Because it was expected that an invasion of Japan would entail thousands of casualties, U.S. policy was to gain a pledge from Stalin that the Soviets would enter the war, taking some of the burden from the Americans.

The Soviet leader was already suspicious of Truman, for he expected American investment to aid the rebuilding of the destroyed areas of his nation. Instead, on the day after the German surrender, Truman, equally unsure of Stalin, ordered all monetary and military aid to the Soviet Union stopped.

In the United States and Great Britain there was an expectation that the governments of East Europe would be freely elected. Diplomats were also aware that Stalin had his own plans and fretted that little could be done to aid eastern European governments with the Soviet army in occupation.

A wartime conference held at Yalta in the Crimea during February 1945 offered a guarantee of elections. Stalin, however, had no intention of allowing anticommunist governments to be elected in the eastern European states. He knew well that Russians and their communist ideology were universally hated there.

The Big Three at Yalta: Churchill, Roosevelt, and Stalin.

Earlier in the war, Stalin and Churchill had met in Moscow, and their conversations determined the future status of East Europe. Percentages of control were initialed on a map that allowed the Soviets a free hand in Romania and Hungary and a 50% stake in Yugoslavia. Great Britain should hold a 90% position of influence in Greece. Recall that at this time, Greek communists were actually in control of the country. United States' foreign policy was to leave the eastern European settlement to the British.

At Yalta both Churchill and Roosevelt agreed that Stalin should regain the Russian territories lost after World War I. This affected the three Baltic states, (Estonia, Latvia, and Lithuania), eastern Poland, and the Romanian province of eastern Moldavia. As compensation, Poland should receive territories to the west, at the expense of the Germans.

Communist East Europe

The Soviet army, as it made its advance through Poland, brought with it a group of communist Poles, who had sat out the war in the Soviet Union. Known as the **Lublin Poles,** they took the name after they set up their first government in that eastern Polish city. The Lublin Poles held power only because they had Soviet bayonets to keep them in office.

Great Britain and the United States insisted that members of the democratic parties be joined to the Lublin Poles. Together they would form a coalition when the government was again located in Warsaw. This coalition proved to be no more than a facade. In 1948 a staged election removed the members of the democratic parties from office.

What happened in the Polish scenario occurred throughout most of East Europe. For a time there was a coalition, but the communists always held the Interior Ministry. This agency controlled the police and the voting procedures. When elections occurred the various communist parties won with huge majorities.

As in the Soviet Union, policy was made in the local party, or in Moscow, not by government officials in East Europe. All opposition was quelled, except in Poland where the Catholic church and nationalism were so identified that the communists held back from an open conflict. By 1948 all East Europe was in the hands of communist governments, with the exception of Finland and Greece.

Yugoslavia also had a communist ruler, but he was a communist with a difference. The leader of the party here was Josip Broz, better known as Tito. During the German occupation of his country, Tito organized a military unit known as the **Partisans.** The Chetniks were a rival organization, composed of Serbians loyal to the Yugoslav dynasty. When the Partisans were not fighting the Germans, they turned on the Chetniks.

Josip Broz Tito, leader of the Yugoslav Partisans.

The Soviet Red Army did not play a major role in liberating Yugoslavia. It was Tito's Partisans who deserved the credit. When Tito learned that Stalin intended to treat Yugoslavia in the same way as the other eastern European nations, he rebelled. Stalin boasted, "I will shake my little finger, and there will be no more Tito." However, Tito's popularity with his countrymen and women was too great. Stalin was frustrated. In 1948 he expelled Yugoslavia from the East Europe's communist bloc and tried to isolate Tito.

The Truman Doctrine

In 1947, the United States and Great Britain faced two major problems in the Mediterranean region. One was in Greece where a native communist army held most of the north, supported by the Yugoslavs and the Bulgarians, but not by Stalin. The other was Turkey, where the Soviets now demanded a position on the Dardanelles that would give Stalin a major role in Turkish affairs.

For many decades the British were the major power in the East Mediterranean, but a war-weary Britain could no longer sustain a major presence. As a result, in February 1947 the London government told the United States it was pulling out of its commitments to restore the Greek democracy.

President Truman, already convinced that any further communist gains must be resisted, declared in a speech to Congress, "It must be the policy of the United States to support free peoples who are resisting subjugation by armed minorities or by outside pressure." The president asked and received from Congress a $400,000,000 appropriation to shore up the Greek and Turkish governments. The **Truman Doctrine** put the United States into the lead in resisting the spread of communism in a struggle with the Soviets in what became known as the **Cold War.**

The Truman Doctrine was soon followed by the **Marshall Plan.** In June 1947 the Secretary of State, George Marshall, in a speech at Harvard University, noted that the nations of Europe were in dire need of investment in order to recover from the war. Marshall held out an offer for economic assistance to all European governments, but Stalin would have none of it. He was convinced that it must be a capitalist plot. The Soviet leader also forbade any of the eastern European countries to participate, but the western European nations were enthusiastic.

The Marshall Plan was a life saver for Europe. Over the next four years, about $13,000,000,000 went overseas. It was used for repairs to highways, port facilities, bridges, and railroads and for getting factories back into production.

Occupied Germany

In defeated Germany, the four conquering armies set up zones of occupation. Along with the British, Soviet, and American armies, a contingent of Free French troops participated in the final assault. This participation allowed France to have its occupation zone along with the others. All four armies shared in the administration of Berlin.

The Soviets in East Germany began dismantling everything of value that they could find. It was then shipped eastward, impoverishing the already destitute population. Tens of thousands of Germans in the Soviet Zone fled to the western nations' occupation zones, creating a massive refugee population. The hard line of the Soviets delayed any talks of a peace treaty with Germany and nudged the Americans, British, and French toward a common policy in West Germany. The Allies brought to justice those Nazis still living, charged with war crimes for the part they played in Hitler's Germany.

In 1948 a major crisis shook Germany, and the possibility of World War III seemed on the horizon. In West Germany, over Soviet objections, the Allies issued a common currency, the *deutschmark*. Stalin was so angered that he closed the highway that connected Berlin to the West. With its land route blockaded, the western states decided on supplying Berlin by air. For months cargo planes landed at the Berlin airport with food, fuel, and the necessities of life. In May 1949 Stalin relented allowing the Berlin artery to reopen when he judged that the West intended to continue the airlift indefinitely.

Conclusion

The interwar period in Europe seemed hopeful in the first decade after the Paris peace conference. The bitterness of the war began to fade, and rebuilding commenced. Germany under the Weimar Republic demonstrated a willingness, after its reparation payments were renegotiated, to cooperate in the community of western European nations.

However, the Great Depression, with its unemployment problem so serious in Germany, brought a new element into the picture. Many of the German people were faced with economic ruin, prompting them to look for a savior to lead them out of their despair. Unfortunately they found Adolf Hitler, a man who promised economic recovery, a spiritual renewal based on nationalism, and an intense racism. Hitler was a very able orator and skillfully played up to the fears and the aspirations of a large segment of the Germans who welcomed authoritarian rule.

World War II was the result of Hitler's plan to annex the Slavic lands to the east. For awhile all went well, but the invasion of the Soviet Union was a major blunder. The Nazis began the extermination of all the Jews in the lands they conquered in what they called the Final Solution; their horrible actions still haunt many. As in World War I, U.S. participation along with the courage of the Soviet Union's armies doomed Hitler's plans.

In the Pacific the Allies fought the Japanese from island to island in preparation for a frontal assault on the Japanese homeland. After two atomic bombs were dropped, the Japanese surrendered, and the attack on the island was never necessary.

After the war the formation of the United Nations gave promise of a better world. However, the Cold War, between the United States with its allies and the Soviet Union with the governments of communist eastern European nations, delayed any solid peace for the next four decades. The threat of a Cold War turning hot hung over the world like a great dark cloud.

CHAPTER 22 REVIEW
WORLD WAR II

Summary

- The Nazi leader, Hitler, used the excuse that German minorities in East Europe were persecuted, especially in the Sudetenland.
- Hitler commenced World War II when he directed German armies to invade Poland.
- Hitler went from victory to victory, but he did not have sufficient sea power to cross the English Channel to invade Great Britain.
- The German invasion of the Soviet Union bogged down before Moscow.
- Japan attacked Pearl Harbor, bringing the United States into war in the Pacific, which gave Hitler a reason to declare war on the United States for its aid to Great Britain.
- The United States and its allies slowly turned the tide of Axis victories and defeated Japan, Germany, and their allies.
- During the war Hitler gave orders to exterminate Europe's Jews, creating the Holocaust.
- At the end of the war, Europe had suffered immense losses of people and property.
- The Allies sought to build a more efficient organization, the United Nations, to keep the peace.
- At the conclusion of World War II, a Cold War between the West and the Soviet Union and its eastern European satellites set in.
- The Truman Doctrine announced that the United States intended to contain communism, and the Marshall Plan sought to rebuild West Europe.

Identify

People: Hitler, Mussolini, Stalin, de Gaulle, Franklin D. Roosevelt, Churchill, Eisenhower, Truman, Tito

Places: Sudetenland, Polish corridor, Danzig, Tokyo, East Indies, Stalingrad, Hiroshima, Yalta

Events: battle of Britain; attack on Pearl Harbor; battle of Midway; dropping the atomic bomb; Marshall Plan; Berlin blockade

Define

lebensraum	Cold War	United Nations
Holocaust	blitzkrieg	Lublin Poles
Molotov-Ribbentrop Pact	Free French	Truman Doctrine
Partisans	Resistance	

Multiple Choice

1. Drawing the map of Europe after World War I
   - (a) kept Germany's borders exactly as they were in 1914.
   - (b) left German ethnic minorities in many East European states.
   - (c) allowed the Soviet Union to regain the territory lost by the Treaty of Brest-Litovsk.
   - (d) ignored the pleas of the Poles to recreate a state.

2. The Scandinavian countries occupied by Nazis were:
   (a) Sweden and Denmark
   (b) Sweden and Norway
   (c) Norway and Finland
   (d) Norway and Denmark

3. He led the French government in Vichy:
   (a) Petain
   (b) de Gaulle
   (c) Daladier
   (d) Blum

4. He followed Chamberlain as the British prime minister:
   (a) Lloyd George
   (b) McDonald
   (c) Macmillan
   (d) Churchill

5. The Italian invasion of Greece came to Hitler
   (a) as a well-conceived plan.
   (b) as a surprise.
   (c) in coordination with his plans to invade Poland.
   (d) in coordination with his plans to invade Yugoslavia.

6. The German invasion of Russia failed to capture
   (a) Moscow.
   (b) Leningrad.
   (c) Gorkiy.
   (d) all the above.

7. Pearl Harbor was attacked in December 1941, but
   (a) the United States suffered no major losses.
   (b) the United States was prepared for the attackers.
   (c) the United States launched a counterattack on Kobe.
   (d) no aircraft carriers were in port at the time.

8. A turning point in the U.S. naval war against Japan occurred at
   (a) Guadalcanal.
   (b) Okinawa.
   (c) Guam.
   (d) Midway.

9. General Rommel's wars were fought in
   (a) Normandy.
   (b) Italy.
   (c) Sicily.
   (d) North Africa.

10. On D-Day Allied troops landed on the beaches of
    (a) Sicily.
    (b) Brittany.
    (c) Belgium.
    (d) Normandy.

11. East Europe was liberated from the Nazis by
    (a) the Soviet's Red Army.
    (b) General Patton.
    (c) General Eisenhower.
    (d) the British army operating out of Greece.

12. The racism of the Nazis required the extinction of
    (a) homosexuals.
    (b) Jews.
    (c) Gypsies.
    (d) all the above.

13. The U.S. general in the Pacific arena was
    (a) Patton.
    (b) Clark.
    (c) Eisenhower.
    (d) MacArthur.

14. Atomic bombs struck these two Japanese cities:
    (a) Tokyo and Osaka
    (b) Hiroshima and Kyoto
    (c) Tokyo and Kobe
    (d) Hiroshima and Nagasaki

15. On the home front all national governments in Europe
    (a) assumed control over all manufacturing industries.
    (b) issued paper money.
    (c) encouraged freedom of dissent.
    (d) used slave labor to work in factories.

16. Most German prisoners of war in the Soviet Union
    (a) were immediately released at the end of the war.
    (b) emigrated to the United States after peace came.
    (c) settled in East Germany.
    (d) disappeared.

17. The United Nations has two houses:
    (a) the General Assembly and the Security Council
    (b) the General Assembly and the Executive Board
    (c) the Security Council and the Chamber of Deputies
    (d) the House of Representatives and the Senate

18. The Cold War broke out after the war because of
    (a) mutual suspicion between the West and the Soviet Union.
    (b) the U.S. refusal to allow the Soviets access to the Marshall Plan.
    (c) the downing of an American spy plane over Russia.
    (d) the U.S. rejection of Soviet demands to share the ingredients of the atomic bomb.

19. The Yugoslav Partisans were led by
    (a) Mihailovich.
    (b) Pasić.
    (c) Andrić.
    (d) Tito.

20. The Marshall Plan
    (a) guaranteed the borders of Greece and Turkey.
    (b) took Trieste from Yugoslavia and gave it to Italy.
    (c) divided Germany into an East and West.
    (d) none of the above.

Essay Questions
1. What were the causes of World War II?
2. What mistakes did Hitler make in directing the Nazi war effort?
3. Why did eastern Europe fall into communist hands?
4. Why did Truman use the atomic bomb? Was it a correct moral decision, or does war have any rules?
5. What caused the alliance between the Soviets and the western powers to break up so soon after the war?

Answers

1. b	6. d	11. a	16. d
2. d	7. d	12. d	17. a
3. a	8. d	13. d	18. a
4. d	9. d	14. d	19. d
5. b	10. d	15. a	20. d

CHAPTER 23

Rebirth of Europe

Throughout western Europe new parties and personalities appeared on the political scene at the conclusion of the war. Many familiar politicians of prewar Europe disappeared along with their parties. Both socialists and communists gained strength because during the war they were prominent in the Resistance. More conservative voters clustered about Christian Democratic parties. Although the word *Christian* usually appeared in their titles, the leaders of these parties had only tenuous connections to the institutional churches of their countries.

The Berlin Blockade of 1948 caused the United States and Canada to forge a new alliance system with ten European democratic nations, the **North Atlantic Treaty Organization** (NATO). In 1955 the Soviets replied with a combination of the eastern European states known as the Warsaw Pact. As a result, an armed border ran the length of the continent and divided Germany into two nations.

Great Britain After the War

Despite the fact that Churchill and his Conservative Party led Great Britain to victory, the electorate wanted a change. In July 1945 a Labour government, socialist in ideology, came to power in Parliament. It delivered on its promise to nationalize utilities and the major industries. A National Health Service offered free medical care for all.

These measures, along with the promotion of subsidized public housing, were politically popular but economically did little to enhance the nation's productive capacity. In addition, the colonial empire of the nineteenth century slowly crumbled, and the demands of the Cold War brought hardships that the British people did not foresee. In 1951 a Conservative government returned to power when British citizens tired of social change.

The economy of Great Britain lagged behind the continental nations for a number of reasons. British industry failed to modernize, and much of the British merchant fleet was obsolete. Labor unions were insistent on pay raises, but production remained low. There were 600 unions in the country, many with leaders who constantly demanded higher wages at a time when production was in decline.

In 1979 British voters chose Margaret Thatcher and the Conservative Party in a major retreat from socialism. She was the first woman to be chosen to lead a major nation in western Europe.

Thatcher's plans involved lopping off the subsidies that financed Britain's welfare state. She reduced taxes with the intent that people should

*Margaret Thatcher,
British Prime Minister
in the 1980s.*

invest more of their money. Industries nationalized under Labour governments were sold to private entrepreneurs.

Conservative policies were not an overnight success because many people
found themselves unemployed. Fortunately the economy began to make a
comeback, helped by a major discovery of oil reserves beneath the North
Sea. In 1983 and 1987 Mrs. Thatcher, the Iron Lady, remained in power as
Conservatives continued to win majorities in Parliament.

Like most political leaders who stay in power too long, rivals began to
appear who sought to replace her. The upshot came in 1990 when John Major
was elected to head the Conservatives, and Thatcher returned to private life.

British foreign policy included a brief conflict in 1982 with Argentina
over the Falkland Islands, a group of desolate drops of land in the
Atlantic. The London government took a hard line on Northern Ireland.
Thatcher supported a program that allowed the Protestant majority to
continue to hold power at the expense of the sizable Catholic minority.
The British army in the north fought an undeclared war with Irish
nationalists in the Irish Republican Army. Car bombings, assassinations,
and arrests without trial became a frequent occurrence in a three-sided
conflict. The army, the IRA, and Protestant paramilitary organizations
frequently used terrorism to promote their goals.

*Young Catholics stone
a British vehicle in
Northern Ireland.*

France Rebuilds

At the close of the war, France had one more opportunity to experiment
with a form of government. General Charles de Gaulle, commander of the

Free French forces during the war, now assumed the leadership of the country in peace. De Gaulle was convinced of the need for a strong presidency, but the assembly summoned to draw up the constitution held a majority of communists and socialists. They were well aware of de Gaulle's plans to become president and thwarted the general's will in the document they approved. In a huff, de Gaulle resigned from the government and retired to private life.

In November 1946 the constitution was finished; it provided for a Fourth Republic with the legislature, the **Chamber of Deputies,** in control. Coalition governments rose and fell over the following years, because majorities were always short-lived.

The colonial problem vexed all governments of the Fourth Republic. Even though politicians believed that France must regain control of its territories in Asia and Africa, reality soon dawned. The colonies did not want the French to return. The most vigorous resistance was met in Indochina, where Ho Chi Minh's nationalist, communist army effectively checked the French efforts. In 1954, after a major defeat at Dien Bien Phu, the French retired from the country, handing over the war to the United States.

Algeria, much closer to home, was deemed essential for France's future. It was the country's oldest colony, and over a million French citizens lived there. Many of them were grandchildren of the first settlers and were adamantly opposed to the native, Arab-speaking Berbers, who wanted independence. A bitter armed conflict broke out with atrocities on both sides. By 1958 France was on the verge of a civil war between those who supported the war in Algeria and the army's efforts and those who wanted an end to it all, giving Algeria its freedom.

There was only one man in whom most Frenchmen and women believed. That was de Gaulle. His prestige allowed him to return to Paris and to convince the politicians that the country must have a new constitution, if a solution to the Algerian problem was to be reached. The response was positive and the country entered into a **Fifth Republic.** This time the constitution put real power in the hands of the president.

With this authority de Gaulle negotiated a settlement despite the opposition of the army and the French settlers in Algeria. In July 1962 Algeria became an independent country.

Two leaders of postwar Europe: Konrad Adenauer of Germany and Charles de Gaulle of France.

Charles de Gaulle's plans emphasized his goal of making France the leading power in western Europe. He thought that the United States had too great a presence on the continent and was determined to demonstrate that France could go it alone. For that reason he withdrew France from most joint military commitments and canceled leases for American bases in France.

From 1958 to 1968 de Gaulle, with the constitution of the Fifth Republic giving him legitimacy, guided French destinies. Then a monetary crisis and student unrest caused him to retire a second time.

Conservative governments followed de Gaulle's departure from public life. For the most part the economy continued to do well, with a mixture of state and private enterprises. In 1981 the Socialist Party, led by François Mitterand, came to power.

Italian Developments

Italy has been described as a country that has no need of a government. In fact, it has had a long series of premiers, with political turmoil and infighting the rule rather than the exception.

Italy, like Germany, sought to make a new political start after World War II. As in Germany, the Christian Democrats, under the leadership of Alicide de Gasperi, formed the government with the moral and financial support of the United States.

The Christian Democrats promised reform, but they were beholden to the powerful families of prewar times, who contributed to their campaigns. The Christian Democrats usually had to depend on a coalition with smaller parties, which made political stability on the national level impossible. On the local level, where it counted, the same volatility did not appear.

The Italian Communist Party was the largest outside the Soviet Union, with its strength in the industrialized North. In Sicily the Mafia held a dominant position, unchallenged because of its shadowy power and links to the region's politicians.

The Christian Democrats remained in power from the close of the war until 1981, seeking to stabilize an economy marked by fits and starts. The Italian public managed to keep afloat through the many crises and in the 1990s reached a living standard comparable to that of Great Britain.

Spain and Portugal under Authoritarian Regimes

In 1975 the long tenure of General Francisco Franco ended with his death. Spanish history entered a new and happier phase. A constitution that protected human rights was drafted, and as a symbol of unity, Juan Carlos, a descendent of the Bourbon kings, was invited to sit on the Spanish throne. His influence, as a constitutional monarch, has been remarkably benificent. In 1981 he successfully thwarted a coup when a group of disgruntled nationalists seized the Cortes, the Spanish parliament. The king went on television to rally the people and army to support Spanish democracy.

The Portuguese were Europe's poorest people living in the West. They lived under the totalitarian rule of Prime Minister Antonio de Oliveira Salazar, whose policies had one purpose in mind, keeping his nation firmly under control.

Two Germanys

As a result of the Soviet threat, in 1955 the western powers agreed to the establishment of the German Federal Republic with its capital in Bonn. The Allied occupation of the country ended, although, because of the NATO alliance, foreign miliary units remained in West Germany, for the Germans were now part of the organization.

After the war the Allies in West Germany sought out politicians who were not compromised by a Nazi past. Among these was Konrad Adenauer, former mayor of Cologne, and a staunch opponent of Nazism during the war.

Adenauer reconstituted the Christian Democratic Party from men and women who once belonged to the Catholic Center Party. The Social Democrats also regrouped, forming the main opposition party. Communists in the West were a handful. In East Germany the communists established the German Democratic Republic with Walter Ulbricht, head of the party, serving as its leader.

East Germany's experience, with its population behind an armed border, resembled a prison. The apparatus of the police state remained in force, with a host of informers spying upon other informers.

The Soviet Union After Stalin

In 1953 Josef Stalin died. His death was officially lamented in the Soviet Union, but in fact the long-suffering citizens of that country were at last free of the terror he inspired. At once a contest began over the succession. Three groups—the army, the secret police, and the Communist Party—sought to dominate.

Nikita Khrushchev makes a point at the United Nations.

After some months of jostling, the Communist Party won out. Nikita Khrushchev ascended to the top post as general secretary. In 1956 Khrushchev did the unthinkable. At the **Twentieth Party Congress,** in a speech that lasted for two days, he denounced Stalin and the tyranny of his rule. Officially the denunciation was to be kept secret, but details soon leaked out.

Revolution in East Europe

Khrushchev's de-Stalinization was risky. The party leadership in eastern European nations came under attack for its support of the Soviet dictator. In Poland for years people suffered from police brutality and shortages of everything from food to housing. Demonstrations broke out demanding change. One of the protests turned into a riot, and over a hundred people died.

The agitation spread to East Germany and Hungary. In October 1956 Hungarian workers commenced tearing down the statues of Stalin that stood on Budapest streets. They searched out members of the hated secret police, beating some and killing others. For several days the Soviet army in Hungary hesitated to act and then began to pull out of the country.

In Moscow, when the party chiefs realized that Hungary intended to leave the Warsaw Pact, they changed their minds. They feared that if one block of their empire was lost, the whole building might collapse, so they ordered the tanks to turn around.

The Hungarians appealed for help because in numbers and weapons they could never match the Soviets. In Washington, London, and Paris the appeals were answered with diplomatic protests. The West was not prepared to start a war to save Hungary. Soviet tanks slaughtered thousands of the Hungarians, and more were arrested. Many Hungarians, over 100,000, fled into Austria for sanctuary.

Hungary's efforts to break free of the Soviet Union brought tanks into Budapest.

Khrushchev's Gambles

The Hungarian revolt put a chill on Soviet relations with the West for the next few years. Then, as tensions lessened, a new point of friction appeared. East Germans discovered that coming to Berlin gave them an opportunity to escape the drabness and tyranny that dominated their lives in the East. What once was a stream of refugees became a river and threatened the East German economy. To halt this flow, on the night of August 13, 1961, workers in East Berlin began the construction of the **Berlin Wall,** whose purpose was to stop the refugees. More than the hammer and sickle on the Soviet flag, the Berlin Wall became the symbol for communism in the West.

A year later a major confrontation once more took place. The United States set up an embargo of Cuba, after it fell into the hands of Fidel Castro, who proclaimed himself a Marxist. In the fall of 1962, Khrushchev decided to test the U.S. resolve by arming the island with missiles that were pointed in the direction of Florida.

President John F. Kennedy demanded that the Soviets dismantle their missiles. For a few days the world seemed destined to plunge into nuclear catastrophe as the two superpowers, armed with hydrogen bombs, faced off. Khrushchev then had to accept the fact that his armed forces were no match for American might. The missiles came down, and a year later, because of his failure, so did Khrushchev.

The Soviet Union appeared to be one of the two superpowers of the world, but all was not well in that huge nation. Because communist ideology required concentration on heavy industry, consumer goods were always in short supply. When Soviet citizens saw a line, they automatically got into it because shortages were so chronic.

Food production was a recurring problem. Both nature and the communist system combined to thwart efforts to produce enough agricultural products. In the United States, the 45° north latitude cuts through Minnesota, one of the northernmost states. In the Soviet Union the same 45° dissects the Crimea, the southernmost part of Ukraine. This meant that crops in the Soviet Union had to be grown in a climate that was often too cold for grains to mature.

One of Khrushchev's ideas was to plow the arid regions of Inner Asia in Kazakhstan. Instead of enabling grains to grow, however, the plowing merely created a huge dust bowl.

Just as industry was controlled by communist authorities in Moscow, so was agriculture. There were two types of farms: *kolkhozes*, collectives, and *sovkhozes*, state farms. The collectives were made up of units averaging 440 families and 15,000 acres. The government took the crops grown on these farms according to assigned quotas. On state farms, workers held jobs as if they were in a factory.

As an exception each rural family was allowed a plot of one to three acres where it could grow whatever it pleased. These small parcels produced a remarkable amount of the nation's milk, butter, and eggs, which were then sold in private markets. The communists conveniently overlooked this exercise in capitalism.

Economic Recovery in Western Europe

The Marshall Plan changed Europe's economic prospects in the West. American aid was used to rebuild the transportation and communication network essential for an industrial economy. Where old factories were destroyed, Marshall Plan dollars replaced them with new and more efficient machinery.

Nearly all western European states prospered in the 1950s. The French and German recovery led the way. Both countries improved their production in increments between 5 and 10% annually. A prosperous middle class in both countries appeared with a living standard that improved each year. The increase in the number of automobiles on European highways gave evidence of the new prosperity.

The demand for industrial workers was so great that a migration of people from the poorer Mediterranean regions moved into northern Europe. Known as *guest workers*, the laborers were expected to return home after several years, but in fact many decided to stay. Within the major cities of France, Switzerland, and Germany, Moroccan, Spanish, Greek, and Turkish sections appeared.

European Integration

One of the differences between Europe and the rest of the world is the great diversity of peoples who live there and their cultures. Yet there has always been a vague feeling among people in every age who believed that European unity was a goal worth pursuing.

After the war several efforts appeared in western Europe to coordinate activities. In 1948 the Council of Europe was formed, but the British wanted no part of it. On the military scene, cooperation came easier because of the Soviet threat to all the states in the West.

In 1950 the French Foreign Minister, Robert Schuman, suggested that France and Germany cooperate in the production of coal and steel. He announced that his actions were based not only on economic considerations but also on political ones. Joint enterprise in these industries would make war between the two countries "not only unthinkable but materially impossible." In 1953 Schuman's dream was realized: Germany, France, and their neighbors Belgium, Netherlands, and Luxembourg formed the **European Coal and Steel Community.** Within five years production increased 42%.

The success of this venture prompted the nations involved to move a step closer toward economic integration. Therefore their leaders broadened its base and formed the **European Economic Community** (EEC), better known as the Common Market. Today it is called the **European Union.** Its purpose was to slowly eliminate tariffs, coordinate currency policies, and, in general, oversee the broad financial and industrial concerns of the member states. With a population of 175 million people, the EEC became the third largest economic unit in the world.

In 1972 the EEC admitted Great Britain, Ireland, and Denmark and in subsequent years Greece, Spain, and Portugal. Its success gave a major impetus to economic growth in West Europe.

The Soviets sought to do something similar in the nations they controlled in East Europe. However, the benefits were all to go to them, not to the nations of East Europe. In 1949 they set up their **Council of Mutual Economic Assistance** (Comecon). Comecon never worked very well, especially in those countries where agriculture defied all efforts to increase production. In the cities, the standard of living improved, but it still was only half that of western Europe.

Soviets under Stress

In 1964 his fellow Politburo leaders brought Nikita Khrushchev down, blaming him for his failure to solve the nation's agricultural problems and his retreat during the Cuban missile crisis. For a time there was collective leadership. At length one man, Leonid Brezhnev, rose to the top.

Brezhnev was not the kind of person to take unnecessary risks, with the result that, on the surface, relations with the United States and the West improved. In 1972 the two nations agreed to talk about reduction of armaments. Known as SALT, the **Strategic Arms Limitation Talks,** progress was made in limiting the number of long-range missiles. The Soviets began purchasing grain from the United States, creating an important bond between the two nations.

Tensions continued to be reduced. In 1975 at Helsinki, the Conference on Security and Cooperation in Europe brought all the continent's nations, Albania excepted, into an agreement that required signatories to respect human rights in their nations. Unfortunately, no adequate means of enforcing the accord was set up, but throughout eastern Europe human rights organizations—Charter 77 in Czechoslovakia was the most active—formed to monitor violations.

There were still opportunities to cause trouble. The Brezhnev Doctrine announced that the Soviets intended to support other communist regimes in the world from threats to their rule. Therefore, communist Cuba remained viable because of Soviet subsidies. In 1968, when it appeared that Czechoslovakia was on the verge of dumping its communist government, the Soviets and the Warsaw Pact nations invaded the country.

The occupation of Prague by the Soviets in 1968 demonstrated Moscow's resolve to dictate policy in East Europe.

Again in 1979 the Soviets intervened to support a Marxist regime in Afghanistan. Although the Soviets had an army with overwhelming fire power and complete control of the air, the Afghan terrain limited the Red Army's effectiveness. Instead of a quick victory, the war bogged down in a stalemate. The United States responded to the Afghan invasion by stopping grain shipments to the Soviet Union and boycotting the Olympic Games in Moscow.

Soviet war materials arrive in Kabul to support the Afghan government.

Conclusion

In Churchill's phrase, an Iron Curtain divided Europe in the postwar years. To the west were the democratic states, which were allied with the United States and Canada and determined to keep communism on its side of the curtain. To the east were those nations of East Europe that had communist governments placed over them because of the strength of the Red Army and the secret police who took their orders from Moscow.

As long as Stalin lived, a reign of terror hovered over the people of the Soviet Union. The Russian people had sacrificed so much to defend their nation from Hitler's armies; yet for all of their sufferings there were no rewards. Communist theory pretended that all was well, but the reality was very different. Khrushchev's Twentieth Party Speech acknowledged the horrors of Stalinism, but too little changed in Moscow because party and army officials did not want to loosen their grip on power and privileges.

The 1956 Hungarian revolt was ample demonstration of the true sentiments of the people in eastern Europe, as well as the unwillingness of the West to act on Hungary's behalf if a general war was to result.

In western Europe, democracy and respect for civil rights expanded to Spain and Portugal. On the negative side, the loss of their colonies came as a major blow to those countries that had created an empire in Asia and Africa, as grudgingly the empire had to be given up. With more attention paid to events in Europe, the steps that led to the European Economic Community were the most positive indication in western Europe and Greece that a third world war would never occur.

CHAPTER 23 REVIEW
REBIRTH OF EUROPE

Summary
- Europe polarized into a democratic West and a communist East after World War II.
- Great Britain lost its empire, and at home industrial production lagged behind other European countries.
- De Gaulle sought to restore French prestige, but the nation's colonial territories also vanished in a wave of nationalism.
- After a short retirement, de Gaulle returned to politics when conflict in Algeria threatened civil war in France.
- Christian Democrats led Italy's postwar government.
- In Spain and Portugal authoritarian regimes continued to hold power immediately after the war.
- Germany was divided into West and East. The West made a remarkable postwar recovery.
- The Soviet Union had a succession of rulers arising from the ranks of the Communist Party after Stalin's death.
- In 1956 Hungarian workers revolted against their communist government in a doomed effort to escape their totalitarian system.
- The Soviets and the United States came close to war over Khrushchev's plans to put missiles in Cuba.
- European economies began to integrate production in the European Economic Community.

Identify
People: de Gaulle, Thatcher, Franco, Adenauer, Khrushchev, de Gasperi, Schuman, Juan Carlos, Ulbricht, Brezhnev
Places: Falkland Islands, Dien Bien Phu, Algeria, Budapest, Berlin Wall, Cuba, Afghanistan
Events: Thatcher turned the British away from the welfare state; de Gaulle saved France from civil war; Christian Democrats governed West Germany and Italy; Twentieth Party Congress in the Soviet Union begins de-Stalinization; Hungarian revolt of 1956; European Union formation

Define

Warsaw Pact
Hungarian revolt
kolkhozes
French Fifth Republic

North Atlantic Treaty Organization
European Economic Community
Strategic Arms Limitation Talks

Multiple Choice
1. The Soviet response to NATO was
    (a) Comecon.
    (b) the Warsaw Pact.
    (c) the Berlin Wall.
    (d) the invasion of Afghanistan.

2. Margaret Thatcher's Conservative government marked a retreat from
   (a) socialist programs of the Labour Party.
   (b) free trade.
   (c) free enterprise.
   (d) NATO.

3. Northern Ireland remained a problem because of
   (a) IRA demands for union with Ireland.
   (b) Protestant insistence on keeping a political monopoly in the region.
   (c) both Catholic and Protestant unhappiness over the British army in the North.
   (d) all the above

4. The death-knell of French colonialism in Southeast Asia came at the battle of
   (a) Saigon.
   (b) Hanoi.
   (c) Hue.
   (d) Dien Bien Phu.

5. Because of de Gaulle's prestige
   (a) the French Fifth Republic rooted strong presidential powers in the constitution.
   (b) the war in Vietnam ended.
   (c) Algerian revolutionaries were suppressed.
   (d) France joined NATO.

6. De Gasperi was the Christian Democratic premier in
   (a) Portugal.
   (b) Spain.
   (c) Italy.
   (d) Germany.

7. After Franco's death this king returned to Spain as a constitutional monarch:
   (a) Louis XVIII
   (b) Charles X
   (c) Henry IV
   (d) Juan Carlos

8. Walter Ulbricht headed
   (a) East Germany.
   (b) West Germany.
   (c) Poland.
   (d) Czechoslovakia.

9. The Twentieth Party Congress of the Soviet Union shocked its members when
   (a) they were requested to resign.
   (b) Khrushchev announced he was putting missiles in Cuba.
   (c) Khrushchev announced the shooting down of an American spy plane.
   (d) Khrushchev announced that Stalin was a tyrant.

10. In 1956 agitation in East Europe over the failures of their communist regimes caused
    (a) Poland's withdrawal from Comecon.
    (b) Romanian coal miners to march on Bucharest.
    (c) Hungarians to begin a revolution.
    (d) the Czechs to sever connection with Moscow.

11. A constant problem in the Soviet economy was
    (a) not enough natural resources.
    (b) not enough food.
    (c) not enough oil.
    (d) overproduction of consumer goods.

12. Guest workers arrived in West Europe
    (a) to alleviate a labor shortage.
    (b) to escape fascist regimes in their own countries.
    (c) to enjoy a better climate.
    (d) to seek citizenship in Germany and France.

13. Robert Schuman's idea was to get
    (a) France and Germany to integrate their armed forces.
    (b) France and Germany to integrate their coal and steel industries.
    (c) de Gaulle to resign the presidency.
    (d) Algerian independence.

14. The purpose of SALT was to
    (a) limit the number of U.S. troops in Germany.
    (b) encourage United States and Soviet cooperation in space.
    (c) limit the deployment of long-range missiles.
    (d) lower tariffs.

15. The Soviet invasion of Afghanistan was meant to
    (a) keep a Marxist government in power.
    (b) support a government of mujadheen.
    (c) keep the United States from invading Afghanistan first.
    (d) secure the oil reserves of the country.

Essay Questions
1. Churchill said in a speech that Europe was divided by an iron curtain. What did he mean by this remark?
2. How did the Berlin Blockade originate? Was the airlift solution a good one?
3. Explain why the Cold War never became a hot one.
4. Why did the 1956 Hungarian Revolution fail?
5. What were the reasons for Khrushchev's willingness to give his Twentieth Party Congress speech? Explain whether it was a good idea.

Answers

1. b	6. c	11. b
2. a	7. d	12. a
3. d	8. a	13. b
4. d	9. d	14. c
5. a	10. c	15. a

Europe in Modern Times

Europe in the 1990s was a different continent than what it was 20 years earlier. A dramatic change occurred in 1989 when the Soviet Union collapsed and its eastern European satellites ousted their communist regimes. The sudden fall of communism seemed hard to explain because the Soviets were judged to be one of the world's two superpowers.

Unfortunately, the end of communism did not mean a new era of peace for all Europeans. Extreme nationalists in Yugoslavia violently cracked that nation apart, and once more the sound of rifle fire and artillery sounded on the continent. Northern Ireland, an old European problem, also remained unstable because of religious and economic strife, but the threat of a nuclear confrontation between East and West was now ended.

Poland Leads the Way

Of all the nations of eastern Europe, the Polish people remained firmly opposed to communism. Nationalism and the Catholic church combined to keep the Poles constantly restive under the communist government.

The gray world that the Communists produced in Poland made the population look for something to cheer about. That happened in 1978 when one of their native sons, Karol Wotilja, was elected to the Catholic papacy.

He was the first man, who was not an Italian, to be chosen pope in over 400 years. He took the name John Paul II.

In July 1980 a wave of strikes hit Poland over the lack of consumer goods and the low wages paid workers in the shipyards of Gdansk (formerly Danzig) and Gdynia. The workers, who sat-in at their places of employment instead of organizing a street demonstration where police could get the upper hand, formed a group known as **Solidarity.** Its leader was a charismatic electrician, Lech Walesa.

Solidarity was able to secure many economic changes and made real progress in rallying the nation. During a visit back to Poland, Pope John Paul II reminded his countrymen and women, "Don't be afraid." His challenge began the crumbling of Poland's police state.

Government officials, alarmed at what the Soviet Union might do, declared martial law. Walesa and many of Solidarity's leaders were arrested or went into hiding.

Lech Walesa was a hero for the Solidarity workers.

Problems in the Soviet Union

As the Soviet Union entered the 1980s, the leaders of the Communist Party were increasingly aware of many challenges. As long as Leonid Brezhnev held power as general secretary, nothing was done to seriously address the needs of the Soviet Empire. In his last years only heavy doses of medication allowed him to function.

High on the list of matters needing attention was the arms race. In an effort to keep Soviet military forces in a state of readiness comparable to the United States, fully 25% of the national income was devoted to armaments and military personnel. This was happening at a time when tensions growing out of the Cold War were supposed to be on the decline. Such was the power of the generals that, before any other need, the military held first place. At the same time, the Red Army continued to fight its costly campaign in Afghanistan.

There was also constant irritation over relations with the countries of eastern Europe. The Brezhnev Doctrine, which stated that armed force would be used against any threat to a friendly socialist country, had some dissenters. These argued that such a policy might well prove more damaging to the Soviets than to the regimes they came to rescue. In 1982 Brezhnev died, and Konstantin Chernenko suceeded as general secretary of the party.

Gorbachev's Election

In March 1985 a meeting of the Politburo in the Kremlin discussed who should be chosen to replace Yuri Andropov. Andropov was not in office much longer than his predecessor, Chernenko, who had served but 13 months. It was obvious that the age of the Politburo leaders was showing. If there was to be stability in the party, a younger man must be chosen general secretary.

The Politburo settled on its youngest member, Mikhail Gorbachev, who was only 54 years of age. He was the first general secretary of the party to be born after the October Revolution, which brought the communists to power. Gorbachev was trained in law, advanced through the party's ranks, and in 1980 was first elected to a seat in the Politburo.

Gorbachev took charge with a determination to make changes. He wanted the Soviet Union to adopt policies that would lighten its heavy military burdens and allow its men and women to be free of police repression.

On the domestic front Gorbachev resolved on two programs: *glasnost* and *perestroika,* openness and restructuring. The openness sought in glasnost meant reining in the KGB, the secret police, and lifting the censorship that hovered over the media. Gorbachev believed that the Soviet people should be rid of the fear that pervaded society since Stalin's days.

Mikhail Gorbachev explains his program to the Russian people.

Soviet citizens discovered a whole new world. Newspapers began printing the truth, movies showed life as it was, and churches reopened. Novels by Russian exiles were printed in the Soviet Union, and western music, once denounced as corrupt, appeared on public television. Gorbachev permitted the well-known dissident, Andrei Sakharov, long suffering under internal exile, to return home.

The idea of perestroika was especially welcome. Everyone recognized that central planning had failed. It was impossible for the architects of the **State Planning Commission,** even with computers, to oversee an economy, producing over 70,000 items from jet planes to toys. In Russian markets often there was little food to buy other than staples such as bread and milk. Russian workers, who could afford it, had to wait seven years before they could purchase an automobile.

Gorbachev announced that henceforth there would be competition in industry. Managers could fire unproductive workers. More authority was vested in local regions to make decisions rather than depend on Moscow's central planners. Profits were to be the test of a factory's efficiency and productivity, not the filling of quotas. Ironically, one of Gorbachev's rules, forbidding vodka sales in the morning hours, unleashed a fury from laborers used to tippling through the day. Despite these reforms, or because of them, the Russian economy continued to decline.

Gorbachev visited the United States on a wave of popularity because he seemed to be a genuine person open to the public. With the United States an agreement was reached limiting nuclear missiles. In April 1989 Gorbachev announced the Soviet withdrawal from Afghanistan, a very welcome move.

Gorbachev also decided to attack the monopoly held by the party. Obviously there was a great amount of dead wood, for a large number of party officials did nothing but collect a paycheck. He announced that elections to the Congress of People's Deputies would be contested. Candidates of all persuasions were welcome to compete, even if they were not communists.

Much to the surprise of world observers, Gorbachev meant what he said. The result was the sacking of many old party leaders and the election of well-known opponents of the regime. Foremost among these was Sakharov and the dismissed party chief of Moscow, Boris Yeltsin, now an outspoken critic of communist rule.

The worst nuclear accident of the postwar years took place in the power plant at Chernobyl, Ukraine.

To demonstrate the lack of central control occurring in the Soviet Union, in the Caucasus regions clashes between Armenians and Azerbaijanis broke out, but the Soviet army did not intervene. Obviously, the Union was in danger of breaking up. Then in Armenia there was a terrible earthquake, 6.9 on the Richter scale. A half million people were left homeless, over 25,000 died. Gorbachev welcomed foreign aid to alleviate the suffering of the Armenians, a tacit admission that the task was beyond Soviet ability to respond.

The Baltic Secession

With the smell of freedom in the air, the Baltic peoples, the most advanced of the Soviet Union and those with the highest standard of living, talked of secession. On the fiftieth anniversary of the Molotov-Ribbentrop

Pact, which put the Balts under Stalin's rule, a human chain of protest stretched across the three nations of Estonia, Latvia, and Lithuania.

In March 1990 the Lithuanian Parliament voted to leave the Soviet Union, a measure that was permitted by the Soviet Constitution but that had never been tested. Gorbachev was upset, but found it hard to make a response. The Politburo, under his direction, responded with economic sanctions because Lithuanian industry depended on oil and natural gas delivered from other Soviet states. The Lithuanians, however, refused to budge and so did the Soviet army units stationed in their country.

Tension reached a climax on the night of January 13, 1991, when Soviet tanks plowed through a crowd of civilians guarding the Lithuanian radio and television station in the capital city of Vilnius. The tanks killed 14 people and injured another 150. Throughout the world, even in Moscow where 100,000 people marched in protest, the Soviet government stood condemned.

Meanwhile, elections were held on a new plan of political action, which entailed giving power to a popularly chosen Supreme Soviet. Gorbachev barely made it to the presidency because by now he had lost favor on both sides of the political spectrum. Conservatives disliked the changes, and liberals thought they did not go far enough.

East Europe Freed from the Soviet Union

In 1989 unrest began to grip East Germany in the wake of Gorbachev's loosening the reins of the Communist Party in the Soviet Union. Groups of people, especially those attached to the Evangelical church, plotted strategy to demand change. Huge crowds demonstrated their disenchantment with the regime on a nightly basis, overwhelming the ability of the police to react. Finally the unthinkable happened.

Germans demonstrate outside the Brandenburg gate for the unification of Berlin.

Erich Honecker, the East German party chief and head of the government, stepped down. The climax of the communist retreat occurred as men and women charged the hated Berlin Wall and began its demolition.

This was the first step toward a united Germany. It caused euphoria among all segments of the population. The country was again a single nation. As months passed, the politicians of East Germany were placed under arrest, the police state was dismantled, and the socialist economic program was abandoned.

After a while, the West Germans discovered that all was not peace and light. East Germany, under communist rule for so long, had become a different nation. Obstacles to unification appeared. This was especially true in the economy because East German factories were inefficient as was its labor force. The infrastructure of highways and railroads was in serious decay and needed to be rebuilt. West Germans discovered that their taxes would have to bail out their eastern cousins, a prospect that left many people grumbling.

The brutal suppression of Solidarity appeared to thwart reforms in Poland, but after the Poles saw what was happening in the Soviet Union, they felt free to oust their regime. The nation set forth on the path to democracy and a capitalist economy. A grateful people elected Walesa president, but once in power the enthusiasm for Solidarity waned, and many other parties claimed their share of the electorate.

Thousands of Czechs crowd the interior of Prague demanding the end of the communist government.

The collapse of communist regimes also took place in Hungary and Czechoslovakia. In Hungary, western nations found good reason to invest because economic changes were already in place. The new-found freedom in Czechoslovakia aroused the nationalist spirit in the Slovakian part of the nation. Despite the fact that only a minority in the country wanted it, Slovak politicians mustered enough political support to demand their own nation. The Czech president, Vaclav Havel, reluctantly agreed to the division of the nation into the Czech and Slovak republics.

Romania's path to independence was bloodier than the rest of the East European states. While pursuing a foreign policy independent of the Soviet Union, at home the Romanian leader, Nicolae Ceausescu, was a mirror image of Stalin at his worst. He bankrupted the economy in a rush to pay off the country's debts and tore out the heart of old Bucharest on a whim to create a palace for himself and his family. A huge police force guaranteed his safety, but even the loyalists in this group, after bitter skirmishes with those demanding change, could not save their leader. An army officer shot Ceausescu and his wife when he attempted to flee the country.

Bulgaria, once the most subservient of Soviet allies, also threw out its communist rulers and turned toward democracy. In Albania, the last of the

Balkan dictators and probably the worst, Enver Hoxha, died before the revolution repudiated the communists. His successors continued his policies until a wave of discontent overwhelmed them.

Gorbachev's Problems

Despite five years of perestroika, the living standards of the average Soviet citizen had gone down, not up, as promised. There was special unhappiness in the military as Soviet troops exited eastern Europe to find poorer accommodations at home than they had in East Germany. On the glasnost front, greater freedom continued. In September 1990, the Supreme Soviet voted for freedom of conscience, declaring all religions equal and allowing the Russian Orthodox church to regain its church structures lost during the communist regime. A quarter million Jews took advantage of the moment to leave the country.

President Gorbachev now became aware that there was no halfway point between freedom and subjugation. He still believed that the Soviet Union could and should be maintained, but the leaders of the 15 Soviet Republics were not so sure. Efforts to curtail the nationalism now reborn everywhere were too difficult. In elections held in June 1991, Boris Yeltsin became the president of the Russian Federation.

In August a new and potentially very dangerous moment occurred. While Gorbachev was vacationing in the Crimea, a group of his opponents in Moscow decided that he must resign. They dispatched a courier to the Crimea with a statement that Gorbachev was to sign, giving up his position. Contrary to what the conspirators expected, Gorbachev refused. He was then put under house arrest.

In Moscow the state television announced that Gorbachev had handed over his authority to an Emergency Committee. This committee in its first public act banned all strikes and demonstrations. Tanks began rolling down Moscow's streets.

The citizens of Moscow had tasted freedom and were not ready to give it up. They gathered about the White House, the Parliament building, to await developments. Then Boris Yeltsin climbed aboard a tank and announced his opposition to the coup leaders. He called for a general strike. Some of the tank commanders took up positions defending the White House and refused an order to attack it.

After some fighting during the night of August 19, the coup collapsed. The plotters were arrested, and Gorbachev flew back to Moscow. Neither the army nor the KGB, gave their support to return the Soviet Union to its Stalinist past. A huge rally welcomed Gorbachev and Yeltsin as saviors of democracy. The Supreme Soviet voted to ban the Communist Party.

The next few days, while confusion persisted, the Baltic states took the opportunity to declare themselves independent. They were soon followed by Ukraine, Moldavia (now Moldava), the Caucasian nations, Belarus, and finally the Asian republics. All 15 declared their independence, and the best that could be salvaged was a loose confederation of some of the former Soviet states that became known as the **Commonwealth of Independent States.**

Soldiers brought into Moscow to support the coup against Gorbachev instead joined forces with those opposing a return to hard-line communism.

On Christmas Eve 1991, the red flag of the Soviet Union with its hammer and sickle was lowered at the Kremlin and in its place soldiers raised the red, white, and blue flag of Russia. President Gorbachev resigned as president of the union that no longer existed.

Russian Independence

It was now Boris Yeltsin who held the limelight in Moscow. Immensely popular for his role in support of democracy in October, Yeltsin had hard decisions to make.

Early in 1993 he ended price controls and cut the state subsidies to factories. Immediately inflation soared to over 100%, and the ruble lost much of its value overnight. Unemployment and crime spread throughout the nation. Yeltsin soon lost the good will he once enjoyed, and his promises of quick recovery were treated with disdain.

In the Russian Soviet, Yeltsin's opponents hammered away at his reforms, accusing him of illegal actions. The Soviet's leaders claimed that they were the highest organ of the government, not the president. Yeltsin narrowly missed a recall. The president scheduled elections for September, after he decreed the dissolution of the Congress of People's Deputies and the Supreme Soviet.

The members of the Soviet called Yeltsin's actions null and void. They elected their head, Alexander Rutskoy, as prime minister and his ally, Ruslan Khasbulatov, as president and proceeded to barricade themselves in the White House. Armed supporters soon joined them, and the sides were drawn. Yeltsin ordered the army to attack. Tanks and soldiers began shelling the White House, killing 200 people and taking the rebel Soviet leaders prisoner.

The elections went forward with 21 parties participating. Voters ratified the new constitution, which gave the president the right to choose the prime minister, to control the army, and to veto any measure passed by a simple majority in the newly established parliament. This parliament held two houses, the lower house, known as the **Duma,** and the upper house, called the **Federation Council.**

Countries of the Former Soviet Union

The largest party elected to the Duma was the Liberal Democrats. The Liberal Democratic leader was Vladimir Zhirinovsky, a strident nationalist and one of Yeltsin's most vigorous opponents. To show its independence, the Duma voted an amnesty to the leaders of the White House revolt against the president.

In late 1994 Yeltsin sent troops against the small Caucasian Muslim region of Chechnya, which had declared itself independent of the Russian Federation. In December Russian planes leveled the Chechnyan capital, Grozny. In late 1996 an agreement was reached with the Chechens to stop the fighting, allowing them to elect a president, even though their exact relationship to Moscow remained to be decided.

Present and Future

The Russian Federation today holds 150 million people. It is the world's largest country, extending over ten time zones from the Pacific Ocean to East Europe.

Although the top 10% of the 150 million people have profited from the breakup of the Soviet state, the vast majority of people have not. Russia now has its millionaires, but at the bottom of the economic ladder 18% of the people now live in dire poverty.

Industrial production has fallen each year since Gorbachev announced perestroika. In 1994 it declined by 27%. Despite efforts to privatize agriculture, in 1995 the state still controlled 90% of farmland. In manufacturing, government-controlled industries make up 50% of the work force.

The effort to move from a controlled to a private economy has caused much misery to the Russian people, well known for its afflictions. The West promised $13,000,000,000 in aid to the government, but no one is sure if the money will be spent other than for subsidies.

If perestroika has, up to the present, failed, glasnost is a success. Few Russians miss the terror of Soviet days. Democratic values seem to be taking firm root in the general populace. Over many protests, the KGB still exists, raising the possibility of a return to the police state of the past.

Moscow consumers must stand in line for oranges, always in short supply.

In foreign affairs Yeltsin has opposed the bid of eastern European countries to seek admission to NATO. In the Bosnian conflict, Moscow deplored NATO attacks on the Bosnian Serbs besieging Sarajevo. Nuclear weapons still rest in Russian silos, causing apprehension in the rest of the world over their security.

Russian democracy remains fragile. The economic hardships of so many people could easily turn the nation toward one-man autocracy. Unless the economic picture brightens in the future, democracy remains threatened.

The irony of these events comes from the fact that at the time of its collapse, the Soviet Union had one of the strongest military machines in the world. Its army, navy, and air force were all armed to the teeth so that the Soviet leadership could play a dominant role on the world scene. Yet all this was happening at the expense of the Russian people who were denied the consumer goods that were commonplace in other industrial countries. Today the once mighty Red Army is in shambles.

Western Democracies

As Great Britain entered the 1990s, John Major and the Conservatives continued to hold a majority in Parliament. Local elections, however, showed voter dissatisfaction rising. The British were still undecided concerning how closely they want to be attached to the continent. In the parliamentary elections of 1997, the Labour Party trounced the Conservatives, and their leader, Tony Blair, became the new prime minister.

Northern Ireland looms as a problem unsolved. In 1994 talks between Dublin and London gave some hope of settling the issue, and a cease-fire was announced and held for several months. In the Republic of Ireland, economic issues remain troublesome. There are not enough jobs for young people, leaving one out of five persons unemployed. As a result, emigration continues at a sizable rate. Change is happening. The influence of bishops in the Catholic church has come under scrutiny in the increasingly secular society of the country. Ireland has elected a very popular woman president, Mary Robinson, in a turn from the patriarchal society of the past.

In France, Mitterand held the presidency almost as long as de Gaulle, leaving office only in 1995. His successor, Jacques Chirac, turned the country back to a more conservative mode, and France could boast of having the fourth largest economy in the world.

In a great about-face, Spain has become a respected member of the European Union. Moreover, public polls now show that the Spaniards have the most liberal views of all Europeans. Portugal also went through a dramatic change. After years of authoritarian government, democratic forces came to power. The loss of the extensive Portuguese empire had discredited the Salazar regime. In 1976, for the first time in half a century, free elections took place. Later both Portugal and Spain entered NATO and the European Union.

It has been said that country is happiest that has no history. If that is the case, then the Scandinavian nations of Sweden, Norway, Denmark, and Finland rank close to bliss because the past 50 years have been very uneventful. People here live in welfare states that provide security from cradle to grave. They have the highest standard of living among all Europeans, and, for that matter, their standard is the highest in the world. Switzerland has an equally favorable economic position.

Perhaps life in Scandinavia is too uneventful. The result is one of the most serious problems with alcoholism in all Europe. Sweden has the highest rate of suicide on the continent. Such statistics show that not all individuals find happiness in their present condition.

The Christian Democratic Party, with only a few years of socialist interruptions, remains the majority party in West Germany. The Social Democrats, as a matter of policy, moved toward the center, rejecting Marxist ideology. Germans concerned about the environment have formed the Green Party, whose policies concentrate on protecting people and the land from pollution. The German example has spawned other green parties in several other countries.

Greece, the one Balkan state that escaped communist rule, prospered when peace returned. Party politics was vigorous in this nation where democracy was first born. This did not mean that the government was very stable. In 1967 a coup brought three colonels to power on the excuse that the communists were preparing a coup. For several years the country became a military dictatorship.

While the colonels ruled, the island of Cyprus, over 70% Greek in background and less than 30% Turkish, erupted into communal strife. The Turkish government landed an army in Cyprus, while the Athens' colonels stood by, fearful of intervention because of Turkish military strength. Their inaction brought down the colonels, and Greece became a democratic state once more.

The Turkish invasion divided Cyprus into a Greek and a Turkish part. A United Nations force patrolled the boundary between the two sectors. All efforts to find a way to keep the island a single nation have foundered because of the uncompromising demands of both communities.

The European Union has abolished passports and most tariffs between its members. On the horizon is a proposal to have a single European Union currency. A member state must first demonstrate that it is willing to balance its budget in such a way that its currency will approach the value of the deutschmark, the strongest currency in Europe.

Yugoslavia at War

As long as Marshal Tito governed his country with an iron hand, the Federal Republic of Yugoslavia remained remarkably stable. Prisons filled with anyone who challenged him. He ruthlessly crushed any sign of nationalism, even among Communist Party members. The day came, however, when death claimed the marshal. He left his legacy in a cumbersome joint presidency with the leadership passing among the representatives of the five republics and two regions that made up the federation.

In 1991, when the Slovene delegation walked out of the joint presidency, the breakup of the country commenced. In Belgrade, the Serbian leader, Slobodan Milesović, refused to admit the dissolution of Yugoslavia. Skirmishes between the Slovenes and the Yugoslav army took place, but the army's intervention was minimal, and Slovenia announced its independence.

Break-up of Yugoslavia

Soon Croatians, Macedonians, and Bosnians also declared independence from Belgrade. Both Croatia and Bosnia held unhappy Serbian minorities. Within these two nations the Serbians declared themselves autonomous. They were successful because Milosević armed them from Serbia and Montenegro, the two remaining states of Yugoslavia.

The situation in Bosnia was especially critical because about 35% of the Bosnians were Muslims. They refused to agree to a partition of their country into Serbian, Croatian, and Muslim regions, and war commenced among the three factions. The Bosnian Serbs were intent upon **ethnic cleansing** of the regions they held. This meant that the Serbs expelled all Muslims and Croatians who lived in Serbian regions. Atrocities occurred on all sides on the excuse that past wrongs could now be made right.

The United Nations acted as a humanitarian buffer, but neither the United States, Russia, nor the European states found a formula to bring peace to the region, until President Bill Clinton put American servicemen and women into Bosnia under United Nations command to separate the combatants. Bosnian Croatians and Muslims agreed to form a confederation that held a little more than 50% of the country. Bosnian Serbs held the rest, awaiting the moment when they will declare union with Yugoslavia, which now is made up of Serbia and Montenegro.

A Croatian woman leaves a Sarajevo church destroyed during the Bosnian conflict.

Europe's New Society

Ironically, in the late 1990s in many eastern European countries, former communist politicians returned to power, even though communism did not. These politicians have more familiar faces than the people who replaced them. The former communists were always insistent that they have had a conversion. Part of their popularity stems from the headlong rush to introduce capitalism into eastern Europe with only a few months of transition. The process left many people behind. Higher prices hit the elderly especially hard because they lived on fixed incomes. Goods were plentiful in the stores, but only the new rich could afford them.

A society that kept crime low and guaranteed employment was torn down so quickly that a class of rugged capitalists, intent on making their fortunes in a hurry, trampled upon the poor of East Europe. Unknown in communist times, a well-armed criminal element that practiced intimidation appeared. This caused dismay among those who thought a turn to democracy and capitalism would be quick and painless, guaranteeing a better life for all.

In western Europe scientists and technocrats have assumed crucial roles in government bureaucracies. They work together with the politicians to form policy. Experts run the modern European world. Thanks to their education, they have risen to positions of importance both in the economy and in government. Usually this class is made up of the children of the wealthy because they are the ones who can afford the cost of a university education.

To a large extent, at least in theory, Europeans now embrace the concept of equality for all citizens. People dress the same, homes have the same appliances, and nearly every family has access to an automobile and a television set. Yet class lines remain, the result of birth or wealth.

Although there is still interest in religious topics in the media, the number of Europeans who attend church is constantly declining. The theological issues of the past no longer seem relevant.

Vatican Council II opened new vistas for Catholicism, which included adopting a vernacular liturgy and allowing greater opportunities for laymen and women to hold church ministries. A willingness to dialog with other Christian denominations was a major change from former Catholic attitudes.

St. Peter's Basilica in Rome was filled with bishops at the Second Vatican Council.

Pope John Paul II is known throughout the world as a personality who deserves attention. His visits outside the Vatican draw huge crowds, even if people ignore his message. A shortage of recruits for the priesthood has become a major problem in keeping the Catholic church viable. Only 20% of baptized Catholics may now be counted as practicing.

The situation in Protestant countries has also become bleak. In Scandinavia, church attendance is less than 5% of the region's people. In Orthodox Russia and the Balkans many churches reopened after the fall of communism, but the level of religious education is low. Church activists in all countries have their idealists who volunteer for organizations at home and abroad to help refugees, the poor, and the sick. Their witness is in contrast to much of the selfishness of secular society.

In recent times the legal position of women has improved in all countries of Europe. Immediately following the war, French and Italian women were given the vote, but this right, until the 1970s, was denied to Spanish and Portuguese females.

The best record for women's advancement was found in Sweden, Norway, France, and the Netherlands. In these countries women's earning power was 80% of men's wages. The total number of women wage-earners in western Europe is approximately 40% of the population.

Matrimony is still the usual choice for European women. Couples now make the choice of whom they shall marry in contrast to the arranged marriages so common in past decades.

Contraception has increasingly meant that families have fewer children than in past decades. In communist eastern Europe, abortions were the most commonly used form of birth control. Divorce is now available in all European countries.

Health and Population

In no other period of human history has there been such progress in providing better health care. Dramatic developments have appeared in the past decades: the artificial heart, bypass surgery, synthetic arteries, dialysis machines, organ transplants, and radiation and chemotherapy.

Far more important for the spectacular reduction of mortality has been the ability to control bacteria and immunize people against disease. Today it is taken for granted that cities will provide clean water, adequate sanitation, and inspection of food. The result has been the most phenomenal increase in life expectancy in recorded history. A person born in 1997 can expect to outlive his or her parents by a decade or more, to 75 years of age except in Russia where life expectancy has actually declined.

Open-air markets are a familiar scene in European cities.

Paralleling the control of adult illnesses has been the elimination of many childhood diseases. Babies, once born at home, are now usually delivered in hospitals. There are vaccines for childhood killers such as diphtheria, polio, and whooping cough.

Unfortunately, despite the risks, many Europeans are heavy smokers. Campaigns against the use of tobacco have fallen on deaf ears. The Poles are first among the number of smokers, and the Greeks are second, but all over Europe smoking is a serious health problem.

Leisure

The people of Europe in the last three decades have had opportunities for leisure never before experienced in history. Part of each day and each week could be enjoyed as men and women saw fit. By 1980 the 40-hour work week and several weeks of paid vacation were common throughout Europe. Modern technology made it possible for people to work shorter amounts of time and still earn enough money to live and to have funds left over.

Families spent their time in different ways. More than any other amusement, going to the movies was the most popular diversion. Although each country has its own film industry, many of the films are made in the United States, giving Europeans an image of this country that hardly mirrors the reality.

The most popular sport in Europe is certainly soccer. Loyal fans follow their team from city to city, and famous players are celebrities wherever they go. A nation with a team in the World Cup championship literally comes to a standstill during tournament play. In addition there is skiing, cycling, swimming, and hiking for the more athletic. During July and August visitors from the north of Europe inundate the beaches of the Mediterranean.

The airplane and bullet train make getting around easier than ever before. Historic sites and buildings receive millions of visitors from Europe, North America, and now Asia.

Automobiles, once a rarity, by 1980 were within the financial reach of ordinary citizens. Cities have a hard time coping with traffic on streets built for pedestrians and horses. Finding a parking place is a major challenge for any commuter.

Conclusion

It came as a major surprise to most European observers that Gorbachev, when elected to head the Communist Party of the Soviet Union, actually meant it when he promised *glasnost* and *perestroika*. Gorbachev obviously had no intention of dismantling the Soviet Union when he announced his policies, yet there could be no turning back, and today the Soviet Union is no more.

A debate goes on as to the reasons for the collapse. Some would credit Ronald Reagan's military buildup that threatened to bankrupt the Soviet Union when it tried to match it. Others look at the inherent weaknesses of a command economy that was unable to compete against capitalism. More important than all was the courage of the men and women of East Europe who fearlessly demanded freedom despite the risk of imprisonment and perhaps even death. The collapse of the Soviet empire in East Europe was surely the most important historical event in the past half century.

Unfortunately, economic progress in East Europe and Russia has been a much more elusive goal to achieve than political independence. An antiquated and inefficient industry, the inability to change the psychology of people accustomed to the communist system, and the rise of a wealthy, irresponsible upper class are all current challenges facing the governments of Russia and East Europe.

Europe approaches the future with both confidence and hesitation. The menace of communism is over, and nuclear war on the continent is no longer a threat. In the West, economic integration has brought great advantages to the countries within the European Union. Border checks have become a thing of the past. Despite some reluctance Great Britain finds itself tied closer to the continent, for a tunnel now links it to France. There are plans for the European Union to issue a common currency in 1999, yet nationalism remains a strong force in all countries, threatening to derail the movement toward European unification.

CHAPTER 24 REVIEW
EUROPE IN MODERN TIMES

Summary
- Two major events helped to pull Poland out of the doldrums: the election of John Paul II, the first Polish pope, and the founding of a labor movement, Solidarity.
- In the Soviet Union Gorbachev was elected general secretary of the party.
- Gorbachev urged the party to encourage glasnost and perestroika, openness and restructuring of the Soviet Union.
- The Baltic states—Estonia, Latvia, and Lithuania—clamored to leave the Soviet Union.
- On Christmas Eve 1991 the red, white, and blue flag of Russia replaced the flag of the Soviet Union.
- Elections for the presidency brought Yeltsin to that office, but economic problems plagued the new nation.
- The Western democracies had problems from unemployment as their economies slowed.
- Eastern Europe, free of Communist Party control, had difficulties moving to a capitalist economy.
- In Bosnia, the weakest of the republics that once made up Yugoslavia, Muslim Bosnians fought Catholic Croatians and Orthodox Serbs.
- European culture has opened greater opportunities for women. Health care and education are free or cost very little, extending life expectancy.

Identify
People: Walesa, John Paul II, Brezhnev, Gorbachev, Yeltsin, Havel, Tito, Robinson, Blair
Places: Armenia, Azerbaijan, Lithuania, Russia's White House, Chechnya, Slovenia
Events: popularity of Solidarity in Poland; Gorbachev elected secretary of the Soviet Communist Party; breakup of the Soviet Union; political independence but economic distress in East Europe; Turkish invasion of Cyprus; changing role of women; war in Bosnia

Define

Solidarity	ethnic cleansing	Commonwealth of Independent States
glasnost	perestroika	Russian Duma

Multiple Choice
1. The labor organization that encouraged resistance to the Polish Communist government was known as
   (a) Solidarity.
   (b) Politburo.
   (c) Presidium.
   (d) Polish Union.

2. The first Polish pope was
   (a) Paul VI.
   (b) John XXIII.
   (c) Walesa.
   (d) John Paul II.

3. Gorbachev gambled that the party in the Soviet Union could stay in power despite
   (a) putting limits on KGB activity.
   (b) opening industry to competition.
   (c) removing censorship.
   (d) all the above.

4. The first republic of the Soviet Union to vote to leave was
   (a) Armenia.
   (b) Azerbaijan.
   (c) Latvia.
   (d) Lithuania.

5. The Commonwealth of Independent States temporarily replaced
   (a) the Soviet Union.
   (b) Comecon.
   (c) the Duma.
   (d) the Supreme Soviet.

6. Yeltsin, elected president, had to put down a rebellion in
   (a) the Russian Parliament.
   (b) Azerbaijan.
   (c) Lithuania.
   (d) the Kremlin.

7. The Chechens demanded that their relation to Russia should be
   (a) federation.
   (b) linked closely to Moscow's economic decisions.
   (c) statehood.
   (d) independence.

8. Russia's economy has faltered for many reasons, one of them is
   (a) the power of the Russian Mafia.
   (b) the revival of the KGB.
   (c) the cost of maintaining the Red Army.
   (d) the cost of modernizing its oil industry.

9. The first woman president of Ireland is
   (a) Thatcher.
   (b) Geraghty.
   (c) McCarthy.
   (d) Robinson.

10. The highest standard of living in Europe is in
    (a) Scandinavia.
    (b) the Baltic.
    (c) Germany.
    (d) the Balkans.

11. The unification of the two Germanies has been
    (a) very easy for West Germans.
    (b) very costly for West Germans.
    (c) impossible because of the Berlin Wall.
    (d) still in the process of negotiation.

12. Vaclav Havel oversaw the division of his country:
    (a) Yugoslavia
    (b) Bulgaria
    (c) Finland
    (d) Czechoslovakia

13. Tito's Yugoslavia came apart with most republics declaring
    (a) union with Germany.
    (b) independence.
    (c) that they wanted a looser federation.
    (d) union with Austria.

14. Serbians living in Bosnia refused to live under a government of
    (a) Catholic Croatians.
    (b) Catholic Slovenes.
    (c) Germans.
    (d) Muslims.

15. The modern European states depend very much on
    (a) royalty.
    (b) capitalists.
    (c) experts.
    (d) armies.

16. Life expectancy in Europe today is approaching
    (a) 80 years.
    (b) 60 years.
    (c) 55 years.
    (d) 75 years.

17. The great passion of European sports fans is
    (a) basketball.
    (b) baseball.
    (c) rugby.
    (d) soccer.

Essay Questions
1. What were the steps that led to the collapse of communism in the Soviet Union?
2. Assess the leadership of Gorbachev and Yeltsin.
3. Why has the unification of Germany presented many problems?
4. How has the role of women changed in the 1990s?
5. Why did the breakup of Yugoslavia lead to war?

Answers

1. a	6. a	11. b	16. d
2. d	7. d	12. d	17. d
3. d	8. d	13. b	
4. d	9. d	14. d	
5. a	10. a	15. c	

Southwest Asia in Conflict

Since World War II, Southwest Asia has been one of the most volatile regions of the world. The most serious problem emerged as the result of the creation of Israel, a Jewish state in Palestine. This placed a foreign entity, with a European outlook, in the midst of a traditional society that resisted its creation.

A series of wars between Israel and its neighbors occurred from 1948 to 1973. These wars gave Israel more territory, but no peace. Public opinion in the Arab countries was strongly opposed to compromise. In 1987, however, a major step toward reconciliation was taken when the Egyptian president, Anwar Sadat, offered Israel a peace treaty. It took almost 20 years for the next Arab leader to work out an agreement with Israel.

The other major development in recent times is the rise of Islamic traditionalism, often called **fundamentalism.** In almost every nation of Southwest Asia, a segment of the population advocates the restoration of Islamic law. In Iran Shi'ite traditionalists now hold power; their country is officially known as an **Islamic Republic.** In other nations fundamentalist attempts to take over the government have so far failed.

Britain and France Dominate Southwest Asia

During World War I the Allied governments made contradictory promises to both Arabs and Jews. Their real interests were in carving out Southwest Asian empires for themselves. In 1919 French troops entered Syria. They were not welcome. Arab nationalists claimed that Syria was an independent nation and that Amir Faisal was its king, but military strength was with the French. The British government assured Paris that it would not stand in the way of a French occupation. This assurance meant the end of Faisal. Later the League of Nations confirmed that France should enjoy a **mandate** to govern Syria and Lebanon, Syria's next door neighbor.

The British were not idle in carving out a piece of Southwest Asia for themselves. Iraq was their goal. The London government agreed to allow the ousted Amir Faisal to make his way to Baghdad, there to govern the nation under British supervision. A high commissioner, appointed in London, oversaw the monarch's activities, and a British general commanded the armed forces. By 1930 Iraq obtained nominal independence and the post of high commissioner was abolished.

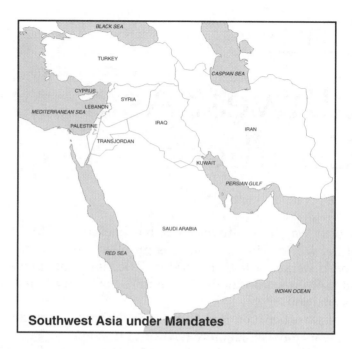

Southwest Asia under Mandates

The British also were anxious to find a throne for the brother of King Faisal. With this in mind, they lopped off the eastern part of Palestine, declaring it to be Transjordan. Then they nominated Faisal's brother, Abdullah, to be its monarch. Transjordan, like Iraq, was in fact a British protectorate with a king who reigned but did not rule.

Three major nations remained independent in the region. One was in the Arabian peninsula, where the family of Ibn Saud held the throne. Another was Persia, later called Iran, where the military leader, Reza Shah Pahlavi, governed with an iron hand. The third was Turkey, a nation formed out of what was left of the Ottoman Empire.

Turkey came under the popular leadership of Mustafa Kemal, once a general in the Ottoman army. The **Treaty of Sèvres,** between the Allies and the sultan's government, left little territory within Turkish borders. Kemal came to the rescue. He defied the treaty, raised an army, and kept the heartland of the Turks intact. His grateful countrymen and women gave him the title Ataturk, Father of the Turks.

Kemal Ataturk, father of modern Turkey.

Both Reza Shah and Ataturk were secular in their outlook. They wanted to break with the past traditions of their nations and to create new modern states on the pattern of the Western world. Ataturk's popularity carried with him the majority of his countrymen and women, but in Iran Reza Shah received only grudging support.

Origins of Zionism

The idea of a Jewish homeland was born late in the nineteenth century in the mind of Theodor Herzl, an Austrian journalist of Jewish descent. While he was covering the Dreyfus trial in France, he recognized how anti-Semitism was the driving force behind the prosecution. Herzl began to dream of a nation that Jews could call their own. He founded an organization called **Zionists,** because Mt. Zion once was the site of King David's palace in Jerusalem during the golden age of ancient Israel.

The Zionist movement was not able to win the support of all Jews throughout the world. Many had worked hard to be accepted in the countries where they lived and saw no need for a Jewish nation. This was especially true in the Americas where freedom to practice the Jewish faith met no hindrances.

Herzl's Zionist movement did enlist some of the wealthy and powerful Jewish families of western Europe. One of the outspoken Zionists in Great Britain was Chaim Weizmann, a man who devoted much of his energies toward the pursuit of the Zionist goal.

In the midst of World War I, the British Foreign Secretary, Sir Arthur Balfour, met with Weizmann. Out of their discussions, Balfour agreed to support the creation of a Jewish homeland and confirmed this in the 1917 Balfour Note.

In 1920, when London assumed its mandate in Palestine, Zionists were anxious to begin the process of reclaiming the land that once had been ancient Israel. There was a difficulty. For 1,700 years this land had been in the hands of people who were not Jews.

In the seventh century Muslim Arabs took Palestine away from the Byzantine Empire. They made it one of the territories of the **caliphates.** Later, in the eleventh century Seljuk Turks occupied the land, followed by European Crusaders, the Egyptians, and finally the Ottoman Turks.

During all this time a small community of Jews continued to live in the region of the Sea of Tiberias in the north, holding to their old traditions and keeping continuity with the past. Nevertheless, by 1920 Palestine was Arabic-speaking and about 80% Muslim and 20% Christian.

Financed by the **Jewish Agency,** an organization devoted to buying property in Palestine, European Jews arrived in Palestine in ever-increasing numbers. Many were socialists and were inspired by ideologies that made farming the ideal occupation. With great enthusiasm they created agricultural communes, called *kibbutzim.*

The Palestinian population viewed their Jewish neighbors with apprehension. Their ways were foreign, and the growing number of the kibbutzim frightened them. They were convinced that the quotas for Jewish immigrants set by the London government were far too generous.

In 1929 Jews and Arabs clashed in Jerusalem, and over the next few years the tension grew worse. Palestinians saw that they were losing their country to the immigrants and blamed the British and the Zionists. By 1936 both Arab and Jewish paramilitary factions were at war with the British troops stationed in Palestine.

World War II in Southwest Asia

After France surrendered to Hitler, the Syrian and Lebanese governments pledged allegiance to the Vichy regime. Because this was no more than a puppet state of Hitler, in July 1941 British and Free French forces successfully invaded both countries and set up regimes loyal to the Allies. Syria and Lebanon were promised that, at the end of the war, they would be completely independent.

Jews arrive on a crowded ship to seek new homes in Palestine.

In Palestine the war changed those Jewish forces bent upon ousting the British through guerrilla warfare into allies. Only a small group, led by Abraham Stern, refused to cooperate. Hitler's treatment of Jews in the Axis-controlled areas of Europe caused a steady stream of Jewish immigrants to seek refuge in Palestine. The British tried to hold their numbers down, but the task was beyond them. World opinion favored a place for Jewish refugees to escape the horrors of Europe.

After the War

By the end of the war, Syria and Lebanon did gain their independence, although for a time it appeared that the French were in no hurry to leave. The British surrendered their former mandates, and the modern nations of Iraq and Transjordan (now Jordan) gained independence.

Although politicians in these first administrations were natives, they reflected the special interests of the colonial elite. By the 1950s there was a strong demand for change, especially among members of the armed forces. The result was the toppling of monarchs in Iraq and of prewar politicians in Syria. A new challenge now confronted the Arab world.

Creation of Israel

In 1945 peace came to Europe, and the enormity of the **Holocaust** became apparent. A collective guilt spread throughout the world in the capitals of Europe and the United States, paralleling the Zionist cry, "Never again!"

In Palestine a three-sided war began once more. The Arab population resisted the idea that they should be made the scapegoat for the sins of Europeans. Arabs fought Jews, Jews fought Arabs, and both sides fought the British. In London the British could not find a solution and so, in November 1947, handed over the Palestine problem to the United Nations.

The United Nations sent a commission to Palestine to examine the best way to solve the conflict between Arabs and Jews. This commission recommended partition of Palestine into Jewish and Arab states. Jerusalem should become an international city under the trusteeship of the United Nations.

As expected, neither side agreed that their interests had been well served, and both Jews and Arabs began building up their armed forces. In the United Nations, a vote that found both the United States and the Soviet Union on the same side accepted the creation of the new nation of Israel.

David Ben-Gurion announces the creation of Israel.

On May 14, 1948, Israel's elected Prime Minister David Ben-Gurion, declared his nation's existence. Within hours of the announcement, all the Arab neighbors of Israel went to war with the new country. The Israelis had no choice but to battle for their lives because they had nowhere to go. Their leaders had long recognized that this moment would come and had made plans on how best to defend themselves. On the other hand, the invading Arab armies and the Palestinians did not coordinate their strategy.

Within a period of several months the Israelis had won, and in 1949 a truce went into effect. Israel now held half of Palestine. Willingly or unwillingly almost a million Palestinians left the Israeli-occupied area. These people settled in refugee camps in Jordan, Syria, Lebanon, and Egypt, waiting for the day they could return. Many Palestinians are still there because that day has still not come.

As a result of the war, Egypt took control of the Gaza Strip, and Jordan occupied a 2400 square mile area of Palestine called the West Bank and the Arab section of Jerusalem.

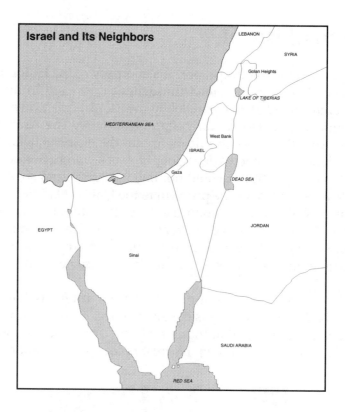

Israel and Its Neighbors

Israel's First Years

Having won its dramatic military victory, Israel could now turn to domestic issues. A State Council of 38 members served as the provisional government until a parliament could be elected. In preparation for this event, Israelis pondered their options. There was a wide choice of parties. From religious parties that were ultra-Orthodox, the spectrum moved all the way to communists. All participated in the election for seats in the **Knesset,** the Israeli parliament of 120 members. Voting was according to proportional representation so that even small parties had at least several members in the Knesset.

In this election and most that followed, the Labor Party won a plurality but never a majority. The result has been that Labor must build coalitions with smaller parties. Although only about 15% of the Israelis supported religious parties, they became the swing votes in the Knesset, allowing their representatives to enjoy more importance than their numbers should merit.

Israel in Combat

The need for national security put a severe strain on the economy of Israel. Approximately 30% of the national budget was earmarked for the armed services. Everyone, male and female, except for Jewish Orthodox women, was drafted for a period of several years. No Arab citizen, except those who belonged to the Druze religion, served in the army.

Israeli leaders review the armed forces.

In 1956 Israel's military forces went on the attack during the British and French Suez invasion. A dozen years later, in 1967, responding to President Nasser's threats, the Israelis struck Egypt again in the **Six Days' War.** Israeli planes and army units simultaneously attacked Syria and Jordan. In less than a week the Israelis reached their objectives. Israel took the Sinai Peninsula and the Gaza Strip from Egypt. They occupied the Jordanian areas on the West Bank and East Jerusalem and seized the Golan Heights from Syria. All of Israel was dizzy with joy.

The wars of Israel, however, were not over. The next time Israel was taken by surprise. On the Jewish holy day of Yom Kippur, in October 1973, Egypt launched an attack. With the country's defenses down, the Israelis had to withdraw. The army suffered severe losses in the Sinai until it recovered and struck back. A truce ended the conflict, but Israeli military invincibility had been plucked.

Israel in Transition

After 1973 there was a massive depression as Israelis turned inward. Questions were raised over the direction of the country's economic and social order. Prior to 1951 immigrants had come from eastern Europe, primarily Poland and the Soviet Union. Then the source of immigrants changed. A majority arrived from Africa and Asia, with an altogether different cultural background. A social, political, and economic gap grew between the European and African and Oriental Jews. Even though the country was once proud of its equality, now there were Israeli bankers, industrialists, and military contractors who were millionaires.

The Israelis also became disenchanted with the Labor Party. In 1977 and again in 1981 the main opposition party, *Likud* (Unity), received a plurality of votes.

Then, to a stunned world audience, Egyptian President Sadat offered peace to Israel. In November 1977 he flew to Jerusalem and addressed the startled Knesset: "We used to reject you . . . . But today we agree to live with you in permanent peace and justice."

President Jimmy Carter seized the opportunity for peace. He invited Sadat and the Israeli Prime Minister Menachem Begin, to meet at Camp David, the U.S. presidential retreat. Hard bargaining went on for 13 days, but at the conclusion it was agreed that Egypt would recognize Israel and exchange ambassadors. In return, the Israelis agreed to return the Sinai Peninsula to Egypt. For the first time, an Arab state agreed to admit Israel as a neighbor.

The Camp David Accord brought Sadat and Begin together to agree on peace terms between Israel and Egypt.

For Palestinians, Egypt's reconciliation was bitterly resisted. They turned to their own leadership, forming a coalition known as the **Palestine Liberation Organization** (PLO). Its leader, Yassir Arafat, directed activities against Israel both inside and outside the country. To the Israelis he was a terrorist, but to the Palestinians he was a hero. An attack on Israeli athletes at the Munich Olympics killed 11 members of the team and exasperated public opinion in Israel.

In 1982, frustrated by PLO raids launched from Lebanon, Israel attacked that country. Planes poured bombs upon the camps that were used as recruiting grounds for the PLO. World opinion harshly condemned Israel, especially after one of the Lebanese factions, under Israeli eyes, sought revenge in a massacre of men, women, and children in a Palestinian camp.

Five years later the Israelis had another uprising to handle. It was known as the **Intifada.** This time it came from within Israel. Palestinian young men, frustrated by unemployment and harsh living conditions, took to the streets to battle Israeli police and soldiers. Whenever a police vehicle came within range, Palestinians peppered it with stones. The Israelis arrested thousands of people and put them in prison in an effort to curtail the violence.

The Gulf War of 1991 brought a new sense of urgency for Israel to seek peace. The Israeli electorate was divided. Should territory be given up for peace or should every inch of ancient Israel be held, no matter the cost? At Madrid in 1991, Israeli representatives sat down for the first time with negotiators from the neighboring Arab states to discuss conditions for peace. Negotiations were expected to continue for years, but once again a surprise was in store.

Direct talks in Oslo in September 1993 between the PLO and Israeli government officials produced a further agreement. Israeli charges of terrorism against the PLO were buried amid an attempt at reconciliation. The Israelis offered Arafat an opportunity to provide local government and police in the Gaza Strip and a small area around the city of Jericho on the West Bank.

In all, Palestinian control extended over only 140 square miles. For its part, the PLO promised to halt all operations against Israel. The parties announced further negotiations over territorial change for the future.

An Israeli town sits above a Bedouin camp.

After the PLO agreed on peace, Jordan followed. In October 1994 the border between Israel and Jordan was opened. Only Syria remained a holdout, demanding immediate evacuation of the Golan Heights in return for recognition of Israel. The Labor government of Yitzhak Rabin wanted instead a phased withdrawal.

Complicating the peace process was the reality of hundreds of Israeli settlements in the occupied territories. The settlers were adamant that they should stay. A wave of terror struck inside Israel as extremists both among Jews and Arabs sought to wreck the peace process. Believing so strongly in their cause, they were willing to die for it.

Palestinian youths joined in the Intifada *to protest the Israeli occupation.*

In September 1995 Arafat and Rabin signed a settlement that provided for the Israeli army to withdraw from 450 towns and villages on the West Bank. Prime Minister Rabin commented, "Faced with crazy suicide attackers, we must learn how to endure." Rabin's words were prophetic. In early November 1995 an Israeli student assassinated him.

Two hard-line groups contested the right of Arafat to speak for the Palestinians. These were **Islamic Jihad** and **Hamas.** In forthcoming elections Arafat's strength was to be tested, but he prevailed.

For the Labor government peace was a gamble. Many Israelis resented Labor's willingness to abandon the Zionist dream of the restoration of all ancient Israel. At the polls the electorate voiced its discontent, once more choosing a Likud government, which elected a new prime minister, Benyamin Netanyahu.

All Israelis remained firm in their determination to hold on to Jerusalem. The path to peace has many hurdles ahead, now that Likud is back in power.

The Arab World

Syria, Lebanon, Jordan, Iraq, Saudi Arabia, Yemen, Oman, the Gulf States, and the Palestinians make up the Arab world of Southwest Asia. Their populations are united by language, culture, geography, and an abiding hatred of Israel.

Over 90% of the people are Muslim, but they are divided into a number of separate groups. Even though mainstream Sunnis are the majority among the Arabs, Shi'ites, Druzes, and Alawites are in large enough numbers that in some localities they constitute a majority.

The Alawites are a sect of Shi'ites who believe that Ali's descendants are the true leaders of Islam. Certain extended families dominate this group, with the rest owing them allegiance. The Druzes are a religious community that occupies villages scattered across Lebanon and an area in Syria known as *Jebal Druze*, where they comprise 80% of the population. They are a very close-knit group, allowing no converts and keeping their beliefs hidden from outsiders.

Arab Christians are found in all countries of Southwest Asia with the exception of Saudi Arabia. They represent a broad variety of churches: Orthodox, Catholic, and a small number of Protestants. A large Armenian church is also present.

Oil

More than any political decision, oil has been the major factor in changing life in the Arab world. Oil and the products made from it fuel the industries of western Europe, Japan, and the Americas. After World War II those countries that provided oil became some of the wealthiest nations of the world.

Oil divided the haves from the have-nots in Southwest Asia. Those countries with oil were Iran, Iraq, Kuwait, the smaller states of the Persian Gulf, and Saudi Arabia. Two-thirds of the known oil reserves on earth are found beneath the surface of the Southwest Asian countries.

In 1960, convinced that they were not getting as much as they should from the sale of oil, most Southwest Asian governments joined together to form **OPEC,** the **Organization of Petroleum Exporting Countries.** This organization was able to keep prices high by limiting oil production. In 1973 OPEC flexed its muscles during the Israeli war with the Arabs when it cut back production in order to punish the Western states' support of Israel.

Society

A small majority of people in the Arab world live in small villages, in flat-roofed houses built of mud bricks. Their standard of living is hardly any better than that had by their ancestors a hundred years ago. Many are sharecroppers, working on land owned by someone else. Bedouin nomads who herd camels are now less than 3% of the total population.

A farmer in Turkey harvests his wheat field without the benefit of modern machinery.

Although over half the population of Southwest Asia still depends on agriculture, the other half has moved to the cities in hopes of finding a better life. Because few new jobs in these cities exist, vast shanty towns now occupy the suburbs of the metropolitan areas. Cairo now has 10,000,000 people; Tehran, 6,000,000; and Baghdad, 3,000,000.

Lacking resources for industrialization, the poorer countries of Southwest Asia have had overwhelming problems in trying to provide services for the people who have flocked into the cities in recent years. They have no electricity, no running water, and the bare minimum of sanitary facilities. Governments urge parents to promote their children's education, but many schools are overcrowded and poorly equipped. City streets are clogged with cars and buses, yet not a single automobile factory is located in Southwest Asia.

The richer oil states do not have the same problems. The Gulf States of Kuwait and Saudi Arabia have new modern highways and airports. Education is universal, and free health care is available. Newspapers, radio, and television stations abound, but censors make sure that people hear the news that the government wants them to hear. Too much of the revenues gained from oil finance the numerous armies of Southwest Asia.

The culture of the Arab people has been and remains shaped by Islam. For the general public hospitality is the highest of virtues, followed by courage. The extended family is all important, and family celebrations vie with religious ones affording holidays. The elite who adopt Western customs have changed some attitudes, but basically most have remained rooted in their past.

In the *souks* or bazaars of the towns, native handicrafts are sold along with food items. These handicrafts include rugs, copper utensils, and clothing. Tourism accounts for a large percentage of Jordanian income. Banking was once the lifeblood of Beirut, Lebanon's capital, but the civil war severely damaged its position as the financial capital of the region.

Carpet weaving is one of the skills of Southwest Asian women.

Syria Independent

After World War II the creation of a stable government in Syria proved an impossible task. Each region of the country had its own chiefs who wanted nothing to do with a strong centralized government in Damascus. Most of Syria's rural population was illiterate and understood little of the political battles in Damascus.

In 1949 a group of army officers decided to "save" the country from the civilian politicians. This began an almost endless series of coups and counter-coups in Damascus that lasted over the next several decades. In all, there were 12 of these coups and 6 constitutions during this period. Colonel followed colonel in the Syrian presidency.

During this time of instability one political party appeared to have some promise. It called itself the **Ba'ath Party,** which stood for the Arab Socialist Revolutionary Party. Founded by a Christian Arab, Michael Aflaq, its program urged a single Arab nation and a socialist economic system. Highly idealistic and attractive to the middle class, only the Syrian communists were as well organized.

An Aleppo street scene mixes the traditional with the modern.

United Arab Republic

The threat of a communist Syria or even a Turkish invasion caused Ba'ath politicians to make a deal with President Nasser of Egypt. In 1956 Nasser could do no wrong in the Arab world, and Syrian politicians believed they had found a savior. After a series of talks with the Egyptian president, in February 1958 a union between Syria and Egypt was proclaimed in Cairo and Damascus. The union was called the **United Arab Republic,** but it did not work well. In September 1961 Syrian officers politely told their Egyptian generals that they were taking back their country.

Syrian Arab Republic

The new regime proclaimed a constitution and a change in the name of the country to the Syrian Arab Republic. Socialist ideas were put into the background for the moment. Politicians scurried about suggesting new ways to deal with Israel and the social and economic problems of the country.

In June 1967 during the Six Days' War the Israelis attacked the Syrians in the Golan Heights. Frequently the Palestinians, with Syria providing the munitions, used these hills to shell Israeli settlements in Galilee. The Syrian army could not hold back the Israelis and withdrew. The Damascus regime was once more frustrated.

The villagers of remote Maloula still speak Syriac.

Israeli armed forces came within 30 miles of Damascus, displacing over 100,000 refugees from the Golan Heights. They had to join the Palestinians in refugee camps. These camps were already overflowing with bitterness, hatred, and hopelessness.

One of the Ba'ath air force officers, Hafez Assad, won out over his rivals. In 1971 a new constitution gave him the presidency with dictatorial powers. Assad is now serving his fourth term in office. Most Syrians have given him credit for at last stopping the merry-go-round of Syrian politics that preceded his coming to power.

Assad is an Alawite from the north of Syria. He soon brought other members of his family and his religion into the government. These are the people he can trust, but for Sunnite Muslims this did not meet with approval. Early in the 1980s a number of demonstrations against the president occurred. The army proved loyal to Assad when the worst rioting took place in Hama. Soldiers opened fire, shelling the city and killing thousands of people. The show of force had the desired effect of suppressing any and all dissent from the president's policies.

Lebanon Occupied

For Syrians the nation of Lebanon has always been a matter of concern. Syrian nationalists regarded the French establishment of a separate Lebanese nation, which allowed the Maronite Christians to rule the country, an insult. In the 1970s the Muslim population of Lebanon challenged Maronite predominance. The Muslims, divided into several armies, along with the Lebanese Druzes, fought a civil war with the Maronite military forces. In fact, Lebanon had so many local military groups operating inside the country that not even a scorecard could keep the combatants identified.

This proved a golden opportunity for Syrian intervention. Acting on a request from some of the factions, but certainly not all, 30,000 Syrian troops entered Lebanon to keep order. At first part of a joint Arab force, the Syrians became the sole occupying force after time. Lebanon, while professing to be an independent nation, has, in fact, become a Syrian satellite. The reunification of Lebanon with Syria was accomplished.

Recent Events

President Assad, with his Soviet policy destroyed by events in Moscow, joined the West during the Gulf War against Iraq. Syria never was on good terms with Saddam Hussein. In a highly symbolic gesture, Assad sent soldiers to Saudi Arabia, although they did not see combat.

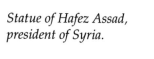

Statue of Hafez Assad, president of Syria.

At the end of the Gulf War, Syria reassessed its relations with Israel. In 1991 at the Madrid negotiations, Syria's position was simply stated. Israel must withdraw completely from the Golan Heights if it wants recognition.

The demand is a difficult one for Israel to accept. Thousands of Jewish settlers now live on the Golan Heights and would have to find new homes. Because the Golan Heights contain the headwaters that supply the Sea of Tiberias, Israel's water supplies would be at risk. Finally Israel must consider the possibility of the Golan's use as a supply base for militant Islamic groups such as *Hezbollah,* intent on continuing the war with Israel.

Syria's political life presently appears placid on the surface. President Assad's security forces keep a tight watch on any dissent. During the last elections he received 99.9% of the vote. The parliament's members are in no mood to challenge him. In every office Assad's picture is on the wall, and a statue of the president stands in every public square.

Syria now has almost 14,000,000 people, many still living in poverty. In villages where most farmers are sharecroppers, they receive between 20% and 40% of the harvest, barely enough to sustain them through the year.

Traffic jams of cars and buses, shoppers in the bazaars, Bedouins in native costumes, and donkey traffic give the cities a cosmopolitan flavor of great vitality. Since the Gulf War, the government has lifted earlier restrictions on the economy.

Efforts to create industry tend to bog down in red tape and inefficiency. Lack of managerial skills and a well-trained labor force are also problems along with a lack of capital. Wisely a major investment has been made in education, which in the future will provide the nation with talent.

Iran's Revolution

When peace came to Southwest Asia after World War II, Muhammad Reza Shah, son of the first Pahlavi monarch, returned to the Iranian throne. Reza Shah, like his father, promoted the rapid modernization of his nation. He also believed in crushing all opposition in his country. The shah's secret police terrified any who stood in the way.

Traditional Muslims were especially alienated because the shah believed that the power of the Muslim Shi'ite *mullahs,* the religious leaders, needed to be broken if his policies were to succeed. The mullahs ruled in the name of the last **imam,** the leader of the Muslim community until his disappearance. Certain distinguished mullahs carried the title of *ayatollah.*

The Ayatollah Ruhollah Khomeini, leader of the Iranian revolution against the shah.

Ayatollah Ruhollah Khomeini, who was widely respected among fervent Muslims, led the opposition to the shah. Khomeini went into exile in France, but his agents in Iran kept up agitation against the shah, who, losing his nerve in January 1979, fled the country. Khomeini returned and announced the formation of an Islamic Republic.

This republic was bitterly antagonistic toward Israel and all things western. In the eyes of the western world, Iran had fallen into the hands of fanatics. Its view was confirmed when Iranian revolutionaries held the personnel of the U.S. embassy in Tehran as hostages. The crisis between Iran and the United States lasted for over a year. Since that time Iran and the United States remain at odds, with no diplomatic relations between the two countries. Much of the content of the Iranian revolution is now gone, but the rhetoric remains.

The Gulf War

In 1980 Iraq commenced hostilities with Iran over oil rich territories in the Tigris Valley. The war lasted for eight years and ended in a stalemate, with huge losses on both sides.

Then, in August 1990, the Iraqi leader, Saddam Hussein, invaded his neighbor to the south, the Sheikdom of Kuwait, the richest of the Gulf States. President George Bush committed the United States to repulse the Iraqis. Under the banner of the United Nations, in January 1991 the United States won a stunning victory in the Gulf War. Once more Kuwait became independent and quickly repaired the damage done during the Iraqi occupation. An American fleet was left in the Persian Gulf to assure the states on its shores of U.S. interest in their welfare.

Before leaving, the Iraqis set the oil fields of Kuwait on fire.

The Kurds

The Kurds make up a large segment of the population of Southwest Asia, numbering about 17,000,000 people. Their language, like Iranian Farsi, is Indo-European, but it is written in Arabic script. It has been Kurdish misfortune that they are presently located in four nations: Turkey, Iraq, Iran, and Syria, preventing them from forming their own state. Factions of the Kurds in both Iraq and Turkey have formed military forces against the governments in Baghdad and Ankara. The United States used its air force to offer protection to the Kurds of Iraq, but in Turkey the Kurds remained on their own to work out a settlement with the Ankara government.

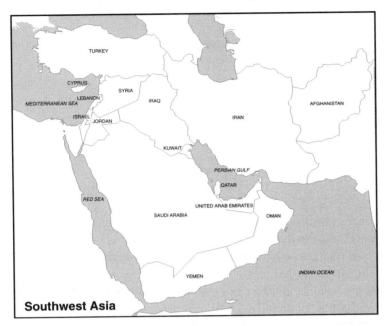

Southwest Asia

Fundamentalists

In all the Muslim nations of Southwest Asia, there is opposition from fundamentalists who resent their present condition. These groups are totally devoted to Islam. They believe that their religion makes demands that, since colonial times, have been ignored. Recruited from lower middle-class people in the cities, often unemployed or underemployed, in some areas the fundamentalists have taken over education and health services. Because the national governments do so little for the poor, the fundamentalists fill the vacuum. The more radical, extremely anti-Western in their outlook, are quite willing to use violence and terrorism to get their way.

Conclusion

Observers of the Southwest Asian scene are divided between optimists and pessimists. Both have good reason for their views. The optimists point to the spirit of reconciliation between the Israeli government and the PLO. Few could have imagined that this would ever occur. Pessimists note that on both sides bitter resentment that will take generations to pass before it is gone still breathes in the hearts of Palestinians and Jews.

Optimists point to economic development in the oil-rich nations; pessimists respond that not all the countries have oil. In the future there is bound to be such a demand for water that conflict is inevitable. Those who regard democratic institutions the hope of the region see progress in Lebanon, Jordan, and Kuwait. Others look at the regimes in Iraq and Iran and are tempted to despair.

CHAPTER 25 REVIEW
SOUTHWEST ASIA IN CONFLICT

Summary
- The major action during World War II was a failed attempt of a German-Italian force to reach the Suez Canal.
- Jews in large numbers left Europe and the countries of Southwest Asia to settle in Palestine, where they met resistance from the Arab population.
- The idea of creating a Jewish state began in the late nineteenth century in a movement known as Zionism.
- In 1948 the state of Israel was declared by the Jewish settlers, and immediately Arab states invaded the country.
- A series of wars between Israel and its neighbors continued to give the Jewish state more territory, but this did not bring it peace.
- Syria obtained independence from the French but plunged into instability until Assad became president.
- Civil war broke out in Lebanon between Maronite Christians and various Muslim parties.
- The Arab world is divided between those countries that have oil and those that do not.
- Iran had a revolution that brought traditionalist Shi'ite religious leaders to power.
- Iraq fought a war with Iran over land rich in oil on their border. Later Saddam Hussein, the Iraqi ruler, occupied Kuwait and sought to overwhelm the Kurdish population in his country.
- During the Gulf War, a coalition of nations led by the United States drove the Iraqis from Kuwait.
- Fundamentalism, a belief that Islam should set the goals and values of governments and societies, is now a major force in most Southwest Asian countries.

Identify
People: Herzl, Balfour, Ben-Gurion, Sadat, Arafat, Rabin, Alawites, Druzes, Assad, Maronites, Hussein, Khomeini
Places: Golan Heights, Gaza, Jordan, Damascus, Jerusalem, Kuwait, Gulf States
Events: exit of colonial powers from Southwest Asia; creation of Israel; Israel's wars with its Arab neighbors; Camp David accords; Iran's revolution; Gulf War

Define

mandate	Islamic Republic	Organization of Petroleum
fundamentalism	Intifada	Exporting Countries (OPEC)
kibbutzim	Knesset	
Zionists	Treaty of Sèvres	

Multiple Choice
1. The goal of most fundamentalists is to
    (a) establish Islamic republics.
    (b) revive the caliphate.
    (c) oust all foreigners from their countries.
    (d) return their countries to Islamic law.

2. At the end of World War II, the French turned over their mandates to native politicians in
   (a) Iraq.
   (b) Iran.
   (c) Syria and Lebanon.
   (d) Iraq and Syria.

3. The British tried to limit Jewish immigration into Palestine before 1948 through
   (a) military action.
   (b) treaties with Zionists.
   (c) quotas.
   (d) closing the ports of Palestine.

4. The idea of a Jewish state was formed first by
   (a) Balfour.
   (b) Dreyfus.
   (c) Ben Gurion.
   (d) Herzl.

5. The Balfour Note of 1917 promised Jews
   (a) access to settlement in the Ottoman Empire.
   (b) a homeland in Palestine.
   (c) territory on Cyprus.
   (d) complete political and economic rights in Great Britain.

6. A kibbutz is
   (a) a Jew born in Israel.
   (b) a Jew born in Asia.
   (c) a party in the Israeli parliament.
   (d) a collective farm.

7. The United Nations commission sent to Palestine recommended
   (a) an Arab state.
   (b) a Jewish state.
   (c) continued British occupation.
   (d) partition.

8. The Israeli parliament is called the
   (a) White House.
   (b) Duma.
   (c) Kibbutz.
   (d) Knesset.

9. Israel's major political parties are
   (a) Likud and Labor.
   (b) Orthodox and Conservative.
   (c) Labor and Conservative.
   (d) Likud and Orthodox.

10. The Camp David accords meant
    (a) Egyptian recognition of Israel.
    (b) the return of the Gaza Strip to Egypt.
    (c) Jordanian recognition of Israel.
    (d) Syrian recognition of Israel.

11. Israel, in its agreement with Arafat, offered the PLO territory
    (a) on the West Bank around Jericho.
    (b) in Jerusalem.
    (c) in Tel Aviv.
    (d) on the Sea of Tiberias' borders.

12. The dominant Christian church in Lebanon is
    (a) Melkite.
    (b) Coptic.
    (c) Shi'ite.
    (d) Maronite.

13. He brought stability to Syria:
    (a) Arafat
    (b) Sadat
    (c) Hussein
    (d) Assad

14. For a short time the United Arab Republic joined
    (a) Syria and Jordan.
    (b) Syria and Iraq.
    (c) Iraq and Jordan.
    (d) Syria and Egypt.

15. Syria refuses to make peace with Israel
    (a) while the Likud Party is in power.
    (b) as long as Israel taps the Jordan River for water.
    (c) as long as it occupies the Golan Heights.
    (d) while the Labor Party is in power.

16. Most Arab farmers in Southwest Asia are
    (a) landowners.
    (b) women.
    (c) sharecroppers.
    (d) renters.

17. The richest of the Arab Gulf States is
    (a) Yemen.
    (b) Oman.
    (c) Bahrain.
    (d) Kuwait.

18. The Gulf War was fought to oust the Iraqis from
    (a) Iran.
    (b) Turkey.
    (c) Syria.
    (d) Kuwait.

19. Iran is now an Islamic Republic thanks to a revolution whose spiritual leader was
    (a) Reza Shah.
    (b) Khomeini.
    (c) Rabin.
    (d) Rasfanjani.

20. The dominant cultural influence in Southwest Asia is provided by
    (a) humanism.
    (b) scientific investigation.
    (c) political secularism.
    (d) religion.

Essay Questions

1. What were the events that led to the creation of Israel?
2. Many Arab people who left Palestine in 1948 still live in refugee camps. What do you see as a solution?
3. What do you expect to see as Iran's revolution unfolds?
4. How do you assess the causes and results of the Gulf War?

Answers

1. d	6. d	11. a	16. c
2. c	7. d	12. d	17. d
3. c	8. d	13. d	18. d
4. d	9. a	14. d	19. b
5. b	10. a	15. c	20. d

CHAPTER 26

India in the Modern Period

India's history from 1914 to the present does much to justify the Hindu belief that time is circular rather than linear. What has happened in the past will occur again as surely as the sun rises and sets each day. The circle of Indian life requires that political leaders come and go, but that the problems of daily life continue to be much the same for the millions of people living in the country's villages and cities.

From 1914 until 1947 attention focused on a drive for independence from British rule. When the British left, interest was directed to domestic problems, especially how to alleviate the grinding poverty of so many men and women in the country. India's leaders advocated modernization as the key to economic progress. Now, with over 50 years of independence concluded, the Indian economy has made remarkable progress and a sizable middle class has emerged. However, for millions of Indians, religious loyalty still dominates their values, holding an emotional appeal far surpassing political concerns.

The Gateway to India, a symbol of British rule in Bombay.

India's great gift to the world through this period are two remarkable people. Both are known for their humanitarian concerns. The one, Mohandas K. Gandhi, led Indians in their struggle for freedom from Great Britain, practicing nonviolence as his weapon to inspire his countrymen to resist foreign rule. Gandhi gave his life promoting the importance of every human person. The other Indian, by choice if not by birth, was Mother Teresa, a nun whose sisters work in the Calcutta slums and other towns of India to help the terminally ill. Like Gandhi, the lesson she taught was the dignity of life, even for the most abandoned of India's poor.

World War I and After

India on the eve of World War I had two major parties that sought change in the country's status. The older was the **Congress Party,** which had long been the major force in promoting better opportunities for native Indians under the **British** *raj,* or government. In its early years Congress did not advocate self-rule from Great Britain, but little by little its position changed from accommodation to demands for the British to withdraw.

Officials in the Congress Party held that all Indians were welcome under its banner. However, Hindu leaders predominated, causing Muslims concern. The result was the formation of the autonomous Muslim League. After 1913 the leader of the Muslim League was Muhammad Ali Jinnah, a lawyer trained, like Gandhi, in London and who later practiced in Bombay.

Ali Jinnah, leader of India's Muslim League.

When World War I commenced the British governor-general simply announced to the Indian people that they were also at war with Germany. No effort was made to confer with Indian national leaders. Despite this high-handed approach, Indians rallied around Great Britain, and soon soldiers were embarking for the Western Front where they took positions with the Allied forces.

A German cruiser sailed into the Indian Ocean, bombing Madras and thereby bringing the war closer to home. Because Germany, after Great Britain, was the largest purchaser of Indian exports, the war caused a major depression in the economy.

As the war dragged on, Indian soldiers in the British armies suffered thousands of casualties. Over a million served in Europe. The expectation of Indian leaders was that for all the sacrifices their nation made, rewards at the conclusion of the war would be great. They were to be disappointed.

Mohandas Gandhi

In 1914, at the very beginning of the war, Mohandas Gandhi arrived back in India. Gandhi had studied law in Great Britain and then traveled to South Africa to practice law in Durban. There were some 40,000 Indians then living in the Natal province, where discrimination against them was rampant. While acting as a legal advisor, Gandhi developed a personal belief that to change unjust laws required *satyagraha*, a conviction that a person must always pursue truth as the most important moral task of life.

In addition Gandhi advocated **ahisma,** doing no violence to any living thing, a tenet long held by followers of India's Jain religion. Therefore Gandhi advocated passive resistance to injustice, for such a response inflicted no physical harm on one's opponents but made a powerful appeal to their conscience. In time Gandhi felt certain that the justice of a person's cause, advocated through nonviolence, was a much more powerful weapon than the use of force.

When he returned to India from South Africa, Gandhi enlisted in the fight for independence. His simplicity, his dress, which was that of a poor peasant, and his sincerity brought him hundreds and then tens of thousands of followers. They recognized him as a **sadhu,** an Indian holy man and began to call him *Mahatma,* the Great Soul. Along with his support of Indian independence, Gandhi sought to abolish the difficulties of India's untouchables, arguing that they must have the same rights as caste Hindus.

In March 1919 Gandhi called on his followers to pray and fast in response to the **Rowlett Acts,** passed in the British Parliament in response to the independence movement. This outraged the Indian nationalists, for the acts' measures were more repressive than any that preceded them. Hindus and Muslims joined together in demonstrations against further British control over their country.

British troops using batons place Indian demonstrators under arrest in 1930.

General Reginald Dyer, in charge of keeping order in the Punjab, forbade all demonstrations. A month after the passage of the Rowlett Acts a large group of people gathered in a walled park in Amritsar to celebrate a Hindu festival. Among them were some nationalists. Dyer ordered his soldiers to blockade the only entrance to the park and commanded his men to fire into the unarmed crowd. About 400 people died and more than 1,000 were wounded. After word spread about the massacre, masses of people poured into the streets looting British shops and attacking Europeans. His superiors sent Dyer back to England, but there he received a welcome from conservatives as the Savior of the Punjab. His legacy left a bitter taste among all Indians. Those who in the past held aloof from the national struggle now enlisted in the cause.

In December 1919 a new Government of India Act passed the British Parliament. It provided a governor-general with executive powers and an Indian legislature. London kept control over India's security and foreign affairs. Such half-way measures did nothing to still the revolutionary mood in the Congress Party.

Gandhi was now in charge. He urged a boycott of all British goods and refusal to obey discriminatory laws. Indians should spin the thread to make their own cloth, a lesson he taught through working at this task himself. For the first time in world history, the spinning wheel became a symbol of revolution, an unlikely combination.

Not all Gandhi's supporters heeded his call for nonviolence against the raj. Strikes and riots sometimes resulted in bloodshed. In February 1922 Gandhi called for an end to civil disobedience, but this did not save him from arrest. A British court sentenced him to prison for six years. After only two years government officials released him because of his poor health. He emerged from confinement to find that Hindus and Muslims were now fighting each other instead of the British. By 1930 the Muslims demanded that if and when independence came, they must have their own state.

In London, new Government of India Acts kept Parliament busy in order to blunt the independence movement. An act passed in 1935 promised each province its own legislature for internal matters. Once more the Congress Party rejected it. Gandhi's own campaign was now directed against the hated salt tax that fell so heavily on the poor. Hundreds of thousands of his supporters followed him in refusing to pay it, and the jails of India filled with political prisoners. Gandhi led a march to the sea where he gathered salt crystals in defiance of British law.

Jawaharlal Nehru meets with Mohandas Gandhi to seek ways to gain Indian independence.

World War II in India

World War II then interjected itself. Once more the British governor-general simply announced that India was at war. Congress politicians demonstrated their disapproval when they resigned their governmental positions throughout the nation. Jinnah seized the opportunity to argue that a separate independent state was now on the horizon for the

80,000,000 Muslims of the country. Gandhi retorted, "The vast majority of Muslims of India are converts to Islam or are descendants of converts. They did not become a separate nation as soon as they became converts." To prove the point that a united India was possible, Congress elected a Muslim president.

Gandhi did not give his support to the war effort. Throughout the country his partisans continued to frustrate British plans to ensure that India should be a major source of supplies, especially iron and steel. Gandhi instead launched a new "Quit India" campaign. His more ardent followers, against his will, waged a guerilla war against the Europeans.

Independence Achieved

World War II sapped whatever resolve Great Britain had to continue its rule over India. The Labour government, elected soon after the war ended, was known to be opposed to colonialism. London dispatched a commission to India to talk over measures needed to be taken for a transition to independence. The Congress Party rejected the **two-Indias plan** of the Muslim League, so that negotiations with the British were made more difficult.

In July 1946 Jinnah called for a day of direct action. Muslim crowds jammed Calcutta's streets killing and looting Hindu homes and businesses, while Hindu mobs retaliated on Muslim establishments. In one day, 5,000 people were killed, and 100,000 were left homeless. For the rest of 1946, terror and violence between Muslims and Hindus spread throughout the nation.

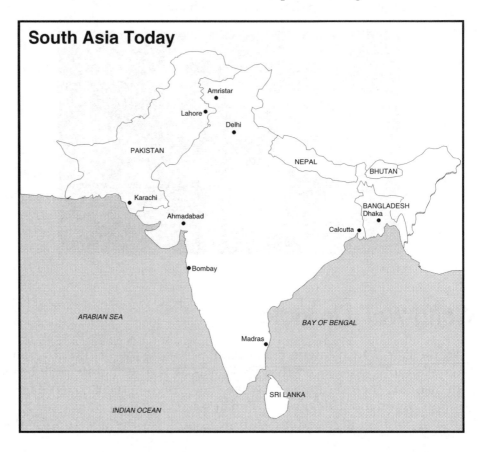

In February 1947 London announced its definite intention to leave India. Negotiating the withdrawal's terms were Jinnah and Jawaharlal Nehru, now representing the Congress Party. Jinnah let it be known that "The only thing the Muslim has in common with the Hindu is his slavery to the British." The Sikh population also demanded a separate state. Gandhi sought to allay Muslim fears. He began to pray from the Qur'an, but this did little to soothe the divisions among his countrymen and women.

All over India communal fighting racked the country. The level of violence convinced the British that partition was the only answer and agreed to the establishment of Pakistan, where a Muslim majority would exist.

On August 15, 1947, India and Pakistan became independent. Nehru assumed the office of prime minister of India; Jinnah, of Pakistan. An uneasy peace existed along the border, especially in Kashmir, for here Muslims were a majority, but India claimed it for its own. Pakistan had two parts, a western nation where Muslims had been a majority for centuries, and an eastern part, the region of Bengal. Fully 10,000,000 people moved out of the countries where they were in the minority. Between 500,000 and 1,000,000 people died, never finding the sanctuary they sought. Gandhi was overwhelmed. He started a fast to protest the deaths of Muslims in Delhi.

India's constitution provided for a secular, democratic state, favoring neither Hindus nor Muslims. Local government was in the hands of the states that made up the federation. Nehru was extremely popular at the time, so successful that he convinced the remaining maharajahs in the country to hand over their territories to a now united country.

On January 30, 1948, a young Brahman shot and killed Gandhi. The assassin and other extremists were firmly opposed to giving untouchables equal status and chose to kill their champion. All India mourned. Nehru expressed his feeling, "The light has gone out of our lives and there is darkness everywhere."

Thousands of people throng Gandhi's funeral.

India After Independence

Nehru set India on a path that he felt best satisfied its role for the future. He was especially proud that his nation had become the largest democracy in the world. He believed in nonalignment and consistently refused to take sides between the United States and the Soviet Union during the Cold War. Nehru was also a firm advocate of socialism; he felt that this economic system better provided for the welfare of the population than capitalism. The government nationalized India's major industries and transportation facilities. Even though measures were enacted to aid the rural poor, there was no confiscation of private wealth because many rich donors were in the Congress Party's ranks.

There were gains and losses on India's frontiers. In 1954 Nehru convinced France to hand over its last colony on Indian soil. The Portuguese wanted no compromise on Goa, so in 1961 the Indian Defense Minister sent the army into that region. Goa's "liberation" attached it as a separate state within India.

On the domestic front, in 1955 the Indian parliament focused on giving equality to women and untouchables. In that year the law permitted women to sue for divorce, and it became illegal to discriminate against anyone because of untouchability. Therefore, the two most disadvantaged groups of India's citizens on legal grounds, if not cultural, became equal with all the others. At that time 60,000,000 men and women were defined as untouchables. They then became *dalits*, or disadvantaged, but no longer untouchables.

In May 1964 Nehru died, creating a major vacuum in Indian politics. During this period a short war with Pakistan broke out over the boundary in Kashmir, in which the Indian army proved the better. Later, a failed revolt in Tibet caused the Dalai Lama and his close followers to seek refuge in India, putting more strain on Indian relations with China.

Mother Teresa

The best-known person in contemporary India came upon the scene in the 1960s. Americans have voted her the most admired woman in the world several times, as late as a 1995 survey.

Agnes Bojaxhiu was born in Skopje, Macedonia, in 1910 of Catholic Albanian parents. When she was 18, she joined a community of nuns, the Congregation of Loreto, and chose the name Teresa when she took her vows. The nuns ran a girls' high school in a town close to Calcutta, and Sister Teresa was sent there to teach. Eventually she became the school principal.

In 1946 she made the decision that changed her life. Sister Teresa asked for permission to leave her community to take up a call to serve India's poor. Two years later she left the convent, dressed now in a sari of white with a simple blue border. She started a school for poor children from the slums of Calcutta. Soon her mission expanded to feeding and caring for homeless people. Several of her former students volunteered to help, so she formed a community of nuns, the Missionaries of Charity.

Mother Teresa, advocate for India's homeless.

The Missionaries spread throughout India, opening hospices for the terminally ill, orphanages for abandoned children, and leper asylums for those afflicted with this dread disease. Her sisters follow her admonition that no one should die without love, affirming that, "Being unwanted is the worst disease that any human being can experience."

The Missionaries of Charity, now with a male branch, share their lives with the poor. Mother Teresa, as she was now known, captivated the world for her work in India. In 1979 she was awarded the Nobel Peace Prize. There are now over 100 foundations in India and other countries with over 1,500 sisters and 400 brothers. Mother Teresa died in September 1997.

Political Scene

In 1966 Nehru's daughter, Indira Gandhi, who was no relation to Mohandas, became prime minister. She held that office for the next ten years. During her tenure, India made significant progress. Thanks to the **Green Revolution,** the development of new strains of wheat and rice, the Indian population managed to feed itself without importing food.

Under Indira Gandhi the Congress majority had its problems. Opponents accused its officials of corruption and indifference to reform. As a result, in 1977 Congress lost the election, and Mrs. Gandhi was out of office, only to be returned as prime minister again in 1980.

Mrs. Gandhi's new government was confronted by Sikh nationalists of the Punjab with more insistent demands that they must have a separate state. Because Punjab was the most prosperous state in India, the disturbances caused by the nationalists presented a serious problem to the Delhi government. Extremists among the Sikhs occupied the Golden Temple of Amritsar, the most sacred sanctuary of the religion, to demonstrate their resolve. They refused to leave until their demands were met.

In July 1984 Mrs. Gandhi ordered the army to oust the Sikh militants, and a bloody battle took place. Four months later, two of her Sikh bodyguards killed Mrs. Gandhi. In retaliation during the next three days Hindu partisans murdered some 2,500 Sikhs and destroyed their property worth millions of dollars. The police looked the other way, and no one was ever brought to trial.

The Golden Temple of Amritsar is the center of Sikh devotion.

Indira Gandhi's son, Rajiv, took his mother's place, once more proving the strength of family prestige within the Indian Congress Party. Rajiv spent much of his time encouraging industrial development, especially in electronics. Factories sprouted in the suburbs of Indian cities as private investors found India a good place to put their money. Nevertheless, in 1989 the Congress Party lost the elections to opposition parties, but Rajiv did not give up easily. He was on campaign in 1991 when a suicide bomber took her own life as well as his.

In the elections that followed, the Congress Party once more came into power, narrowly defeating a new Hindu religious party, the Baharatiya Janata. The prime minister, P. V. Narasimha Rao, summed up his program, "The only way to exist in India is to coexist."

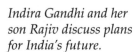

Indira Gandhi and her son Rajiv discuss plans for India's future.

Opposition to Congress' secular attitudes among the Hindu masses became evident in an incident that occurred a year later. In December 1992 Hindu extremists called on their followers to destroy a mosque that they claimed marked the spot where Vishnu was born as Lord Rama. In the sixteenth century the Moghul emperor had built a mosque on the site. Some 200,000 Hindus marched on the mosque in Ayodha and frantically tore down the structure.

Prime Minister Rao for a time weathered all attacks to bring down the Congress Party. Accused of rampant corruption in its ranks, it lost the elections of 1996 to the Baharitya Janata, but a coalition of parties kept it from holding power for long. In the space of a year, India had three prime ministers as the nation's former political stability began to unravel.

Hindu fundamentalism is a very powerful and growing force, making it difficult for the 10% of Indians who are Muslim, Buddhist, Christian, Jain, Parsee, or Sikh. In fact, the minorities of India, many of whom are in the highest ranks of society, must remain fearful that their security might change overnight if militants demand that India become a completely Hindu state.

India has always had differences among its people. Today the population numbers over 900,000,000 men and women. The birth rate continues to soar, making population control the most serious problem facing the country. In Bombay alone there are 6,000,000 homeless families that must live on a blanket placed on the sidewalk. There are so many contrasts, for next door to a homeless family, the home of a rich industrialist may have dozens of rooms and a bevy of servants.

A Hindu festival at a temple in south India draws a huge crowd.

India now has enough food for its population, and its electronics industry is one of the world's finest. All over India new investment has created factories and industry, making it one of the world's top ten economies. Yet choking pollution in the cities and a rapid destruction of the environment has been a high price to pay for the nation's economic growth.

In Indian villages old customs die slowly. Dalits remain outcasts, and a bride whose family has failed to pay her dowry lives in jeopardy. The danger of political fragmentation remains a fact of life.

Pakistan

The nation of Pakistan, born a twin of India in 1947, came into existence because of the Muslim fear of living in a nation where the Hindus would compose a large majority. From the very beginning the new nation had its problems because its two parts were separated by a distance of over a thousand miles. Into the poorer part of colonial India, millions of Muslim refugees now had to be fed and housed, and meaningful employment could hardly be found for such a multitude.

Because U.S. foreign policy sought to build barriers against expansion of either Communist China or the Soviet Union, it found an ally in Pakistan. In return for its anticommunist stance and later its assistance to the Afghan fighters, the *mujahadin,* against the Soviet-sponsored regime in their country, the United States poured economic and military aid into Pakistan.

In 1971 the fragile union between East and West Pakistan broke apart, and civil war ensued. India came to the aid of the East Pakistanis, who resented the dominant role of their western countrymen. With this help East Pakistan won its battle and became a new nation, Bangladesh.

The history of Bangladesh and Pakistan since then has witnessed a struggle for political stability and economic progress. A birth rate similar to India's continues to eat up much of the small gains in the economy. Military dictatorships appeared in both nations beneath a facade of democratic government. Pakistan, to please its Muslim clergy, has declared itself an Islamic Republic, with the promise, however, that the rights of minorities would be respected.

Conclusion

The struggle for independence in India was one of the great epics of the modern world. Ghandi's use of nonviolence as a strategy for revolution proved its value for the first time in world history. Independence has yet to improve the lives of the poor of India, but progress has created a growing middle class. India's development is progressing, both in industry and agriculture as western and local investment create new enterprises.

Bangladesh remains the poorest of Asian nations with a long path ahead for its people to reach a decent standard of living. Nature does not cooperate; flooding bedevils the country, wiping out thousands of people and their small farms all too often. Pakistan, although not as desperate, is a fellow traveler on the same road.

CHAPTER 26 REVIEW
INDIA IN THE MODERN PERIOD

Summary
- India's two major parties before World War I were formed on religious identity, the Congress, and the Muslim League.
- Indian soldiers fought in Europe in the British army during World War I, expecting concessions from London at the conclusion of the conflict.
- While the war was in progress, Mohandas Ghandi returned to India to lead the independence movement in nonviolent ways.
- British repression failed to keep the drive for independence curtailed.
- Ghandi was jailed for several years.
- At the end of World War II, an exhausted Great Britain agreed to Indian independence.
- By this time Muslims and Hindus were clashing with one another. Muslims demanded their own separate nation.
- In 1947 the Indians gained independence, collected in two states. Pakistan was the Muslim nation and India was predominantly Hindu.
- A huge migration of people occurred as Hindus hurried out of Pakistan and Muslims left India.
- Jawaharlal Nehru became India's first prime minister.
- Indira Ghandi's tenure as prime minister ended when her Sikh body-guards killed her.
- Mother Teresa, who founded a religious order to care for the dying, may well be India's most famous citizen.
- Pakistan, born in turbulence, continues on that path.

Identify
People: Gandhi, Jinnah, Dyer, Jawaharlal Nehru, Mother Teresa, Indira Gandhi, Rao
Places: Bombay, Madras, Amritsar, Kashmir, Bengal, Goa, Calcutta, Bangladesh, Pakistan
Events: Gandhi's drive for independence; government of India Acts; communal violence between Hindus and Muslims; Sikh nationalists demand a separate state

Define

Rowlett Acts	sadhu
British raj	Congress Party
two-Indias plan	Green Revolution
ahisma	

Multiple Choice
1. Ali Jinnah was the leader of the
   (a) Congress Party.
   (b) Muslim League.
   (c) All-India Party.
   (d) Hindu Reform Party.

2. During World War I, Indians fought in
   (a) Europe.
   (b) Southwest Asia.
   (c) East Asia.
   (d) Russia.

3. Hindus and Muslims quarreled over
   (a) having a single state after independence.
   (b) allowing the British to stay.
   (c) continuing the maharajahs in power.
   (d) supporting ahisma.

4. Gandhi's experience taught him to avoid
   (a) Muslims.
   (b) jail.
   (c) red meat.
   (d) violence.

5. General Dyer is famous for
   (a) jailing Gandhi.
   (b) bringing Gandhi and Jinnah to agree on a single state.
   (c) firing on an unarmed crowd in Amritsar.
   (d) repressing the Muslim League.

6. India's independence occurred while this party governed in London:
   (a) Labour
   (b) Conservative
   (c) Socialist
   (d) Social Democrat

7. The declaration of independence for India and Pakistan resulted in
   (a) a huge exodus of Muslims from India.
   (b) a large migration of Hindus into Bangladesh.
   (c) attacks on the British troops remaining in India.
   (d) Gandhi's resignation from the Congress Party.

8. The Indian constitution favors
   (a) Hindus.
   (b) Christians.
   (c) Muslims.
   (d) none of the above.

9. The Brahman caste in India resented Gandhi's willingness to
   (a) allow British garrisons to remain in India.
   (b) favor the creation of Pakistan.
   (c) allow Goa to remain Portuguese.
   (d) give equality to the untouchables.

10. One of India's guests living in exile is
    (a) the first prime minister of Pakistan.
    (b) the Dalai Lama.
    (c) the Archbishop of Ceylon.
    (d) the Iranian shah.

11. A Green Revolution allows India to
    (a) maintain a large army.
    (b) quiet all Muslim dissent.
    (c) thwart Chinese border adjustments.
    (d) grow enough food to feed its population.

12. Hindu fundamentalism wants the government to do more
    (a) to promote Hindu values.
    (b) to assist Bangladesh.
    (c) to limit the Sikhs to the Punjab.
    (d) to force foreigners out of India.

13. Bangladesh once was a part of
    (a) Pakistan.
    (b) Kashmir.
    (c) Afghanistan.
    (d) Iran.

14. India's most famous citizen known for her aid to the poor is
    (a) Indira Gandhi.
    (b) Mother Teresa.
    (c) Sister Carey.
    (d) Mother Marie.

Essay Questions
1. Provide an estimate of Gandhi's role in the independence movement.
2. Why were the British willing to leave India in 1947 and not in 1918?
3. Explain the violence among the different religious groups in India.

Answers

1. b	6. a	11. d
2. a	7. a	12. a
3. a	8. d	13. a
4. d	9. d	14. b
5. c	10. b	

CHAPTER 27

Communist China and Korea

The major dividing line in twentieth-century East Asian history originates in the events that followed World War II and the rise of communism. Its success in China and North Korea can be traced to native party leaders, convinced that its program offered a solution to the political and economic problems that faced their countries. Mao Zedong in China and Kim Il Sung in North Korea shared a common ambition to gain absolute power over their people.

China Between Nationalists and Communists

The 1920s were crucial for Chinese history. Sun Yat-sen, who established the Chinese Republic, soon discovered how difficult it was to rule the country. Too many war lords refused to pay attention to the government. Taxation was chaotic, leaving the government strapped for money. In southern China the Communists set up an independent state. The Nationalist government believed that they were a very dangerous threat. Attacks on the Communists became so frequent that their leader Mao Zedong determined to lead his followers to sanctuary in the far north.

This Long March was one of the most difficult in world history. As many as 100,000 people began the journey, but only 3,000 survived. The distance covered over several years was 6,000 miles. Mao then established his communist state.

The Japanese invaded Chinese Manchuria while the Long March was in progress. Opposing them was the Nationalist leader, Chiang Kai-shek (his name in the new Chinese spelling is Jiang Jie-shi), who became the heir of Sun Yat-sen. At first Chiang and Mao cooperated in the fight against the Japanese, but they had a falling out by the war's end.

By the summer of 1949, it was obvious that Chiang Kai-shek and his Nationalist forces were on the verge of collapse. Despite the infusion of millions of American dollars to assist him, Chiang was unable to turn his armies into effective fighting forces. More than money, the Nationalists required a boost in morale, but the peasants of China were much more likely to cast their lot with the Communists of Mao Zedong. The Nationalists offered the peasants a return to the past, which meant more of the same, whereas the Communists promised them a new and brighter future. In December the last Nationalists withdrew to Taiwan, and the Chinese mainland was left in the hands of Mao's People's Liberation Army.

Chinese Communist troops enter a city once held by the Nationalists.

Even before the Nationalists were gone, the leaders of the Communists announced on October 1, 1949, that China was now a **People's Republic.** Mao became chairman of the state, and Zhou Enlai, the prime minister as well as the foreign minister. Power was in the Communist Party, which numbered about 4,500,000 people.

China was in shambles as a result of decades of violence, natural disasters, and corruption among the country's leaders. Of the people, 80% or 550,000,000, were peasant farmers who were barely able to survive. This did not discourage Mao and his cohorts, for they counted on the strength of the long-suffering peasants of China to make the country a strong industrialized nation. It would not happen at once, but then the Chinese were well known for patience.

Land Reform

The first task the Beijing government undertook was to reward the peasants for their support through land redistribution. With a complete disregard for legality or individual rights, from 1950 to 1952, the People's Liberation Army arrested and violently disposed of about 3,000,000 landowners. The peasants were permitted to take out their rage on them before they died in farcical trials.

The peasants did not long enjoy the small plots of land that they held from the redistribution, for the Chinese leaders were well aware that private ownership violated Marxist theory. Therefore, after 1953, the peasants were herded onto **collectives,** numbering 200 to 300 people.

The Chinese Communists looked to the Soviet Union's example in destroying the landowning class and in establishing collectives. It was equally true for the Stalinist model that all industries and businesses must be nationalized. In 1953 the central planning officials in Beijing produced the first Five Year Plan. This outline described targets in all major industries of the country. Marx had argued that it was the urban worker, not the peasant, who was the true revolutionary. Chairman Mao reluctantly turned his attention to the cities.

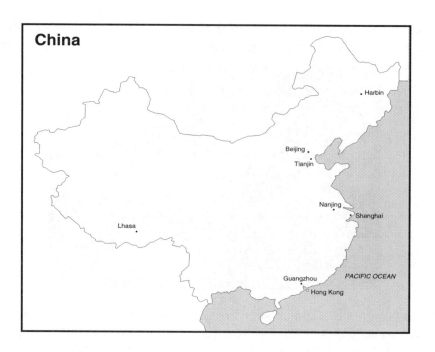

China

Harbin

Beijing
Tianjin

Nanjing
Shanghai

Lhasa

Guangzhou
Hong Kong

PACIFIC OCEAN

Foreign Policy

The basis of Chinese foreign policy was also a close alliance with the elder brother of communism, the Soviet Union. Mao and Stalin were quick to create an understanding that guaranteed Soviet aid for the rebuilding of the country. Soviet advisors with **rubles** in their pockets arrived in China to assist in the nation's industrialization. However, it soon became evident that the Soviets regarded the Chinese as clients and second-class communists.

After Stalin's death and Khrushchev's coming to power, the number of rubles began to decline, although the haughty attitude of the Russians did not. They scolded the Chinese when they took unsanctioned trips to other Asian or African nations. In 1959 Khrushchev refused a Chinese request for information on making nuclear weapons. A year later, it was obvious on both sides that the two communist giants could no longer work together. Moscow called back its advisors, and no more financial aid went to the Chinese.

Korean War

It might have been expected that after so many years of war, the People's Liberation Army deserved a rest. This was not, however, to be the case. In October 1950, only a year after coming to power, the army was sent to aid the North Koreans.

At the close of World War II, the United States and the Soviets agreed to divide Korea into a north and south. The dividing line was at the thirty-eighth parallel. Little by little the U.S. occupying forces withdrew until, by 1949, only 500 troops were left.

Unknown to the West, North Korean leaders intended to unify the country through force. After consultation with both the Soviets and the Chinese, who gave them assurances of support, the North Korean army crossed into South Korea on June 29, 1950. The presumption in Pyongyang, the North Korean capital, was that the United States was not that interested in defending South Korea.

President Harry Truman surprised them. He ordered American troops in Japan to deploy into Korea. The United Nations, urged on by Washington, declared its intention to resist the aggression. However, momentum was with North Korea, and by September all Korea except its southeast corner was in communist hands.

U.S. troops move to the front in Korea.

At this critical moment, General Douglas MacArthur, the United Nations commander, landed an army behind the battle lines on the Korean coast. The surprised North Koreans withdrew from their forward positions. The United Nations' success so frightened the Chinese that they thought they must intervene. Mao Zedong did not want an American army on the Chinese border. Chinese troops, numbering 300,000 men, poured into Korea and canceled the early United Nations' success.

MacArthur wanted to use nuclear weapons, but Truman said no and dismissed him. By 1952 the United Nations army was back at the thirty-eighth parallel, and a year later the combatants signed a cease fire.

More Battles

At the same time as the Korean War, Mao was so rich in manpower that he could order his troops to occupy Tibet. This was done in November 1950 on the excuse that the territory of Tibet was historically a province of imperial China. That nation was no match for the Chinese. The Tibetans would not willingly accept Chinese rule and, in 1959, went into open revolt. The Dalai Lama and 100,000 Tibetans took refuge in India. As a further goal, the Communists intended an invasion of Taiwan to dislodge the Nationalists from their refuge. (The Nationalists continued to call their government the Republic of China.) On this matter, they had to take into consideration the U.S. resolve to defend the independence of Taiwan. Despite numerous threats and bombardments of two small Nationalist-held island fortresses, Taiwan remained outside the grasp of the Communist regime.

Buddhist monks from Tibet play their horns as part of a service.

Mao Pushes Ahead

In June 1957 Chairman Mao had unexpectedly announced a new policy of government toleration. Even though opposition to the Party and government was crushed ruthlessly in the past, now he proclaimed, "Let a hundred flowers bloom. Let a hundred schools of thought contend." Looking back on what happened next shows either Mao's cleverness or his duplicity, for hidden opponents who believed themselves to be safe came out from hiding. Within a year the chairman clamped down on the easily identified dissenters, and repression returned in one more program, the year of the **Great Leap Forward.**

The essence of this "leap" was the establishment of still larger agricultural units, **communes.** The communes averaged 15,000 acres and held 25,000 people. Mao was convinced that such consolidation would increase production and focus the Party's interest on the peasant once more. Party leaders put the peasants into batallions that marched into the fields singing revolutionary songs. They ate in communal mess halls, slept in dormitories, and left their children in nurseries. Every bit of privacy was denied them.

Mao also had a plan for workers. Industry was to be decentralized, moved to communes or backyards. Here eager workers constructed small steel mills.

Neither of these projects succeeded. The peasants quietly resisted, spending long hours in pretending to work but doing little. The backyard steel mills produced worthless metal. Starvation was the result for both farmers and workers. Between 1958 and 1961 almost 25,000,000 people died as famine overwhelmed the country.

Mao Zedong reviews the Chinese Red Army.

Mao's failures were evident enough to all in the Party to allow, for a time, a change in direction. He stepped down as chairman, but held on to his position as head of the Party. The pragmatists who now governed the country allowed people to leave the communes. Private homes and garden plots returned to the countryside, and agricultural productivity increased. Factories reopened with salaried workers receiving pay based on merit.

It was not easy for Mao, or his increasingly active wife, Jiang Qing, to let China alone. What had become of the revolution?

Among China's young people, a cult of Mao elevated the chairman to a role a little less than divine. His picture hung in every classroom as China's savior. It was now time to use this adulation. Mao called on his devotees to come forward to "save the Revolution" and, less apparently, Mao's own skin as China's political head. Come forward they did, and with a vengeance. The year 1966 became the year of the Cultural Revolution.

Cultural Revolution

There are times in history when something amounting to mass hysteria seizes a nation. It happened in China during the **Cultural Revolution.** Mao's appeal to renew the revolution brought forth a response from the youth that was remarkable for its violent intensity. Armed with the little *Red Book,* filled with Mao's sayings, young men and women poured out of their classrooms to attack everyone and everything that smacked of privilege or hated "Western corruption."

The leaders formed **Red Guards,** which were kept in line with strict military discipline. Soldiers in the Red Guards burst into private homes and public buildings in search of "enemies of the people." Mao's party rivals were accused of betrayal, publicly humiliated, put on trial, and imprisoned or executed according to the seriousness of their alleged crimes. Professors of the universities, lawyers, doctors, writers, bankers, factory managers, and in fact, anyone who had a higher education or a position of authority, suffered as Mao's Red Guards sought to purify the country.

China was in chaos. Even Mao became alarmed. Only the army remained untouched thanks to the prestige it enjoyed. At last the generals intervened, disbanding the Red Guards, and after two years of havoc, the Cultural Revolution was over. Zhou Enlai took charge of the reconstruction while Mao, once more, stepped aside.

Red Guards shout out their loyalty to Mao Zedong during the Cultural Revolution.

The Opening of China

Besides restoring what was left of domestic Chinese life untouched by the Cultural Revolution, Zhou became active in foreign affairs. He realized that, in the world of superpowers, China had enemies both in the Soviet Union and the United States. His first tentative move in 1971 was to invite an American table tennis team to compete in China, and he personally greeted the players in Beijing. Ping-pong, long a favorite sport in China, now became the basis for renewed ties to the United States.

The thawing of relations between the two countries progressed from step to step. The United States agreed to the People's Republic replacing Nationalist China in the United Nations. In February 1972 President Richard Nixon surprised the American public when he visited China. In his talks with Zhou and Mao, they agreed that China and the United States should open cultural exchanges in order to pave the way for full diplomatic relations. This occurred seven years later because American politicians insisted that America's ally, Taiwan, should not be abandoned.

The Second Revolution

In 1976 another period of Chinese history commenced when Zhou and Mao both died. Power now passed to one of the last of the Old Revolutionaries, Deng Xiaoping. Deng solidified his role when he had the leaders of the Cultural Revolution arrested, among them Mao's wife. They were known as the **Gang of Four** and were put on trial, convicted, and sentenced to death. Later their sentence was commuted to life imprisonment. Deng, who had himself been jailed during the Cultural Revolution, had his revenge.

Deng preferred to keep out of the limelight, allowing others to hold government posts and party offices. Nevertheless, it was Deng who now shifted the Chinese economy toward capitalism. The remaining communes were dissolved, and farmers returned to growing crops for profit. Several inefficient industries were closed, and competition returned among some businesses; however, in other areas of the economy, government enterprises continued to function. Foreign investment and corporations were welcomed. Hotel chains opened, some of them financed from outside the country, and tourism soon became a major industry.

Ordinary people's standard of living rose as did their aspirations to buy refrigerators, televisions, western clothes, and even shares of companies in a Chinese stock exchange. City streets filled with bicycles as people discovered a new freedom in their lives.

One aspect of central planning did not change. This was the government's concern that the growth of the Chinese population be limited. In less than 20 years there had been an increase of 200,000,000 people. Demographers estimated that the country would have at least another 300,000,000 by the year 2000. As early as the 1960s, government regulations ordered that rural families were allowed but one child, city families were allowed two, with exceptions allowed the small ethnic minorities living in China. This did not entirely slow down births sufficiently, so that by 1980 only one child per family was permitted.

Abortions, especially of female babies, became the norm in Chinese families. Even with these rules, China's population will approach over 1,000,000,000 people by the year 2000.

China's Search for Democracy

It is not certain that there is a direct connection between economic and political reform, but this seems to be the case. It is more certain that one generation of students will differ a great deal from the one before it. In the 1980s, the children of the Red Guards who attended the nation's universities may have nodded to the statues of Mao Zedong as they passed, but his values and those of their parents were certainly different. The students wanted more than comfortable lives. They talked about change in the Party and greater freedom of expression. They were insistent that civil rights be respected and that the corruption among the Party elite be rooted out.

In April 1989 over 100,000 students marched into Beijing's downtown to Tiananmen Square, the vast plaza in front of the Forbidden City. There were cries for more freedom, democracy, and the ouster of corrupt officials. The demonstrators pledged to stay in the square until their demands were met.

Government officials were not quite sure how to handle this outburst. Perhaps they expected it to evaporate in a short time, but instead ordinary citizens joined the demonstrators, to such a number that 1,000,000 people were now out in the streets. The Party chieftains held many meetings. Deng believed there should be a crackdown. On the other hand, the general secretary of the party, Zhao Ziyang, was sympathetic to reform.

Deng's party of hard-liners won out. Martial law was declared, and army troops surrounded Beijing but did not move into the city. Despite some defections from their cause, 10,000 students held firm, constructing a 30-foot statue named the Goddess of Liberty.

A brave Chinese tries to delay the tanks rolling into Tiananmen Square.

Tension remained high. Then on June 4, tanks began to move into the city, crushing through the barricades. Soldiers and tank crews fired point blank into the crowds in Tiananmen Square. Pandemonium erupted as people fled for safety. Hundreds died; thousands were wounded. During the next week in police sweeps, over 10,000 people were arrested. The Chinese media proclaimed that "criminals and thugs" had sought to overthrow the government.

After Tiananmen

The events of the night of June 4 cast a shadow over China that was not easy to dissipate. Despite its economic gains, the country was obviously still in the grip of a totalitarian clique of politicians. Eventually a shakeup occurred, bringing Jiang Zemin into the role of party head and Li Peng as prime minister. In the background Deng Xiaoping continued to be China's most powerful man until February 1997 when he died at 92 years of age.

Major charges of corruption among party officials were once more shaking the People's Republic in Deng's last years. It is hard to keep enthusiasm for Marxism alive when it is well known that Party officials live a lavish lifestyle because of bribery and embezzlement. In 1996 over 20,000 people came under arrest for illegal activities.

China's economy continued to surge as more people entered the middle class. Especially in South China, a prosperity never before seen in the nation now exists. Dissent, however, remains a crime, and anyone who would criticize the party chiefs is in critical danger.

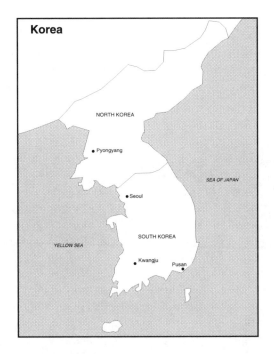

Korea

After the Korean shooting war concluded, North and South Korea went their separate ways. In North Korea the Chinese were the government's ally, while the United States played the same role in the South. South Korea, thanks to American and Japanese investment, and government policies that encouraged development, created a vibrant economy. In the North, by contrast, communist orthodoxy did not permit the same kind of economic growth.

Talk of reunification of Korea's two parts was frequent, but the communist demand that all foreign troops leave South Korea delayed any progress. The United States still keeps 35,000 troops in South Korea and intends to keep them there.

A cemetery in Korea holds the graves of the American soldiers who died during the war.

South Korea's economic success was not matched by an extension of democracy or protection of civil liberties. The result of authoritarian rule and obvious corruption in the wealthy class of Koreans brought student demonstrations against the government on numerous occasions. The riot police in South Korea have had their hands full. In the late 1990s a host of former Korean officials, including past presidents, were put on trial, found guilty, and imprisoned.

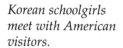

Korean schoolgirls meet with American visitors.

In 1961 South Korea was still basically an agricultural country, with less than $100 a year per capita. By 1970 the national average reached $1,000, and manufacturing had replaced agriculture as the country's economic mainstay. Since then, South Korea's success story continues. Despite its size, in 1997 it had the twelfth largest economy in the world. The nation is fifth in automobile production and third in semiconductors and builds one third of the world's ships.

One remarkable phenomenon in South Korea has been the turn of the population to Christianity, especially to the Presbyterian church. In addition, a native of Korea, Sun Myong Moon, founded the Unification Church, which now has spread throughout the world.

In North Korea in 1995 Kim Il Sung died and his son, Kim Jong Il, has become heir apparent to the communist legacy. The economy has become a disaster, and a serious shortage of food in 1997 put 8,000,000 North Korean people in danger of mass famine.

Society and Culture

In the communist countries of China and North Korea, party officials hold the top positions in society. Wealthy families of the past are either dead or in exile; now a person's rank in the party determines social status. Today wealthy communists are in government and business in these countries and are difficult to distinguish from their capitalist counterparts in other parts of the world.

Education is held in high regard in both communist states, for it is the key to social advancement. Except in very remote areas, universal primary education is now the rule. As a young man or woman approaches higher grades, the number of students diminishes. Governments believe that higher education is for the privileged few who can pass all the required examinations. Unemployed, highly educated people are a threat to stability, a fact well recognized in Beijing and Pyongyang.

In the communist East Asian nations all religions suffered from government persecution for decades. The Chinese government ruthlessly closed hundreds of Buddhist monasteries, Daoist temples, and Christian churches. In recent years, authorities have lifted some of the restrictions on religious practice. Nevertheless, anyone who is a religious person in North Korea or China assumes a certain amount of risk.

Tourists visit a Buddhist temple in Korea.

Conclusion

For centuries the teachings of Confucius and Buddhism determined the values held by people on the East Asian mainland. These values established norms for relationships within the family, giving near absolute authority to the father and keeping women in an inferior position. Despite the efforts to push Confucianism aside, it continues to affect family life in both China and Korea. The willingness of the masses to accept authoritarian rule, as Confucius insisted, in those countries actually benefits the communist leadership.

It can safely be said of East Asia that change, already rapid, is bound to accelerate. The booming economic ties between China and the United States are on the increase. Hardly a week goes by without an American corporation announcing plans to build a new factory in China.

The trend toward greater freedom for individuals stalled in 1996, with all dissidents either in prison or exile. Chinese foreign policy remains riveted on bringing Taiwan under its sovereignty.

In North Korea, the all-powerful Communist Party rules with an iron hand. Its leaders remain adamantly opposed to capitalism and all things western. As a result, North Korea remains one of the world's poorest countries, in sharp contrast to the prosperity of South Korea.

CHAPTER 27 REVIEW
COMMUNIST CHINA AND KOREA

Summary
- After the communists gained control of China, the country became a partisan in the Cold War.
- Intervention in the Korean War was the first test of communist resolve, with the United States and China sponsoring South and North Korea, respectively, and then committing their own troops.
- Land reform commenced in China under government direction with private landowners displaced in favor of collective farms.
- China pulled away from the Soviet Union because Moscow was not willing to treat the Chinese as equals.
- The Cultural Revolution, inspired by Mao, was an attempt to reinvigorate the revolutionary spirit.
- China settled into more peaceful ways after 1976 when Deng Xiaoping replaced Mao.
- Chinese students, discouraged at the lack of democracy, staged demonstrations, but the army was called in, and its guns were used to extinguish their resistance.
- China's economic situation constantly improves as a result of privatization.

Identify
People: MacArthur, Chiang Kai-shek, Mao Zedong, Zhou Enlai, Deng Xiaoping, Jiang Zemin, Kim Il Sung
Places: Seoul, Panmunjong, Tiananmen Square
Events: Communists seized power in China; industry and agriculture were nationalized; China committed troops to the Korean War; Mao directed China's Cultural Revolution; students demanded democracy

Define

Long March	collectives
Great Leap Forward	Cultural Revolution
communes	Red Guards

Multiple Choice
1. Disenchantment with the Nationalist government in China caused
   (a) workers and peasants to join the Communists.
   (b) a migration of Chinese people to the South.
   (c) workers and peasants to form a separate political party.
   (d) a general strike throughout China.

2. North Korea invaded the South because
   (a) it wanted its rich oil fields.
   (b) it felt no other nation would come to its aid and it could win a quick victory.
   (c) it hoped to gain its wealthy agricultural lands.
   (d) it needed its gold reserves.

3. The United Nations commander in Korea was
   (a) Eisenhower.
   (b) Marshall.
   (c) Clark.
   (d) MacArthur.

4. The Nationalist officials withdrew here after their expulsion from mainland China:
   (a) Philippines
   (b) Korea
   (c) Taiwan
   (d) Japan

5. In the years after their victory over the Nationalists, the foreign policy of China was closely geared to
   (a) the United States.
   (b) Japan.
   (c) Manchuria.
   (d) the Soviet Union.

6. In 1950 Mao ordered troops into Tibet because
   (a) he feared that the Nationalists would establish a base here.
   (b) he feared Indian ambitions in the country.
   (c) he wanted to obtain the oil fields of the country.
   (d) this country had once been a province of China.

7. The Red Guards were in the forefront of the
   (a) Great Leap Forward.
   (b) the Tiananmen demonstrations.
   (c) the Cultural Revolution.
   (d) the Korean War.

8. In 1972 Chinese foreign policy shifted toward
   (a) restoration of ties to the United States.
   (b) closer relations with the Soviets.
   (c) peace with the Nationalists.
   (d) withdrawal of troops from Tibet.

9. After Mao's death the leadership of the party passed to
   (a) Zhou Enlai.
   (b) Chiang Kai-shek.
   (c) Deng Xiaoping.
   (d) Kim Il Sung.

10. In order to control population growth, China has instituted
    (a) resettlement of much of the population.
    (b) collective farms.
    (c) rapid industrialization.
    (d) limitation on the number of children in each family.

11. The capitals of the two Koreas are
    (a) Beijing and Panmunjong.
    (b) Seoul and Pyongyang.
    (c) Seoul and Mukden.
    (d) Pyongyang and Penang.

12. South Korea has shown remarkable
    (a) economic progress.
    (b) student unrest.
    (c) government corruption.
    (d) all the above.

Essay Questions
1. Explain the collapse of Nationalist China.
2. What stratagems did Mao Zedong employ to keep the revolution alive?
3. Why did the Korean War take place?
4. Why is democracy difficult to obtain in China?
5. What should be the stance of the United States in its relations with China?

Answers

1. a	5. d	9. c
2. b	6. d	10. d
3. d	7. c	11. b
4. c	8. a	12. d

CHAPTER 28

Japan and Southeast Asia

Some of the fastest economic growth in the world occurred in Japan and Southeast Asia after World War II. Strong gains in industry and shipping of textiles, electronics, televisions, and automobiles has given the region a major economic push. Low wages paid to workers is one reason industry is making such advances, but personal income has risen for nearly everyone as the economy expands.

The Japanese Experience

At the close of World War II, the future of Japan seemed very bleak. Much of the country was in ruins. The U.S. army occupied the country under the command of General Douglas MacArthur. The United States intended that Japan should have a new democratic political system, and women were to enjoy equal rights with men. By 1947 the constitution was in place. It allowed Emperor Hirohito to stay on the throne, but he was to be a constitutional monarch. All adult Japanese could vote for members of the *Diet*, the Japanese parliament. The Diet chose a prime minister, who then formed a cabinet.

MacArthur stands next to Emperor Hirohito of Japan.

The demilitarization of Japan was a further goal of the United States. The constitution put strict limits on armaments and the number of soldiers and sailors recruited for the armed forces. An alliance with the United States permitted American troops to remain in Japan, even after 1952, when the official occupation ended.

517

The postwar years were concentrated on rebuilding. The nation's resources remained low. Then there was a major turnaround. During the next four decades Japan became the most dynamic country in Asia. In 1953 the Japanese economy began to surge, averaging 9.7% growth on an annual basis over the next 20 years. Prosperity extended over the country's population in a way never before experienced in the island nation.

The obvious question appears: What made it possible for Japan to turn from poverty to wealth so rapidly? The transition is even more remarkable when it is weighed against the fact that Japan has little in the way of natural resources. Oil, natural gas, iron ore, copper, bauxite, wool, cotton, and most lumber must be imported from other countries.

There are several reasons. The constitution provided a stable government, restoring confidence in the yen. Because the constitution limited the Japanese military, little money in the national budget went to armaments. A large labor market appeared as farmers moved into the cities by the thousands. Finally, the Japanese worker proved to be extraordinarily productive. Japanese companies demanded and received strong loyalty from their employees. Once hired, the Japanese worker could count on a job for life.

The Kobe Harbor, a major port of Japan, needed to be rebuilt after a devastating earthquake.

When the Korean War opened, the Japanese found that there was a pressing demand for trucks and other heavy equipment. Companies poured money into modern and efficient steel mills to satisfy this demand. Shipyards soon followed, undercutting British and U.S. production.

Next the Japanese entered the automobile market, with cars especially designed for export. In the 1950s the first Japanese cars were not much competition in the North American market. Japanese executives of the automobile companies—Toyota, Honda, Mitsubishi, and Datsun—soon learned what cars attracted buyers in the United States and Canada. By the late 1970s Japanese car production bounded ahead of the U.S. companies.

This was not to be the end of Japanese expansion in the world market. Radios, televisions, cameras, and consumer electronics gave Japan a huge favorable balance of payments. Japan also became the world leader in the use of robots. Engineers programmed the robots to weld, assemble, drill holes, or form metal parts. The Japanese economy seemed to have nothing but success ahead of it, when in the spring of 1992 the economy stalled. People, worried about the soundness of the banks, began to withdraw their money. The stock market headed downward, and in 1997, economists spoke of a dual economy: a weak domestic market, but a powerful multinational element. Tokyo is now a city of over 20,000,000 people. Despite its tremendous growth there is little crime or violence.

Japan, with its large economic surpluses, does not have a corresponding political role in world politics. Asian neighbors still remember the events of World War II with great bitterness. Fifty years after the close of the conflict, Japanese officials have a hard time admitting what happened.

The Four Tigers

The example of Japan's economic success acted as a stimulus on other Pacific Rim countries of Asia. South Korea, Taiwan, Singapore, and Hong Kong became known as the **Four Tigers.** When industrialists in these countries studied Japanese methods of production, they found ways to imitate them and became economically aggressive in their own right.

Taiwan's success was such that in the 1970s its industrial output was higher than that of mainland China. Hong Kong, the British enclave in the south of China, took in 4,000,000 refugees from Communist China. The people of this exodus were put to work in the specialties of the colony, textiles and electric goods. Singapore had similar growth, with overseas Chinese leading the way.

Hong Kong's 1996 per capita income stood at about $20,200 per person, Singapore's was at $19,300. This compares to mainland China's $2,200. In July 1997 Hong Kong returned to the communist mainland's rule, and predictions about its future are on hold. Beijing has assured the people in Hong Kong that it does not intend to stifle their booming capitalist economy.

The Hong Kong skyline is overshadowed by skyscrapers.

These Asian successes are remarkable because Taiwan and South Korea are small nations and Singapore and Hong Kong are only large cities. All are relatively poor in natural resources. Their success should be sought in other factors. Among them must be the Confucian ethic that dominates both business and labor, a stable political system, and the ability to achieve a high rate of savings. Workers in the Four Tigers work long hours at low wages, giving an edge to their companies. The investment that the governments of these nations have made in education is one more reason for their success.

Taiwanese troops march past the monument to Chiang Kai-shek.

Nations of the Southeast Asian Mainland

Late in the nineteenth century the French occupied Indochina, making it one of its most important colonial possessions. Several thousand French men and women moved into Vietnam and into neighboring Laos and Cambodia. The cities of the country took on a French look, while Chinese cultural influence in the country waned.

During World War II the Japanese replaced the French as the colonial power. In 1945 at the end of the war, the Japanese surrendered Vietnam to the Chinese Nationalists. The Chinese government had to deal with a strong Communist Party that had fought the Japanese during the war. Its leader was Ho Chi Minh, a man who had worked in France and there espoused the communist cause as an antidote to colonialism.

The Chinese allowed Ho to declare Vietnam a democratic republic, the title communists used to label their type of government. In reality it was neither democratic nor republican because all major decisions were made by a few party leaders.

The French had no intention of allowing Vietnam to become independent. In 1946 Paris sent troops to Southeast Asia to regain the country. The superior weapons of the French enabled them to hold the cities, but in the countryside Ho Chi Minh's communists could not be driven out. United States' foreign policy was to support the French for fear that a Vietnamese victory would encourage communism to spread through all of Southeast Asia.

The communist army, as a result of sheer numbers, slowly turned the tide in eight years of fighting the French. In 1955 the two sides met in Geneva where they agreed upon a settlement that divided the country at the seventeenth parallel. Ho Chi Minh's government took over Hanoi and the north, while Ngo Dinh Diem, with French support, governed the south from Saigon.

French soldiers on patrol in Vietnam.

The communists were not content with only half of Vietnam. Before long, guerrillas, known as Viet Cong, became active in the south. They won over many peasants to their cause either through persuasion or intimidation. The inefficiency and corruption in Saigon increased the communist appeal. In 1963 a military coup overthrew Diem, but it did little to spark enthusiasm among the peasants for its policies.

At this time, President Lyndon Johnson decided that American forces had to go to Vietnam or the country would be lost to the communists. In 1964 Americans took over the war in Vietnam as allies of the South Vietnamese government. Despite its advanced weapons and massive air power, the U.S. forces could not secure a victory. Peasants remained disenchanted with the South Vietnamese government. It appeared to them that the United States had simply replaced the French as outside invaders.

In the United States much of the country grew frustrated that the war was taking so many American lives and there was no sign that the conflict would ever end. President Richard Nixon thought bombing of neighboring Cambodia, where the Viet Cong had a supply line to the north, might shift the balance, but his plan failed. The aerial attacks brought Cambodians into the war, but supplies from the north kept coming. The United States, considering its options, began to withdraw its troops.

U.S. troops took over the war in Vietnam after the French left.

In early 1975 with President Gerald Ford in the White House, it became evident that the American hope for South Vietnam's survival had ended. Washington informed President Nguyen Van Thieu that he must resign. Thieu commented, "You ran away and left us to do the job that you could not do." Within weeks communist troops entered Saigon and crashed through the gates of the presidential palace. The war came to an end, and Ho Chi Minh gave his name to the city of Saigon.

For the following decade, orthodox communism was the rule. Life became so difficult that 200,000 people fled the country in boats. The communists rounded up South Vietnamese soldiers and government workers and sent them to "reeducation camps."

Inflation in Vietnam reached 700% despite a subsidy that cost the Soviets up to $4,000,000 per day. The Soviets were willing to pay this sum because it gave them, rather than the Chinese, the predominant role in Southeast Asia. Clashes with the Chinese on its border were meant to draw the Vietnamese army out of Cambodia, but Hanoi did not budge.

In 1986 the Vietnamese government relaxed some of its earlier rules on the economy, as relations with China improved. Hanoi returned land to the farmers and withdrew financial aid to several state-owned industries. The government announced that foreign investment would be welcome. These measures, coupled with lowering inflation, helped the economy considerably.

By 1993 Vietnam had so recovered that it exported $2,850,000,000 in goods. The United States lifted its economic embargo in 1994 and a year later restored diplomatic relations.

Vietnam today holds 73,000,000 people. It enjoys stability and independence, but the government allows no opposition or dissent. The present party leader, Du Muoi, follows Ho Chi Minh's tradition of authoritarian rule. A bloated bureaucracy delays any reforms.

Despite its economic progress, Vietnam has a long way to go. The country's per capita income is the lowest in Southeast Asia at approximately $1,000 a year. Half of the population lives below the poverty level.

Cambodia

In 1975 civil war erupted in Cambodia between the Cambodian communists, the **Khmer Rouge**, under Pol Pot and the military regime sponsored by the American government. The Khmer Rouge began a reign of terror in the country, starving millions of people to death through the confiscation of rice supplies and executing everyone thought to oppose them. Despite a common communist background, Vietnam intervened in 1978 and overthrew the Khmer Rouge, establishing its own puppet government.

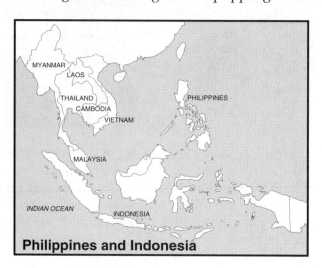

Philippines and Indonesia

Indonesia and the Philippines

Both Indonesia and the Philippines have enjoyed growth, but not so rapidly as to place them among the Tigers. In 1949 Indonesia became independent, when the Netherlands gave up on its struggle to keep the islands of the East Indies part of a Dutch empire. Ahmed Sukarno became the nation's first president. His successor, President Suharto, has held power so long he has taken the opportunity to become a dictator. Oil keeps the Indonesian future bright.

At the end of World War II, the United States left the Philippines peacefully but held on to some important military bases. Elections were held to give the nation a democratic government. From 1965 to 1986 Ferdinand Marcos ruled; he was famous for his authoritarian government and corruption. His wife Imelda was noted for her purchase of shoes, totaling in the thousands.

In 1983 Marcos's most prominent opponent Benigno Aquino was shot. Three years later his widow Corazon ran and was elected president. Marcos claimed victory, but popular opinion knew better, and he and his wife fled the country. Unfortunately, Corazon Aquino's rule did not live up to expectations.

In 1992 Fidel Ramos was elected president. His government has offered stability sufficient for the nation to improve its economic standing. The United States has removed its bases, taking away a major reason for dissent. A smoldering insurrection continues in Muslim parts of the country but now appears to be under control. Volcanic eruptions are not under control, and in recent years they have done much damage to the Philippines.

President and Mrs. Marcos, the Philippine first family.

Social Structure in East Asia

The East Asian countries provide a wide range of societies. In Japan, the Philippines, and the Four Tiger nations, a wealthy capitalist elite now dominates society. These are the executives who run the companies, the bankers, and the insurance managers who predominate in their fields.

Politicians come out of this elite, solidifying the joining of forces of government and business.

A growing middle class is made up of office workers, government employees, and professionals such as doctors and lawyers. The ready entry to the middle class allows these nations to enjoy remarkable political stability.

The industrial working people of these nations are found in factories and service industries. Their hours are often long, and their pay is low. Labor unions are not yet strong enough to provide security and safety for their members.

Growing rice, the major cereal grain of East Asia, requires intensive cultivation, yet rural farm workers receive few benefits for their long hours at work. Young girls in large families are especially vulnerable to exploitation.

Religion

The predominant religion of East Asians is Buddhism. For over 2,000 years in China and 1,500 years in Japan, people have looked to the teachings of the Buddha as the key to understanding the purpose of life.

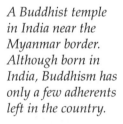

A Buddhist temple in India near the Myanmar border. Although born in India, Buddhism has only a few adherents left in the country.

More recent religions that have entered East Asia are Islam and Christianity. Large pockets of Muslims live in eastern China, and Indonesia has a predominantly Muslim population. In fact, Indonesia holds the largest Muslim population in the world, but significant Hindu and Christian minorities are also present. In the Philippines, on the island of Mindanao, Muslims also are found in large numbers.

Christians are a majority in only one country, the Philippines; they are minorities in all other Southeast Asian countries. Taiwan and South Korea are regions of special growth due to western missionary activity.

Culture

The culture of Japan and the countries of Southeast Asia are caught up in rapid transformation. In the cities tall skyscrapers and ultraexpensive hotels give evidence of a city population rapidly modeling itself on American and European life. Businessmen and women dress in exactly the same clothes as westerners, they use the same cellular phones, and computers are found in every office. Automobiles crowd the streets.

Japan and Indochina have long literary traditions, making book publishing a major industry with their own literature. The Japanese are especially fond of poetry. Poems with 31 syllables are known as *tanka;* those with 17 syllables are called *haiku.* Bookstores also carry books and magazines published in the United States and Europe.

A food market in the Philippines offers customers a wide variety.

Traditional East Asian music still competes with popular musicians who play western songs for young audiences. Each country has unique musical instruments including drums, stringed instruments such as the zither, and woodwinds. In Indonesia the gangalong band is very popular.

In Japan the *no* play continues to entertain the upper classes, while *kabuki* is a more popular presentation. Actors use elaborate costumes and overly dramatic gestures to tell their stories in their performances, similar to Chinese opera.

Conclusion

The recent turbulent history of Southeast Asian nations contrasts remarkably with the experience of Japan. The people of Vietnam, Laos, and Cambodia suffered terrible deprivation as war tore their countries apart. They are only now emerging from their travail, as their commitment to Marxism wanes.

Japan's economic recovery after World War II was remarkable for its rapid success. Today its people enjoy the highest standard of living in Asia, and Japanese financial advisors are widely consulted throughout the world. Economic growth, however, is not everything. The human spirit demands much more.

CHAPTER 28 REVIEW
JAPAN AND SOUTHEAST ASIA

Summary
- After World War II Japan began reconstruction under a constitution drawn up to make it a democracy.
- Japan began to experience an economic boom as automobile and electronic equipment exports soared.
- Japan's industrial success was picked up by other Asian neighbors that came to be known as the Four Tigers.
- The Philippines gained independence from the United States.
- Indonesia joined the industrialized world.
- In the Southeast Asian mainland, the end of French colonialism meant the growth of communist nationalist armies.
- The United States came to the aid of South Vietnam resulting in the Vietnam War.
- The United States withdrew its troops, and all Vietnam came under a communist government.
- Cambodia was torn apart by civil war.

Identify
People: Hirohito, Sukarno, Suharto, Marcos, Ho Chi Minh, Pot, Muoi, Ramos
Places: Indonesia, Philippines, Vietnam, Cambodia, Hanoi, Saigon, Laos, Singapore
Events: economic surge in Japan; capitalist success of the Four Tigers; Vietnam War; Cambodian civil war

Define
Four Tigers   Khmer Rouge   Viet Cong

Multiple Choice
1. Although Emperor Hirohito remained on the throne after being defeated in World War II, Japan became
   (a) a democratic nation.
   (b) a communist nation.
   (c) a fascist state.
   (d) an authoritarian state.

2. The constitution of Japan puts strict limits on its
   (a) economy.
   (b) police.
   (c) military.
   (d) colonies.

3. Japan's economic recovery was remarkable because it had
   (a) little capital to rebuild.
   (b) few natural resources for industrialization.
   (c) too many people working in agriculture.
   (d) no experience in manufacturing.

4. The Four Tigers are
   (a) North Korea, South Korea, Taiwan, and Singapore.
   (b) Singapore, Cambodia, Malaysia, and Vietnam.
   (c) Hong Kong, Japan, Taiwan, and Singapore.
   (d) South Korea, Taiwan, Singapore, and Hong Kong.

5. Imelda Marcos became famous for her collection of
   (a) spoons.
   (b) hats.
   (c) furs.
   (d) shoes.

6. Corazon Aquino was elected president of
   (a) Pakistan.
   (b) Vietnam.
   (c) Indonesia.
   (d) the Philippines.

7. The cultural tradition of mainland East Asia is principally that of
   (a) Hinduism.
   (b) Islam.
   (c) Christianity.
   (d) Buddhism.

8. Saigon was the capital of
   (a) South Korea.
   (b) South Vietnam.
   (c) Indonesia.
   (d) North Vietnam.

9. The boat people were refugees from
   (a) Cambodia.
   (b) Laos.
   (c) Philippines.
   (d) Vietnam.

10. The Khmer Rouge was a communist army operating in
    (a) Laos.
    (b) Malaysia.
    (c) Vietnam.
    (d) Cambodia.

Essay Questions
1. Explain the economic recovery of Japan.
2. Some American military believe Japan's constitution should be amended so as to counter the growing strength of China. What do you think? Explain.
3. How do you assess the Vietnam War?

Answers

1. a	3. b	5. d	7. d	9. d
2. c	4. d	6. d	8. b	10. d

CHAPTER 29

The New Africa

Although sub-Saharan Africa was not the scene of actual fighting during World War II, Africans eagerly followed the news of what was happening in Europe. If Great Britain, Belgium, and France were all threatened by Hitler's conquests, what would this mean to their African empires? In the minds of many black African nationalists, the war confirmed that they must work to overthrow the prewar colonialism as soon as the conflict ended.

End of Colonialism

Most African nationalists were educated in Great Britain or France prior to the war. Others served in the armed forces in Europe. Now they were ready to use their skills to bring an end to the foreign rule of their countries. They correctly judged that the European governments would be exhausted after the war.

At first, no European politician agreed to turn over his country's African possessions to the native peoples. Despite war-weariness there was a sense that the African colonies should remain in place. Churchill made the statement that the British did not fight the war to dismantle the empire. European military units and civilian officials stationed in Africa acted as though business must continue as if nothing had happened.

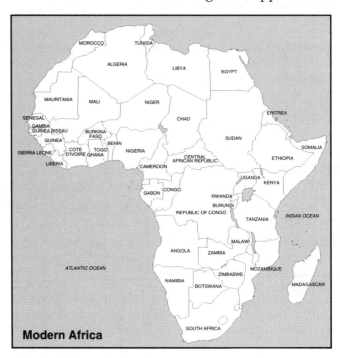

Modern Africa

It was not long, however, before the Europeans realized that conditions had changed. All over Africa political parties were forming; they were headed by native leaders demanding independence. Sometimes they were Marxists, which gave the colonial administrators an additional excuse to have them jailed. Nearly all espoused some sort of socialist ideology, which, they claimed, was more consonant with African tradition.

As prisons filled with nationalist leaders and strikes and boycotts of European goods increased, politicians in the European capitals urged more direct action. Slowly, however, the tide began to turn. In London, Paris, and Brussels realists argued that it was not worth the effort to keep their colonies; the drain on wealth, manpower, and world opinion was too much. After Parliament gave India its independence, it made no sense to argue that the British possessions in Africa should not follow the same path.

Egypt Seeks Direction

In Egypt the decade after World War II witnessed a search for direction. A group of military officers decided the country had no more need of a monarch. They sent King Farouk, the last of the dynasty begun by Muhammad Ali, into exile. For a while there was hesitation over who would assume the leadership. Eventually a colonel in the army, Gamal Abdel Nasser, won out. He was a charismatic figure, who promised to bring Egypt out of the past into a new and vigorous present.

Nasser counted on investment from the United States and Great Britain to make his plans come true. The Americans and British, however, balked at financing his proposal to put up a new dam across the Nile at Aswan. Rejected by the West, Nasser turned to the Soviet Union. He also announced the nationalization of the Suez Canal. The British were determined that this should not happen. In alliance with France and Israel, they made plans to intervene.

Gamal Abdel Nasser, hero of the Egyptian revolution.

In October 1956 the three nations attacked Egypt. Within ten days the canal was in European hands, but worldwide condemnation of the attack, especially in the United Nations, caused the western powers and Israel to withdraw. Nasser's influence, far from being damaged, was enhanced throughout the Arab world.

In early 1967 it appeared that Nasser was on the verge of an attack upon Israel. Before that happened the Israelis struck first. In this Six Days' War the Egyptians lost the Sinai Peninsula.

Egypt became a different nation under Nasser's successor, Anwar Sadat. In 1973 Sadat restored Egypt's reputation in a short war that, for the first time in recent history, brought Egyptian victories. Four years later Sadat surprised the world when he announced that his government was prepared to talk peace. An agreement that gave back the Sinai to Egypt followed. Afterwards, while reviewing a military parade, Sadat's enemies, angered by his peace treaty with Israel, assassinated him.

His successor, Hosni Mubarak, then assumed the presidency, with a pledge to continue Sadat's policies. Mubarak, now in power for over 20 years, has tilted Egypt back to a pro-Western course; therefore, Egypt receives substantial foreign aid from the United States.

North Africa

In the three countries that made up French North Africa, independence appeared in different circumstances. In 1956 Tunisia became a one-party republic at the same time that Morocco acquired independence under its king, Hassan. At once Morocco demanded recognition of borders that were much more generous than its neighbors would agree to admit. The result was tension and open clashes on its boundaries.

The war in Algeria caused large losses among the civilian population.

Algeria was another matter. A million Europeans lived in the nation; they demanded that Algeria stay joined to France. Guerrilla warfare, which was marked by atrocities, commenced. Both the natives and the Europeans were convinced that every effort had to be made for victory. The loss of so many men and the huge price of continuing the war divided the French homeland. Was it worth the cost? In Paris there was talk of civil war. General Charles de Gaulle came out of retirement; he was the one person who had sufficient prestige to convince his countrymen and women that

Algeria must be allowed its freedom. In 1962 the Algerian people became free of French rule.

As in Tunisia a one-party republic was declared in Algeria, and efforts commenced to rebuild the country. Oil was a major factor in improving the economy. In the late 1990s the government of army generals felt strong enough to hold elections, only to discover in the first round that Muslim fundamentalists, rather than their candidates, had won majorities. The military officers, now recognizing how unpopular they were, canceled any further voting. Outraged at this development, the fundamentalists of the Islamic Salvation Front took up arms against the government. Their methods were to slit the throats of rural villagers and to explode car bombs in the cities to get their way. By 1997 the toll of dead stood at 60,000 with little hope of the sides reaching a peaceful settlement.

A peaceful scene in Algeria does not show the bitter war in the country between the government and the Islamic fundamentalists.

South of the Sahara

The first British colonies freed were those that had few Europeans living in them. In 1957 Kwame Nkrumah led the way, when he became the first prime minister of Ghana, and subsequently its president. Three years later Nigeria also obtained independence. Then the smaller British-controlled states of West Africa followed. All joined the British Commonwealth, a loose federation of states that were once under London's rule.

In East Africa a considerable number of white settlers made their homes in Kenya and the two Rhodesias. They were altogether opposed to cutting their ties with the European homeland. They feared for their future under governments where blacks would form large majorities.

In Kenya, among the Kikuyu people, a militant organization called Mau Mau dedicated itself to forcing the British to leave. Between 1952 and 1961 a very one-sided war went on. It left 75 whites dead, but 13,000 Kenyans were killed. The Kikuyu leader, Jomo Kenyatta, was kept in prison, but this did not deter his followers. In Tanganyika, Julius Nyere promoted a quiet revolution. In the Rhodesias, independence came more slowly because the whites there were more numerous and determined. South Africa, the bulwark of white minority rule, sent aid to keep the white regimes in power.

In the Ivory Coast, Felix Houphouet-Boigny effectively led resistance against the French. In Senegal, the poet Leopold Sedar Sengor was equally effective as a political leader and, after independence, became the nation's first president.

One of the most traumatic developments happened in the Belgian Congo. The Belgians held the country with a firm hand during the colonial period, making sure that no native Congolese received any training in politics or economic affairs. By 1957, however, it was evident in Brussels that unless the Congo became a military camp, the days of Belgian rule were over. In 1960 the Belgian government announced that it would grant independence to the Congo.

With undue haste the Belgians pulled out of the Congo, taking with them whatever was of value. The white managerial class, who ran the copper mines that made the Congo rich, abandoned the country.

The Congolese chose Patrice Lumumba to become the country's first prime minister. Throughout the Congo, separatist governments appeared, arguing that they had no need of a centralized, national state. In Katanga, the region where the copper mines were located, Moise Tshombe declared an independent state.

A canoe on the Congo River provides transportation.

Chaos erupted in the Congo, and in 1961 Lumumba was assassinated. The United Nations voted to send a multinational peacekeeping force in an effort to bring order to the situation. Later, after four years of struggle, the Congo was again a single nation. Its leader, Mobutu Sese Seko, established a personal dictatorship holding power through terrorizing the opposition. Mobutu changed the name of the country to Zaire, a translation of the European name for Congo. In May 1997 a rebel force, led by Laurent Kaliba, toppled Mobutu after a seven-month insurrection that ended Mobutu's long tenure.

Nigeria also fell into a bitter civil war. With over 250 different peoples, it was not easy to form a national consciousness. In the southeast region of the country, holding the country's oil fields, the Ibo people announced their secession. They formed the state of **Biafra**. From 1967 to 1970 the national government of Nigeria, led by a majority of Muslims from the north, fought the Christian Ibo. Over a million people died, many from famine, until the war ended with the abolition of the Biafran state.

Military dictators appeared elsewhere in central Africa. In Uganda Idi Amin took power using the army for his support. The armed forces murdered over a million of his opponents until Amin crumbled and went into exile.

The Portuguese were not involved in World War II. They expected that, even if other European nations were leaving Africa, their colonies might be kept intact. Such was not to be. Nationalism, once ignited, spills over borders. In 1961 the first attacks began on the Europeans, and for the next 15 years the conflict continued. For the Portuguese, it was a losing game. In June 1975 Mozambique gained independence, followed a year later by Angola.

In both countries civil war soon broke out. On one side were forces that advocated Marxist regimes; on the other side were nationalists who advocated capitalist economies. The West and the Soviets sent arms to advance their clients, for the Cold War was still in progress. Cuban troops, in considerable numbers, defended the Angolan communist government.

Shape of the Government

Despite the fact that most African governments immediately after independence professed to be democracies, it was not long before military dictatorships became the rule. There were just too many problems. History has shown that decades are needed to foster mature, stable democracies.

In nearly all the newly independent countries of Africa, only a small percentage of the population was sufficiently educated to become politically active. These were the elite who went off to European and American universities and had become the leaders of the nationalist movements on their return. In fact, they had little contact with ordinary people, especially villagers who lived in rural areas.

African chiefs must find a new role in the modern nation states of Africa.

Loyalty to their families and their local chiefs gave most Africans an identity; they had no loyalty to a national government in some distant city they had never seen. Africans had no chance under the colonial regimes to learn the skills of democracy. The young governments collapsed when it became obvious that they had no way to meet popular expectations.

Europeans, for their own convenience during the colonial era, drew up the borders of the African nations. Often this split peoples of the same nation into two different countries.

Economic problems were abundant. The Europeans made sure that African colonies should provide their home countries with raw materials and little else. No effort was made to develop internal markets or local industry. Therefore, Africa's new states were born into an industrialized world where they found it difficult to compete.

The new African nations desperately needed investment capital, but the instability of governments and frequent civil strife caused private investors to shy away from putting their money there. The Africans, therefore, had to turn to the World Bank and foreign governments for financial aid. Exceptions were in mining, lumber, and the production of cocoa and cotton in a few select countries. Often the companies that were present in colonial times were able to hold on to their businesses because they had access to foreign markets.

Most Africans remained subsistence farmers, living in small villages and caring for their fields in ways that have not changed over centuries. The soils of Africa are not rich, and drought has been a constant problem in the sahel area of the continent. Overgrazing of the land, plagues of insects, the arrival of hundreds or even thousands of refugees from other regions have placed a major strain on African resources. Ethiopia and Somalia are prime examples of massive starvation among the population.

Society

African population doubled in the period from 1950 to 1980, reaching 500,000,000 people. It would have doubled again in the next 20 years had not a new element entered the scene, the infection of large numbers of people with AIDS. In some countries, those infected have reached 25% of the people. As a result, all projections of future population growth have been put on hold.

Some of the most promising advances in Africa have been made in education. When independence came, 80% of the people were illiterate. Today that number has been cut in half. In some nations, such as Tanzania, the numbers are completely reversed, and 80% of the people are literate.

Tanzanian students prepare themselves for entering the job market.

Great advances have also occurred in providing better sanitary facilities and housing. Except for the problem with AIDS, public health measures have eradicated or at least lessened age-old problems of sickness, such as cholera. Even though doctors and nurses are nowhere in adequate supply, there has been a great improvement in medical training. Obtaining clean water sources would make a major difference in the health of the continent's people.

The pressure of population in rural areas has caused, as in other developing nations, a massive immigration of people into the cities. Lagos, capital of Nigeria, held 600,000 people in 1960. Today there are over 10,000,000 people. The burden of supplying services and jobs is staggering. When urbanization happened in the United States and western Europe, the process was much slower, and industry was expanding. African nations have not been as fortunate.

During the Cold War both the West and East poured arms into the African states to support the series of wars that erupted in many countries. These arms were never returned. Wars are now fought throughout the continent with machine guns and rocket-propelled grenades left over from the Cold War.

Somalia is the best example of factions armed with the most modern weaponry fighting each other and making life miserable for everyone else. So grim was the conflict in 1993 that the United Nations, with the United States in the forefront, placed an army in the country to provide emergency relief. Trying to disarm the rival clans, however, proved beyond the ability of the United Nations. Still another ongoing war continues in the Sudan. Here the Islamic government is in a brutal struggle against the Christian South.

In 1994 the most recent conflict shocked the world when thousands of individuals of the Tutsi nation were slaughtered in Rwanda. Here the Hutus, who share this small country with the Tutsi, sought to avenge past grievances through massive killings; the Tutsi replied in kind.

Rwanda is home of the world's remaining mountain gorillas. Many people throughout the world were concerned over the animals' fate. Apparently the gorillas have survived, coming out of the war much better than the numerous people who now survive with the memory of human slaughter fresh in their minds.

One of Africa's success stories has been the growth of a tourist industry that is concerned over the future of wildlife. Elephants appear to be making a comeback all over Africa after ivory-hunting poachers once endangered their population. East Africa supports the largest group of wild animals in the world. On the expansive Serengeti Plain tens of thousands of animals still migrate each year as they have for millions of years.

The Serengeti Plain is the largest wildlife reserve in the world.

African Culture

African culture is very rich in music, song, art, and sculpture. Over the centuries each ethnic group has preserved its history in story and dance. Celebrations that involve whole village communities are frequent.

In the cities, television and radio are within the reach of the upper classes. Theaters showing western films are everywhere. In capitals such as Nairobi in Kenya, foreign flights link Africa to the rest of the world as planes bring in passengers and newspapers from abroad.

Today African writers are included in all collections of world anthologies of contemporary literature. Nigeria's Wole Soyinka was the first African author to receive a Nobel prize. Senegal's president, Leopold Sedar Senghor, enjoyed an international reputation in literature. Many African authors use English or French, thereby reaching a wider audience. Others are content to write in their native tongue and trust in future translations of their work.

Religion

Religion is a major concern for most Africans. Even those leaders who today profess Marxism or atheism probably went to mission schools. Christianity is growing faster in Africa than on any other continent. Traditional animist religions are disappearing, but for many Africans adopting Christianity has meant combining it with much of their earlier beliefs.

In all major Christian denominations, there is great concern for acculturation, to keep as many native traditions as possible. Because most African societies were polygamous before the colonial regimes came into the country, many Africans find the Christian teaching on monogamy difficult to incorporate into their own religious views. Should polygamy, therefore, be allowed or rejected? Over a thousand Christian churches now exist, for many Africans see no need to hold onto the ties that once bound them to Europe and therefore start their own denominations.

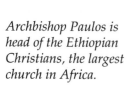

Archbishop Paulos is head of the Ethiopian Christians, the largest church in Africa.

Islam is also on the march in Africa, with tens of thousands of new converts enrolled each year. In a contest with Christianity for African allegiance,

Islam has certain advantages. For example, Muslim countries are not identified with the recent colonial past, and Islam permits polygamy.

Unfortunately, Christianity has not convinced Africans to be rid of ethnic hatreds. Rwanda was over 80% Christian at the time the ethnic slaughters took place.

Ghana

Ghana is fairly representative of the new states of Africa. It borders on the Atlantic, and during the era of slave trading, it was a center for the shipment of men and women to the Americas. Today it is important for the cocoa it supplies to the rest of the world. In times past, its major product was gold; therefore, it carried the name Gold Coast until the modern state was created.

World War I gave the Gold Coast people an opportunity for greater political activity. A small, black middle class that wanted self-rule appeared. As early as 1918 members formed a **National Congress of British West Africa.** The goal of the congress was to pressure authorities to allow the formation of native legislative assemblies in the colonies. The British rejected these ideas, claiming that they were too far ahead of their time.

More important for the future of the Gold Coast was the enrollment of native men and women in European and American universities. Among those who sought higher education abroad was Kwame Nkrumah. After ten years away from his homeland, Nkrumah returned to lead the movement for independence, founding the **Convention People's Party.** To pressure the British, he urged a boycott of their products.

By this time the Gold Coast had 4,500 native university graduates, many of them politically active. Through threats and frequent arrests British authorities tried to dam the growth of nationalism. Compromise was also tried. In 1951 it was agreed that Africans should have their own legislative assembly and be admitted into positions in the government.

Independent Ghana

Finally in 1957 the British Parliament voted to allow the Gold Coast to be free. On the stroke of 12 midnight, on March 6, 1957, all over the Gold Coast the bells of churches rang out to proclaim the birth of the nation. In Accra, the capital, a beaming Kwame Nkrumah took the oath of office as prime minister.

Parliament agreed to rename the country Ghana, after the first of West Africa's medieval kingdoms. The new constitution kept much of the political and legal system of the British in place. In Ghana's courts judges still wore the traditional wigs.

In 1960 elections gave Nkrumah the presidency. Visitors from all over the world poured into Accra to observe the workings of Africa's first post-colonial nation. Ghana's independence was a model for black politicians throughout the rest of British and French colonial possessions.

Hopes were high for a modern, democratic Ghana that would lead the rest of Africa to independence.

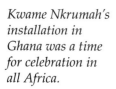

Kwame Nkrumah's installation in Ghana was a time for celebration in all Africa.

Unfortunately, these hopes were pitched too high. There were so many problems waiting in the shadows. Economic progress was slow. The cocoa crop depended on fickle world markets. Ethnic problems were troublesome. There were 25 different peoples in Ghana, all of them demanding attention. Akan-speaking people, including the Ashante, made up only a slight majority. The existence of such a large number of different languages meant that Parliament declared that English should be Ghana's official language.

Nkrumah's personality made him more and more the autocrat. He sought and obtained the title of president-for-life, hardly a reassuring move. Corruption plagued the civil bureaucrats who sought to make their lives comfortable no matter what the cost.

In 1966, while Nkrumah was on a state visit to China, the officers in the Ghanian army seized power, warning the president not to return. A new constitution proclaimed that Ghana was now in a Second Republic. Six years later another coup inaugurated the Third Republic. It happened again in 1978, 1979, and 1981. In that year the winner was Flight Lieutenant Jerry Rawlings.

Rawlings banned all political parties, dissolved parliament, and arrested his predecessor. Rawlings has proven to be more lasting than those before him, for he is still in office, now holding the title of president.

In 1992 Rawlings proposed a new constitution, which was approved by 90% of the voters. His National Democrats received 58% of the vote, but claimed 189 of the 200 seats in Parliament. This made it possible, in January 1993, to announce that Ghana was in its Fourth Republic.

The population of the country, now approaching 17,000,000 has $1,500 income per capita each year. Moreover, a full 46% of the population is under 15 years of age, and these children will enter a labor force already saturated. To the government's credit, education is required by law, but with insufficient teachers only a slight majority of the population has had formal schooling. Medical facilities are totally inadequate, with 25,000 persons per doctor.

The government remains the largest employer in the country, sapping the national income. Industrial and agricultural companies are typically state-owned and generally inefficient. Borrowing by the government has created a major debt crisis for the nation, delaying further investment. Capitalism is best seen in the very active Accra stock market. Akwame Pianim, head of the New Patriotic Party has assessed Ghana's future: "What you see here is not our progress. It is our potential . . . . We have to build our middle class to protect democracy—because only a middle class has something to protect."

One third of Ghana is forest, a major resource, which if managed correctly, can do much to help the economy. The country's rivers are harnessed to provide hydroelectric power. Gold mining provides 15% of the national income.

Like many African countries, problems seem more in evidence than solutions. Yet Ghana has three universities, showing that it wants to invest in its most important resource, its people.

South Africa

As Africa's richest country, South Africa was watched with interest not only on the continent but also around the world after the conclusion of World War II. Observers predicted that the white population, Afrikaners and British, would lessen their animosity toward each other. However, due to poor economic conditions, unemployment remained high. Whenever economic conditions are difficult, there are always "others" to blame, and in this case, poor Afrikaners and British whites found consolation in accusing each other of provoking the situation.

A black man passes by a beach sign restricting the area for whites.

Black South Africans were even poorer than the Europeans. They found themselves excluded from many jobs so that whites would receive priority in the few jobs that were available.

The **Nationalist Party** led by Daniel Malan urged the nation to cut loose from its ties with Great Britain and to rigorously separate blacks and whites in the life of South Africa. In 1948 the Nationalists won the election and began the construction of a South Africa that fit their view.

Nationalist Rule

The goal of the Nationalist Party was to ensure the economic and political preeminence of the whites in South Africa. A policy known as *apartheid* was adopted. It was meant to separate whites from blacks in as many ways as possible. Racism was written into the legal structure of the country. Whites and blacks were to have separate schools, hospitals, neighborhoods, parks, playgrounds, and beaches.

The South African government was completely in the hands of Europeans. Blacks had no vote and no representatives in the Parliament, and the law forbade them to form political parties. These measures galvanized black politicians to fight the apartheid laws.

Black resistance to government policies actually was in place as early as 1912. In that year the **African National Congress (ANC)** was formed to promote the interests of the Bantu people. The South African government refused to recognize the ANC's existence and frequently imprisoned its leaders.

In 1959 the government took apartheid a step farther. It announced the creation of national homelands for blacks, *Bantustans,* where in theory they would have autonomy, if not complete independence. The Bantustans composed about 13% of the country's territory. Thousands of blacks migrated into them, some willingly but most ruthlessly uprooted from their homes. It should not be a surprise that the land in the Bantustans was the poorest in the country.

World opinion became more and more outraged over the blatant racism of South African whites. The British Commonwealth expelled South Africa, and in 1974 the United Nations also excluded South Africa from membership. Three years later, a resolution forbade the sale of military equipment to the country and imposed economic sanctions that were meant to isolate South Africa.

In 1960 blacks fought the police in what became known as the **Sharpeville Massacre.** Police fired into a crowd of protestors, killing 69 people. The government response was to jail the ANC leaders. Nelson Mandela, its president, was sentenced to life in prison. His wife, Winnie Mandela, then took up her husband's cause.

After the Sharpeville massacre, the wounded and the dead lay side by side.

In the late 1980s apartheid began to show cracks. The black Anglican bishop of Cape Town, Desmond Tutu, became an active spokesman for blacks. His denunciation of apartheid made him an international figure, but authorities feared to silence him. The government allowed formerly segregated sports teams to be integrated. It also agreed that the Asian community of 900,000 and the Coloured population of 3,200,000 might establish parliaments for their internal affairs. The national Parliament, however, retained the right of veto over whatever action they took.

Apartheid Collapses

In the 1989 elections F. W. de Klerk was chosen president. He was known as a moderate, open to change so as to remove South Africa's isolation from the world community. Economic sanctions were, after many years, having an effect, and businessmen in the country were anxious to have the sanctions removed. In February 1990 de Klerk lifted the ban on the ANC and freed Nelson Mandela from prison.

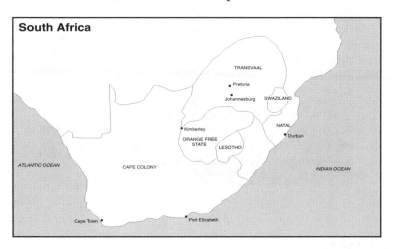

Remarkably Mandela showed little bitterness over his long confinement. His triumphant return to political life, speaking of black and white cooperation, was just the right note to encourage the majority of South Africans that his view of the future was a promising one.

In 1991 and 1992 the South African Parliament voted to abolish the laws that apartheid spawned, ending legal racism. The government also withdrew its troops from Southwest Africa, allowing that nation to close its colonial past. It entered the free world as the country of Namibia.

Elections in 1994 brought forth a three-way contest. De Klerk ran on the Nationalist ticket, Mandela was the natural candidate of the ANC, but the Zulus, under Chief Mangosuthu Buthelize, formed their own party, the **Inkatha.** Because Zulus are the largest black nation in South Africa, numbering about 7,500,000 people, conflict with the ANC commenced.

The election result was a strong vote for Mandela, who became South Africa's first black president. De Klerk assumed the vice presidency. A new constitution guaranteed that Mandela's slogan, "Let us build together," *Masakhane,* would be more than words.

The remarkably peaceful transition to black majority rule brought new investment. Nearly $24,000,000,000 came into the country. The Gross Domestic Product rose an astonishing 23%. These economic gains principally benefitted the whites, without doubt helping them to accept that they were now a political minority.

Whites still own 75% of South African land, and black unemployment runs about 40%, a figure that is evident in the shantytowns surrounding the major cities. Crime and violence are on the rise, but there is hope. Mandela has promised a huge housing and electrification program and major water projects. A school lunch program means that the next generation of blacks will not suffer from malnutrition.

Mandela and de Klerk are both very popular figures. Working together they have taught South Africans to sing the same national anthem. The transition to majority rule in South Africa is one of the most impressive democratic victories of the twentieth century.

The new South African leadership, de Klerk and Mandela, become vice president and president.

Conclusion

There are times when Africa appears to arrive at a better day. This occurred in the nineteenth century when slavery came to an end. It happened a second time when colonialism collapsed. Now a third better day awaits, with South Africa in the lead. This day should bring economic prosperity and political guarantees of civil rights to peoples long familiar with their opposites.

The African present is not easy to assess. Even though certain nations prosper, among them Cameroon and the Côte d'Ivoire, others groan under military dictatorships that are completely immune to any other consideration than staying in power. These dictators are very similar to the African chieftains that promoted slavery in earlier times. As long as they prospered, nothing else mattered. It is the same today. The generals who run the dictatorships use every type of violence against their opponents, and the African people suffer.

CHAPTER 29 REVIEW
THE NEW AFRICA

Summary
- World War II demonstrated that colonialism was doomed in Africa.
- Egypt's Nasser sought to make Egypt the major power of the Arab world.
- In Kenya the Mau Mau sought to expel the British.
- Chaos struck the Congo after the Belgians precipitously pulled out of the country.
- Civil war exploded in the Portuguese territories of Angola and Mozambique.
- A new elite of native Africans, many of them from the armed forces, replaced the colonial rulers.
- Progress came in the form of greater educational opportunities.
- Both Christianity and Islam are growing very quickly in Africa as animism declines.
- Ghana's history is representative of many West African states.
- South Africa went from apartheid to a multiracial government.

Identify
People: Nasser, Sadat, Mubarak, Nkrumah, Mau Mau, Kenyata, Nyere, Mobutu, Hutus, Tutsi, Senghor, Rawlings, Tutu, de Klerk, Mandela
Places: Aswan, Nigeria, Somalia, Rwanda, Nairobi, Accra, Sharpeville, Biafra
Events: end of colonialism; Nasser's Egypt became the leading state of the Arab world; Biafra revolt in Nigeria; AIDS epidemic; fall of apartheid in South Africa

Define
apartheid
Masakhane
African National Congress
　(ANC)

National Congress of British
　West Africa
Convention People's Party

Multiple Choice
1. Most African nationalists were educated in
　(a) Europe.
　(b) Southwest Asia.
　(c) local universities.
　(d) India.

2. Colonial governments in the 1940s sought to head off nationalism by
　(a) negotiations in London and Paris.
　(b) encouraging more investments.
　(c) sending more European colonists into Africa.
　(d) putting its leaders in prison.

3. The last of Muhammad Ali's royal descendants in Egypt was replaced by
　(a) Sadat.
　(b) Mubarak.
　(c) Nasser.
　(d) Ben Gurion.

4. This Egyptian leader agreed on peace with Israel with the Sinai returned to Cairo's care:
   (a) Begin
   (b) Mubarak
   (c) Nasser
   (d) Sadat

5. Algeria's government has been at war with Muslim fundamentalists since
   (a) it lost the 1997 elections.
   (b) France gave Algeria independence.
   (c) it cancelled the final elections.
   (d) Libya began attacks on its eastern borders.

6. The Mau Mau sought to be rid of
   (a) British rule over Kenya.
   (b) British rule over the Rhodesias.
   (c) British rule over Nigeria.
   (d) French rule over Senegal.

7. Mobutu Sese Seko was the undisputed ruler of
   (a) Tanzania.
   (b) Ivory Coast.
   (c) Zaire.
   (d) Zambia.

8. In Nigeria the Ibo people declared independence in
   (a) Biafra.
   (b) Rwanda.
   (c) Gabon.
   (d) Benin.

9. Many Africans were most discouraged to find that independence did not
   (a) bring new investments.
   (b) improve transportation and communications.
   (c) raise everyone's standard of living.
   (d) enhance the number of African exports.

10. Since gaining independence, most African states have seen
    (a) rapid industrialization.
    (b) rapid urbanization.
    (c) a rise in commerce.
    (d) none of the above.

11. In 1996 Hutus and Tutsi began killing each other in
    (a) Botswana.
    (b) Namibia.
    (c) Burundi.
    (d) Rwanda.

12. The first prime minister of Ghana was
    (a) Nyere.
    (b) Kenyatta.
    (c) Senghor.
    (d) Nkrumah.

13. Apartheid supporters in South Africa called for
    (a) white and black cooperation.
    (b) school integration.
    (c) separation of blacks and whites.
    (d) expulsion of British mining interests from the country.

14. A Bantustan was a territory reserved for
    (a) Indians of South Africa.
    (b) whites of South Africa.
    (c) blacks of South Africa.
    (d) Afrikaaners of South Africa.

15. The first black elected president of South Africa:
    (a) de Klerk
    (b) Kruger
    (c) Malan
    (d) Mandela

Essay Questions

1. Discuss the process of decolonization in Africa.
2. Explain the health concerns of modern Africans and their causes.
3. Why has investment been slow to come to Africa?
4. Compare the career of Nasser with that of Sadat.

Answers

1. a	6. a	11. d
2. d	7. c	12. d
3. c	8. a	13. c
4. d	9. c	14. c
5. c	10. b	15. d

The United States and Canada in an Era of Prosperity

After the end of the First World War, the United States and Canada had much in common. Both contributed to a successful conclusion of World War I, both enjoyed a time of economic development during the **Roaring Twenties,** and then both fell into despair during the difficult years of the Depression.

Roaring Twenties in the United States

Although the United States Senate had rejected participation in the **League of Nations,** the country was recognized throughout the world as having joined the Great Powers. America had sent 2,000,000 of its young men into World War I, and their contribution to the Allied victory was evident. It was understandable that many Americans now wanted to avoid further troubles in Europe.

The 1920s witnessed accelerating changes in American life that had already started before the war. More and more farmers and their families packed up their belongings and headed for the city, where the men looked for jobs in industry as wage earners. The women in the household appreciated the modern conveniences newly available to them: a washing machine, a refrigerator, a telephone, and an improved sewing machine. A family car could be used for trips to visit relatives and friends and for Sunday drives into the country. The neighborhood grocery store carried more items than ever before.

Some Americans, especially members of the more rigorous Protestant churches, were discouraged as they looked about their cities and found increased crime, prostitution, gambling, and the consumption of alcoholic beverages. To remedy this situation, they pressed their legislators to pass the **Eighteenth Amendment** to the Constitution prohibiting the sale of alcohol. Congress and state legislators obliged and, in January 1920, made it unlawful to buy or sell alcoholic drinks. Not all Americans supported **Prohibition** and they sought ways to get around the law by making gin in the bathtub or beer in the basement or by buying homemade alcoholic drinks from enterprising **bootleggers.**

Federal agents destroy barrels of illegal whiskey.

Women made progress politically as well as in the home. At long last, in August 1920, the **Nineteenth Amendment** to the Constitution permitted women to vote. They were now full citizens and the more active sought political office, but old habits persisted in many states. The number of women legislators remained very small in proportion to men. Less politically oriented women turned to a carefree lifestyle that earned them the name **flappers.**

Americans appreciated the growth in the movie industry, and going to the neighborhood theater was a diversion nearly everyone enjoyed. In 1927 the *Jazz Singer* introduced sound to films. The radio brought the weather, the latest news, and a variety of programs to eager listeners.

Racism was still very much a part of the American life. The Ku Klux Klan, or KKK, which had waned since the nineteenth century, experienced a rebirth in the 1920s. It counted 2,000,000 members anxious to don sheets that gave them anonymity as they burned crosses in front of homes of the people they considered undesirable: blacks, Jews, and Catholics.

The presidents of the decade of the 1920s were all Republicans who had no desire to pursue activist government policies. These presidents were Warren Harding, Calvin Coolidge, and Herbert Hoover, and they believed that they were elected to encourage business. In 1922 a high tariff on foreign goods made it easier for local manufacturers to gain market share.

Henry Ford sits in one of his early model automobiles.

Of all industries, automobile manufacturing expanded the most. Henry Ford, who gave his name to the cars he produced, brought down the price of manufacturing autos so that every middle-class family could afford one. His secret was the assembly line. Factory workers specialized in working on only one part of the automobile as it made its way through the factory.

The Great Depression and the Roosevelt Era

Forgetting that economic trends tend to be cyclical, most Americans seemed to think that the good times of the 1920s were here to stay. However, times of expansion, when jobs are plentiful and businesses have a rise in profits, are almost always followed by overproduction, unemployment, and slim earnings. For many Americans the New York Stock Exchange was the place to put their money, where they could watch their shares double or triple in a year. Buying stocks on credit became a national pastime.

Then in October 1929 a day of reckoning arrived. Prices plummeted, wiping out past gains and more. Panic set in as people who once were rich had nothing left. Unemployment struck the factory workers, and the low prices offered farmers for their produce meant that many lost their land to the banks who had put up the money for their purchase. Then the banks failed because they had no way to collect on outstanding loans. No one was there to buy the land gained through foreclosures. By 1933 over 33,000,000 Americans were unemployed. Doom settled upon the nation.

The election of 1932 brought two very different candidates to the fore. The Republicans renominated Herbert Hoover, convinced that the economic problems besetting the country would in time heal themselves. The Democratic nominee was Franklin Delano Roosevelt, who promised a **New Deal** of government action to end the Depression.

The voters gave Roosevelt his chance, and the New Deal went into effect. The president proposed legislation to Congress to inaugurate a public works program to hire the unemployed, a bank reform that guaranteed no further loss of savings, and easier credit facilities for the nation's farmers and business men and women. Congress went along with these measures because it was solidly Democratic. However, the Supreme Court declared much of the New Deal legislation unconstitutional.

The Great Depression caused thousands to lose their jobs.

Without doubt the New Deal restored confidence to the men and women of the United States, but the effects of the Great Depression and the Stock Market crash hung on for the next six years. It was only the stimulus to provide goods for World War II that lifted the country out of the economic slump into which it had fallen.

Roosevelt's New Deal changed the way government and people interacted by inaugurating government activism in the economy. Prior to the New Deal Washington simply observed, but did not interfere in, private farming and industry. Americans now expected the government to solve their problems. With every crisis Washington was called on to intervene. The president's wife, Eleanor, toured the country whipping up support for her husband's policies and reporting back to him on the mood of the people.

The role of government was further enhanced because of World War II. From the beginning of the conflict, Roosevelt was anxious to put the resources of the United States behind the Allied war effort, although the United States only became a direct participant after Japan bombed Pearl Harbor in Hawaii on December 7, 1941, and Hitler declared war on the United States three days later.

Franklin D. Roosevelt, president of the United States, inaugurated the New Deal.

World War II

There was little doubt in American public opinion that the United States was engaged in combat with two enemies representing totalitarian, fascist regimes of the worst kind. Young men and women volunteered for the military services by the millions. Those men less eager to fight were drafted. Factories in the country transferred their domestic production to making war materials: aircraft, naval vessels, tanks, and munitions. Women took the place of men in the factories when they were called up for military service.

American troops crossed the Atlantic in great convoys, landed in Great Britain, and from there participated with the Allies in the North African, Italian, and finally the Normandy campaigns that forced the surrender of Nazi Germany. On the Pacific front the navy and marines fought on the Pacific islands as they prepared to launch an expected frontal assault on Japan.

While the war was still in progress in Europe, President Roosevelt died, and the office passed to Vice President Harry S. Truman. Roosevelt had been elected to four terms, the only U.S. president to be so honored. It was, therefore, left to Truman to make the fateful decision whether or not to drop the **atomic bomb.** When the Japanese, already severely weakened from incessant bombing on their cities, still refused to surrender, on August 8, 1945, Truman agreed to use the weapon against Hiroshima. Three days later a second atomic bomb was dropped on Nagasaki.

The bomb's destruction was unbelievable, instantaneous, and long-term. It was the most powerful weapon ever devised. Its use against civilian targets, and the dropping of a second bomb, created a moral question that is still debated. The horror of nuclear warfare so impressed itself on world leaders that no atomic or hydrogen bombs have been used since 1945.

The Cold War

It was not long after the Japanese surrender in September 1945 that the Allies who had fought together during the war realized they had quite different agendas. The Soviet leader, Josef Stalin, never really trusted the United States and its European allies. In the western view, communism was the great evil of the world, threatening to impose its political and economic systems everywhere possible. The result of this mistrust was at the heart of the **Cold War.**

In every country of the world where opportunities to spread communism existed, Soviet military and financial aid arrived. The United States reacted by sending its help to communist opponents. The **Truman Doctrine** spelled out U.S. commitment, sending aid to Greece and Turkey. In China, Southeast Asia, Africa, and Latin America, the Soviet Union and the United States fought each other using proxies. Billions of dollars went into the arms industry to provide the latest technological weaponry to limit communist gains. Hydrogen bombs that dwarfed the atomic bomb that fell on Hiroshima were produced. Both the Soviets and the United States kept intercontinental missiles on the ready, aimed at each other's cities so that the advantage of a first strike would be canceled. Somehow there was supposed to be a winner if a contest of mutual annihilation ever took place.

In 1950 the United States found its resolve tested when North Korea invaded South Korea. President Truman, strengthened by a United Nations' resolution, sent American troops into battle for the next three years.

Harry Truman, the U.S. president at the time the Cold War commenced.

Fear of communist infiltration into the government convinced many Americans of the validity of the investigations of Senator Joseph R. McCarthy. This Wisconsin senator made sweeping charges against a number of officials in the government and movie industry, accusing them of promoting communism and betraying their country. By the time McCarthy finished, most Americans decided that he had gone too far, destroying the reputations of many innocent people and providing little, if any, actual evidence of treasonous behavior.

Economic Growth

The period after World War II was one of impressive growth in the American economy. The experience of industries improving productivity during the war enabled them to transfer this skill to domestic output. Factories introduced hundreds of new items, from jet aircraft to frozen foods.

Good wages and an expanding population created extraordinary demand from consumers. The housing industry was especially busy as new families were created. Suburban life around cities attracted the middle class, while the core downtown areas were left to poorer people. Commuting between home and work became a way of life for millions, creating a huge demand for automobile production, gasoline stations, car repair shops, and dozens of other auxiliary businesses. The two- or even three-car family became the norm for suburbanites.

Americans took longer vacations and traveled farther than ever before. Congress led by President Eisenhower financed an ambitious program of super highway construction permitting people to travel from city to city without seeing a traffic signal. Motels and fast food outlets proliferated at the junctions of the super highways, offering more opportunities for employment.

During the 1950s radio networks began airing television shows into American homes, revolutionizing the way people used their leisure time. The whole family could watch nightly quiz, news, drama, and comedy programs.

Children are entertained by the new invention of television.

One of the great American success stories was known as the **GI Bill of Rights.** This congressional legislation rewarded veterans with grants to attend college and low-interest loans to finance new homes, businesses, and farm purchases for young families. Millions of men and women who never would have had such opportunities flooded into colleges and universities, graduating with degrees in the sciences, humanities, and arts.

Higher education expanded to meet these new students with new campus buildings or the establishment of entirely new institutions of learning. Thousands of foreign students also enrolled in universities as the reputation of U.S. and Canadian institutions came to be recognized throughout the world.

The Civil Rights Movement

The general prosperity of the United States did not reach poor Americans in the 1950s and 1960s. Even though poverty and unemployment could be found in all segments of the population, the most extreme cases were found among African Americans. Fortunately, they found a voice in a Baptist minister, Martin Luther King, Jr., who organized demonstrations against discrimination. In August 1963 King sponsored a freedom march of 200,000 people on the nation's capital and urged an end to inequality between whites and blacks in the United States.

Martin Luther King, Jr., leads a civil rights march.

President John F. Kennedy, working in conjunction with Congress, approved several pieces of legislation to end discrimination because of race. The **Civil Rights Act of 1964** guaranteed equality for African Americans in areas of voter registration, public accommodations, and employment. Four years later a second Civil Rights Act forbade any type of discrimination in renting and selling housing.

Legislation, without economic improvement, can lead to despair. Such despondency overwhelmed residents of inner cities during the 1960s, when rioting broke out in a number of locations. Businesses and stores were looted and burned in a self-defeating effort to call attention to the ills of inner city poor. Commissions were quickly set up to study the causes of the riots, but few practical outcomes resulted.

The Kennedy Years

In 1961 John F. Kennedy was elected president. Born into a wealthy Massachusetts family, he was the youngest man and the first Catholic elected to the office. The charm and wit of the president and the popularity of his wife Jackie and their children combined to make them the ideal first family. One of his accomplishments was to create a **Peace Corps** of American volunteers to serve people in other countries of the world.

President John Kennedy's son, John, Jr., breaks ranks to greet his father.

Kennedy pushed for strong American commitment to space exploration and was delighted when Alan B. Shepard, Jr., became the first American in space. The Soviet space program had already put a man into orbit, an achievement that goaded the United States to allocate more resources into its own space program. In July 1969 the reward for this commitment appeared when the American astronaut, Neil Armstrong, stepped onto the surface of the moon.

Kennedy's foreign policy decisions were crucial for the on-going confrontations between the United States and the Soviet Union. First, Kennedy allowed an invasion of Cuba, planned during the Eisenhower years, to go forward. Led by Cuban expatriates, troops landed in the **Bay of Pigs.** Without air support, the invaders were destined to fail. Second, the **Cuban**

Missile Crisis, which terrified the world, developed after Nikita Khrushchev put missiles in Cuba, only several minutes flying time away from the Florida coast.

Kennedy demanded their removal at a time when Soviet ships were in transit to Havana. The world situation was extremely tense; no one was sure which of the superpowers would back down. Khrushchev blinked, recalled the Soviet ships, and the launching stations were dismantled. Kennedy had won.

Thirdly, Kennedy increased the number of military advisors and the amount of aid in Vietnam in order to support the war of the South Vietnamese against the communist North and the Viet Cong, the communist opposition in the South. This decision began the deep involvement of the United States in that area for the next decade.

While Kennedy's administration was still not fully matured, the President made a visit to Dallas, Texas, on November 22, 1963. An assassin was waiting for his motorcade to pass. Two shots were fired, killing Kennedy at once. Lee Harvey Oswald was arrested, but his motives remain unknown because Oswald himself was killed while he was in custody. The country plunged into deep mourning.

The Years of the Vietnam War

Vice President Lyndon B. Johnson followed Kennedy in the presidency until 1969 when he did not seek reelection. Johnson was known for his legislative skills in the House of Representatives where he had served as Speaker. His relationship with President Kennedy was never close, but it was expected that he would continue to espouse the late president's program.

A critical choice had to be made concerning American involvement in Vietnam. Johnson believed that he had to pursue the course already taken and support South Vietnam. Therefore, he increased the American presence, and in 1965 Johnson sent combat troops into battle in Vietnam.

Most people supported this policy in Vietnam, believing that no more countries should fall under communist control. In 1965 Americans knew little about Vietnamese history and supposed that the Vietnamese were acting on behalf of Communist China. In fact, for centuries Vietnam and China had been traditional enemies.

As television, for the first time in history, recorded the war for American viewers, disenchantment set in. Critics of the war charged that it was a struggle over national concerns, not communism. Soon demonstrations, especially on college campuses, took place calling for an end to U.S. participation. A peace movement gathered thousands of recruits for marches against the war in Washington. The troubled Johnson declined to run for office again. The next president would be a Republican, Richard M. Nixon.

A U.S. soldier in Vietnam cautiously leaves his bunker.

The Nixon Presidency

Richard M. Nixon won the presidency on promises to halt the inflation that plagued the country's economy through the last years of the Johnson administration and to withdraw American forces from the unpopular Vietnam War. Inflation was especially bad at this time, because the country was in a recession with high unemployment that continued until the middle 1970s.

Nixon's foreign policy marked a dramatic shift in the relationship between the United States and China. After learning that a visit to China would be welcome, in 1972 Nixon visited Beijing, meeting with the communist leaders who for years had claimed that the Americans were their worst enemies. Nixon also went to Moscow as a growing spirit of *détente,* or relaxation of tension, developed between the United States and the Soviet Union.

Nixon, like Johnson before him, was convinced that "there was a light at the end of the tunnel" in Vietnam. He made the fateful decision to bomb the Vietnamese supply lines in Cambodia in complete disregard of the consequences for the people of that nation. Finally, in 1973, Nixon ordered combat troops out of Vietnam, responding to the momentum for peace in every stratum of American society.

Nixon was always known for his suspicion of others, even of friends. During his campaign for reelection in 1972, the president approved a secret group working on his behalf to break into the Democratic Party's offices in the Watergate Hotel in Washington, D.C. This covert operation's goal remains undefined. Unfortunately for Nixon, newspapers picked up the story, and Congress demanded an inquiry. Nixon had tapes made of his conversations with his staff during this time that unwittingly gave his critics ammunition to prove that the president was involved in a cover-up.

The Watergate break-in resulted in the resignation of President Richard M. Nixon.

In July 1974 the Judiciary Committee of the House of Representatives voted articles of impeachment, and it was evident that the president's denial of wrongdoing no longer was credible. Rather than face removal by action of the Senate, on August 9, 1974, Nixon resigned, the first president ever to do so. Vice President Gerald Ford completed Nixon's unfinished term. Over the criticism of many, Ford gave Nixon a pardon for his activities in the White House scandal.

In 1976 Jimmy Carter took office, having defeated Ford's efforts to stay in office for four more years. This year, 1976, was the bicentennial year of the country, marked by celebrations all over the United States. The festivities helped people forget about the trying times of the Vietnam War and Nixon's forced resignation.

Carter tried to improve relations with the Soviet Union, China, and Panama. A treaty with the latter promised to turn over the canal to Panama at the end of 1999. Carter also signed an agreement with the Soviets on the limitation of nuclear weapons and oversaw the negotiations between Menachem Begin of Israel and Anwar Sadat of Egypt that brought peace to their two countries. Carter's efforts to relax tension in Southwest Asia were dealt a setback when, in November 1979, Muslim militants in Tehran seized the U.S. embassy and took its employees hostage. This embarrassment lasted until January 1981 and contributed to Carter's defeat when seeking a second term.

Ronald Reagan in Office

Inflation again rose during the Carter years, partly as a result of higher oil prices. Ronald Reagan, formerly governor of California, who had made his reputation as an actor in Hollywood, assured voters that his election would turn the economy around. Reagan proposed and Congress voted approval of income tax reductions to begin in 1981. At the same time, the president urged a massive increase in spending on a military buildup and a space defense system called Star Wars. These two measures combined to cause record deficits in the federal budget.

In 1983 the economy began to recover, but many individual workers were not aware of it. New machines and technology replaced semiskilled workers in many factories. A computer could do the work of a white-collar worker faster and more efficiently, with the result that middle-class workers also entered the jobless ranks. Many of the large multinational companies preferred moving their operations abroad to South Korea, Taiwan, Hong Kong, or Mexico where labor costs were much lower, contributing to unemployment in the United States.

Ronald Reagan and George Bush, president and vice president of the United States after the election of 1980.

Reagan pursued a very active anti-communist foreign policy, especially against the Soviet Union, which he dubbed "the evil empire." In Central America, U.S. advisors and money aided the government of El Salvador against its rebels. Similar assistance was sent to the **Contras,** a rebel force fighting the Marxist regime of Nicaragua. Many observers credited Reagan's policies as contributing to the collapse of the Soviet Union in 1989.

The Bush and Clinton Presidencies

Both George Bush and Bill Clinton inherited budget problems because deficits began to run to $150,000,000,000 annually during Reagan's administration. Part of the deficit was due to the failure of hundreds of savings and loan institutions. They had loaned money for real estate development and small businesses that subsequently collapsed. Congress had to appropriate funds in the billions of dollars so that investors would not see their savings evaporate.

In efforts to lower the budget on both the national and the state levels, legislators sought ways to get people off welfare and into jobs. Homeless people, often mentally ill or addicted to drugs, relied heavily on public funds in every major city. In 1996 Congress passed one more welfare "reform" law that shifted money away from Washington to the states.

In foreign policy, the Bush administration executed a raid on Panama in December 1989 to remove its military leader, Manuel Noriega, from office for his complicity in drug dealing and other illegal activities. The armed forces brought Noriega to the United States to stand trial. Later Bush sent troops to Somalia in an effort to allay famine and stop clan warfare.

Bush's major initiative in foreign affairs came out of his decision to put U.S. forces into the Gulf War that had as its goal the expulsion of Saddam Hussein's troops from Kuwait. The rousing success of the American armies in Kuwait brought the popularity of the president to new heights in 1991, but economic problems a year later caused Bush to lose the election to Clinton.

Clinton's foreign policy was a cautious one. Looking at the disenchantment caused by the Somali occupation, the president was loath to commit troops to Bosnia. Without the lead of the United States, the Europeans held back. Eventually a United Nations force separated the sides in Bosnia with the United States supplying the bulk of the military forces.

The Computer Revolution

The past three decades have witnessed a bewildering succession of new products that have altered the lives of people living within the United States and Canada. None has been more important than the computer. In the 1940s the first models were put into use in research laboratories. Initially, the computers were very large, filling a room, but when the transistor chip was developed, computers became smaller, faster, and cheaper.

By the 1990s a personal computer could be found in many homes as well as in factories, offices, banks, and universities. The computer, now enhanced by the Internet and the World Wide Web, has initiated a new age where information is the driving force of economic life in the United States, Canada, and the world.

Society

The demands of contemporary society can often be difficult for women in the United States and Canada. With a divorce rate approaching half of all marriages, a particular burden falls on them. In nine out of ten divorces, the children stay with their mothers. This means that American women, especially those who are homemakers, defend themselves by having fewer children and trying to keep one foot in the labor force, even when their children are very young.

In the 1970s, women took jobs that once were limited to men.

In the 1970s numbers of American women joined in support for equality in every aspect of social and economic life. An organization, the **National Organization of Women (NOW),** focused on this goal, but the feminism of that time appears to be in decline in the 1990s. Most women today reject the label, although young women still espouse feminist goals. Naturally women want equality between the sexes, opportunities for equal education, pay, and promotion. They want respect for being mothers of the future generation.

The sexual revolution has taken a toll on women with a large increase in births outside of marriage. So has the need for caretakers of elderly people, a task that pays little but demands much.

Education and the environment are two issues that receive a great deal of vocal attention but painfully slow action in some areas. The Environmental Protection Agency has worked at cleaning air and water with some success in the United States. It has not done as well in removing toxic chemicals and oil from the ground. Lawyer fees became as much a part of the budget as bulldozers and pumps.

A much publicized war on drugs promoted by both the White House and Congress has had mixed, if not negative, results. Despite years seizing huge quantities of home-made and imported drugs, the amount sold on American streets has not diminished. The major effect of the war on drugs has been to increase prison populations.

Abortion has been a major divisive issue in American politics. In 1973 the Supreme Court in **Roe v Wade** struck down all state legislation regarding abortion and affirmed a woman's right to abort a fetus without breaking the law during the first three months of pregnancy. For those Americans who regard human life to begin at conception, rather than birth, strenuous efforts have been made to overturn, or at least modify, the court's decision.

The American public spends million of dollars on entertainment. Film stars, popular musicians, and players in professional sports receive the highest salaries in the nation. The annual Superbowl, which pits the two most successful football teams in the nation against each other, commands millions of viewers.

The American space effort put a man on the moon, enabling him to photograph the earth.

Society became increasingly more secular in the 1990s, with only one third of Americans now attending weekly services in church, synagogue, or mosque. Even though over 95% of the population claims to believe in

God, there is suspicion over the way his message reaches them through religious institutions. Christian conservatives, especially Evangelicals, now claim a large segment of the Protestant population, while attendance at the more traditional churches is on the decline.

Canada

The history of Canada after World War I parallels that of the United States. At first there had been an economic boon during the 1920s, but then came the Great Depression. This downturn in the economy was every bit as serious as in the United States.

In September 1939 Canada became part of World War II when it followed Great Britain into the conflict against Hitler, and later against Japan. Canadian armed forces fought both in Europe and in the Pacific, with 100,000 men and women killed or wounded in battle.

After the war Canada took in over 1,000,000 immigrants, refugees from postwar Europe. They joined the urban labor force, which by 1950 found more Canadians in industry and business than in farming. In 1959 the opening of the St. Lawrence Seaway gave inland Canada access to the Atlantic and new opportunities for development.

During the 1960s a wave of nationalism swept through French-speaking Québec. The Liberal Party of the province agitated for more government jobs and for French to be accepted with English on an equal footing as an official national language. Several French Canadian extremist groups appeared, using bombings and kidnapping to get their way. The Parti Québécois after 1968 seemed to be on the way to gaining a separate status within Canada, but a vote showed only 40% of the Québec electorate wanted to separate from the rest of Canada. The issue remains alive, and separatists believe that eventually they will prevail.

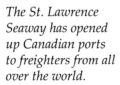

The St. Lawrence Seaway has opened up Canadian ports to freighters from all over the world.

In 1982 Canada severed its last ties with Great Britain in a **Constitution Act.** Canada is now completely independent of Great Britain.

Canada is well known for its humanitarian activities throughout the world. Its soldiers always participate in the United Nations' peacekeeping efforts. Canada is also a signatory to NAFTA, the North American Free

Trade Association, which lowers the economic barriers between its neighbors, the United States and Mexico.

Conclusion

No one in the world today doubts that the United States is the leading world power. English, its language, has become a universal means of communication, building on the foundation of England itself and the countries colonized by its men and women.

Decisions made in Washington have far-reaching results in every corner of the globe. With the demise of the Soviet Union, the United States has the responsibility to shoulder the role of world leadership. This is not necessarily something the American people want; their concerns are much closer to home.

The values of the American people may best be reflected in an election poll taken after the 1996 voting. Those interviewed said their greatest concern was keeping their jobs and trusting that the trend in the economy was heading upward. Medicare and Social Security benefits came second and third as the generation of baby-boomers think more and more about retirement. In fourth and fifth place education and taxes were mentioned. Less than 5% of the people checked foreign affairs as a significant concern.

Canadians pursue many of the same goals. Their economic well being is assured because the natural resources of the country are so great. Most believe that a compromise between the English- and French-speaking part of the nation will eventually be worked out.

CHAPTER 30 REVIEW
THE UNITED STATES AND CANADA IN AN ERA OF PROSPERITY

Summary
- The Roaring Twenties, which followed World War I, was a time of restlessness and change.
- A movement of social reform caused Prohibition to be added to the Constitution.
- The Ku Klux Klan made a negative impact on American political and social life.
- The automobile revolutionized the way men and women traveled.
- The Great Depression caused widespread unemployment and financial grief.
- President Roosevelt promised his New Deal would reinvigorate the economy.
- The United States entered World War II after Japan bombed Pearl Harbor.
- The Cold War between the democratic and communist countries preoccupied the United States.
- A period of prosperity raised the standard of living for most Americans and Canadians.
- The Civil Rights Movement convinced Congress to strike down the laws allowing segregation.
- The war in Vietnam divided the nation and brought about a realization that the U.S. military had limitations.
- President Nixon was the first U.S. chief executive to resign from office.
- Bush increased his popularity with the Gulf War, while Clinton improved his by war on welfare and sponsoring a balanced budget.
- Québec's French-speaking population is looking for a special position in Canada.

Identify
People: Ku Klux Klan, Hoover, Truman, McCarthy, King, Kennedy, Shepard, Johnson, Reagan
Places: New York Stock Exchange, Pearl Harbor, Hiroshima, Tehran, Bosnia, St. Lawrence Seaway, Quebec
Events: Great Depression; World War II; dropping the atomic bomb; Kennedy assassination; Vietnam War; Nixon resignation; Gulf War; Canada's Constitution Act

Define

Nineteenth Amendment	Eighteenth Amendment
Roaring Twenties	flappers
New Deal	bootleggers
GI Bill of Rights	détente
Contras	Peace Corps
National Organization of Women (NOW)	Cuban Missile Crisis
	NAFTA
Prohibition	Roe v. Wade
Cold War	*Jazz Singer*
Civil Rights Act of 1964	

Multiple Choice

1. The 1920s were a period when Americans turned to
   (a) intervention in European affairs.
   (b) isolation.
   (c) involvement in the League of Nations.
   (d) seeking foreign investment.

2. The *Jazz Singer* was unique because
   (a) it added sound to the movies.
   (b) it was the first film in Technicolor.
   (c) it was the longest movie ever filmed.
   (d) it was the first film of Cecil B. DeMille.

3. The Eighteenth amendment
   (a) prohibited gambling.
   (b) prohibited abortion.
   (c) gave women the right to vote.
   (d) prohibited sale of alcoholic beverages.

4. This organization sought to intimidate blacks, Jews, and Catholics during the 1920s:
   (a) the flappers
   (b) the Alien Nation
   (c) the League for White Supremacy
   (d) the Ku Klux Klan

5. The popularity of the automobile in America owes much to
   (a) Frank Peugeot.
   (b) Ernst Benz.
   (c) Andrew Carnegie.
   (d) Henry Ford.

6. A stock market crash in New York was the first step toward
   (a) the Great Depression.
   (b) deficit spending.
   (c) the break-up of Standard Oil.
   (d) the delay of reparations.

7. Roosevelt's New Deal promised
   (a) active government involvement in the economy.
   (b) to take government out of business.
   (c) to initiate Civil Service examinations.
   (d) to reform the New York Stock Exchange.

8. This president agreed to drop the atomic bomb:
   (a) Dwight Eisenhower
   (b) Ronald Reagan
   (c) Franklin Roosevelt
   (d) Harry Truman

9. The Cold War refers to the tension created between the democratic nations and
   - (a) the Third World.
   - (b) the communist states.
   - (c) Vietnam.
   - (d) Hitler's Germany.

10. Senator Joseph McCarthy claimed that
    - (a) there was need to build defenses along the American border.
    - (b) the U.S. government had been infiltrated by communists.
    - (c) Congress must act with the president to balance the budget.
    - (d) taxes were too high.

11. The GI Bill offered tuition for
    - (a) buying books.
    - (b) poor children in public schools.
    - (c) poor children in private schools.
    - (d) college education.

12. The Civil Rights Movement found a leader in
    - (a) Robert Kennedy.
    - (b) John F. Kennedy.
    - (c) Martin Luther King, Jr.
    - (d) Booker T. Washington.

13. The Cuban Missile Crisis pitted the wills of
    - (a) Kennedy and Stalin.
    - (b) Castro and Reagan.
    - (c) Truman and Khrushchev.
    - (d) Kennedy and Khrushchev.

14. The peace movement of the 1960s urged the United States to withdraw troops from
    - (a) Vietnam.
    - (b) the League of Nations.
    - (c) Cuba.
    - (d) Kuwait.

15. The first president to visit Communist China was
    - (a) Kennedy.
    - (b) Johnson.
    - (c) Nixon.
    - (d) Reagan.

16. In 1979 Islamic militants seized the U.S. embassy in
    - (a) Cairo.
    - (b) Beijing.
    - (c) Jerusalem.
    - (d) Tehran.

17. The United States sent help to the Contras in a civil war in
    (a) Honduras.
    (b) Chiapas.
    (c) Costa Rica.
    (d) Nicaragua.

18. American women could join a feminist movement in the 1970s called
    (a) NOW.
    (b) WON.
    (c) AFL.
    (d) WFP.

19. The Constitution Act of 1982
    (a) made French the official language in Canada.
    (b) severed Canada's ties to Great Britain.
    (c) lowered economic barriers with the United States.
    (d) sent troops to Vietnam.

20. The major concerns of Americans during the Clinton presidency have been on
    (a) education.
    (b) foreign affairs.
    (c) jobs and the economy.
    (d) drugs.

Essay Questions
1. What were the effects of the Great Depression on the United States and Canada?
2. How have women's issues come to the fore since World War II?
3. What justified the dropping of the atomic bomb on two Japanese cities?
4. Explain the Cold War and its causes.
5. Why have many of the people of Québec wanted a special status in Canada?
6. Discuss the role of Martin Luther King, Jr. in the Civil Rights movement.

Answers

1. b	6. a	11. d	16. d
2. a	7. a	12. c	17. d
3. d	8. d	13. d	18. a
4. d	9. b	14. a	19. b
5. d	10. b	15. c	20. c

Latin America

The Latin American people entered the twentieth century with promises of a better life yet unfulfilled. From the Rio Grande in northern Mexico to the cold Antarctic waters that flow through the Straits of Magellan at the tip of South America, there is a world of fabulous natural riches. Yet only a few wealthy families and a rather larger middle class enjoy a life of comfort.

Many observers blame the unique ethnic mix and class structure in Latin America for its problems. More than in any other region of the world, social and racial diversity endure. In Argentina, Uruguay, and Costa Rica the population is nearly all of European ancestry. In Chile, El Salvador, and Mexico a mixed people are predominant. Bolivia, Ecuador, Peru, and Paraguay have Indian majorities. In Haiti and most Caribbean islands, descendants of African peoples form the largest segment of society.

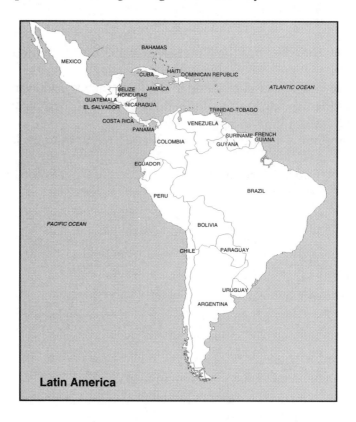

Latin America

In every one of the nations of Latin America, there exists an elite that has its origins in the colonial past. It is not only skin color, but also family inheritance, education, and social connections that establish rigid class structures. Because class distinctions are so firmly drawn, it is much easier for a rich family to become richer than for a poor family to become rich.

The Latin American population has soared in the twentieth century. Today the region holds 421,000,000 people with over 40% of the population under 15 years of age. Modern medicine has done wonders in prolonging life and reducing illness. High birth rates also contribute to the increase. Poor women generally have large families, for ignorance of birth control and traditions that make them subservient to their husbands result in large families. One estimate holds that a majority of children born in Latin America do not know their fathers.

Political Scene

In 1900 the overwhelming number of countries were in the hands of strong men, *caudillos,* who ruled their countries on behalf of their families and friends. Today about 90% of Latin Americans live under democratically elected governments, but the threat of military coups still hovers over the region. Many elections are fraudulent because of graft and bribery. Armies in Latin America still command resources far beyond their need and many a general has strong ambitions to "save" his country.

One of the most colorful was Juan Perón and his wife Evita in Argentina. Together, while he was president from 1946 to 1952, they organized a populist regime, dependent upon the strength of the country's labor unions. Evita saw to women's suffrage and many welfare plans that endeared her to the Argentine poor. The death of Evita in 1952 predicted a decline in Perónist popularity, and three years later a coup forced Perón into exile. He returned to office in 1973 but lasted only a year before death removed him from the political scene.

Evita and Juan Perón came to power in Argentina backed by the labor union of the country.

In the Latin American past, political parties divided along class lines, but often the opposition was little more than a label. The usual pattern put military leaders in conjunction with a small group of aristocratic families to provide the Latin American countries with their governments.

Both civilian and military regimes of the last two decades burdened the region with huge debts. Borrowing money on future prospects was so popular that no politician felt any need to think through how these debts would be repaid. In 1970 Latin American governments owed $15,000,000,000; in 1990 the total was $420,000,000,000. Many national budgets must send a large portion of revenues to New York and London banks instead of using it within the national borders. Recovery is made more difficult because in many countries the tax system is inadequate and poorly enforced.

In the past 30 years peasant uprisings have appeared in the Central American countries of Guatemala, El Salvador, and Nicaragua and in Mexico's Chiapas province. Often accused of favoring communism, the United States was quick to send aid to their opposition. When the Sandanistas, a Marxist party came to power in Nicaragua, the Americans patronized the **Contras,** the army of the old regime and its supporters. The Guatemalan civil war started in 1954 and only concluded in December 1996, making it the longest conflict of North America in recent times.

Economic Realities

In the early twentieth century Latin American agriculture supported the economy. Large landowners, with their plantations and haciendas worked by peasant laborers, dominated the region. In Argentina some ranches held over a million acres. Often a nation produced but a single crop, leaving it vulnerable to changing world markets. For example, Colombia exported coffee; Venezuela, oil; Cuba, sugar; Argentina, beef; Chile, copper; and Honduras, bananas. When prices for these **commodities** fell, so did the economic well-being of the nations.

Prices for Latin American products are determined in Chicago and London where commodity traders balance buy or sell orders on sheets of paper. The drop of a few cents in these markets may spell disaster for a Latin American farmer.

Merchants in Ecuador display their crop of bananas.

In 1997 the livelihood of 40% of Latin Americans still depends on agriculture, and one-third of the men and women in some nations earn less than the equivalent of $2 a day. The Indians hold the poorest land. In Peru and Bolivia they live in the Andes where high winds and cold keep their harvests small. Little mechanization is possible because of the terrain. In the Atlantic region, northeastern Brazil is particularly poor because rainfall is so meager.

Latin America is noted for its mineral wealth. Most European colonists emigrated here on the promise of getting rich from gold and silver mining. Today oil is the major resource. Mexico and Venezuela are major producers, sitting on reserves that geologists estimate to be 12% of the world's supply.

Industrialization in Latin America has been slow to develop in some regions. In others, significant progress has occurred. Brazil and Mexico are the two countries that have profited the most from developing local industries. These include processing chemicals, cement, food products, and automobiles.

The interior of South and Central American countries suffer from inadequate highways and railroads. In recent years air traffic has improved the situation, but it has not solved all the problems for manufacturers. Investors are slow to put money into local industries.

The service industry, as in the United States, makes a major contribution to the incomes of the regions. Tourism in the West Indies and Mexico contributes millions of dollars to the economy of those nations. Panama is fortunate because it collects revenue from its canal.

Communications in many nations remain inadequate. The postal system is not dependable, and governments have no money for introducing modern equipment. Owning a phone in some countries is a well-known status symbol. However, better times are predicted as radio and telecommunications begin to invade even remote areas.

As the twenty-first century approaches, the major crop of several South American countries is drugs. Poor farmers are quite willing to produce the raw materials that are needed to provide cocaine, heroin, and marijuana for addicts of major cities in the United States and Europe.

Latin American Society

The Indians of Latin America remain poor and marginalized. Often they grow corn and more corn, their small fields eroding the topsoil with each planting. Medical and dental care are almost unknown, because few physicians or dentists choose to live in rural areas. Illiteracy, especially among women, is very high. Haiti and Honduras rank as countries with the highest illiteracy. Fidel Castro's Cuba, on the other hand, is very proud of its record in bringing elementary education to all children in the country.

Education for the elite is quite another matter. From the very beginning colonial governments sponsored higher education, with a university in Santo Domingo started as early as 1538. Its foundation is close to a century before the settlement of Jamestown. Every country has its own national university, but a student can attend only after passing rigorous examinations. Attendance is free for the fortunate few who enter.

The educated middle class continues to grow in most countries as modernization advances. People in this group provide the businessmen and white-collar workers of the governments. They now compete with their skills for privileges once reserved for the wealthy.

In all major towns there are numerous public libraries and museums. The anthropological museum in Mexico City is one of the world's outstanding institutions.

Sports play a significant role in Latin America, with soccer leading the list of favorite pastimes. Baseball has increased its share of sports fans in the Dominican Republic, Cuba, and Mexico. Theatrical productions, movies, and opera are available in all major cities.

The bullfighting tradition of Spain is alive and well in Mexico. Each year every large and small town celebrates a fiesta, a colorful holiday that brings out the whole population for sports, dancing, and religious processions.

Religion

For centuries the Catholic leadership, usually born in Spain or Portugal, supported the upper classes in their privileges. After the Second Vatican Council in the 1960s, there was a major shift in church allegiance. Several conferences of Latin American bishops announced their support for social change. They urged their governments to help impoverished peasants to gain ownership of the land that they farmed. The result has been resentment on the part of the ruling elite toward the church because its members feel betrayed. In some parts of Latin America, police and locally organized militias of the landowners do their best through imprisonment, assassinations, and harassment to keep troublesome priests silenced.

In many countries people of Indian and African culture blend their traditional beliefs with Catholicism. The result is a fascinating variety of folk religions, shaped to meet the needs of everyone.

At the turn of the twentieth century, Protestant missionaries decided to make a major effort to convince Latin Americans to join their churches. They have enjoyed remarkable success. Even though a hundred years ago Latin American Protestants numbered several hundred, today they are counted in the millions. If present trends continue, Guatemala will become the first Latin American country to have a Protestant majority. The clergy of these churches say little about social revolution, preferring to take a conservative stance on such matters.

International Affairs

Latin America has not played a large role in international affairs since World War II. Isolated by two oceans from European and Asian problems, Latin American nations have seen no reason to become involved.

Fidel Castro, second from the left, joins comrades celebrating his victory in Cuba.

Despite an environment where poverty is commonplace, Cuba is the one country where communism has succeeded in installing a Marxist regime. Fidel Castro, the architect of the Cuban Revolution, has weathered all attempts to oust him. The United States placed an embargo on Cuba to thwart Castro, but it did not bring him down. For decades the Soviet Union poured money into Cuba while receiving its sugar in partial payment. With the dissolution of the Soviet Union, the embargo is still in place. Thousands of Cubans have fled to the United States, allowing Castro to be rid of his opposition.

Latin American Culture

Latin American countries have numerous writers and painters who are well known nationally and internationally. Several have received Nobel Prizes in literature for their work. One of the most recent choices was Gabriel Garcia Marquez of Colombia.

More than any other art, Latin Americans enjoy music. They have made major contributions to the outside world: calypso from Trinidad, reggae from Jamaica, tango from Argentina, and the samba from Brazil. Classical ballet and folk dance groups supplement the musical scene.

Latin American artists are also known for painting, pottery, leatherwork, and wood sculptures. Brasilia, the new capital of Brazil, is noted for its architecture.

The history of two representative countries of the region, Brazil and Mexico, will demonstrate the search for political stability and economic development in Latin America.

Brazil: Giant of South America

After the declaration of its republic in 1889, Brazilian politics changed very little. The same wealthy landowning families determined the course of the country. The population continued to increase, cities grew larger, but the rigid class lines remained very much in place.

In the 1920s some political reformers appeared, but for the most part, their voices were isolated. It was only when the Great Depression struck that the nation was jolted out of its complacency. Brazil had no market for its coffee, and millions of dollars worth of unsold coffee beans filled Brazilian warehouses.

This shock to the nation caused serious problems within the country. Fascist groups developed; they promised to lead Brazil using Nazi Germany as their model. Out of the confusion, Getulio Vargas appeared, calling on Brazilians to support a new order, *Estado Novo*.

During World War II the Brazilian economy once more came to life, and Vargas found an opportunity to enhance the nation's prestige. Brazil declared war on the Axis Powers, and its troops saw action on the Italian front. Vargas's leadership during the war was not enough to save his presidency. In 1945 a coup deposed him. His detractors, however, were not successful in guiding the country through the postwar doldrums. As a consequence, after five years in political limbo, Vargas resumed the nation's presidency. In an appeal to the labor unions and the nationalists, Vargas engineered a limitation on the profits of foreign corporations in Brazil. He also made a state-owned monopoly of the oil industry. The president's career came to an unexpected conclusion in 1954 when he committed suicide.

The skyline of Sâo Paulo. This city is Brazil's largest with over 10 million people.

During the 1950s Brazil's population showed tremendous growth. Especially around Sâo Paulo, industries and businesses expanded at a huge rate. Peasants from the countryside flocked to the cities in search of work. The lucky few found employment. The rest, who remained unemployed, lived in shanty towns called *favelas*, without electricity, water, or sanitation. An observer noted, "Year after year, the favelas continue to grow as landless peasants exchange the grinding poverty of the countryside for urban squalor."

In 1956 a new president, Juscelino Kubitschek, came into office promising a better program. One of his ideas was to promote the construction of a new capital in the Brazilian interior. Officials chose a site for the federal complex, named Brasilia, located about 800 miles northwest of Rio de Janeiro. An army of workers poured into this isolated area to begin the construction. Today Brasilia holds over a million people, the only planned city to be built on such a massive scale since World War II.

Brasilia is the new capital of Brazil.

In 1964 the military felt that partisan politics had done too little to solve the nation's problems. The generals overthrew the civilian government. They cut wages and instituted price controls in an effort to stem inflation. Their officials suppressed opposition parties and ignored civil liberties. Imprisonment and torture of prisoners became routine. Oil, mining, and telecommunications were made monopolies, but nothing worked very well. The nation labored under a $100,000,000,000 debt to foreign banks.

The generals finally decided that they could do no better than the civilians in solving the major economic problems of the country. In 1989 they stepped down to make way for new presidential elections. Election fever caused 19 political parties to present candidates. The victor was Fernando Collor de Mello.

Collor de Mello discovered that the Brazilian Congress had its own ideas on running the country. Composed of 595 legislators, each member felt it was his duty to sponsor expensive projects in his home district. Allegations of corruption against Collor de Mello were so frequent that in October 1992 the Congress threatened impeachment and the president resigned. New elections brought Fernando Henrique Cardoso to the office.

Cardoso previously served as finance minister and had slashed the inflationary spiral that seemed out of control for so long. In 1994 inflation stood at a rate of 5,000%. The problems of the nation came from many sides. The government had a bloated bureaucracy where patronage was the key to a job. Subsidies and pensions consumed large chunks of the budget, and state and local governments received up to 65% of all national revenues. This happened in a country where the wealthiest families paid almost no taxes and the burden fell upon the productive members of society. Working people gave over half of their salaries to taxes, while the rich owed $40,000,000,000 in unpaid revenues. Cordoso turned the economy around, collecting more revenue, cutting government expenses, and striking down existing trade barriers.

In 1995 Brazilian inflation was under control, and investment in the country was increasing when the Mexican monetary crisis spilled over to Brazil. In a few short weeks investors pulled $6,000,000,000 out of the country.

The Present and Future

Both positive and negative forces are now at work in Brazil. The large gap between rich and poor is at the root of the problem. An oligarchy of the wealthy controls the government in its interests. Anyone who suggests land reform, giving tenants farmers some of the land, is met with cries of "Communist!"

The church in Brazil, whose numbers are so large that they make the country the most populous Catholic nation in the world, has made a turnaround in recent years. Theologians have become spokespersons for the poor. Inspired by what is known as **liberation theology,** clergy have formed base communities where the Bible's demands for social justice are emphasized. Several bishops have joined the struggle for a more equitable distribution of wealth. In the words of the Archbishop of Pernambuco, Dom Helder da Camera, "The trouble with Brazil is not an excess of communist doctrine, but a lack of Christian justice."

Brazilian women have only had the right to vote since 1932. Their enfranchisement shows how strongly patriarchal traditions held on. Today women number about 10% of the country's office holders. As in most countries of the world, women are paid much less than men; their work is called unskilled. Rural women have large families, averaging six children, who share in the hard work of farming.

Those who live in the favelas live without hope. Young children who cannot be fed drift from the favelas into the cities. Here they live as best they can, sleeping on the streets and begging for handouts. They both add to crime and are themselves victims. Twenty murders each day occur in Rio de Janeiro.

People in a Brazilian favela have yet to participate in the country's prosperity.

On the positive side, Brazil is in the midst of rapid industrialization. Its burgeoning labor force is well trained and productive, and Brazil now is the fourth largest auto manufacturer in the world. In agricultural production Brazil ranks as the world's leading supplier of coffee and sugar.

Brazil's people are rich in culture. The mixture of whites, blacks, and browns allows every cultural group to contribute to the literature, music, and dance of the country. In Brazil everyone knows the samba.

Rio de Janeiro and its Cococabana Beach is famous around the world for its charm. Nowhere is Carnival celebrated with such enthusiasm as in Rio. Mardi Gras in New Orleans is a pale reflection. Over 500,000 people dress in costume while some 80,000 people march in a day-long parade competing for the Championship of the Avenue. The costumes are most lavish and require months of preparation.

The Rio de Janeiro carnival offers everyone a chance to get in the parade.

Perhaps Carnival explains why the Brazilians are so tolerant. Despite their difficulties, ordinary people have been remarkably unrevolutionary. The class structure is too strong and the police too vigilant for political activists to succeed.

The headlong drive to develop the Amazon River region is destroying the rain forest and the Indians who make it their home. Some areas are now deserts. Poor farmers, cattle ranchers, and loggers feel they have little choice but to push farther and farther into the rain forest. The Trans-Amazonia Highway, which extends 3,480 miles through the forest, allows the settlers access into the interior.

Brazil's future rests in the hands of a very young population. The need to provide jobs, education, financial stability, and social justice are immense tasks for the future. The common good demands that the privileged few learn to share, but this demands a change in heart for an oligarchy in power for centuries. Brazil's great resource is its people, its tolerance of racial differences, and the general optimism found in the population. With these virtues in mind, Brazil's future may well be brighter than its many unsolved problems might admit.

The World of Mexico

From 1910 to 1920 Mexico lost 500,000 people because of constant civil war. The result was the impoverishment of the people, especially the peasants, and the loss of any sense of security.

Successive presidents made efforts at land redistribution, but the process of breaking up the large estates proved slow and tedious. The establishment of credit facilities and irrigation projects in various localities did aid some in the peasant class.

Pancho Villa, astride his horse, became a hero to many Mexicans.

One more crisis erupted in 1926 when the Archbishop of Mexico City told Catholics that they should not obey the constitution. The government responded by nationalizing all church property; closing religious schools, convents, and monasteries; and expelling all foreign clerics. The Vatican placed the country under interdict, forbidding all religious services throughout the nation. For three years armies favorable to the church, the **Cristeros,** fought the government in a losing struggle.

Mexico under the National Revolutionary Party

After the Cristero Rebellion concluded, the National Revolutionary Party dominated the country's politics. Its leadership, vested in a president with a 6-year term, shared the government with a Congress of legislators. Because much of the party's support came from labor unions, this group tended to be favored. Land reform accelerated; 40,000,000 acres changed hands from 1934 to 1940.

In 1938 the government took a major economic gamble when it decided on the nationalization of the American and British oil companies. Although the move was immensely popular in Mexico, it was vigorously denounced in Washington and London. The government set up its own company, PEMEX, to extract and market the nation's oil. For a time, trade between the United States and Mexico came to a standstill.

This period of Mexican history, marked by strong populism, was given visual representation in a flourishing of artists and writers. Two painters, Diego Rivera and David Sigueiros, created murals that showed the victory of the peasant over the clergy and the landowners in graphic form. The Indian base of Mexican culture was exalted at the expense of the European.

The outbreak of World War II brought the United States and Mexico back together. With so many U.S. citizens involved in industry, the governments commenced the *bracero* program to bring Mexican farm workers into the United States to support U.S. agriculture. This began a major influx of immigrants into the United States.

A parade through Mexico City emphasizes the country's rich heritage.

At the conclusion of the war, the name of the ruling party was changed to the PRI, the Institutional Revolutionary Party. The tradition of one 6-year term for the presidency continued to be enforced, but despite changes in this office, a small clique of party managers actually controlled elections. Up to the present, the PRI remains dominant on the national scene. Unfortunately, corruption and illegal activities as well as assassinations have plagued national life as a result of the monopoly the PRI has held since 1946.

Mexico Today

Because of a better diet and medical improvements, the life span of the average citizen has increased considerably in the past 40 years. Although Mexico is now the fourth largest oil-producing nation in the world, the wealth from this resource is dependent on world markets. In times of high prices, Mexico flourishes. In times of low prices, the economy suffers.

Mexico has a serious population problem. There are not enough jobs for all the people entering the job market. From 1940 to 1990 the population has risen from about 20,000,000 to 80,000,000 people. Educational facilities have not kept pace with the tide of children entering school. Of 100 children only 60 will finish elementary school, only 5 will complete secondary school, and 1 will receive a university degree. Therefore the large social and economic dichotomy that plagues the country is institutionalized by the educational system.

Emigration to the United States has acted as a safety valve for Mexico. As many as 10,000,000 Mexicans have come, legally or illegally, into the United States in this generation. Here they take jobs that native-born Americans shun, working very hard to improve their living standard. Failure to learn English has caused many Mexicans to remain outside the American mainstream and in recent years inspired an anti-immigrant reaction.

The immigration has created an opportunity for American politicians to argue that Mexicans in the United States represent a serious problem for schools and social services. Although unproven, this charge has captured a majority of voters' sympathies in California.

An Aztec calendar has a prominent place in Mexico City's National Archaeological Museum.

In early 1994 the **North American Free Trade Agreement (NAFTA)** went into effect. This was considered to be a major boost for the Mexican economy because low wages in that country were expected to entice increased industrial investment south of the border.

In late 1994 Ernesto Zedillo became president. Zedillo received the nomination of the PRI only after the first nominee, Luis Donaldo Colosio, was assassinated.

Mexico's most recent difficulties arose from a government decision in December 1994 to devalue the peso to such an extent that the economic progress of the country was put in serious jeopardy. Although there was little doubt that inflation was growing very quickly, the cure proved worse than the disease. The economic crisis struck the emerging middle class, the very foundation upon which the future of the country rested. President Clinton in the United States came to the rescue, raising a loan of $52,000,000,000, of which one-third came from the United States. The loan has since been repaid, but Mexico in 1997 remains a rich nation where the majority of the people live in poverty.

Conclusion

Latin American countries appear to be in their adolescence among the world's nations. Although old in some ways, the continent's peoples, so young in age, are still on the edge of reaching maturity. Unsolved economic and social problems remain serious for too many countries.

Brazil provides a good example of how the wealthy keep the nation's prosperity limited to themselves. Brazil is now the sixth largest industrial nation in the world. Yet the gains of industrialization have not reached the ordinary citizen. The average salary remains under $200 per month. A secure future requires this imbalance to change.

CHAPTER 31 REVIEW
LATIN AMERICA

Summary
- Latin America has a unique mix of people and class structure.
- Most nations have passed through military government to stable democracies in the past generation.
- Heavy debts burden most of the region.
- Indian populations are at the bottom of the class structure, while a growing middle class continues to improve its standard of living.
- Evangelical Protestant missionary activity has gained many converts away from Catholicism.
- Cuba, the only communist country in Latin America, suffers from a U.S. boycott.
- Brazil, the most populous state in Latin America, is now on its way to becoming the major economic power of South America.
- Mexico has had a unique history, passing through a period of civil war and the ascendancy of a single political party.
- Devaluation of the peso in 1994 triggered a crisis in the Mexican economy.

Identify
People: Castro, Vargas, Evita Perón, Cardoso, Cristeros, Zedillo
Places: Argentina, Panama, West Indies, Guatemala, Brazil, Brasilia
Events: Cuba's turn to communism; industrialization in Brazil; Peronism in Argentina; the challenge to the Mexican Institutional Revolutionary Party

Define
caudillos

North American Free Trade
 Agreement (NAFTA)

favelas

liberation theology

commodities

Multiple Choice
1. These countries of Latin America have a predominant Indian population:
   (a) Argentina and Uruguay
   (b) Chile and Mexico
   (c) Ecuador and Bolivia
   (d) Argentina and Mexico

2. The leaders of Latin American states prior to 1990 were usually from
   (a) the clergy.
   (b) the mestizo population.
   (c) the military.
   (d) the industrialists.

3. A major problem for most governments in Latin America is
   (a) holding elections.
   (b) revising the constitution.
   (c) subsidizing agriculture.
   (d) paying off enormous debts.

4. Venezuela gets most of its income from exports of
   (a) sugar.
   (b) coffee.
   (c) oil.
   (d) bananas.

5. The West Indies' economy is heavily dependent on
   (a) oil.
   (b) tourism.
   (c) mining.
   (d) forestry.

6. In 1999 the Panama Canal will be operated entirely by the
   (a) Colombian Company.
   (b) Panamanians.
   (c) Americans.
   (d) Costa Ricans.

7. The oldest university in the Americas was started in
   (a) Santo Domingo.
   (b) Veracruz.
   (c) Rio de Janeiro.
   (d) Cambridge, Massachusetts.

8. Many Latin Americans are recent converts to
   (a) Islam.
   (b) Evangelical Protestantism.
   (c) the Episcopal church.
   (d) Scientology.

9. For a long time Castro's Cuba had to depend on subsidies from
   (a) Great Britain.
   (b) Spain.
   (c) France.
   (d) the Soviet Union.

10. The favorite dance of Argentina is the
    (a) samba.
    (b) reggae.
    (c) calypso.
    (d) tango.

11. A Brazilian favela is home for the nation's
    (a) middle class.
    (b) wealthy.
    (c) military officers.
    (d) poor.

12. Carnival in this city is Brazil's most elaborate:
    (a) Sâo Paulo
    (b) Montevideo
    (c) Rio de Janeiro
    (d) Brasilia

13. In the 1920s the Mexican government began its fight with the
    (a) Catholic church.
    (b) oil companies.
    (c) cattle ranchers.
    (d) American investors.

14. Mexico's PRI
    (a) has held a national political monopoly since 1946.
    (b) welcomes political opposition.
    (c) encourages immigration into Mexico.
    (d) has its major supporters in the Indian population.

15. The adoption of NAFTA was meant to
    (a) control the value of the peso.
    (b) ensure an election victory for the PRI.
    (c) come to terms with revolutionaries in Chiapas.
    (d) increase investment in Mexican manufacturing.

Essay Questions
1. Why is there such a large gap between rich and poor in Latin America?
2. Explain ways to solve the debt crisis in Latin America.
3. Compare the recent history of Brazil with Mexico.
4. Why have Protestant Evangelical churches prospered in Latin America?

Answers

1. c	6. b	11. d
2. c	7. a	12. c
3. d	8. b	13. a
4. c	9. d	14. a
5. b	10. d	15. d

CHAPTER 32

Australia, New Zealand, and the Pacific Islands

The one-third of the world that the Pacific Ocean covers has had its own distinctive history in the nineteenth and twentieth centuries. Basically, the story is easily told. The coming of Europeans into the Pacific region meant a major change in the environment and the human populations that had no way to respond adequately to this challenge from outside.

Australian Settlement

The colony of convicts that first landed in Botany Bay in 1788 had to support itself through farming in its first years. The soldier guards were given tracts of land, as were those prisoners who had finished serving their sentences. Other shiploads of passengers, both convicts and free men and women, continued to arrive in Botany Bay from England. It soon became a major town that, in time, received the name Sydney. The transport of convicts continued until 1868, when the last ship reached Western Australia with its human cargo.

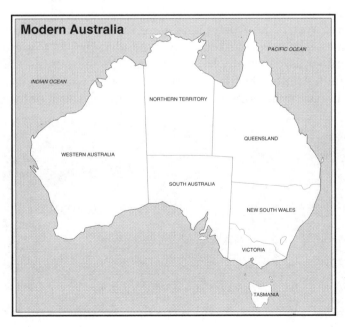

The introduction of sheep into Australia meant that the colony prospered in the 1820s from wool sent off to Great Britain. Ranches were kept within certain perimeters because the colonial government claimed to own all the remaining land of New South Wales. There were no ways to enforce this prohibition with the result that many settlers became **squatters** on government land. Settlers later established colonies at Melbourne and Perth.

The discovery of gold in 1851 brought a surge of prospectors to the continent, raising the population close to 500,000 people. This expansion of the white population did not bode well for the Aborigines of the country, who received the same treatment as the Indians of North America.

In the nineteenth century, Sydney became a major commercial city in the South Pacific.

By 1890 the colonies were self-governing with their own administrations and legislatures. Great Britain provided for the defense and international affairs of the Australians, but the distance from London to Sydney demanded that most decisions should be made on the local level. There was also a need to do more to unite the colonies, with the result that a constitutional convention met and produced a document for the people to vote on. This was done, and on New Years' Day 1901 Australia became a single commonwealth.

In 1908 politicians reached an agreement to locate Australia's capital in Canberra. However, the buildings were not ready for occupancy until 19 years later.

After World War II the Australians were involved in numerous international activities. The domestic economy expanded thanks to significant discoveries of minerals, especially bauxite for making aluminum and uranium for nuclear fuel. Another factor in economic growth was the immigration of Greeks and Italians who hoped to make a new home south of the equator.

The Opera House of Sydney has become Australia's most famous landmark.

The usual problems of capitalist cycles of boom and bust resulted in frequent changes of mood in voters who vacillated between the two major parties, Liberal and Labor. The European population continues to keep to the coastline of the continent, creating prosperous urban life, but 20 miles outside the cities a traveler enters a world empty of life except for ranches. Miles and miles of desert fill the Australian interior, quite a contrast to Melbourne, Adelaide, Perth, and Sydney with its spectacular opera house.

New Zealand

New Zealand immigrants from Europe brought a large variety of new plants and animals with them; the more important were sheep, deer, and opossums as well as potatoes and grain. Because the Royal Navy had need of the lumber, the country's hardwood trees fell to the ax. By 1840 half the forested area of the island was gone.

Sheepherding is the lifeblood of New Zealand agriculture.

People paid scant attention to the rapid depletion of New Zealand's resources. Ranchers burned off trees and grasslands so that they could keep cattle and sheep. New Zealand sheep growers sent huge amounts of wool to the factories of Great Britain. Then in 1882 the use of refrigerated ships also made it possible to send meat and dairy products to European markets. This opened a meat packing industry that rapidly developed. By 1940 New Zealanders had the most efficient agricultural production in the world.

Pacific Islands

In the nineteenth century a large drop in human population occurred on the Pacific Islands. Many men took jobs on ships sailing from European and American ports. Others signed on with labor recruiters. Melanesians worked in Australian cane fields in such numbers that the population on their islands declined by 20%. All over the Pacific, the building and maintenance of fields for agriculture were abandoned. Some studies show a decline of as much as 90%, allowing second-growth forest to establish itself on once bare islands.

The introduction of grazing animals, however, impeded the return of trees and all other forms of native plant and animal life. Today Hawaii has over 5,000 **alien species,** introduced by choice or by accident. Australia provides the best example of what can happen as a result of the introduction of a new species. Europeans brought rabbits with them to Australia for eating and fur. Today they number over 500,000,000 animals, and their numbers are still expanding.

In the ocean, seals and whales felt the brunt of unlimited slaughter. Ignoring any concern for conservation, hunters were as anxious to kill as many animals as possible before rivals could take a greater share.

Timber, especially sandalwood, was the preferred material for Chinese chests, boxes, and furniture. Merchants found in Hawaii just what they wanted, for a royal monopoly existed on its export. The Hawaiian rulers made great profits sending it off to China. By the close of the nineteenth century, only 10% of the sandalwood was still growing in remote corners of the islands.

Late in the nineteenth century, Europeans and Americans took an interest in the islands because of their importance as potential colonies and places to service their naval vessels. American missionaries in Hawaii are said to have come to do good, and then did very well. Many, like the Dole family, became wealthy, creating an island aristocracy that sought U.S. protection.

Honolulu Harbor became a major port for U.S. shipping.

Because of the deposing of Queen Liliuokalani in 1893, the Americans hoped for annexation to the United States. Five years later, this was done; Hawaii became a territory of the United States, and in 1959 the islands became a state.

During World War II the islands of Guadalcanal and Okinawa were the scene of the most bitter fighting between the Americans and Japanese. After the war the United States decided to use the Pacific islands for nuclear testing. An atomic bomb was set off on the Bikini atoll in the Marshall Islands and in 1952 the first hydrogen bomb explosion took place on Eniwetok, an atoll northwest of the Marshall Islands. The number of nuclear tests of the United States, Great Britain, and France has now reached 250, leaving a permanent scar on the Pacific Islands.

Conclusion

The history of Australia in the nineteenth century transformed that continent from isolation to participation in the world economy. Ranching, mining, and local industry attracted thousands of new immigrants from Europe who hoped to share in the economy of a land still thinly populated. Here they created a dynamic society and all the forms of a democratic state. New Zealand had a similar experience.

Australians will demonstrate their coming of age in 2000 when they host the Olympic Games in Sydney. They look upon their country, still young, on its way to make its mark in the third millennium. For the Pacific islanders tourism may well change their rather bleak past into a happier future.

CHAPTER 32 REVIEW
AUSTRALIA, NEW ZEALAND, AND THE PACIFIC ISLANDS

Summary
- Great Britain for many years used Australia as a place to transport criminals.
- In New South Wales raising sheep for wool created a major export industry.
- In 1901 Australia's colonies became a single commonwealth.
- Australia is a major producer of minerals in the present world economy.
- Major environmental changes occurred in New Zealand with European settlement and sheep ranching.
- The Pacific Islands went through a major ecological shift as alien plants and animals tended to overwhelm native species.
- The Americans, British, and French conducted nuclear tests on sites in the Pacific adding to environmental changes.

Identify
People: Melanesians, Aborigines, Liliuokalani
Places: Eniwetok, Sydney, Melbourne, Perth, Canberra
Events: transporting convicts to Australia; gold discovery in Australia; environmental changes

Define

sandalwood	squatters	alien species

Multiple Choice
1. The first use of Australia by the British was
   (a) for colonizing the Pacific.
   (b) as a place to settle homeless people.
   (c) as a place of exile for convicts.
   (d) as a coaling station for naval ships.

2. Australia and New Zealand ranchers specialize in
   (a) hogs.
   (b) horses.
   (c) cattle.
   (d) sheep.

3. The first major city in New South Wales was
   (a) Perth.
   (b) Melbourne.
   (c) Adelaide.
   (d) Sydney.

4. Australia's capital is at
   (a) Perth.
   (b) Canberra.
   (c) Sydney.
   (d) Alice Springs.

5. Sandalwood in Hawaii found a major market in
   (a) China.
   (b) the United States.
   (c) Japan.
   (d) Australia.

Essay Questions
   1. What were the stages of Australian development?
   2. What environmental changes have affected the Pacific Islands in the past 200 years?

Answers
1. c   2. d   3. d   4. b   5. a

Index